Lecture Notes in Artificial Intelligence 4106

Edited by J. G. Carbonell and J. Siekmann

Subseries of Lecture Notes in Computer Science

Thomas R. Roth-Berghofer
Mehmet H. Göker
H. Altay Güvenir (Eds.)

Advances in Case-Based Reasoning

8th European Conference, ECCBR 2006
Fethiye, Turkey, September 4-7, 2006
Proceedings

 Springer

Series Editors

Jaime G. Carbonell, Carnegie Mellon University, Pittsburgh, PA, USA
Jörg Siekmann, University of Saarland, Saarbrücken, Germany

Volume Editors

Thomas R. Roth-Berghofer
Deutsches Forschungszentrum für Künstliche Intelligenz DFKI GmbH
Erwin-Schrödinger-Straße 57, 67663 Kaiserslautern, Germany
E-mail: thomas.roth-berghofer@dfki.de

Mehmet H. Göker
2189 Sharon Road, Menlo Park, CA 94025, USA
E-mail: mgoker@sbcglobal.net

H. Altay Güvenir
Bilkent University
Computer Engineering Department
06800 Ankara, Turkey
E-mail: guvenir@cs.bilkent.edu.tr

Library of Congress Control Number: 2006930094

CR Subject Classification (1998): I.2, J.4, J.1, F.4.1

LNCS Sublibrary: SL 7 – Artificial Intelligence

ISSN   0302-9743
ISBN-10   3-540-36843-4 Springer Berlin Heidelberg New York
ISBN-13   978-3-540-36843-4 Springer Berlin Heidelberg New York

Springer is a part of Springer Science+Business Media

springer.com

© Springer-Verlag Berlin Heidelberg 2006
Printed in Germany

Typesetting: Camera-ready by author, data conversion by Scientific Publishing Services, Chennai, India
Printed on acid-free paper   SPIN: 11805816   06/3142   5 4 3 2 1 0

Preface

This volume contains the papers presented at the 8th European Conference on Case-Based Reasoning (ECCBR 2006).

Case-Based Reasoning (CBR) is an artificial intelligence approach where new problems are solved by remembering, adapting and reusing solutions to a previously solved, similar problem. The collection of previously solved problems and their associated solutions is stored in the case base. New or adapted solutions are learned and updated in the case base as needed.

ECCBR and its sister conference ICCBR alternate every year. ECCBR 2006 followed a series of seven successful European Workshops previously held in Kaiserslautern, Germany (1993), Chantilly, France (1994), Lausanne, Switzerland (1996), Dublin, Ireland (1998), and Trento, Italy (2000), and two European Conferences in Aberdeen, UK (2002), and Madrid, Spain (2004). The International Conferences on Case-Based Reasoning (ICCBR) were previously held in Sesimbra, Portugal (1995), Providence, Rhode Island, USA (1997), Seeon, Germany (1999), Vancouver, Canada (2001), Trondheim, Norway (2003), and Chicago, USA (2005). These meetings have a history of attracting first-class European and international researchers and practitioners. Proceedings of ECCBR and ICCBR conferences are traditionally published by Springer in their LNAI series.

The ECCBR 2006 conference was held at the conference center of the Lykiaworld Resort hotel in ldeniz/Fethiye, Turkey. The now traditional Industry Day started the program giving insight into fielded CBR applications. The second day was devoted to workshops on specific areas of interest to the CBR community such as Textual CBR: Reasoning with Texts, CBR in Health Sciences, Uncertainty and Fuzziness in Case-Based Reasoning, and CBR and Context-Awareness. The remaining two days featured invited talks, presentations and posters on both theoretical and applied research in CBR.

The accepted papers were chosen based on a thorough and highly selective review process. Each paper was reviewed and discussed by at least three Program Committee members and revised according to their comments.

We believe that the papers of this volume are a representative snapshot of current research and contribute to both theoretical and applied aspects of CBR research. The papers are organized into three sections: invited talks (two papers and two abstracts), research papers (31) and application papers (5).

The chairs would like to thank the invited speakers Edwina Rissland, David McSherry, and Gholamreza Nakhaeizadeh for their contribution to the success of this conference. With their invited talks on CBR in business, Michel Manago and Stefan Wess added substantially to Industry Day. Particular thanks go to the Program Committee and additional reviewers for their efforts and hard work in the reviewing and selection process.

We are also grateful for the work of the Industry Day Chairs, Bill Cheetham and Kareem S. Aggour, the Workshops Coordinator, Mirjam Minor, as well as the Chairs of the four workshops and their various committee members for preparations for Industry Day and the Workshops. We thank all the authors who submitted to the conference to make this program possible and gratefully acknowledge the generous support of the sponsors of ECCBR 2006 and their, partly long-time, sponsorship of ECCBR and ICCBR.

This volume has been produced using the EasyChair system[1]. We would like to express our gratitude to its author Andrei Voronkov. Finally, we thank Springer for its continuing support in publishing this series of conference proceedings.

June 2006   Thomas R. Roth-Berghofer
                                                                  Mehmet H. Gker
                                                                  H. Altay Gvenir

---

[1] http://www.easychair.org

Conference Organization

Program Chairs

Mehmet H. Gker, PricewaterhouseCoopers, USA
Thomas R. Roth-Berghofer, TU Kaiserslautern/DFKI GmbH, Germany

Local Organization

H. Altay Gvenir, Bilkent University, Turkey

Industry Day Coordination

Bill Cheetham, General Electric Co. NY, USA
Kareem S. Aggour, General Electric Co. NY, USA

Workshop Coordination

Mirjam Minor, University of Trier, Germany

Program Committee

Agnar Aamodt, Norwegian University of Science and Technology, Norway
David W. Aha, Naval Research Laboratory, USA
Esma Aimeur, University of Montreal, Canada
Vincent Aleven, Carnegie Mellon University, USA
Ethem Alpaydin, Bogazii University, Istanbul, Turkey
Klaus-Dieter Althoff, University of Hildesheim, Germany
Josep Llus Arcos, IIIACSIC, Spain
Kevin Ashley, University of Pittsburgh, USA
Brigitte Bartsch-Spoerl, BSR Consulting, Germany
Ralph Bergmann, University of Trier, Germany
Isabelle Bichindaritz, University of Washington, USA
Enrico Blanzieri, University of Trento, Italy
L. Karl Branting, BAE Systems, Inc., USA
Derek Bridge, University College Cork, Ireland
Stefanie Bruninghaus, University of Pittsburgh, USA
Robin Burke, DePaul University, USA
Hans-Dieter Burkhard, Humboldt University Berlin, Germany
Bill Cheetham, General Electric Co. NY, USA

Additional Reviewers

Daniel Duarte Abdala   Mobyen Ahmed   Stella Asiimwe
Shahina Begum   Ralf Berger   Enrico Blanzieri
Kalyan Moy Gupta   Alexandre Hanft   Stewart Massie
Rainer Maximini   David McDonald   Petri Myllymki
Jason M. Proctor   Joes Staal   Alexander Tartakovski
Ning Xiong

Conference Sponsors

DaimlerChrysler, Germany
DFKI GmbH, Germany
empolis, Germany
kaidara software, France
Microsoft, Turkey
PricewaterhouseCoopers, USA

Table of Contents

Application Papers

The Fun Begins with Retrieval:
Explanation and CBR

Edwina L. Rissland

Department of Computer Science, University of Massachusetts
Amherst, Massachusetts, U.S.A. 01003

Abstract. This paper discusses the importance of the post-retrieval steps of CBR, that is, the steps that occur after relevant cases have been retrieved. Explanations and arguments, for instance, require much to be done post-retrieval. I also discuss both the importance of explanation to CBR and the use of CBR to generate explanations.

1 Introduction

Some of the most interesting aspects of CBR occur after relevant cases have been retrieved. Explanations—and here I include argument—are some of the most important, and they play a central role in CBR. They are needed to elucidate the results of the case-based reasoning—why a case was interpreted or classified in a particular way, how a new design or plan works, why a particular diagnosis is most compelling, etc.—and explanations can themselves be created using CBR. For CBR to create arguments, designs, plans, etc., much work must be done, and most of it begins after relevant cases have been retrieved [18], [23]. That is, a good part of the core of case-based reasoning occurs post-retrieval.

Since some systems like Branting's GREBE [5] and Koton's CASEY [19] create their explanations using adaptive mechanisms, it is not clear how to draw a line between so-called interpretive and adaptive CBR systems. However, it is abundantly clear that in both types the lion's share of the work is done post-retrieval. While explanation is not the focus of other adaptive CBR systems like Hammond's CHEF [16] or Cheetham's FORM TOOL [8], they do indeed accomplish their tasks post-retrieval. That is, retrieval is only an initial step in case-based problem-solving, and the fun—and most of the hard work—occurs post-retrieval.

The ability to explain one's reasoning is a hallmark of intelligence, and is—or should be—one of the keystones of CBR systems. This is so whether CBR is being used to interpret or classify a new case, or to adapt an old solution in order to solve a new problem. Too often our CBR systems—particularly those used to classify new cases—de-emphasize or even forget about the post-retrieval "R's" in CBR, like "reuse, revise, retain" [1]. Retrieval is, of course, an absolutely crucial step in CBR, but it is only one of several: it is one of the six R's in Göker & Roth-Berghofer's formulation [14] and one of the eleven in Derek Bridge's [7].

Explanation is really a kind of teaching, and can be viewed as the other side of the coin of learning. Both explanation and learning are inextricably intertwined with

T.R. Roth-Berghofer et al. (Eds.): ECCBR 2006, LNAI 4106, pp. 1–8, 2006.

concepts, conceptual emergence, and concept change. We really thus have a longterm cycle in which cases play an integral role. Although I won't really consider the closely related problems of similarity assessment and credit assignment in this presentation, they are indeed very important to both this overarching cycle and to the inner workings of CBR, including retrieval.

Most of us know how critical the choices of similarity metric and case space structure are in CBR. Both choices are motivated by what we want to bring to the fore in the reasoning. They also dictate what will be possible to accomplish in it or explain about it. That is, there is another inescapable intertwining in CBR between notions of similarity and explanation. One can thus say that the fun also begins before retrieval.

This is especially true in systems that stop at retrieval or a slight bit beyond—what we might call CB-little-r systems—for instance, those that use retrieved examples to classify a new case (e.g., with nearest neighbor methods), or that use the results of the early steps of CBR to initiate other types of processing, like information retrieval. For instance, the SPIRE system stopped short of argument creation, but used retrieval and similarity assessment (e.g., HYPO-style claim lattices) to generate queries for a full-text IR engine [9], [44], [45]. In CB-r systems there is perhaps a more critical dependence on getting the space and metric "right" than in CBR systems that keep on processing or that can explain themselves.

In fact, explanations can help lessen the burdens of CBR systems since they make their reasoning less opaque, a requirement, I believe, for intelligent systems. Explaining the behavior of CBR systems to users is receiving new attention in recent work, with goals such as enabling systems to explain their questions [31] or to explain the space of retrieval possibilities [37]. Leake & McSherry's [24] collection on CBR and explanation demonstrates new activity in a number of directions, but current work just scratches the surface of possibilities. Even with regard to similarity and retrieval, we don't, in my opinion, have enough variety in our ideas. So, in addition to pressing for more consideration of the post-retrieval R's, I would also press for more research on the first R: retrieval.

2 Cases as Both Drivers and Aids

Cases (called exemplars or examples in other contexts) not only are drivers of the inter-looped processes of explanation and concept evolution, but they can also serve as central elements in the representation of concepts and the teaching of the art of explanation. For instance, examples can be used by themselves to produce a totally extensional representation; that is, a concept is simply considered to be the set of its positive exemplars. They can participate in hybrid representations in concert with other mechanisms like rules or prototypes or statistical models. Examples can serve as extensional annotations on rules; these can serve to help resolve ambiguities in rules or terms and to keep them up to date with new interpretations and exceptions. Concrete examples can be used to capture some of the information that statistics summarize but cannot explicitly represent. Cases—like atypical borderline examples, anomalies, penumbral cases—are particularly useful in the tails of distributions where data can be sparse.

Hybrid approaches, both in representation and reasoning, have been used in a variety of systems from the earliest days of CBR to the present: CABARET, GREBE,

ANAPRON, CAMPER, CARMA, and FORM TOOL, for instance. (For concise overviews of such hybrids, see [27], [28].) Cases in many of these systems serve to complement and supplement other forms of reasoning and representation. For example, ANAPRON used cases to capture exceptions to rules [15]. An early landmark system in AI and Law by Anne Gardner to model the issue-spotting task issue on problems of the kind found on law school and bar exams used examples as sanity checks on rule-based reasoning and when rule-based reasoning failed, or when as Gardner puts it, "the rules run out" [12]. CABARET used cases in these ways as well [46]. In addition CABARET used cases to help carry out a repertoire of strategies and tactics for performing statutory interpretation, that is, determination of the scope and meaning of legal rules and their ingredient predicates [51]. CAMPER used cases and rules to generate plans for nutritional menus [26]. CARMA used cases and rules together with models [17].

Related to our interests are two paradigms from psychology concerning reasoning with and representing concepts and categories: the *prototype* and *exemplar* views [34]. (Murphy's *The Big Book of Concepts* provides an extensive overview.) Pioneered by Rosch, Medin and others about thirty years ago, the prototype paradigm focuses on the "typicality" of examples [49], [32], [33], [52]. Sometimes a prototype is taken to be a maximally typical actual example; other times it is more of a summary or a model like a frame in AI. Prototypes have been extensively investigated in psychology. In the exemplar view, a concept is represented by the set of its positive examples. It has not been as thoroughly considered, and it is nowhere as sophisticated as our own work in CBR to which it is obviously closely related. For instance, we have many highly elaborated and computationally well-defined mechanisms for case retrieval and comparison. Hybrid representations—of prototypes and examples, say— have not been used much at all in psychology. On the other hand, hybrid approaches have been extensively explored in CBR and closely related fields like AI and Law. For example, McCarty and Sridharan early on proposed a hybrid "prototype-plus-deformation" approach [29]. (For an overview of AI & Law, see [43].)

3 The Centrality of Explanation

Explanation is central to all types of CBR. In interpreting a new case using past interpretations from the case base, many CBR systems reason with relevant similarities and differences. Such interpretive CBR can involve analogically mapping over explanations from existing precedents, for instance by structure mapping, or by constructing a completely new rationale, for instance, by HYPO-style dimensional analysis.

Many of the earliest CBR systems focused on explanations. For instance, HYPO used highly relevant previously interpreted cases—that is, precedents—to interpret the case at hand and generate arguments both for and against a particular conclusion [4]. HYPO elucidated interpretations with explanatorily-relevant hypotheticals. Branting's GREBE re-used and mapped over past explanations to new situations [5], [6]. It employed the structure mapping model of analogical reasoning developed by Gentner and others [10], [11], [13]. Koton's CASEY used a causal model of heart disease and a calculus of explanatory differences to adapt a previous explanation to diagnose a new patient's symptoms [19]. Kass, Leake and Owen's SWALE directly addressed the problem of explaining a phenomenon—particularly an unexpected one like the collapse of a racehorse in the prime of its life—by recalling and adapting relevant past explanations [50]. Leake's work also illustrated the centrality of explanations by showing how they can serve many different goals, for system reasoning as well as external performance tasks [22].

More recently, CBR has been used to foster learning of how to perform specialized types of explanation like appellate argument. Aleven and Ashley's CATO tackled the task of teaching law students how to make good precedent-based arguments [2], [3]. McLaren's SIROCCO used examples to help explain ethics principles [30]. In his research, Aleven demonstrated that CATO-trained law students do as well as those trained in the traditional ways involving written and oral exercises [2]. This comports well with what has been found experimentally in psychology.

Psychologists have shown that explicit comparison of past exemplars with a new instance can promote more nuanced and better learning. This is true across a whole range of learners from toddlers to business school students. For instance, Gentner showed that exploring explicit analogical mappings in a concept categorization task can lead to better categorization in the sense that the children focused more on deep properties (like functionality) rather than on shallow ones (like appearance) [20], [35]. Business school students were better able to choose the appropriate negotiation strategy for a new problem case when they had already practiced making analogical comparisons [25].

The examples and cases so vital to CBR and explanation can themselves be constructed using CBR. Example generation is the twin task to example interpretation. In it one creates examples that meet specified criteria; these typically serve the needs of other processes like explanation, argument, teaching, supervised learning, etc. CEG can be viewed as a design task. In my lab, we developed a "retrieval-plus-modify" architecture for creating examples satisfying such prescribed constraints, and called it *Constrained Example Generation* or CEG [39], [47]. In CEG, a person or machine tries to satisfy as many of the desiderata as possible by retrieval—that is, finding examples that possess as many of them as possible, and then trying to satisfy the remaining properties through modification. This is essentially "adaptive" CBR. However, given the nasty way that constraints can interact, this is not easy. A fuller model of example generation should integrate techniques from constraint satisfaction problem (CSP) solving into CEG. There has been important work on CSP and on integrating CBR and CSP since CEG was developed (See [27], [28]).

CEG was initially directed at generating counter-examples in mathematics and grew into a larger effort to explore the use of examples in other types of explanations (e.g., on-line help systems) and arguments (e.g., appellate-style legal argument) [48]. Counter-examples are like designs having specified properties. For instance, if one wants to show that not all continuous functions are necessarily differentiable, that not all quadrilaterals are necessarily convex, that not all primes are odd, one needs examples that possess precise mathematical properties. Such closely crafted examples are pivotal in the dialectic of proofs and refutations—they can annihilate conjectures and force concept change, for instance [21], [36], [41]. Examples of various types—startup, reference, counter, etc.—play a very important role in developing understanding in mathematics [38]. Where such interesting examples come from is an intriguing question. One answer is through an adaptive process like CEG.

Generating hypotheticals can also be viewed as a kind of CEG task, and thus amenable to adaptive methods. For instance, hypos can be created by taking a seed case and making it more extreme, or by combining two hypos to create a conflict hypo [42]. Hypos can be used with surgical precision in oral argument and law school dialogues to show the limits of a line of reasoning or to uncover fatal flaws in its logic [40]. The reasoning context provides the desiderata for the hypos and a CBR process can be used to produce them. The HYPO system actually grew out of our work on examples and hypos using the CEG approach [48].

The study of legal explanations, including argument, is a rich area for study and it can provide us both with interesting data to "explain" and learn from, and with interesting techniques to borrow and apply in other domains. For instance, if we want to build CBR systems that can analogize and distinguish cases as a way of explaining why a particular outcome should obtain, there is a plethora of examples from law that we can examine. There are many kinds of legal argument moves and strategies—slippery slope, strawman, chicken-turkey-fish, reduction loop—that can profitably be used in non-legal domains as well [51].

While there have indeed been many insightful landmark systems on explanation and argument, they have by no means exhausted the topic. It's time to push the envelope further.

4 Conclusion

In summary, in my talk I focus on explanations and CBR, and the larger issue of what can be accomplished in the post-retrieval stages of CBR. This is not to diminsh the importance of similarity assessment and of retrieval in CBR, but rather to suggest that we cannot ignore what happens once relevant cases have been retrieved. Some of the most interesting work for CBR—adapting old solutions to solve new problems, using existing precedents to interpret new facts—is done post-retrieval. Of late, we have shied away from these stages of CBR, some of which I grant can be quite difficult. But for us to miss out on all the post-retrieval fun in CBR would indeed be a shame.

Acknowledgments

I acknowledge the support of the US National Science Foundation in preparing this article. Any opinions, findings, conclusions, or recommendations expressed in this material are my own and do not necessarily reflect the views of the NSF. I also thank David Leake for his generous feedback.

References

1. Aamodt, A. & Plaza, E. "Case-Based Reasoning: Foundational Issues, Methodological Variations, and System Approaches." *Artificial Intelligence Communications*, IOS Press, 7(1): 39-59, 1994.
2. Aleven, V. "Using background knowledge in case-based legal reasoning: A computational model and an intelligent learning environment." *Artificial Intelligence*. 150(1-2): 183-237, 2003.

3. Aleven, V. & Ashley, K.D. "Automated Generation of Examples for a Tutorial in Case-Based Argumentation." *Second International Conference on Intelligent Tutoring Systems* (ITS-92), pp. 575-584, 1992.
4. Ashley, K.D. *Modeling Legal Argument: Reasoning with Cases and Hypotheticals.* MIT Press, 1990.
5. Branting, L.K. "Building Explanations from rules and structured cases." *International Journal of Man-Machine Studies,* (34)6: 797-837, June, 1991.
6. Branting, L.K. *Reasoning with Rules and Precedents.* Kluwer, 2000.
7. Bridge, D. "The Virtue of Reward: Performance, Reinforcement, and Discovery in Case-Based Reasoning." Invited talk, *Proceedings 6th International Conference on Case-Based Reasoning (ICCBR 2005).* Chicago, August, 2005.
8. Cheetham, W. "Tenth Anniversary of the Plastics Color Formulation Tool." *AI Magazine,* 26(3): 51-61, 2005.
9. Daniels, J.J., & Rissland, E.L. "What You Saw Is What You Want: Using Cases to Seed Information Retrieval." *Case-Based Reasoning Research and Development* (Springer Lecture Notes in Artificial Intelligence No. 1266) the *Proceedings Second International Conference on Case-Based Reasoning, ICCBR-97,* Providence, July 1997, pp. 325-337.
10. Falkenhainer, B, Forbus, K.D. & Gentner, D. "The structure-mapping engine: algorithm and examples." *Artificial Intelligence.* 41(1): 1-63, 1989.
11. Forbus, K., Gentner, D., & Law, K. "MAC/FAC: A model of similarity-based retrieval." *Cognitive Science,* 19, pp.141-205, 1994.
12. Gardner, A vdL. *An Artificial Intelligence Approach to Legal Reasoning.* MIT Press, 1987.
13. Gentner, D. "Structure-mapping: A theoretical framework for analogy." *Cognitive Science,* 7(2): 155-170, 1983.
14. Göker, M., & Roth-Berghofer, T. "Development and utilization of a Case-Based Help desk Support Sytem in a Corporate Environment." *Proceedings Third International Conference on CBR,* pp. 132-146, 1999.
15. Golding, A.R. & Rosenbloom, P.S. "Improving rule-based systems through case-based reasoning." *Proceedings of the Ninth National Conference on Artificial Intelligence* (AAAI-91), pp. 22-27, 1991.
16. Hammond, K. J. *Case-based planning.* Academic Press, 1989.
17. Hastings, J., Branting, L.K., & Lockwood, J. "CARMA: A case-based rangeland management advisor." *AI Magazine,* 23(2): 49-62, 2002.
18. Kolodner, J.L. *Case-Based Reasoning.* Morgan-Kaufman, 1993.
19. Koton, P. "Reasoning about evidence in causal explanation." *Proceedings Seventh National on Artificial Intelligence (AAAI-88),* pp. 256-261.
20. Kotovsky, L., & Gentner, D. "Comparison and categorization in the development of relational similarity." *Child Development,* 67, 2797-2822, 1986.
21. Lakatos, I. *Proofs and Refutations: The Logic of Mathematical Discovery.* Cambridge University Press, 1976.
22. Leake, D. B. *Evaluating Explanations: A Content Theory.* Lawrence Erlbaum, 1992.
23. Leake, D. B. (ed). *Case-Based Reasoning: Experiences, Lessons, & Future Directions.* AAAI Press/MIT Press, 1996.
24. Leake, D.B., & McSherry, D. (eds). *Artificial Intelligence Review:* Special Issue on Case-Based Reasoning and Explanation, 24(2), 2005.
25. Loewenstein, J., Thompson, L. & Gentner, D. "Analogical encoding facilitates knowledge transfer in negotiation." *Psychonomic Bulletin & Review,* 6, pp. 586-597, 1999.
26. Marling, C.R., Petot, G.J., & Sterling, L.S. "Integrating case-based and rule-based reasoning to meet multiple design constraints." *Computational Intelligence* 15(3): 308-332, 1999.

27. Marling, C., Muñoz-Avila, H., Rissland, E.L., Sqalli, M., & Aha, D. "Case-Based Reasoning Integrations." *AI Magazine*, 23(1): 69-86, Spring 2002.
28. Marling, C., Rissland, E.L., & Aamodt, A. "Integrations with case-based reasoning." *Knowledge Engineering Review*, 20(3), Special issue on Case-Based Reasoning, 2006.
29. McCarty, L.T. & Sridharan, N.S. "The Representation of an Evolving System of Legal Concepts: I. Logical Templates." *Proceedings Third National Conference of the Canadian Society for Computational Studies of Intelligence*, Victoria May 1980, pp. 304-311.
30. McLaren, B.M. "Extensionally defining principles and cases in ethics: An AI model." *Artificial Intelligence*. 150(1-2): 145-181, 2003.
31. McSherry, D. "Explanation in Recommender Systems." In Leake, D.B., and McSherry, D. (eds). *Artificial Intelligence Review*: Special Issue on Case-Based Reasoning and Explanation, 24(2), 2005.
32. Medin, D. "Concepts and conceptual structure." *American Psychologist*, 44, pp.1469-1481, 1989.
33. Medin, D.L. & Shaffer, M.M. "Context theory of classification learning." *Psychological Review*, 85, pp.207-238, 1978.
34. Murphy, G.L. *The Big Book of Concepts*. MIT Press, 2002.
35. Namy, L.L., & Gentner, D. "Making a silk purse out of two sows' ears: Young children's use of comparison in category learning." *Journal of Experimental Psychology: General, 131*, pp. 5-15, 2002.
36. Polya, G. *Mathematical Discovery*. Volume 2. John Wiley & Sons, 1965.
37. Reilly, J., McCarthy, K., McGinty, L., & Smyth, B. "Explaining Compound Critiques". In Leake, D.B., and McSherry, D. (eds). *Artificial Intelligence Review*: Special Issue on Case-Based Reasoning and Explanation, 24(2), 2005.
38. Rissland, E. (Michener) "Understanding Understanding Mathematics." *Cognitive Science*, 2(4): 361-383, 1978.
39. Rissland, E.L. "Example Generation." *Proceedings Third National Conference of the Canadian Society for Computational Studies of Intelligence*, Victoria, May 1980, pp. 280-288.
40. Rissland, E.L. "Examples in Legal Reasoning: Legal Hypotheticals." *Proceedings Eighth International Joint Conference on Artificial Intelligence (IJCAI-83)*. Karlsruhe, August 1983, pp. 90-93.
41. Rissland, E.L. "The Ubiquitous Dialectic." *Proceedings Sixth European Conference on Artificial Intelligence* (ECAI-84), Pisa, pp. 367-372, North Holland, 1984.
42. Rissland, E.L., & Ashley, K.D. "Hypotheticals as Heuristic Device." *Proceedings Fifth National Conference on Artificial Intelligence (AAAI-86)*, Philadelphia,, pp. 289-297, 1986.
43. Rissland, E.L. & Ashley, K.D., & Loui. R.P. "AI and Law: A Fruitful Synergy." *Artificial Intelligence*. 150(1-2): 1-15, 2003.
44. Rissland, E.L. & Daniels, J.J. "Using CBR to Drive IR." *Proceedings Fourteenth International Joint Conference on Artificial Intelligence (IJCAI-95)*, Montreal, pp. 400-407, 1995.
45. Rissland, E.L. & Daniels, J.J. "The Synergistic Application of CBR to IR". *Artificial Intelligence Review*: Special Issue on the use of AI in Information Retrieval, 10, pp. 441-475, 1996.
46. Rissland, E.L., & Skalak, D.B. "CABARET: Statutory Interpretation in a Hybrid Architecture." *International Journal of Man-Machine Studies*, 34(6): 839-887, June 1991.
47. Rissland, E.L., & Soloway, E.M. "Overview of an Example Generation System." *Proceedings First National Conference on Artificial Intelligence (AAAI-80)*, Stanford, pp. 256-258, 1980

48. Rissland, E.L., Valcarce, E.M., & Ashley, K.D. "Explaining and Arguing with Examples." *Proceedings Fourth National on Artificial Intelligence (AAAI-84),* Austin, pp. 288-294, 1984

49. Rosch, E, & Mervais, C.B. "Family resemblance: Studies in the internal structure of categories." *Cognitive Psychology* 7: 573-605, 1975.

50. Schank, R.C., & Leake, D.B., "Creativity and Learning in a Case-Based Explainer." Artificial Intelligence, 40(1-3): 353-385, 1989.

51. Skalak, D.B. & Rissland, E.L. "Arguments and Cases: An Inevitable Intertwining." *Artificial Intelligence and Law,* 1(1): 3-44, 1992.

52. Smith, E.E., & Medin, D.L. *Categories and Concepts.* Harvard University Press, 1981.

Completeness Criteria for Retrieval in Recommender Systems

David McSherry

School of Computing and Information Engineering
University of Ulster, Coleraine BT52 1SA, Northern Ireland
dmg.mcsherry@ulster.ac.uk

Abstract. Often in practice, a recommender system query may include constraints that must be satisfied. Ensuring the retrieval of a product that satisfies any hard constraints in a given query, if such a product exists, is one benefit of a retrieval criterion we refer to as *completeness*. Other benefits include the ease with which the *non-existence* of an acceptable product can often be recognized from the results for a given query, and the ability to justify the exclusion of any product from the retrieval set on the basis that one of the retrieved products satisfies at least the same constraints. We show that in contrast to most retrieval strategies, compromise driven retrieval (CDR) is complete. Another important benefit of CDR is its ability to ensure the retrieval of the *most similar* product, if any, which satisfies all the hard constraints in a given query, a criterion we refer to as *optimal* completeness.

1 Introduction

In case-based reasoning (CBR) approaches to product recommendation, descriptions of available products are stored in a product case base and retrieved in response to user queries. The standard CBR approach to retrieval in recommender systems is k nearest neighbor (k-NN) retrieval. In contrast to traditional database retrieval, k-NN does not insist on exact matching, thus having the advantage that the retrieval set (i.e., the k most similar cases) is never empty [1].

Regardless of the strategy on which the retrieval of recommended cases is based, a query can also be seen as a set of *constraints*. For example, the preferred attribute values in a k-NN query are *equality* constraints that may or may not be satisfied by a given case. One approach to retrieval in CBR that takes account of the constraints satisfied by a given case is compromise driven retrieval (CDR) [2-3]. For example, no case that is less similar than another case which satisfies the same constraints is included in the CDR retrieval set.

While no account is taken of satisfied constraints in k-NN, cases which satisfy more constraints may also tend to be more similar. However, there is often a conflict between the goals of retrieval strategies like k-NN which reward cases on the basis of overall similarity and those which take account of the constraints satisfied by a given case. As we show in Section 2, for example, it is possible for a case that satisfies a proper subset of the constraints satisfied by another case to be more similar. Also, an

T.R. Roth-Berghofer et al. (Eds.): ECCBR 2006, LNAI 4106, pp. 9–29, 2006.
© Springer-Verlag Berlin Heidelberg 2006

issue that k-NN only partly addresses by offering the user a choice of k alternatives is that often in practice a given query may include constraints that must be satisfied.

In a holiday recommender, for example, a user seeking a skiing holiday for two persons in December may be unable to compromise on the number of persons and unwilling to compromise on holiday type. If the k most similar cases do not include a skiing holiday for two persons then the system has failed to recommend an acceptable case. It might be considered that even with $k = 3$ there is a good chance that an acceptable case, if one exists, will be retrieved. However, k-NN is known to be limited in its coverage of cases that may be acceptable to the user, or *compromises* that the user may be prepared to consider (e.g., the timing of the holiday) [2-5]. A related problem is that the most similar cases also tend to be very similar to each other, with the result that the user may be offered a limited choice [6-8].

Ensuring the retrieval of a case that satisfies any hard constraints, if such a case exists, is the weaker of two *completeness* criteria for retrieval in recommender systems that we present in this paper. Of course, it is a simple matter to ensure the retrieval of a case that satisfies any *known* hard constraints in a given query if such a case exists. However, requiring users to identify hard constraints in advance may not be a realistic solution. Often in practice, a user may not have a clear idea of what she is looking for when constructing her query, and may begin to consider hard constraints only when faced with the need to compromise. Instead we assume that any hard constraints in a given query are *unknown* to the recommender system and therefore that no distinction is made between hard and soft constraints in the retrieval process.

In the formal definition of completeness that we now present, we refer to a case that satisfies all the hard constraints in a given query as a *feasible* case for the query. Whether such a case is acceptable to the user may of course depend on the extent to which it satisfies any soft constraints in her query. However, the non-existence of a feasible case in the case base implies the non-existence of an acceptable case. Equally, the non-existence of a feasible case in the retrieval set means that none of the recommended cases are acceptable.

Completeness. *We say that a retrieval strategy is complete if the retrieval set for any query is guaranteed to include a feasible case if such a case exists.*

Ensuring the retrieval of a case that may be acceptable to the user whenever possible is just one advantage of completeness. In Section 3, we show that *only* in a complete retrieval strategy can the exclusion of any case from the retrieval set always be justified on the basis that one of the retrieved cases satisfies at least the same constraints as the non-retrieved case. As we show in Theorem 1, another benefit of completeness is the ease with which the *non-existence* of an acceptable case can often be recognized from the results for a given query — an issue often neglected in recommender systems.

Theorem 1. *In a complete retrieval strategy, the non-existence of a feasible case in the retrieval set implies the non-existence of an acceptable case in the case base.*

Proof. Immediate from the definition of completeness.

As we show in Section 4, k-NN is incomplete regardless of the size of the retrieval set. We also show that it is possible for a retrieval strategy that takes no account of a retrieved case's similarity to be complete. An important question, therefore, is whether the benefits of completeness can be combined with those to be gained by taking account of similarity knowledge. For example, enabling an otherwise competitive case to *compensate* for its failure to satisfy one or more of the constraints satisfied by another case is an important advantage of k-NN. Moreover, a complete retrieval strategy that fails to retrieve the *most similar* case ignores the possibility that it may be the best option for the user if none of her requirements are hard constraints.

The role of similarity in balancing trade-offs between competing products is implicit in our definition of *optimal* completeness, the second of our completeness criteria for retrieval in recommender systems.

Optimal Completeness. *We say that a retrieval strategy is optimally complete if the retrieval set for any query is guaranteed to include a case that is maximally similar among the feasible cases, if any, in the case base.*

Ensuring the retrieval of the most similar feasible case, or one that is maximally similar, is likely to be of most benefit when there are many feasible cases for a given query — which is not unlikely if most of the constraints in a given query are soft constraints. As we show in Theorem 2, optimal completeness also ensures the retrieval of the most similar case in the case base.

Theorem 2. *In an optimally complete retrieval strategy, the retrieval set for any query must include the most similar case.*

Proof. It suffices to observe that if none of the constraints in a given query are hard constraints, then all the available cases are feasible cases.

As we show in Section 4, CDR [2-3] is optimally complete, thus ensuring the retrieval of the most similar case as in k-NN. Enabling an otherwise competitive case to compensate for its failure to satisfy one or more of the constraints satisfied by another case is another important feature that CDR shares with k-NN.

In Section 2, we use an example case base to illustrate some of the limitations of k-NN that are well known and others that have received less attention. We also show that some of the problems highlighted can be attributed to the incompleteness of k-NN. In Section 3, we present necessary and sufficient conditions for completeness and optimal completeness that can be used to determine whether these criteria are satisfied by a given retrieval strategy. In Section 4, we show that while most retrieval strategies used in CBR recommender systems are incomplete, CDR is optimally complete. Related work is discussed in Section 5, and our conclusions are presented in Section 6.

2   Limitations of k-NN

Increasing awareness of the limitations of k-NN in CBR recommender systems has prompted significant research interest in alternative retrieval strategies (e.g., [2-16]). A detailed account of the issues addressed by this important body of research is beyond the scope of the present discussion. Instead we use an example case base in the property domain to illustrate some of the limitations of k-NN that are well known and others that have received less attention. We also show that some of problems highlighted can be attributed to the incompleteness of k-NN.

For example, an issue often neglected in recommender systems is that none of the available cases (i.e., products) may be acceptable to the user. If none of the available cases satisfies all the hard constraints in a given query, it is reasonable to expect that the *non-existence* of an acceptable case should be clear to the user from the system's response to her query. As shown in Section 1, an important benefit of completeness is that the non-existence of an acceptable case can always be inferred from the non-existence of a feasible case in the retrieval set for a given query.

Although k-NN is incomplete, it may be possible for a user with a good understanding of similarity to infer the non-existence of an acceptable case from the non-existence of a feasible case in the k-NN retrieval set. For example, it may be clear to such a user that a feasible case, if one existed, would be more similar than any of the recommended cases and would thus be included in the k-NN retrieval set. In general, however, the non-existence of an acceptable case cannot be inferred from the non-existence of a feasible case in the k-NN retrieval set. Before presenting the example that we use to clarify this important point, we outline a typical approach to similarity assessment in CBR recommender systems.

Global Similarity Measure. The similarity of a case C to a given query Q is typically defined as:

$$Sim(C, Q) = \frac{\sum_{a \in A} w_a \times sim_a(C, Q)}{\sum_{a \in A} w_a} \tag{1}$$

where A is the set of attributes for which preferred values are specified in Q. For each $a \in A$, w_a is an importance weight assigned to a and $sim_a(C, Q)$ is a *local* measure of the similarity between the attribute's values in C and Q.

Local Similarity Measures. Local similarity measures are often defined in terms of an attribute's values without reference to a specific query or case. For example, the similarity of two values x and y of a numeric attribute is typically defined as:

$$sim(x, y) = 1 - \frac{|x - y|}{max - min} \tag{2}$$

where max and min are the attribute's maximum and minimum values in the case base.

2.1 Example Case Base

Fig. 1 shows an example case base and query in the property domain that we use to illustrate some of the limitations of k-NN. The equally weighted attributes in the case base are location (A, B, or C), bedrooms (2, 3, or 4), type (detached, semi-detached, or terraced), and reception rooms (1, 2, or 3). The user is looking for a 4 bedroom detached property in location A with 3 reception rooms (RRs). The similarity of each case to the target query is shown in the rightmost column. Similarity assessment with respect to location and type is based on the similarity scores: $sim(A, A) = 1$, $sim(B, A) = 0.5$, $sim(C, A) = 0$, $sim(det, det) = 1$, $sim(sem, det) = 0.5$, $sim(ter, det) = 0$. The standard similarity measure for numeric attributes (2) is used for bedrooms and reception rooms.

	Loc	Beds	Type	RRs					
Query	A	4	det	3	**Constraints**				**Similarity**
Case 1	B	4	det	3	N	Y	Y	Y	0.88
Case 2	C	4	det	3	N	Y	Y	Y	0.75
Case 3	A	3	sem	2	Y	N	N	N	0.63
Case 4	A	3	ter	2	Y	N	N	N	0.50
Case 5	A	2	det	1	Y	N	Y	N	0.50

Fig. 1. Example case base and query in the property domain

Constraints in the example query that each case satisfies, or fails to satisfy, are indicated by the entries (Y or N) in the four columns to the right of each case in Fig. 1. No case satisfies all the constraints, a situation that would result in a query failure in traditional database retrieval. In the following sections, we briefly examine some of the issues highlighted by the 3-NN retrieval set for the example query (i.e., the three cases that are not shaded in Fig. 1).

2.2   Recognizing the Non-existence of an Acceptable Case

If $loc = A$ and $beds = 4$ are hard constraints in the example query, then *none* of the available cases are acceptable to the user. But the user is unable to tell from the system's response to her query that there is no acceptable case. For example, she might be prepared to consider a 4 bedroom terraced property in location A with one reception room. But if such a case existed, it would not appear in the 3-NN retrieval set as its similarity to the user's query (0.50) would be less than the similarities of Cases 1, 2, and 3.

2.3   Coverage of Available Cases

As mentioned in the introduction, k-NN is known to be limited in its coverage of cases that may be acceptable to the user [2-5]. For example, if $loc = A$ and $type = det$ are hard constraints in the example query, then 3-NN has failed to retrieve the only case that might be acceptable to the user (i.e., Case 5). However, it can be seen from our definition of completeness (Section 1) that no complete retrieval strategy can fail to retrieve Case 5, the only feasible case in this situation. Thus k-NN's limited coverage of cases that may be acceptable to the user can be attributed to its incompleteness.

2.4 Explaining Why a Case is Not Recommended

If asked to explain why Case 5 is not recommended in 3-NN, the system could point to three recommended cases that are more similar than Case 5, including two that match the given query exactly on bedrooms, type and reception rooms and one that matches it exactly on location. However, such an explanation is unlikely to satisfy a user who is unwilling to compromise on location or type. Of course, one reason why current recommender systems are seldom required to explain their failure to recommend a case which — in the user's opinion — should have been recommended is that the only cases that most users see are those recommended by the system. Nevertheless, explaining why a given case is not recommended is an important test of a system's ability to justify its recommendations [10, 12].

As we show in Section 3, it is *only* in a complete retrieval strategy that the exclusion of a given case from the retrieval set can always be justified on the basis that one of the retrieved cases satisfies at least the same constraints. As the above example shows, k-NN's failure to retrieve a given case cannot always be justified in this way — another limitation of k-NN that can be attributed to its incompleteness.

2.5 Recommendation Diversity

The first two cases in the 3-NN retrieval set are very similar to each other, and both satisfy the same constraints. One might argue, of course, that this makes good sense in a domain in which the recommended cases (i.e., properties) are sought in competition with other users. However, the recommendation engineering technique of providing the user with a link from each retrieved case to non-retrieved cases which satisfy the same constraints provides a simple solution to this problem in any retrieval strategy [14].

Retrieval strategies that aim to increase recommendation diversity by combining measures of similarity and diversity in the retrieval process [7-8] are discussed in Section 4. Instead of relying on a measure of diversity to guide the retrieval process, CDR [2-3] addresses the issue of recommendation diversity by ensuring that no two cases in the retrieval set satisfy the same constraints. Thus for the example query in Fig. 1, the CDR retrieval set would include Case 1 (N Y Y Y) and Case 3 (Y N N N) but not Case 2 (N Y Y Y) or Case 4 (Y N N N).

3 Completeness and Optimal Completeness

In this section, we formally define the concepts on which our completeness criteria are based. We also establish necessary and sufficient conditions for completeness and optimal completeness that can be used to determine whether or not these criteria are satisfied by a given retrieval strategy.

Retrieval Set. *Given a retrieval strategy S, we denote by r(S, Q) the set of cases that are retrieved in response to a given query Q.*

For example, $r(k\text{-NN}, Q)$ is the set of k cases that are most similar to Q. To distinguish k-NN from the unrealistic strategy of retrieving all the available cases, we assume that $1 \leq k < n$, where n is the number of cases.

Query Constraints. *For any query Q, we denote by constraints(Q) the set of all constraints in Q.*

In addition to the *equality* constraints supported by any retrieval strategy, the constraints in a recommender system query might include upper and/or lower limits for numeric attributes and *sets* of preferred values for nominal attributes [2, 10, 13].

Hard Constraints. *For any query Q, we denote by hard-constraints(Q) the set of hard constraints in Q.*

As mentioned in the introduction, we assume that any hard constraints in a given query are *unknown* to the recommender system.

Satisfied Constraints. *For any case C and query Q, we denote by satisfied-constraints(C, Q) the set of constraints in Q that are satisfied by C.*

Feasible Case. *For any case C and query Q, we say that C is a feasible case for Q if hard-constraints(Q) $\subseteq$ satisfied-constraints(C, Q).*

Exactly Matching Case. *We say that a case C exactly matches a given query Q if satisfied-constraints(C, Q) = constraints(Q).*

As well as providing a necessary and sufficient condition for completeness, Theorem 3 confirms our claim that *only* in a complete retrieval strategy can the exclusion of any case from the retrieval set always be justified on the basis that one of the retrieved cases satisfies at least the same constraints as the non-retrieved case.

Theorem 3. *A retrieval strategy S is complete if and only if for any query Q and $C_1 \notin r(S, Q)$, there exists $C_2 \in r(S, Q)$ such that satisfied-constraints(C_1, Q) $\subseteq$ satisfied-constraints(C_2, Q).*

Proof. If the latter condition holds, and C_1 is a feasible case for a given query Q, then *hard-constraints(Q) $\subseteq$ satisfied-constraints(C_1, Q)* and there exists $C_2 \in r(S, Q)$ such that *satisfied-constraints(C_1, Q) $\subseteq$ satisfied-constraints(C_2, Q)*. We have established as required the existence of $C_2 \in r(S, Q)$ such that *hard-constraints(Q) $\subseteq$ satisfied-constraints(C_2, Q)*. Conversely, if S is a complete retrieval strategy then for any query Q and $C_1 \notin r(S, Q)$ we can construct another query Q' that differs from Q, if at all, only in that *hard-constraints(Q') = satisfied-constraints(C_1, Q)*. As *satisfied-constraints(C_1, Q') = satisfied-constraints(C_1, Q)*, C_1 is a feasible case for Q', so it follows by the completeness of S that there exists $C_2 \in r(S, Q')$ such that *hard-constraints(Q') $\subseteq$ satisfied-constraints(C_2, Q')*. As we assume that no distinction is made between hard and soft constraints in the retrieval process, $r(S, Q') = r(S, Q)$, and so we have established the existence of $C_2 \in r(S, Q)$ such that *satisfied-constraints(C_1, Q) = hard-constraints(Q') $\subseteq$ satisfied-constraints(C_2, Q') = satisfied-constraints(C_2, Q)*.

As we show in Theorem 4, a necessary and sufficient condition for *optimal completeness* is that the exclusion of any case from the retrieval set can always be justified on the basis that one of the retrieved cases is at least as similar as the non-retrieved case, and satisfies at least the same constraints.

Theorem 4. *A retrieval strategy S is optimally complete if and only if for any query Q and $C_1 \notin r(S, Q)$, there exists $C_2 \in r(S, Q)$ such that similarity(C_1, Q) ≤ similarity(C_2, Q) and satisfied-constraints(C_1, Q) ⊆ satisfied-constraints(C_2, Q).*

Proof. Assuming that the latter condition holds, let Q be any query for which a feasible case exists, and let C_1 be a feasible case of *maximal* similarity to Q. If $C_1 \in r(S, Q)$ there is nothing more to prove, while if $C_1 \notin r(S, Q)$ then there exists $C_2 \in r(S, Q)$ such that *similarity*(C_1, Q) ≤ *similarity*(C_2, Q) and *satisfied-constraints*(C_1, Q) ⊆ *satisfied-constraints*(C_2, Q). Since *hard-constraints*(Q) ⊆ *satisfied-constraints*(C_1, Q) ⊆ *satisfied-constraints*(C_2, Q), C_2 is a feasible case and so *similarity*(C_2, Q) ≤ *similarity*(C_1, Q). It follows that *similarity*(C_2, Q) = *similarity*(C_1, Q), so we have established as required the existence of a feasible case of maximal similarity $C_2 \in r(S, Q)$.

Conversely, if S is optimally complete then for any query Q and $C_1 \notin r(S, Q)$ we can construct another query Q' that differs from Q, if at all, only in that *hard-constraints*(Q') = *satisfied-constraints*(C_1, Q). As C_1 is a feasible case for Q', it follows by the optimal completeness of S that there exists $C_2 \in r(S, Q')$ of maximal similarity among all cases C such that *hard-constraints*(Q') ⊆ *satisfied-constraints*(C, Q'). In particular, *hard-constraints*(Q') = *satisfied-constraints*(C_1, Q) = *satisfied-constraints*(C_1, Q') and so *similarity*(C_1, Q) = *similarity*(C_1, Q') ≤ *similarity*(C_2, Q') = *similarity*(C_2, Q). As we assume that no distinction is made between hard and soft constraints in the retrieval process, $r(S, Q') = r(S, Q)$, and so we have established the existence of $C_2 \in r(S, Q)$ such that *similarity*(C_1, Q) ≤ *similarity*(C_2, Q) and *satisfied-constraints*(C_1, Q) = *hard-constraints*(Q') ⊆ *satisfied-constraints*(C_2, Q') = *satisfied-constraints*(C_2, Q).

When the number of constraints in a given query is small, is not unusual for one or more exactly matching cases to be available. In this situation, a single recommended case (i.e., any exactly matching case) is enough to satisfy the condition for completeness in Theorem 3. Equally, a single recommended case (i.e., the most similar of the exactly matching cases) is enough to satisfy the condition for optimal completeness in Theorem 4.

4   Comparison of Retrieval Strategies

In this section we compare six possible approaches to retrieval in recommender systems with respect to the following criteria:

1. Is the most similar case always retrieved?
2. Is a feasible case always retrieved if such a case exists?
3. Is the most similar feasible case always retrieved if there is more than one feasible case?

Ensuring the retrieval of the most similar case, the first of the above criteria, is of course a feature of most retrieval strategies in CBR recommender systems. Criteria 2 and 3 are the criteria for completeness and optimal completeness that we use to assess the effectiveness of retrieval when, as often in practice, a given query may include constraints that must be satisfied.

4.1 k-NN Retrieval

As discussed in Section 1, the standard approach to the retrieval of recommended cases in CBR has some important advantages, such as ensuring the retrieval of the most similar case for a given query. As we show in Theorem 5, however, k-NN is incomplete regardless of the size of the retrieval set; that is, the existence of a feasible case does not guarantee that such a case will be retrieved.

Theorem 5. k-NN *is incomplete regardless of the size of the retrieval set.*

Proof. For any $k \geq 3$, we can construct a case base with $k + 1$ cases $C_1, C_2, ..., C_{k+1}$ and $k + 1$ equally weighted attributes $a_1, a_2, ..., a_{k+1}$ such that for $1 \leq i \leq k + 1$, $a_i = 1$ in all cases with the following exceptions: (1) for $1 \leq i \leq k$, $a_i = 0$ in C_{k+1}, (2) for $1 \leq i \leq k$, $a_i = 0$ in C_i, and (3) for $1 \leq i \leq k$, $a_{k+1} = 0$ in C_i. For $k = 3$, the cases in the resulting case base are:

$$C_1 = (0, 1, 1, 0), \ C_2 = (1, 0, 1, 0), \ C_3 = (1, 1, 0, 0), \ C_4 = (0, 0, 0, 1)$$

Now consider the query $Q = \{a_i = 1: 1 \leq i \leq k + 1\}$. It can be seen that for $1 \leq i \leq k$, $Sim(C_i, Q) = \dfrac{k-1}{k+1}$ while $Sim(C_{k+1}, Q) = \dfrac{1}{k+1}$. The k-NN retrieval set therefore includes all cases in the case base except C_{k+1}. It can also be seen that while *satisfied-constraints*$(C_{k+1}, Q) = \{a_{k+1} = 1\}$, there is no case in the k-NN retrieval set which satisfies the constraint $a_{k+1} = 1$. There is therefore no case C in the k-NN retrieval set such that *satisfied-constraints*$(C, Q) \subseteq$ *satisfied-constraints*(C_{k+1}, Q). It follows from Theorem 3 that for $k \geq 3$, k-NN is incomplete. It remains only to observe that as k-NN is incomplete for $k = 3$ it must also be incomplete for $k = 2$ and $k = 1$.

An important corollary of Theorem 5 is that any retrieval strategy in which the cases retrieved for a given query are selected from the k-NN retrieval set is incomplete.

Theorem 6. *Any retrieval strategy S in which the retrieved cases are selected from the* k-NN *retrieval set is incomplete.*

Proof. As k-NN is incomplete by Theorem 5, there exists for any $k \geq 1$ a case base, a query Q, and a case $C_1 \notin r(k$-NN, $Q)$ for which there is no case $C_2 \in r(k$-NN, $Q)$ such that *satisfied-constraints*$(C_1, Q) \subseteq$ *satisfied-constraints*(C_2, Q). As $r(S, Q) \subseteq r(k$-NN, $Q)$ it follows that $C_1 \notin r(S, Q)$ and there can be no case $C_2 \in r(S, Q)$ such that *satisfied-constraints*$(C_1, Q) \subseteq$ *satisfied-constraints*(C_2, Q). Thus S is incomplete as required.

4.2 Database Retrieval

Often referred to as filter based retrieval, traditional database retrieval (DBR) insists on exact matching:

$$r(DBR, Q) = \{C: \textit{satisfied-constraints}(C, Q) = \textit{constraints}(Q)\}$$

If there is no case (or database object) that satisfies all the constraints in a given query, then the DBR retrieval set is empty and the user has no alternative but to start again with a modified query [1, 17].

Theorem 7. DBR *is incomplete.*

Proof. It suffices to observe that if none of the constraints in a given query are hard constraints then *any* case is a feasible case but the DBR retrieval set may still be empty.

DBR is not guaranteed to retrieve the most similar case for a given query, or indeed any case. Another drawback is that for queries with only a few constraints, the user may be swamped by a large number of exactly matching cases (or database objects) [17].

4.3 Retrieval of Non-dominated Cases

In database research, there is increasing interest in the retrieval of database objects that are Pareto optimal with respect to the preferences expressed in a given query (i.e., not *dominated* by another object) as an approach to addressing the limitations of retrieval based on exact matching [17-18]. Elimination of dominated alternatives is also a strategy sometimes used to reduce the number of candidates to be compared by other methods in multiple criteria decision making [19-20]. With respect to each constraint in a recommender system query, it is reasonable to assume that any case that satisfies the constraint is preferred to one that does not satisfy the constraint. A possible approach to retrieval of recommended cases is therefore one in which the retrieval set consists of all cases that are not dominated with respect to the constraints they satisfy. We will refer to this strategy as retrieval of non-dominated cases (RNC).

	Constraints				Similarity	RNC	3-NN	CDR
Case 1	N	Y	Y	Y	0.88	•	•	•
Case 2	N	Y	Y	Y	0.75	•	•	
Case 3	Y	N	N	N	0.63		•	•
Case 4	Y	N	N	N	0.50			
Case 5	Y	N	Y	N	0.50	•		•

Fig. 2. Cases retrieved (•) by RNC, 3-NN, and CDR for the example case base and query in the property domain

Dominance Criterion. *We say that a given case C_1 is dominated by another case C_2 with respect to a given query if C_2 satisfies every constraint that C_1 satisfies and at least one constraint that C_1 does not satisfy.*

It is worth noting that RNC is equivalent to retrieving the maxima with respect to a partial order induced by a given query Q on the case base:

$C_1 \leq_Q C_2$ if and only if *satisfied-constraints*$(C_1, Q) \subseteq$ *satisfied-constraints*(C_2, Q)

It is therefore also related to order based retrieval, a general framework for retrieval in CBR recommender systems in which a partial order constructed from user preferences is applied to the case base to retrieve the maxima [6, 10].

Fig. 2 shows the cases retrieved by RNC for the example case base and query used to highlight limitations of *k*-NN in Section 2. The retrieval sets for 3-NN and CDR [2-3] are also shown. Case 3 (Y N N N) and Case 4 (Y N N N) are dominated by Case 5 (Y N Y N), but none of the other cases are dominated. The RNC retrieval set for the example query is therefore {Case 1, Case 2, Case 5}.

As we show in Theorem 8, RNC is complete. However, it is not optimally complete; that is, it is not guaranteed to retrieve the *most similar* feasible case if there is more than one feasible case. If the only hard constraint in the example query is the first constraint, then Cases 3, 4, and 5 are all feasible cases. But Case 5, the one retrieved by RNC, is not the most similar.

RNC is also not guaranteed to retrieve the most similar case. For example, if Case 1 and Case 2 were removed from the case base, then Case 3 would be the most similar of the remaining cases. However, it would still be dominated by Case 5 and therefore not retrieved by RNC. On the other hand, the RNC retrieval set may include more cases than are needed for completeness. For each $C_1 \in r(RNC, Q)$, the retrieval set must also include all cases C_2 such that *satisfied-constraints*(C_1, Q) = *satisfied-constraints*(C_2, Q). In the RNC retrieval set for the example query, only Case 1 and Case 5 are needed to satisfy the condition for completeness in Theorem 3.

Theorem 8. RNC *is complete.*

Proof. It suffices by Theorem 3 to show that for any query Q and $C_1 \notin r(RNC, Q)$, there exists $C_2 \in r(RNC, Q)$ such that *satisfied-constraints*$(C_1, Q) \subseteq$ *satisfied-constraints*(C_2, Q). If $C_1 \notin r(RNC, Q)$ there must be at least one case C such that *satisfied-constraints*$(C_1, Q) \subset$ *satisfied-constraints*(C, Q). Among such cases, let C_2 be one for which |*satisfied-constraints*(C_2, Q)| is maximal. As there can be no case that dominates C_2, we have established the existence of $C_2 \in r(RNC, Q)$ such that *satisfied-constraints*$(C_1, Q) \subset$ *satisfied-constraints*(C_2, Q).

4.4 Compromise-Driven Retrieval

In CDR, the constraints satisfied by a given case and its similarity to the target query play complementary roles in the retrieval process [2-3]. The first step in the construction of the retrieval set is to rank all cases in the case base in order of decreasing similarity. Among cases that are *equally* similar to the target query, any case that satisfies a superset of the constraints satisfied by another equally similar case is given priority in the ranking process. The algorithm used to select cases to be included in the CDR retrieval set from the ranked list of candidate cases is shown in Fig. 3.

```
algorithm CDR(Q, Candidates)
begin
    RetrievalSet ← φ
    while |Candidates| > 0 do
    begin
        C₁ ← first(Candidates)
        RetrievalSet ← RetrievalSet ∪ {C₁}
        Candidates ← Candidates - {C₁}
        for all C₂ ∈ rest(Candidates) do
        begin
            if satisfied-constraints(C₂, Q) ⊆ satisfied-constraints(C₁, Q)
                then Candidates ← Candidates - {C₂}
        end
    end
    return RetrievalSet
end
```

Fig. 3. Constructing the retrieval set in compromise driven retrieval

First, the most similar case is placed in the retrieval set and any cases that satisfy a subset of the constraints satisfied by this case are eliminated from the list of candidate cases. The most similar of the remaining cases is now added to the retrieval set and any cases that satisfy a subset of the constraints satisfied by that case are eliminated. This process continues until no further cases remain.

A detail not shown in Fig. 3 is that for each case added to the CDR retrieval set, any cases that satisfy the *same* constraints are placed in a separate *reference set*. A link from the retrieved case to the reference set is also created, thus ensuring that cases which satisfy the same constraints are available for immediate inspection at the user's request. In this way, a retrieved case acts as a *representative* for all cases that satisfy the same constraints. This recommendation engineering technique [14] helps to keep the size of the CDR retrieval set within reasonable limits while also addressing the needs of users who are not just seeking a single recommended item, but would like to be informed of all items (e.g., jobs, rental apartments) that are likely to be of interest [2-3].

Theorem 9. CDR *is optimally complete.*

Proof. For any query Q, a given case C_1 can fail to be included in the CDR retrieval set only if there exists $C_2 \in r(\text{CDR}, Q)$ such that $similarity(C_1, Q) \leq similarity(C_2, Q)$ and $satisfied\text{-}constraints(C_1, Q) \subseteq satisfied\text{-}constraints(C_2, Q)$. The optimal completeness of CDR immediately follows from Theorem 4.

It follows from Theorem 2 (and is clear from Fig. 3) that in common with k-NN, the most similar case is always retrieved in CDR. Another important feature that CDR shares with k-NN is that an otherwise competitive case can often compensate for its failure to satisfy one or more of the constraints satisfied by another case. As shown in

Fig. 2, the CDR retrieval set for our example case base and query in the property domain is {Case 1, Case 3, Case 5}. Although Case 3 (Y N N N) fails to satisfy one of the constraints satisfied by Case 5 (Y N Y N), the greater similarity of Case 3 ensures that it is not excluded from the CDR retrieval set.

That the CDR retrieval set may include more cases than are needed for completeness can be seen from the fact that only Case 1 and Case 5 are needed to satisfy the condition for completeness in Theorem 3. However, Case 3 must also be included in the retrieval set for *optimal* completeness. If the first constraint is the only hard constraint in the example query, then Case 3 is the most similar of the feasible cases Case 3, Case 4, and Case 5.

4.5 Bounded Greedy

Bounded Greedy (BG) combines measures of similarity and diversity in the retrieval process to achieve a better balance between these often conflicting characteristics of the retrieved cases [8]. It selects r cases from the $b \times r$ cases that are most similar to the target query, where r is the required size of the retrieval set and b is an integer parameter which is usually assigned a small value such as 2 or 3.

BG has been shown to provide significant gains in diversity at the expense of relatively small reductions in similarity [8]. As we show Theorem 10, however, BG is incomplete regardless of the size of the retrieval set or number of candidate cases from which the retrieved cases are selected.

Theorem 10. BG *is incomplete regardless of the size of the retrieval set or number of candidate cases from which the retrieved cases are selected.*

Proof. For any values of the parameters b and r, BG selects r cases from the k-NN retrieval set for $k = b \times r$. Its incompleteness immediately follows from Theorem 6.

A feature that BG shares with k-NN is that the most similar case for a given query is always retrieved.

4.6 Diversity Conscious Retrieval

Usually diversity can be increased only at the expense of some loss of average similarity relative to the k-NN retrieval set. Diversity conscious retrieval (DCR) aims to increase recommendation diversity while ensuring that any loss of similarity is strictly controlled [7]. The approach is based on the idea that for any integer $r \geq 2$, a given query partitions the set of cases with non-zero similarities according to the *similarity intervals* in which their similarities lie:

$$(0, \ 1-\frac{r-1}{r} \ ], \ (1-\frac{r-1}{r}, \ 1-\frac{r-2}{r} \ ], \ldots, (1-\frac{1}{r}, \ 1]$$

The retrieval process also depends on k, the required size of the retrieval set, and case selection is guided by the measure of relative diversity used in BG [8]. However, the DCR retrieval set is allowed to differ from the k-NN retrieval set only in cases whose similarities lie in the *leftmost* similarity interval that contributes to the k-NN retrieval set. This ensures that loss of average similarity relative to the k-NN retrieval set can never be more than $\frac{1}{r}$, the width of the similarity intervals on which retrieval

is based. For $r = 20$, the loss of average similarity cannot be more than 0.05. With this level of protection against loss of similarity, DCR has been shown to be capable of delivering worthwhile gains in diversity [7]. As we show in Theorem 11, however, DCR is incomplete.

In common with k-NN and BG, the most similar case for a given query is always retrieved in DCR.

Theorem 11. DCR *is incomplete regardless of the size of the retrieval set or width of the similarity intervals on which retrieval is based.*

Proof. For $r \geq 2$ and $k \leq 6$, we can construct a case base with $k + 1$ cases $C_1, C_2, ..., C_{k+1}$ and equally weighted attributes $a_1, a_2, ..., a_7$ such that for $1 \leq i \leq 7$, $a_i = 1$ in all cases with the following exceptions: (1) for $1 \leq i \leq 6$, $a_i = 0$ in C_{k+1}, (2) for $1 \leq i \leq k$, $a_i = 0$ in C_i, and (3) for $1 \leq i \leq k$, $a_7 = 0$ in C_i. For $k = 1$, the cases in the resulting case base are:

$$C_1 = (0, 1, 1, 1, 1, 1, 0), \ C_2 = (0, 0, 0, 0, 0, 0, 1)$$

Now consider the query $Q = \{a_i = 1: 1 \leq i \leq 7\}$. As $Sim(C_i, Q) = \frac{5}{7}$ for $1 \leq i \leq k$,

and $Sim(C_{k+1}, Q) = \frac{1}{7}$, the k-NN retrieval set includes all cases in the case base except

C_{k+1}. It is also clear that the similarities of all cases in the k-NN retrieval set must lie in same similarity interval. For C_{k+1} to be eligible for retrieval in DCR, $Sim(C_{k+1}, Q)$ must therefore be in the *only* similarity interval that contributes to the k-NN retrieval set. However, this cannot be the case as the difference in similarity between C_k and C_{k+1} exceeds the width of the similarity intervals on which retrieval is based:

$$Sim(C_k, Q) - Sim(C_{k+1}, Q) = \frac{5}{7} - \frac{1}{7} = \frac{4}{7} > \frac{1}{2} \geq \frac{1}{r}$$

The DCR retrieval set for Q is therefore the same as the k-NN retrieval set. As there is no case C in the DCR retrieval set such that *satisfied-constraints*$(C, Q) \subseteq$ *satisfied-constraints*(C_{k+1}, Q) it follows by Theorem 3 that DCR is incomplete for $r \geq 2$ and $k \leq 6$.

For $r \geq 2$ and $k > 6$, we can construct as in the proof of Theorem 5 a case base with $k + 1$ cases $C_1, C_2, ..., C_{k+1}$ and $k + 1$ equally weighted attributes $a_1, a_2, ..., a_{k+1}$, and a

query Q such that for $1 \leq i \leq k$, $Sim(C_i, Q) = \frac{k-1}{k+1}$ while $Sim(C_{k+1}, Q) = \frac{1}{k+1}$. Once

again, the k-NN retrieval set includes all cases in the case base except C_{k+1}, and the latter case is not eligible for inclusion in the DCR retrieval set because:

$$Sim(C_k, Q) - Sim(C_{k+1}, Q) = \frac{k-2}{k+1} = \frac{7k-14}{7(k+1)} = \frac{3k+4k-14}{7(k+1)} > \frac{18+4k-14}{7(k+1)} = \frac{4(k+1)}{7(k+1)} = \frac{4}{7}$$

There is therefore no case C in the DCR retrieval set such that *satisfied-constraints*$(C, Q) \subseteq$ *satisfied-constraints*(C_{k+1}, Q). Thus DCR is also incomplete for $r \geq 2$ and $k > 6$.

4.7 Discussion

The results of our comparison of retrieval strategies are summarized in Table 1. Of the six retrieval strategies included in our analysis, only RNC and CDR are complete (i.e., guaranteed to retrieve a feasible case if one exists), and only CDR is optimally complete (i.e., guaranteed to retrieve the most similar feasible case if there are two or more feasible cases). All except DBR and RNC are guaranteed to retrieve the most similar case for a given query.

As shown by our analysis, the effectiveness of some retrieval strategies may be open to question when, as often in practice, a given query may include constraints that must be satisfied. In terms of assumptions about the nature of the constraints in a given query, DBR and k-NN can be seen to represent two extreme positions. In DBR, all the constraints in a given query are treated as hard constraints, whereas in k-NN they are essentially treated as soft constraints. However, recognizing that any combination of hard and soft constraints is possible in practice — as in a complete retrieval strategy — seems a more realistic basis for the retrieval of recommended cases. While the completeness of RNC ensures the retrieval of a feasible case if such a case exists, no account is taken of a retrieved case's similarity in the retrieval process. In contrast, the optimal completeness of CDR ensures the retrieval of the most similar feasible case, if any, for a given query.

Table 1. Comparison of retrieval strategies with respect to completeness, optimal completeness, and retrieval of the most similar case

Retrieval Strategy	Feasible Case?	Most Similar Feasible Case?	Most Similar Case?
Database Retrieval (DBR)	N	N	N
k-NN	N	N	Y
Bounded Greedy (BG)	N	N	Y
Diversity Conscious Retrieval (DCR)	N	N	Y
Retrieval of Non-Dominated Cases (RNC)	Y	N	N
Compromise Driven Retrieval (CDR)	Y	Y	Y

5 Related Work

5.1 Recommendation Dialogues

We have focused in this paper on approaches to the retrieval of recommended cases in response to a query provided by the user in advance. In approaches related to conversational CBR [21], a query is *incrementally* elicited in an interactive dialogue with the user, often with the aim of minimizing the number of questions the user is asked before a recommended product is retrieved (e.g., [22-30]).

Incremental nearest neighbor (iNN) is one such strategy that uniquely combines a goal-driven approach to selecting the most useful question at each stage of the recommendation dialogue with a mechanism for ensuring that the dialogue is terminated only when it is certain that the most similar case (or cases) will be the same regardless of the user's preferences with respect to any remaining attributes [25-28]. One important benefit is that recommendations based on incomplete queries can be justified on the basis that any user preferences that remain unknown cannot affect the recommendation. However, like any retrieval strategy in which only a single case (or set of equally similar cases) is recommended, and no attempt is made to identify constraints that must be satisfied, iNN is incomplete.

In any recommender system, of course, more than a single recommendation cycle may be needed to retrieve a case that is acceptable to the user. As we have seen, a complete retrieval strategy ensures the retrieval of a feasible case whenever possible, but whether such a case is acceptable to the user may depend on the extent to which it satisfies any soft constraints in her query — or additional constraints not mentioned in her query. Approaches to extending recommendation dialogues beyond an initially unsuccessful recommendation include critiquing approaches to elicitation of user feedback (e.g., [2, 10, 20, 31-32, 41]), referral of the user's query to other recommender agents [26], and the recommendation engineering technique of providing the user with a link from each recommended case to other cases that satisfy the same constraints [2-3, 14].

5.2 Retrieval Failure and Recovery

By ensuring the retrieval of a case that satisfies any hard constraints in a given query whenever possible, a complete retrieval strategy avoids the need to identify constraints in a given query that must be satisfied. In some retrieval strategies, the non-existence of an exactly matching case (i.e., one that satisfies all the constraints in a given query) is treated as a query *failure* (or retrieval failure) that triggers a recovery process based on query relaxation (e.g., [30, 32-37]). Usually the aim of the relaxation process is to identify constraints in the user's query that need *not* be satisfied and can thus be treated as soft constraints.

For example, the Adaptive Place Advisor [30] is an in-car recommender system for restaurants that converses with the user through a spoken dialogue interface. If there is no restaurant that exactly matches the user's requirements, the system suggests a constraint to be relaxed (e.g., *price range* or *cuisine*) based on its current understanding of the user's preferences. If the suggested constraint is one that must be satisfied, the system may suggest another constraint to be relaxed (i.e., treated as a soft constraint). In the Intelligent Travel Recommender [37], the choice of constraint to be relaxed is left to the user.

However, recovery may not be possible by relaxing a *single* constraint, or at least not one that the user is willing to relax [33-36]. To address this issue, McSherry [34] proposes an *incremental* relaxation process that aims to minimize the number of constraint relaxations required for recovery. An explanation of the query failure is followed by a mixed-initiative dialogue in which the user is guided in the selection of one or more constraints to be relaxed. If the constraint suggested for relaxation at any stage is one that must be satisfied, the user can select another constraint to be relaxed.

Expressed in terms of minimally failing sub-queries, the explanations of query failure provided in the approach are adapted from research on co-operative responses to failing database queries (e.g., [38-40]).

5.3 Compromise Driven Retrieval in First Case

First Case is a CDR recommender system that supports queries involving attributes and constraints of different types [2-3]. A *nominal* attribute is one whose values do not have a natural ordering that determines their similarity (e.g., the type or make of a personal computer). A *more-is-better* (MIB) attribute is one that most users would prefer to maximize (e.g., memory). A *less-is-better* (LIB) attribute is one that most users would prefer to minimize (e.g., price). A *nearer-is-better* (NIB) attribute is one for which most users have in mind an ideal value and prefer values that are closer to their ideal value (e.g., screen size). A query in *First Case* may include upper limits for LIB attributes (e.g., $price \leq 500$), lower limits for MIB attributes (e.g., $memory \geq 256$), and ideal values for NIB or nominal attributes (e.g., screen = 15, $type$ = laptop).

An ideal value for a NIB or nominal attribute, if any, is treated as an equality constraint and also provides the basis for assessment of a given case's similarity with respect to the attribute. Assessment of similarity with respect to LIB/MIB attributes for which upper/lower limits are provided in a given query is based on *assumed* preferences [3, 28]. That is, the preferred value of a LIB attribute is assumed to be the *lowest* value in the case base, while the preferred value of a MIB attribute is assumed to be the *highest* value in the case base.

McSherry [3] investigates the potential benefits of also taking account of assumed preferences with respect to *non-query* attributes in CDR. One such benefit is that competitive cases that might otherwise be overlooked can more easily *compensate* for their failure to satisfy one or more of the constraints in a given query. Assumed preferences also play an important role in a CDR recommender system's ability to explain the benefits of a recommended case relative to another case that is less strongly recommended [2-3].

5.4 Balancing User Satisfaction and Cognitive Load

Balancing the trade-off between user satisfaction (or solution quality) and cognitive load is an important issue in recommender systems (e.g., [3, 5, 9]). A simple measure of cognitive load is the number of cases, on average, recommended in response to user queries, while possible measures of solution quality include precision and recall [13, 25]. The aspect of user satisfaction on which we have focused in this paper is the ability to ensure the retrieval of a case that may be acceptable to the user if such a case exists. As we have shown in Section 4, the optimal completeness of CDR ensures the retrieval of the most similar feasible case, if any, for a given query. In contrast, the existence of a feasible case does not guarantee that such a case will be retrieved regardless of the size of the k-NN retrieval set.

While the size of the k-NN retrieval set is the same for all queries, the size of the CDR retrieval set depends on the query and cannot be predicted in advance. That retrieval set size increases in CDR as query length increases is confirmed by our empirical results on the digital camera case base [41], with average retrieval set sizes of 1.5 for short queries (3 attributes), 3.0 for longer queries (6 attributes), and 5.6 for queries of maximum length (9 attributes) [3]. Taking account of assumed preferences with respect to non-query (LIB/MIB) attributes had only a minor effect on cognitive load, with average retrieval set sizes increasing to 1.9 for short queries (3 attributes) and 3.3 for longer queries (6 attributes).

For queries of maximum length (8 attributes) on the well-known Travel case base, the average size of the CDR retrieval set was 7.7 [2]. Even for $k = 30$ in this experiment, k-NN was unable to match CDR's ability to ensure the retrieval of a case that satisfies any hard constraints in a given query if such a case exists. This provides empirical confirmation of our analysis in Section 4 showing that k-NN is incomplete regardless of the size of the retrieval set.

6 Conclusions

Completeness is a term used in search and planning, and other areas of artificial intelligence, to describe an algorithm's ability to guarantee that a solution will be found if one exists [42-44]. In this paper we have extended the notion of completeness to retrieval in recommender systems. We say that a retrieval strategy is *complete* if it ensures the retrieval of a product that satisfies any hard constraints in a given query if such a case exists.

We have shown that incompleteness is a limitation that k-NN shares with most retrieval strategies, and highlighted other limitations of k-NN which can be attributed to its incompleteness. One such limitation that appears not to be widely recognized is that the *non-existence* of an acceptable case cannot always be inferred from the non-existence of a feasible case (i.e., one that satisfies any hard constraints in a given query) in the k-NN retrieval set. Also in contrast to a complete retrieval strategy, k-NN's failure to retrieve a given case cannot always be justified on the basis that one of the retrieved cases satisfies at least the same constraints.

On the other hand, k-NN has important advantages that are not necessarily shared by a complete retrieval strategy, such as enabling an otherwise competitive case to *compensate* for its failure to satisfy one or more of the constraints satisfied by another case. However, the role of similarity in balancing trade-offs between competing cases is implicit in our definition of *optimal* completeness. A retrieval strategy is optimally complete if it ensures the retrieval of the *most similar* case, if any, which satisfies all the hard constraints in a given query. Optimal completeness also has the advantage of ensuring the retrieval of the most similar case as in k-NN.

Finally, we have shown that the ability to justify the exclusion of any case from the retrieval set on the basis that one of the retrieved cases is at least as similar, and satisfies at least the same constraints, is one of several benefits of CDR [2-3] that can be attributed to its optimal completeness.

Acknowledgements

The author would like to thank Chris Stretch for his insightful comments on an earlier version of this paper.

References

1. Wilke, W., Lenz, M., Wess, S.: Intelligent Sales Support with CBR. In: Lenz, M., Bartsch-Spörl, B., Burkhard, H.-D., Wess, S. (eds.): Case-Based Reasoning Technology. Springer-Verlag, Berlin Heidelberg New York (1998) 91-113

2. McSherry, D.: Similarity and Compromise. In: Ashley, K.D., Bridge, D.G. (eds.): Case-Based Reasoning Research and Development. LNAI, Vol. 2689. Springer-Verlag, Berlin Heidelberg New York (2003) 291-305

3. McSherry, D.: On the Role of Default Preferences in Compromise-Driven Retrieval. Proceedings of the 10th UK Workshop on Case-Based Reasoning (2005) 11-19

4. McSherry, D.: Coverage-Optimized Retrieval. Proceedings of the 18th International Joint Conference on Artificial Intelligence (2003) 1349-1350

5. McSherry, D.: Balancing User Satisfaction and Cognitive Load in Coverage-Optimised Retrieval. Knowledge-Based Systems 17 (2004) 113-119

6. Bridge, D., Ferguson, A.: Diverse Product Recommendations using an Expressive Language for Case Retrieval. In: Craw, S., Preece, A. (eds.): Advances in Case-Based Reasoning. LNAI, Vol. 2416. Springer-Verlag, Berlin Heidelberg New York (2002) 43-57

7. McSherry, D.: Diversity-Conscious Retrieval. In: Craw, S., Preece, A. (eds.): Advances in Case-Based Reasoning. LNAI, Vol. 2416. Springer-Verlag, Berlin Heidelberg New York (2002) 219-233

8. Smyth, B., McClave, P.: Similarity vs. Diversity. In: Aha, D.W., Watson, I. (eds.): Case-Based Reasoning Research and Development. LNAI, Vol. 2080. Springer-Verlag, Berlin Heidelberg New York (2001) 347-361

9. Branting, L.K.: Acquiring Customer Preferences from Return-Set Selections. In: Aha, D.W., Watson, I. (eds.): Case-Based Reasoning Research and Development. LNAI, Vol. 2080. Springer-Verlag, Berlin Heidelberg New York (2001) 59-73

10. Bridge, D., Ferguson, A.: An Expressive Query Language for Product Recommender Systems. Artificial Intelligence Review 18 (2002) 269-307

11. Burkhard, H.-D.: Extending Some Concepts of CBR - Foundations of Case Retrieval Nets. In: Lenz, M., Bartsch-Spörl, B., Burkhard, H.-D., Wess, S. (eds.): Case-Based Reasoning Technology. Springer-Verlag, Berlin Heidelberg New York (1998) 17-50

12. Ferguson, A., Bridge, D.: Partial Orders and Indifference Relations: Being Purposefully Vague in Case-Based Retrieval. In: Blanzieri, E., Portinale, L. (eds.): Advances in Case-Based Reasoning. LNAI, Vol. 1898. Springer-Verlag, Berlin Heidelberg New York (2000) 74-85

13. McSherry, D.: A Generalised Approach to Similarity-Based Retrieval in Recommender Systems. Artificial Intelligence Review 18 (2002) 309-341

14. McSherry, D.: Recommendation Engineering. Proceedings of the 15th European Conference on Artificial Intelligence. IOS Press, Amsterdam (2002) 86-90

15. McSherry, D.: The Inseparability Problem in Interactive Case-Based Reasoning. Knowledge-Based Systems 15 (2002) 293-300

16. McSherry, D., Stretch, C.: Automating the Discovery of Recommendation Knowledge. Proceedings of the 19th International Joint Conference on Artificial Intelligence (2005) 9-14

17. Kießling, W.: Foundations of Preferences in Database Systems. Proceedings of the 28th International Conference on Very Large Databases (2002) 311-322

18. Balke, W.-T., Günzer, U.: Efficient Skyline Queries under Weak Pareto Dominance. IJCAI-05 Workshop on Advances in Preference Handling (2005) 1-6

19. Hong, I., Vogel, D.: Data and Model Management in a Generalised MCDM-DSS. Decision Sciences **22** (1991) 1-25

20. Linden, G., Hanks, S., Lesh, N.: Interactive Assessment of User Preference Models: The Automated Travel Assistant. Proceedings of the 6th International Conference on User Modeling (1997) 67-78

21. Aha, D.W., Breslow, L.A., Muñoz-Avila, H.: Conversational Case-Based Reasoning. Applied Intelligence **14** (2001) 9-32

22. Doyle, M., Cunningham, P.: A Dynamic Approach to Reducing Dialog in On-Line Decision Guides. In: Blanzieri, E., Portinale, L. (eds.): Advances in Case-Based Reasoning. LNAI, Vol. 1898. Springer-Verlag, Berlin Heidelberg New York (2000) 49-60

23. Kohlmaier, A., Schmitt, S., Bergmann, R.: A Similarity-Based Approach to Attribute Selection in User-Adaptive Sales Dialogues. In: Aha, D.W., Watson, I. (eds.): Case-Based Reasoning Research and Development. LNAI, Vol. 2080. Springer-Verlag, Berlin Heidelberg New York (2001) 306-320

24. McSherry, D.: Minimizing Dialog Length in Interactive Case-Based Reasoning. Proceedings of the 17th International Joint Conference on Artificial Intelligence (2001) 993-998

25. McSherry, D.: Increasing Dialogue Efficiency in Case-Based Reasoning without Loss of Solution Quality. Proceedings of the 18th International Joint Conference on Artificial Intelligence (2003) 121-126

26. McSherry, D.: Conversational CBR in Multi-Agent Recommendation. IJCAI-05 Workshop on Multi-Agent Information Retrieval and Recommender Systems (2005) 331-345

27. McSherry, D.: Explanation in Recommender Systems. Artificial Intelligence Review **24** (2005) 179-197

28. McSherry, D.: Incremental Nearest Neighbour with Default Preferences. Proceedings of the 16th Irish Conference on Artificial Intelligence and Cognitive Science (2005) 9-18

29. Shimazu, H.: ExpertClerk: A Conversational Case-Based Reasoning Tool for Developing Salesclerk Agents in E-Commerce Webshops. Artificial Intelligence Review **18** (2002) 223-244

30. Thompson, C.A., Göker, M.H., Langley, P.: A Personalized System for Conversational Recommendations. Journal of Artificial Intelligence Research **21** (2004) 393-428

31. Burke, R., Hammond, K.J., Young, B.: The FindMe Approach to Assisted Browsing. IEEE Expert **12** (1997) 32-40

32. Hammond, K.J., Burke, R., Schmitt, K.: A Case-Based Approach to Knowledge Navigation. In: Leake, D.B. (ed.): Case-Based Reasoning: Experiences, Lessons & Future Directions. AAAI Press/MIT Press, Menlo Park, CA (1996) 125-136

33. McSherry, D.: Explanation of Retrieval Mismatches in Recommender System Dialogues. ICCBR-03 Workshop on Mixed-Initiative Case-Based Reasoning (2003) 191-199

34. McSherry, D.: Incremental Relaxation of Unsuccessful Queries. In: González-Calero, P., Funk, P. (eds.): Advances in Case-Based Reasoning. LNAI, Vol. 3155. Springer-Verlag, Berlin Heidelberg New York (2004) 331-345

35. McSherry, D.: Maximally Successful Relaxations of Unsuccessful Queries. Proceedings of the 15th Conference on Artificial Intelligence and Cognitive Science (2004) 127-136

36. McSherry, D.: Retrieval Failure and Recovery in Recommender Systems. Artificial Intelligence Review **24** (2005) 319-338

37. Ricci, F., Arslan, B., Mirzadeh, N., Venturini, A.: ITR: A Case-Based Travel Advisory System. In: Craw, S., Preece, A. (eds.): Advances in Case-Based Reasoning. LNAI, Vol. 2416. Springer-Verlag, Berlin Heidelberg New York (2002) 613-627

38. Gaasterland, T., Godfrey, P., Minker, J.: An Overview of Cooperative Answering. Journal of Intelligent Information Systems **1** (1992) 123-157

39. Godfrey, P.: Minimisation in Cooperative Response to Failing Database Queries. International Journal of Cooperative Information Systems **6** (1997) 95-149

40. Kaplan, S.J.: Cooperative Responses from a Portable Natural Language Query System. Artificial Intelligence **19** (1982) 165-187

41. McCarthy, K., Reilly, J., McGinty, L., Smyth, B.: Experiments in Dynamic Critiquing. Proceedings of the 10th International Conference on Intelligent User Interfaces (2005) 175-182

42. Lieber, J., Napoli, A.: Correct and Complete Retrieval for Case-Based Problem Solving. Proceedings of the 13th European Conference on Artificial Intelligence. Wiley, Chichester (1998) 68-72

43. Muñoz-Avila, H.: Case-base Maintenance by Integrating Case-Index Revision and Case-Retention Policies in a Derivational Replay Framework. Computational Intelligence **17** (2001) 280-294

44. Russell, S., Norvig, S.: Artificial Intelligence: A Modern Approach. Prentice Hall, Upper Saddle River, New Jersey (1995)

Is Consideration of Background Knowledge in Data Driven Solutions Possible at All?

Gholamreza Nakhaeizadeh

DaimlerChrysler Research and Technology,
Data Mining Solutions
P.O.Box 2360, 89013 Ulm, Germany
gholamreza.nakhaeizadeh@daimlerchrysler.com

Abstract. In Data Driven Solutions using CBR or Data Mining approaches the optimal results can be achieved if one can consider and use, besides available data and texts, all other available information sources like general and background knowledge. Formalization and integration of such kind of knowledge in the knowledge extracted from data and texts is not, however, a simple task. For this reason, a lot of approaches, among them Bayesian Networks and Inductive Logic Programming, have been suggested in the literature to solve this problem.

In the talk, this topic is discussed pragmatically by reviewing the personal experiences of the speaker in the last 20 years using concrete examples from the automotive industry.

T.R. Roth-Berghofer et al. (Eds.): ECCBR 2006, LNAI 4106, p. 30, 2006.
© Springer-Verlag Berlin Heidelberg 2006

Reality Meets Research

Stefan Wess

empolis GmbH, Europaallee 10, 67657 Kaiserslautern, Germany
stefan.wess@empolis.com

Back in the late 1980ies in Kaiserslautern we became serious in doing CBR research. The focus of our work was on understanding and algorithms for CBR as well as its application. Both topics had an academic perspective rather than an eye on actual business benefits for users. Later at Inference and empolis this focus shifted, i.e., from research to reality.

In reality most users do not care whether a solution deploys CBR or not as long as it solves the problem and has a clear business benefit. Actually, most do not know that it is CBR. This coincided with the insight that the CBR engine forms only a fraction of the solution. Our early tools, e.g. PATDEX and even CBRWorks, were appropriate to understand the principles, but insufficient for real world deployment. Hence, we took our experience and built a new tool from scratch, i.e. orenge or e:IAS, as it is called today.

Since then, we had to add a multitude of ingredients to make it a success, for example:

- textual and structured CBR, rules and decision trees (the obvious)
- lingustics for information extraction and full text search
- associative search and classification
- text summarisation and keyword extraction
- language detection
- distributed processing and load balancing for scalability
- interfaces for all sorts of data sources
- interfaces for building applications
- APIs for all sorts of front ends
- a component architecture to plug it all together
- services to fit it into the SOA world

The above list is in no way complete. However, it illustrates how much rather boring stuff must be added when reality hits research. What are the lessons learned? Or, more precise: What can 15 years of reality feed back into research? Here are some issues:

- It must scale: Millions of cases are the rule, not the exception
- Adaptation still is not a killer feature.
- Distributed collaborative modeling is not yet state of practice, i.e. a research issue.
- And last but not least, if the Semantic Web will play a role in the future, then what is the role of CBR in the Semantic Web?

The latter, sounding academic again, is an issue for the CBR research community, since it asks the question for future directions. From realities perspective this could become an important one.

T.R. Roth-Berghofer et al. (Eds.): ECCBR 2006, LNAI 4106, p. 31, 2006.

Multi-agent Case-Based Reasoning
for Cooperative Reinforcement Learners

Thomas Gabel and Martin Riedmiller

Neuroinformatics Group
Department of Mathematics and Computer Science
Institute of Cognitive Science
University of Osnabrück, 49069 Osnabrück, Germany
{thomas.gabel, martin.riedmiller}@uni-osnabrueck.de

Abstract. In both research fields, Case-Based Reasoning and Reinforcement Learning, the system under consideration gains its expertise from experience. Utilizing this fundamental common ground as well as further characteristics and results of these two disciplines, in this paper we develop an approach that facilitates the distributed learning of behaviour policies in cooperative multi-agent domains without communication between the learning agents. We evaluate our algorithms in a case study in reactive production scheduling.

1 Introduction

A reinforcement learning (RL) agent must acquire its behavior policy by repeatedly collecting experience within its environment. Usually, that experience is then processed into a state or state-action value function, from which an appropriate behaviour policy can be induced easily [21]. When applying RL approaches to complex and/or real-world domains, typically some kind of function approximation mechanism to represent the value function has to be used. While in previous work [5], we have explored the use of case-based methods for that specific task, the CBR component will play a similar, yet more prominent role in this paper.

Just like a reinforcement learner, a CBR system's competence is based upon the *experience* it comprises. One main difference is, however, that this experience is not processed mathematically into some kind of value function, but explicitly stored in the system's case base. Furthermore, it is rather unusual to speak of autonomous agents in CBR settings. This difference, however, is of minor importance, since it represents a question of notion and reflects only two different views of describing how the system acquires its experience.

Multi-agent domains in which autonomous agents act entirely independently are faced with the problem that the agents behave without any form of central control in a shared environment, having the goal to learn a behaviour policy that is optimal for the respective environment. This heavily increases the degree of difficulty of learning compared to single-agent scenarios. In earlier work [9], we presented an experience- and Q learning-based reinforcement learning

T.R. Roth-Berghofer et al. (Eds.): ECCBR 2006, LNAI 4106, pp. 32–46, 2006.

algorithm for multi-agent learning of independent learners in general stochastic environments. In a data-efficient version, this algorithm has been proven to feature convergence to the optimal joint policy. In that version, however, it is applicable to problems with finite and small state spaces and has been shown to perform well for a small "climbing game" [4], only.

In this paper, we will extend that algorithm and embed it into a CBR framework. Despite losing guarantees of theoretical convergence to the optimum, we will show that our approach can be applied successfully to larger-scale, real-world tasks. For the purpose of evaluation, we focus on complex application scenarios of reactive production scheduling, in particular on job-shop scheduling tasks [16].

The remainder of this paper is structured as follows. In Section 2 we clarify the problem statement for this paper by focusing on multi-agent reinforcement learning, highlighting its difficulties and reviewing in short the experience-based multi-agent learning algorithm mentioned. Furthermore, relevant related work is highlighted. Section 3 introduces our multi-agent CBR approach and discusses issues of case modelling and distributed case-based value function approximation. In Section 4 we introduce and explain in detail our case-based reinforcement learning algorithm for independent learners. Section 5 depicts the application field of reactive production scheduling and summarises the results of a set of experimental evaluations, applying our approach to job-shop scheduling problems. Finally, Section 6 concludes and points to ongoing and future work.

2 Distributed Reinforcement Learning

Promising a way to program agents without explicitly encoding problem-solving routines, reinforcement learning approaches have been attracting much interest in the machine learning and artificial intelligence communities during the past decades. Traditional reinforcement learning approaches are concerned with single agents that act autonomously in their environment and seek for an optimal behaviour. In many applications, however, interaction and/or coordination with other agents is of crucial importance to achieve some goal.

2.1 From One to m Agents

The standard approach to modelling reinforcement learning problems is to use Markov Decision Processes (MDP). An MDP is a 4-tuple (A, S, r, p) where S and A denote the state and action spaces, respectively, $p : S \times A \times S \rightarrow [0, 1]$ is a probabilistic state transition function with $p(s, a, s')$ describing the probability to end up in s' when taking action a in state s. Moreover, $r : S \times A \rightarrow \mathbb{R}$ is a reward function that denotes the immediate reward that is obtained when taking a specific action in some state. In search of an optimal behaviour, the learning agent must differentiate between the value of possible successor states or the value of taking a specific action in a certain state. Typically, this kind of ranking is made by computing a state or state-action value function, $V : S \rightarrow \mathbb{R}$ or $Q : S \times A \rightarrow \mathbb{R}$. For more basics and a thorough review of state-of-the-art reinforcement learning methods we refer to [21].

If there is no explicit model of the environment and of the reward structure available, Q learning is one of the reinforcement learning methods of choice to learn a state-action value function for the problem at hand [26]. It updates directly the estimates for the values of state-action pairs according to

$$Q(s,a) := (1 - \alpha)Q(s,a) + \alpha(r(s,a) + max_{b \in A(s')}Q(s',b)) \qquad (1)$$

where the successor state s' and the immediate reward $r(s,a)$ are generated by simulation or by interaction with a real process. For the case of finite state and action spaces where the Q function can be represented using a look-up table, there are convergence guarantees that say that Q learning converges to the optimal value function $Q^\star$, assumed that all state-action pairs are visited infinitely often and that α diminishes appropriately. Given convergence to $Q^\star$, the optimal policy $\pi^\star$ can be induced by greedy exploitation of Q according to $\pi^\star(s) = \arg\max_{a \in A(s)} Q^\star(s,a)$.

If there are multiple agents acting concurrently, actions are *vectors* of individual actions. Each agent i contributes its own action component a_i – to be termed *elementary action* subsequently – to the joint action vector $\boldsymbol{a}$. Given the current state and the joint action vector the environment transitions to a successor state s', while at the same time all agents receive the (global) reward signal r. The agents' overall goal is to find an optimal joint behaviour policy, i.e. a mapping from states to actions, that maximises the sum of expected rewards [1].

In [4] the distinction between joint-action learners and independent learners is introduced. While the former know about the actions taken by the other agents, the latter only know about their own contribution a_i to the joint action. As a consequence of their lack of action information, the attempt to estimate an elementary action's value in a specific state would most likely fail: The reward signals for different joint action vectors (differing in the action contributions of the other agents) would mix for any state s and any elementary action a_i. In this paper, we focus on independent learners: As argued before, the key problem of independent reinforcement learners is that they must somehow be enabled to distinguish between different joint actions to which they contributed the same elementary action. We shall explore that issue more thoroughly in the following.

2.2   Core Ideas of a Learning Algorithm for Independent Learners

In [9] we presented an algorithm that realises the idea of implicit agent co-ordination: Each agent is endowed with the capability to differ between joint action vectors without knowing what the joint actions are, i.e. without knowing which elementary actions are taken by the other agents. As follows, we briefly summarise the core ideas of that algorithm, while in Sections 3 and 4 we further-develop and fully integrate it into a CBR framework.

Implicit Coordination: Each agent i manages for each state $s \in S$ an experience list $E_i(s)$, which on the one hand contains exactly one entry e for every joint action vector and on the other hand for reasons of efficiency is sorted with respect to the estimated value of that piece of experience. The list entry

e is a 3-tuple $e = (Q, a_i, n)$. Here, Q denotes the actual value of e and thus the value of taking the corresponding, not explicitly known action vector in state s (the sorting is done w.r.t. Q), a_i is the elementary action taken by agent i and n stands for the number of times the estimated value Q of this experience has already been updated.

If it can be assured, that at every point of time each agent choosing an action uses the same index x to access its experience list, i.e. selecting $e := E_i(s)[x]$, and moreover, selects the action $e.a_i$ given by that experience, then the reward signal generated by the environment can be related correctly to the (implicitly) referenced joint action vector. Accordingly, the corresponding Q value $e.Q = E_i(s)[x].Q$ may be updated appropriately.

Index Selection Harmonisation: The procedure to select index x within an experience list $E_i(s)$ must be implemented in exactly the same manner in every agent. It has to guarantee that at each instant of time each agent selects the same index, which implies that all agents must be aware of the same time.

Efficient Exploration: Due to the sorting of all experience lists, the best actions are to be found at their beginnings. Therefore, an index selection mechanism that aims at greedily exploiting the knowledge contained in its lists, would always select the first index. However, to trade off exploration and exploitation it is suitable to select the top entries more frequently, but also to choose the last entries with a non-zero probability. The implementation of a corresponding procedure is straightforward.

For further details of the algorithm as well as for a proof of its theoretical convergence properties we refer to [9]. An obvious limitation of this algorithm is its usability for discrete state-action spaces, only. However, the application of generalisation techniques, to deal with large state/action spaces, is of great importance, in particular in multi-agent domains where the size of the joint action spaces can grow exponentially with the number of agents [4]. Therefore, taking the learning algorithm sketched so far as a starting point, in the next section we will present an extended, case-based version of it that may be employed for larger-scale problems.

2.3   Related Work

Different authors have investigated the use of case-based technology in RL-related and multi-agent settings. Powell et. al [17] introduce automatic case elicitation (ACE), a learning technique where the CBR system initially starts without domain knowledge and incrementally gains competence through real-time exploration and interaction within the environment. Their system is successfully applied in the domain of checkers. Macedo [13] focuses in depth on the issue of efficient CBR-based exploration of an autonomous agent in an eventually non-stationary environment an evaluates his approach in the context of robotics. The aspect of agent-cooperation is highlighted, for example, in the work of Ontanon and Plaza on ensemble CBR [14]. The focus there is on case retention of collaborative agents trying to solve some analytical classification task while having different degrees of competence. In a later work, Plaza spots the issue of distributed case-based reuse, assuming cooperation of multiple agents in problem-solving and tackling configuration tasks [15]. There has also been much work into the direction of multi-case-based reasoning (MCBR [10]), where case bases contain knowledge collected in different contexts and for different tasks or where each case base may specialise on certain regions of the problem space.

A comprehensive article reviewing and comparing a number of memory-based approaches to value function approximation in reinforcement learning is the one by Santamaria and Sutton [20]. With our case-based Q function representation we are in line with these authors as well as with the work of Bridge [3], since we will consider the actions as a part of the cases' solutions.

Multi-agent learning has been an important topic in the RL literature for years. Foundational issues and algorithms as well as a number of approaches to extend the Q learning algorithm into the area of multi-agent domains can be found, e.g., in [7,11,23]. While most of these works focus on discrete problems with finite state spaces, there have also been attempts to tackle larger multi-agent problem domains in conjunction with function approximation. Focusing not on cooperative MA learning, but on adversarial settings with one agent and one opponent, Uther [25] uses a piecewise linear function approximator similar to decision trees in an abstracted soccer game. For the domain of Robotic Soccer Simulation we have learnt a number of strategic behaviors in which multiple agents are involved using neural networks for value function representation [18]. Bowling and Veloso [2] use the CMAC for function approximation in adversarial multi-robot learning in conjunction with policy gradient RL. Cooperative multi-agent learning of independent learners (as we do) and the aspect of inter-agent communication is investigated in the work of Szer and Charpillet [22] where, however, mutual communication between the agents is allowed.

In the evaluation part of this paper we will focus on the application field of reactive production scheduling. For a deeper understanding of that domain we refer to [16] and to our own previous work in that area [19,6] using RL with neural net-based function approximation. Moreover, there have been also attempts to solve scheduling problems with case-based methods (e.g. [8,24,12]).

3   A CBR Approach to Multi-agent Reinforcement Learning

The CBR paradigm tells that similar problems have similar solutions. We may transfer that statement to a terminology that is more closely related to reinforcement learning tasks and say it is likely that in similar situations similar or identical actions are of similar utility. Based on that assumption, case-based techniques have been employed at times to generalise and approximate value functions for RL problems in large/continuous state-action spaces. The same principle also holds when multiple agents are involved: In similar situations a collective of agents will obtain similar rewards when taking similar joint actions.

3.1   Distributed Case-Based Value Function Approximation

For large and/or continuous state spaces S it is impossible to store the expected value of all state-action pairs explicitly (e.g., in a Q table). So, we suggest to utilize the capability to generalise that can be achieved via CBR: We intend to cover S by a finite number of cases, where the expected values (Q values) of different actions are stored in a special form in the cases' solution parts.

Each agent manages its own case base to cover the state space. When a new state is entered, the best-matching representative (nearest neighbour) from the case base is retrieved and the action which promises to yield the highest reward is selected for execution. For single-agent scenarios the implementation of appropriate algorithms seems intuitive, but when multiple agents are involved in decision-making, a number of substantial problem arise:

- Since we consider independent learners that have no idea of the actions taken by their colleagues, we must find a way to enable each agent to differentiate between different joint action vectors in the light of case-based Q value function approximation.
- Efficient and effective exploration of the joint action space are indispensable to learn good policy behaviours. Accordingly, some synchronisation mechanism is required.
- Lack of adequate (state) information in some agents might imply that learning proceeds differently than in other agents. Consequently, retrieval and reuse of experience could not be made in a harmonised way.

The issues raised above manifest necessary conditions for a distributed case-based value function approximation to work successfully. Regarding the last problem we emphasise that we always assume all agents to have the same information on the current global state. We stress that the state information may very well be incomplete, i.e. the environment may be partially observable only (as in our experiments in Section 5), which adds further difficulty to the learning problem. However, then for each agent the same parts of the global state are hidden. As a consequence of the identical global view each agent has and assuming identical case-base management and retrieval algorithms to be used by all agents, it can easily be guaranteed that all agents have case bases with identical contents and that retrieval produces the same results across all agents.

3.2   Case Representation and Retrieval

Pursuing the traditional way to model the case representation, we consider cases that are made up of a problem and a solution part, in the following. Note, that each agent present in our multi-agent settings has its own case base and has no access to any other agent's case base and that no inter-agent communication is allowed. The overall case structure is sketched in Figure 1.

3.2.1   The Problem Part

The cases problem parts are meant to represent the instances s of the state space S. Our algorithms do not pose any requirements on the modelling of the

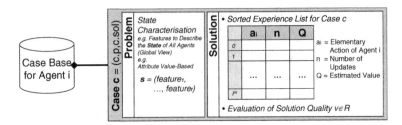

Fig. 1. Case Representation

case problem parts as long as adequate similarity measures can be defined, which reflect similarities between states. So, we assume the existence of some similarity measure $sim : S \times S \rightarrow [0,1]$ that assesses the degree of similarity between two states. Consequently, given a case base CB, the nearest neighbour $\nu \in CB$ of any query $q \in S$ can be determined easily, and[1] it holds $NN(q) := \nu.p = \arg\max_{c \in CB} sim(c.p, q)$. In Figure 1 the cases' problem parts are exemplarily realised by a number of features (attribute-value based representation).

3.2.2 The Solution Part

For the cases' solution parts we need to define some specific data structures that are aligned with the distributed learning algorithm sketched in Section 2.2. A solution $c.sol$ of a case c consists of two parts, $c.sol = (E, v)$. Whereas $v \in \mathbb{R}$ represents an evaluation value of the solution quality, E is a list into which the experience is compressed the agent has made within its environment. Specifically, $E = (E[1], \ldots, E[l^m])$ contains exactly l^m entries (with m the number of agents and l the number of elementary actions selectable by each agent[2]). Hence, an experience list reserves one entry to implicitly reference each possible joint action vector. Each list entry $e = E[x]$ of E can be accessed by its index x (for ease of notation we will also allow the shortcut $e = c.sol[x]$ instead of $c.sol.E[x]$) and is a 3-tuple, $e = (a_i, n, Q)$ as indicated in Section 2.2. The key point of this representation is that, no matter which case is considered and no matter which list entry of the case's solution is regarded, the agent only knows its own elementary action a_i. Despite that, it is enabled to implicitly differentiate between all l^m joint action vectors by means of the mechanism that shall be explained subsequently.

4 Multi-agent CBR for Independent Learners

In this section we present our case-based multi-agent RL algorithm in a threefold way. First, in Figure 2 we provide a coarse overview over its components involved. Second, Algorithm 1 gives a possible realisation of its main functionality in

---

[1] We use the notation $c.p$ and $c.sol$ to access the problem and solution part of case c, respectively.

[2] We assume the number of elementary actions to be finite or, in the case of continuous actions, that an appropriate action discretisation has been introduced.

pseudo-code. And finally, the text describes all elements and their interplay in a much more detailed way.

Since our focus is on multi-agent learning, in the following we must clearly distinguish between the agents' learning and application phases. During the former, the agents interact with their environment, collect experience and extend and refine the contents of their case bases. During the latter (the reuse or application phase), the results of learning are exploited, which means that for each state the best action possible is considered by all agents and collectively executed.

Many practical problems are of episodic nature, characterised by some set G of goal states (an episode ends, when an $s \in G$ has been reached). In order to not complicate Algorithm 1 it has been given in a non-episodic realisation, though it may easily be adapted to handle episodic tasks.

4.1 Solution Index Addressing and Exploration

Each time an agent is provided with a new observation, i.e. a new state s, it takes this state as query and searches its case base for the nearest neighbour ν. Most of our considerations to be made in the rest of this and the following sections will refer to the appending solution $\nu.sol$.

For the moment we ignore the question if the agent ought to add a new case for state s to the case base (cf. Section 4.3). The method `selectIndex(i,t)` (step 3 in Figure 2 and 2b-iii in Algorithm 1), as already indicated in Section 2.2, selects an index x to access the solution's experience list $\nu.sol$ and must be implemented in such a way that it returns the same list index in each agent. For this to happen each agent needs the same implementation and moreover, if random accessing is required, for instance, identical random number generator seedings in each agent. Let $x_i :=$ `selectIndex(i,t)` with t as current time, then the agent will choose $\nu.sol[x_i].a$ as its next elementary action[3].

Using a clever implementation of `selectIndex`, this way an efficient exploration mechanism can be realised. For example, ε-greedy exploration can be implemented by returning index 1 with probability $1 - \varepsilon$ (greedy action choice) and a random index from $[1, \ldots, l^m]$ with probability ε.

After all agents have decided for their elementary action the composite action vector is executed and the successor state s' and reward r are observed by all agents (steps 2c and 2d in Algorithm 1 and steps 5 and 6 in Figure 2).

4.2 Distributed Q Learning Updates

Standard Q learning, as briefly introduced in Section 2.1, converges for MDPs with finite state and action spaces to the expected true rewards, when the learning rate $\alpha_i = \alpha_{n(s,a)}$ in the update rule (Equation 1) is sensitive to the number of updates $n(s, a)$ that have already been made to the state-action pair (s, a) and it holds:

---

[3] Note, that $x_i = x_j$ for all $i, j \in \{1, \ldots, l^m\}$, but in general it holds $a_i \neq a_j$ for many $i, j \in \{1, \ldots, l^m\}$.

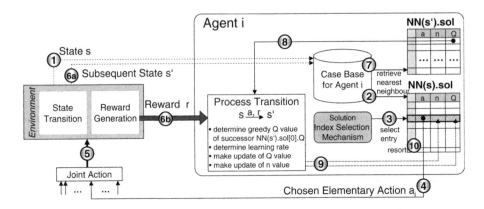

Fig. 2. Procedural View on CBR-Based Multi-Agent Reinforcement Learning

a) the sequence $(\alpha_i)_{i=1}^{\infty}$ fulfills $\alpha_i \in [0, 1]$, $\sum_{i=1}^{\infty} \alpha_i = \infty$, $\sum_{i=1}^{\infty} \alpha_i^2 < \infty$, and
b) each state-action pair is visited an infinite number of times.

Although our implementation of the procedure `getLearningRate` (cf. Algorithm 1, step 2e-ii) fulfills the first requirement, convergence to the theoretical optimum could even under fulfillment of b) not be expected, since we do use a case-based function approximator (with a finite number of instances in memory) to cover the state space. Nevertheless, good policies can be learnt even in presence of this kind of generalisation (cf. our empirical result in Section 5).

For an independent learner with a case-based and experience list-based representation of its Q function, the update rule, originally provided in Section 2.1, can now be rewritten with respect to the data structures and case representation we have introduced. Let $T = (s, a_i, s', r)$ be a transition perceived by agent i consisting of state s, (elementary) action a_i of agent i (where a_i corresponds to the previously selected index x_i, i.e. $\nu.sol[x_i] = a_i$), the successor state and the reward, let ν and ν' denote the nearest neighbours of s and s' with respect to CB_i, respectively, and let α_i denote the learning rate calculated by `getLearningRate` (e.g. $\alpha_i := \frac{1}{1+\nu.sol[x_i].n}$), then the agent performs the following updates:

$$\nu.sol[x_i].Q := (1 - \alpha_i) \cdot \nu.sol[x_i].Q + \alpha_i(r + \gamma \cdot \nu'.sol[1].Q)$$
$$\nu.sol[x_i].n := \nu.sol[x_i].n + 1 \qquad (2)$$

After having performed this kind of update, the experience list in $\nu.sol$ is resorted with respect to increasing Q values (see steps 9 and 10 in Figure 2). It is easy to prove by induction that at each instant of time the contents of all agents' case bases and hence, their Q functions, are identical. Due to limited space we omit the proof here.

4.3   Case Base Management

Of course, when the case base is empty the agent has to insert a new, blank case for the state s provided. Otherwise, predicate `addCaseCriterion(s)` must

1. let t be the global time, m be the number of agents, l the number of elementary actions, $CB_i = \varnothing$ an empty case base for each agent, γ the discount factor, and set $s = s' \in S$ to the initial state of the system
2. **repeat**
   (a) **set** $s := s'$
   (b) **for all** agents $i \in \{1, \ldots, m\}$ **do**
       i. **if** $CB_i = \varnothing$ or addCaseCriterion(s) is true
          then $CB := CB \cup c$
              with $c.p = s$ and $c.sol =$ emptySolution(i)
       ii. **retrieve** nearest neighbour $\nu_i := \arg\max_{c \in CB_i} sim(s, c.p)$ of state s
       iii. **set** index $x_i :=$ selectIndex(i,t)
       iv. **select** elementary action $a_i := \nu_i.sol[x_i].a_i$
   (c) **apply** joint action $a = (a_1, \ldots, a_m)$
   (d) **observe** successor state $s' \in S$ and reward $r \in \mathbb{R}$
   (e) **for all** agents $i \in \{1, \ldots, m\}$ **do**
       i. **retrieve** nearest neighbour $\nu_i' := \arg\max_{c \in CB_i} sim(s, c.p)$ of state s'
       ii. **set** learn rate $\alpha_i :=$ getLearningRate($\nu_i.sol[x_i].n$)
       iii. **set** $\nu_i.sol[x_i].Q := (1 - \alpha_i)\nu_i.sol[x_i].Q + \alpha_i(r + \gamma\nu_i'.sol[1].Q)$
       iv. **increment** $\nu_i.sol[x_i].n$ by one
       v. **resort** the experience list in $\nu_i.sol$
   until stopCriterion() becomes true

Algorithm 1. Case-Based Multi-Agent Reinforcement Learning in a Non-Episodic Realisation

make the decision whether to add a new case for s. Here, it must be deliberated whether the experience already contained in CB can be considered reusable for the current situation. In particular, the similarity between s and the problem part of its nearest neighbour in the case base may be a meaningful indicator, provided that appropriate, knowledge-intensive similarity measures have been defined for the task at hand. In our current implementation, addCaseCriterion(s) returns true, if the case base size limit has not been exceeded and the similarity between s and its nearest neighbour in CB is less than some threshold ς. Note, that the addition of a new case incurs some necessary follow-up operations:

- Let C_{new} be a case added at time t_{new}. Assume that the transition (s, a, s_{new}, r) has to be processed at $t = t_{new} + \delta$ (with some small δ) where $c := NN(s)$ has been added at time $t_s < t_{new}$. Then, the update according to Equation 2 should take into account that the solution of the nearest neighbour case of s_{new} is most likely rather "uninformed". Therefore, we omit making updates when $NN(s_{new}).sol[1].n = 0$, i.e. when no update for the greedy action in the case responsible for s_{new} has been made, yet. This clearly reduces the speed of learning as long as new cases are added repeatedly.
- After having added a new case c_{new}, the solution parts of all cases in $C := \{c \in C | c_{new} = NN(c)\}$ have to be reinitialised: Let $S_{c_{new}} := \{s \in S | c_{new} = \arg\max_{c \in CB} sim(c.p, s)\} \subset S$ be the subset of the state space, for queries

from which c_{new} is the nearest neighbour in CB. Then, before c_{new} was added to CB, the nearest neighbours of all $s \in S_{c_{new}}$ were elements of C. Hence, the solution parts of all $c \in C$ are no more valid and must be reset.

When resetting as well as initialising a case's solution $c.sol$, i.e. when creating empty solutions (procedure emptySolution in Algorithm 1), of course all Q value entries and entries telling the number of updates are set to zero: $c.sol[x].Q = c.sol[x].n = 0$ for all $x \in \{1, \ldots, l^m\}$ in all agents. The field for the elementary action $c.sol[x].a$, however, must be set with some care: The implementation of emptySolution(i) must guarantee that – when combining the elementary actions of all agents i over all list entries – there is exactly one entry for each possible joint action, which can be easily achieved by a careful design of the corresponding programming. Given this kind of initialisation and the solution index selection mechanism described, the preconditions for the proof shown in Section 4.2 are satisfied.

Case Base Quality Evaluation: After each learning update step the changed solution $c.sol$ is evaluated with respect to its usability for new problems and the corresponding evaluation is stored in $c.sol.v$. A possible indicator of its quality may be the sum $\sum_{j=1}^{l^m} c.sol[j].n$ of Q learning updates that have already been made for this solution. Currently, however, we employ a simpler, boolean solution evaluation: We consider a solution of a case valid and usable if and only if each of the entries in the belonging experience list has been updated at least once. In other words, each joint action vector possible must have been tried once for each $c \in CB$, until the corresponding case solution is unlocked for use.

5   Experimental Evaluation

To evaluate our case-based and experience list-based approach to multi-agent reinforcement learning we chose the application domain of reactive production scheduling. The learners' task is to autonomously find a cooperative dispatching policy to assign jobs to a limited number of resources, where each job consists of a number of operations that must be performed on specific resources in a pre-defined order. Most classical approaches to solve scheduling problems perform search in the space of possible schedules (e.g. tabu search [16], but also GA-based solutions [12]). By contrast, we take an alternative, reactive approach to job-shop scheduling: We model the environment (the plant) as an MDP and have a learning agent at each resource that decides which job to process next based on its current view on the entire plant (see [19] for more details). A fundamental advantage of this reactive approach is that the agents will also be able to react quickly and appropriately in new, unforeseen situations (e.g. in case of a machine breakdown), whereas most classical scheduling algorithms will have to discard their calculated schedule and start recomputing it. Since, job-shop scheduling problems are well-known to be NP-hard, this can become a time-critical problem.

5.1 Experiment Setup

In our modelling of the scheduling environment a state s must describe the situation of all resources at that point of time – so, s characterises the sets of waiting jobs at all resources. In our current implementation we use an attribute-value based state representation where the state description is made up of $4m$ features, i.e. the sets of waiting jobs at each resource are characterised by four properties. This way, of course, not all of the properties of the currently waiting jobs can be captured, why the environment is perceived as partially observable by each agent. To calculate the similarity between two states we have made use of the local-global principle, defined appropriate local similarity measures for the features and amalgamated them to the global similarity $sim(s_1, s_2)$ using suitable feature weights.

The overall goal of learning is to minimise production costs. Costs arise each time a job is *tardy*, that means when it has not been finished until its due date. So, the overall learning goal is to minimise summed tardiness over all jobs in the system, $\sum_t \sum_j jobTardy(t, j)$. Accordingly, each time one or more tardy jobs are in the system, a negative reward is incurred; if there are no jobs that have violated their due date, the immediate reward is zero.

The actions our agents are allowed to take are decisions to act according to one out of l rather simple, established dispatching priority rules (DPR). A DPR chooses a job j out of a set of waiting jobs J subject to some specific criterion. There is a variety of more or less complex DPRs: For example, the EDD rule chooses the job $j \in J$ which has the earliest due date. The MS rule picks the job with minimal processing slack and the SPT rule, for instance, chooses a job whose next operation has the shortest processing time. In the scope of our evaluation we will focus on the mentioned three DPRs, i.e. the set of available elementary actions for each agent is $A = \{a^{EDD}, a^{MS}, a^{SPT}\}$. Furthermore, in all our experiments we consider two cooperative scheduling resources/agents that work according to the algorithms discussed in the previous sections.

5.2 Results

Each experiment is divided into a training and a testing phase: A random set S_a of training scheduling scenarios and an independent set S_b of testing scenarios are generated (all of them differing in the properties and numbers of jobs to be processed, $|S_a| = 10$, $|S_b| = 50$). During training, the scenarios in S_a are processed repeatedly[4] where the agent picks random actions with $p = 0.5$ (explores) and that way gathers experience. During testing, the scenarios in S_b are processed once, where now all agents behave greedily w.r.t. their current Q functions, stored distributedly in their case bases. The performance is measured in terms of the average summed tardiness on the scheduling scenarios from $S_{a/b}$.

Comparison to DPR-based Agents: We compared the final scheduling capabilities of our learning agents to nine different agent-constellations in which both agents

---

[4] We call the processing of one scenario an *episode*.

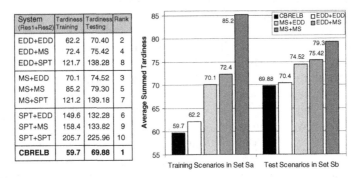

System (Res1+Res2)	Tardiness Training	Tardiness Testing	Rank
EDD+EDD	62.2	70.40	2
EDD+MS	72.4	75.42	4
EDD+SPT	121.7	138.28	8
MS+EDD	70.1	74.52	3
MS+MS	85.2	79.30	5
MS+SPT	121.2	139.18	7
SPT+EDD	149.6	132.28	6
SPT+MS	158.4	133.82	9
SPT+SPT	205.7	225.96	10
CBRELB	**59.7**	**69.88**	**1**

Fig. 3. Performance of the CBR-based Scheduler vs. the Top 4 Heuristic Ones

worked according to some fixed DPR. To be exact, we evaluated each combination of each agent working with one of the rules from $\{EDD, MS, SPT\}$ (see Figure 3). Obviously, the setting when the first as well as the second agent worked with the EDD rule, was the best-performing one (on set S_a as well as on S_b). When both agents were learning, however, the resulting scheduling quality could be increased (data row $CBRELB$ in Figure 3). The resulting scheduling system (using a case base of 500 instances) outperformed the best of all DPR-based systems by 4.2% on the training scenarios (average tardiness of 59.7 instead of 62.2). Even on the independent test set, i.e. on 50 entirely different scheduling scenarios the best combination of heuristically acting agents is beaten (average tardiness of 69.88 instead of 70.4). So, one may conclude that the learning agents have discovered and learnt regions of the problem space in which certain joint actions are of extremely high usefulness. We allowed the $CBRELB$ agents to learn for 20000 episodes to reach those results.

Case Solution Utilisation: Working within an 8-dimensional problem space, it may happen that for some (query) state q the similarity σ to its nearest neighbour in CB is rather low. Therefore, we allowed each agent to use a fallback action in case that no well-matching case in CB could be found. To be exact, during evaluation an agent used the EDD rule as fallback action in situations when $\sigma < 0.8$ or when the nearest neighbour's solution part had an evaluation value v that marked this solution as not usable (cf. Section 4.3). Of course, the more comprehensive the case base and the longer the learning process has been going on, the less often these situations occur. It is clear that the amount of stored experience must not be too sparse. When experimenting with case bases of sizes 100 and 200 only, the $CBRELB$-setting still outperformed $EDD + EDD$ on the training instances (tardiness of 60.1 and 60.6, respectively), but on the test set an average tardiness of 75.68 and 70.36, respectively, could be achieved only.

6   Conclusions

We have developed and evaluated a CBR-approach that allows for the distributed learning of behaviour policies of independent reinforcement learners. To tackle the complexity and high-dimensionality inherent in multi-agent settings we employed case-based reasoning as the core technology to facilitate generalisation. Moreover, we combined CBR with a mechanism to achieve implicit coordination of the agents involved which is a necessary prerequisite to make a correct processing of rewards obtained from the environment possible. Our results of a series of experiments in the application domain of reactive job-shop scheduling are very promising, since our approach was able to outperform all schedules generated by a larger number of scheduling systems that worked with fixed dispatching priority rules.

Our research has raised a number of interesting issues to be investigated in on-going and future work. In a next step, we want to evaluate our approach in even larger application scenarios, involving more cooperative learning agents and a larger number of elementary actions. Another interesting issue concerns efficient and effective routines for case base management, case addition and case relocalisation, which need to be developed and further-developed, respectively. Finally, we also seek to design an offline variant of the Q learning update employed which makes more efficient use of gathered experience and, hence, is likely to bring about faster and presumably better learning results.

Acknowledgements. This research has been supported by the German Research Foundation (DFG) under grant number Ri 923/2-1.

References

1. D. Bertsekas and J. Tsitsiklis. *Neuro Dynamic Programming*. Athena Scientific, Belmont, USA, 1996.
2. M. Bowling and M. Veloso. Simultaneous Adversarial Multi-Robot Learning. In *Proceedings of the Eighteenth International Joint Conference on Artificial Intelligence (IJCAI-03)*, pages 699–704, Acapulco, Mexico, 2003. Morgan Kaufmann.
3. D. Bridge. The Virtue of Reward: Performance, Reinforcement and Discovery in Case-Based Reasoning. In *Proceedings of the 6th International Conference on Case-Based Reasoning (ICCBR 2005)*, page 1, Chicago, USA, 2005. Springer.
4. C. Claus and C. Boutilier. The Dynamics of Reinforcement Learning in Cooperative Multiagent Systems. In *Proceedings of the Fifteenth National Conference on Artificial Intelligence (AAAI-98)*, Menlo Park, USA, 1998. AAAI Press.
5. T. Gabel and M. Riedmiller. CBR for State Value Function Approximation in Reinforcement Learning. In *Proceedings of the 6th International Conference on Case-Based Reasoning (ICCBR 2005)*, pages 206–221, Chicago, USA, 2005. Springer.
6. T. Gabel and M. Riedmiller. Reducing Policy Degradation in Neuro-Dynamic Programming. In *Proceedings of ESANN2006*, Bruges, Belgium, 2006. To appear.
7. J. Hu and M. Wellman. Nash Q-Learning for General-Sum Stochastic Games. *Journal of Machine Learning Research*, 4:1039–1069, 2003.
8. J. Kim, D. Seong, S. Jung, and J. Park. Integrated CBR Framework for Quality Designing and Scheduling in Steel Industry. In *Proceedings of the 7th European Conference on CBR (ECCBR 2004)*, pages 645–658, Madrid, Spain, 2005. Springer.
9. M. Lauer and M. Riedmiller. Reinforcement Learning for Stochastic Cooperative Multi-Agent Systems. In *Proceedings of AAMAS 2004*, pages 1514–1515, New York, NY, July 2004. ACM Press.

10. D. Leake and R. Sooriamurthi. Managing Multiple Case Bases: Dimensions and Issues. In *FLAIRS Conference*, pages 106–110, Pensacola Beach, 2002. AAAI Press.
11. M. Littman. Friend-or-Foe Q-learning in General-Sum Games. In *Proceedings of the Eighteenth International Conference on Machine Learning (ICML 2001)*, pages 322–328, Williamstown, USA, 2001. Morgan Kaufman.
12. S. Louis and J. McDonnell. Learning with Case-Injected Genetic Algorithms. *IEEE Trans. Evolutionary Computation*, 8(4):316–328, 2004.
13. L. Macedo and A. Cardoso. Using CBR in the Exploration of Unknown Environments with an Autonomous Agent. In *Proceedings of the 7th European Conference on CBR (ECCBR 2004)*, pages 272–286, Madrid, Spain, 2005. Springer.
14. S. Ontanon and E. Plaza. Collaborative Case Retention Strategies for CBR Agents. In *Proceedings of the 5th International Conference on Case-Based Reasoning (IC-CBR 2003)*, pages 392–406, Trondheim, Norway, 2003. Springer.
15. S. Ontanon and E. Plaza. Cooperative Reuse for Compositional Cases in Multi-agent Systems. In *Proceedings of the 6th International Conference on Case-Based Reasoning (ICCBR 2005)*, pages 382–396, Chicago, USA, 2005. Springer.
16. M. Pinedo. *Scheduling. Theory, Algorithms, and Systems*. Prentice Hall, 2002.
17. J. Powell, B. Hauff, and J. Hastings. Evaluating the Effectiveness of Exploration and Accumulated Experience in Automatic Case Elicitation. In *Proceedings of ICCBR 2005*, pages 397–407, Chicago, USA, 2005. Springer.
18. M. Riedmiller and A. Merke. Using Machine Learning Techniques in Complex Multi-Agent Domains. In I. Stamatescu, W. Menzel, M. Richter, and U. Ratsch, editors, *Adaptivity and Learning*. Springer, 2003.
19. S. Riedmiller and M. Riedmiller. A Neural Reinforcement Learning Approach to Learn Local Dispatching Policies in Production Scheduling. In *Proceedings of ICJAI'99*, pages 764–771, Stockholm, Sweden, 1999.
20. J. Santamaria, R. Sutton, and A. Ram. Experiments with RL in Problems with Continuous State and Action Spaces. *Adaptive Behavior*, 6(2):163–217, 1998.
21. R. S. Sutton and A. G. Barto. *Reinforcement Learning. An Introduction*. MIT Press/A Bradford Book, Cambridge, USA, 1998.
22. D. Szer and F. Charpillet. Coordination through Mutual Notification in Cooperative Multiagent Reinforcement Learning. In *Proceedings of AAMAS 2004*, pages 1254–1255, New York, USA, 2004. IEEE Computer Society.
23. G. Tesauro. Extending Q-Learning to General Adaptive Multi-Agent Systems. In *Proceedings of NIPS 2003*, Vancouver and Whistler, Canada, 2003. MIT Press.
24. P. Tinkler, J. Fox, C. Green, D. Rome, K. Casey, and C. Furmanski. Analogical and Case-Based Reasoning for Predicting Satellite Task Schedulability. In *Proceedings of ICCBR 2005*, pages 566–578, Chicago, USA, 2005. Springer.
25. W. Uther and M. Veloso. Adversarial Reinforcement Learning. Technical Report CMU-CS-03-107, School of Computer Science, Carnegie Mellon University, 2003.
26. C. Watkins and P. Dayan. Q-Learning. *Machine Learning*, 8:279–292, 1992.

Retrieving and Reusing
Game Plays for Robot Soccer

Raquel Ros[1], Manuela Veloso[2], Ramon López de Màntaras[1],
Carles Sierra[1], Josep Lluís Arcos[1]

[1] IIIA - Artificial Intelligence Research Institute
CSIC - Spanish Council for Scientific Research
Campus UAB, 08193 Barcelona, Spain*
[2] Computer Science Department, Carnegie Mellon University
Pittsburgh, PA 15213, USA**
veloso@cs.cmu.edu, {ros, mantaras, sierra, arcos}@iiia.csic.es

Abstract. The problem of defining robot behaviors to completely address a large and complex set of situations is very challenging. We present an approach for robot's action selection in the robot soccer domain using Case-Based Reasoning techniques. A case represents a snapshot of the game at time t and the actions the robot should perform in that situation. We basically focus our work on the retrieval and reuse steps of the system, presenting the similarity functions and a planning process to adapt the current problem to a case. We present first results of the performance of the system under simulation and the analysis of the parameters used in the approach.

1 Introduction

The problem of defining robot behaviors in environments represented as a large state space is very challenging. The behavior of a robot results from the execution of actions for different states, if we define acting as the execution of a policy $\pi : s \rightarrow a$ (where s is the current state and a, the action to execute in the given state). Defining each possible state and the actions to perform at each state, i.e. defining the policy, is challenging, tedious and impossible to be done completely manually. Furthermore, we have to deal with a second issue: the nature of the environment. We are working with real robots that interact with non controllable elements of the environment, which are constantly moving.

We illustrate our work in the robot soccer domain (Robocup)[2]. In this domain, we do not deal with an independent action (e.g. turn 30 degrees, kick,

---

* Partial funding by the Spanish Ministry of Education and Science project DPI2003-05193-C02-02. Raquel Ros holds a scholarship from the Generalitat de Catalunya Government

** This research was partially sponsored by BBNT Solutions, LLC under contract no. FA8760-04-C-0002 with the US Air Force. The views and conclusions contained herein are those of the authors and should not be interpreted as necessarily representing the official policies or endorsements, either expressed or implied, of the sponsoring institutions, the U.S. Government or any other entity.

T.R. Roth-Berghofer et al. (Eds.): ECCBR 2006, LNAI 4106, pp. 47–61, 2006.

walk forward 100cm), but with a sequence of actions that the robots execute to accomplish their goals (e.g. dribble and shoot). We call this sequence a *game play*. Hence, the problem we address is to find out which game plays the robots should execute during a match. We focus our work on the application of Case-Based Reasoning techniques to define the actions the robots should perform in this environment, i.e. we use the CBR approach to generate the π function. We believe that reproducing game plays from similar past situations (similar environment's description) solves the robot behavior definition problem in an easy and fast way. The approach followed in this work is to define action cases for robots to provide them with a set of cases and then have them autonomously select which case to replay.

The work we present in this paper is centered on modelling the main steps of a Case-Based Reasoning system [1]: the retrieval step and the reuse step. For this purpose, we first analyze the environment to choose the main features that better describe it and then we define an appropriate similarity function. We use different functions to model the similarity for each feature domain and then an aggregation function to compute the overall similarity. We also introduce some initial experiments to test the current implementation based on a single player with no teammates.

The organization of the paper is as follows. Section 2 presents related work. Section 3 describes the robot soccer domain. Section 4 introduces the features of the environment and the formal representation of a case. Section 5 and 6 detail the retrieval and reuse steps respectively. Section 7 shows the analysis and first results of the performance of the system. Section 8 discusses the extension of the current case representation in order to model the dynamics of the game plays. Finally, Section 9 concludes the work and describes future work.

2   Related Work

Some researchers have already focused their work on using Case-Based Reasoning techniques for deciding the best actions a player should execute during a game. Karol et al. [5] present a model to build high level planning strategies for AIBO robots. For any game situation, game plays are chosen based on the similarity between the current state of the play and the cases in the case base. The paper only presents the general model without any experiment and does not describe the different steps of the CBR approach. Wendler et al. [15] describe an approach to select soccer players' actions based on previously collected experiences encoded as cases. The work is restricted to the Simulation League. Thus, many parameters they take into account are not considered in our domain, and also they do not have to deal with the major problems involved when working with real robots. Regarding the retrieval step, they apply a *Case Retrieval Net* model to improve the retrieval of cases in terms of efficiency. Marling et al. [9] introduce three CBR prototypes in their robots team (RoboCats, in the Small Size League): the first prototype focused on positioning the goalie; the second one, on selecting team formations; and the third one, on recognizing game states. All three systems are mainly based on taking snapshots of the game and extracting features from the positions of the robots during the game.

We can also find some bibliography dedicated to solve the action selection problem, but applying other learning techniques. Riedmiller et al. [11] focus their work on Reinforcement Learning techniques applied to two different levels: moving level and tactical level. The former refers to learning a specific move, for example, learning to kick. While the latter refers to which move should be applied at a certain point, as *pass the ball*. The work is restricted to the Simulation League, and they only used the moving level during a competition. With respect to the tactical level, they experimented with two attackers against one or two defenders. The attackers used the approach presented, while the defenders used a fixed policy. Similarly, Sarge et al. [13] present a RL approach to learn low-level skills. These skills can later be put together and used to emulate the expertise of experienced players. More precisely, they work on the *intercepting the ball* skill. They performed experiments with hand-coded players vs. learning players. They obtained positive results after one hour of learning. Finally, Lattner et al. [7] present an approach that creates patterns based on the qualitative information of the environment. The result of learning is a set of prediction rules that give information about what (future) actions or situations might occur with some probability if certain preconditions satisfy. Patterns can be generalized, as well as specialized. As in the previous papers, this is used in the Simulation League.

Finally, CBR techniques have been also used for purposes other than action selection. Wendler et al. [14] present a case-based approach for self-localization of robots based on local visual information of landmarks. The approach is used in robot soccer, and once again, they use the *Case Retrieval Net* model. Gabel and Veloso [3] model an online coach in the Simulation League to determine the team line-up. Based on previous soccer matches the coach reasons about the current state of the match and decides which player of his team line-up is assigned to which of the available players type. Haigh and Veloso [4] solve a path planning problem with a system that plans a route using a city map. The global path is created using different cases from the case base. Kruusmaa [6] develops a system to choose routes in a grid-based map that are less risky to follow and lead faster to the goal based on previous experience. Ros et al. [12] present an approach for robot navigation in semistructured unknown environments. Cases represent landmarks configurations that the robot should avoid in order to reach its target. Ram and Santamaría [10] and Likhachev and Arkin [8] focus their work on a CBR approach to dynamically select and modify the robot's behaviors as the environment changes during navigation.

3   Robot Soccer Description

The Robocup Soccer competition involves several leagues. One of them is the one we focus our work on: the Four-Legged League. Teams consist of four Sony AIBO robots. The robots operate fully autonomously, i.e. there is no external control, neither by humans nor by computers. The field dimensions are 6m long

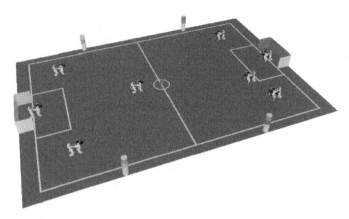

Fig. 1. Snapshot of the Four-Legged League (image extracted from [2])

and 4m wide. There are two goals (cyan and yellow) and four colored markers the robots use to localize themselves in the field. There are two teams in a game: a red team and a blue team. Figure 1 shows a snapshot of the field. The robots can communicate with each other by wireless or even using the speakers and microphones (although this is not common).

A game consists of three parts, i. e. the first half, a half-time break, and the second half. Each half is 10 minutes. The teams change the goal defended and color of the team markers during the half-time break. At any point of the game, if the score difference is greater than 10 points the game ends. For more details on the official rules of the game refer to [2].

4   Case Definition

In order to define a case, we first must choose the main features of the environment (from a single robot's point of view) that better describe the different situations the robot can encounter through a game. Given the domain, we differentiate between two features' types, common in most games:

Environment-based features. They represent the spatial features of a game. In robot soccer we consider the positions of the robots and the ball as the basic features to compare different situations, which represent the dynamics of the environment. These positions are in global coordinates with respect to the field (the origin corresponds to the center of the field). Regarding the robots, we consider the heading as a third parameter to describe their positions. It corresponds to the angle of the robot with respect to the x axis of the field, i.e. which direction the robot is facing to.

Game-based features. They represent the *strategy* applied in the game. We use the time and the score as the main features. As time passes and depending on the current score, the strategy should be more offensive if we are losing, or a more defensive if we are winning. These features are beyond robot soccer and are applicable to other games.

In the work we present in this paper we always refer to a main robot (we could think of it as the team's *captain*; hereafter we will refer to it either as the captain) who is responsible for retrieving a case and informing the rest of the players (teammates) the actions each of them should perform (including himself). We divide the description of a case in two parts: the problem description and the solution description. The former refers to the description of the environment and the game features at time t from the captain's point of view (we can talk about a snapshot of the game), while the latter refers to the solution to solve that problem. Thus, within the soccer domain a case is a 2-tuple:

$$case = ((R, B, G, Tm, Opp, t, S), A)$$

where:

1. R: robot's position (x_R, y_R) and heading θ (captain's information).

$$x_R \in [-2700..2700] \text{mm.} \quad y_R \in [-1800..1800] \text{mm} \quad \theta \in [0..360) \text{degrees}$$

2. B: ball's position (x_B, y_B).

$$x_B \in [-2700..2700] \text{mm.} \quad y_B \in [-1800..1800] \text{mm}$$

3. G: defending goal
$$G \in \{\text{cyan, yellow}\}$$

4. Tm: teammates' positions.

$$Tm = \{(id_1, R_1), (id_2, R_2), (id_3, R_3)\}$$

where id_i corresponds to the teammate identification for teams of 4 robots.
5. Opp: opponents' positions.

$$Opp = \{opp_1, opp_2, ..., opp_n\}$$

where opp_i is a point (x, y) and $n \in \{1, 2, 3, 4\}$ for teams of 4 robots.
6. t: timing of the match. Two halves parts of 10 min.

$$t \in [0..20] \text{min}, t \in \mathbb{N}$$

7. S: difference between the goals scored by our team and the opponent's team. The maximum difference allowed is 10. The sign indicates if the team is losing or winning.
$$S \in [-10..10]$$

8. A: sequence of actions (also seen as behaviors) to perform. Some examples of individual actions are $Turn(\phi)$, $Kick(\text{right})$, $Dribble$, etc. The combination of these actions result in different sequences.

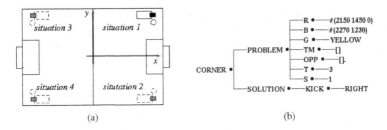

(a)   (b)

Fig. 2. (a) Situation 1 corresponds to the original description of the case. While situation 2, 3 and 4 correspond to the symmetric descriptions. (b) Example of a case.

4.1 Case Properties

We can observe two symmetric properties of the ball's and robot's positions and the defending goal: one with respect to the x axis, and the other one, with respect to the y axis and the defending goal. That is, a robot at point (x, y) and defending the yellow goal describes *situation 1*, which is symmetric to *situation 2* $((x, -y)$, defending the yellow goal), *situation 3* $((-x, y)$, defending the cyan goal) and *situation 4* $((-x, -y)$, defending the cyan goal) (Figure 2(a)).

Similarly, the solution of a problem has the same symmetric properties. For instance, in a situation where the solution is *kick to the left*, its symmetric solution with respect to the x axis would be *kick to the right*. Thus, for every case in the case base, we compute its symmetric descriptions, obtaining three more cases. Figure 2(b) shows an example of the case previously described.

Because of the inevitable spatial nature of robots domains, interestingly a particular case can be mapped into multiple ones through different spatial transformations. Thus, from a small set of cases, we easily generate a larger set.

5   Retrieval Step

To retrieve a case we must define a similarity function that computes the similarity degree between the current problem $P_c = ((R_c, B_c, G_c, Opp_c, t_c, S_c), \langle\rangle)$ and the cases in the case base $C_i = ((R_i, B_i, G_i, Opp_i, t_i, S_i), A_i)$ in the interval $[0..1]$ (with 0 meaning no similarity at all, and 1 meaning maximum similarity). Next we introduce the different similarity functions used to compare the features of a case. We first compute the similarities along each feature (assuming feature independence). Then we use a filtering mechanism based on these values to discard non-similar cases and finally, we use an aggregation function to compute the overall similarity obtaining a set of similar cases (if any).

5.1   Similarity Functions

We next define two types of similarity functions based on the features' types described in Section 4:

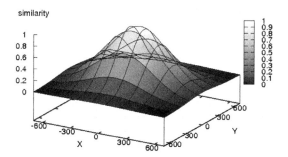

Fig. 3. 2D Gaussian function with $\tau_x = 300$ and $\tau_y = 250$

Environment-based features. We use a 2D Gaussian function to compute the degree of similarity between two points, $p_1 = (x_1, y_1)$ and $p_2 = (x_2, y_2)$ in a 2D space. Unidimensional Gaussian functions are defined by two parameters: one represents the reference value x_r with respect to which we compare any other value x, and the other, the maximum distance τ allowed between two values to consider to be similar. Hence, low values for τ model very restrictive similarities, and high values, very tolerant similarities. As we work on a 2D plane, to define the Gaussian function we have to consider four parameters instead of two: x_r, y_r, τ_x and τ_y:

$$G(x, y) = Ae^{-(\frac{(x - x_r)^2}{2\tau_x^2} + \frac{(y - y_r)^2}{2\tau_y^2})}$$

where x_r, y_r are the reference values, τ_x, τ_y, the maximum distance for each axis and A is the maximum value of $G(x, y)$. In our case, since we model the similarities in the interval $[0..1]$, $A = 1$. Figure 3 shows a 2D Gaussian.

We define the similarity function for two points as:

$$sim(x_1, y_1, x_2, y_2) = e^{-(\frac{(x_1 - x_2)^2}{2\tau_x^2} + \frac{(y_1 - y_2)^2}{2\tau_y^2})}$$

where the point (x_1, y_1) refers to either the robots' or the ball's position in the problem and (x_2, y_2) refers to the positions in the case. We do not use the heading of the robots to compute the similarity value, but for the reuse step.

Regarding the defending goal feature we define a simple binary function:

$$sim(G_1, G2) = \begin{cases} 1 & \text{if } G_1 = G_2 \\ 0 & \text{if } G_1 \neq G_2 \end{cases}$$

where G_1 is the defending goal in the problem and G_2, the one described in the case.

Game-based features. We are interested in defining a function that combines time and score since they are extremely related. As time t passes, depending on the score of the game, we expect a more offensive or defensive behavior. We consider as critical situations those where the scoring difference S is minimum,

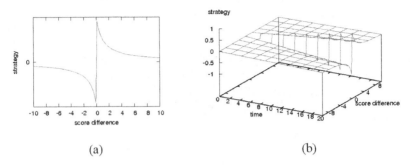

Fig. 4. (a) Strategy function for time $t = 5$. (b) Strategy function over time.

i.e. when the chances for any of the two teams of winning or losing the game are still high, and thus the strategy (or behavior) of the team might be decisive. We model the strategy for a 20 minutes game as:

$$strat(t, S) = \begin{cases} \frac{t}{20(S-1)} & \text{if } S < 0 \\ \frac{t}{20} & \text{if } S = 0 \\ \frac{t}{20(S+1)} & \text{if } S > 0 \end{cases}$$

where $strat(t, S) \in [-1..1]$, with -1 meaning a very offensive strategy and 1 meaning a very defensive strategy.

Figure 4(a) depicts the behavior of the team at time t. Positive and negative scoring differences mean that the team is winning or losing respectively. The higher the absolute value of S is, the lower the opportunity of changing the current score and the behavior of the team. For extreme values of S (in the interval $[-10..10]$) the outcome of the function approaches zero. Otherwise, the function value indicates the degree of intensity, either for a defensive or an offensive behavior. As time passes, the intensity increases until reaching maximum values of 1 and -1, (defensive and offensive, respectively). Figure 4(b) shows the behavior of the function combining both variables.

We define the similarity function for time and score as:

$$sim_{tS}(t_1, S_1, t_2, S_2) = 1 - |strat(t_1, S_1) - strat(t_2, S_2)|$$

where t_1 and S_1 corresponds to the time and scoring features in the problem and t_2 and S_1, the features in the case.

5.2   Retrieving a Case

Case retrieval is in general driven by the similarity metric between the new problem and the saved cases. We introduce a novel method to base the selection of the case to retrieve. We evaluate similarity along two important metrics: the similarity between the problem and the case, and the cost of adapting the problem to the case. Before explaining in more detail these metrics we first define two types of features: *controllable* indices and *non-controllable* indices.

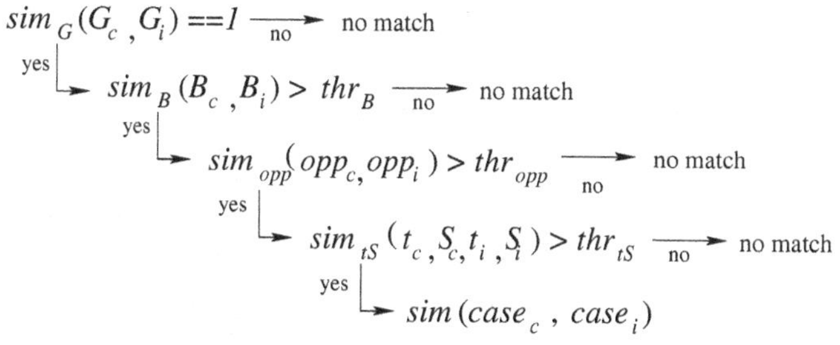

$$sim_G(G_c, G_i) == 1 \xrightarrow{\text{no}} \text{no match}$$

$$\text{yes} \quad sim_B(B_c, B_i) > thr_B \xrightarrow{\text{no}} \text{no match}$$

$$\text{yes} \quad sim_{opp}(opp_c, opp_i) > thr_{opp} \xrightarrow{\text{no}} \text{no match}$$

$$\text{yes} \quad sim_{tS}(t_c, S_c, t_i, S_i) > thr_{tS} \xrightarrow{\text{no}} \text{no match}$$

$$\text{yes} \quad sim(case_c, case_i)$$

Fig. 5. Filtering mechanism to compute the similarity between cases. The subindex c refers to the current problem, and i, to a case in the case base.

The former ones refer to the captain's and teammates' positions (since they can move to more appropriate positions), while the latter refers to the ball's and opponents' position, the defending goal, time and score (which we cannot directly modify).

The idea of separating the features into controllable and non-controllable is that a case can be retrieved if we can modify part of the current problem description in order to adapt it to the description of the case. Given the domain we are working on, the modification of the controllable features leads to a planning process where the system has to define how to reach the positions (or adapted positions as detailed in Section 6) of the captain and the teammates indicated in the retrieved case in order to reuse its solution.

Similarity Value. We compute the similarity between the current problem P_c and a case C_i using the non-controllable features. For this purpose, we filter the case based on the individual features similarities (Figure 5). If the similarities are all above the given thresholds, we then compute the overall similarity value between the case and the problem. Otherwise, we consider that the problem does not match the case. We discuss the values of these thresholds in Section 7.

In order to compute the opponents' similarity value we first must determine the correspondence between the opponents of the problem and the case, i.e. which opponent opp_i from the problem description corresponds to which opponent opp_j in the case description. For this purpose, we use a *Branch&Bound* search algorithm in a binary tree. Each node of the tree represents either the fact of considering a match between the pair (opp_i, opp_j), or the fact of not considering the match between this pair. As soon as the algorithm finds the optimal correspondence, we obtain the similarity value for each pair of opponents using the Gaussian function.

Finally, we compute the overall similarity sim between the current problem and the case:

$$sim = f(sim_B, sim_{tS}, sim_{Opp_1}, \ldots, sim_{Opp_n})$$

where n is the number of opponents in the case, and each argument of f corresponds to the similarity value obtained for each feature. In Section 7 we discuss the most appropriate aggregation function f.

Cost Value. This measure defines the cost of modifying the controllable features of the problem P_c to match the case C_i. We represent the cost of adapting the problem to a case as the maximum Euclidean distance $dist$ between the players' positions in the current problem and the adapted positions in the case (after obtaining the correspondence between the players using the same method as for the opponents):

$$cost(P_c, C_i) = \max_{j \in \{R\} \cup Tm} \{dist(pos_j, pos'_j)\}$$

where R corresponds to the captain, $Tm = \{tm_1, tm_2, tm_3\}$, to the teammates, pos_j represents the position of j in the problem description and pos'_j, the position of j in the case description.

After computing the similarities between the problem and the cases, we obtain a list of potential cases from where we must select one for the reuse step. We consider a compromise between the similarity degree between the problem and the case and the cost of adapting the problem to the case. The properties for the best choice are to have a very similar case and to apply little adaptations to the problem to reuse the solution of the case, while the worst choice would be low similarity and high cost (the opposite situation). But we also have to avoid those situations where even though the similarity is high, the problem also needs a big adaptation (high cost) before reusing the selected case.

We then select the most similar case from the list of cases with cost lower than a threshold thr_{cost}:

$$C_r = \arg\max\{sim(P_c, C_i) \mid cost(P, C_i) < thr_{cost}\}, \quad \forall C_i \in \text{LS}$$

where LS is a list of cases with similarity over 0.4 and C_r is the case retrieved.

6   Case Reuse

After selecting the best case, the next step is to reuse its solution. Before executing the actions indicated in the case, we first adapt the current problem to the description of the case. To this end we modify the controllable features (captain and teammates) to those positions where the relation between the features is the same as the one described in the case. We take the ball as the reference point in the field. From the case retrieved we obtain the relative positions of the players with respect to the ball. Hence, the adapted positions of the players for the current problem are the transformations of these relative coordinates to global coordinates, having the current position of the ball as the new reference point.

Figure 6 shows an example. The relative position of the robot with respect to the ball ($B_i = (750, 300)$) in the case retrieved is $R_i^r = (-300, 0)$. Thus, the

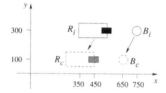

Fig. 6. The case description depicted in solid lines (R_i, B_i), and the problem description, in dashed lines (R_c, B_c). Adapting the position of the robot with respect to the ball's position described in the problem.

robot's adapted global position in the current problem is $R_c = (350, 100)$ since the ball's position is $B_c = (650, 100)$. Briefly, the adaptation of the problem description is based on positioning the controllable features with respect to the ball's position, instead of maintaining the original positions indicated in the case. Once we compute these new locations, the robot retrieving the case (captain) informs the rest of the teammates about the positions they should take.

7 Empirical Evaluation

We discuss the different values for the thresholds, the aggregation function we have introduced in Section 5.2 and the first results of the system.

Environment-based features. We have used a Gaussian to model the similarity function for this type of features. As we already mentioned, the function has two parameters, τ_x, τ_y, which are used to model the maximum distance between two points that we consider to be similar. These parameters define an ellipse (the projection of the Gaussian in the plane XY) with radius τ_x and τ_y. All points contained in this ellipse have a $G(x, y) > 0.6$. Thus, we use this value as the threshold for the ball, thr_B, and opponents similarity, thr_{opp}. To set the τ values for the ball, we empirically observed that the maximum distance we consider the ball's position is similar to a reference point is 30cm. for the x axis, and 25cm. for the y axis (since the field has a rectangular shape). Thus, $\tau_x = 300$ and $\tau_y = 250$. Regarding the opponents' we consider a more flatter function because the imprecision of their positions is higher than the one for the ball. We then fix both τ_x and τ_y to 350.

Game-based features. We are specially interested in distinguishing between those situations that take place at the end of the game with score difference close to 0 from those that happen at the beginning of the game, since the strategy can be very different in each of these situations. After analyzing the values obtained by the strategy function described in Section 5.1, we observed that comparing two situations, fixing one to $t_1 = 0$ and $S_1 = 0$ and varying the other one through all the possible values, the following situations occur:

- first half of the game and no matter which score:

$$t_2 \in [0..10) \wedge S_2 \in [-10..10], sim_{tS}(t_1, S_2, t_2, S_2) > 0.7$$

– first part of the second half and equal scoring:

$$t_2 \in [10..14] \wedge S_2 = 0, sim_{tS}(t_1, S_2, t_2, S_2) < 0.7$$

– second part of the second half and 1 goal difference:

$$t_2 \in [15..18] \wedge S_2 \in [-1..1], sim_{tS}(t_1, S_2, t_2, S_2) < 0.7$$

– ending game and 2 goals difference:

$$t_2 \in [19..20] \wedge S_2 \in [-2..2], sim_{tS}(t_1, S_2, t_2, S_2) < 0.7$$

As we can see, fixing the threshold thr_{tS} to 0.7 allows us to separate the situations previously mentioned.

Aggregation function. We tested four different functions: the mean, the weighted mean, the minimum and the harmonic mean. The minimum function results in a very restrictive aggregation function since the overall outcome is only based on the lowest value. Hence, lower values penalize high values rapidly. Regarding the harmonic mean, for similar values, its behavior is closer to the mean function. While for disparate values, the lower values are highly considered and the outcome decreases (although not as much as with the minimum function) as more lower values are taken into account. On the contrary, the mean function rapidly increases the outcome for high values, and does not give enough importance to low values. Finally, the weighted mean does not make difference between low and high values either, since the importance of each value is given by their weights. If a low value has a low weight and the rest of the values are all high, the outcome is slightly affected and results high anyway.

We are interested in obtaining an aggregation function that considers all values as much as possible but highlighting the lower ones. This is an important property as the values we are considering are similarity values. Hence, if one of the features has a low similarity, the overall similarity has to reflect this fact decreasing its value. Therefore, we use the harmonic mean as the aggregation function f:

$$f(x_1, ..., x_n) = \frac{n}{\sum_{i=1}^{n} \frac{1}{x_i}}$$

where x_i corresponds to the individual similarity values of the features.

Cost threshold. We consider worth adapting a problem to a case if the distances the robots have to travel from their original positions to the adapted ones are short enough so the environment changes as little as possible during this time. After observing the robots movements, we fixed the maximum distance to translate them to 1m. Their current average velocity is 350 mm per second. Hence, walking for 1m. takes around 2.8 seconds. Even though for now we are fixing this value to test the current system, we have to take into account that the threshold also depends on the opponents we are playing with. The faster they are, the lower the threshold should be.

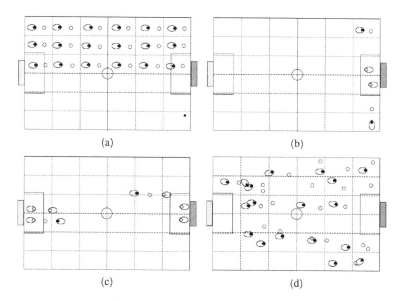

Fig. 7. (a) shows simple cases which allow the robot (depicted with filled head) to kick the ball towards the goal at every point of the field, (b) and (c) correspond to more complex situations where we have included one or two opponents (depicted with non-filled heads) and our robot attacking either from the front or the corners, and (d) shows some of the problems we used to test the system so far

Experiments. We manually defined 90 cases with one player, i.e. no teammates so far, varying the number of opponents (from 0 to 2), the time and the score difference. We also tested 50 problems created randomly and then manually labeled them to verify if the correct cases were retrieved using the system. We indeed obtained always the right ones, i.e. the system retrieved the case indicated in the labeled problem. It also computed the adapted position the robot should take and the actions to perform from that point on. Figure 7 depicts a set of the cases and problems created.

8   Extending the Case Definition

As previously mentioned, the solution of a case is a sequence of actions. So far we have been comparing snapshots of the current game with cases that describe the initial state of a game play. We believe that it would be also interesting to consider parts of a game play (the solution of a case) as part of the problem description of a case. The solution represents the (discrete) trajectory performed by the robots with their related actions. Thus, instead of comparing the current problem with the initial state of the case, we could compare it with the execution of the solution and reuse the solution from the closest point. This way, we can also avoid useless movements (e.g. going backwards to reach the initial position and then going forward again executing the solution's actions).

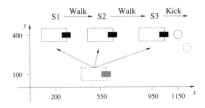

Fig. 8. Case description (solid lines) and problem description (dashed lines)

To this end, cases should have a more complex structure. We should define them by means of a graph structure or a sequence of nodes, where each node represents a situation S_i (description of the environment at time t) and arcs represent the associated actions to go from one node to the other. Then the retrieval step would have to consider each node S_i as a potential similar case to solve the new problem.

Given the problem and the case depicted in Figure 8, instead of positioning the robot in the initial state of the case ($S1$), we could move it to the adapted position indicated in $S2$ and then continue reusing the solution from this point.

9   Conclusion and Future Work

We have presented the initial steps towards a Case-Based Reasoning system for deciding which actions a robot should execute in the robot soccer domain. More precisely, we have focused our work on the retrieval and reusing steps of the system. While we contribute concretely to robot soccer, several of the features of the approach are applicable to general game-based adversarial environments.

We have defined the concept of *case* as well as the features that describe the state of a game, dividing them in two types: the *environment-based features* and the *game-based features*. We have discussed the similarity functions for the different features and we have tested different aggregation functions to compute the overall similarity. We have introduced a separation between the *controllable* and the *non-controllable* case indices to compute two metrics: the similarity and the cost. We select the retrieved case based on a compromise between the similarity and the cost of adapting the current problem to a case. Regarding the case reuse, we have detailed the adaptation of the description of the problem to the case retrieved and the reusing process of the solution. To test these first steps, we have designed a simulation interface to easily modify the different functions and parameters described.

As future work, we will continue on finishing the extension of the case description we have proposed in Section 8. After further testing the proposed approach in simulation, we will move our case-based approach to real robots.

References

1. A. Aamodt and E. Plaza. Case-based reasoning: Foundational issues, methodological variations, and system approaches. *Artificial Intelligence Communications*, 7(1):39–59, 1994.
2. RoboCup Technical Committee. *Sony Four Legged Robot Football League Rule Book*, Dec 2004.
3. T. Gabel and M. Veloso. Selecting heterogeneous team players by case-based reasoning: A case study in robotic soccer simulation. Technical report CMU-CS-01-165, Carnegie Mellon University, 2001.
4. K. Haigh and M. Veloso. Route planning by analogy. In *International Conference on Case-Based Reasoning*, pages 169–180, October 1995.
5. A. Karol, B. Nebel, C. Stanton, and M. Williams. Case Based Game Play in the RoboCup Four-Legged League Part I The Theoretical Model. In *RoboCup*, 2003.
6. M. Kruusmaa. Global navigation in dynamic environments using case-based reasoning. *Auton. Robots*, 14(1):71–91, 2003.
7. A. Lattner, A. Miene, U. Visser, and O.Herzog. Sequential Pattern Mining for Situation and Behavior Prediction in Simulated Robotic Soccer. In *9th RoboCup International Symposium*, 2005.
8. M. Likhachev and R. Arkin. Spatio-temporal case-based reasoning for behavioral selection. In *ICRA*, pages 1627–1634, 2001.
9. C. Marling, M. Tomko, M. Gillen, D. Alexander, and D. Chelberg. Case-based reasoning for planning and world modeling in the robocup small size league. In *IJCAI Workshop on Issues in Designing Physical Agents for Dynamic Real-Time Environments*, 2003.
10. A. Ram and J. C. Santamaria. Continuous case-based reasoning. *Artificial Intelligence*, 90(1-2):25–77, 1997.
11. M. Riedmiller, A. Merke, D. Meier, A. Hoffmann, A. Sinner, O. Thate, and R. Ehrmann. Karlsruhe brainstormers — A reinforcement learning approach to robotic soccer. *Lecture Notes in Computer Science*, 2019, 2001.
12. R. Ros, R. López de Màntaras C. Sierra, and J.L. Arcos. A CBR system for autonomous robot navigation. *Proceedings of CCIA'05*, 131, 2005.
13. A. Sarje, A. Chawre, and S. Nair. Reinforcement Learning of Player Agents in RoboCup Soccer Simulation. In *Fourth International Conference on Hybrid Intelligent Systems*, pages 480–481, 2004.
14. J. Wendler, S. Brüggert, H. Burkhard, and H. Myritz. Fault-tolerant self localization by case-based reasoning. In *RoboCup*, 2001.
15. J. Wendler and M. Lenz. CBR for Dynamic Situation Assessment in an Agent-Oriented Setting. In *Proc. AAAI-98 Workshop on CBR Integrations*, 1998.

Self-organising Hierarchical Retrieval
in a Case-Agent System

Ian Watson and Jens Trotzky

Dept. of Computer Science
University of Auckland
New Zealand
{ian@cs, jtro012@ec}.auckland.ac.nz

Abstract. This paper describes the implementation of a distributed case-agent system where a case-base is comprised of a set of agents, where each computational agent is a case, rather than the standard case-base reasoning model where a single computational agent accesses a single case-base. This paper demonstrates a set of features that can be modelled in a case-agent system focusing on distributed self-organising hierarchical retrieval. The performance of the system is evaluated and compared to that of a well recognised hierarchical retrieval method (i.e., footprint-based retrieval). The emergent properties of the case-agent architecture are discussed.

1 Introduction

The majority of case-based reasoning (CBR) systems have taken what Plaza and McGinty (2006) call a: *"single agent, single case base problem solving approach where one, usually well-maintained, case base functions as the central knowledge resource"* (Plaza & McGinty, 2006). They cite classic examples of this approach such as: "Entree" (Hammond et al., 1997) and "FAQ Finder" (Burke et al.,1997). Research in the area of *distributed CBR* they categorised with two key criteria (Figure 1):

1. how knowledge is organized or managed within the system (i.e., single vs. multiple case bases), and
2. how knowledge is processed by the system (i.e., single vs multiple processing agents).

The case-agents architecture, first proposed by Watson (2004), takes the most extreme position possible in this categorisation. Namely, the number of case bases is exactly equal to the number of agents, or in other words, each case is an individual computational agent. We will introduce the idea of the case-agent approach and discuss features of our implementation. The performance of the resulting system is compared to a k-nearest neighbour (k-NN) algorithm, compressed nearest neighbour (CNN) and the footprint-based retrieval algorithm (Smyth & McKenna, 1999).

Typically, a CBR system has a single case-base accessed by a single retrieval algorithm (most commonly k-NN) and an adaptation system (Aamodt & Plaza, 1994). In the case-agent architecture each case is itself an agent. Each agent can act

T.R. Roth-Berghofer et al. (Eds.): ECCBR 2006, LNAI 4106, pp. 62–75, 2006.

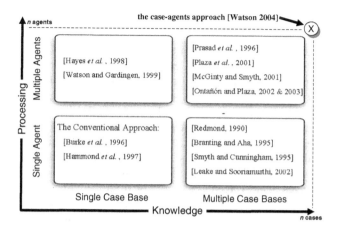

Fig. 1. The distributed CBR landscape (after Plaza & McGinty, 2006)

independently with its own similarity metrics and adaptation methods. Communication and co-operation between agents; for example, deciding which case is the most similar to a query-case, is managed by broker-agents.

2 Implementation Decisions

The implementation of case-agents would naturally benefit from an object-oriented design since individual case-agents would be instances of a general class of case-agent. Instances could inherit general functionality but show heterogeneity (Jaczynski & Trousse, 1998). Microsoft .NET and C# were used. The application consists of three major parts modelling the case-agent approach:

1. the case-agent representing a case from the case-base;
2. the similarity metrics, providing information on similarity to other case-agents and the query-case; and
3. the broker-agent, who creates case-agents using a case-reader, maintains communication between the agents, provides methods to determine the best case for a given query, and is central in hierarchically organising the case-agents.

In addition, two classes providing input and output methods to the user:

1. the case-reader which reads the cases from a given data file and creates agents;a
2. a case drawing class that visualises the agents based on their values, thresholds, status and similarity towards other case-agents in the case-base.

Our initial implementation was on a single computer and meant that we didn't have to deal with distribution of agents across multiple machines. Once we had proven that the basic case-agent architecture worked, we distributed the case-agents across a network of machines. For simplicity we use TCP/IP as the communications protocol with all the case-agents listening on the same open port. We realise that for a fully robust and secure implementation this approach may not be sufficient, but it was sufficient for us to evaluate the self organising properties of the system.

3 Case-Agents

A case-agent is modelled as an instance of the case-agent class. Each case-agent holds a set of value-attribute pairs taken from a case in the case-base. These values are used to measure the similarity of a case-agent to other case-agents. Given the fact that a case-agent has its own similarity metrics and adaptation methods, there is no global object that computes similarity or performs adaptation. In the distributed environment individual cases can exist on different machines with communication occurring across the network. However, it is not necessary for an individual case-agent to communicate with all other case-agents and so case-agents can be members of *domains* (effectively partitions of the case-base). Case-agents are prevented from comparing themselves against agents that are not from the same domain. A broker-agent is responsible for each domain   The following sections describe the implementation of the main features and methods of a case-agent.

Creation – Case-agents are created by the case-reader that reads information about a case from file and determines the set of value-attribute pairs that form the attributes of the case. The case-agent keeps a list of the attributes as well as their values. All case-agents are active by default, meaning that they are all potential candidates to satisfy a query in their domain.

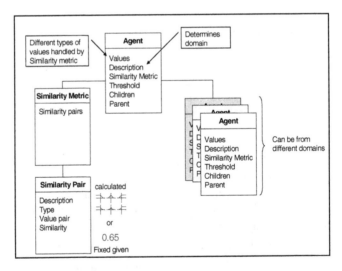

Fig. 2. The case-agent object structure

Upon creation of a new case-agent instance new similarity metrics are created for the case-agent. Default similarity metrics are inherited from the case-agent class but these can be exchanged or modified as a result of interaction with other case-agents, queries or adaptations. The case-agent is identified as part of a *domain* by its attribute set. Different domains have different attribute sets that are not comparable.

Similarity metrics – A similarity metric is an object that is created for each case-agent. It determines how values stored in the agent can be compared against other values from the same domain. We provide seven different default similarity metrics of two types (Amato, et al., 2003):

1. Numeric similarities that can be calculated by comparing two numbers. This is implemented in six ways defining a linear drop in similarity in three ways or an exponential decline in similarity in three ways. Symmetry and asymmetry are supported.
2. Symbolic similarity is implemented in two ways: (1) by a similarity matrix, where each cell contains a similarity value, or (2) by a similarity function $sim(v_1,v_2)$ where a similarity value is computed by some (possible knowledge intensive) method. Symbolic symmetry can be symmetric or asymmetric.

Activation and deactivation – Case-agents can be activated and deactivated during runtime. This feature can be used in various situations to increase performance or to decrease the density of case-agents at certain regions of the case base or to archive cases. Deactivation is a useful tool with inter-case-agent communication and is essential to create hierarchies of case-agents to improve retrieval efficiency.

4 Inter-agent Communication

To provide communication between agents across a network TCP/IP is used. Broker-agents maintain a directory of connected agents within their domain and of other brokers.

Similarity metric/Distance measure – Agents use a distance measure to determine their similarity towards another case-agent or towards a query-agent. Distance measures are an important feature that allows case-agents to locate themselves in the problem space (Amato, et al., 2003). The distance measure:

♦ determines the similarity between a case-agent and query-agent;
♦ determines the distance between each case-agent within a domain; and
♦ is used to hierarchical organise case-agents.

Because similarity can be asymmetric it is important to recognise that the distance between case-agents can depend on the direction of comparison. Comparing agent 1 with agent 2 might return a different similarity than comparing agent 2 with agent 1 and hence a different distance measure.

Parent-child relationships – In order to decrease the number of active case-agents performing similarity comparisons building hierarchies is efficient. Figure 3 illustrates a common problem that one might face with all case-agents being active; the left set of agents is not close to the query agent, whereas the right set of agents is a possible solution to the query-agent. In this example however, every single agent is active and needs to compare themselves against the query-agent.

A more efficient approach would be to have parent-agents measure similarity first and if their distance to the query falls below some threshold their children would not measure their similarity.

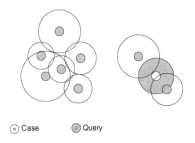

Fig. 3. All case-agents measure similarity

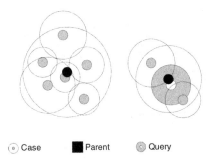

Fig. 4. A hierarchical organisation of case-agents

In Figure 4 only the parent-agents initially measure their similarity to the query. Then since the parent-agent of the right group sees the query within its neighbourhood it directs its children to measure their similarity to the query. This is directly analogous to the hierarchical organisation of cases in Smyth & McKenna's footprint-based retrieval (Smyth & McKenna, 1999), with parent-agents being equivalent to footprint cases.

Parent-agents – Parent-agents have special access to the *active* status of their children. Certain methods can be called from the parent-agents to modify the behaviour of the children. The parents themselves are identified as parent-agents by the domain's broker-agent. The broker-agent makes sure that the correct case-agents are invited to compare themselves against a query-agent. A flat hierarchy with no parent-child relationships could be characterised as the broker-agent being the only parent in the domain.

5   The Broker-Agent

The broker-agent is responsible for hierarchically organising the agents within its domain. The algorithm used for identifying the parent-agents is a modification of the CNN/IB2 algorithms [Hart, 1967; Aha *et al.*, 1991; Dasarathy, 1991; Brown, 1994) described in Smyth & McKenna (1999). During retrieval case-agents return a similarity value to their broker-agent who ranks the case-agents accordingly. The broker-agent would usually choose the highest ranking case-agent. However, other behaviours are possible, for example the broker-agent could select a set of case-agents and request that the set calculate their similarity each to the other. In this way a maximally diverse retrieval set could be obtained. The broker-agent:

♦ keeps basic information about the domain and assures that agents hosted by the broker comply with the domain specification through the given attribute set;
♦ keeps information about the parent-agents and family (competence) groups;
♦ stores similarity values from case-agents and typically selects the highest ranking (i.e., most similar) case-agent;
♦ gives feedback to case-agents about their overall ranking; and
♦ facilitates communication between the case-agents on their performance.

User feedback – Interaction with the user can give feedback to the case-agents. As the case-base is a multi-dimensional space of possible solutions it is sometimes useful to give directional feedback rather than binary feedback in terms of yes or no. A user interface to the broker-agent allows more detailed feedback (Ciaccia & Patella, 2002). A user can select a case as the most appropriate one even though it doesn't score the highest similarity value and may give additional reasons for the choice. This feedback gives the agents in the case-base a means of adjusting attribute weightings.

6   Case-Agent Visualisation

Visualising case-agents is a complex task of displaying multi-dimensional information. Case-agents created in our implementation have ten dimensions (taken from the travel case-base). To show parts of the problem space agents are drawn in two dimensions only (i.e., focusing on just two of the ten dimensions). Our initial implementation only visualises numeric dimensions. Case-agents are drawn in different colours depending on their status. A case-agent consists of the actual body, indicated by a circle that represents the set of attributes of the case-agent. The diameter of the circle represents the similarity threshold of that particular case-agent within which the case-agent considers another case-agent or a query-agent as being close by and therefore similar.

Our system draws the case-agents with a simple circle only. This does not handle asymmetry (i.e., that the similarity threshold might vary depending on the direction of comparison between case-agents) the true picture could be more complex. Moreover, this would be even more complex for symbolic attributes that may be highly non-linear in nature. Figure 5 shows a screenshot of the application displaying a query-agent and case-agents from the travel case-base. The application provides a set of tools to modify the similarity metrics as well as create query-agents and provides methods to display regions of the case base. For better understanding parent-child links can be displayed as well as the IP address of individual case-agents.

7   Evaluation

To allow comparisons with other CBR approaches the travel case-base (available from www.ai-cbr.org) was chosen to evaluate our prototype. The travel case-base consists of approximately 1,400 holidays with information on geographical regions, holiday type, price, accommodation class, duration, commencement date, etc. Attributes range from simple numeric attributes, like price, where similarity can be modelled by a simple asymmetric linear function to complex symbolic attributes, like geographic regions with complex similarity. As a consequence the travel case-base is a good evaluator for CBR systems.

The travel case-base was modified to meet the requirements of our evaluation. Case-agents are created based on the data of each case but the travel case-base doesn't include any domain information. This information needs to be defined as different agents can belong to different domains. Our implementation adds domain information to the case description, grouping case-agents into twelve geographic region domains.

Tests were performed by creating query-agents and analysing the behaviour of the system. The query-agent is marked as such and can be identified by broker-agents, that initiate retrieval. Any case-agent can be transformed into a query-agent as well, enabling leave-one-out testing.

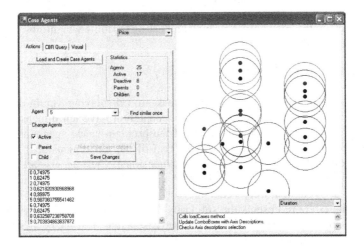

Fig. 5. Screenshot of the implementation

Our evaluation aims to demonstrate that the case-agent architecture works and that a similar architecture could be used in future to create CBR systems for highly distributed cases without having to aggregate cases into a single case-base with a single physical locality. Note that this differs from the virtual-case base model proposed by Brown et al. (1995) where data from disparate heterogeneous databases could be temporarily aggregated into a central virtual case repository.

7.1 Experimental Methodology

Our hierarchical case-agent architecture (HCA) was compared to three other retrieval algorithms. The first, k-NN, is the standard brute force nearest-neighbour algorithm where the target (query) case is compared to every case in the case-base and the most similar case is retrieved. k-NN therefore provides a benchmark against which to compare performance. The second algorithm, CNN, is a standard way to reduce retrieval time by generating an edited subset of cases. The third algorithm, FPBR, was an implementation of Smyth & McKenna's (1999) footprint based retrieval algorithm. This algorithm has been shown to more efficient than k-NN without sacrificing retrieval quality like CNN. We would expect our case-agent architecture to show similar retrieval results to FPBR. The travel case-base was randomly divided into 10 different case-base sizes, ranging from 100 cases to 1000 cases, with accompanying sets of 400 target problems.

7.2 Efficiency

The first experiment evaluated the efficiency of the retrieval algorithms over the range of case-base sizes. Efficiency is measured as the inverse of the number of cases examined during retrieval. The fewer the number of cases examined the greater the efficiency. k-NN will provide a benchmark for inefficiency as it examines every case.

Method: Case-bases of size n were tested with respect to their target problem sets and the average retrieval cost for the targets was computed. This produces an average retrieval cost per target problem for each case-base of size n.

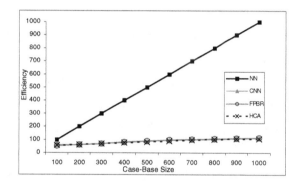

Fig. 6a. Efficiency vs. Case-Base Size

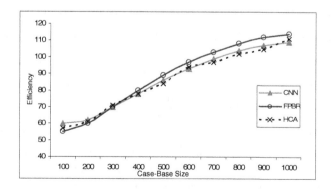

Fig. 6b. Efficiency vs. Case-Base Size (detail)

Discussion: Figure 6 shows that FPBR, CNN, and hierarchical case-agents (HCA) are all clearly much more efficient than standard k-NN. Figure 6b shows the detail for CNN, FPBR and HCA and indicates some slight variation between the three with FPBR being perhaps slightly more efficient. This may be due to the random selection of cases in the test case-bases or to differences in the selection of footprint cases and parent agents.

7.3 Competence

Since CNN discards cases from the case-base we would expect the competence of CNN to suffer. However, since FPBR and HCA do not discard any cases we would not expect their competence to suffer in a similar way.

Method: Each case-base of size n is tested with respect to its set of target problems, and the percentage of target problems that can be correctly solved using each retrieval method is measured. This cost is averaged for each of the case-bases of size n to compute a mean competence for each case-base size and retrieval method.

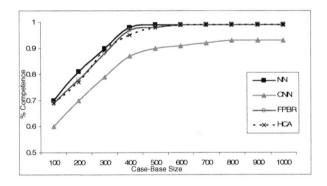

Fig. 7. % Competence vs. Case-Base Size

Discussion: As expected CNN performs poorly, particularly at smaller case-base sizes. k-NN, FPBR and HCA seem to perform similarly as shown in Figure 7.

7.4 Quality

In CBR solution quality is most usually thought of as a function of the distance between the target and the retrieved case. As the distance increases (i.e., similarity decreases), the amount of adaptation needed also increases and solution quality tends to decrease (Leake, 1996). This experiment shows how close CNN, FPBR, and HCA methods get to the benchmark quality level of standard k-NN.

Method: Each case-base of size n is tested with respect to its target problem set. The average similarity between target and retrieved case is computed. This similarity is then averaged over the case-bases of size n to produce a mean similarity per target problem for each case-base size. A similarity of 1.0 is an exact match and therefore of the highest quality.

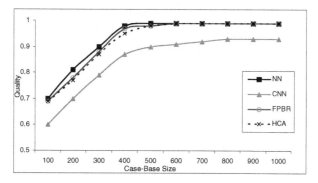

Fig. 8. Quality vs. Case-Base Size

Discussion: Once again CNN as expected performs worse with the quality of its retrieved cases suffering because of important cases being edited out of its case-base. k-NN, FPBR and HCA once the case-base size is around 500 perform at around 0.99 (i.e., very similar). From this size upwards the case-bases are sufficiently densely populated for a very close match to be retrieved. HCA does seem to perform slightly worse around the 400 cases size but again this is probably due to the random way the case-bases were selected or to differences in the selection of footprint cases and parent-agents.

7.5 Optimality

Here we are seeking to measure the ability of a retrieval algorithm to select the closest case to a target problem. Standard k-NN is used as a benchmark and we assume it retrieves the optimal case. This will not be so for CNN since it may have discarded the optimal case and therefore not have access to it.

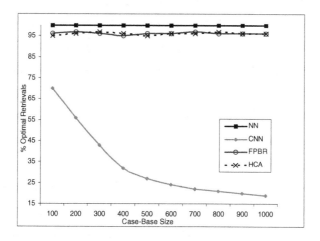

Fig. 9. Percentage of Optimal Retrievals vs. Case-Base Size

Method: As before each case-base of size n is tested with respect to its target problem set. This time we measure the percentage of times each of CNN, FPBR and HCA select the same optimal case for a target problem as the standard k-NN algorithm.

Discussion: As expected CNN is very poor with respect to optimality, particularly as the case-base size increases and more and more cases are discarded. FPBR and HCA both perform well with minor differences probably being due to small differences in the selection of footprint cases and parent agents.

7.6 Case Distribution

With the case-agent architecture there are numerous ways agents could be distributed across a network. At one extreme all the agents could reside on a single computer; at the other extreme each agent could be on a separate computer. We would envisage a commodity or product supplier probably keeping all their cases on a single server. The purpose of this experiment was to see if the distribution of cases influenced performance. A network of 10 computers was used. In *random* the case-agents were assigned to a machine randomly. In *logical* all the cases from a domain were assigned to the same computer, thus agents were distributed by domain simulating a product supplier offering numerous similar products. The efficiency of the retrieval (i.e., the number of cases examined) was compared for each approach.

Method: As before, case-bases of size n were tested with respect to their target problem sets and the average retrieval cost for the targets was computed. This produces an average retrieval cost per target problem for each case-base of size n.

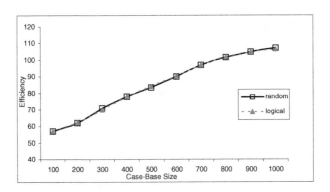

Fig. 10. Efficiency vs. Case-Base Size for randomly and logically distributed case-agents

Discussion: There was no discernable difference in efficiency between random and logical as shown in Figure 10. The very minor variations are probably due to differences between the randomly generated case-bases. Thus, we can conclude that the physical location of the case-agents is irrelevant with respect to retrieval efficiency.

7.7 General Performance

The general performance of the system relies on the number of cases and especially the number of individual similarity comparisons (Gennaro, et al., 2001). The comparisons of agents has a runtime of at least polynomial time with a power of two or higher depending on the complexity of the similarity metric definitions. With such poor performance for large case-bases using a two stage hierarchical retrieval process will significantly improve performance. Moreover, we do not need to limit ourselves to just two stages, hierarchies could be much deeper, improving performance more.

8 Conclusion

We have shown that case-agents can self organise into retrieval hierarchies with performance characteristics similar to a two stage retrieval method like footprint-based retrieval. Treating cases as agents is a novel approach with emergent potential enabling distributed systems to model real world problems closer than normal CBR systems do. Cases can reside as agents on the servers of disparate commodity providers, yet can still act as a cohesive case-base with regard to retrieval. In competitive environments case-agents would permit a commodity provider to individualise their case-agents configurations. Another interesting possibility is the fact that cases from different domains can be hosted on the same system. For example, in a travel agency, separate domains for flights, hotels, car hire and activity bookings could all co-exist on the same system and respond independently to different aspects of a single query.

Similarity metrics can be copied, exchanged and modified easily with potentially interesting applications. A variety of dynamic behaviour can be envisaged; for example, in the travel case-base case-agents could behave as commodities (i.e., holidays) and once sold or consumed, they would be deleted since they are no longer available. Moreover, as the commencement date of a holiday approached a case-agent can lower its similarity threshold and adapt its price (by lowering it) to make it more likely to be retrieved. This mimics the practice of discounting holidays booked at the last minute.

Visualising the similarity relationships of symbolic values is a significant challenge but even visualising numerical values is not simple. In our implementation similarity thresholds have been illustrated by circles with a certain radius. However, this doesn't give much insight into the behaviour of the threshold nor does it give any idea of whether the threshold is the same for each agent, since each agent could have a different similarity metric and therefore a different threshold. To find a more suitable solution to illustrate the similarity thresholds of cases would be of interest. This includes the shape of the threshold which is not necessarily symmetrical.

This paper has described the first implementation of a case-agent system. Further work will investigate the emergent properties of this novel architecture and in particular will investigate more complex agent topologies and the use of different similarity metrics and adaptation methods within an agent community.

References

Aamont, A. & Plaza, E. (1994). Case-Based Reasoning: Foundational Issues, Methodological Variations, and System Approaches. AICOM 7(1): pp. 39-58.

Aha, D.W., Kibler, D., & Albert, M.K (1991). Instance-Based Learning Algorithms. Machine Learning 6: pp.37-66.

Amato, G.F., Rabitti, F., Savino, P. & Zezula, P. (2003). Region proximity in metric spaces and its use for approximate similarity search. ACM Trans. Inf. Syst. 21(2): pp.192-227

Branting K. & Aha, D. (1995). Stratified Case-Based Reasoning: Reusing Hierarchical Problem Solving Episodes. In, Proc. of the 14th Int. Joint Conf. on Artificial Intelligence, Montreal, Canada, pp.20-25.

Brown, M.G. (1994). An Underlying Memory Model to Support Case Retrieval. In, Topics in Case-Based Reasoning. Springer LNAI 837: pp.132-43.

Brown, M.G., Watson, I. & Filer, N. (1995). Separating the Cases from the Data; Towards More Flexible Case-Based Reasoning. In, Case-Based Reasoning Research and Development Veloso, M., & Aamodt, A. (Eds.) Springer LNAI 1010.

Burke, R., Hammond, K., Kulyukin, V., Lytinen, S., Tomuro, N. & Schoenberg, S. (1997). Question answering from frequently-asked question files: Experiences with the FAQ Finder system. AI Magazine 18(2): pp. 57–66.

Ciaccia, P. & Patella, M. (2002). Searching in metric spaces with user-defined and approximate distances. ACM Trans. Database Syst. 27(4): pp.398-437.

Dasarathy, B.V. (1991). Nearest Neighbor Norms: NN Pattern Classification Techniques. IEEE Press, Los Alamos, California, US.

Gennaro, C., Savino, P. & Zezula, P. (2001). Similarity search in metric databases through hashing. In, Proc. of the 2001 ACM workshops on Multimedia: multimedia information retrieval, Ottawa, Canada, ACM Press, pp.1-5.

Hammond, K., Burke, R. and Young, B. (1997), The FindMe approach to assisted browsing. IEEE Expert 12(4): pp.32–40.

Hart, P.E. (1967).The Condensed Nearest Neighbor Rule. IEEE Trans. on Info. Theory, 14: pp.515-16.

Hayes, C., Cunningham, P. & Doyle, M. (1998). Distributed CBR using XML. In Proc. of the UKCBR Workshop: Intelligent Systems & Electronic Commerce.

Jaczynski, M., & Trousse, B. (1998). An object-oriented framework for the design and the implementation of case-based reasoners. In, Proc. of the 6th German Workshop on Case-Based Reasoning, L. Gierl & M. Lenz (Eds.), Berlin, Germany.

Leake, D. (1996). Case-Based Reasoning: Experiences, Lessons and Future Dirctions. AAAI Press/MIT Press.

Leake, D. & Sooriamurthi, R. (2001). When two case bases are better than one: Exploiting multiple case bases. In, Proc. of the 4th Int. Conf. on Case-Based Reasoning, D.W. Aha & I. Watson, eds., Springer LNAI 2080: pp.321–35.

McGinty, L. & Smyth, B. (2001). Collaborative case-based reasoning: Applications in personalized route planning. In, Proc. of the 4th Int. Conf. on Case-Based Reasoning, D.W. Aha & I. Watson, eds., Springer LNAI 2080: pp.362–76.

Ontanon, S. & Plaza, E. (2002). A bartering aproach to improve multiagent learning, In, Proc. of the 1st Int. Joint Conf. on Autonomous Agents & Multiagent Systems, pp.386–93.

Ontanon, S. & Plaza, E. (2003). Learning to form dynamic committees. In, Proc. of the 2nd Int. Joint Conf. on Autonomous Agents and Multiagent Systems, pp.504–11.

Plaza, E. & McGinty, L. (2006). Distributed Case-Based Reasoning. The Knowledge Engineering Review (to appear).

Plaza, E. & Ontanon, S. (2001). Ensemble case-based reasoning: Collaboration policies for multiagent cooperative CBR, in Proc. of the 4th Int. Conf. on Case-Based Reasoning, D.W. Aha & I. Watson, eds., LNAI 2080, Springer: pp.437–51.

Prasad, M.V.N., Lesser, V.R. & Lander, S.E. (1996). Retrieval and reasoning in distributed case bases, Journal of Visual Communication & Image Representation, Special Issue on Digital Libraries 7(1): pp.74–87.

Redmond, M. (1990). Distributed cases for case-based reasoning: Facilitating use of multiple cases. In, Proc. of the 18th National Conf. on Artificial Intelligence, T. Dietterich & W. Swartout, eds., AAAI Press/The MIT Press, pp.304–9.

Smyth, B. & Cunningham, P. (1996). The utility problem analysed: A case-based reasoning perspective. In, Proceedings of the 3rd European Workshop on Case-Based Reasoning, I. Smith and B. Faltings, eds, Springer LNAI 1168: pp.392–99.

Smyth, B. & McKenna, E. (1999). Footprint Based Retrieval. In, Proc. of the 3rd Int. Conf. on Case-based Reasoning. K-D Althoff, R Bergmann & K Branting (Eds.), Springer LNAI 1650: pp.343-57.

Watson, I. (2004). Case-Agents: A Novel Architecture for Case-Based Agents. In, Proc. of the 17th Int. Florida Artificial Intelligence Research Society Conf., AAAI Press, pp.202-6.

Watson, I. & Gardingen, D. (1999), A distributed case-based reasoning application for engineering sales support. In, Proc. of the 16th Int. Joint Conf. on Artificial Intelligence, T. Dean, ed., Morgan Kaufmann, 1: pp.600–5.

COBRAS: Cooperative CBR System for Bibliographical Reference Recommendation

Hager Karoui, Rushed Kanawati, and Laure Petrucci

LIPN, CNRS UMR 7030, Université Paris XIII
99, avenue Jean-Baptiste Clément
F-93430 Villetaneuse, France
{hager.karoui, rushed.kanawati, laure.petrucci}@lipn.univ-paris13.fr

Abstract. In this paper, we describe a cooperative P2P bibliographical data management and recommendation system (COBRAS). In CO-BRAS, each user is assisted by a personal software agent that helps her/him to manage bibliographical data and to recommend new bibliographical references that are known by peer agents. Key problems are:
- how to obtain relevant references?
- how to choose a set of peer agents that can provide the most relevant recommendations?

Two inter-related case-based reasoning (CBR) components are proposed to handle both of the above mentioned problems. The first CBR is used to search, for a given user's interest, a set of appropriate peers to collaborate with. The second one is used to search for relevant references from the selected agents. Thus, each recommender agent proposes not only relevant references but also some agents which it judges to be similar to the initiator agent. Our experiments show that using a CBR approach for committee and reference recommendation allows to enhance the system overall performances by reducing network load (i.e. number of contacted peers, avoiding redundancy) and enhancing the relevance of computed recommendations by reducing the number of *noisy* recommendations.

1 Introduction

Maintaining an up-to-date annotated bibliographical database is a central activity of research teams. However the multiplication of document sources (e.g. workshops, conferences, journals, etc.) as well as the on-line availability of most documents have contributed in making the task more complex and more time-consuming. Actually, in addition to the classical information overload problem, researchers have now direct access to papers text that are seldom coupled with the complete bibliographical data. It is frequent now to start a new search session in order to find the exact reference of an interesting paper that we have found earlier. Fortunately, researchers usually work in like-minded teams. It is highly possible that information we are looking for is already obtained or known to one or more colleagues. In addition, colleagues may have useful hints about the quality of papers and what to read if interested in a given topic. It is obvious that sharing the team bibliographical knowledge could not only enrich each

T.R. Roth-Berghofer et al. (Eds.): ECCBR 2006, LNAI 4106, pp. 76–90, 2006.

member knowledge but also reduce time and efforts required to manage personal databases. Two key issues to handle are: which colleague (peer) to collaborate with? and what to recommend to others? In this work, we propose a COoperative Bibliographic Recommendation Agent System (COBRAS).

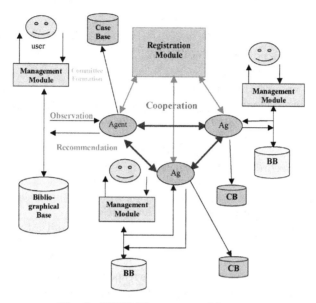

Fig. 1. COBRAS system architecture

COBRAS has a peer-to-peer architecture (depicted in figure 1) and aims at: providing help for users to manage their local bibliographical databases and to exchange bibliographical data among like-minded users' groups in an *implicit* and *intelligent* way. We consider a context of small groups (e.g. members of laboratory, members of a research team...). Each user is associated with a personal software agent that provides different types of help such as: filling bibliographical records, verifying the correctness of the information entered and more importantly, recommending the user with relevant bibliographical references. To perform these tasks, the personal agent collaborates with a set of peers in order to get relevant recommendations. The CBR [1] problem solving methodology has been successfully used by a number of recommender systems [4], [7], [9]. COBRAS is based on two CBR approaches: the first one searches for a given user's interest, a set of appropriate peers to collaborate with, and the second one searches for relevant references from the selected agents. Thus, each recommender agent proposes not only relevant references but also some agents which it judges to be similar to the initiator agent. The agents are supposed to be willing to cooperate for simple reasons, e.g.: they can improve their performances, their results and their knowledge about their colleagues. Since each agent has its own base, having various references from other peers and an idea about their relevance for a given interest will be of great benefit.

The paper is organised as follows. First, we give an overview of our global system in section 2. Then, we focus on both COBRAS CBR components: the reference recommendation system and the committee recommendation system in section 3. Some experimental results for system validation are presented in section 4 and related work is discussed in section 5. Finally, in section 6, we conclude and give some directions for future work.

2   COBRAS: System Overview

COBRAS is a cooperative bibliographical reference recommendation system. It aims at sharing references between a group of like-minded users and allows to take advantage of past experiences of a single user or even a group of users. In COBRAS, each agent disposes of a reference base which is an XML base containing references related to different topics. Each bibliographical reference is described by a record containing the principal following information:

- Bibliographical data: classical data composing a reference such as the type (e.g. Article, In Proceedings, etc), authors, title, etc.
- Keywords: list of keywords describing the reference and introduced by the user.
- Topics: a list of topics the reference is related to, according to the user's point of view. The user chooses the corresponding reference topics from a shared topic hierarchy. This hierarchy has a tree structure and is based on the ACM[1] hierarchy related to the Computer Science domain (for more details, see [11]). However, we stress that the same hierarchy will be used differently by different users, i.e. the same reference can be related to different topics by different users. For example one may index all CBR-related papers with the same topic, e.g. CBR, while another user may index the same papers differently: some related to memory organisation in CBR systems and others for CBR case maintenance. A third may index the same references as all related to lazy learning.

The recommendation process includes the following steps:

- The initiator agent observes its user's actions on his own local database and determines its interests. The agent applies a simple algorithm (described in [10]) in order to compute the hottest topics of its user's interest.
- For each hot topic, the initiator agent sends a recommendation request to a "committee" of peers. A committee is a set of agents that are likely to have references related to the current hot topic. We use a CBR approach to compute the committee at which we add new agents from a Recommended Agent List (RAL) (see section 3.2). The CBR technique is used in a cooperative way in order to allow reuse and sharing of past knowledge between users.

---
[1] http://www.acm.org/class/1998.

- Each contacted agent (recommender agent) searches for references related to the received request and sends result to the initiator agent. Reference search is done using an other CBR approach in order to reuse the solution for future similar problems and to accelerate the reference search process (see section 3.1).
- The initiator agent handles the results received from the recommender agents. The results contain not only recommended reference lists, but also recommended agents. The initiator agent applies a voting scheme in order to rank recommended references. The k highly ranked recommended references will be proposed to the user. Then, it reevaluates them according to its user's behavior with respect to the recommended references. The agent's committee and the Recommended Agent List are updated according to this reevaluated results. Finally, it sends a feedback about the evaluated references to the recommender agents.
- Each recommender agent learns from the received feedback and updates its reference case base.

3 CBR for Reference and Committee Recommendation in COBRAS

A recommendation request message is a triple: $R = < A, T, KL >$ where:

- A is the sender agent identifier (initiator agent),
- T is the hot topic detected by the initiator agent,
- KL is a list of keywords that is computed from the set of keywords lists describing references related, directly or indirectly to the topic T in the local reference database.

A reference is indirectly related to a topic T if it is related to a topic T' more specific than T.

3.1 Reference Recommendation System

When the initiator agent finds the appropriate committee, it asks all agents belonging to this committee for references. Each contacted agent applies a CBR cycle in order to find relevant references. A case has the following structure:

- The problem part is composed by the hot topic and the list of keywords of the recommendation request. $Problem = (T, KL)$.
- The solution part ($Solution = (TL_s, KL_s, A, E)$) is composed by four elements: a topic list TL_s indicating where to search for references in the database, a keyword list KL_s describing the references found related to TL_s, an identifier of the previous initiator agent A and the evaluation of the case by the initiator agent E. The A attributes of the different similar cases form the list of agents to recommend by each recommender agent. This information is used by the second CBR system for committee recommendation and presents an example of collaboration between the two CBR components.

The cycle is described as follows: informally the topic and the keyword list contained in the request form the target problem (T, KL). The search phase is based on a case similarity function (see equation 1) between the target case (TC) and each source case (SC) in the reference case base. If this similarity is above a given specified threshold σ_c, then the case will be recalled.

$$Sim_{Case}(TC, SC) = \alpha \ Sim_{Topics}(TC.T, SC.T) +$$
$$\beta \ Sim_{Keywords}(TC.KL, SC.KL) \qquad (1)$$

We face two cases: the first case happens when the recommender agent does not find similar cases in its reference case base, so it searches directly in the bibliographical base for references that match the received query by applying a specific search algorithm (see 3.1) and sends only a list of recommended references to the initiator agent. The second one is when the recommender agent finds similar cases in its reference case base, then it goes to the reuse phase. Having all similar cases, we apply a simple heuristic retaining only cases having their case similarity greater than the average one. The solution of the reuse phase is a set of signs facilitating the search in the bibliographical base. Sign set includes topics and keywords lists used to search for reference in the bibliographical database. The solution of the target problem is composed by the topic and keyword lists of the different selected source cases. In the next step, the new case is evaluated by the initiator agent according to the user behavior faced with the proposed references. This evaluation indicates the relevance of the application of that case solution on the bibliographical base and also its importance according to the other solutions. $E = (LP, AP)$ where LP is the local precision (defined in Heuristics 2 in section 3.2) of the solution of the agent and AP is the average precision of all the solutions suggested by the other recommender agents. Each agent will learn by adding in its case base new well evaluated cases or by updating existing cases. If there is no solution found in the search phase, the new formed case will be added to the reference case base. Else, if the case exists already in the case base for the same agent (A), then the case, specifically, the evaluation part will be updated with the new values (i.e. LP, AP). If A is not the same, then if the case is well evaluated (i.e. LP is close to AP), then it will be added to the case base.

The new case elaboration is done as follows: the problem part is the target problem, the solution part corresponds to the topic list where the proposed references are found, the keyword list describing these references, the identifier of the initiator agent and its evaluation.

Note that the final request's solution (reference list) presents the application of each agent CBR solution on the bibliographical database and not the brute solution returned by the CBR cycle.

Search Algorithm. When receiving a request, an agent starts to search its local database for references that match the pair (T, KL). Informally, the keyword list is treated as a query, the designated target topic T indicates the start point of the document research in the local database. The agent will retrieve from the local database references that match the received query. Reference/query matching is evaluated by a simple similarity function $sim_{Ref}(R, r)$ that measures the similarity between a request R and a reference r. A reference r matches a request R if their similarity is above a given specified threshold σ_r. The similarity function is a weighted aggregation of two basic similarity functions: topic similarity (Sim_{topic}) and keywords similarity ($Sim_{keywords}$). Formally we have:

$$Sim_{Ref}(R, r) = \alpha Sim_{topic}(R.T, r.topics) + \beta Sim_{keywords}(R.KL, r.keywords) \tag{2}$$

where α and β are the basic similarity weights. We have $\alpha + \beta = 1$. The used keyword similarity function is a simple function measuring the number of common words between two lists. Formally:

$$Sim_{Keywords}(A, B) = \frac{|A \cap B|}{|A \cup B|} \tag{3}$$

The topic similarity measure uses the topics hierarchical structure. The applied heuristics is the following: the similarity between two topics depends on the length of the path that links the two topics and on the depth of the topics in the hierarchy [7]. Recall that in a tree, there exists only one path between any two nodes. The deeper the nodes are, the more they represent specific topics, hence the more similar they are. Formally we have:

$$Sim_{Topics}(T_1, T_2) = 1 - \frac{path(T_1, MSCA(T_1, T_2)) + path(T_2, MSCA(T_1, T_2))}{path(T_1, root) + path(T_2, root)} \tag{4}$$

where $path(a, b)$ is the path length between nodes a and b, $root$ is the topic's tree root and $MSCA(a, b)$ returns the most specific common ancestor of nodes a and b in the topic tree. Using these similarity functions, the local agent returns the m most relevant references that match the received request. Starting from the target topic $R.T$, the agent will search for related references which similarity is above the threshold σ_r. If no sufficient references are found, it examines references related to more specific topics, then it moves to more general topics. The retrieval process ends when m relevant references are found or when no more topic is left.

3.2   Committee Recommendation System

A case has the following structure: $Case = (T, C)$ where:

- $Problem = T$ is a detected hot topic,
- $Solution = C$ is a committee composed of interesting peer agents according to the topic T.

Search Phase. For each topic T of the computed hot topic list, the assistant agent applies a CBR cycle. The committee search is based on a topic similarity (equation 4) which compares the target topic with the one of the case in the agent's case base. If this similarity value is above a given threshold σ_t, then the case will be recalled. At the beginning, since the committee case base is empty, the initiator agent sends the recommendation request to all available agents.

Reuse Phase. This phase aims at finding a solution to the target problem from a set of source cases found in the previous phase. The solution presents an interesting peer agents committee, to which the recommendation request will be forwarded. Based on the idea that the more the case is similar to the target case, the more the associated agents are relevant because they were evaluated according to that topic, we make a selection of the similar cases found at the previous phase by retaining only cases having their similarity to the target problem greater than the average similarity of all the source cases. The solution takes the union of the different committees of the selected source cases C at which we add the list of recommended agents for this topic $(RAL(T))$. The *target case =* (T, C), is such that: T is the initial topic, $C = \cup C_i + RAL(T)$, where C_i is the solution of the source case i. Then, the recommendation request is broadcasted to all peer agents composing the committee C. The Recommended Agent List (RAL) is a list of agents recommended by the recommender agents and which are not evaluated by the initiator agent yet. This list contains new agents to be discovered by the related agent. It aims at ensuring some dynamicity to the committee in order to try to track the user's interest changing over time and to avoid always having the same committee to solicit.

Revision Phase. The solution computed in the previous phase is then evaluated by the initiator agent according the its user's behavior with respect to the recommended references. If the user is interested in a set of recommended references (e.g. the user adds some references to its local base), then their associated cases and agents will be well evaluated.

Learning Phase. This step consists of adding new committee cases to the local agent committee case base and the selected recommended agents to the Recommended Agent List. It is the most important step in the CBR cycle. In fact, the selection of retained agents for future similar problems is done at this stage. As we have explained before, the peer selection is achieved so as to reduce committee size while preserving the result quality (result in the case of solliciting all peers). The elaboration of the new case must be accurate in order to store the relevant information. This phase is based on the agent addition strategy, i.e. the criteria used in order to decide if a given responding agent will be added to the newly formed committee or not. A natural idea is to choose all agents which propose some relevant references. Although this simple strategy gives encouraging preliminary results, it does not optimise the committee size. In order to reduce the number of contacted agents, we define criteria which evaluate each agent contribution within the selected committee. We define two criteria-based strategies: heuristics 1 and heuristics 2.

1. **Heuristics 1:** consists of retaining only agents with a local recall value greater than or equal to the average recall value of the references recommending agents. The recall represents the rate of good recommended references among the good existing references ($Recall = \frac{Good\_recommended\_references}{Good\_references}$).
2. **Heuristics 2:** consists of retaining only agents with a local precision value greater than or equal to the average precision value of the recommended

references. The precision represents the rate of good recommended references among all the recommended ones ($Precision = \frac{Good\_recommended\_references}{All\_recommended\_references}$).

Preliminary experimental results show that $Heuristics$ 2 and $Heuristics$ 1 give very similar results, so we choose $Heuristics$ 2 to retain agents from all recommender agents. Concerning the second adding in the Recommended Agent List, we retain only new agents, i.e. agents not yet contacted or not already evaluated by the initiator agent for that topic. This allows for discovering new agents and updating the committee.

4   System Validation

This section describes the evaluation of the committee formation strategy proposed in section 3.2. We suppose that our Multi-Agent System (MAS) is composed by n agents. All agents have the same references but they are distributed differently and randomly among the topics of the topic tree. We fix a hot topic, which is considered as a query and we apply our strategy in order to find appropriate agents. We vary each time the number of interesting agents in the MAS and we compute the recall and the precision. By interesting agent, we mean an agent having at least x% of the references associated with the hot topic. To evaluate the whole system, we considered three evaluation criteria. These criteria are of two types :

- Quality criteria: presented by the recall and the precision measures (already described in $Heuristics$ 1 and $Heuristics$ 2).
- Performance criteria: presented here by the reduction rate. It is the quotient of the committee size over the number of all available agents (Reduction rate $= \frac{Contacted\_agents}{Available\_agents}$).

The simulation is performed with three different settings:

- All: we use a naive approach where the recommendation request is broadcasted to all available agents (in our case the n agents).
- $Random$: we apply a simple peer selection algorithm, which randomly selects m agents knowing that m always corresponds to the number of interesting agents (m varies from 1 to n).
- $Committee$: the set of agents returned by the previous described committee CBR approach.

In our experiments, we fixed the MAS size to 10 agents, the used topic similarity threshold σ_t has the value of 0.7 in order to return the most similar references. We suppose that an interesting agent is an agent having at least 70% of the reference set associated with the hot topic. A single simulation consists of fixing the minimum number of good references for the interesting agents. Interesting agents do not necessarily have the same set of good references. The set is chosen randomly. The other references are dispersed among the other topics in a random manner.

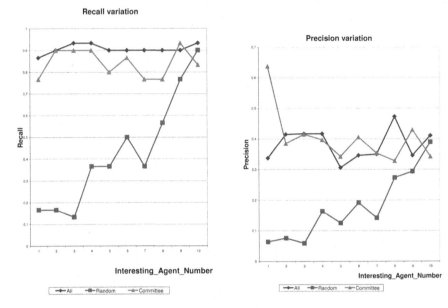

Fig. 2. Recall variation

Fig. 3. Precision variation

Figure 2 shows the recall variation according to the number of interesting agents. We notice that the recall for the *committee* strategy is very close to the *all* strategy and clearly better than the *random* strategy. The recall is often improved by the increase of the number of interesting agents when we randomly choose the agents.

The precision variation is described in figure 3 for the three settings. The *all* and *committee* strategies present more or less similar results, which are better than the naive approach based on random peer selection. However, the precision value is fairly weak with an average of 0.403. This is due to the same content of the agent's bases: we considered that all agents have the same references which are distributed differently and randomly among the topics. The precision value will be considerably improved when each agent has its own different base.

Then, in order to evaluate the performance of the system using the proposed committee formation strategy, figure 4 shows the number of contacted agents among ten available agents. We notice that the number of contacted agents is reduced. For example in the case of 1 interesting agent, we solicit only 1 agent instead of 10, for 6 and 7 interesting agents, we solicit 5 agents. The committee is more useful when the interesting agent number is important, we contact only 6 agents while there is 9 interesting agents in the MAS and only 4 agents in the case of 10 interesting agents while preserving similar system's performances (even an increase of the precision value in the case of 9 interesting agents). This shows that our approach allows not only to contact interesting agents but also to determine the best agents from the interesting ones. This allows to reduce noisy recommendations and decreases the redundancy between agent's references.

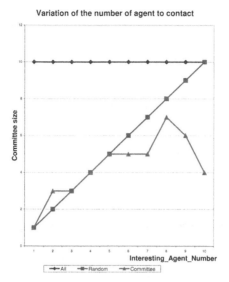

Fig. 4. Committee Size

Finally, we can say that our committee formation strategy improves the system performance by reducing the number of contacted agents, while it gives similar quality results (i.e. recall and precision) as when all available agents are contacted.

Because of the dynamicity of the P2P networks, the committee found by COBRAS contains some agents unavailable at that time. So, in the following experimentation, we suppose that when we solicit the computed committee, some random agents (designed by off in the figures) are off-line. We vary each time the rate of the unavailable agents in the MAS and we compute the recall and the precision. *Committee* presents the committee obtained without taking into account the recommended agents while Committee ($off = 0\%$) presents the committee returned by the CBR system with the recommended agents. Committee ($off = x\%$) means that $x\%$ of the MAS agents are off-line when the request is sent. All the curves have nearly the same trend for the recall and the precision values according to the increasing number of interesting agents in the MAS (see figures 5, 6). We note that the recall value decreases as the rate of disconnected agents increases (off). For example, in the case of 10 interesting agents, the recall falls from 0.9 to 0.766 when $off = 50\%$, and from 0.766 to 0.00 in the case of one interesting agent. Conversely, precision values are increasing according to the decreasing of the contacted agents. Obviously, the increase and decrease amounts of the criteria values depend on the type of the off-line agent: if the given agent is interesting, this will often descrease the recall of the system (e.g. the case of one interesting agent with $off = 50\%$, the case of 4 interesting agents with $off = 50\%$, $off = 30\%$, $off = 20\%$), else, this will on the contrary improve the system precision (e.g. the case of 2 interesting agents with $off = 30\%$, $off = 50\%$).

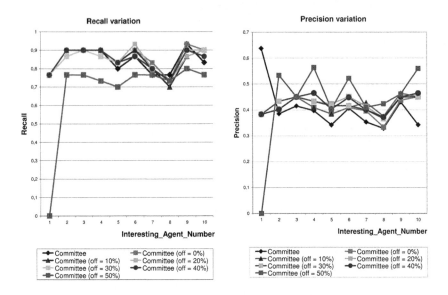

Fig. 5. Recall variation   **Fig. 6.** Precision variation

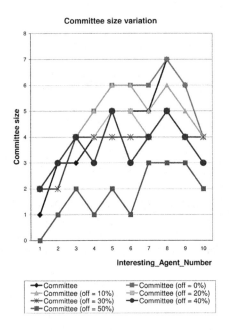

Fig. 7. Committee Size

Figure 7 shows that the number of contacted agents decreases according to the increase of the off-line agents. The effect is very clear when the off rate is very important (greater than 40% for this example).

Experimental results show that using an appropriate CBR approach for reference and committee recommendation enhances the system performances while preserving similar result quality (e.g. recall and precision).

5 Related Work

One interesting work directly related to our proposed system COBRAS is the Bibster system (standing for Semantic-Based Bibliographic Peer-to-Peer System, [3]). The main goal of Bibster is to allow a group of people to search for bibliographical references in each other personal database. A peer-to-peer architecture is used. However, only exact searching is supported. Our system represents, in a way, an extension of Bibster where similarity-based searching is used. In addition the search is made by software agents instead of being initiated by the users themselves. Collaborative bookmarking systems address a similar problem [8]. However in the peer-to-peer collaborative bookmarking system [9], we lack a unified hierarchy of topics making the matching evaluation harder to compute. Another similar work is the I-SPY information searching engine [2]. The goal of the I-SPY system is to allow a group of like-minded people to share their searching results in an implicit way. The system is built in a centralised way where a hit matrix records for each submitted query the documents selected by the user. When a new query is submitted, results that have been selected by other users in response to similar past queries are provided by the system. In our system, the set of topics can be viewed as a set of pre-specified queries. The overlap between the users queries is more likely to happen than in the case of open vocabulary queries.

In [12], McGinty and Smyth describe a collaborative case base reasoning (CCBR) architecture, which allows problem solving experiences to be shared among multiple agents by trading cases. This approach was applied in personalised route planning and it promises a solution by allowing a given user agent to borrow cases from similar agents that are familiar with the target territory. Plaza et al. investigate in [14] possible modes of cooperation among homogeneous agents with learning capabilities. They present two modes of cooperation among agents: Distributed Case-Based Reasoning (DistCBR) and Collective Case-Based Reasoning (ColCBR). In the DistCBR cooperation, an originating agent delegates authority to another peer agent to solve the problem. In contrast, ColCBR maintains the authority of the originating agent, since it decides which CBR method to apply and merely uses the experience accumulated by other peer agents. They prove that the result of cooperation is always better than no cooperation at all. However, these protocols are domain dependent and are the result of a knowledge modeling process.

One fundamental issue is our system concerns the choice of appropriate peers to collaborate with. Different approaches are proposed in the literature. Some are based on the notion of agent reputation [5] or agent expertise [3]. Others propose to apply automatic learning techniques in order to enable each agent to determine if it needs to increase the committee of peers and, if it is the case, which peer agent to invite [13]. For our purposes, the idea consists of providing each peer agent with the capacity of selecting a subset of peer agents having good results according to a given recommendation request type (in our case, the recommendation of bibliographical references). The goal is to improve the performance of the whole system by reducing the network and the agents load. Bibster system [3] has a peer-to-peer architecture and aims at sharing bibliographic data between researchers. The peer selection is based on the *expertise* notion [6]. The expertise is a set of ACM topics. All system peers share a common ontology for publishing semantic descriptions of their expertise in a peer-to-peer network. This knowledge about the other peers expertise forms the semantic topology, which is independent of the underlying network topology. When a peer receives a request, it decides to forward the query to peers whose expertise is similar to the subject of the query. Peers decide autonomously to whom advertisements should be sent and which advertisements to accept. This decision is based on the semantic similarity between expertise descriptions. This strategy gives good results compared with broadcasting the query to all or to a random set of peers but does not exploit past experience to learn and improve the formed semantic topology. Ammar et. al. [5] propose a reputation system for decentralised unstructured P2P networks like Gnutella [2] for searching and information sharing. The peer selection strategy is based on the agent *reputation* notion. A reputation score is intended to give a general idea of the peer's level of participation in the system. Reputation scores are based on two essential factors: the peer capability and its behavior. The capability of a peer depends on its processing capacity, memory, storage capacity, and bandwidth. The behavior of a peer is determined by the level of contribution offered by it for the common good of the P2P network. Having reliable reputation information about peers can form the basis of an incentive system and can guide peers in taking decisions. Ontañón and Plaza [13] propose another strategy of selection of the agents that join a committee for solving a problem in the classification tasks. The committee organization improves (in general) the classification accuracy with respect to individual agents. It is a learning framework that unifies both the when and the who issues. In fact, the agent learns to assess the likelihood that the current committee will provide a correct solution. If the likelihood is not high, the agent has to invite a new agent and has to decide which agent to invite. The agent learns to form a committee in a dynamic way and to take decisions such as whether it is better to invite a new member to join a committee, when to individually solve a problem, when it is better to convene a committee.

We have chosen to propose a new strategy of committee formation which will be dynamic, extensible and adaptable. The proposed strategy exploits as much as possible past experiences and will be adaptable with the new real constraints. To ensure this, our strategy relies on a case-based reasoning system. It aims at computing committee's recommendations. In fact, when an agent detects a hot topic, it applies a CBR cycle to find some committee recommendation associated with the request type. The reference recommendation request will then be forwarded to peer agents composing the recommended committee.

---

[2] http://gnutella.wego.com/.

6   Conclusion

We have presented a cooperative P2P bibliographical recommendation system COBRAS. It aims at finding the most relevant references from the appropriate agents. The system is based on two CBR components collaborating each other in order to provide good recommendations. The first CBR reasoner aims at finding an appropriate committee to ask for a given recommendation request. The second CBR reasoners aims at finding the most relevant references from the previous computed committee. The experiments show that the combination of the two collaborative reasoner enhance COBRAS' performances while preserving similar result quality as when contacting everybody. The obtained results are encouraging. Different tracks however should be explored in order to improve all the working process system. We will propose a strategy to maintain the agent committee and reference case bases, and to learn forming an optimal committee for each recommendation request type.

References

1. A. Aamodt and E. Plaza. Case-based reasoning: Foundational issues, methodological variations, and system approaches. *In AI Communications IOS Press*, 7(1):39–59, 1994.
2. E. Balfe and B. Smyth. Case-based collaborative web search. In *7th European Conference on Advances in Case-based Reasoning, Madrid*, pages 489–503, 2004.
3. J. Broekstra, M. Ehrig, P. Haase, F. Harmelen, M. Menken, P. Mika, B. Schnizler, and R. Siebes. Bibster -a semantics-based bibliographic peer-to-peer system. In *Proceedings of SemPGRID'04, 2nd Workshop on Semantics in Peer-to-Peer and Grid Computing*, pages 3–22, New York, USA, may 2004.
4. Robin Burke. Hybrid recommender systems with case-based reasoning. In *Advances in Case-based Reasoning, 7th European Conference, ECCBR 2004, LNAI.*, number 3155, pages 91–105, 2004.
5. M. Gupta, P. Judge, and M. Ammar. A reputation system for peer-to-peer networks. In *Proceedings of ACM Networks and Operating System Support for Digital And Video NOSSDAV 2003*, Monterey, CA, 2003.
6. P. Haase, R. Siebes, and F. Harmelen. Peer selection in peer-to-peer networks with semantic topologies. In *International Conference on Semantics of a Networked World: Semantics for Grid Databases.*, Paris, 2004.
7. M. Jaczynski and B.Trousse. www assisted browsing by reusing past navigations of a group of users. In *Proceedings of EWCBR'98, Lecture Notes on Artificial Intelligence*, number 1488, pages 160–171, 1998.
8. R. Kanawati and M. Malek. Informing the design of shared bookmark systems. In *Proceedings of RIAO'2000: Content-based Multimedia Information Access*, 2000.
9. R. Kanawati and M. Malek. Cowing: A collaborative bookmark management system. In *Proceedings of CIA'02: International workshop on cooperative information agents, LNAI 2182*, pages 34–39, 2001.
10. H. Karoui, R. Kanawati, and L. Petrucci. An intelligent peer-to-peer multi-agent system for collaborative management of bibliographic databases. In *Proceedings of the 9th UK Workshop on Case-Based Reasoning*, pages 43–50, Queens' College, Cambridge, UK, December 2004.

11. Hager Karoui. Agent RàPC pour la gestion coopérative de bases bibliographiques personnelles. In *Plate-forme AFIA' 2005, 13 ème atelier de Raisonnement à Partir de Cas*, Nice, FRANCE, Mai 2005.

12. L. McGinty and B. Smyth. Collaborative case-based reasoning: Applications in personalised route planning. In *LNCS ICCBR*, pages 362–376, 2001.

13. S. Ontanon and E. Plaza. Learning to form dynamic committees. In *Proceedings of the second international joint conference on Autonomous Agents and Multi-Agent Systems*, pages 504–511, Melbourne, Australia, 2003. ACM Press, NEW YORK, USA.

14. E. Plaza, J. L. Arcos, and F. Martin. Cooperation modes among case-based reasoning agents. In *Proceedings of ECAI'96 Workshop on Learning in Distributed Artificial Intelligence Systems*, 1996.

A Knowledge-Light Approach to Regression Using Case-Based Reasoning

Neil McDonnell and Pádraig Cunningham

Department of Computer Science, Trinity College Dublin, Ireland
{neil.mcdonnell, padraig.cunningham}@cs.tcd.ie

Abstract. Most CBR systems in operation today are 'retrieval-only' in that they do not adapt the solutions of retrieved cases. Adaptation is, in general, a difficult problem that often requires the acquisition and maintenance of a large body of explicit domain knowledge. For certain machine-learning tasks, however, adaptation can be performed successfully using only knowledge contained within the case base itself. One such task is regression (i.e. predicting the value of a numeric variable). This paper presents a knowledge-light regression algorithm in which the knowledge required to solve a query is generated from the differences between pairs of stored cases. Experiments show that this technique performs well relative to standard algorithms on a range of datasets.

1 Introduction

Case-based reasoning (CBR) systems solve new problems by re-using solutions from similar, previously solved cases. Solutions may be directly copied from old to new cases, or may be *adapted* to match the requirements of new problems more precisely [1]. The adaptation of old solutions is a difficult process that generally requires detailed knowledge of both the problem domain and the task at hand. For that reason, most deployed CBR systems do not attempt adaptation, but instead limit themselves to the retrieval of past cases.

In general, the complexity of the adaptation task increases with the complexity of the problem domain. Highly complex domains require the addition of explicit adaptation knowledge, often in the form of rule-sets [2]. CBR systems that rely on this knowledge have been described as 'knowledge-intensive'; those that seek to minimize the use of domain-specific knowledge have been called 'knowledge-light' [3].

One application amenable to a knowledge-light approach is regression, where the goal is to predict the value of a numeric variable. The knowledge required to solve a problem case may be garnered locally from neighbouring cases at run-time, e.g. using the k-NN algorithm. Alternatively, adaptation knowledge may be compiled into a global domain model, e.g. a neural network or linear model. This paper describes a knowledge-light approach to regression that utilizes both global and local adaptation knowledge. Global adaptation knowledge is automatically generated from the differences between stored cases in the case base (CB). When a new problem case is received, global and local knowledge are combined to predict its solution.

T.R. Roth-Berghofer et al. (Eds.): ECCBR 2006, LNAI 4106, pp. 91 – 105, 2006.

In a previous paper [4], we introduced the idea of mining adaptation knowledge from case differences. This paper details how case differences can be used to construct a robust, effective regression system. It also describes how regression can be performed on datasets with nominal attributes, and presents new experimental results.

Section 2 introduces case differences and shows how they can be used in a simple regression system. It identifies some limitations that impair this system's performance in many real-world domains. Section 3 addresses these and describes how case differences can form the basis for a practical regression algorithm. Finally, section 4 presents an experimental evaluation of the technique by comparing its performance with standard algorithms on a range of datasets.

2   Case Differences

This section describes what we mean by case differences, and shows how they can be applied to solve regression problems in a simple domain. This 'first attempt' at using case differences is subject to a number of limitations that must be overcome before the technique can be applied in real-world domains. These limitations are discussed, and solutions proposed in Section 3.

2.1   Introduction to Case Differences

Let us assume for the moment that each case is stored as a vector of numeric attributes. The difference between any two cases can then be calculated simply by subtracting one from the other.

Suppose we have a simple artificial housing domain where the value of a house is a function of its number of bedrooms and location:

$$housePrice = f(numBedrooms, location)$$

where problem attributes $numBedrooms$ and $location$ have range 1 to 6. Given two sample cases of form ($numBedrooms, location, housePrice$),

$$C_1: (4, 1, 320000), \quad C_2: (3, 2, 300000),$$

the differences between them can be calculated and stored in a $difference\ case$:

$$\Delta(C_1, C_2) = C_1 - C_2 = (1, -1, 20000).$$

This difference case states that an increase of 1 in $numBedrooms$ and a decrease of 1 in $location$ results in an increase of 20000 in $housePrice$. It encapsulates specific adaptation knowledge that may be applied to solve new problems. A difference case can be generated from each pair of cases in the CB, $C_i - C_j$. All difference cases can then be stored together in their own $Difference\ CB$.

2.2   Naïve Application of Case Differences for Regression

Case differences can be used to solve a new query problem as follows: calculate the differences between the query and a neighbouring case, then account for these differences using a stored difference case.

Let us take an example from the housing domain: suppose we receive a query case **Q** = (*4, 2, ?*), so that our task is to predict the value of a house with 4 bedrooms in location 2. The problem-solving process then proceeds as follows (see Fig. 1):

1. Retrieve the nearest neighbour to **Q**: **NN** = (*5, 1, 350000*)
2. Find the difference between their problem descriptions: Δ(**NN, Q**) = (*1, -1*)
3. Retrieve a difference case from the Difference CB to account for these differences: Δ(**C₁, C₂**) = (*1, -1, 20000*) for some **C₁, C₂** in the original CB
4. Predict the target value for **Q**: *350000 – 20000 = €330,000*

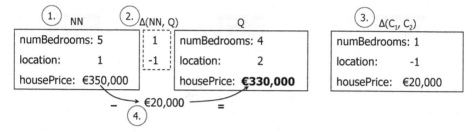

Fig. 1. Solving a query using case differences

The problem-solving process involves calculating the differences between **Q** and **NN**, then using a difference case to predict the effect that these differences will have on the solution. We will refer to the three cases used for each prediction, (**NN, C₁, C₂**), as an *adaptation triple*. (These cases are referred to as an 'estimation triple' in [5].)

The knowledge within a CBR system can be conveniently divided into four 'knowledge containers' [6]. Generating adaptation knowledge from case differences involves transferring knowledge between two of them, the CB and the solution transformation. Re-using knowledge in this way eases construction and maintenance of the overall CBR system.

The idea of mining adaptation knowledge from case differences has been considered in previous research. Hanney & Keane [7] generated adaptation rules from case differences and applied these rules to regression problems. McSherry [5] used case differences for regression in linear domains where all cases in the CB strictly dominate one another. Jarmulak et al. [8] and Craw [9] consider the application of case differences for a synthesis task in the medical domain. They also proposed storing case differences together in their own CB.

2.3 Problems Associated with Naïve Application of Case Differences

The process demonstrated above has many positive aspects: it utilizes adaptation knowledge easily generated from the original CB; it is intuitive and easily understood. Unfortunately, it suffers from one major drawback: it will only work correctly in linear domains, i.e. domains that can be accurately represented by a linear model. Many real-world domains do not exhibit global linearity, including the real-world housing domain. For example, increasing the number of bedrooms from 1 to 2 in one location will very probably have a different impact on house price than an increase from 5 to 6 in another location. Non-linearity has two root causes:

1. The influence from each attribute on the target value may not be linear throughout its range. E.g. increasing *numBedrooms* from 5 to 6 may generally lead to a greater increase in *housePrice* than an increase from 1 to 2.
2. There may be interaction between problem attributes. E.g. the effect of changing *numBedrooms* may vary depending on *location*.

Summing up, the simple application of case differences to solve regression problems makes the assumption that the target domain is linear – it assumes that the differences between any pair of stored cases can be used to account for the differences between the query and a neighbouring case.

Previous research has recognized the problem caused by non-linearity within the problem domain, and some partial solutions have been proposed to address it. Jarmulak et al. [8] made the assumption of local linearity around the query, and limited the search for difference cases to this region of domain space. McSherry [5] proposed holding all but one of a set of interacting attributes constant during problem-solving.

The difficulty with such attempts to avoid non-linearity is that they greatly reduce the search space for difference cases. Furthermore, the restrictions imposed are inflexible in that they do not take into account the individual characteristics of different domains and queries. What is needed is some way to deal with non-linearity that maximizes the number of difference cases that can be considered when searching for solutions, and that adapts automatically to the topology of the problem domain and the specific characteristics of the query. Such a method is proposed in Section 3. As we shall see, it requires a greater degree of care when choosing difference cases to bridge the gap between a query and its neighbour.

3   Using Case Differences for Regression

We have shown that difference cases provide a simple method for performing regression using CBR. Unfortunately, their naïve application may not perform well in non-linear domains, because differences between cases in one part of domain space may not have the same effect on the target value as differences in another.

Having calculated the differences between the query and a neighbour, then, our aim is to find a difference case that correctly accounts for these differences while also taking non-linearity in the problem domain into account. Local linear regression (LLR) can help us achieve this goal (see [10] for an introduction to local linear modeling). In particular, LLR can act as a useful heuristic in two ways:

1. LLR can identify those difference cases most likely to be useful in solving any particular query;
2. LLR can reduce prediction error by helping to avoid noisy cases.

Sections 3.1 and 3.2 discuss each of these aspects in turn. Section 3.3 describes how overall prediction error can be reduced by combining several predictions. Section 3.4 looks at how nominal attributes can be accommodated in the problem-solving process.

3.1 Using Local Linear Regression to Help Choose Difference Cases

Let us begin by re-examining the example used in Section 2.2. The differences between query $\mathbf{Q}$ and neighbouring case $\mathbf{NN}$ were calculated as:

$$\Delta(\mathbf{NN}, \mathbf{Q}) = (1, -1).$$

A difference case was found to predict the effect of these differences on *housePrice*:

$$\Delta(\mathbf{C_1}, \mathbf{C_2}) = (1, -1, 20000).$$

The question is: can this difference case actually be applied here? Logically, the answer is that it applies if the impact that changes in *numBedrooms* and *location* have on *housePrice* is the same in the area of domain space around $\mathbf{Q}$ as in the area around $\mathbf{C_1}$ and $\mathbf{C_2}$. More generally, *difference cases can be applied to solve a query if the cases used in their construction come from an area of domain space similar to that around the query, where similar areas of domain space are those where changes in problem attributes have the same impact on target value.* That is, similar areas of domain space have similar rates of change of target value with respect to each problem attribute.

Suppose our problem domain has problem attributes $a_1, a_2, ..., a_n$ and solution y, i.e. $y = f(a_1, a_2, ..., a_n)$. This represents a scalar field in which target function f maps $\mathbf{R}^n$ to $\mathbf{R}$. At any point, the rate of change of f with respect to each problem attribute a_i is defined as the *gradient* of f:

$$grad(f) \equiv \nabla \mathbf{f} = \left(\frac{\partial y}{\partial a_1}, \frac{\partial y}{\partial a_2}, ..., \frac{\partial y}{\partial a_n} \right) \qquad (1)$$

This vector cannot be calculated precisely because the actual form of the target function is unknown. However, since the gradient is defined as the best linear approximation to f at any particular point in $\mathbf{R}^n$, *it can be approximated at any point by constructing a local linear model and taking the slope for each problem attribute.* So local linear modeling allows us to calculate the gradient at any point, and gradients help us to choose difference cases that are likely to be applicable to the query. The updated problem-solving process can be summarized as follows:

To solve a query case, use a difference case from an area of domain space with similar gradient to that around the query, where gradients are approximated using local linear modeling.

The gradient in those regions of domain space containing $\Delta(\mathbf{NN}, \mathbf{Q})$ and $\Delta(\mathbf{C_1}, \mathbf{C_2})$ can be approximated by taking the gradient at points $\mathbf{Q}$ and $\mathbf{C_2}$ respectively.

Using gradients to guide the search for difference cases allows the case-differences algorithm to be used in non-linear as well as linear domains. Given $\Delta(\mathbf{NN}, \mathbf{Q})$, we are looking for a closely matching difference case $\Delta(\mathbf{C_1}, \mathbf{C_2})$, where gradients around the query and difference case also match. These twin objectives can be handled in four different ways during the search process, reflecting different levels at which they can be combined.

3.1.1 Approach 1: Don't Consider Gradients at All

In Section 2.3 it was stated that many real-world domains are non-linear. Many domains *are* roughly linear, however, and can be tackled using the basic case-differences algorithm described in Section 2.

Let us present this algorithm a little more formally. Given query $\mathbf{Q}$, the problem-solving process involves two search steps and an adaptation step:

1. A neighbouring case to the query, $\mathbf{NN}$, is found in the original CB;
2. A difference case $\Delta(\mathbf{C_1}, \mathbf{C_2})$ matching $\Delta(\mathbf{NN}, \mathbf{Q})$ is found in the Difference CB for some $\mathbf{C_1}, \mathbf{C_2}$ in the original CB;
3. Target values from $\mathbf{NN}$, $\mathbf{C_1}$ and $\mathbf{C_2}$ are used to predict a target value for $\mathbf{Q}$.

Steps 1 and 2 involve searches in the original and Difference CBs, whereby a search case is compared with each stored case to find the most similar. Both CBs have the same set of problem attributes, A. The similarity between any two cases τ and ρ in either CB is calculated as follows:

$$Sim(\tau, \rho) = \sum_{a \in A} sim(\tau_a, \rho_a) \qquad (2)$$

Steps 1 and 2 constitute a twin-objective search where the optimal adaptation triple $(\mathbf{NN}, \mathbf{C_1}, \mathbf{C_2})$ to solve a particular query $\mathbf{Q}$ simultaneously maximizes the similarity between $\mathbf{NN}$ and $\mathbf{Q}$, and between $\Delta(\mathbf{NN}, \mathbf{Q})$ and $\Delta(\mathbf{C_1}, \mathbf{C_2})$. These objectives can be incorporated into a score for each potential triple:

$$Score_0 = Sim(\mathbf{NN}, \mathbf{Q}) + Sim(\Delta(\mathbf{NN}, \mathbf{Q}), \Delta(\mathbf{C_1}, \mathbf{C_2})) \qquad (3)$$

In Step 3, the triple with the highest score is used to predict the target value for the query, $y_p^{\mathbf{Q}}$:

$$y_p^{\mathbf{Q}} = y^{\mathbf{NN}} - (y^{\mathbf{C_1}} - y^{\mathbf{C_2}}) \qquad (4)$$

3.1.2 Approach 2: Consider Difference Cases and Gradients Separately

In arbitrary non-linear domains, performance is likely to be improved if difference cases are chosen from areas of domain space with similar gradients to that around the query. This requirement can be supported by adding an additional term to Eq. (3):

$$Score_1 = Score_0 + Sim(\nabla \mathbf{Q}, \nabla \mathbf{C_2}) \qquad (5)$$

Each prediction now involves a multi-objective search with three objectives: maximize the similarity between $\mathbf{NN}$ and $\mathbf{Q}$, $\Delta(\mathbf{NN}, \mathbf{Q})$ and $\Delta(\mathbf{C_1}, \mathbf{C_2})$, and $\nabla \mathbf{Q}$ and $\nabla \mathbf{C_2}$. Note that in linear domains where all gradients are very similar, Eq. (5) defaults to Eq. (3). As non-linearity increases in the problem domain, the area of domain space where applicable difference cases may be found gradually reduces in size. This is the flexibility that we were looking for in Section 2.3; it is also shared by the two search strategies described below.

3.1.3 Approach 3: Combine Difference Cases and Gradients in a Vector

It can be noted that difference cases and gradients are intimately related to one another. Given query $\mathbf{Q}$ and neighbouring case $\mathbf{NN}$, suppose we achieve a perfect match between $\Delta(\mathbf{NN}, \mathbf{Q})$ and $\mathbf{DC} = \Delta(\mathbf{C_1}, \mathbf{C_2})$. If the gradient at $\mathbf{C_2}$ is higher than that at $\mathbf{Q}$ for each attribute, then $\mathbf{DC}$ is likely to overestimate the effect of attribute differences at $\mathbf{Q}$ on the target value. If it is lower, $\mathbf{DC}$ is likely to underestimate their impact. From this we can see that difference cases and gradients may offset one another, so that even if $\mathbf{DC}$ has smaller attribute differences than those in $\Delta(\mathbf{NN}, \mathbf{Q})$, it may still yield a correct prediction if the gradient at $\mathbf{C_2}$ is higher than that at $\mathbf{Q}$. It therefore makes sense to consider difference cases and gradients together when searching for the optimal adaptation triple.

The differences between any two cases τ and ρ can be stored in a difference case:

$$\Delta(\tau,\rho) = (\tau_1 - \rho_1, \tau_2 - \rho_2,..., \tau_n - \rho_n) = (\Delta a_1^{\tau,\rho}, \Delta a_2^{\tau,\rho},..., \Delta a_n^{\tau,\rho})$$

The predicted increase in target value y resulting from each attribute difference is

$$\Delta \mathbf{y}_p^{\tau,\rho} = (\Delta y_{1p}^{\tau,\rho}, \Delta y_{2p}^{\tau,\rho},..., \Delta y_{np}^{\tau,\rho})$$

where $\Delta y_{ip}^{\tau,\rho} = \left.\dfrac{\partial y}{\partial a_i}\right|_\rho .\Delta a_i^{\tau,\rho}$, and $\left.\dfrac{\partial y}{\partial a_i}\right|_\rho$ is the slope of attribute a_i at point ρ.

In looking for the optimal adaptation triple $(\mathbf{NN}, \mathbf{C_1}, \mathbf{C_2})$, the search process again has two objectives. We want to maximize the similarity between $\mathbf{NN}$ and $\mathbf{Q}$, as well as the similarity between predicted changes in target value resulting from differences in each problem attribute:

$$Score_2 = Sim(\mathbf{NN}, \mathbf{Q}) + Sim(\Delta \mathbf{y}_p^{NN,Q}, \Delta \mathbf{y}_p^{C_1,C_2}) \qquad (6)$$

This strategy can be summed up as follows: a difference case is applicable if each of its attribute differences has the same impact on target value as each of the attribute differences in $\Delta(\mathbf{NN}, \mathbf{Q})$.

3.1.4 Approach 4: Combine Difference Cases and Gradients in a Scalar

Let us restate the objective of our search: we are looking for a difference case that correctly predicts the impact of $\Delta(\mathbf{NN}, \mathbf{Q})$ on the target value. If $\Delta(\mathbf{NN}, \mathbf{Q})$ and $\Delta(\mathbf{C_1}, \mathbf{C_2})$ have a similar predicted impact, then the actual difference in target value given by $y^{C_1} - y^{C_2}$ can be used to predict the target value for $\mathbf{Q}$ (using Eq. (4)).

For any two cases τ and ρ, the overall impact of their differences on the target value can be predicted by taking the scalar product of $\Delta(\tau, \rho)$ and the gradient at ρ:

$$\Delta y_p^{\tau,\rho} = \sum_{a \in A} (\tau_a - \rho_a).\left.\frac{\partial y}{\partial a}\right|_\rho = \Delta(\tau,\rho) \bullet \nabla \rho$$

Difference case/gradient pairs can therefore be reduced to simple scalar values before being compared:

$$Score_3 = Sim(\mathbf{NN}, \mathbf{Q}) + Sim(\Delta y_p^{NN,Q}, \Delta y_p^{C_1,C_2}) \qquad (7)$$

3.1.5 Discussion

The preceding subsections describe four different ways to consider gradients when searching for the optimal adaptation triple to solve query **Q**; which one works best will depend on the nature of the problem domain. Approach 1 is simplest and is adequate in linear domains. Constructing a traditional linear model is even simpler, however, and is to be preferred when working with domains known to be globally linear. Approach 2 is likely to perform best in highly non-linear or noisy domains, where gradients may offer only limited assistance in choosing difference cases. These are domains where k-NN has also been shown to perform well. Approach 4 is designed to perform well in domains that exhibit strong local linearity, i.e. domains where local linear regression performs well as a prediction algorithm. Approach 3 takes a middle path between 2 and 4, and is probably the best general-purpose approach for most problem domains.

Note that when gradients are used to help find adaptation triples, the similarity function used to compare cases does not need to use global attribute weights or scaling factors (see Eq. (2)). Attributes' influence on the target value may vary throughout domain space, and the algorithm correctly accounts for this.

Note also that in the best-scoring adaptation triple (**NN**, **C₁**, **C₂**), case **NN** may not be the nearest neighbour to the query. Instead, **NN**, **C₁** and **C₂** are chosen together so as to maximize their likely usefulness in solving a particular query **Q**. This is an example of adaptation-guided retrieval [11] – the adaptability of neighbouring cases is considered in addition to their proximity to the query.

3.2 Using Local Linear Regression to Reduce Prediction Error

Let us assume that in the original CB, errors in target values are distributed normally about their true values with variance v^2. Let us also assume that errors are independent of problem attribute values (i.e. the error function is homoschedastic). Each prediction uses target values from three stored cases (see Eq. (4)). Since each has error variance v^2, the prediction error has variance $3 \times v^2$. If we can reduce the error among these three cases, variance in prediction error will be reduced threefold.

Eq. (4) shows that the case-differences algorithm is highly *local* in that each prediction is based on only three cases. But in using LLR to help choose difference cases, the algorithm also assumes some degree of local linearity in the problem domain. This local linearity can act as a useful guide when choosing cases (**NN**, **C₁**, **C₂**). Recall from Section 3.1 that estimating the gradient at each case involves constructing a local linear model at that point in domain space. This local model can be thought of as an approximation of the target function's mean throughout that area of domain space. Cases lying further from the linear model are more likely to be noisy than those close to it. This provides a simple heuristic: when choosing (**NN**, **C₁**, **C₂**), prefer cases that lie closer to the local linear model constructed around them. Variance is reduced by biasing the choice of cases towards the local mean.

For any case τ, the normalized residual $r^{\tau} = (y^{\tau} - y_p^{\tau}) / (y_{max} - y_{min})$ is the difference between actual and predicted target values, normalized to lie in the range -1 to 1. For **NN**, we simply want a low residual r^{NN}. For **C₁** and **C₂**, we want to minimize the difference of their residuals, $(r^{C_1} - r^{C_2})$ – if both cases are offset from their local linear model by the same distance, their predictive quality will not be affected. Each of the score formulas in Eq.s (3), (5), (6) and (7) can be altered to take case quality into account:

$$Score_i = Score_i \times (3 - (abs(r^{NN}) + abs(r^{C_1} - r^{C_2}))) \tag{8}$$

As before, the triple with the highest score is used to predict the target value for **Q**.

3.3 Combining Multiple Predictions to Reduce Prediction Error

Each prediction is made following a search for the highest-scoring adaptation triple. A list of triples ordered by score can easily be maintained during this search. The best n triples can each be used to make a prediction, and these predictions averaged to reduce the variance in overall prediction error.

If all triples were of equally high quality, averaging the first n predictions would reduce the variance of the prediction error from v^2 to $\dfrac{v^2}{n}$. This gain is not in fact achieved because the first prediction uses the highest scoring adaptation triple; predictions based on subsequent triples will, in general, have higher error. Nevertheless, a suitable n can be found using cross validation so that overall prediction error is minimized. Eq. (4) is modified to take an average of n predictions, where each is weighted by its score:

$$y_p^Q = \frac{\sum\limits_{i=1}^{n} Score_i \times (y^{NN_i} - (y^{C_{1i}} - y^{C_{2i}}))}{\sum\limits_{i=1}^{n} Score_i} \tag{9}$$

3.4 Adding Support for Nominal Attributes

So far, we have assumed that cases are represented as vectors of numeric attributes. The case-differences algorithm can be extended to support nominal problem attributes, provided at least one remains numeric. Some minor changes are required to the algorithm described above, starting with the construction of the Difference CB. Differences between numeric values are found by subtracting one from the other. Differences between any two nominal values v_1 and v_2 are calculated as follows:

$$\Delta(v_1, v_2) = \begin{cases} v_1 = v_2 & 'u' \\ v_1 \neq v_2 & v_1' \rightarrow 'v_2 \end{cases} \tag{10}$$

I.e. the values of v_1 and v_2 are concatenated with the symbol '$\rightarrow$' between them. E.g. if $C_1 = $ ('a', 3, 'no') and $C_2 = $ ('a', 5, 'yes'), then $\Delta(C_1, C_2) = $ ('u', -2, 'no$\rightarrow$yes'). The operation of the basic case-differences algorithm (as presented in Section 3.1.1) is largely unchanged in the presence of nominal problem attributes:

1. Given query $\mathbf{Q}$, a neighbouring case $\mathbf{NN}$ is found using Eq. (2). Nominal attributes may have their own custom comparators, or may be treated more simply, e.g. *sim=1* for equal values, *sim=0* for unequal values.
2. $\Delta(\mathbf{NN}, \mathbf{Q})$ is calculated using Eq. (10), and matching difference case $\Delta(\mathbf{C_1}, \mathbf{C_2})$ is found using Eq. (2). For any two nominal values, *sim=1* for equal values, *sim=0* for unequal values.
3. A prediction is made using target values from $\mathbf{NN}$, $\mathbf{C_1}$ and $\mathbf{C_2}$ as before.

Sections 3.1 – 3.3 describe improvements to the basic algorithm to accommodate non-linearity in the problem domain and to improve the robustness of predictions. Sections 3.1 and 3.2 require construction of local linear models around each case in the original CB. These are then used as a heuristic to help choose difference cases likely to apply to the query, and to help avoid noisy cases. LLR only works with numeric values, so how can this heuristic be used in the presence of non-numeric attributes? The answer is that nominal attributes can simply be ignored, and local linear models constructed using only those attributes that are numeric. This approach is reasonable because local linear models are not used directly to make predictions. They simply guide the search for cases ($\mathbf{NN}$, $\mathbf{C_1}$, $\mathbf{C_2}$), and continue to perform a useful role even when they are constructed using only a subset of problem attributes. This is borne out in the experimental results shown below.

4   Experimental Evaluation

Experiments were carried out using five standard regression datasets that vary in size, and in number and type of problem attributes. None has any missing values. All numeric attributes (including target values) were normalized to the range 0–1. Leave-one-out cross validation was used for all testing, with the exception of the Abalone dataset where a 90%/10% training/test split was made. The datasets are summarized in Table 1.

Two sets of experiments were conducted. The first set comprised an ablation study in which different variants of the case-differences algorithm were compared[1]. This

Table 1. Datasets used for experimental evaluation

Dataset Name	Problem Att. Types – Numeric + Nominal	Number of Instances (Train + Test)	Source
Boston Housing	13 + 0	506	UCI [12]
Tecator	10 + 0	195	StatLib [13]
Abalone	7 + 1	4177 (3759 + 418)	UCI
CPU	7 + 1	209	UCI
Servo	2 + 2	167	UCI

---

[1] The implementation of the case-differences algorithm differed from the description above in one respect: when constructing the Difference CB, each case in the original CB was compared with its 10 nearest neighbours instead of with all other cases. For a CB of size n, this limits the size of the Difference CB to $(10 \times n)$.

showed how improvements in performance were related to different parts of the algorithm. The second set of experiments compared the case-differences approach with a number of standard regression techniques.

Experiment 1 – comparing different variants of the case-differences algorithm

Different variants of the case-differences algorithm were compared for each dataset in turn. These results were then aggregated to show the overall performance of each variant relative to the basic algorithm (variant 1). Results are shown in Fig. 2.

The following variants of the algorithm were compared (left to right in each chart in Fig. 2):

1. Basic case-differences algorithm (see Section 3.1.1). A single adaptation triple was used for each prediction. Difference case $\Delta(C_1, C_2)$ was chosen from any part of domain space to provide the closest match to $\Delta(NN, Q)$.

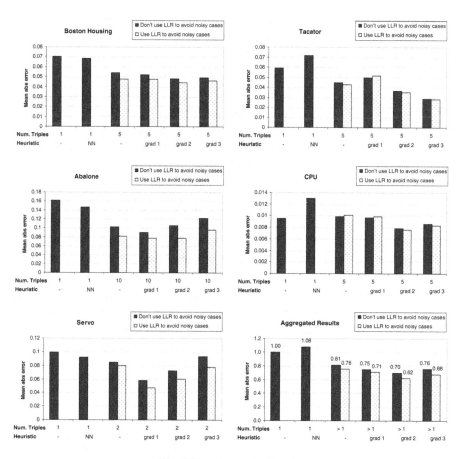

Fig. 2. Experiment 1 – Results

2. Basic case-differences algorithm with a nearest-neighbour heuristic. A single triple was used for each prediction, but difference cases $\Delta(C_1, C_2)$ from close to the query were preferred. This heuristic has been suggested in prior research, and serves as a useful baseline for comparison (see Section 2.3).
3. Several adaptation triples were averaged for each prediction (see Section 3.3) – the actual number used is indicated for each dataset. In a second variation of this experiment, LLR was used to avoid noisy cases (see Section 3.2).
4. As 3, but with a preference for difference cases from areas of domain space with a gradient similar to that around the query. The use of gradients was based on Eq. (5) (see Section 3.1.2).
5. As 4, but with treatment of gradients based on Eq. (6) (see Section 3.1.3).
6. As 4, but with treatment of gradients based on Eq. (7) (see Section 3.1.4).

The following conclusions may be drawn from Experiment 1:

1. The nearest-neighbour heuristic did not improve results over the basic case-differences algorithm. As discussed in Section 2.3, the benefit of choosing difference cases from close to the query was more than offset by the reduction in search space for these cases.
2. All enhancements to the basic algorithm improved results: using gradients to guide the search for difference cases, using LLR to avoid noisy cases, and averaging results from several predictions.
3. The best approach to using gradients depended on the dataset concerned: 'grad 1', 'grad 2' and 'grad 3' were best twice, twice and once for the five datasets. Overall, the best-performing was 'grad 2' (described in Section 3.1.3).

Experiment 2 – comparing case-differences with standard regression techniques
The second set of experiments compared the use of case-differences with the following standard regression techniques: k-NN[2], Global Linear Regression (GLR), Local Linear Regression (LLR)[3], and MP5 regression trees[4]. Results are shown in Fig. 3. Points to note are:

- For all experiments involving the case-differences algorithm, LLR was used to avoid noisy cases and results were averaged from a number of predictions.
- 'Diffs – No Gradient' is the result for the case-differences algorithm where gradients were not used to guide the search for adaptation triples (see Section 3.1.1).
- 'Diffs – Mean Gradient' is the average result from all three approaches to using gradients to select adaptation triples (see Sections 3.1.2–3.1.4).

---

[2] The optimal k for each dataset was found using cross-validation.
[3] GLR and LLR only work with numeric attributes. On datasets with nominal attributes, they were run twice: once with nominal attributes removed, and once with each nominal attribute replaced by an ordered set of synthetic binary attributes [14]. The better of the two results is shown in Fig. 3.
[4] The Weka implementation of MP5 was used with default parameter settings [14].

- • 'Diffs – Best Gradient' is the best performing of the three approaches to using gradients (see Sections 3.1.2–3.1.4). The optimal approach for any particular dataset can be found using a subset of test cases from the original CB.

The first chart in Fig. 3 shows the performance of all regression algorithms on each dataset; the second shows their performance relative to 1-NN.

Experiment 2 prompts the following conclusions:

1. On the datasets tested, the case-differences algorithm performed well relative to other regression techniques.

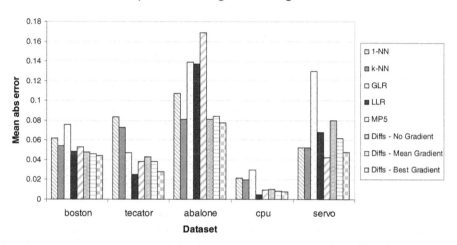

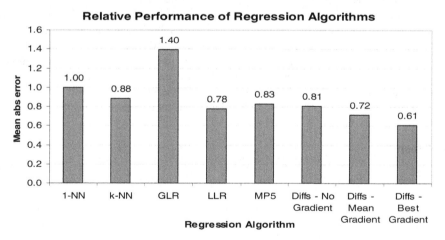

Fig. 3. Experiment 2 – Results

2. The main issue when using case-differences is deciding how to treat gradients during the search for adaptation triples. Fig. 3 shows that significantly better results are obtained using gradients than without them ('Diffs – Mean Gradient' versus 'Diffs – No Gradient'). The optimal approach for each dataset ('Diffs – Best Gradient') significantly outperformed the mean, showing the benefit of setting this parameter correctly prior to problem-solving.

The case-differences algorithm includes 'lazy' and 'eager' elements: difference cases and gradients are calculated in advance, but most of the problem-solving process is delayed until a query is received. The algorithm also incorporates local and global elements: it is highly local in that each prediction is ultimately based on only a few cases, but global in that difference cases may come from any part of domain space. These characteristics may explain its good performance across contrasting datasets – it is best-performing on two of the five datasets, and second best on the remaining three. These results suggest that it may be a useful general-purpose regression algorithm.

5   Conclusions

Within CBR systems, the knowledge required for successful adaptation is most difficult to acquire. Adaptation knowledge tends to be highly domain-dependent – knowledge collected for one problem domain cannot generally be applied in another. In addition, it is often stored in structures that are tightly integrated into application-specific adaptation processes. There is no general, re-usable adaptation framework in existence today that supports different types of applications and problem domains.

This paper has focused on the problem of acquiring adaptation knowledge for regression. It describes a generic framework for predicting numeric values given a set of cases with numeric and nominal problem attributes. For regression problems, enough knowledge is contained within the case base to enable successful adaptation. Global case knowledge is first converted to adaptation knowledge and stored in the form of difference cases and gradients. This is combined with local knowledge to predict a solution for new query cases. Adaptation knowledge is stored within its own CB, with case structure and retrieval mechanisms identical to those of the original CB. Adaptation therefore integrates naturally into the overall CBR system. As a working algorithm, the case-differences approach has proved both effective and robust, performing well relative to standard algorithms on a range of datasets.

References

1. Aamodt, A., Plaza, E.: Case-based reasoning: foundational issues, methodological variations, and system approaches. *AI Communications* 1994, 7(i):39-59
2. Leake, D., Kinley, A., Wilson, D.: Learning to Improve Case Adaptation by Introspective Reasoning and CBR. In *Proc First International Conference on Case-Based Reasoning*, pages 229-240, 1995. Springer Verlag
3. Wilke, W., Vollrath, I., Althoff, K.-D, Bergmann, R.: A framework for learning adaptation knowledge based on knowledge light approaches. In *Proc 5th German Workshop on Case-Based Reasoning*, 1997

4. McDonnell, N., Cunningham, P.: Using Case Differences for Regression in CBR Systems. In *Proc 25th Annual International Conference of the BCS SGAI*, pages 219-232, 2005. Springer

5. McSherry, D.: An adaptation heuristic for case-based estimation. In *Proc 4th European Workshop on Case-Based Reasoning*, pages 184-195, 1998. Springer

6. Richter, M.: Introduction. In *Wess S., Lenz M., Bartsch-Spörl B., and H.D. Burkhard H. D. (Eds.) Case-Based Reasoning Technology: From Foundations to Applications*. LNAI 1400. Springer, 1998

7. Hanney, K., Keane, M.: Learning Adaptation Rules from a Case-Base. In *Proc Third European Workshop on Case-based Reasoning*, pages 179-192, 1996. Springer Verlag

8. Jarmulak, J., Craw, S., Rowe, R.: Using Case-Base Data to Learn Adaptation Knowledge for Design. In *Proc 17th International Conference on Artificial Intelligence*, pages 1011-1020, 2001. Morgan Kaufmann

9. Craw, S.: Introspective Learning to Build Case-Based Reasoning (CBR) Knowledge Containers. In *Proc 3rd International Conference on Machine Learning and Data Mining in Pattern Recognition*, pages 1-6, 2003. Springer

10. Atkeson, C., Moore, A., Schaal, S.: Locally weighted learning. *AI Review*, 1996

11. Smyth, B., Keane, M.T.: Adaptation-guided retrieval: Questioning the similarity assumption. *Artificial Intelligence*, 102:249–293, 1998

12. Hettich, S., Blake, C.L., Merz, C.J.: UCI Repository of machine learning databases. University of California, Irvine, CA, 1998

13. Tecator dataset originally compiled by Hans Henrik Thodberg, Danish Meat Research Institute, Maglegaardsvej 2, Postboks 57, DK-4000 Roskilde, Denmark. Available from StatLib: http://lib.stat.cmu.edu/datasets/tecator

14. Witten, I.H., Eibe, F.: Data Mining: Practical machine learning tools with Java implementations, page 246. Morgan Kaufmann, San Francisco, 2000

Case-Base Maintenance for
CCBR-Based Process Evolution

Barbara Weber[1], Manfred Reichert[2], and Werner Wild[3]

[1] Quality Engineering Research Group, University of Innsbruck, Austria
Barbara.Weber@uibk.ac.at
[2] Information Systems Group, University of Twente, The Netherlands
m.u.reichert@utwente.nl
[3] Evolution Consulting, Innsbruck, Austria
werner.wild@evolution.at

Abstract. The success of a company more and more depends on its ability to flexibly and quickly react to changes. Combining process management techniques and conversational case-based reasoning (CCBR) allows for flexibly aligning the business processes to new requirements by providing integrated process life cycle support. This includes the adaptation of business processes to changing needs by allowing deviations from the predefined process model, the memorization and the reuse of these deviations using CCBR, and the derivation of process improvements from cases. However, to effectively support users during the whole process life cycle, the quality of the data maintained in the case base (CB) is essential. Low problem solving efficiency of the CCBR system as well as inconsistent or inaccurate cases can limit user acceptance. In this paper we describe fundamental requirements for CB maintenance, which arise when integrating business process management (BPM) and CCBR and elaborate our approach to meeting these requirements.

1 Introduction

The economic success of an enterprise more and more depends on its ability to flexibly align its business processes to quickly react to changes, e.g., in the market or in technology requiring flexible "process-aware" information systems (PAIS) [1] to effectively support this alignment [2,3]. Authorized users must be allowed to deviate from the pre-defined process model to deal with unanticipated situations. For example, in a specific patient treatment process the patient's current medication may have to be changed due to an allergic reaction, i.e., the process instance representing this treatment procedure may have to be dynamically adapted (e.g., by deleting, adding or moving process activities). In addition to such instance-specific changes, PAIS must be able to adapt to changes of the underlying business processes themselves, e.g., due to reengineering efforts [4] or the introduction of new laws. For instance, it might become necessary to inform not only newly admitted patients about the risks of a medical treatment, but also patients with an ongoing treatment process who have not obtained their medication yet.

T.R. Roth-Berghofer et al. (Eds.): ECCBR 2006, LNAI 4106, pp. 106–120, 2006.

The need for more flexible PAIS has been recognized for several years [2,3]. Existing technology supports ad-hoc changes at the process instance level (i.e., run time adaptations of individual process instances) as well as changes at the process type level (i.e., changes of a process model) [5]. In CBRFlow [6], for example, we have applied conversational case-based reasoning (CCBR) to assist users in defining ad-hoc changes and in capturing contextual knowledge about these changes; furthermore, CBRFlow supports the reuse of information about ad-hoc changes when defining new ones. CCBR is an extension of the CBR paradigm, which actively involves users in the inference process [7]. A CCBR system can be characterized as an interactive system that, via a mixed-initiative dialogue, guides users through a question-answering sequence in a case retrieval context (cf. Fig 3). In [8,9] we have extended our approach to a complete framework for integrated process life cycle support as knowledge from the case base (CB) is applied to continuously derive improved process models.

To provide adequate process life cycle support, the quality of the data maintained in the CB is essential. For example, the presence of inconsistent or inaccurate cases in the CB is likely to reduce problem-solving efficiency and solution quality and limit user acceptance. The need for CB maintenance arises as cases covering ad-hoc deviations are added by users and not by experienced process engineers and the CB incrementally evolves over time. New cases are added in exceptional situations which have never been dealt with before. To ensure accuracy of the cases and to improve the performance of the CB, CB maintenance becomes crucial when the CB grows. Due to environmental changes and process evolution updates of the CB itself become necessary. Potential process improvements are suggested by the CCBR system, leading to changes in the process model. To maintain consistency of the cases in the CB and to avoid redundancies between the updated process model and the CB, cases leading to or affected by these updates must be revised or possibly removed from the CB version. The process engineer must be supported by suitable maintenance policies and tools.

In our previous work we focused on the integration of business process management (BPM) and CCBR. We developed detailed concepts for memorization and reuse of process instance changes, which allow to derive process (model) improvements from cases [6,9,10]. So far, CB maintenance issues have not been considered in detail, but are a logical next step to provide comprehensive support for process life cycle management. Section 2 introduces basic concepts related to process life cycle support. Section 3 discusses fundamental requirements for CB maintenance in the BPM domain. How we meet these requirements in our approach is described in Section 4. Section 5 discusses related work. We conclude with a summary and an outlook in Section 6.

2 Integrated Process Life Cycle Support Through CCBR

2.1 Business Process Management Fundamentals

PAIS enable users to model, execute, and monitor a company's business processes. In general, orchestration of a business process is based on a predefined process model, called a *process schema*, consisting of the tasks to be executed (i.e., activities), their dependencies (e.g., control and data flow), organizational entities performing these tasks (i.e., actors) and business objects which provide data for the activities. Each business case is handled by a newly created *process instance* and executed as specified in the underlying process schema.

For each business process (e.g., booking a business trip or handling an order) a *process type* T has to be defined. One or more *process schemes* may exist reflecting different versions of T. In Fig. 1, for example, process schemes S and S' correspond to different versions of the same process type. Based on a process schema new *process instances* $I_1, \ldots, I_m$ can be created and executed.

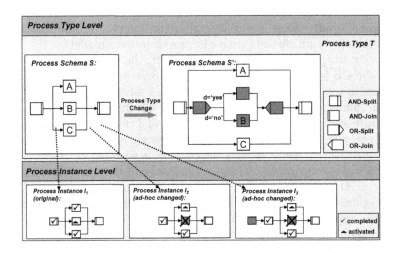

Fig. 1. Different Levels of Process Change

As motivated above PAIS must support process type as well as process instance changes. Changes to a process type T that are necessary to cover the evolution of real-world business processes are performed by the process engineer [5,11,12]. As a result we obtain a new schema version S' of the same type T (cf. Fig. 1) and the execution of future process instances is then based on S'. In contrast, ad-hoc changes of individual process instances are performed by process participants (i.e., end users). Such changes become necessary to react to exceptional situations [2,6,13]. The effects of such instance-specific changes are kept local to the respective process instance, i.e., they do not affect other process instances of the same type. In Fig. 1 instance I_2 has been individually modified by dynamically deleting activity B. Thus the respective execution schema of I_2 deviates from the original process schema S this instance was derived from.

2.2   Integrated Process Life Cycle Support - Overview

Fig. 2 shows how integrated process life cycle support can be achieved by combining BPM technology and CCBR. At build time an initial representation of a business process is created either by process analysis or by process mining (i.e., by observing process and task executions) (1). At run time new process instances can then be created from the predefined process schema (2). In general, process instances are executed according to the process schema they were derived from, and activities are assigned to process participants to perform the respective tasks (3). However, when exceptional situations occur at the process instance level, process participants must be able to deviate from the predefined schema. Users can either define an ad-hoc deviation from scratch and document the reasons for the changes in the CB, or they can reuse a previously specified ad-hoc modification from the CB (4). The PAIS monitors how often a particular schema is instantiated and how often deviations occur. When a particular ad-hoc modification is frequently reused, the process engineer is notified that a process type change may have to be performed (5). The process engineer can then evolve the process schema (6). In addition, existing cases which are still relevant for the new process schema version are migrated to a new version of the CB (7).

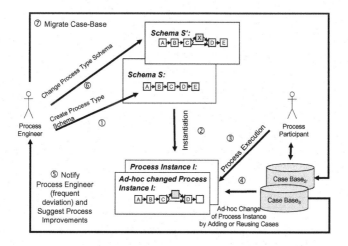

Fig. 2. Integrated Process Life Cycle Support (adapted from [10])

2.3   Case Representation and Reuse

In this section we describe how CCBR is used to capture the semantics of process instance changes, how these changes are memorized, and how they can be retrieved and reused when similar situations occur (for details see [8]).

Case Representation. In our approach a case c represents a concrete ad-hoc modification of one or more process instances. It provides the context of and the reasons for the deviation (cf. Fig. 3). If no similar cases can be found when introducing a process instance change, the user adds a new case with the respective change information to the system. A case consists of a textual problem description pd which briefly describes the exceptional situation that led to the

ad-hoc deviation. The reasons for the change are described as question-answer
(QA) pairs $\{q_1a_1, \ldots, q_na_n\}$ each of which denotes one particular condition; QA
pairs are also used to retrieve cases when similar problems arise in the future. The
solution part *sol* (i.e., the action list) contains the applied change operations.

Definition 1 (Case). *A case c is a tuple (pd, qaSet, sol) where*

- *pd is a textual problem description*
- *qaSet = $\{q_1a_1, \ldots, q_na_n\}$ denotes a set of question-answer pairs*
- *sol = { op_j | $op_j = (opType_j, s_j, paramList_j)$, j = 1, ..., k} is the solution
  part of the case denoting a list of change operations (i.e., the changes that
  have been applied to one or more process instances)[1].*

The question of a QA pair is usually free text, however, to reduce duplicates it
can also be selected from a list of already existing questions in that CB. The
answer can either be free text or a structured answer expression (cf. Fig 3).
Answer expressions allow using contextual information already kept in the PAIS
(e.g., due to legal requirements), thus avoiding redundant data entry. Questions
with answer expressions can be evaluated automatically by retrieving values for
their context attributes from existing data in the system, i.e., they do not have to
be answered by users, thus preventing errors and saving time. Free text answers
are used when no suitable context attributes are defined within the system or the
user is not trained to write answer expressions. For instance, the second QA pair
in Fig. 3 contains an answer expression using the context attribute *Patient.age*
and can be evaluated automatically. In contrast, the answer in the first QA pair
is free text provided by the user.

All information on process instance changes related to a process schema version S is stored as cases in the associated CB of S.

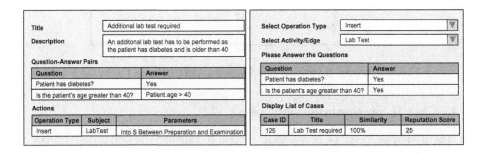

Fig. 3. Sample CCBR Dialogs - Adding a New Case and Retrieving Similar Cases

Definition 2 (Case Base). *A case base CB_S is a tuple (S, $\{c_1, \ldots, c_m\}$, freqs)
where*

- *S denotes the schema version the case base is related to*

---

[1] An operation $op_j := (opType_j, s_j, paramList_j)$ (j = 1, ..., m) consists of operation
type $opType_j$, subject s_j of the change, and parameter list $paramList_j$.

- $\{c_1, \ldots, c_m\}$ denotes a set of cases (cf. Def. 1)
- $freq_S(c_i) \in \mathbb{N}$ denotes the frequency with which case c_i has been (re-)used in connection with schema version S, formally: $freq_S: \{c_1, \ldots, c_m\} \mapsto \mathbb{N}$

Case Retrieval. When deviations from the predefined process schema become necessary the user initiates a case retrieval dialogue in the CCBR component (cf. Fig 3). The system then assists her in finding already stored similar cases (i.e., change scenarios in our context) by presenting a set of questions. Questions with an answer expression are evaluated by automatically retrieving the values of the context attributes. Based on this the system then searches for similar cases by calculating the similarity for each case in the CB and it displays the top n ranked cases (ordered by decreasing similarity) with their reputation score (for details see Section 4.1). Similarity is calculated by dividing the number of correctly answered questions minus the number of incorrectly answered questions by the total number of questions in the case. The user then has different options:

1. The user can directly answer any of the remaining unanswered questions (in arbitrary order), similarity is then recalculated and the n most similar cases are displayed to the user.
2. The user can apply a filter to the case-base (e.g., by only considering cases whose solution part contains a particular change operation). Then all cases not matching the filter criteria are removed from the displayed list of cases.
3. The user can decide to review one of the displayed cases. The case description is then shown to the user.
4. The user can select one of the displayed cases for reuse. The actions specified in the solution part of the case are then forwarded to and carried out by the PAIS. The reuse counter of the case is incremented.

3   Requirements for CB Maintenance

In this section we derive fundamental requirements for CB maintenance in the described scenario. The requirements are aligned with the three top-level performance objectives for CBR systems (cf. [14]): problem-solving efficiency (i.e., average problem solving time), competence (i.e., range of target problems solved) and solution quality (i.e., average quality of a proposed solution).

Req. 1 (Accuracy of the Cases): When using CCBR for memorization and reuse of ad-hoc modifications the CB incrementally evolves over time as new cases are added by end users when exceptions occur. Our approach already guarantees syntactical correctness of the solution part, i.e., the application of change operations to a process schema always results in a syntactically correct process schema [2]. However, semantical correctness of cases must be ensured as well. When cases are added to the CB by inexperienced users it can not always be prevented that inaccurate or low quality cases are added to the CB; however, it must at least be ensured that incorrect cases will not be reused.

Req. 2 (Refactoring QA Pairs): Whenever possible, answer expressions which can be automatically evaluated should be used instead of free text to ease the retrieval process and to increase problem solving efficiency. However, in practice free text QA pairs are entered for good reasons, e.g., the user is unaware of relevant context attributes, she is not trained to formulate answer expressions, or there are no suitable context attributes available in the system when entering the case. The process engineer should be supported in all of the scenarios described above to refactor free text to answer expressions later on.

Req. 3 (Detecting and Handling Inter-Case Dependencies): Occasionally, more than one case may have been applied to a particular process instance. Such dependencies between cases can be observed by analyzing log data (e.g., whenever case c_1 has been applied to a process instance, case c_2 has been applied to this instance as well, i.e., inter-case dependencies exist). When two cases are only used in combination they should be merged to increase problem solving efficiency. When two cases are not always used in combination, but their co-occurrence is frequent, the system should remind users to consider applying the dependent case(s) as well (e.g., by displaying dependent cases).

Req. 4 (Support for CB Migration): Even if cases have been accurate when they were added to the CB, they can become outdated over time. For instance, the evolution of a process schema S (i.e., continuous adaptation schema S to organizational and environmental changes) may reduce the accuracy of parts of the schema-specific CB. After a process type change a subset of the knowledge encoded in the cases may now be captured in the new process schema version S'. The challenge is to migrate only those cases to the new CB version which are still relevant. Cases affected by the process change must be revised by the process engineer or removed from the CB if they are no longer needed.

Additional Requirements. When a CB evolves iteratively, the risk of inconsistencies due to duplicate cases increases and should be mitigated. *Duplicate* cases are either identical, or have the same semantics but are expressed differently. In addition, QA pairs with the same semantics, but different wording, should be avoided, e.g., when entering a new case the user should be supported to reuse already existing QA pairs.

4   Approach to CB Maintenance

In this section we present our approach to CB maintenance and describe how we address the requirements from Section 3.

4.1   Accuracy of the Cases

The accuracy of the cases maintained within a CB is crucial for the overall performance of the CBR system and consequently for the trust users have in it. Particularly, if cases are added by end users adequate evaluation mechanisms for ensuring quality become essential. Like Cheetham and Price [15] we propose to augment the CBR cycle with the ability to determine the confidence users have in the accuracy of individual solutions. In [8], we use the concept of reputation to indicate

Fig. 4. Feedback forms

how successfully an ad-hoc modification – represented by a case – was reused in the past, i.e., to which degree that case has contributed to the performance of the CB, thus indicating the confidence in the accuracy of this case.

Whenever a user adds or reuses a case she is encouraged to provide feedback on the performed process instance change. She can rate the performance of the respective ad-hoc modification with feedback scores 2 (highly positive), 1 (positive), 0 (neutral), -1 (negative), or -2 (highly negative); additional comments can be entered optionally (cf. Fig. 4); the reputation score of a case is then calculated as the sum of feedback scores. While a high reputation score of a case is an indicator of its semantic correctness, negative feedback probably results from problems after performing a process instance change. Negative feedback therefore results in an immediate notification of the process engineer, who may deactivate the case to prevent its further reuse. The case itself, however, remains in the system to allow for learning from failures as well as to maintain traceability.

During case retrieval the CCBR system displays the overall reputation score (cf. Fig. 3) and the ratings for the past 7 days, the past month, and the past 6 months are also available to the user (cf. Fig. 4). Upon request the user can read all comments provided in the past and decide whether the reputation of the case is high enough for her to have confidence in its accuracy.

4.2   Refactoring QA Pairs

As mentioned cases are used to support memorization and reuse of ad-hoc deviations, whereas QA pairs describe the reasons for the deviation. A question is always free text, an answer can be free text or a structured answer expression (cf. Section 2.3). Whenever possible, answer expressions should be used instead of free text to increase problem solving efficiency. While answer expressions can be automatically evaluated by the system (i.e., answer values are automatically inferred from existing data), free text answers have to be provided by the user. However, in practice it is not always feasible to use answer expressions instead of free text. In the following we describe three scenarios where free text QA pairs are entered into the system, and we sketch maintenance policies for refactoring free text answers to formal answer expressions.

Scenario 1: The end user applies CCBR to handle an exception, but is not knowledgeable enough to specify formal answer expressions. As the exceptional situation has to be resolved quickly, the user enters free text QA pairs to capture the reasons for the deviation and applies the case immediately. In order to increase problem solving efficiency the respective QA pair should be refactored to a formal answer expression later on, if feasible. Thus, whenever the frequency of answering a particular QA pair exceeds a predefined threshold a notification is sent to the process engineer to accomplish this refactoring.

Scenario 2: The end user is unaware of the application context and cannot find suitable context attributes for specifying answer expressions even though they are available in the system. Therefore, the user enters free text to capture the reasons for the deviation. The process engineer is not informed immediately, but only when the respective QA pair has been answered frequently enough, exceeding a threshold value. He can then refactor the free text to an equivalent answer expression to be used during case retrieval instead.

Scenario 3: No suitable context attributes are available within the system to describe the concrete ad-hoc modification. In this scenario, the user must specify the QA pair using free text. As in Scenarios 1 and 2 the process engineer is informed when the QA pair has been answered frequently enough. He can then decide whether to extend the application context and to add the required context attribute. When a new context attribute is inserted into the system, suitable software components (adapters) for retrieving the context attribute values during run time must be provided.

4.3   Detecting and Handling Inter-case Dependencies

Generally, several ad-hoc changes may be applied to a particular process instance over time, and consequently several cases may exist which affect this instance. In Figure 5, case c_1 and c_2 were both applied to process instance I_1. Case c_1 led to the insertion of an additional activity Z between activities B and C, while the application of case c_2 resulted in the deletion of activity D.

Cases applied to the same instance may be independent of each other, or inter-case dependencies may exist. In a medical treatment process, for example, magnet resonance therapy (MRT) must not be performed if the patient has a cardiac pacemaker. However, a different imaging technique like X-ray may be applied instead. As the deletion of the MRT activity triggers the insertion of the X-ray activity, a semantic dependency between these two ad-hoc changes exists. Discovering such inter-case dependencies is crucial to better assist users in defining changes for other instances later on. In order to discover inter-case dependencies we apply process mining techniques and analyze change logs. In our example the change log reveals that cases c_1 and c_2 were not coincidentally applied together to I_1 only, but always appear in combination.

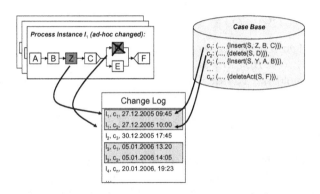

Fig. 5. Discovery of Inter-Case Dependencies

Definition 3 (Strong Inter-Case Dependency). *Let S be a process schema with associated case base CB_S and process instance set $InstanceSet_S$. Further, for case $c \in CB_S$ let $InstanceSet_c \subseteq InstanceSet_S$ denote the set of all process instances to which case c was applied. Then:*

A strong inter-case dependency between $c_1 \in CB_S$ and $c_2 \in CB_S$ exists if $InstanceSet_{c_1} = InstanceSet_{c_2}$, i.e., case c_2 has been applied to all process instances to which c_1 has been applied and vice versa.

If a strong inter-case dependency between c_1 and c_2 exists and the total number of co-occurrences of these two dependent cases exceeds a given threshold n, the process engineer is notified about the option to merge c_1 and c_2. In this situation a new case c' will be created and the original cases c_1 and c_2 be deactivated.[2] The problem description and the QA pairs of c_1 and c_2 are manually merged by the process engineer; the solution parts sol_1 and sol_2, in turn, can be automatically merged by combining the change operations of the original cases in the correct order.

Very often cases co-occur frequently, but do not always co-occur; i.e., there is no strong inter–case dependency between them (cf. Def. 3). In such a scenario the cases cannot be merged. Nevertheless advanced user support can be provided when reusing a case. Assume, for example, that case c_2 has been frequently reused for process instances on the condition that case c_1 has been applied to these instances as well (but not vice versa). When a user applies case c_1 to a process instance and the (conditional) co-occurrence rate $CO(c_2|c_1)$ (see below) exceeds a predefined threshold $m <= 1$, our system will suggest to also consider applying case c_2 to this instance as well.

Definition 4 (Conditional Co-Occurrence Rate). *Let S be a process schema with case base CB_S and let $c_1, c_2 \in CB_S$ be two cases. The conditional co-occurence rate $CO(c_2|c_1)$ denotes the relative frequency of case c_2 on the condition that case c_1 has been applied as well. Formally:*

---

[2] For traceability reasons respective cases are not deleted, but only deactivated.

$$CO(c_2|c_1) \equiv \frac{|instanceSet_{c_1} \cap instanceSet_{c_2}|}{|instanceSet_{c_1}|}$$

Generally, when reusing a case $c \in CB_S$ at the instance level we present the user all cases $c_k \in CB_S \setminus \{c\}$ with a conditional co-occurence rate $CO(c_k|c)$ exceeding threshold m. The qualified user can then select one or more of the displayed cases and apply them in addition to the previously applied one.

4.4   Support for CB Migration

As discussed in Section 2.1 a PAIS must not only support ad-hoc changes of individual process instances, but also cope with changes at the process type level. An adaptation of process type T may become necessary to react to environmental changes (e.g., the introduction of a new law) or to cover the evolution of business processes. It may also be triggered by the monitoring component of the PAIS, if a particular ad-hoc instance modification has been frequently reused and the process engineer decides to pull this change up to the type level.

Formally, a process type change $\Delta_T = op_1 \ldots op_n$ comprises a sequence of parameterized change operations which are applied to the original type schema S. As a result we obtain a new schema version $S' = S + \Delta_T$ for this type. The challenging questions are how to treat already running process instances of this type and how to evolve case base CB_S.

The execution of future process instances is based on S' whereas already running instances are either continued according to the old schema S or migrated to the new one. Among other constraints the ability to migrate a particular process instance from S to S' depends on its current state; i.e., process instances which have not progressed too far may be migrated to S' and then be executed according to the new schema, whereas instances whose state is not compliant with S' are still executed according to S [5]. On the one hand this enables flexibility when dealing with environmental changes, on the other hand it ensures consistency and correct execution behavior after the change [16,2].

When changing process schema S to $S' = S + \Delta_T$ and migrating selected process instances to S' we must evolve the case base CB_S too. A naive solution would be to ignore all "old" cases for S' (i.e., $CB_{S'} := \emptyset$); another extreme is to associate all existing cases with S' as well (i.e., $CB_{S'} = CB_S$). While the former approach discards all experiences gathered in the past, the latter leads to an inaccurate (i.e., outdated) case base. Note that when applying change $\Delta_T = op_1 \ldots op_n$ to process schema S a subset of the knowledge encoded in the cases from CB_S may then be captured by S'. This particularly holds true if the type change has been triggered by the PAIS itself when the reuse counter of a particular ad-hoc modification (i.e., case) has exceeded a given threshold.

The challenge is to migrate only those cases to $CB_{S'}$ (i.e., to add them to $CB_{S'}$) which remain relevant for future reuse scenarios. This necessitates advanced mechanisms that allow to decide which cases from CB_S can be retained unchanged for $CB_{S'}$, which cases have to be adapted before adding them to $CB_{S'}$, and which cases shall be left out of $CB_{S'}$. In order to answer these questions we have to differentiate whether the process type change triggered by one or more cases is relevant for all process instances based on S' or only for a particular subset of instances (e.g., an additional activity is only conditionally inserted) [9]. In the following we focus on the former scenario where the solution parts of the triggering cases are directly reflected in the new process schema S' and take a closer look at the relationship between the solution part of a case and the type change Δ_T. Let $\Delta_T = op_1 \ldots op_n$ be a process type change applied to schema S with associated case base CB_S, resulting in the new type schema S'. We consider an arbitrary case $c = (pd_c, qaSet_c, sol_c) \in CB_S$ (with solution part $sol_c = a_1, \ldots, a_k$) and compare it with Δ_T. As the changes are relevant for all instances we can factor out $qaSet_c$ and focus on sol_c only. comparison of parameterized change operations.

- sol_c **and** Δ_T **are equivalent** (i.e., $k = n \land a_\nu \equiv op_\nu$, $\nu = 1 \ldots n$): Cases whose solution part equals Δ_T are not added to $CB_{S'}$. Their "effects" are the same as those of the type change (e.g., case c_1 in Fig 6).
- sol_c **is a subset of** Δ_T (i.e., $\exists\ \mu_1 \ldots \mu_k : 1 \leq \mu_1 < \ldots < \mu_k \leq n : a_\nu \equiv op_{\mu_\nu}, \nu = 1 \ldots k$): Cases whose solution part is a subset of Δ_T are not added to $CB_{S'}$ as their effects are completely covered by the type change (e.g., case c_3 in Fig 6).
- sol_c **and** Δ_T **are disjoint** (i.e., $a_\nu \neq op_\mu, \nu = 1 \ldots k, \mu = 1 \ldots n$): Since the effects of case c are not covered by S' c should be added to $CB_{S'}$. Later reusability requires that actions $a_1, \ldots, a_k$ remain correctly applicable to S'. Note that this might not always be possible due to conflicting change operations. Change Δ_T, for example, might delete an activity from S (e.g., (delete, B)) to which another operation a from sol_c refers (e.g., $a = $ (insert, X, Between A and B)). We use advanced conflict tests to detect such situations. If no conflicts between sol_c and Δ_T exist, case c can be added to $CB_{S'}$ without further adaptation. Otherwise, the process engineer has to adapt the case in a way that it becomes applicable to S' as well (e.g., by changing the parameterization of actions from sol_c) (e.g., case c_2 in Fig 6).
- sol_c **is a superset of** Δ_T (i.e., $\exists\ \nu_1 \ldots \nu_n : 1 \leq \nu_1 < \ldots < \nu_n \leq k : op_\mu \equiv a_{\nu_\mu}, \mu = 1 \ldots n$): Cases whose solution part is a proper superset of the type change are not directly migrated to $CB_{S'}$. Instead, the process engineer decides whether to add c to $CB_{S'}$ and, if so, how to adapt it. The default adaptation in our system suggests (logically) removing those actions from the solution part of the case whose effects are already captured by S' (i.e., $sol'_c := sol_c \neg \{a_{\nu_1} \ldots a_{\nu_n}\}$) (e.g., case c_4 in Fig 6).
- sol_c **and** Δ_T **are partially overlapping**: Cases in this category are not automatically migrated to $CB_{S'}$. The system supports the process engineer by determining those actions of sol_c whose effects are not reflected by S' (i.e., by calculating the difference set $sol_c \neg \Delta_T$). The process engineer might then decide to migrate case c, after adapting its solution part from sol_c to $sol_c \neg \Delta_T$.

Generally, it is not sufficient to only compare the solution parts of the cases and the process type change. When a process type change triggered by a case is only relevant for a particular subset of process instances (e.g., a lab test should only be performed for patients older than 40 years suffering from diabetes), we must also look at the corresponding QA pairs and their semantics. Reusing a case at the instance level applies the change operations in its solution part only; the context for this ad-hoc modification is reflected in the case's QA pairs and must be considered by the process engineer when pulling the solution part of the case up to the process type level. Currently we only provide CB migration policies when a process type change is relevant for all process instances. However, we are also investigating migration policies for the scenario just described.

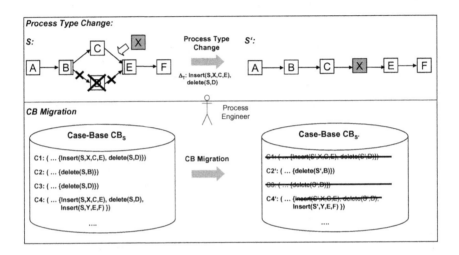

Fig. 6. CB Migration

5   Related Work

Previous research has addressed many aspects of CB maintenance. In general, research on CB maintenance is driven by performance concerns [17] (i.e., problem solving efficiency, CB competence and solution quality of problems solved [18]).

   To improve problem solving efficiency while preserving CB competence, strategies for controlling the growth of the CB [19] as well as for selective case retention have been proposed (e.g., [20,21]). In our approach, cases are used for the memorization and the reuse of ad-hoc changes due to exceptions in the business process. In this scenario cases cannot be deleted or only selectively added as traceability of ad-hoc changes must be guaranteed. However, case base migration as proposed by our approach tries to tackle the same problems, aiming to keep the size of the CB compact while preserving competence. When performing CB migration the size of the CB is compressed without reducing the competence of the overall system. Only cases that are still relevant are migrated to the new version of the CB, the removed cases are covered by the new version of the process schema (cf. Section 4.4).

Although a significant body of research exists on CB maintenance none of these approaches deals with inter-case dependencies (i.e., the application of one case triggers the application of another case). In our approach CCBR is not used as a standalone application, but in the broader context of a process management system. This allows us to provide additional context information (e.g., two cases have been applied to the same process instance, i.e., business transaction) facilitating the detection of inter-case dependencies (cf. Section 4.3).

The accuracy of the cases in the case base is crucial for the overall performance of the CB. Therefore Cheetham and Price [15] proposed to augment the CBR cycle with the ability to determine the confidence in the accuracy of individual solutions. However, in our approach accuracy cannot be determined automatically as the semantics of the QA pairs are unknown to the system. Instead, we use the concept of reputation to indicate how successfully a case has been reused in the past, thus indicating the degree of confidence in the accuracy of this case (cf. Section 4.1).

To our knowledge refactoring of free text to answer expressions in a CCBR system has not yet been addressed by existing approaches. They either support structured or unstructured QA pairs, but not both at the same time.

While systematic approaches to CB maintenance like SIAM [22] provide a general framework for building better maintainable CBR systems, this paper focuses on the specifics of the BPM domain.

6 Summary and Outlook

We have derived basic requirements for CB maintenance in the BPM domain (accuracy of cases, refactoring of QA pairs, detecting and handling of inter-case dependencies, and support for CB migration), and we have presented our approach to meeting these requirements. To maintain case quality we apply the concept of reputation score indicating how successfully a case has been applied in the past. Refactoring QA pairs from free text to answer expressions and our approach to dealing with inter-case dependencies contribute to increased problem solving efficiency. Finally, in the context of process evolution we suggest CB migration to deal with outdated cases, keeping the CB compact, while preserving its competence. Ongoing work includes the evaluation of our prototype in a real world scenario. Future work will address the problem of inconsistencies due to redundant cases as we currently only support the reuse of QA pairs by displaying existing ones to the user when adding a new case. We further plan the extension of our CB maintenance approach to also provide policies for CB migration when process type changes are not relevant for all process instances, but only for a particular subset. In this situation the semantics encoded in the QA pairs must be considered when performing a process type change. In summary, CCBR techniques contribute significantly to enriching BPM systems with more semantics and to improving process life cycle support.

References

1. Dumas, M., ter Hofstede, A., van der Aalst, W., eds.: Process Aware Information Systems. Wiley Publishing (2005)
2. Reichert, M., Dadam, P.: ADEPT$_{flex}$ - Supporting Dynamic Changes of Workflows Without Losing Control. JIIS **10** (1998) 93–129
3. Jørgensen, H.D.: Interactive Process Models. PhD thesis, Norwegian University of Science and Technology, Trondheim, Norway (2004)
4. Hammer, M., Stanton, S.: The Reengineering Revolution – The Handbook. Harper Collins Publ. (1995)
5. Rinderle, S., Reichert, M., Dadam, P.: Correctness Criteria for Dynamic Changes in Workflow Systems – A Survey. DKE **50** (2004) 9–34
6. Weber, B., Wild, W., Breu, R.: CBRFlow: Enabling Adaptive Workflow Management Through Conversational Case-Based Reasoning. In: ECCBR'04, Madrid (2004) 434–448
7. Aha, D.W., Muñoz-Avila, H.: Introduction: Interactive Case-Based Reasoning. Applied Intelligence **14** (2001) 7–8
8. Weber, B., Rinderle, S., Wild, W., Reichert, M.: CCBR–Driven Business Process Evolution. In: ICCBR'05, Chicago (2005) 610–624
9. Rinderle, S., Weber, B., Reichert, M., Wild, W.: Integrating Process Learning and Process Evolution - A Semantics Based Approach. In: BPM 2005. (2005) 252–267
10. Weber, B., Reichert, M., Rinderle, S., Wild, W.: Towards a Framework for the Agile Mining of Business Processes. In: BPM 2005 Workshops. (2005) 191–202
11. Casati, F., Ceri, S., Pernici, B., Pozzi, G.: Workflow Evolution. Data and Knowledge Engineering **24** (1998) 211–238
12. Weske, M.: Workflow Management Systems: Formal Foundation, Conceptual Design, Implementation Aspects. Univ. of Münster, Germany (2000) Habil Thesis.
13. Luo, Z., Sheth, A., Kochut, K., Miller, J.: Exception Handling in Workflow Systems. Applied Intelligence **13** (2000) 125–147
14. Smyth, B., McKenna, E.: Footprint-Based Retrieval. In: ICCBR'99. (1999) 343–357
15. Cheetham, W., Price, J.: Measures of Solution Accuracy in Case-Based Reasoning Systems. In: ECCBR'04. (2004) 106–118
16. Rinderle, S., Reichert, M., Dadam, P.: Flexible Support of Team Processes by Adaptive Workflow Systems. Distributed and Parallel Databases **16** (2004) 91–116
17. Leake, D.B., Wilson, D.C.: Remembering Why to Remember: Performance-Guided Case-Base Maintenance. In: EWCBR'00. (2000) 161–172
18. Smyth, B., McKenna, E.: Footprint-Based Retrieval. Lecture Notes in Computer Science **1650** (1999) 343–357
19. Smyth, B., Keane, M.T.: Remembering to Forget: A Competence-Preserving Case Deletion Policy for Case-Based Reasoning Systems. In: IJCAI'95. (1995) 377–383
20. Smyth, B., McKenna, E.: Building Compact Competent Case-Bases. Lecture Notes in Computer Science **1650** (1999) 329–342
21. Zhu, J., Yang, Q.: Remembering to Add: Competence-preserving Case-Addition Policies for Case Base Maintenance. In: IJCAI'99. (1999) 234–241
22. Roth-Berghofer, T.: Knowledge maintenance of case-based reasoning systems. The SIAM methodology. PhD thesis, University of Kaiserslautern (2002)

Evaluating CBR Systems Using Different Data Sources: A Case Study

Mingyang Gu and Agnar Aamodt

Department of Computer and Information Science, Norwegian University of Science and Technology, Sem Saelands vei 7-9, N-7491, Trondheim, Norway
{mingyang, agnar}@idi.ntnu.no

Abstract. The complexity and high construction cost of case bases make it very difficult, if not impossible, to evaluate a CBR system, especially a knowledge-intensive CBR system, using statistical evaluation methods on many case bases. In this paper, we propose an evaluation strategy, which uses both many simple case bases and a few complex case bases to evaluate a CBR system, and show how this strategy may satisfy different evaluation goals. The identified evaluation goals are classified into two categories: domain-independent and domain-dependent. For the evaluation goals in the first category, we apply the statistical evaluation method using many simple case bases (for example, UCI data sets); for evaluation goals in the second category, we apply different, relatively weak, evaluation methods on a few complex domain-specific case bases. We apply this combined evaluation strategy to evaluate our knowledge-intensive conversational CBR method as a case study.

1 Introduction

As summarized in [1], AI research is an empirical process: selecting a task incorporating intelligence features, building a system exhibiting these features, and evaluating the system in different task environments. After an intelligent system is constructed, it is necessary to evaluate whether it does what we expect it to do and how good its performances is. Cohen and Howe [2] extend the importance of evaluation from assessing the performance to guiding the different AI research phases.

Evaluation methods for intelligent systems include statistical evaluation (inductive evaluation), theoretical analysis, ablation evaluation, tuning evaluation, limitation evaluation, direct expert evaluation and characteristic analysis [3,4,5]. The ideal evaluation method among them is statistical evaluation; that is, to execute the constructed system in different task environments in order to investigate its performance in different application contexts. This method is difficult to apply, in general, to case-based reasoning (CBR) [6,7] because of the typical complexity of CBR applications. The complexity comes from two aspects [8]: the CBR system itself is complex, and the task domain where it operates is also typically complex and ill-structured. The complexity of the application domain makes it difficult and expensive to construct a case base, especially for

T.R. Roth-Berghofer et al. (Eds.): ECCBR 2006, LNAI 4106, pp. 121–135, 2006.
© Springer-Verlag Berlin Heidelberg 2006

knowledge-intensive CBR systems [9] that demand a significant knowledge engineering effort. Because of the complexity and heterogeneity of CBR systems, transplanting a case base from one CBR system to another also needs considerable adaptation work. Therefore, it is very hard to construct or transplant a number of complex case bases to use in a statistical evaluation. For these reasons, the evaluation of a CBR system is, to a large extent, based on one or a few case bases, which can only provide limited evidence.

Aha [10] provides a method to generalize the evaluation result of an AI system, which is based on one (or a few) data sets. In this method, a set of dimensions are identified to describe the original data set, and a data set generator is created to produce many artificial data sets with predefined values on the identified dimensions. The target system is executed on the artificial data sets, and its performances are recorded. The relations between differences of the system performance and changes of the dimension values are studied, and a set of rules are generated to describe the conditions under which the performance differences hold. Applying this method into CBR researches needs substantial efforts since it is difficult to artificially construct a set of complex case bases with the predefined dimension values.

When we look into the details of the evaluation process for CBR research, we find that there are usually multiple evaluation goals. For instance, this includes the efficiency of the similarity calculation method, the validity of the adaptation method, the problem solving efficiency on the target application domain, the usability or human friendliness, and the individual contributions of various system components. Further, different evaluation goals are related to different application scopes. Some goals are domain-dependent; that is, they need to be evaluated on the target specific application domain, for example to determine whether the general domain knowledge can improve, for instance, the similarity matching using a knowledge-intensive method [11], or make an explanation to the user more understandable [12]. Other goals are domain-independent, for instance whether the sustained learning process in CBR can improve problem solving capability. For the domain-independent goals, we can evaluate them on either complex case bases or simple case bases. There are plenty of such simple case bases, for instance, the data sets available at the UCI repository [13], and there are many examples of research contributions evaluated by this data sets within CBR community [14,15,16,17].

We propose an evaluation strategy for CBR research aiming to assess these two types of evaluation goals (domain-dependent and domain-independent) based on different data sources and using different evaluation methods. For the domain-independent evaluation goals, we use the statistical evaluation over many simple data sets, while domain-dependent goals are evaluated on one or a limited number of complex case bases using multiple weak evaluation methods. That is, this strategy combines a statistical evaluation method with many simple case bases, and alternatively combines limited number of complex case bases with multiple weak evaluation methods. This evaluation strategy can provide solid evidence for both the domain-independent goals and the domain-dependent goals. For the domain-independent goals, the evaluation power comes from the statistical justification. For the domain-dependent goals, the solidity comes from whether all the multiple weak evaluation methods can output positive outcomes.

As part of our current research, we have designed and implemented a knowledge-intensive conversational case-based reasoning (KI-CCBR) system which can capture and utilize general domain knowledge to support an efficient and natural conversation process to complete the case retrieval task. In this paper, we use our proposed evaluation strategy to evaluate this KI-CCBR method as a case study.

In the next section, we give a short introduction to the evaluation methods we have used. In Section 3, we briefly introduce our KI-CCBR method and identify the relevant evaluation goals. In Section 4, we report how we use 36 UCI data sets to show that the two domain-independent evaluation goals, lazy dialog learning and query-biased similarity calculation, can improve conversation efficiency of CCBR in general. We also evaluate the KI-CCBR method on a case base of image processing software components, within a system designed to support component reuse in software design. Three different evaluation methods are used: a characteristic analysis is used to see whether the system meets the requirements of a conversational diagnosis system; a direct domain expert assessment is used in order to see whether the KI-CCBR method can provide a natural conversation process; and a simulated ablation study is adopted to evaluate whether KI-CCBR can improve the conversation efficiency and how much each knowledge-intensive module contributes to the total improvement. We conclude in Section 6.

2   Introduction to the Evaluation Methods

The purpose of an evaluation process is to assess a system, with reference to some selected baseline, to see whether the performance of the system is accepted or improved. In this section, we introduce the evaluation methods used in our study.

2.1   Statistical Evaluation (Inductive Evaluation)

The basic statistical evaluation process is one in which we define one or more performance measures, execute both the new system and the baseline system on many different data sets, and calculate the percentage of the data sets on which the new system gives better performance, or test statistical significance in relation to predefined hypotheses. Statistical evaluation is a proper method to support the claim of generality of a system's benefits or advantages. This method is a strong evaluation method and is frequently used in many scientific disciplines such as psychology or biology. Cohen [4] gives detailed information about how to apply this evaluation method for AI research.

2.2   Characteristic Analysis

For a certain type of intelligent system, what characterizes it are usually discussed and gradually agreed upon by researchers in that field. Analyzing whether and to what degree a system can support the relevant characteristics is one approach to evaluate the system with respect to its possible performance. For example, if a CBR system support all the four 'RE-' phases [6], we may claim that this system is a full-cycle CBR system.

2.3 Direct Expert Evaluation

When a test system can produce more acceptable solutions than we can possibly generate beforehand as a baseline [3], or the evaluation measures involve human common sense or psychology aspects, one method is to invite domain experts to use the system and report back their subjective assessments. This is a weak evaluation method because of experts' overly generosity and their unrepresentativeness of typical users. One way to balance this shortcoming is to select experts using different criteria, or experts from different related domains.

2.4 Ablation (Lesion, Substitution) Evaluation

Ablation evaluation [2,8] is a method for analyzing the contributions of different modules of a system to the total performance improvement. In this type of evaluation, one or more modules are de-activated, removed or replaced by other comparable modules to observe changes on system performance. This method was used to evaluate the PROTOS system [18] and the SIROCCO system [19]. One difficulty in applying this evaluation method is that it is not always feasible to remove or de-active particular modules in a system because of the interdependence among modules.

3   Knowledge-Intensive Conversational Case-Based Reasoning

3.1 Research Overview

Conversational case-based reasoning (CCBR) [20] is a special type of CBR, which emphasizes the difficulty to appropriately describe a new problem, i.e. to define a new case. CCBR alleviates it through providing a mixed-initiative interactive process to guide users to incrementally construct a new case description that is sufficient to complete the case retrieval task.

In CCBR, an initial new case (only one or few features) is specified and used to retrieve a set of most similar cases from the case base. A group of discriminative questions are identified based on the returned cases (transformed by the features that have values in the returned cases but not in the current new case), and ranked according to their capabilities to discriminate the stored cases. Both the returned cases, sorted according to their similarity values, and the ranked questions are displayed to the user. The user either finds a satisfactory stored case, which then terminates the case retrieval phase, or chooses a question to answer. The newly gained answer and the current new case are combined together to construct an updated new case. A new round of retrieval and question-answering is started, and this continues until the user finds a satisfactory stored case or there are no discriminative questions left for the user to choose.

A major research concern in CCBR is how to select the most discriminative questions [14,21] and ask them in a natural way [20,22,5] to alleviate users' cognitive load demanded in the conversation process. Most of the methods used to select questions now are knowledge-poor (KP); that is, only statistical metrics are used. In our research, we study the possibility of using general domain knowledge in the conversation process [23]. We identify the following four tasks for which general domain knowledge can be used to improve the conversation process:

- **Feature Inferencing:** The features that can be inferred from the current new case description should be added into the new case description, instead of posting users questions.
- **Knowledge-Intensive Question Ranking:** The semantic relations among discriminative questions should be taken into account during question ranking. For instance, if one answer of question A, A_a, can be inferred out by one answer of question B, B_a, question B should be asked before question A.
- **Consistent Question Clustering:** The questions that are connected by some semantic relations, for example, a causal relation or subclass relation, should be grouped and displayed together, so that users can inspect them together and select which one to answer first.
- **Coherent Question Sequencing:** If a question from a higher level node in a taxonomic structure is asked in the current question answering cycle, the question one level lower should be asked in the next cycle, instead of inserting other unrelated questions between them.

We classify similarity calculation methods in CBR into three categories, according to the scope of the features that are taken into account during similarity calculation:

- **Query-Biased Similarity Methods:** Only the features appearing in the current new case (query) are taken into account during similarity calculation.
- **Case-Biased Similarity Methods:** Only the features appearing in the current stored case are considered during similarity calculation.
- **Equally-Biased Similarity Methods:** All the features appearing in both the current new case and the current stored case are taken into account during similarity calculation.

We emphasize the special characteristic of the new case, partially specified, in CCBR. If the features which have not yet been assigned values in the new case, are considered in the similarity calculation, the similarity method will be biased to those cases with fewer such features, instead of to those that most satisfy the current new case (users' attention focus). So in order to avoid the negative influence of these features, we argue that the query-biased similarity calculation method is more suitable for CCBR than the case-biased or equally-biased similarity calculation methods [24].

In addition, we introduce a lazy dialog learner into CCBR [25], which is capable of capturing and storing previous successful conversational case retrieval processes and reusing them in the later conversational case retrieval tasks.

The implemented KI-CCBR method has been recently tested in an image processing software component retrieval application [26].

3.2 Identified Evaluation Goals

As discussed in Section 1, the evaluation goals of this KI-CCBR method are classified into two categories. The first category contains the evaluation goals that are valid for CCBR research in general; that is, domain-independent: whether the query-biased similarity calculation method and the lazy dialog learner can improve the efficiency of CCBR. The second category includes the evaluation goals that rely on a specific application domain, the image processing component retrieval application. This includes whether the KI-CCBR method meets the requirements of a conversational diagnosis system, whether the KI-CCBR method can provide users with a natural question answering process, whether the KI-CCBR method can achieve higher efficiency compared to the knowledge-poor CCBR method, and how the different knowledge-intensive modules contribute to the total achievement.

In Section 4 and Section 5, we will report how we choose different evaluation methods and test case bases for the identified evaluation goals.

4 Statistical Evaluation on UCI Data Sets

In an attempt to evaluate whether the query-biased similarity calculation method and the lazy dialog learner can improve the efficiency of CCBR in general, we choose the statistical evaluation method to see whether these methods can achieve higher efficiency than their competitors on multiple simple case bases.

In order to evaluate which similarity calculation method (query-biased, case-biased, or equally-biased) is more suitable for CCBR, we implement three variants of CCBR within Weka [27], each of which uses a particular similarity calculation method. In order to evaluate whether the dialog learning mechanism can improve the conversation efficiency, we implement two more variants of CCBR also within Weka, one of them using our dialog learning mechanism and the other not. We summarize the statistical evaluation to these two topics in this paper, and more detailed information can be found in our earlier studies [24,25].

The simple case bases we test are 36 classification data sets[1] provided by Weka, originally from the UCI repository [13]. Some of these case bases have been used to test conversational CBR methods in [14,16,17]. Aha, McSherry and Yang [28] argued that the typical case bases in CCBR applications are irreducible and heterogeneous. From our perspective, it is not necessary for case bases in CCBR to have these characteristics. For instance, in one typical CCBR

---

[1] For the evaluation of the lazy dialog learner, we drop off the 4 biggest case bases simply because they need too much execution time.

application domain, fault diagnosis, it is natural for two types of faults to share the same solution, which means the case base is reducible. Heterogeneity is only the characteristic of one type of case bases in CCBR, which is the necessary condition to apply the occurrence-frequency metric [20] in discriminative question selection. However, the entropy based question selection methods, which are adopted by more CCBR researches [29,21,30], require all the cases having the same structure (homogeneous).

The human-computer conversation process is simulated using leave-one-out cross validation (LOOCV). LOOCV is an extreme variant of K-fold cross validation, which splits the entire n cases in one case base into n subsets, each containing only one case. In each evaluation cycle of LOOCV, the test case, q, is taken as a description of a new problem, referred to as the target case. Before the retrieval starts, a part of the problem description of q, a subset of the $< feature, value >$ pairs (10%), is taken out to construct an initial new case. This initial new case is used for retrieval from the test case base containing the remaining cases in the original case base. If the base case, with respect to the target case, is returned as the most similar case, or is in the returned most similar case group, the retrieval process is terminated successfully. Otherwise, the question generating and ranking module will output a set of sorted discriminative questions. A predefined question selection strategy is used to select a question from the discriminative question list, for example selecting the first question. The $< feature, value >$ pair corresponding to the selected question is chosen from the target case q and added into the current new case to form an updated new case. Based on the updated new case, a new round of retrieval is started. The retrieval, question selection and answering process will continue until the successful condition or failed condition (there are no $< feature, value >$ pairs left to choose) is met.

The average session number of the conversations simulated by the total set of cases in one case base is taken as the main criterion to assess the performance of a CCBR method on that case base [20,14].

The successful termination condition of LOOCV is that the base case appears in the first returned case group (k cases). If the query biased similarity method is used, especially in the beginning phase of the retrieval process, the number, m, of the cases that exactly match the partially-specified new case (and are thus equally similar) may be larger than k. In this situation, the simulated process randomly returns k out of them. This setting may be arbitrary. Ferguson and Bridge [31] suggest a method to abandon exact similarities in favor of preference relations between cases. In our case, the successful termination condition is acceptable since the final statistical result is computed from multiple cases and case bases using the same successful condition.

For the evaluation of the similarity calculation methods, in 31 out of total 36 case bases, the CCBR using query-biased similarity method gets better performance than the other two methods (case-biased and equally-biased similarity methods). For the assessment of the lazy dialog learner, in 29 out of total 32 case bases, the CCBR process with the lazy learner gets better performance than that without the learner. In this experiment, we execute the LOOCV two rounds with the aim to evaluate the ability of the lazy learner to learn in a long term. The results show that the lazy dialog learner is sustainable and the dialog case base is maintainable; that is, with the dialog learning going on, the dialog learner achieves better performance and the lazy learner requires fewer dialog cases to be stored in the dialog case base. For all the above comparisons, we have carried out the significance tests on the tested case bases (t-test with the significance level 0.01), and the results give us supportive evidence (all the observed differences in performance are significant).

5   Evaluating the KI-CCBR Method on an Image Processing Software Component Retrieval Application

We have implemented our KI-CCBR within the CREEK system [26][2]. We choose image processing software component retrieval, exemplified by retrieving components from the DynamicImager system [32], as the evaluation domain to assess the domain-dependent evaluation goals. DynamicImager is an image processing development and visualization environment, in which different image processing components can be combined in various ways. Currently, the components in the system are categorized according to their functions, and users select each component by exploring the category structure manually. A knowledge base has been constructed through combining image processing domain knowledge with 118 image processing components extracted from DynamicImager. In this knowledge base, there are 1170 concepts, 104 features and 913 semantic relationships, using approximately 20 relation types (e.g. has subclass, has part, causes).

As illustrated in Fig. 1, a conversational retrieval process contains one or several conversation sessions, and for each session, there are three window panes to move between in the computer interface. The ExtendedQuery pane is used to show how a new case is extended through feature inferencing, and to display a detailed explanation of why a new feature is added into the case. Based on the extended new case, a set of stored cases are retrieved and displayed in the RetrieveResult pane. In this pane the user can inspect the explanations about how the similarity values are computed. If a user is not satisfied with the retrieved cases, she can go to the Dialogue pane, where the discriminative questions are ranked using both the knowledge-intensive question ranking method and statistical metrics, and adjusted by the consistent question clustering and coherent question sequencing processes. After the user selects a discriminative question and submits her answer, a new conversation session is started based on the updated new case by combining the newly gained answer with the previous new case.

5.1   Characteristic Analysis as a Sequential Diagnosis System

The CCBR process is basically a sequential diagnosis process: as more and more problem features (evidence) are identified and added into the new case, the system can identify the correct diagnosis (the base case) with more confidence.

---

[2] The dialog learning mechanism is not implemented in our KI-CCBR.

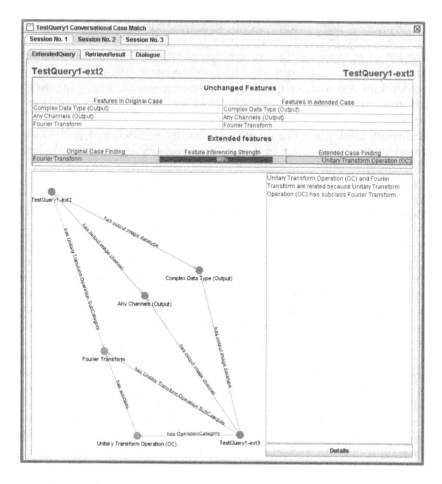

Fig. 1. The conversational case retrieval process in our KI-CCBR

McSherry [5] identifies seven desirable features (or characteristics) of an intelligent sequential diagnosis system. Our implemented system supports all of these characteristics.

- **Mixed-Initiative Dialogue:** Users, particularly professional users, are unlikely to accept a conversation partner (or intelligent system) who keeps asking a lot of questions. Instead, users prefer playing a positive role in the conversation, i.e. to control the conversation or to volunteer data at any stage of the conversation. Permitting users to select a question to answer from a list is a form of mixed-initiative dialogue which is supported by most CCBR applications. In addition, our method allows users to cancel or modify their answered questions (go to the specific session window and remove or reselect the answered entities). Furthermore, our method clusters related questions together, so that users can inspect the questions with different difficulty levels, and select one to answer according to their expertise levels.

- **Feedback on the Impact of Reported Evidence:** It is unacceptable if users get no feedback from an expert (or intelligent system) after they provide more evidence. In our method, after the user answers a question, or modifies the initial new case or previous answered questions, the case retrieval process and the question ranking, sequencing, clustering processes will run immediately. The returned cases and discriminative questions will be based on the updated evidence.

- **Relevant Dialogue:** The questions asked by an intelligent partner should be relevant to the context of the problem provided by the user. We assume that only the features appearing in the most similar cases are relevant. Therefore, our method generates discriminative questions based only on the most similar cases, instead of all the cases in the case base.

- **Consistent Dialogue:** The questions that can be answered implicitly by the current partially specified new case should not be prompted again. Otherwise, the conversation efficiency is reduced, and users are unlikely to trust a conversation partner that repeats previously implicitly answered questions. Furthermore, if a user provides an answer to a question that is not consistent with that inferred from the current new case, the content of the new case is not consistent any more. The feature inferencing process in our method guarantees that this type of dialog inconsistency will not occur, by ensuring that these types of questions will not be asked.

- **Explanation of Reasoning:** In order to improve users' confidence in the results of an intelligent system, it is important to provide an explanation of how results are derived [33,34,5,12]. Our KI-CCBR method provides the following explanations: why a new feature is added into the current new case description through feature inferencing, why two different feature values are partially matched through knowledge-intensive case matching [11], why a question is ranked with highest priority in the coherent question sequencing, and why two questions are grouped and displayed together through consistent question clustering.

- **Tolerance of Missing Data:** Missing data stem from two aspects. First, the cases in the case base may contain missing features. Our system's partial matching process can tolerate this type of missing data. We adopt the occurrence-frequency metric [20] as the knowledge-poor question ranking method, which basically takes the advantage of the presence of missing features. In addition, our explanation-driven reasoning process [23] exploits general domain knowledge, which may itself be incomplete. Another source of missing data is the user's incapability to answer every question due to the unavailability of some observations, the user's lack of expertise, or need for an expensive test to obtain the answer. Our method tolerates this type of missing data through permitting the user to choose candidate questions to answer, instead of forcing her to answer them in a fixed sequence.

- **Sensitivity Analysis:** The uncertainty that is inherent in the dialogue process, as well as the possible uncertainty in the user's answers to questions, means that support for sensitivity analysis is essential. Our method supports sensitivity analysis through allowing users to modify previously specified features (answered questions) and re-execute the retrieval and question-answering process in order to inspect the possible influences of the updated information.

5.2   Domain Expert Evaluation of the Psychological Goals

Evaluation Goals of KI-CCBR related to psychology include the user's cognitive load, the 'natural' question-answering process, and the user's confidence in the final results. We adopt a relatively simple or weak evaluation method, a so-called direct expert evaluation [2], for these evaluation goals.

We invited two experts from the software engineering domain, and two experts from the image processing domain, to test our system. Given a set of image processing tasks, these domain experts were asked to retrieve image processing components using both a one-shot CBR-based retrieval method and the multiple shots KI-CCBR method. After doing so, they were required to fill in a form to describe their subjective evaluation of the implemented system[3]. The resulting analysis of the collected feedback forms suggests that:

- Based on the same initial new case, the KI-CCBR method can achieve more useful results;
- The reasoning transparency provided by the explanation mechanisms in KI-CCBR improves user confidence in the retrieved results;
- The feature inferencing, consistent question clustering and coherent question sequencing mechanisms provide users with a natural question-answering process, which helps to alleviate their cognitive loads in retrieving components interactively;
- The straightforward question-answering query construction process helps to reduce users' cognitive load in constructing queries, thus enabling users with limited domain knowledge to retrieve suitable components.

5.3   Ablation Evaluation Using Leave-One-In Cross Validation

In order to show that the KI-CCBR method does improve the conversation efficiency by reducing the length of conversation sessions compared to knowledge-poor CCBR, we execute another cross validation on the image processing component retrieval application. Unlike the LOOCV we introduced in Session 4, we adopt leave-one-in cross validation (LOICV) to simulate the human-computer conversation. The difference between them is that, in LOOCV, the test case (target case) is taken away from the case base during the case retrieval process, while in LOICV, the test case is kept in the case base, and acted as the base case for the simulated retrieval process[4]. The LOICV has been successfully used in the CCBR community [20,22].

---

[3] The hypotheses list and the feedback form can be found at
   http://www.idi.ntnu.no/~mingyang/research/CCRM_Evaluation.pdf

[4] The query-biased similarity method ensures that the test case is always included in the case group with highest similarity value, so the successful termination condition in LOICV, unlike that in LOOCV, is that the case group with the highest similarity value only contains the test case itself.

The reason why we switch from LOOCV to LOICV lies in that:

- In the UCI case bases we use in LOOCV, many of the cases in a case base have the same solutions, so we can evaluate variant CCBR applications in a classification context. In this context, we can choose a case, which shares the same solution as the target case, as the base case of the target case. That is, it is possible to execute a simulated CCBR retrieval with the target case out of the case base.
- In the image processing software component case base, each software component has a unique solution (i.e., the software component itself). McSherry [21] refers to a case base with this property as an *irreducible* case base. The component retrieval problem is basically an identification problem rather than a classification problem. It is impossible to carry out a simulated CCBR retrieval with the target case being removed from an irreducible case base, as its unique solution is no longer represented in the case base.

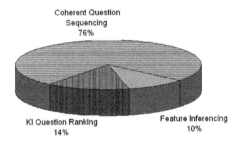

Fig. 2. Relative contribution of each KI-CCBR module to overall improvement in conversation efficiency

In our KI-CCBR method, if we disable the four knowledge-intensive modules, Feature Inferencing, Knowledge-Intensive Question Ranking, Consistent Question Clustering, and Coherent Question Sequencing, the system becomes a knowledge-poor CCBR system (use only the statistical metric (occurrence frequency) to rank questions). Instead of enabling all these four modules at the same time, we enable them in a sequence of Feature Inferencing, Knowledge-Intensive Question Ranking, and Coherent Question Sequencing[5], respectively. With the above module enabling sequence, the average conversation session numbers needed to find the base case are 3.70, 3.64, 3.56, and 3.12, respectively, the latter with all modules enabled. That is, our knowledge-intensive CCBR method improves the efficiency by using 16% fewer conversation sessions (questions) to find the base case compared with the knowledge-poor CCBR method. Fig. 2 shows us that the relative improvements from Feature Inferencing, Knowledge-Intensive Question Ranking, and Coherent Question Sequencing are 10%, 14%,

---

[5] In the simulated question-answering process, only the question with the highest priority is selected to be answered, so the enabling status of the consistent question clustering module has no influence on the evaluation results.

and 76%, respectively. The underlying reason why the coherent question sequencing module has such a major impact is that it guides users to answer the discriminative questions using a sequence ranging from general to specific and insisting on one description aspect instead of allowing a jump from one aspect to another which may be unrelated. However, the degree to which each module contributes to overall performance may depend on the different application domains and the contents of the knowledge bases.

6   Conclusion

In this paper, we note the difficulty of evaluating CBR systems using multiple case bases, and propose an evaluation strategy to use different data sources to assess different evaluation goals of a CBR system. First, all the evaluation goals are divided into two categories: domain-independent goals and domain-dependent goals. For domain-independent goals, we can choose many simple case bases and a statistical evaluation method for testing. For domain-dependent goals, we can choose one or a few target domain case bases and use multiple weak evaluation methods for testing. This evaluation strategy is applied to a knowledge-intensive conversational CBR method as a case study. The results of our case study indicate that such a combination of evaluation methods and test data sources can provide more solid evaluation results than is possible with a single evaluation method.

References

1. Simon, H.A.: Artificial Intelligence: an Empirical Science. Artif. Intell. **77** (1995) 95–127
2. Cohen, P.R., Howe, A.E.: How Evaluation Guides AI Research. AI Mag. **9** (1988) 35–43
3. Cohen, P., Howe, A.: Toward AI Research Methodology: Three Case Studies in Evaluation. Systems, Man and Cybernetics, IEEE Transactions on **19** (1989) 634–646
4. Cohen, P.R.: Empirical Methods for Artificial Intelligence. MIT Press, Cambridge, MA, USA (1995)
5. McSherry, D.: Interactive Case-Based Reasoning in Sequential Diagnosis. Applied Intelligence **14** (2001) 65–76
6. Aamodt, A., Plaza, E.: Case-Based Reasoning: Foundational Issues, Methodological Variations, and System Approaches. AI Communications **7** (1994) 39–59
7. Kolodner, J.: Case-Based Reasoning. Morgan Kaufmann Publishers Inc. (1993)
8. Santamaria, J.C., Ram, A.: Systematic Evaluation of Design Decisions in CBR Systems. In: Proceedings of the AAAI Case-Based Reasoning Workshop, Seattle, Washington (1994) 23 – 29
9. Díaz-Agudo, B., González-Calero, P.A.: An Architecture for Knowledge Intensive CBR Systems. In: Proceedings of the 5th European Workshop on Case-Based Reasoning. Trento, Italy (2000) 37–48

10. Aha, D.W.: Generalizing from Case Studies: A Case Study. In Sleeman, D.H., Edwards, P., eds.: Proceedings of the Ninth International Workshop on Machine Learning, Aberdeen, Scotland, UK, Morgan Kaufmann (1992) 1–10

11. Aamodt, A.: Knowledge-Intensive Case-Based Reasoning in Creek. In Funk, P., González-Calero, P.A., eds.: 7th European Conference on Case-Based Reasoning. Madrid, Spain, (2004) 1–15

12. Sørmo, F., Cassens, J., Aamodt, A.: Explanation in Case-Based Reasoning-Perspectives and Goals. Artificial Intelligence Review **24** (2005) 109 – 143

13. Newman, D., Hettich, S., Blake, C., Merz, C.: UCI Repository of Machine Learning Databases [http://www.ics.uci.edu/ mlearn/mlrepository.html] (1998)

14. Doyle, M., Cunningham, P.: A Dynamic Approach to Reducing Dialog in On-line Decision Guides. In: European Workshop on Advances in Case-Based Reasoning, Trento, Italy (2000) 49–60

15. Tong, X., Öztürk, P., Gu, M.: Dynamic Feature Weighting in Nearest Neighbor Classifiers. In: Proceedings of the 3rd International Conference on Machine Learning and Cybe (ICMLC2004). Volume 4., Shanghai, China, (2004) 2406 – 2411

16. Yang, Q., Wu, J.: Enhancing the Effectiveness of Interactive Case-Based Reasoning with Clustering and Decision Forests. Applied Intelligence, **12** (2001) 49 – 64

17. Bogaerts, S., Leake, D.: Facilitating CBR for Incompletely-Described Cases: Distance Metrics for Partial Problem Descriptions. In: Proceedings of the 7th European Conference on Case-Based Reasoning, Springer - Verlag (2004) 62–76

18. Bareiss, R.: The Experimental Evaluation of a Case-Based Learning Apprentice. In: the proceedings of the Case-Based Reasoning Workshop, Pensacola Beach, Florida (1989) 162 – 167

19. McLaren, B.M.: Extensionally Defining Principles and Cases in Ethics: an AI Model. Artificial Intelligence Journal **150** (2003) 145 – 181

20. Aha, D.W., Breslow, L., Muñoz-Avila, H.: Conversational Case-Based Reasoning. Applied Intelligence: The International Journal of Artificial Intelligence, Neural Networks, and Complex Problem-Solving Technologies **14** (2001) 9

21. McSherry, D.: Minimizing Dialog Length in Interactive Case-Based Reasoning. In: International Joint Conferences on Artificial Intelligence. (2001) 993–998

22. Gupta, K.M., Aha, D.W., Sandhu, N.: Exploiting Taxonomic and Causal Relations in Conversational Case Retrieval. In: European Conference on Case Based Reasoning, Aberdeen, Scotland, UK (2002) 133–147

23. Gu, M., Aamodt, A.: A Knowledge-Intensive Method for Conversational CBR. In Muñoz-Avila, H., Ricci, F., eds.: Case-Based Reasoning Research and Development, Proceedings of the 6th International Conference on Case-Based Reasoning. Chicago, Illinois, Springer Verlag (2005) 296–311

24. Gu, M., Tong, X., Aamodt, A.: Comparing Similarity Calculation Methods in Conversational CBR. In Zhang, D., Khoshgoftaar, T.M., Shyu, M.L., eds.: Proceedings of the 2005 IEEE International Conference on Information Reuse and Integration, Hilton, Las Vegas, Nevada, USA, (2005) 427 – 432

25. Gu, M., Aamodt, A.: Dialog Learning in Conversational CBR. To appear in the Proceedings of the 19th International FLAIRS Conference, Melbourne Beach, Florida, AAAI Press (2006)

26. Gu, M., Bø, K.: Component Retrieval Using Knowledge-Intensive Conversational CBR. To appear in the Proceedings of the 19th International Conference on Industrial, Engineering and Other Applications of Applied Intelligent Systems. Annecy, France, Springer (2006)

27. Witten, I.H., Frank, E.: Data Mining: Practical Machine Learning Tools and Techniques, Second Edition. 2 edn. Morgan Kaufmann Series in Data Management Systems. Morgan Kaufmann Publishers (2005)
28. Aha, D.W., McSherry, D., Yang, Q.: Advances in Conversational Case-Based Reasoning. Knowledge Engineering Review **20** (2006) 7
29. Göker, M.H., Thompson, C.A.: Personalized Conversational Case-Based Recommendation. In: the 5th European Workshop on Case-Based Reasoning(EWCBR 2000), Trento, Italy (2000)
30. Shimazu, H.: Expertclerk: A Conversational Case-Based Reasoning Tool for Developing Salesclerk Agents in E-Commerce Webshops. Artificial Intelligence Review **18** (2002) 223 – 244
31. Ferguson, A., Bridge, D.G.: Partial Orders and Indifference Relations: Being Purposefully Vague in Case-Based Retrieval. In: EWCBR '00: Proceedings of the 5th European Workshop on Advances in Case-Based Reasoning, London, UK, Springer-Verlag (2000) 74–85
32. Gu, M., Aamodt, A., Tong, X.: Component Retrieval Using Conversational Case-Based Reasoning. In Shi, Z., He, Q., eds.: Intelligent Information Processing II, Volume 163 of IFIP International Federation for Information Processing., Springer Science + Business Media Inc (2004)
33. McSherry, D.: Explanation in Recommender Systems. Artificial Intelligence Review **24** (2005) 179 – 197
34. Reilly, J., McCarthy, K., McGinty, L., Smyth, B.: Explaining compound critiques. Artificial Intelligence Review **24** (2005) 199 – 220

Decision Diagrams: Fast and Flexible Support for Case Retrieval and Recommendation*

Ross Nicholson, Derek Bridge, and Nic Wilson

University College Cork,
Cork, Ireland
rn1@cs.ucc.ie, d.bridge@cs.ucc.ie, n.wilson@4c.ucc.ie

Abstract. We show how case bases can be compiled into Decision Diagrams, which represent the cases with reduced redundancy. Numerous computations can be performed efficiently on the Decision Diagrams. The ones we illustrate are: counting characteristics of the case base; computing the distance between a user query and all cases in the case base; and retrieving the k best cases from the case base. Through empirical investigation on four case bases, we confirm that Decision Diagrams are more efficient than a conventional algorithm. Finally, we argue that Decision Diagrams are also flexible in that they support a wide range of computations, additional to the retrieval of the k nearest neighbours.

1 Introduction

Speed of response is important in Case-Based Reasoning (CBR). It is important in embedded case-based systems: in a rapidly changing environment, actions must be timely. It is important in interactive case-based systems: users will only wait so long for an answer. The challenges of providing timely responses to users of interactive case-based systems are increasing because the systems must now support a wider range of computations. In conversational recommender systems, for example, systems must increasingly support question selection [4] and the computation of explanations [6].

Compilation has a long history in Computer Science as a way of improving performance. But it is rarer in CBR. One example is Case Retrieval Nets, where we can think of the case base as having been compiled into a graph of information entities [3]. Another example is any system that automatically constructs an index structure into the case base (e.g. the k-d trees described in [8]).

In this paper, we compile the case base into a *Decision Diagram*. Decision Diagrams are described by Wilson [9], extending the approach of [1]. They, along with [1,2], represent a strand of research into compiling Constraint Satisfaction Problems (CSPs). Our contribution is to apply them to CBR, especially case-based retrieval and to current conversational recommender systems.

---

* The support of the Informatics Commercialisation initiative of Enterprise Ireland is gratefully acknowledged; this work was also supported by Science Foundation Ireland under Grant No. 00/PI.1/C075. We are grateful to Dr. Lorraine McGinty and Mr. James Reilly for making their Laptops and Cameras data available to us.

T.R. Roth-Berghofer et al. (Eds.): ECCBR 2006, LNAI 4106, pp. 136–150, 2006.

Location	Bathrooms	Furnished	Bedrooms
Chelsea	1	Yes	2
Chelsea	1	No	2
Chelsea	2	Yes	4
Chelsea	2	Yes	3
Clapham	2	Yes	2
Clapham	1	Yes	2
Clapham	1	No	2

Fig. 1. Example case base

In Section 2.1, we explain how to compile a case base into a Decision Diagram; in Section 2.2 we use the Decision Diagram to efficiently count properties of the case base; in Section 2.3 we show how to use the Diagram to efficiently compute the distance between a user's query and every case in the case base; and in Section 2.4 we explain how to efficiently retrieve the best k cases from the Diagram. Section 3 reports empirical results on four case bases, comparing operation counts and timings, and showing much improved performance when using Decision Diagrams. Finally, in Section 4, we argue that Decision Diagrams are also extremely flexible in that they support a wide range of useful computations.

2   Decision Diagrams

A Decision Diagram is a directed graph, having distinguished Source and Sink nodes. Each complete path, i.e. from Source to Sink, represents a solution to the Constraint Satisfaction Problem (CSP), or a case in the case base, from which the Decision Diagram was compiled. Values representing the degree to which constraints are satisfied, or the degree to which cases match a user's query, are propagated and aggregated across the graph to efficiently implement key CSP and CBR operations.

In our work, we assume that cases are 'flat' vectors of attribute-value pairs. The case base we use as a running example is shown in Figure 1. The example case base contains seven case descriptions of the kind used in case-based recommender systems. Here, each is a London property rental.

Figure 2 shows one possible Decision Diagram for the example case base. For m attributes, there are $m + 1$ layers (columns) of nodes, which we will refer to as layers 0 to m. In the example, four attributes gives five layers of nodes. There is only one node in layer 0, referred to as Source, and one node in layer m, referred to as Sink. In our specialisation of the Decision Diagram formalism [9], each of layers 0 to $m - 1$ is associated with a case attribute, and the edges that connect to the next layer are labelled with values for that attribute. In the example, Source is associated with the *Location* attribute and so edges that connect to the next layer are labelled with values *Chelsea* or *Clapham*; the next layer is associated with the *Bathrooms* attribute and so edges that connect to the next layer are labelled with values 1 or 2; and so on. Sink is not associated with any attribute. Each complete

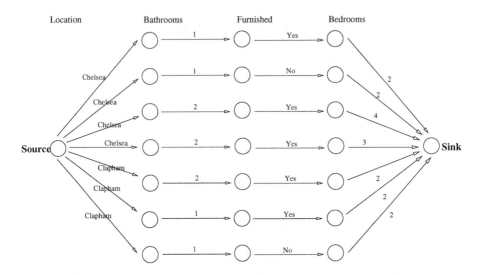

Fig. 2. DD(7): One possible Decision Diagram for Figure 1's case base

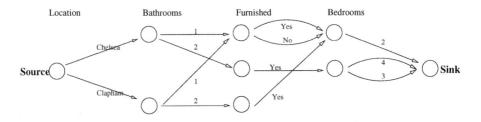

Fig. 3. DD(3): Another possible Decision Diagram for Figure 1's case base

path through the graph, from Source to Sink, corresponds to a case in the case base. In Figure 1 there are seven cases; in Figure 2 there are seven complete paths.

Now consider Figure 3, which is another Decision Diagram for the same case base. Nodes which were separate in Figure 2 have, in effect, been *merged* in Figure 3. The number of layers is the same and, crucially, there are still seven paths through the Decision Diagram, corresponding to the seven cases.

We define the width of a Decision Diagram at any point to be the number of edges connecting layer i to layer $i + 1$. For example, in Figure 3, the width between layers 0 and 1 is two. We define the width of the Decision Diagram *as a whole* to be the average of the widths between each layer, rounded to the nearest integer. The width of Figure 2 is therefore seven: it is this wide at all points. The width of Figure 3 is three: $(2 + 4 + 4 + 3)/4$. In this paper, we use the width as a concise way of referring to a Diagram: the Diagram in Figure 2, we call DD(7); and the one in Figure 3, we call DD(3). Obviously, DD(3) is more compact than DD(7): it is narrower at all points. It is this reduction in redundancy that will give us performance improvements over traditional case retrieval algorithms.

Algorithm 1. Building a Decision Diagram from case base CB, whose set of attributes is $A = \{a_0, \ldots, a_{m-1}\}$

---

insert a new node, Source, at layer 0
for all $c \in CB$ **do**
  $current :=$ Source
  $R := \{\,\}$
  $P := A$
  for $i := 0$ upto $m - 1$ **do**
    insert attribute-value pair $\langle a_i, v \rangle$ from case c into set R
    remove attribute a_i from set P
    if there is already an edge, labelled by value v, from $current$ to some node $next$
    then
      $current := next$ {i.e. traverse the edge}
    else {i.e. need a new edge}
      $slice := \pi_P(\sigma_R(CB))$
      if there already exists a node $next$ at layer $i + 1$ for which slice($next$) = $slice$
      then
        insert an edge $current \xrightarrow{v} next$
      else {i.e. need a new node as well}
        insert a new node $next$ at layer $i + 1$
        slice($next$) := $slice$
        insert an edge $current \xrightarrow{v} next$
      end if
    end if
  end for
end for

2.1   Compiling a Decision Diagram from a Case Base

Our algorithm for creating a Decision Diagram from a case base, Algorithm 1, is a novel specialisation of the one described in [9] for compiling a Decision Diagram from a CSP. We will explain this algorithm with reference to the first two cases in the case base shown in Figure 1.

Figure 4 depicts the Decision Diagram after we have processed the first case in the case base. The Decision Diagram initially contained only the Source node. Hence, edges were created for each attribute-value pair in the first case. Alongside the nodes, we show case base 'slices'. These are explained in the next paragraph.

Now consider processing the second case in the case base. If possible, we follow an existing path through the Decision Diagram; we only insert new edges and nodes if necessary. We start at Source. The case's first attribute-value pair is $\langle Location, Chelsea \rangle$ and there is an edge in Figure 4 labelled $Chelsea$ emanating from Source; so we follow this edge. The next attribute-value pair in the case is $\langle Bathrooms, 1 \rangle$. There is an edge in Figure 4 labelled 1, and so we are able to follow this edge. We are now at the third node from the left in Figure 4.

The next attribute-value pair is $\langle Furnished, No \rangle$. There is no edge in Figure 4 labelled No emanating from our current node. One thing is certain: we will need to insert a new edge into the Diagram. The question is: will we also insert a new

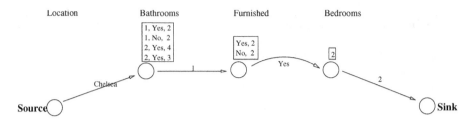

Fig. 4. Building the Decision Diagram: the result of processing the first case

node as the destination of this edge, or will we be able to use an existing node? This is where the case base slices are used.

In our specialisation of the Decision Diagrams in [9], slices are computed using σ and π, which are the standard select and project operators of relational algebra [5]. In the *select* operator, $\sigma_R(S)$, R is a Boolean condition. The operator returns all tuples (cases) in S that satisfy R: a kind of horizontal subset. In the *project* operator, $\pi_P(S)$, P is a set of attributes. The operator returns all tuples (cases) in S but confined to the attributes in P: a kind of vertical subset.

In our algorithm, R contains the attribute-value pairs that we have looked at so far from the case that we are processing. In the example, we have looked at $\{\langle Location, Chelsea\rangle, \langle Bathrooms, 1\rangle, \langle Furnished, No\rangle\}$. So, in forming our new slice, we select cases that agree with these attribute-value pairs. In our algorithm, P is the set of attributes that we have not looked at so far in the case that we are processing. In the example, there is just one attribute that we have not yet looked at: *Bedrooms*. So, in forming our new slice, we project the result of the selection operator on this attribute. Hence, in this example, we are computing:

$$\pi_{\{Bedrooms\}}\left(\sigma_{\{\langle Location, Chelsea\rangle, \langle Bathrooms, 1\rangle, \langle Furnished, No\rangle\}}(CB)\right)$$

The resulting slice contains just one tuple, having one attribute, and the value of this attribute in that tuple is 2. Figure 5 shows that, because this new slice equals a slice already associated with a node in the destination layer, we do not need to insert a new node. Instead, we insert an edge to the node whose slice equals the new slice.

This concludes processing of the second case in the case base. The other cases are each processed in a similar fashion, giving rise to the Decision Diagram that we showed in Figure 3.

Of course, as can be seen in Figure 5, each slice can be computed incrementally from the previous one; it does not need to be computed 'from scratch'.

When we run our algorithm, we employ a heuristic that generally increases the opportunities for merging of nodes, thereby reducing the size of the Diagram. Specifically, we sort the *attributes* by ascending domain size. We have already done this in Figure 1: the *Bedrooms* attribute, whose domain size is three, comes after the other attributes, all of which have domain sizes of two. The order of the *cases* in the case base, however, is not significant: irrespective of their order, the algorithm produces the same Decision Diagram.

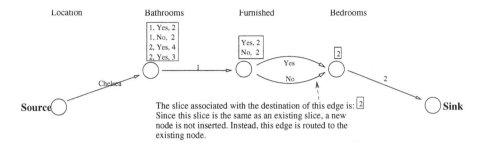

Fig. 5. Building the Decision Diagram: the result of processing the second case

A newly-retained case can easily be incorporated incrementally into the Decision Diagram. In essence, this involves running just the inner for-loop in Algorithm 1. However, computing and comparing slices means inserting a case into a Decision Diagram will be slower than inserting a case into a flat case base.

2.2 Counting Cases

We have shown how we compile a case base into a Decision Diagram, which is usually more compact than the original case base. What remains to be shown is how we can efficiently compute with the Decision Diagram. This involves the propagation and aggregation of values across the graph. We begin with something simple: counting properties of the case base from its Decision Diagram. We look at this first because doing so aids the exposition: it has the virtue of being readily understandable and it generalises to more useful operations.

Each node n in a Decision Diagram is associated with two values, which we refer to as its f-value and its g-value. We define $f(n)$ inductively as follows:

$$f(n) =_{\text{def}} \begin{cases} 1 & \text{if } n = \text{Source} \\ \sum_{n' \longrightarrow n} f(n') & \text{otherwise} \end{cases} \tag{1}$$

where $n' \longrightarrow n$ signifies an edge from n' to n. In other words, the f-value of n is the sum of the f-values of its 'parents' over all edges entering n.

We define g-values analogously, this time summing g-values of 'child' nodes over all edges leaving n:

$$g(n) =_{\text{def}} \begin{cases} 1 & \text{if } n = \text{Sink} \\ \sum_{n \longrightarrow n'} g(n') & \text{otherwise} \end{cases} \tag{2}$$

We can use a breadth-first 'search' from Source to Sink to compute f-values. A breadth-first 'search' from Sink to Source will compute g-values. The complexity of these procedures is linear in the size of the Decision Diagram.

Figure 6 shows f- and g-values computed in this way. For example, the node labelled by an asterisk has three edges entering it. We obtain its f-value by summing, for each edge entering the node, the f-values of the parent: $2+2+1 = 5$

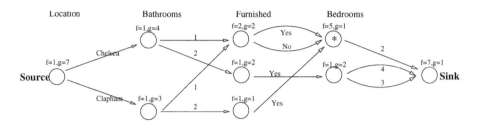

Fig. 6. Decision Diagram with f- and g-values for counting solutions. (The asterisk is referred to in the text.)

(by Equation (1)). We obtain its g-value by summing, for each edge leaving the node, the g-values of the child: 1 (by Equation (2)).

We see that $f(\text{Sink})$ and $g(\text{Source})$ both denote the number of paths (cases) in the graph, in this case seven.

The f-value at a node n summarises information about paths from Source to n; the g-value at n summarises information about paths from n to Sink. For example, the node labelled with an asterisk in Figure 6 is reached by five paths from Source and by one path to Sink.

Why would we want to compute *both* f- and g-values? Together, they allow us to compute how many complete paths pass through a *node* n. We do this by multiplying $f(n) \times g(n)$. For example, the number of complete paths passing through the node labelled with an asterisk is $5 \times 1 = 5$. In a similar vein, we can find out how many complete paths include a particular *edge* $n \longrightarrow n'$ by multiplying $f(n) \times g(n')$. For example, the number of complete paths that include the edge between the node with an asterisk and Sink is $5 \times 1 = 5$.

This can be used to compute how many complete paths (cases) contain a particular attribute-value pair. For example, we can determine in how many of the rental properties *Furnished* = *Yes*. We sum the number of complete paths that pass through each edge labelled *Yes*. There are three such edges, and the value we compute is $2 \times 1 + 1 \times 2 + 1 \times 1 = 5$. Assuming f- and g-values have already been computed, the complexity of this computation is proportional to the width of the Diagram at this point. While this may, in the worst-case, be equal to the number of cases, it will often, as in the example, be much lower.

In the next section, we will generalise these ideas to similarity-based retrieval.

2.3   Similarity-Based Retrieval

A user's query or probe q is a set of attribute-value pairs. We may wish to compute, for each case c in the case base, its degree of similarity to the query. In fact, our presentation will be in terms of distance, rather than similarity. We assume a set of local distance measures dist_a, one for each attribute $a \in A$. We take global distance dist to be a weighted sum of the local distances:

$$\text{dist}(q, c) =_{\text{def}} \sum_{a \in A} w_a \times \text{dist}_a(q.a, c.a) \tag{3}$$

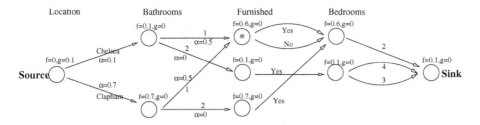

Fig. 7. Decision Diagram with f- and g-values for computing distances. The user query is *Bathrooms* = 2, *Location* = *Pimlico*. Where α-values are not shown, they are 0. (The asterisk is referred to in the text.)

where w_a are the weights and $q.a$ and $c.a$ are q's and c's values for attribute a. We will constrain weights and local distances to be in $[0, 1]$, hence global distance will be in $[0, m]$, where m is the number of attributes, with 0 being the 'best' value and m being the 'worst'.

We use f- and g-values to propagate and aggregate the measures of distance. But, additionally, we associate with every edge $n \longrightarrow n'$ a value, which, following [9], we denote by $\alpha(n \longrightarrow n')$. It is important to appreciate that the α-value of an edge is distinct from the attribute-value of that edge. The attribute-values are the values that label the edges in Figures 2–5, e.g. that the *Location* is *Chelsea*. α-values, by contrast, denote local distances.

Initially, all α-values are set to 0. For each attribute-value pair $a = v$ in the user's query, we update the α-values of all edges that emanate from nodes that are in the layer of the Decision Diagram pertaining to attribute a. Specifically, if node n is in the layer that pertains to attribute a and there is an edge $n \longrightarrow n'$ labelled with attribute-value v', then

$$\alpha(n \longrightarrow n') := w_a \times \text{dist}_a(v, v') \tag{4}$$

Now, f- and g-values are defined inductively as follows:

$$f(n) =_{\text{def}} \begin{cases} 0 & \text{if } n = \text{Source} \\ \min_{n' \longrightarrow n} (f(n') + \alpha(n' \longrightarrow n)) & \text{otherwise} \end{cases} \tag{5}$$

$$g(n) =_{\text{def}} \begin{cases} 0 & \text{if } n = \text{Sink} \\ \min_{n \longrightarrow n'} (\alpha(n \longrightarrow n') + g(n')) & \text{otherwise} \end{cases} \tag{6}$$

As before, a breadth-first search from Source to Sink will compute f-values. But, in fact, we reduce effort by starting, not from Source, but from leftmost nodes entered by an edge with an altered α-value. We compute g-values in the opposite direction and starting from rightmost nodes exited by an edge with an altered α-value. The cost of computing these f- and g-values is, as before, linear in the number of edges in the Decision Diagram.

We show an example in Figure 7. In the example, the user prefers two bathrooms. We take $\text{dist}_{Bathrooms}(2, 1) = 0.5$ and $\text{dist}_{Bathrooms}(2, 2) = 0$. She would

also like to live in Pimlico, and we will assume that $\text{dist}_{Location}(Pimlico, Chelsea)$
$= 0.1$ and $\text{dist}_{Location}(Pimlico, Clapham) = 0.7$. We take all weights to be one.
As shown in Figure 7, the local distances are used to update the α-values of all
edges emanating from layers 0 and 1. The α-values of all other edges remain at
0, and are not shown in the figure in order to reduce clutter.

The node labelled by an asterisk has two edges entering it. We obtain its f-
value by taking the minimum, over each edge entering the node, of the f-values
of the parent added to the α-value of the edge: $\min(0.1 + 0.5, 0.7 + 0.5) = 0.6$
(by Equation (5)).

We see that $f(\text{Sink})$ and $g(\text{Source})$ both denote the distance between the best
case in the case base and the user's query: the two properties in Chelsea with 2
bathrooms are 0.1 distant from the query.

We can use these f- and g-values in ways that are analogous to the uses we
found in Section 2.2. We can compute the distance from the query of the best
complete path that passes through a *node* n by adding $f(n) + g(n)$. For example,
the best complete path passing through the node labelled with an asterisk has
a distance of $0.6 + 0 = 0.6$ from the query. And, we can compute the distance
from the query of complete paths that include a particular *edge* $n \longrightarrow n'$, again
by adding $f(n) + \alpha(n \longrightarrow n') + g(n')$. For example, the best complete path that
includes the edge labelled *Yes* that emanates from the node with an asterisk is
$0.6 + 0 + 0 = 0.6$ distant from the query. And, we can compute the least distance
from the query of complete paths that contain a particular attribute-value pair.
For example, suppose we ask this question of furnished properties. For each edge
$n \longrightarrow n'$ labelled *Yes*, we compute $f(n) + \alpha(n \longrightarrow n') + g(n')$, and we take the
minimum of these values. There are three such edges, and the value we compute
is $\min(0.6 + 0 + 0, 0.1 + 0 + 0, 0.7 + 0 + 0) = 0.1$.

2.4 k Nearest Neighbours

Of course, in CBR rarely would we just want to know how distant the best case
is from the user's query. Rather, we wish to *retrieve* the best case, or the best k
cases, or the cases whose distances are less than some threshold θ.

Algorithm 2 is a new algorithm that efficiently retrieves the best k cases from
the Decision Diagram. An analogous algorithm can extract those cases whose
distances are less than θ.

The algorithm maintains a priority-ordered queue of paths and repeatedly
extends the best of these paths until it has found k paths that reach Sink or it
has run out of paths to extend. It is like an A^* search inasmuch as the items on
the queue are ordered by a combination of their path cost so far and an estimate
of the cost of the cheapest path from the current node to Sink ($\text{cost}(p') + g(n')$
in the algorithm). However, there is a crucial difference. Typically in A^* the
estimated part of the cost is truly an estimate, computed by some heuristic. In
our algorithm, by contrast, it is not an estimate at all: it is the g-value, which
is the *actual* cost of the cheapest path from the current node to Sink.

When a path p' is inserted onto the queue, it should be placed ahead of any-
thing already on the queue of the same or lower priority. Then the algorithm will

Algorithm 2. Retrieving the k best cases from a Decision Diagram

$bestK := \{\}$
create $agenda$, an empty priority-ordered queue
create a path p containing just Source
$\text{cost}(p) := 0$
insert p into $agenda$
while $|bestK| < k \wedge agenda$ is not empty **do**
  remove path p from front of $agenda$
  $n :=$ the last node in path p
  if $n = $ Sink **then**
    insert p into $bestK$
  else
    for all edges $n \longrightarrow n'$ **do**
      $p' := p$ extended by $n \longrightarrow n'$
      $\text{cost}(p') := \text{cost}(p) + \alpha(n \longrightarrow n')$
      insert p' into $agenda$ where the priority of p' is $\text{cost}(p') + g(n')$
    end for
  end if
end while
return $bestK$

unerringly enumerate the best k cases from the Diagram in increasing order of cost. And, assuming f- and g-values have already been computed, its complexity will be approximately linear in k and m (the number of attributes): it will not depend on the size of the Diagram or the number of cases.

3   Efficiency Experiments

We compiled Decision Diagrams from four case bases: Travel, Laptops, Cameras and Lettings. Prior to compiling, we ordered the attributes by ascending domain size. Characteristics of the case bases and the corresponding Decision Diagrams are given in Table 1. We see from the table (row F) that between 83% and 94% of these case bases are repetitions of the same attribute-value pairs. In the Decision Diagrams, this redundancy is reduced to between 68% and 80% (row G). In terms of the representation of attribute-value pairs, the Decision Diagrams save between 23% and 53% of the representation of the case base (row H). However, because Decision Diagrams are more complex data structures, with greater space overheads, their memory footprint is larger than that of a case base in a text file. In two of the case bases, the footprint doubles in size; in one it is a little less than double; in another it is considerably more (row I). However, none of the footprints is unreasonable: all are less than 302kb (row E).

In fact, for each case base, we built *two* Decision Diagrams. In one we disallowed 'merging' of nodes, hence these Diagrams are like the one depicted in Figure 2. In the other, we allowed 'merging', as explained in Algorithm 1, hence these Diagrams are more like the one depicted in Figure 3. It is the latter Diagrams that are characterised in Table 1. (The characteristics of the former are

Table 1. Characteristics of case bases and corresponding Decision Diagrams

	Travel	Laptops	Cameras	Lettings	
Case Bases					
# of cases	1470	693	210	794	
# of attributes	8	14	9	6	
Domain sizes — smallest	4	2	5	2	
— largest	839	438	165	175	
— average	119	37	35	46	
# of attribute-value pairs	11760	9702	1890	4764	(A)
# of distinct attribute-value pairs	954	520	317	273	(B)
Size as text file (kb.)	132	105	15.8	43.1	(C)
Decision Diagrams					
# of edges	3771	2598	1006	1100	(D)
Width — at narrowest point	4	2	5	4	
— at widest point	1387	438	195	601	
— average	471	186	112	183	
Size as serialised Java object (kb.)	301.5	230.5	99.6	62.7	(E)
Build time (ms.) averaged over 10 runs	1156	718	156	266	
Comparison					
Redundancy in case base $(A - B$ as % of $A)$	92%	90%	83%	94%	(F)
Redundancy in DD $(D - B$ as % of $D)$	75%	80%	68%	75%	(G)
Size saving $(D$ as % of $A)$	32%	28%	53%	23%	(H)
Size cost $(E$ as % of $C)$	228%	220%	630%	145%	(I)

basically the same as the characteristics of the case bases themselves, e.g. they have uniform width which is, at every point, the same as the number of cases.)

Recall that we refer to Diagrams using their average width. So the two Travel Decision Diagrams (one without and one with 'merging') are referred to as DD(1470) and DD(471); the two Laptops Decision Diagrams are DD(693) and DD(186); the two Cameras Decision Diagrams are DD(210) and DD(112); and the two Lettings Decision Diagrams are DD(794) and DD(183).

To evaluate efficiency, we ran experiments to compare the number of operations and the times needed to compute twenty nearest neighbours. We used the leave-one-in methodology: each case in the case base is taken in turn and used to form queries. From a given case, we form all queries that comprise just one attribute-value pair taken from the case; then we form all queries that include two attribute-value pairs from the case; and so on until we form a query that involves using all the attribute-value pairs from the case. Hence, the number of queries is $^m C_1 + {}^m C_2 + \cdots + {}^m C_m$, where m is the number of attributes. In the histograms (Figures 8 and 9), we have columns for each query size and also columns (the rightmost) for all queries taken together, irrespective of size.

The queries are evaluated by three different systems. The first, denoted kNN, is an implementation of the nearest neighbours algorithm applied to the

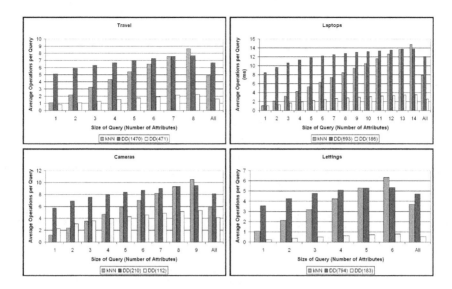

Fig. 8. Average operation counts by query size and for all queries

original case base: it does a linear search through all the cases of the case base, but it includes a degree of caching to give it a fairer chance against Decision Diagrams. The second system uses the Decision Diagram in which merging is disallowed, and the third system uses the Diagram in which merging is allowed.

Operation counts and timings both have well-recognised weaknesses as ways of comparing the efficiency of different algorithms. We hope by including both counts and times that the weaknesses of using one are compensated for by using the other. In any case, both sets of results tell much the same story.

In Figure 8 we show, for each system on each case base, the number of operations needed to compute the global distance between the query and every case in the case base. Hence, we are counting the number of local distances that the systems compute and the number of addition operations needed to aggregate the local distances into global distances. In these operation counts, we exclude any consideration of retrieving the best k cases. We did this because the different systems (kNN on the one hand and Decision Diagrams on the other hand) use such different ways of retrieving the winning cases that we could not find a fair basis for comparison in terms of operation counts. However, retrieval *is* included in the timing results reported in Figure 9 below.

We see in Figure 8, as we would expect, that the narrower Diagrams always perform fewer operations than the other two systems. Taken over all queries, irrespective of size, the narrower Decision Diagrams perform 67%, 68%, 30% and 85% fewer operations than kNN on Travel, Laptops, Cameras and Lettings respectively. Interestingly, Decision Diagram performance is much less variable over different query sizes than is kNN performance.

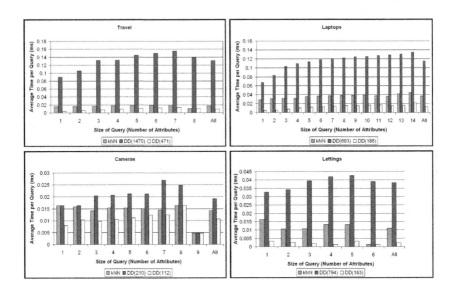

Fig. 9. Average time (ms.) by query size and for all queries

In Figure 9 we show, for each system on each case base, the time in milliseconds needed to retrieve the twenty nearest neighbours of the query. Hence, we are measuring how long it takes to compute distances *and* to retrieve the twenty winning cases. The figures used are averages over ten runs.

The Figure shows that the narrower Decision Diagrams are never outperformed, but there is a handful of query sizes where kNN is competitive on some of the case bases. Taken over all queries, irrespective of size, the narrower Decision Diagrams take 46%, 64%, 25% and 79% less time than kNN on Travel, Laptops, Cameras and Lettings respectively.

4   Concluding Discussion

We have shown two uses of the f- and g-values in Decision Diagrams: efficiently propagating and aggregating counts and distances. But the values can be generalised further for even greater flexibility; this is the way Decision Diagrams are presented in [9]. There it is shown that the f- and g-values can be drawn from any semiring. In [9], a semiring is defined as a set of values S containing different elements **0** and **1**, and two operations on S, $\oplus$ and $\otimes$, that satisfy the following properties: $\oplus$ is associative and commutative with identity **0** (i.e. $a \oplus (b \oplus c) = (a \oplus b) \oplus c$, $a \oplus b = b \oplus a$ and $a \oplus \mathbf{0} = a$); $\otimes$ is associative and commutative with identity **1** (i.e. $a \otimes (b \otimes c) = (a \otimes b) \otimes c$, $a \otimes b = b \otimes a$ and $a \otimes \mathbf{1} = a$); **0** is a null element (i.e. $a \otimes \mathbf{0} = \mathbf{0}$); and $\otimes$ distributes over $\oplus$ (i.e. $a \otimes (b \oplus c) = (a \otimes b) \oplus (a \otimes c)$). It is important to note that **0** and **1** are special elements of set S; they are not necessarily the integers 0 and 1.

Then, in general, f- and g-values are defined as follows

$$f(n) =_{\text{def}} \begin{cases} 1 & \text{if } n = \text{Source} \\ \bigoplus_{n' \longrightarrow n} (f(n') \otimes \alpha(n' \longrightarrow n)) & \text{otherwise} \end{cases} \tag{7}$$

$$g(n) =_{\text{def}} \begin{cases} 1 & \text{if } n = \text{Sink} \\ \bigoplus_{n \longrightarrow n'} (\alpha(n \longrightarrow n') \otimes g(n')) & \text{otherwise} \end{cases} \tag{8}$$

Initially, prior, e.g., to the imposition of user preferences, α-values are $\mathbf{1}$.

In Section 2.2, where we were counting properties of the case base, we were using the following: $S = \mathbb{N}$, the natural numbers (including zero); $\mathbf{0} = 0$; $\mathbf{1} = 1$; $\oplus = +$; and $\otimes = \times$. Equations (1) and (2) are instantiations of Equations (7) and (8) where $\otimes = \times$ and the α-value of every edge is 1.

One way of viewing what we were doing in Section 2.3, where we were using distance measures, is: $S = [0, m]$, the real numbers between 0 and m, where m is number of attributes; $\mathbf{0} = m$; $\mathbf{1} = 0$; $\oplus = \min$; and $\otimes = +$.[1] You can see that Equations (5) and (6) are special cases of Equations (7) and (8). What this also means is that Algorithm 2, our new algorithm for efficiently extracting best paths from a Decision Diagram, can be used for many semirings. The changes required are that path costs be initialised to the semiring's $\mathbf{1}$ element and, where addition occurs in Algorithm 2, it be replaced by the semiring's $\otimes$ operator. However, the semiring must additionally satisfy the *addition-is-max* property [9]: for all $a, b \in S$ either $a \oplus b = a$ or $a \oplus b = b$. This property ensures that there is a total order on S, which is necessary for ordering elements on the queue.

The great advantage of this generalisation is that the same framework (and, indeed, the same software) can be used in multiple ways, requiring only a change of semiring. For example, suppose we wished to do exact-matching, instead of using distance measures. In other words, we want to find cases that *exactly* match the attribute-values in the user's query. We need only switch to the following semiring: $S = \{true, false\}$; $\mathbf{0} = false$; $\mathbf{1} = true$; $\oplus = \vee$; and $\otimes = \wedge$.

In our software, we allow the nodes of the Decision Diagram to have multiple f- and g-values, based on possibly different semirings, so that we can simultaneously compute and store different consequences of the user's query.

In ongoing work, we are using Decision Diagrams to build recommender systems. We believe that the efficiency and flexibility of the Diagrams give an ideal foundation. For example, a number of recommender systems now use a two-stage approach, in which an exact-matching stage precedes an inexact-matching stage (e.g. [7]); as we have explained, both forms of matching are supported by Decision Diagrams. Entropy-based approaches to question selection (e.g. [4]) rely on

---

[1] In fact, strictly, in order to satisfy the requirement that the $\mathbf{0}$ element (in this case, m) be a null element (i.e. $a \otimes \mathbf{0} = \mathbf{0}$), we cannot let $\otimes = +$. Instead, we let $\otimes =\overset{m}{+}$, where $\overset{z}{+}$ is simply addition in which the result is not allowed to exceed z: $x \overset{z}{+} y =_{\text{def}} \min(x + y, z)$. $\overset{m}{+}$ does have m as its null element. However, this nicety plays no part in our software because, the way we are computing with local distances, they will never sum to more than m.

dynamically counting cases, in the light of incrementally-supplied user preferences; as we have shown, counting is efficient in Decision Diagrams; incremental processing is also easy. Explanations of retrieval failure are also important, especially in systems that use exact matching (e.g. [6]). Although not described here, we have generalised the ideas in [1] to allow us to efficiently support computations related to retrieval failure.

References

1. Amilhastre, J., Fargier, H. & Marquis, P.: Consistency restoration and explanations in dynamic CSPs — Application to configuration, *Artificial Intelligence*, vol.135(1–2), pp.199–234, 2002
2. Bryant, R.E.: Symbolic Boolean Manipulation with Ordered Binary Decision Diagrams, *ACM Computing Surveys*, vol.24, no.3, pp.292–318, 1992
3. Burkhard, H.-D. & Lenz, M.: Case Retrieval Nets: Basic ideas and extensions, in H.-D.Burkhard & M.Lenz (eds.), *Procs. of the 4th German Workshop on CBR*, pp.103–110, Humboldt University, 1996.
4. Doyle, M. & Cunningham, P.: A Dynamic Approach to Reducing Dialog in On-Line Decision Guides, in E.Blanzieri & L.Portinale (eds.), *Procs. of the 5th European Workshop on Case-Based Reasoning*, pp.49–60, Springer, 2000
5. Elmasri, R. & Navathe, S.B.: *Fundamentals of Database Systems (5th edn.)*, Addison-Wesley, 2006
6. McSherry, D.: Explanation of Retrieval Mismatches in Recommender System Dialogues, in D.W.Aha (ed.), *Procs. of the Workshop on Mixed-Initiative Case-Based Reasoning*, pp.191–199, Norwegian University of Science and Technology, 2003
7. Ricci, F., Arslan, B., Mirzadeh, N. & Venturini, A.: ITR: A Case-Based Travel Advisory System, in S.Craw & A.Preece (eds.), *Procs. of the 6th European Conference on Case-Based Reasoning*, pp.613–641, Springer, 2002
8. Wess, S., Althoff, K.-D. & Derwand, G.: Using *k*-d Trees to Improve the Retrieval Step in Case-Based Reasoning, in S.Wess et al., (eds.), *Procs. of the 1st European Workshop on Case-Based Reasoning*, pp.167–181, Springer, 1993
9. Wilson, N.: Decision Diagrams for the Computation of Semiring Valuations, *Procs. of the 19th IJCAI*, pp.331-336, 2005

Case-Based Reasoning for Knowledge-Intensive Template Selection During Text Generation

Raquel Hervás and Pablo Gervás

Departamento de Sistemas Informáticos y Programación
Universidad Complutense de Madrid, Spain
raquelhb@fdi.ucm.es, pgervas@sip.ucm.es

Abstract. The present paper describes a case-based reasoning solution for solving the task of selecting adequate templates for realizing messages describing actions in a given domain. This solution involves the construction of a case base from a corpus of example texts, using information from WordNet to group related verbs together. A case retrieval net is used as a memory model. A taxonomy of the concepts involved in the texts is used to compute similarity between concepts. The set of data to be converted into text acts as a query to the system. The process of solving a given query may involve several retrieval processes - to obtain a set of cases that together constitute a good solution for transcribing the data in the query as text messages - and a process of knowledge-intensive adaptation which resorts to a knowledge base to identify appropriate substitutions and completions for the concepts that appear in the cases, using the query as a source. We describe this case-based solution, and we present examples of how it solves the task of selecting an appropriate set of templates to render a given set of data as text.

1 Introduction

Template-based solutions for natural language generation rely on reusing fragments of text extracted from typical texts in a given domain, having applied to them a process which identifies the part of them which is common to all uses, and leaving certain gaps to be filled with details corresponding to a new use. For instance, when conveying the information that John moved to Atlanta, a template such as _ *moved to* _ may be used, filling in the gap with appropriate strings for John and Atlanta. Whereas more complex natural language generation systems based on the use of grammars can have rich stages devoted to selecting fresh combinations of words to convey the same meaning, template-based systems are faced with an additional difficulty. The fact that templates are made up of words that are not accessible to the system makes the system blind to their appropriateness as means of conveying a given idea for a specific set of arguments. Annotating the templates with tags that indicate the circumstances under which it is appropriate to use the template would solve the problem, but it eliminates some of the advantages of the template solution over more knowledge-rich approaches.

T.R. Roth-Berghofer et al. (Eds.): ECCBR 2006, LNAI 4106, pp. 151–165, 2006.

Applying a case-based solution presents the advantage that the information needed to solve the problem can be obtained from the original examples of appropriate use that gave rise to the templates. By associating a case with each template, with case attributes consisting of conceptual descriptions of the arguments that were used for the template in the original instance, a case-based reasoning solution can be employed to select the best template for realizing a particular message. This approach has a certain psychological plausibility. People do not always create new linguistic constructions each time they need to express an idea not used before, but rather they appeal to their memory of expressions they have used or heard in the past looking for the best way to express the new idea. They remember other situations where they have expressed similar ideas, and the phrasing they used in each situation. In this process they take into account existing relations between the elements of the lexicon they already know.

The present paper describes a case-based solution for the task of selecting adequate templates for realizing messages describing actions in a given domain. The goal is to achieve coverage of a broad range of messages by combining instances of a restricted set of templates, providing automated means for dealing with overlaps between the information conveyed by the templates found, and to ensure coherent use of context information - in the shape of a knowledge base for the domain accepted as input - whenever the resulting templates need to mention information that was not explicit in the given query.

Section 2 presents a review of previous work in the relevant fields. Section 3 describes a case-based solution to template selection, outlining the inputs to consider, the construction of the case base, and the main CBR processes involved. Section 4 describes in detail an example of system operation, and section 5 presents conclusions and further work.

2   Lexicalisation and Knowledge Intensive CBR

The general process of text generation takes place in several stages, during which the conceptual input is progressively refined by adding information that will shape the final text [1]. During the initial stages the concepts and messages that will appear in the final content are decided (*content determination*), these messages are organised into a specific order and structure (*discourse planning*), and particular ways of describing each concept where it appears in the discourse plan are selected (*referring expresion generation*). This results in a version of the discourse plan where the contents, the structure of the discourse, and the level of detail of each concept are already fixed. The *lexicalization* stage that follows decides which specific words and phrases should be chosen to express the domain concepts and relations which appear in the messages. A final stage of *surface realization* assembles all the relevant pieces into linguistically and typographically correct text.

The most common model of lexicalisation is one where the lexicalisation module converts an input built from domain concepts and relations organised as a graph into an output built from words and syntactic relations also organised as a graph. Cahill [2] differentiates between "lexicalization" and "lexical choice". The first term is taken to indicate a broader meaning of the conversion of something to lexical items, while the second is used in a narrower sense to mean deciding between lexical alternatives representing the same propositional content. Stede [3] proposes a more flexible way of attaching lexical items to configurations of concepts and roles, using a lexical option finder that determines the set of content words that cover pieces of the message to be expressed. These items may vary in semantic specificity and in connotation, also including synonyms and nearsynonyms. From this set, the subsequent steps of the generation process can select the most preferred subset for expressing the message.

In template-based generation, the selection of templates is part lexicalization and part surface realization, in the sense that it determines some of the words that appear in the final text, but it also defines how they are put together into a (hopefully) correct linguistic statement. For this reason, template selection inherits a distinction equivalent to that pointed out by Cahill: one can talk about *rigid template assignment* - where a given type of message is always realised by the same template -, and *template choice* - where a given type of message can be realised by several templates and mechanisms must be provided for deciding when to use each possible template. A solution similar to that proposed by Stede for pure lexicalization would be a good way of implementing template choice.

Case based approaches have been applied to natural language processing (NLP) problems in the past. These natural language solutions process a text by retrieving stored examples that describe how similar texts were handled in the past. Examples of particular applications are stress acquisition [4], word sense disambiguation [5] and concept extraction [6]. A good review of applications of machine learning techniques in general to NLP tasks can be found in [7].

Knowledge Intensive Case-Based Reasoning (KI-CBR) relies on taxonomical information about the concepts handled by a CBR system in order to improve the results of the processes involved. This taxonomical information usually takes the form of specific ontologies of domain information, sometimes coupled with generic ontologies about CBR concepts [8]. A typical use involves resorting to the taxonomy for computing similarity between cases.

When building knowledge resources for supporting this type of CBR, accepted practice recommends the reuse of previous existing ones. The WordNet lexical database [9] has been widely used for knowledge-based systems, including applications to CBR in domains such as design support [10].

Case Retrieval Nets (CRNs) [11] are a memory model developed to improve the efficiency of the retrieval tasks of the CBR cycle. They are based on the idea that humans are able to solve problems without performing an intensive search process, but they often start from the given description, consider the neighbourhood, and extend the scope of considered objects if required.

The basic item in the context of the CRNs are so-called Information Entities (IEs). These represent any basic knowledge item in the form of an attribute-value pair. A case then consist of a set of such IEs, and the case base is a net with nodes for the entities observed in the domain and additional nodes denoting the particular cases. IE nodes may be connected by similarity arcs, and a case node is reachable from its constituting IE nodes via relevance arcs. Different degrees of similarity and relevance are expressed by varying arc weights. Given this structure, case retrieval is carried out by activating the IEs given in the query case, propagating this activation according to similarity through the net of IE nodes, and collecting the achieved activation in the associated case nodes.

Case retrieval nets have been used for lexicalization before. Hervás and Gervás [12] presented an application of a CRN to heuristic lexicalization in the context of a NLG application. The case base employed was obtained from the set of formalised documents used as input to the generator. The experimental results showed that the use of the case-based reasoning paradigm for the task of lexicalisation is a good approximation whenever enough information is available in the case base to express in an acceptable form any new request. If queries beyond the scope of the input were tried, the system performed poorly. It remained an open question whether the use of a larger case base with broader coverage would improve results.

3   Case Based Solutions for Template Selection

Lexicalization based on templates selects words from the vocabulary to describe the concepts involved in the current draft, using lexical tags for static concepts, as characters and scenarios, and templates for actions and verbs, providing structure to the sentences. Templates partly solve the need for having an explicit grammar, but the knowledge base provides the required information to solve issues like number and gender agreement. This is an acceptable method when operating in restricted domains, but results can be poor if complex actions have to be expressed. Complex actions require the introduction of lexical chains that are employed exclusively for a specific verb in some context. This introduces an unwanted rigidity in the system, because it makes the task of extending the vocabulary an arduous one. This solution also implies that the vocabulary holds no semantic information about actors or objects involved in an action.

As an alternative, we have implemented a case-based lexicalisation module. When human beings talk or write, they do not always invent entirely new sentences whenever they need to express a specific idea that they have never before put into words. Instead, sometimes they search for relations between the new idea to be expressed and other ideas expressed previously, taking the same vocabulary and adapting it as required. They reuse previous experience to solve a new case.

This module relies on subsequent processing of its output by an accompanying surface realization module. This module is in charge of putting together the selected terms and templates. Additionally, it carries out a basic orthographic transformation of the resulting sentences. Templates are converted into strings formatted in accordance to the orthographic rules of English - sentence initial letters are capitalized, and a period is added at the end.

The specific architecture of the NLG application that uses these modules is implemented using cFROGS [13], a framework-like library of architectural classes intended to facilitate the development of NLG applications. It is designed to provide the necessary infrastructure for developing NLG applications, minimizing the implementation effort by means of schemas and generic architectural structures commonly used in these systems.

3.1 Inputs to the NLG Module

Three particular inputs to the NLG module are relevant to the work described here: the knowledge base, the vocabulary and the discourse plan.

The Knowledge Base. The knowledge base contains the relevant conceptual information about the domain, in such a way that the generator can consult it and use it. It is organized as a tree, including individuals, locations, objects, relations between them and their attributes. The facts in the knowledge base are domain concepts that are used to instantiate the templates when representing cases. The concepts appearing in the cases are organized as a taxonomy needed to compute their similarities. Each type of concept is divided into several subtypes.

The Vocabulary. The vocabulary contains all the lexical information essential to write the final text. It is structured as a tree as well, very similar to the knowledge base one, with the difference that each fact or relation has a lexical tag associated to its eventual realization in the final text.

In the vocabulary that the system uses, a lexical tag made up of one or more words is assigned to each concept in the domain. This is used for lexicalising individual concepts, with little choice given. The vocabulary for actions or verbs becomes more complex: it is stored in the form of cases, where each case stores not only the corresponding template but also additional information concerning the type of case, the elements involved in the action, and the role that those elements play in the action. The types of actions that appear in this module are shown in Table 1.

It is important to take into account that the structure of each one of these types is not rigid. They will not always have the same elements, nor in the same order. A clear example is provided by the verbs 'leave' and 'go', both of type Move. The

Table 1. Types of actions

Type	Characteristics of action
Move	a character or an object changes of location
Atrans	possession of a character or an object is transferred
Fight	physical confrontations between characters
Ingest	a character ingests something (either another character or an object)
Propel	a physical force is applied to an object
State	change of state of a character or an object
Use	an element of the domain participates in the action
Feel	involve feelings, both positive or negative
Speak	a character or an object express an idea out loud

first one has an attribute From to indicate where the character is coming from, whereas the second one has an attribute To that indicates his destination.

Verbs are particularly important in the present context because we are considering narrative tales which have little descriptive depth. This implies that verbs carry a significant part of the communication effort.

A case is not an abstract instance of a verb or action, but rather a concrete instance in which specific characters, places and objects appear. These elements are stored in the module's knowledge base. This allows the establishment of relations between them when it comes to retrieving or reusing the cases.

Not all the attributes in a case act later as slot-fillers in the corresponding template. Some attributes - like the specification of initial and final states in a state change - are not explicitly mentioned in a template. For example, the case for *kill* indicates an initial state alive and a final state dead, but these are not mentioned in the surface form of the template. Such attributes appear enclosed in culry brackets in the representation of the case.

Examples of cases for the different types of action are given below. The associated templates are shown below for each case:

```
TYPE:    LEX:    ACTOR:    OBJECT:
FIGHT    attack  witch     Hansel
```

_ *attacked* _

```
TYPE:    LEX:    ACTOR:        OBJECT:       {FEELING:}
FEEL     envy    stepsisters   Cinderella    bad
```

_ *envied* _

```
TYPE:    LEX:    ACTOR1:  ACTOR2:    {INI:}   {FINAL:}
STATE    marry   knight   princess   single   married
```

_ *married* _

The Discourse Plan. The discourse plan is the structure of the information that is to be rendered as text. Each line of this input corresponds to a paragraph sized portion of the text, containing information about a sequence of actions, the place where they take place, the characters involved, and the objects used in them. The solution presented here involves only a particular line of the discourse plan. The rest of the discourse plan would have to be treated in the same way one line at a time. For some complex decisions involved in case adaptation - discussed in section 3.5 - the context as featured in the discourse plan may need to be consulted.

3.2   Building the Case Base

To ensure a broad coverage of possible inputs, the case base has been built by combining two sources: WordNet and a corpus of texts selected as typical examples of the type of text desired as output. In order to provide a broad enough choice of templates - in the sense described above - a set of possible templates must be assigned to each type of action. WordNet is used as a basic source to obtain a set of possible verbs for conveying a given type of action. This set of verbs must be filtered to ensure that the final selection of verbs conforms with typical usage in the desired genre. A corpus of texts is used to filter out the WordNet senses that are inappropriate for the genre of the desired outputs. For the selected senses, the corpus provides examples of use, which are used to generate the cases.

The corpus employed consists of 109 classic fairy tales, which included a total of 9852 sentences. These have been obtained from Internet web sites presenting collections of fairy tales in English, and they include a collection of Aesop's fables, a selection of Afanasiev's collection of Russian fairy tales, and tales from the selections by Andersen, the Grim brothers, and Perrault.

For each case, the concepts appearing in the example found in the corpus - which become information entities in the case retrieval net used to store the cases - must also be inserted into the knowledge base. To ensure appropriate performance, they must be inserted at the correct place in the taxonomy that organises the knowledge base. This is important because the system uses the relative positions in this taxonomy to calculate similarity between the query and the cases during retrieval.

The general process of constructing a particular case is better illustrated by means of an example.

The MOVE type of action is associated with the concept 'move' found in WordNet. Sixteen senses are provided for it. Of those, the first three are relevant in this situation: sense 1 (travel, go, move, locomote), sense 2 (move, displace) and sense 3 (move so as to change position, perform a nontranslational motion). For each one a number of possible words for that sense are listed (132 for sense 1, 90 for sense 2 and 99 for sense 3). These must be filtered with respect to the corpus. For instance, 51 of the possible words for sense 1 do not appear at all in the corpus.

One of the possible words suggested by WordNet as a sense of 'move' is:

```
travel -- (undergo transportation as in a vehicle; "We travelled
North on Rte. 508")
```

The corpus provides the following examples of use of that word:

One day the king went travelling to distant lands
Then we [Simbad (and the merchants)] traveled many days across high mountains until we came to the sea, where we set sail.

These examples give rise to the corresponding cases:

```
TYPE:    LEX:       ACTOR:   TO:
MOVE     travel-to  king     distant-lands
```

```
TYPE:    LEX:            ACTOR:   ACROSS:
MOVE     travel-across   Simbad   mountains
```

The nature of the documents used to build the corpus - children's fairy tales - presents the advantage that the range of concepts involved, both in terms of verbs and nouns, is limited. This results in a certain degree of lexical redundancy which simplifies the knowledge acquisition process. This process is carried out semi-automatically. A dependency analysis is carried out for the sentences in the corpus using MINIPAR [14]. Verbs and the nouns that depend on them are identified. For each verb, and action must be built and a template must be generated. A type is assigned to each action. This type constitutes a strong restriction during retrieval, so it should be used with caution. As discusses in section 4, maximal flexibility in the use of the system is obtained by ommiting this attribute during retrieval. The concepts corresponding to the nouns identified in the corpus must be inserted into the knowledge base. Both action construction and noun concept insertion require human supervision. However, the fact that nouns and verbs are treated asymmetrically reduces the actual effort involved in processing a large corpus: no composite structure is built for representing nouns, and the insertion of verbs into the knowledge base is not subject to positional restrictions.

3.3   The Case Base

Cases are stored in a Case Retrieval Net. This model is appropriate for the problem under consideration, because on one hand our cases consist of attribute-value pairs that are related with one another, and on the other hand the queries posed to the module will not always be complete. To find a lexical tag for a given action, the CRN is queried with the class of elements involved in the action.

The vocabulary of the module is built from the case base. For each attribute-value pair in the cases an information entity is created. For each case, a node is created which holds references to the information entities that are contained. When introducing an IE, if that entity has already appeared in another case it is not duplicated. Instead, another association is created between the new case and the existing information entity.

As IEs are inserted to form the net, it is necessary to establish a measure of similarity between them. This is done by reference to the module's knowledge base, in which the different concepts of the domain are organised into a taxonomy. The similarity between two entities is calculated by taking into account the distance between them in the knowledge base and using Formula 1. H is the maximum height of the taxonomy tree in the knowledge base.

$$sim(c1, c2) = 1 - (1 + distance(c1, c2))/(H * 2) \qquad (1)$$

The distance between two concepts is calculated by finding their first shared ancestor, and adding up the distance between this ancestor and each of the concepts. It can be seen as the number of nodes we have to pass when going from one of the concepts to the other. It is also necessary to have a similarity value for each entity with itself. This value is always 1, the maximum possible.

Each of the IEs is related to the cases to which it belongs with a certain value of relevance. In the implemented module, the maximum relevance within a case corresponds to the attribute Type with value 1, and the rest of the elements have relevance 0.5. This is because when retrieving cases we are mainly interested in the type of action that we are looking for, rather than which elements are involved in it. However, it can occur that the module retrieves a case of a different type, if the similarity weights of the attributes of the case are high enough.

3.4   Case Retrieval

The retrieval task starts with a partial or complete problem description, and ends when a matching previous case has been found. In our module, the retrieval of cases is directly handled by the Case Retrieval Net and its method of similarity propagation. Starting from a partial description of the action we need to lexicalise, the retrieval of the more similar cases is done by calculating an activation value for each case in the case base. The ones with higher activation are the more similar ones to the given query. This calculation is performed in three steps:

1. The IE nodes that correspond to the query are activated. If they are not in the net because they did not belong to any case in the case base, the corresponding nodes are inserted at the time of querying, calculating the similarity and relevance weights using the knowledge base. The nodes corresponding to the query are assigned an activation value of 1, and the rest a value of 0.

2. The activation is propagated according to the similarity values of the arcs. This is performed by looking over all the entity nodes of the net and by calculating for each one its activation value using its own activation and its similarity with the rest of IE nodes. This is achieved by using Formula 2 (where N is the total number of IE nodes).

$$activation(e) = \sum_{i=1}^{N}(sim(e_i, e) * activation(e_i)) \tag{2}$$

3. The achieved activations in the previous step are collected in the associated case nodes, calculating the final activations of the cases also considering the relevance weights of the arcs that connect the cases with their entities. This final activation value of the cases is calculated with Formula 3.

$$activation(c) = \sum_{i=1}^{N}(rel(e_i, c) * activation(e_i)) \tag{3}$$

Once we have the final activation in the cases, the one with the higher value is returned by the net. It would be possible to take not only the most similar one, but a set with the most similar cases to the query.

3.5   Case Reuse

Each retrieved case has an associated template from the vocabulary for the verb or action it represents. In the process of reusing the case we have obtained from the net, we have to substitute the attribute values of the past case with the query values. Here we have three different possibilities: (1) the retrieved case and the query have the same set of attributes, (2) the query has more attributes than the retrieved case, or (3) there are more attributes in the retrieved case than in the query.

For situation 1, the values of the retrieved case are simply replaced with the values in the query. The template corresponding to the retrieved case is filled with the new values. At the end of the reuse process the query has been assigned a correct template to realize as text the message it conveys.

For situation 2, the attributes of the retrieved case are filled with the corresponding query values. The resulting adaptation is a partial solution to the problem posed by the query. A secondary retrieval process is set in motion, using as a query simply the set of attributes in the query that could not be accommodated in the partial solution provided by the first case retrieved by the system. This query includes no specific type of action, and it relies on the ability of the case retrieval net for case completion to provide a case with a type of action that matches the given arguments.

For situation 3, there will be vacant attributes in the corresponding solution. The easiest solution is to keep the values of the past case in the slots for which the query does not specify any value. Better results can be obtained by consulting the system knowledge base for concepts that the knowledge base shows as related to those appearing in the query. In order to be appropriate as fillers for the vacant slots, these concepts must be within a given threshold of similarity - in terms of relative distance within the taxonomy - with respect to the original values given in the retrieved case for those attributes. In situations where lexicalization of a particular message forms part of a larger context - such as a larger text - better results are obtained by searching the neighbouring messages in the discourse.

3.6   Case Revision and Retainment

A very complex set of linguistic, cognitive and pragmatic constraints must be taken into account when validating any natural language solutions generated in this manner. The contribution of an expert in the domain is required to revise the results achieved by the module, and no automated solution to this stage of the CBR cycle is contemplated so far.

4   An Example of System Operation

To show how the system operates, an example is presented. Suppose the system is presented with a query such as:

```
ACTOR: prince, OBJECT: dragon, WITH: sword, INI: alive, FINAL: dead
```

The text that would correspond to this query would presumably be *"The prince killed the dragon with a sword"*.

The retrieval process results in the following case:

```
TYPE:    LEX:    ACTOR:   OBJECT: WHERE:  {INI:}    {FINAL:}
STATE    kill    peasant  snake   forest  {alive}   {dead}
```

This case is chosen because the values for the attributes INI and FINAL are equal, and the similarities between the other concepts, computed using the taxonomy, is high (*'prince'* and *'peasant'* are immediate siblings in the taxonomy - descendants of *'person'* - and *'dragon'* and *'snake'* are descendants of nodes that are immediate siblings - *'flying-creature'* and *'non-flying-creature'*).

The case obtained during the retrieval process contains attributes (TYPE and WHERE) for which no values are given in the query. The TYPE attribute is special and it will be simply inherited by the contribution obtained from this case for the final solution. The absence of TYPE in the query is intentional. The final result provided by the system may have to be built up from several cases of different types in order to account for all the attributes given explicitly in the query. To include an explicit type in the query would restrict the set of possible actions that can be included in the final result to those matching the explicit type. This would defeat the purpose of the technology we are using. The presence of unfulfilled attributes of other kinds - such as the WHERE attribute in this example - triggers a secondary process of searching the knowledge base for possible values for those attributes. Elements in the knowledge base related with those elements appearing in the query are considered as possible candidates to fill the additional attribute slots in the second retrieved case. The most similar ones - according to relative proximity within the taxonomy - are considered. In this instance, the knowledge base is queried for elements related to prince, dragon or sword which are similar to forest. The relations for these three concepts are shown in the paraphrase of the knowledge base[1] given in Table 2.

The system returns cave because the knowledge base contains information about the dragon living in a cave, and cave is similar to forest in the taxonomy. Other choices would have been palace or princess, related in the knowledge base to the prince, but their calculated similarities to forest are lower.

Since there are attributes present in the query for which no slot is available in the retrieved case (WITH), a second retrieval process is triggered with the following query, resulting from a selective restriction of the original query to those attributes not provided in the case retrieved in the first instance (the subject and object of the action are retained, to ensure soundness of the result):

```
ACTOR: prince, OBJECT: dragon, WITH: sword
```

---

[1] Relations in the actual knowledge base are represented in terms of instance identifiers, which would be meaningless for readers in this context.

Table 2. Relations in the knowledge base

```
relations:
    relation(prince,palace,live)
    relation(prince,sword,have)
    relation(prince,princess,love)
    [...]
    relation(dragon,cave,live)
    [...]
```

This second retrieval process returns the following case:

TYPE:	LEX:	ACTOR:	OBJECT:	WITH:
FIGHT	attack	hunter	lion	spear

The final result of the complete process is an adaptation of the set of retrieved cases in all the required retrieval process, together with an assignment of values to their attributes, either from the original attributes in the query or from values related to them obtained from the knowledge base. The fact that the query had no explicit TYPE attribute has permitted that the solution be composed of several instances with different types.

The associated templates are shown below for each case.

TYPE:	LEX:	ACTOR:	OBJECT:	WHERE:	{INI:}	{FINAL:}
STATE	kill	prince	dragon	cave	{alive}	{dead}

_ killed _ in _

TYPE:	LEX:	ACTOR:	OBJECT:	WITH:
FIGHT	attack	prince	dragon	sword

_ attacked _ with _

To improve readability, any attribute slots whose values have already been mentioned in preceding cases within the same response are marked, to indicate that subsequent stages of the generation process should render them as pronouns.

After surface realization, the result provided by the system for the original query would be:

The prince killed the dragon in the cave. He attacked it with a sword.

This result is not exactly what we were looking for, but it conveys all the desired information. The vocabulary does not have the exact template needed in this case, but the system combines the templates and knowledge base resources it possesses to compose an alternative phrasing for the requested message.

5   Conclusions and Future Work

The case-based solution described in this paper presents the advantage of achieving coverage of a broad range of messages by combining instances of a restricted set of templates, providing automated means for dealing with overlaps between the information conveyed by the templates found, and ensuring coherent use of context information - in the shape of a knowledge base for the domain accepted as input - whenever the resulting templates need to mention information that was not explicit in the given query. By resorting recursively to processes of case retrieval with progressively reduced versions of the query till all the data in the query have been covered by at least one case, the system automatically obtains the best set of cases that cover the data with minimal overlap. Whenever the selected cases involve information that was not explicitly available in the query, the use of the input knowledge base guarantees that any additional information drafted into the final result is coherent with the particular set of data under consideration.

The main advantage of this method with respect to other template selection approaches is that the system does not need an exhaustive set of templates, as CRNs work by approximation and can retrieve similar cases for unknown queries due to the automatic semantic relations attained in the net. A classic problem in natural language generation is the "generation gap" described by Meteer [15], a discrepancy between what can be expressed in the text plan and what the particular realization solution can actually convert into text. In terms of templates, the "generation gap" occurs when the input calls for messages not explicitly contemplated in the set of templates in use. The present system ensures that such messages can be conveyed by a combination of simpler templates, adequately linked together by occurrences of coreferring elements. CRNs can handle partially specified queries without loss of efficiency, in contrast to most case retrieval techniques that have problems with partial descriptions. Given only a part of a case, the net can complete the rest of its content. This behaviour is similar to that suggested by Stede [3] for the lexicalization task.

Insertion of new cases (even with new attributes) can be performed incrementally by injecting new nodes and arcs. This is a particular advantage since any extension of the corpus may lead to the addition of new cases.

The difficulties presented by the knowledge acquisition have been partially addressed by the semi-automatization of the analysis of the corpus. We are currently working on improving this aspect of the system. Although it will probably be impossible to fully automate the process of acquisition, the method presented here represents a significant improvement on manual approaches to the development of template-based generators. Both approaches require the construction of the templates and the representation of the concepts. However, whereas an altogether manual approaches requires the additional elaboration of explicit criteria to guide the correct use of templates, the approach presented here provides an automatic case-based decision process for template selection.

The approach employed in this paper for actions may be extended to other elements in a story, such as characters, objects, locations,... This would require a specific notation in which these elements are described as a collection of attribute-value pairs. We have chosen to focus on actions until we have explored the potential of the technique. The exploration of such extensions to other elements will be contemplated as further work. However, the possible effect upon the complexity of knowledge acquisition must be considered.

The representation of actions in the current version of the system is very simple. The resulting texts would improve significantly if a more complex set of actions where considered. Template-based generators have obtained results comparable to more elaborate solutions by resorting to recursive use of templates [16]. In our approach, this would correspond to allowing actions to be represented as nested cases, where a case would be constructed not only of attribute-value pairs, but also attribute-case pairs, where the value for some attribute may itself be a complete case - with an associated template. Recursive nesting of cases would allow recursive use of templates. The retrieval and adaptation stages would have to be adapted to deal with this recursive nature.

In order to tackle the complexity arising from this enhancement, we contemplate two possible sources of inspiration. One is to consider the use of primitives to build complex actions from simple ingredients, along the lines of Schank's Conceptual Dependency theory [17]. Schank proposed an open set of primitives to express the meaning of any sentence in terms of primitives, using a complex system for representing states and relationships. Another is to define a complex conceptual taxonomy of actions, relying for their manipulation on the same techniques employed for handling individual concepts in the current system. This would allow a homogeneous treatment of knowledge through the system, and may lead to easier interactions between the different types of knowledge. To organise such a taxonomy of actions, WordNet would be a valuable source.

Efficiency issues have not been contemplated so far, but as the size of the case base rises, they are becoming relevant. A possible way of reducing this risk would be to implement *lazy spreading activation* [18] in the Case Retrieval Net. Instead of propagating activation to all entity nodes, and then to all case nodes, propagation takes place progressively from most similar nodes to not so similar nodes. Once enough case nodes have been activated to reply to the query, propagation stops.

References

1. Reiter, E., Dale, R.: Building Natural Language Generation Systems. Cambridge University Press (2000)
2. Cahill, L.: Lexicalisation in applied NLG systems. Technical Report ITRI-99-04 (1998)
3. Stede, M.: Lexical options in multilingual generation from a knowledge base. In Adorni, G., Zock, M., eds.: Trends in natural language generation: an artificial intelligence perspective. Number 1036. Springer-Verlag (1996) 222–237
4. Daelemans, W., Gillis, S., Durieux, G.: The acquisition of stress: a data-oriented approach. Comput. Linguist. **20** (1994) 421–451
5. Ng, H.T., Lee, H.B.: Integrating multiple knowledge sources to disambiguate word sense: an exemplar-based approach. In: Proceedings of ACL 1996, NJ, USA, ACL (1996) 40–47

6. Cardie, C.: Integrating Case-Based Learning and Cognitive Biases for Machine Learning of Natural Language. Journal of Experimental and Theoretical Artificial Intelligence **11** (1999) 297–337
7. Daelemans, W.: Introduction to the special issue on memory-based language processing. J. Exp. Theor. Artif. Intell. **11** (1999) 287–296
8. Gervás, P., Díaz-Agudo, B., Peinado, F., Hervás, R.: Story Plot Generation based on CBR. Journal of Knowledge-Based Systems **18** (2005) 235–242
9. Miller, G.A.: Wordnet: a lexical database for English. Commun. ACM **38** (1995) 39–41
10. Gomes, P., Pereira, F.C., Paiva, P., Seco, N., Carreiro, P., Ferreira, J., Bento, C.: Selection and Reuse of Software Design Patterns Using CBR and WordNet. In: Proc. of the 15th International Conference on Software Engineering and Knowledge Engineering (SEKE'03). (2003)
11. Lenz, M., Burkhard, H.D.: Case Retrieval Nets: Basic Ideas and Extensions. In: KI - Kunstliche Intelligenz. (1996) 227–239
12. Hervás, R., Gervás, P.: Case Retrieval Nets for Heuristic Lexicalization in Natural Language Generation. In Cardoso, A., Bento, C., Dias, G., eds.: Progress in Artificial Intelligence (EPIA 05). Number LNAI 1036, (Springer-Verlag)
13. García, C., Hervás, R., Gervás, P.: Una Arquitectura Software para el Desarrollo de Aplicaciones de Generación de Lenguaje Natural. Procesamiento de Lenguaje Natural **33** (2004) 111–118
14. Lin, D.: Dependency-based evaluation of MINIPAR. In: Proc. of Workshop on the Evaluation of Parsing Systems, Granada, Spain (May 1998)
15. Meteer, M.W.: The generation gap: the problem of expressibility in text planning. PhD thesis, Amherst, MA, USA (1990)
16. McRoy, S., Channarukul, S., Ali, S.: A Natural Language Generation Component for Dialog Systems. In Cox, M., ed.: Working Notes of the AAAI Workshop on Mixed-Initiative Intelligence (AAAI99). (1999)
17. Schank, R.: Conceptual Information Processing. Elsevier Science Inc., New York, NY, USA (1975)
18. Lenz, M., Burkhard, H.: Case Retrieval Nets: Foundations, properties, implementation, and results. Technical report, Humboldt University, Berlin (1996)

Rough Set Feature Selection Algorithms for Textual Case-Based Classification

Kalyan Moy Gupta[1], David W. Aha[2], and Philip Moore[3]

[1] Knexus Research Corp.; Springfield, VA 22153; USA
[2] Naval Research Laboratory (Code 5515); Washington, DC 20375; USA
[3] ITT Industries; AES Division; Alexandria, VA 22303; USA
firstname.lastname@nrl.navy.mil

Abstract. Feature selection algorithms can reduce the high dimensionality of textual cases and increase case-based task performance. However, conventional algorithms (e.g., information gain) are computationally expensive. We previously showed that, on one dataset, a rough set feature selection algorithm can reduce computational complexity without sacrificing task performance. Here we test the generality of our findings on additional feature selection algorithms, add one data set, and improve our empirical methodology. We observed that features of textual cases vary in their contribution to task performance based on their part-of-speech, and adapted the algorithms to include a part-of-speech bias as background knowledge. Our evaluation shows that injecting this bias significantly increases task performance for rough set algorithms, and that one of these attained significantly higher classification accuracies than information gain. We also confirmed that, under some conditions, randomized training partitions can dramatically reduce training times for rough set algorithms without compromising task performance.

1 Introduction

Textual case-based reasoning (TCBR) is a case-based reasoning (CBR) subfield concerned with the use of textual knowledge sources (Weber *et al.*, 2005). TCBR systems differ in the degree to which their text content is used; some are *weakly textual* CBR while others are *strongly* textual CBR, meaning that textual information is the focus of reasoning (Wilson & Bradshaw, 2000). Applications such as email categorization, news categorization, and spam filtering require the use of strongly textual CBR methodologies. Most of these systems use a bag-of-words or term-based representation for cases (e.g., Wiratunga *et al.,* 2004; Delany *et al.*, 2005), which can be problematic for textual case bases that have thousands of features. For example, this huge dimensionality could reduce accuracies on classification tasks and/or result in large computational costs.

A variety of feature selection algorithms can be used to address this issue. For example, these include conventional algorithms such as document frequency, information gain, and mutual information (Yang & Pederson, 1997). Wiratunga *et al.* (2004) extended these algorithms to include boosting and feature generalization with considerable success. However, some of these conventional algorithms have high

T.R. Roth-Berghofer et al. (Eds.): ECCBR 2006, LNAI 4106, pp. 166–181, 2006.

computational complexity, which can be a problem when a TCBR system is applied to dynamic decision environments that require frequent case base maintenance.

Feature selection algorithms based on rough set theory (RST) rather than conventional algorithms can potentially alleviate this high computational complexity and also increase the task performance of TCBR systems. RST (Pawlak, 1991) is an approach for decision making with incomplete information. Feature selection algorithms motivated by RST have been applied with much success in non-textual CBR systems (e.g., Pal & Shiu, 2004). Recently, these algorithms have been applied to textual data sets. For example, Chouchoulas and Shen (2001) applied a rough set algorithm called QuickReduct to select features for an email categorization task. Also, we examined a rough set feature selection algorithm, called *Johnson's reduct*, to a multi-class classification problem (Gupta *et al.*, 2005). We empirically demonstrated that this algorithm, for one data set, was an order of magnitude faster than information gain and yet provided comparable classification performance. We also introduced a methodology that randomly partitions a training set, and selects and merges features from each partition. This *randomized training partitions* procedure can dramatically reduce feature selection time. We showed that its combination with Johnson's reduct was effective.

In this paper, we extend our earlier work on feature selection for TCBR classification tasks by exploring additional rough set algorithms. In particular, we introduce a variant of Li *et al.*'s (2006) relative dependency metric, called the *marginal relative dependency metric*, and explore its effectiveness with randomized training partitions. In addition, we introduce the notion of *part-of-speech bias* in textual case bases. This is based on our observation that textual features with different parts of speech may inherently differ in their ability to contribute to reasoning. For example, noun features may contribute more than verb features, as described in Section 3.4. Adapting rough set and conventional feature selection algorithms to incorporate this bias could improve their performance. We empirically investigate these issues on two data sets.

The rest of this paper is organized as follows. Section 2 introduces RST and two of its derivative feature selection algorithms. We also include a description of randomized training partitions and introduce the notion of part-of-speech bias. We present an empirical evaluation of the feature selection algorithms and their interaction with randomized training partitions and part-of-speech bias in Section 3. We review related work on feature selection in Section 4 and conclude with a discussion of our plans for future research in Section 5.

2   Rough Set Theoretic Feature Selection

2.1   Building Blocks of Rough Set Theory

For the sake of clarity for this audience, we use established CBR terminology, such as *cases* and *features*, to present the elements of RST. RST is based on a formal description of an information system (Pawlak, 1991). An information system S is a tuple $S = \langle C, F, V \rangle$ where:

$C = \{c_1, c_2, \ldots, c_n\}$ denotes a non-empty, finite set of *cases*,
$F = \{f_1, f_2, \ldots, f_m\}$ denotes a non-empty, finite set of *features* (or *attributes*), and
$V = \{V_1, V_2, \ldots, V_m\}$ is the set of value domains for the features in F.

A decision table is a special case of an information system where we distinguish two kinds of features: (1) a class (or *decision*) feature f_d, and (2) the standard conditional features F_p, which are used to predict the class of a case. Therefore, $F = F_p \cup \{f_d\}$.

Table 1. A case base fragment for hiring decisions

Cases	f_1 = age	f_2 = experience	f_3 = grades	f_d = hired
c_1 = Anna	21-30	none	good	yes
c_2 = Bill	21-30	none	good	no
c_3 = Cathy	21-30	4-6	average	no
c_4 = Dave	31-40	1-3	excellent	yes
c_5 = Emma	31-40	4-6	good	yes
c_6 = Frank	31-40	4-6	good	yes

We will explain RST concepts using the trivial case base in Table 1, which pertains to making hiring decisions based on three features. Central to RST is the notion of *indiscernibility*. Examining the cases in Table 1, we see that cases c_1=Anna and c_2=Bill have identical values for all the features, and thus are *indiscernible* with respect to the three conditional features f_1, f_2, and f_3. More broadly, a set of cases C' is indiscernible with respect to a set of features $F' \subseteq F$ if the following is true:

$$IND(F',C)= \{ \ C' \subseteq C \ | \ \forall f \in F', \ \forall c_i, c_{j\,(i \neq j)} \in C' \ f(c_i) = f(c_j)\} \tag{1}$$

Thus, two cases are indiscernible with respect to features in F' if they have identical values for all the features in F'.

An indiscernibility relation is an equivalence relation that partitions the set of cases into equivalence classes. Each equivalence class contains a set of indiscernible cases for the given set of features F'. For example, given the hiring decision table:

$$IND(F', C) = \{\{ \ c_1 , c_2\}, \{ \ c_3 \},\{ \ c_4 \},\{ \ c_5 , c_6\}\}$$

where $F'=\{age, experience, grades\}$ and $C=\{c_1,c_2,c_3,c_4,c_5,c_6\}$. The equivalence class of a case c_i with respect to selected features F' is denoted by $[c_i]_F$. Based on the equivalence classes, RST develops two kinds of set approximations. First, given sets $C' \subseteq C$ and $F' \subseteq F$, the *lower approximation* of C' with respect to F' is defined as:

$$lower(C, F', C') = \{c \in C \ | \ [c]_{F'} \subseteq C'\} \tag{2}$$

or the collection of cases whose equivalence classes are subsets of C'. Second, the *upper approximation* of C' with respect to F' is instead defined as:

$$upper(C, F', C') = \{c \in C \ | \ [c]_{F'} \cap C' \neq \varnothing\} \tag{3}$$

or the collection of cases whose equivalence classes have a non-empty intersection set with C'. A set of cases C' is *crisp* (or *definable*) if $lower(C, F',C') = upper(C, F',C')$, and is otherwise *rough*.

For example, in the hiring decision table, consider $C'_{\{hired=yes\}} = \{c_1, c_4, c_5, c_6\}$, then the lower and upper approximations of $C'_{\{hired=yes\}}$ with respect to $F' = \{age, experience, grades\}$ are:

$$lower(C, F', C'_{\{hired=yes\}}) = \{c_4, c_5, c_6\} \text{ and } upper(C, F', C'_{\{hired=yes\}}) = \{c_1, c_2, c_4, c_5, c_6\}$$

Case c_1 is not included in the lower approximation because its equivalence class $\{c_1, c_2\}$ is not a subset of $C'_{\{hired=yes\}}$. However, it is included in the upper approximation because its equivalence class has a non-empty intersection with $C'_{\{hired=yes\}}$.

Another important RST element is the notion of a set called the *positive region*. The positive region of a decision feature f_d with respect to $F' \subset F$ is defined as:

$$POS_F(f_d, C) = \cup \{ lower(C, F', C') \mid C' \in IND(\{f_d\}, C)\} \tag{4}$$

or the collection of the F'-lower approximations corresponding to all the equivalence classes of f_d. For example, the positive region of f_d {hiring} with respect to $F' = \{age, experience, grades\}$, where $lower(C, F', C'_{\{hired=no\}}) = \{c_3\}$, is as follows:

$$POS_F(f_d, C) = lower(C, F', C'_{\{hired=yes\}}) \cup lower(C, F', C'_{\{hired=no\}}) = \{c_3, c_4, c_5, c_6\}$$

The positive region can be used to develop a measure of a feature's ability to contribute information for decision making. A feature $f \in F'$ makes no contribution or is *dispensable* if $POS_F(f_d, C) = POS_{F'-\{fd\}}(f_d, C)$ and is *indispensable* otherwise. That is, removing the feature f_d from F' does not change the positive region of the decision feature. Therefore, **features can be selected by checking whether they are indispensable** with respect to a decision variable. The minimal set of features F', $F' \subset F$, is called a **reduct** if $POS_{F'}(f_d, C) = POS_F(f_d, C)$.

Often, an information system has more than one possible reduct. Generating a reduct of minimal length is a NP-hard problem. Therefore, in practice, algorithms have been developed to generate one "good" reduct. Next, we present our adaptations of two such algorithms: (1) Johnson's heuristic algorithm and (2) the marginal relative dependency algorithm.

2.2 Feature Selection with Johnson's Heuristic Algorithm

We adapted Johnson's (1974) heuristic to compute reducts as follows. It sequentially selects features by finding those that are most discernible for a given decision feature (see Figure 1). It computes a discernibility matrix M, where each cell $m_{i,j}$ of the matrix corresponding to cases c_i and c_j includes the conditional features in which the two cases' values differ. Formally, we define *strict discernibility* as:

$$m_{i,j} = \{\{f \in F_p: f(c_i) \neq f(c_j)\} \text{ for } f_d(c_i) \neq f_d(c_j), \text{ and } \emptyset \text{ otherwise }\} \tag{5}$$

JOHNSONSREDUCT(F_p, f_d, C)
Input F_p: conditional features, f_d: decision feature, C: cases
Output R: Reduct $R \subseteq F_p$

1     $R \leftarrow \emptyset$, $F' \leftarrow F_p$
2     $M \leftarrow$ computeDiscernibilityMatrix(C, F', f_d)
3   **do**
4         $f_h \leftarrow$ selectHighestScoringFeature(M)
5         $R \leftarrow R \cup \{f_h\}$
6   **for** (i=0 to |C|, j=i to |C|)
7             $m_{i,j} \leftarrow \emptyset$ **if** $f_h \in m_{i,j}$
8         $F' \leftarrow F' - \{f_h\}$
9   **until** $m_{i,j} = \emptyset$ $\forall i, j$
10   **return** R

Fig. 1. Pseudocode for Johnson's heuristic algorithm

Given such a matrix M, for each feature, the algorithm counts the number of cells in which it appears. The feature f_h with the highest number of entries is selected for addition to the reduct R. Then all the entries $m_{i,j}$ that contain f_h are removed and the next best feature is selected. This procedure is repeated until M is empty.

The computational complexity of JOHNSONSREDUCT is $O(VC^2)$, where V is the (typically large) vocabulary size and bounds the number of times the **do** loop is executed. However, this is a loose upper bound that is better approximated by $O(RC^2)$, where is $R \ll V$. Comparing this complexity with the computational complexity of information gain, which is $O(MVC)$, where M is the number of classes, the complexity of JOHNSONSREDUCT is lower because, typically, $RC < MV$. However, the worst case space complexity of JOHNSONSREDUCT is $O(VC^2)$, which is significantly greater than Information Gain's space complexity of $O(VC)$.

In TCBR applications, each case may have only a small subset of features. *Strict discernibility* could be implemented as follows: $f(c_i) \neq f(c_j)$ if only one of the cases c_i or c_j contains the term denoted by the feature f. However, such an approach ignores the information contained in the variation of term frequencies (i.e., value) across cases. Hence, a graded or fuzzy notion of indiscernibility, instead of a strict notion, may be more effective (e.g., Skowron, 1995). We extend strict discernibility to *graded or fuzzy discernibility* using a similarity computation as follows. In Equation 5, we consider:

$$f(c_i) \neq f(c_j), \text{ when } sim(f(c_i), f(c_j)) < \tau_f \qquad (6)$$

where ($0 < \tau_f < 1$) is a user defined similarity threshold whose value is determined empirically. We adapt a similarity measure for ordinal scales (Montazemi & Gupta, 1997) to compute the similarity between two non-zero frequency valued features as follows:

$$sim(f(c_i), f(c_j)) = \left\{ \begin{array}{l} 1 - abs((f(c_i) - f(c_j)) / \psi . \sigma_f, \text{ when } abs((f(c_i) - f(c_j)) \leq \psi . \sigma_f \\ 0, \text{ otherwise} \end{array} \right. \qquad (7)$$

where σ_f is the standard deviation of non-zero frequency values for feature f, and $\psi > 0$ is a user-defined parameter for adjusting similarity sensitivity. For example, for a feature f with $\sigma_f = 1.87$ and $\psi = 1$,

$$sim(4, 5) = 1 - abs(4-5)/1.87*1 = 0.465$$

Similarly, the issue of class feature discernibility arises in TCBR for *multiclass* classification tasks in which more than one class can be assigned to a case. For example, topic assignment is a multi-class classification task. In Equation 5, we consider:

$$f_d(c_i) \neq f_d(c_j), \text{ when } sim(f_d(c_i), f_d(c_j)) < \tau_d \tag{8}$$

where $f_d(c_i)$ can be a set of values, $sim(f_d(c_i), f_d(c_j))$ yields the ratio of the intersection of its values to their union, and $0 < \tau_d < 1$ is a user defined similarity threshold.

2.3 Feature Selection Using Marginal Relative Dependency

In Section 2.1, we described how an indiscernibility (or equivalence) relation partitions a case base C into equivalence classes with respect to a set of features F'. Intuitively, with an increase in the number of features in F', we expect the number of equivalence classes to increase and each equivalence class to contain fewer cases. The *degree of relative dependency* of a set of features F' builds on this intuition. For a decision feature f_d and a set of features F', it is defined as (Li *et al.*, 2006):

$$\delta_{F'}^{f_d} = \frac{\left|\Pi_{F'}(C)\right|}{\left|\Pi_{F' \cup f_d}(C)\right|} \tag{9}$$

where $\Pi_{F'}(C)$ is the set of equivalence classes generated over C with respect to features F' and $\Pi_{F' \cup f_d}(C)$ is the set of equivalence classes generated over C with respect to features $F' \cup \{f_d\}$. Clearly, the maximum value of $\delta_{F'}^{f_d}$ is 1. Based on this measure, we compute the marginal contribution of a feature f (i.e., marginal relative dependency), denoted by μ_f, as follows:

$$\mu_f = \delta_{F' \cup \{f\}}^{f_d} - \delta_{F'}^{f_d} \tag{10}$$

In addition to using μ_f as a metric for selecting features, it can also be used as a feature weight because $\sum_{f \in R} \mu_f = 1$, where R is a reduct.

Our variation on this reduct computation algorithm, called the *Marginal Relative Dependency* algorithm (MRD), is as follows (see Figure 2). At each iteration, it computes the marginal relative dependency of all the candidate features T, selects the feature f_m with the maximum marginal relative dependency, and adds it to the reduct R. The algorithm terminates when the relative dependency $\delta_R = \beta$, where β is a user defined parameter in the range $(0 < \beta < 1)$. In a TCBR application, it is possible that beyond a certain point both μ_f and $\delta_{F'}^{f_d}$ may behave asymptotically. Therefore, β can be specified to terminate the feature selection process early.

MRD(F_p, f_d, C)

Input F_p: Conditional features, f_d: Decision feature, C: Cases, β: Threshold
Output R: Reduct $R \subseteq F_p$

```
1        R←∅, F'←Fp, δR←0
3        do
4            <fm, μm> ← selectMaximallyContributingFeatureAndValue(F',C)
5            R ←R ∪ {fm}
6            F' ← F' − {fm}
7            δR ← δR + μm
8        until δR = β
9        return R
```

Fig. 2. Pseudocode for the Marginal Relative Dependency algorithm (MRD)

Like JOHNSONSREDUCT, the determination of equivalence classes in MRD can be based on a strict or graded notion of discernibility. For the graded notion of discernibility we apply Equations 6, 7, and 8.

The worst case computational complexity of MRD is $O(RVC^2)$. For large textual case bases, this is an order of magnitude more complex than JOHNSONSREDUCT and information gain. However, its worst case space complexity is only $O(VC)$.

2.4 Feature Selection with Random Training Set Partitions

The computational complexities of the feature selection algorithms discussed above depend on C, the number of training cases. The complexities of both RST approaches, JOHNSONSREDUCT and MRD, are a function of the square of the number of training cases. Therefore, reducing the number of training cases that need to be considered at one time can dramatically reduce feature selection and training time. We can accomplish this by using randomized training partitions (RTP) (Gupta *et al.*, 2005), which is a procedure with the following steps:

1. Randomly create m equal-sized partitions of the training set.
2. From each partition, select features using a feature selection algorithm (e.g., JOHNSONSREDUCT or MRD).
3. Define the final feature set as the union of features selected from each partition.

This approach could reduce the training time by a factor of m for the RST feature selection algorithms.

2.5 POS-Biaser: A Part-of-Speech Bias Adjustment Method

In TCBR, words or terms are typically used as features. The linguistic attributes associated with such features (e.g., part-of-speech (POS), syntactic roles) could impact feature selection and TCBR task performance. For example, it is likely that noun features are generally more informative than verb features possibly because nouns are an *open class* of words, whereas verbs, adjectives, adverbs, prepositions, and pronouns are *closed classes* of words (Quirk *et al.*, 1985). Open word classes are frequently extended to include new words, whereas closed classes are rarely extended. Thus, a large percentage of terms in a typical vocabulary are nouns. However, each noun feature may occur in relatively fewer cases and thus may contribute more to a decision. In contrast, verbs tend to occur more frequently across many cases. Also, there is considerable flexibility in the choice of verbs used to express the case content. This causes variability in verb expressions that could be inappropriately construed as informative (e.g., by information-theoretic measures) and as a result may be favored by feature selection algorithms. For example, this would adversely affect JOHNSONSREDUCT, which relies on pair-wise case comparisons to construct a discernibility matrix. It is likely to select spurious verbs, as could MRD and information gain (IG) (Yang & Pederson, 1997).

One general-purpose way to counter the effect of this inherent potential bias of textual case bases is to bias the feature selection algorithms accordingly. Thus, we introduce a methodology, called *POS-Biaser*, to use in combination with any feature selection algorithm. POS-Biaser assumes that part-of-speech tagging is performed during the case indexing process. This is feasible because part of speech taggers are publicly available (e.g., Brill, 1993). POS-Biaser uses a POS biasing factor ρ_{pos} for each POS along with a feature selection metric to select features. For example, when $\rho_{noun} = 1.8$, $\rho_{verb} = 0.6$, $\rho_{adjective} = 1$, and $\rho_{adverb} = 0.3$, the feature selection algorithm's values for nouns are inflated to 1.8 times their original value, the values for verbs are deflated to 0.6 times their original value, and so on.

The POS-Biased JOHNSONSREDUCT includes a modification to the step that executes *selectHighestScoringFeature(M)* (Figure 1, line 4), which computes the number of cell entries as the score of each feature (i.e., the feature selection metric). In particular, feature scores are now multiplied by their respective ρ_{pos} values. This would bias JohnsonsReduct to select more noun features than its unbiased version. Likewise, we accommodate a POS bias in MRD by similarly modifying the statement that executes *selectMaximallyContributingFeatureAndValue(F',C)*.

3   Evaluation

3.1   Claims and Empirical Methodology

We evaluated the feature selection algorithms described in Section 2 to explore the following hypotheses, where we focus on the quality of the selected features when all three algorithms select the same number:

1. Rough set methods perform as well as or outperform information gain on our case-based classification tasks.
2. The performances of rough set feature selection algorithms are affected by the POS bias in textual case bases.
3. RTP is an effective way to dramatically reduce feature selection time without compromising case-based task performance.

We selected both a *single* and a *multi*-classification task to evaluate the utility of the feature selection and POS-biasing algorithms for a case-based classifier. Single classification involves assigning exactly one class label to a new text case, while multi-classification involves assigning one or more class labels. For example, sorting emails into a known set of folders is a single classification task and assigning one or more topic to news articles is a multi-classification task.

We selected tasks from two data sets, one for each type of classification task. The first data set is Reuters-21578 (Reuters, 2006); it contains news items and its multi-classification task concerns assigning topics to these items. The second data set is a subset of 20-News Groups (Lang, 2006); it contains news group emails and its single classification task concerns assigning a news group label to each of these emails. Due to the relatively high computational and space complexities of the algorithms being tested, we selected only the first ten news groups for evaluation in this data set; we call this 10-News Groups. Table 2 summarizes the characteristics of both data sets.

Table 2. A summary of the characteristics of the data sets used in the experiments

Characteristic	Reuters-21578	10-News Groups
Number of Cases	11,330 (with more than 0 topics)	10,013
Number of Classes	110	10
Num. Cases per class	103 (Avg.)	1001.3 (Avg.)
Num. Classes per Case	1.26 (Avg.), 1 (min.), 16 (max.)	1
Num. Words per case	137 (Avg.)	200.35 (Avg.)

We used two rough set feature selection algorithms (JohnsonsReduct (JR) and MRD) and one conventional feature selection algorithm, namely IG (Yang & Pederson, 1997). In the experiments, for a fair comparison, we ensured that all the algorithms selected the same number of features, and used JR to determine how many features to select. They were all applied using the same bag-of-words representation for features. Finally, we also incorporated the POS bias in each feature selection algorithm, and refer to them as JRB, MRDB, and IGB, respectively.

Our feature generation algorithm performs tokenization, POS tagging, and morphotactic parsing to create POS-tagged terms as features. Morphotactic parsing is a more involved method than simple stemming; it reduces terms to their baseforms even across different POS (Gupta & Aha, 2004). For example, it reduces the noun "computer" to the verb "compute". Features with document frequency greater than two were considered for feature selection.

We applied a k-nearest neighbor classifier with the fuzzy feature similarity function described in Equation 7 to evaluate classification performance using the selected features. (We set $k=5$ based on feedback from our initial empirical studies.) All features were weighted equally to isolate the *selection* behaviors of the feature selection algorithms in our experiments. Multi-classification task performance was measured using *11-point average precision*, which is the average precision obtained at recall thresholds of (0%, 20%, …100%). The classifier assigns as many topics as needed until a given recall is achieved (Yang & Pederson, 1997). Performance on the single classification task was measured as classification accuracy. We also measured feature selection time (in seconds) for each algorithm.

We used a two-fold cross validation strategy to evaluate the algorithms. Two sets of two folds were randomly created. For RTP, all the algorithms were run with the same set of 10, 20, 30, and 40 randomized training partitions in each fold. We did not experiment without partitions due to the RTS algorithms' high computational and memory requirements.

3.2 Empirical Results

Results with the Reuters-21578 Data Set. The key results for the six algorithms (i.e., JR, IG, MRD, JRB, IGB, and MRDB) on this data set are shown in Figures 3-5. JR selected an average of 95.5, 118, 135, and 139.5 features for partitions of size 10, 20, 30, and 40, respectively. Increasing the number of RTP partitions increases the chance of selecting different features in different partitions, which increases the total number of unique features selected.

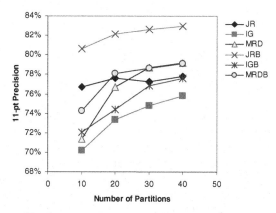

Fig. 3. Precision performance (Reuters-21578)

We compared the algorithms' precisions using one-tailed paired student t-tests. Comparisons of the feature selection algorithms' unbiased versions show that JR significantly outperformed IG for every number of partitions tested (e.g., 76.72% vs. 70.17% at 10 partitions [p=.0006]), as did MRD (e.g., 79.21% vs. 75.86% at 40 partitions [p=.0018]). Therefore, *both the rough set feature selection methods significantly outperformed a conventional feature selection method*. In addition, MRD significantly outperformed JR at partitions of 30 and 40 (e.g., 79.20% vs. 77.83% at 40 partitions [p=.0003]), but the reverse was true for 10 partitions.

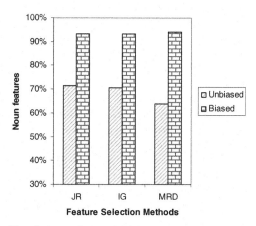

Fig. 4. The effect of POS-bias on the number of noun features selected by the three algorithms for Reuters-21578 using 10 RTP partitions

Comparing the POS-biased versions of the feature selection algorithms with their respective unbiased versions shows that JRB and IGB outperform JR and IG respectively at all RTP sizes. For example, at 30 partitions, JRB significantly outperforms JR (82.61% vs. 77.26% [p=.0007]) and IGB significantly outperforms IG (76.84% vs.74.79% [p=.0019]). However, MRDB significantly outperforms MRD only at 10 and 20 partitions; for 30 and 40 partitions there was no significant difference. Overall, *POS bias had a positive effect on all the feature selection algorithms, including IG.* It was most effective with JR, whose classification accuracy improved by 6.1% on average versus its unbiased version. Finally, *when adjusted for POS bias, JR recorded significantly higher precision results than the other feature selection algorithms we tested.*

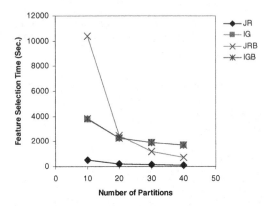

Fig. 5. Feature selection times (Reuters-21578)

Figure 4 shows the effect of POS bias on the three feature selection algorithms for Reuters-21578 at 10 partitions. The proportion of noun features without bias were at comparable levels for JR and IG (each at 71%) and slightly lower for MRD (64%). With this bias, the proportion of noun features increased to 93% for JR and IG and 94% for MRD. The increase in the proportion of noun features was comparable and consistent across the three algorithms, yet its effect on JR's precision performance was most substantial. Thus, we conclude that JR is most sensitive to POS bias.

Figure 5 shows the feature selection times for IG, JR, IGB, and JRB. *JR has the lowest feature selection time*, as predicted by our analyses in Section 2.2. It decreased by 81.92% from 510 seconds at 10 partitions to 92 seconds at 40 partitions, without decreasing average precision, demonstrating that RTP is highly effective. Its biased version (JRB) has higher feature selection times (10,382 sec. at 10 to 738 sec. at 40 partitions) but achieves a similar decrease in feature selection time as the number of partitions increases. JRB's times are higher than JR's because POS bias significantly increases the reduct sizes. In contrast, IG and IGB have the same feature selection times. It reduces by 54% (3780 seconds to 1725 seconds) as the number of partitions is increased from 10 to 40. As expected, MRD has extremely long feature selection times (99,843 sec. at 10 partitions to 22,276 sec. at 40 partitions; not shown in Figure 5), and MRDB times are even longer. However, both had a substantial drop in feature selection time as the number of partitions was increased. Therefore, *RTP effectively reduces feature selection time on Reuters-21578 for the three algorithms tested.*

Results with the 10-News Groups Data Set. As with the Reuters-21578 data set, we again used the number of features selected by JR as a baseline for the other algorithms. It selected an average of 123, 134.75, 141.25, & 153.5 features at 10, 20, 30, and 40 partitions, respectively.

Comparison of the unbiased versions of the algorithms shows that IG attains significantly higher accuracies than the others at all RTP levels data (see Figure 6). For example, at 30 partitions, IG outperformed JR (70.31% vs. 51.74%, [p=.0005]) and MR (70.31% vs. 57.82%, p=.0005]). This contrasts with its comparatively poor precision performance on the Reuters-21578 data set.

Comparing the two rough set methodologies with each other reveals that MRD significantly outperformed JR at 30 and 40 partitions (e.g., 57.82 % vs. 51.74% at 30

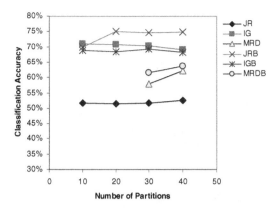

Fig. 6. Classification accuracies (10-News Groups)

partitions, [*p*=.022]). This finding is consistent with those on the Reuters data set. However, MRD's performance could not be objectively compared with JR at 10 and 20 partitions because it selected fewer features than JR at those partitions.

Comparing the algorithms' biased and unbiased versions show that JRB and MRDB attain significantly higher classification accuracies than JR and MRD, respectively. For example, JRB's average accuracy is significantly higher than JR's at 30 partitions (74.68% vs. 51.74%, [*p*=.0006]) and MRDB outperforms MRD (61.47% vs. 57.82%,

[*p*=.022]). In contrast, IG was adversely affected by bias. That is, IG performed slightly better than IGB (e.g., 70.31% vs. 69.36% at 30 partitions), although this difference was small and statistically insignificant. *Overall, JRB significantly outperformed the other algorithms at 20, 30, and 40 partitions.* For example, it attained significantly higher average classification accuracies than IG (74.7% vs. 70.3% at 30 partitions [*p*=.0018]).

One possible reason could be that we used the same POS bias parameter settings for all the algorithms, but IG may require different settings. We gained additional insight into this by examining the effect of POS bias on the algorithms (see

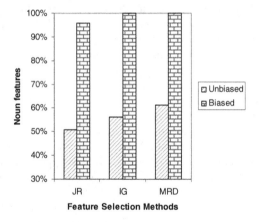

Fig. 7. The effect of POS-bias on the number of noun features selected by the three algorithms for 10-News Groups using 30 RTP partitions

Figure 7). The unbiased versions of the algorithms selected different proportions of noun features; JR selected 51%, IG selected 55%, and MRD selected 61% at 30 partitions. Examining the biased versions shows that JRB selects 96%, while IGB and MRDB select 100%, indicating that the bias factors may be too strong for IG and MRD.

Analyses of the feature selection times shows that JR's times steadily decrease from 325 seconds at 10 partitions to 60 seconds at 40 partitions and is the lowest among all algorithms at 20-40 partitions (see Figure 8). Feature selection times for IG and IGB remain relatively constant (268 seconds, on average) across different partition sizes. In contrast, JRB's feature selection times decreased dramatically from

10 to 20 partitions, but increased from 30 to 40. This occurred because the decrease in the number of cases per partition is offset by larger increases in the reduct sizes, thereby leading to an overall increase in feature selection times. For the same reason MRD and MRDB's times steadily increase from 6291 seconds at 10 partitions to 10,134 seconds at 40 partitions (not shown in Figure 8). In general, MRD selects more features than

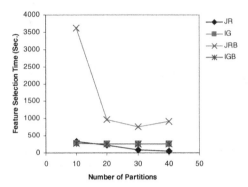

Fig. 8. Feature selection times (10-News Groups)

JR and this is further amplified for higher numbers of partitions. *Thus, RTP significantly reduces feature selection times for only JR and JRB on the 10-News Group data set.*

Results Summary and Discussion. Given that one of the rough set methods, JR with suitable POS bias, outperformed IG on both the data sets, we partially accept our first hypothesis, which claims that rough set methods significantly outperform IG. We also confirmed our second hypothesis, which states that POS-bias has a positive effect on RST feature selection algorithms. In particular, its effect on JR was substantial (6.1% increase in precision in Reuters-21578, and 41.78% increase in accuracy in 10-News Groups). Interestingly, the effect of POS-bias on IG was mixed: positive on Reuters-21578 and negative on 10-News Groups. We conjecture that the reasons for this mixed result are that the bias parameters for IG were too strong for the 10-News Groups set and that IG effectively counters the inherent POS bias when the number of cases per class is large (e.g., 1000 as opposed to 100).

We showed that the RTP was effective in dramatically reducing feature selection time for JR. However, the effect of RTP on MRD was mixed. It was positive on Reuters-21578 and negative on 10-News Groups. Therefore, we cannot fully confirm our third hypothesis that RTP is always effective in reducing training time for rough set methods. However, without RTP it would have been practically infeasible to run MRD and JR. We also observed that RTP has a positive effect on IG, although small compared to RST methods. This is because increasing the number of partitions reduces the effective vocabulary that IG must deal with and IG's computational complexity is linearly dependent on the vocabulary size.

4   Related Work

TCBR systems have been designed to support a variety of applications such as those involving legal reasoning (Brüninghaus & Ashley, 2003), spam filtering (Delany *et al.*, 2005), and news group classification (Wiratunga *et al.*, 2004). Typically, TCBR systems that use knowledge poor approaches (e.g., for email classification) tend to automatically generate features and operate on large data sets. For example, Delany *et al.* (2005) used IG to select features in a spam filtering task and Wiratunga *et al.*,

(2004) used IG to select features with boosted decision stumps. However, unlike us, they did not focus on reducing the computational complexity of their feature selection algorithms. Furthermore, high computational complexity was not a limiting factor because their binary classification task is not particularly demanding of information gain, especially given that their case bases were relatively small, containing only about 1000 cases. We instead investigate multi-classification and n-ary classification tasks involving thousands of cases, which require more attention to computational complexity. Despite these differences, our feature selection algorithms, randomized training partitions, and POS biasing can be effectively integrated with their approach.

Given a set of manually selected features, Brüninghaus & Ashley's (2003) TCBR system induces a set of classifiers that can automatically assign features to text documents. They used ID3 to induce these classifiers. If the number of features is large, its performance would degrade significantly. In such situations, our feature selection algorithms could significantly improve ID3's performance.

While RST-motivated feature selection algorithms have recently been applied to textual case bases on classification tasks, we are the first group to   highlight complexity issues (Gupta et al., 2005). For example, Chouchoulas & Shen (2001) applied their QuickReduct method for email classification. While QuickReduct's complexity (Gupta et al., 2005) is high (i.e., the same as MRD), they did not address complexity because their data included only 1500 cases. Furthermore, they did not compare QuickReduct with any conventional feature selection algorithms, such as IG.

Li et al. (2006) developed a Fast Rough Set Feature Reduction algorithm. Unlike the RST algorithms we evaluated, it is not feasible to isolate the contributions of RST in their hybrid conventional/RST algorithm. In particular, they used IG to rank-order the features for selection and the relative dependency metric *only* to terminate feature selection. Finally, they did not compare the performance of their algorithm with conventional algorithms.

An et al. (2004) developed a rough set feature selection method called ELEM2 and applied it to web page classification. As with the other research groups, they did not address complexity issues and evaluated their algorithm on a relatively small set of 327 web pages. Moreover, they tested their algorithm only with the most frequently occurring 20, 30, and 40 keywords per category. Although this drastically reduces their data set's number of features, frequency-based keyword selection is not always competitive with other feature selection algorithms (Yang & Pederson, 1997).

In our previous research (Gupta et al., 2005), we introduced RST motivated feature selection algorithms for a multi-class classification task. We also noted that the high computational complexity of feature selection algorithms are a limiting factor and introduced randomized training partitions to reduce training time. Finally, we showed that JohnsonsReduct performed comparably to IG on a single data set. In this paper, we extended JohnsonsReduct to work with multi-valued features and introduced the topic of fuzzy discernibility. In addition, we introduced MRD, a pure rough set version of Li et al.'s (2006) Fast Rough Set Reduction Approach. While this increases computational complexity, it is offset through the use of RTP. We also improved our evaluation methodology. For example, we eliminated variances due to differences in feature weighting by weighting all features equally, added a single classification task to improve the reliability of our conclusions, and used a two-fold cross validation methodology rather than random sampling. This has led us to qualitatively new results. For example, we found randomized training partitions to be effective for *both* rough set and conventional feature selection algorithms (for the Reuters-21758 data set), rather than only for the former.

Finally, we introduced the use of a POS-bias in textual case bases and described why it can impact feature selection. This explicit manipulation of bias appears to be novel; we are not aware of any prior research on using background knowledge of this type to assist TCBR systems on classification tasks. We showed that biasing feature selection algorithms can significantly increase classification accuracy of both conventional and RST-motivated feature selection algorithms, and that these increases are more substantial for the rough set algorithms.

5   Conclusion

Until recently, only conventional feature selection algorithms (e.g., IG and its extensions) had been applied to textual CBR with little concern for their computational complexity. In this paper, we rigorously investigated the potential of RST approaches to improve task performance and reduce feature selection times. We considered two RST algorithms: (1) JR with lower computational complexity than IG and (2) MRD with much higher computational complexity than IG. We evaluated the effect of RTP on these algorithms, a method we introduced in our previous research, to dramatically reduce feature selection time. In addition, we introduced a novel idea of part-of-speech bias in textual CBR that could affect both RST and conventional approaches. Evaluation of these methodologies with large multi-class and n-ary classification tasks showed that JR, suitably biased, significantly outperforms IG and significantly benefits from RTP. Furthermore, POS bias significantly improved RST feature selection algorithms.

JR significantly outperformed IG on our data. Thus, we suspect that Wiratunga *et al.*'s (2004) boosted algorithm, which is based on IG, could significantly benefit from our methodologies. We also conjectured that using an appropriate POS bias could consistently improve IG, and that IG effectively counters bias when the number of cases per class is large. In our future work, we will investigate these conjectures.

Acknowledgements

This research was supported by the Naval Research Laboratory. Thanks to the reviewers for their useful suggestions.

References

An, A., Huang, Y., Huang, X., & Cercone, N. (2004). An effective rough set-based method for text classification. *Transactions on Rough Sets*, **2**, 1-13.

Brill, E. (1993). *A corpus-based approach to language learning*. Doctoral dissertation: Department of Computer Science, University of Pennsylvania, Philadelphia, PA.

Bruninghaus, S. & Ashley, K.D. (2003). Combining case-based and model-based reasoning for predicting the outcome of legal cases. *Proceedings of the Fifth International Conference on Case-Based Reasoning* (pp. 65-79). Trondheim, Norway: Springer.

Chouchoulas, A., & Shen, Q. (2001). Rough-set aided keyword reduction for text categorization. *Applied Artificial Intelligence*, **15**, 843-873.

Delany, S.J., Cunningham, P., Doyle D., & Zamolokskikh, A. (2005). Generating estimates of classification confidence for a case-based spam filter. *Proceedings of the Sixth International Conference on Case-Based Reasoning* (pp. 177-190), Chicago, IL: Springer.

Gupta, K.M, & Aha, D.W.(2004). RuMop: A rule-based morphotactic parser. *Proceedings of the International Conference on Natural Language Processing* (pp. 280-284). Hyderabad, India: Allied Publishers.

Gupta, K.M., Moore, P.G., Aha, D.W., & Pal, S.K. (2005). Rough set feature selection methods for case-based categorization of text documents. *Proceedings of the First International Conference on Pattern Recognition and Machine Intelligence* (pp. 792-798). Kolkata, India: Springer.

Johnson, D.S. (1974). Approximation algorithms for combinatorial problems, *Journal of Computer and System Sciences*, **9**, 256-278.

Lang, K. (2006). 20 News group dataset. [http://www.cs.cmu.edu/afs/cs.cmu.edu/project/theo-20/www/data/news20.html]

Li, Y., Shiu, S.C.K., & Pal, S. (2006). Combining Feature Reduction and Case Selection in Building CBR Classifiers. In D.W. Aha, K.M. Gupta, & S.K. Pal (Eds.) *Case-Based Reasoning and Data Mining*. Hoboken, NJ: John Wiley & Sons.

Montazemi, A.R. & Gupta, K.M. (1997). A framework for retrieval in case-based reasoning systems. *Annals of operations research*, **72**, 51-73.

Pal, S.K., & Shiu, S.C.K. (2004). *Foundations of soft case-based reasoning*. Hoboken, NJ: Wiley.

Pawlak, Z. (1991). *Rough sets*. Norwell, MA: Kluwer Academic Publishers.

Quirk, R., Greenbaum, S., Leech, G., & Svartvik, J. (1985). *A comprehensive grammar of the English language*. New York, NY: Longman.

Reuters (2006). Reuters-21578 Evaluation Data. Retrieved on April, 12, 2005 from [http://www.daviddlewis.com/resources/testcollections/reuters21578/]

Skowron, A., (1995). Extracting laws from decision tables. *Computational Intelligence*, **11**(2), 371-388.

Weber, R.O., Ashley, K.D., & Brüninghaus, S. (2005). Textual case-based reasoning. To appear in *Knowledge Engineering Review*, **20**(3).

Wilson, D.C., & Bradshaw, S. (2000). CBR textuality. *Expert Update*, **3**(1), 28-37.

Wiratunga, N., Koychev, I., & Massie, S. (2004). Feature selection and generalization for retrieval of textual cases. *Proceedings of the Seventh European Conference on Case-Based Reasoning* (pp. 806-820). Madrid, Spain: Springer.

Yang, Y., & Pederson, J. (1997). A comparative study of feature selection in text categorization. *Proceedings of the Fourteenth International Conference on Machine Learning* (pp. 412-420). Nashville, TN: Morgan Kaufmann.

Experience Management with Case-Based Assistant Systems

Mirjam Minor

University of Trier,
Department of Business Information Systems II,
54286 Trier, Germany
minor@uni-trier.de

Abstract. In this paper, we present a framework for Experience Management (EM) which is populated with case-based assistant systems for EM. The framework follows the building block model of Probst et al [28] which has been developed as a guidance for knowledge management activities. We taylor the building blocks for the special needs of EM and discuss for each building block the support and automation opportunities by case-based assistant systems based on sample systems from the literature. We take up a holistic point of view, i.e. we regard the psycho-social aspect in an own building block as well as the organizational aspect. The impacts of these efforts are investigated in a case study that has shown significantly increasing access ratios when following some psycho-social findings in the design and organization of a case-based EM system.

1 Introduction

Gilbert Probst demands that knowledge management 'is clearly embedded into an organizational and social context' [27, own translation]. In recent literature [3,4,25,24] case-based reasoning (CBR) has been employed for experience management (EM) to provide technical support by means of assistant systems. Those case-based approaches lack the explicit integration of the social aspect. We follow Probst in our framework for developing, integrating, and maintaining case-based EM systems. We show in an experimental evaluation that it is worth while to consider the socio-psychological aspect of EM systems.

This paper is organized as follows: Section 2 gives a brief intoduction to EM and the holistic point of view. Section 3 reports the building block model for knowledge management from Probst et al. In Section 4, we taylor this model for the special needs of EM, refer to case-based sample systems for the particular building blocks, and discuss the potential for automation. Section 5 contains a case study on the building block *use of knowledge* which deals with the psycho-social aspect of a case-based EM system. In Section 6, we discuss related work and draw a conclusion.

2 Holistic Experience Management

EM is a special kind of knowledge management that is restricted to experience knowledge [4]. *Experience knowledge* (also called *experiential knowledge*) origins

T.R. Roth-Berghofer et al. (Eds.): ECCBR 2006, LNAI 4106, pp. 182–195, 2006.

from the experience of an agent in a previous problem solving situation. It is valid for a certain scope of duties like the configuration of mobile phones or like the guidance of project teams. This understanding of experiential knowledge is in opposite to the idea of general knowledge which has a broad coverage of domains or is even universally valid.

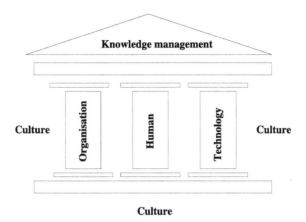

Fig. 1. The three pillars of holistic knowledge management [36]

We will deal with EM in a *holistic* way, i.e. it takes into account not only the technical support of EM but also the organizational and psycho-social aspect. The holistic view is supported by Wolf et al's model of knowledge management [36] in Figure 1. Wolf et al place knowledge management on three pillars: The organization and the human carry the roof together with the technology. If one of the pillars is missing the building is instable. The entire model is embedded into the cultural context of the humans. We transfer the holistic model of Wolf et al. to EM systems. The psycho-social aspect (the human and the culture in Figure 1) is especially important for experiential knowledge as experience is rather personal and revealing it makes the contributor vulnerable.

3   The Building Block Model for Knowledge Management

Gilbert Probst et al [28] have developed a process model for managers who perform knowledge management activities. It has been derived from several case studies by an action research approach that combines theoretical and practical issues. The process model provides a hands-on raster that has become a standard work in the German-speaking part.

Figure 2 shows the six basic building blocks of knowledge management. They build a cycle and are affiliated with each other.

- The *identification of knowledge* aims to make it transparent which knowledge is available. The main task of this building block is to localize useful knowledge within and outside the own organization.

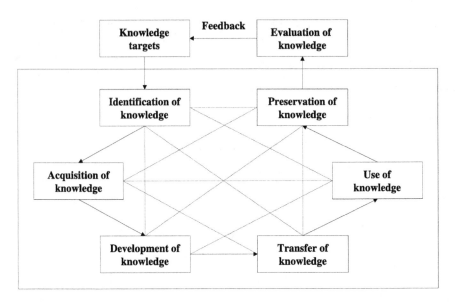

Fig. 2. The building blocks for knowledge management by Probst et al.

- The *acquisition of knowledge* deals with getting access to external knowledge either by recruiting knowledge carriers, or by acquiring the knowledge of other organizations like customer organizations, or by buying knowledge products.
- The *development of knowledge* focuses on creating new knowledge. This is supported, for instance, by a family-friendly atmosphere, by fault tolerance, and by honoring long-term success. In this way, knowledge may emerge during activities that are normally not supposed to be productive. Probst et al's description of the development building block is in accordance with the well-known knowledge creating approach of Nonaka and Takeuchi[26].
- The *transfer of knowledge* concerns the process of spreading knowledge over the organization. It includes very often the face-to-face contact of individuals.
- The *use of knowledge* is the main purpose of knowledge management. However, it may be restricted by a series of barriers, e.g. the commercial barrier of a missing patent.
- The *preservation of knowledge* results in an organizational memory. It consists of three sub-processes, namely to select the valuable knowledge, to store it appropriately, and to ensure that the knowledge is updated.

Two strategic building blocks close the cycle: To determine the *knowledge targets* should mark the beginning of any knowledge management activities. The *evaluation of knowledge* provides a measure for the success of the learning processes and helps to adjust the course of knowledge management activities by means of feedback. Probst et al's process model gives useful guidance for knowledge management activities in practice.

4   The Building Block Model for EM Systems

We have adapted the original model of Probst et al to the special requirements of EM. Figure 3 provides a framework for the development, psycho-social integration, and maintenance of case-based EM systems. It includes the organizational and psycho-social aspect explicitly in the two building blocks *organize* and *maintain*. Furthermore, we discuss for the particular building blocks to what extend they can be supported or even automated by CBR systems.

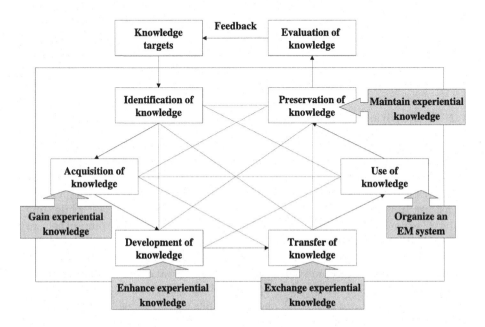

Fig. 3. The building blocks adapted to the special needs of EM

4.1   Identification of Knowledge

The *identification of knowledge* for case-based EM systems is mainly the **identification of knowledge sources** for the contents of the knowledge containers case base, vocabulary, similarity measure, and adaptation knowledge [29]. Knowledge sources may be human beings with a rich treasury of experiences, electronic databases, or even non-electronic material and observed objects or systems as far as there is a mechanism to transform the gained knowledge for the case-based assistant system. We developed the following criteria for the manual selection of appropriate knowledge sources:

- the quality,
- the suitable focus, and
- the topicality of the source

as the three main criteria, and secondarily

- the easy accessibility of the source and
- the networking idea.

The networking idea means - as far as possible – to link the assistant systems with the knowledge sources rather than to copy the contents to the system.

Potential for automation: We have not found any case-based system in the literature that automatically identifies knowledge sources. But there are other assistant systems in the literature that support the knowledge identification process and automate parts of it, e.g. the ontology-based system *ProPer* [33]. *ProPer* supports the human resource management by means of an ontology on the staff of an organization. The effort to identify knowledge sources automatically is quite high, and it is only possible in case there is a complete and structured directory of potential knowledge sources available.

4.2   Acquisition of Knowledge: Gain Experiential Knowledge

The *acquisition of knowledge* for EM systems is the process of **accessing knowledge sources and integrating them with the system**. The borderlines between the building blocks 'acquisition of knowledge' and 'development of knowledge' are variable. As a rule of thumb, to put something down on paper or to transform it syntactically belongs rather to the acquisition process, while something like machine learning of knowledge or enhancing it in some other way belongs rather to the developing process.

Sample applications in [20,23] gain vocabulary and components of the similarity measure from electronic sources like WordNet[8] and the on-line dictionary Leo[15]. [19] describes the SimLex approach that generates cases automatically from emails and continuous texts and cross-links similar cases based on the systems similarity measure.

Potential for automation: The acquisition of knowledge for retrieval purposes can be automated under certain conditions. The required knowledge has to be electronically available, for instance, and the system needs to know which parts of the knowledge should be transformed in what way.

4.3   Development of Knowledge: Enhance Experiential Knowledge

The *development of knowledge* concerning assistant systems may happen in two ways: either **for** the assistant system or **by means of** the assistant system.

The INRECA methodology [5,4] provides guidance for developing knowledge *for* case-based systems (see Section 6). Ontology learning [22] and other machine learning techniques [32,6,11] have been employed to support the development of knowledge *for* case-based systems. [21] describes a life-cycle model for cases and the according case-based authoring support to enhance experiential knowledge. In this way, the humans develop experiential knowledge *by means of* the case-based system.

Potential for automation: The lion's share of developing knowledge for case-based EM systems is still a human task as it includes the externalization of human experience.

4.4   Transfer of Knowledge: Exchange Experiential Knowledge

The *transfer of knowledge* is supported by all case-based systems that let the users share a common case base. More interesting is the **interoperability of case-based systems** that exchange experiential knowledge that is stored in their knowledge containers.

The personal assistant agents in [17] exchange services, i.e. cases, and the according vocabulary and similarity measures to retrieve those services. They perform a shallow kind of ontology mapping to integrate the received knowledge. Agile software development [2] is a prominent – yet non-case-based – example for paying attention on the exchangeability.

Potential for automation: A case-based system can be regarded an agent if it proactively queries another system for knowledge. There is plenty of work on the communication of agents [13] that shows the high potential for the automation of knowledge exchange. There is still much work to be done in CBR research on such agile methods.

4.5   Use of Knowledge: Organize an EM System

To boost the *use of knowledge* means for case-based EM systems to design and organize the system in a way that it is accepted by the users. The **barriers against the use of a case-based EM system** are mainly organizational and psycho-social barriers.

The work on CBR and business processes [10,5] deals with the organizational aspect. Section 5 describes a new approach to take care on the psycho-social aspect.

Potential for automation: Only small parts of a promotional policy can be automated at the moment.

4.6   Preservation of Knowledge: Maintain Experiential Knowledge

To select and to store valuable knowledge within a case-based EM system are the first steps to *preserve this knowledge*. To keep the experiential knowledge valuable, it has to be **maintained carefully**.

Wilson [35] gives a useful review of the CBR literature on maintenance until 2001. The SIAM methodology [30] is a useful hands-on guidance for maintenance (see Section 6). Ferrario and Smyth [9] automate the organization of maintenance processes for structural cases by means of a scoring system. [12] transfer this work to textual CBR. Competence measures [31,7] may support the humans who have to judge experiential knowledge.

Potential for automation: Parts of the organization of maintenance can be automated. However, the execution requires the effort of humans. It may be supported by automatic quality measures.

5 Case Study with Empirical Evaluation

We have performed a case study for our framework that focuses on the building block *use of knowledge*, i.e. on the organizational and socio-technical actions to boost the use of the case-based EM system. An *organizational action* for an EM system means an action that concerns the integration of the system with the organization. A *socio-technical action* is a technical modification of the system to realize some psycho-social findings.

5.1 The Application Scenario

We took the **ExperienceBook II** [18] as an application scenario for our case study. The ExperienceBook II is a case-based assistant system that supports students of computer science in their daily problems. This includes computer science related problems like how to use a certain software but also issues of student life like the best pubs on the campus. Meanwhile, the case base contains about 60 textual cases on the following topics:

- UNIX problems,
- Linux problems,
- Prolog problems,
- problems with the network dial-in at the university's,
- questions concerning the exercise and examination management system Goya,
- the lecture 'Practical computer science I', and
- general problems and questions.

The representation and retrieval of cases follows Lenz et al's approach of textual case-based reasoning [14]. The students may ask questions to retrieve their commillitones' experience. The case-based part of the system is integrated with a discussion forum for the same community of users. The navigation between the two parts is per mouse-click. The ExperienceBook II has been employed at Humboldt University, Berlin, for more than two years. It is on-line accessible for the members of Humboldt's computer science department[1].

5.2 The Psycho-social Findings

We have developed a catalog of organizational and socio-technical actions to boost the use of our sample application. It relies on a psychological study on the main reasons for the failure of knowledge management by Meyer and Scholl[16] which results in three recommendations:

1. **Requirements analysis:** Make a requirements analysis to identify the kind of assistance and the contents that the users really need.
2. **Attitude:** Exert influence on the users attitude towards the system.
3. **Organizational barriers:** Avoid organizational barriers that may prevent the users from using the system.

---

[1] Feel free to send an email to the author for a guest account.

We followed the first recommendation by the early and continuing participation of the users. This included discussions with students before, during, and after the launch of the system as well as interviews to gain written feedback. Additionally, we got hints for the knowledge demand of the students by analyzing the queries that have been posed to the system.

The second recommendation is especially crucial for EM systems as people circulate their personal experience only when they trust the receiver, i.e. the receiving system and the other users of the system. For instance, the fear of being controlled via a system leads to a negative attitude. We exerted influence on the users' attitude towards the system by informing and motivating them on several promotional channels. Our results show that promotion has a measurable impact on the access ratio (see below). This indicates a reduction of the organizational barriers 'fear of control' and 'lack of motivation'.

We identified 'unsatisfying contents', 'defensive attitude', and 'system not tightly integrated with the working environment' as further organizational barriers. Paying regard to these barriers resulted in an improvement of the system measured by the access statistics (see below). Meyer and Scholl mention 'to small resources for knowledge management' and 'restrictive conventions' as further organizational barriers; they do not apply in our case study.

5.3   The Results of the Activities

Table 1 contains the organizational and socio-technical activities that we have taken to follow the above recommendations. We used the following catalog of methods for it:

- discussions,
- oral and written interviews,
- talks,
- links to the system from other Web pages,
- written group work,
- email communication, and
- Web logfile analysis.

A written group work in a seminary provided us with an initial case base and some further topics of interest for which the cases had still to be written. We created some more cases from teaching material and from the Web pages of the system administration group. The whole initial case base contained two dozen cases what has been a first step against the organizational barrier 'unsatisfying contents'.

The advertising activities informed the students on several channels: per email, per links from the Web page of the lecture 'Practical computer science I', and via face-to-face communication by discussing in meetings of the students' self-administration and by giving a talk in the lecture. The access statistics (see below) showed that the face-to-face advertisement has been the most successful promotion as each discussion and talk was followed by a peak of accesses. We used

Table 1. The organizational and socio-technical activites in chronological order

	Requirements analysis	Attitude	Organizational barriers
	written group work to determine topics of interest for cases		initial case base to avoid 'unsatisfying contents'
before the start of the system (Sep 2003)		advertising activities (emails, links, discussions, talks), communication-friendly design	avoid 'lack of motivation'
		only intrinsic motivation, privacy policy	avoid 'defensive attitude'
some weeks after the start of the system (Oct 2003)	Web log analysis and oral interviews for getting feedback, discussion of authoring support requirements		Web page with a list of open cases, new cases from the discussion forum to avoid 'unsatisfying contents'
some months after the start of the system (Jan 2004)	Web log analysis and questionnaire for getting feedback		
		advertising activities	avoid 'fear of control'
before the second turn of the system (Sep 2004)			link from 'GOYA' to avoid that the system is 'not tightly integrated with the working environment'
some months after the second start (Mar 2004)	Web log analysis for getting feedback		new cases from lecturers to avoid 'unsatisfying contents'

all meetings also for the requirements analysis. We developed a communication-friendly design of the system to motivate the students to contribute their experience. The design includes text fields for the author and an email contact address in the cases, a commentary field to extend a case, the right to edit cases for every user, and the integration of the case-based part of the system with the discussion forum.

We decided to abstain from extrinsic motivation like giving the students extra scores for writing a case, for instance. The usage of the system and the authoring of new cases is voluntary, the motivation is intrinsic and has to be done by convincement only. Together with our privacy policy, the intrinsic motivation aims to avoid a *'defensive attitude'*. The privacy is preserved as the system is only accessible for members of the department: There is free access from inside the department's network and password protected access from outside the network. Furthermore, the retrieval is anonymous and the query data is stored not individual-relatedly.

The analysis of the Web log files some weeks after the introduction of the system showed 1,453 accesses (see the value for October 2003 in Figure 4). However, only two authors had written new cases while the discussion forum got many new entries during the same time period. Oral feedback and a discussion of authoring support requirements confirmed that the students felt it difficult to write new cases due to a lack of ideas for topics. They asked for an extra Web page with open cases. Since, we have filled this page regularly with topics from the query log files. Additionally, the discussion forum contributed material for some new cases.

Some months after the introduction of the system, the number of accesses was rapidly decreasing (see the values for December 2003 and January 2004 in Figure 4). We sent a questionnaire to the students of the lecture 'Practical computer science 1'. The return rate was low (15 of 298 students, i.e. about 5%), but the results were rather informative: The target community had installed an own discussion forum meanwhile that was stored outside the university. The students did not mention the reasons for this relocation. They assessed the usability of the system as good. They asked for more cases from the lecturers. The most students knew the system from the lecture. This confirms our above observation that the face-to-face communication is the most effective promotional channel.

For the second turn of the system in October 2004, we repeated our advertising activities with a new generation of students. We put special emphasize on the

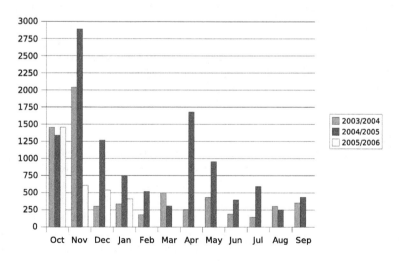

Fig. 4. The access statistics of the ExperienceBook II

organizational barrier 'fear of control' and recurred to say that the lecturers are not reading the students' queries nor the comments and new cases.

We linked the ExperienceBook II from the Web page of the GOYA system to integrate it further with the students' working environment. Since, about a third of all accesses come from the GOYA page.

The analysis of the Web log file had again the result that the users performed little authoring activities. As a countermeasure, we asked lecturers for help. They wrote cases on open topics at the special Web page.

Meanwhile, we have a case base with 59 cases: 8 of them have been written by 5 named students, 5 anonymously, and 46 by 3 different lecturers. 10 comments have been written and 11 cases have been edited. Over 60 authors contributed to the case base and the discussion forum. The contents of the case base are still a bit unsatisfying as such an amount of cases is manageable without any retrieval, e.g. within a catalog structure.

Figure 4 shows a peak of accesses in April 2004 after the new contributions from the lecturers and minor peaks around the examination in July 2005 and at the beginning of the new academic year with the third generation of users in October 2005. In 2005, only mouth-to-mouth communication made promotion for the system.

6   Discussion of Related Work and Conclusion

The INRECA methodology [5] is for the development of industrial applications of CBR. It describes process models on three levels: on the common general level that covers many applications, on the cookbook level for certain kinds of applications, e.g. the class of help desk systems, and on the specific project level. A process is decribed by input values, output values and a set of different methods that can be used to implement it. INRECA is compliant with the ISO 900x standard. It is a powerful framework for huge projects that requires some effort for integrating a case-based EM system with the business processes of the target company. For non-commercial projects, this effort is not achievable sometimes even for lack of specified business processes. However, taking care on the organizational and the psycho-social aspect following our building block model can be done with little effort. We learned from the INRECA methodology that it is important not to be restricted on the technical aspect of a case-based EM system only.

The SIAM (Setup, Initialization, Application, Maintenance) methodology [30] is a framework for case-based systems. SIAM extends the originally four processes of Aamodt and Plaza's CBR cycle [1] by two processes for the application and maintenance of the system. SIAM has been integrated with INRECA and operationalizes a maintenance policy on the general, cookbook, and specific project level. Like SIAM, our framework aims on a systematical approach for the organizational aspect. In addition to SIAM, we allow also light-weight maintenance policies as in [9] and [12].

Weber at al [34] give a survey of knowledge management systems that deal with experiential working knowledge. As one of the first authors they state that such systems, although well-intentioned, are rarely used. They give a categorizing schema that aims to guide the development of improved systems. The scope of this work is still limited to technological and organizational issues.

In this paper, we proposed a framework of EM that is applicable for the development, integration, and maintenance of case-based EM systems in the following way: The designers and managers may select the most important (or all) building blocks for a particular application and take guidance from the referred sample systems how to realize it.

As our results of a case study show, it is measurably worth while to take care on the psycho-social aspect.

Acknowledgments

The author acknowledges the Humboldt University, Berlin, for providing the computational environment for the case study.

References

1. A. Aamodt and E. Plaza. Case-Based Reasoning: Foundational Issues, Methodological Variations , and System Approaches. *AI Communications*, 7(1):39 – 59, 1994.
2. The agile manifest. Internet: http://www.agilemanifesto.org, 2006. [last visited: Feb 2006].
3. K.-D. Althoff, B. Decker, S. Hartkopf, A. Jedlitschka, M. Nick, and J. Rech. Experience management: The fraunhofer iese experience factory. In P. Perner, editor, *Data Mining, Data Warehouse and Knowledge Management. Proc. Industrial Conference on Data Mining*, Institut für Bildverarbeitung und angewandte Informatik IBai Report, pages 12 – 29, Leipzig, Germany, 2001. Institute for Computer Vision and applied Computer Sciences.
4. R. Bergmann. *Experience Management: Foundations, Development Methodology, and Internet Based Applications*. LNAI 2432. Springer-Verlag, Berlin, 2002.
5. R. Bergmann, S. Bree, E. Fayol, M. Göker, M. Manago, S. Schmitt, J. Schumacher, A. Stahl, S. Wess, and W. Wilke. Collecting experience on the systematic development of cbr applications using the inreca methodology. In P. C. Barry Smyth, editor, *Advances in Case-Based Reasoning. Proceedings of the Fourth European Workshop on Case-Based Reasoning (EWCBR-98)*, LNAI 1488, pages 460 – 470, Berlin, 1998. Springer-Verlag.
6. S. Brüninghaus and K. Ashley. The role of information extraction for textual cbr. In D. Aha and I. Watson, editors, *Case-Based Reasoning Research and Development, Proceedings of the ICCBR'01*, LNAI 2080, pages 74 – 89. Springer-Verlag, 2001.
7. S. J. Delany and P. Cunningham. An analysis of case-base editing in a spam filtering system. In P. Funk and P. A. González-Calero, editors, *Advances in Case-Based Reasoning, 7th European Conference, ECCBR 2004, Madrid, Spain, August 30 - September 2, 2004, Proceedings*, LNCS 3155, pages 128 – 141. Springer-Verlag, 2004.

8. C. Fellbaum. *Wordnet: An Electronic Lexical Database*. The MIT Press, Cambridge, Mass., 1998.

9. M. A. Ferrario and B. Smyth. Collaborative maintenance - a distributed, interactive case-base maintenance strategy. In E. Blanzieri and L. Portinale, editors, *Advances in Case-Based Reasoning: 5th European Workshop, EWCBR 2000*, LNAI 1898, pages 393–405, Heidelberg, September 2000. Springer-Verlag.

10. M. H. Göker, T. Roth-Berghofer, R. Bergmann, T. Pantleon, R. Traphöner, S. Wess, and W. Wilke. The development of homer: A case-based cad/cam helpdesk support tool. In B. Smyth and P. Cunningham, editors, *Advances in Case-Based Reasoning, 4th European Workshop, EWCBR-98, Dublin, Ireland, September 1998, Proceedings*, LNAI 1488, pages 346 – 357. Springer-Verlag, 1998.

11. K. M. Gupta and D. W. Aha. Knowledge extraction for conversational case-based reasoning. In D. W. Aha, K. M. Gupta, and S. K. Pal, editors, *Case-Based Reasoning in Knowledge Discovery and Data Mining*, page to appear. John Wiley & Sons, 2005.

12. A. Hanft and M. Minor. A low-effort, collaborative maintenance model for textual cbr. In R. Weber and K. Branting, editors, *Workshop Proceedings of the 6th International Conference on Case-Based Reasoning*, pages 138 – 149, Chicago, Illinois, 2005. DePaul University.

13. The ARPA-sponsored Knowledge Sharing Effort. Internet: http://www.csee.umbc.edu/kse/, 2006. [last visited: Feb 2006].

14. M. Lenz, A. Hübner, and M. Kunze. Textual CBR. In M. Lenz, H.-D. Burkhard, B. Bartsch-Spörl, and S. Weß, editors, *Case-Based Reasoning Technology — From Foundations to Applications*, LNAI 1400, Berlin, 1998. Springer-Verlag.

15. Link everything online. Internet: http://dict.leo.org/, 2005. [last visited: September 2005].

16. B. Meyer and W. Scholl. A Comparison of Paradigmatic Views in Knowledge Management: An Empirical Case Study on Shortcomings in KM. In O. K. Ferstl, E. J. Sinz, S. Eckert, and T. Isselhorst, editors, *Wirtschaftsinformatik 2005: eEconomy, eGovernment, eSociety, 7. Internationale Tagung Wirtschaftsinformatik 2005, Bamberg, 23.2.2005 - 25.2.2005*, pages 1003–1022. Physica-Verlag, 2005.

17. M. Minor. Assistant agents with personal ontologies. In J. van Diggelen, V. Dignum, L. van Elst, and A. Abecker, editors, *Agent Mediated Knowledge Management Workshop*, pages 41 – 51, Utrecht, 2005. Universiteit Utrecht.

18. M. Minor. Introduction strategy and feedback from an experience management project. In K.-D. Althoff, A. Dengel, R. Bergmann, M. Nick, and T. Roth-Berghofer, editors, *Professional Knowledge Management. WM 2005 post-conference proceedings.*, LNAI 3782, pages 284 – 292. Springer-Verlag, 2005.

19. M. Minor and C. Biermann. Case acquisition and semantic cross-linking for case-based experience management systems. In D. Zhang, T. M. Khoshgoftaa, and M.-L. Shyu, editors, *Proceedings of the 2005 IEEE International Conference on Information Reuse and Integration (IRI-2005)*, number 05EX1058, pages 433 – 438, Las Vegas, 2005. IEEE Systems, Man, and Cybernetics Society.

20. M. Minor and J. C. Del Prado. Multilingual textual case-based reasoning. In H.-P. Schnurr, S. Staab, R. Studer, G. Stumme, and Y. Sure, editors, *Professionelles Wissensmanagement: Erfahrungen und Visionen*, pages 281 – 282, Aachen, 2001. Shaker-Verlag.

21. M. Minor and A. Hanft. The life cycle of test cases in a cbr system. In E. Blanzieri and L. Portinale, editors, *Advances in Case-Based Reasoning: 5th European Workshop, EWCBR 2000*, LNAI 1898, pages 455 – 466, Berlin, 2000. Springer-Verlag.

22. M. Minor and K. Schmidt. Automatic transformation and enlargement of similarity models for case-based reasoning. In *Proceedings of the Modellierung 2006*, to appear.
23. F. Müller. Integration von TFBS-Systemen und Ontologien. Diplomarbeit, Institut für Informatik, Humboldt-Universität zu Berlin, Berlin, 2005.
24. M. Nick. *Experience Maintenance through Closed-Loop Feedback*. PhD thesis, Technische Universität Kaiserslautern, 2005.
25. M. Nick, B. Snoek, and T. Willrich. Supporting the it security of eservices with cbr-based experience management. In K. D. Ashley and D. G. Bridge, editors, *Case-Based Reasoning Research and Development, 5th International Conference on Case-Based Reasoning, ICCBR 2003, Trondheim, Norway, June 23-26, 2003, Proceedings*, LNAI 2689, pages 362 – 376. Springer, 2003.
26. I. Nonaka and H. Takeuchi. *The knowledge creating company*. Oxford University Press, 1995.
27. G. Probst. Ganzheitliches Wissensmanagement: Trends und kritische Reflexionen, Eingeladener Vortrag auf der WM 2003. Internet: http://wm2003.aifb.uni-karlsruhe.de/invitedtalk_probst.pdf, 2003. [last visited: November 2004].
28. G. Probst, S. Raub, and K. Romhardt. *Wissen managen: Wie Unternehmen ihre wertvollste Ressource optimal nutzen*. Gabler-Verlag, Wiesbaden, 1999.
29. M. M. Richter. Fallbasiertes Schließen. In G. Görz, C.-R. Rollinger, and J. Schneeberger, editors, *Handbuch der Künstlichen Intelligenz*, chapter 11, pages 407 – 430. Oldenbourg-Verlag, München, 2000.
30. T. Roth-Berghofer. *Knowledge Maintenance of Case-Based Reasoning Systems - The SIAM Methodology*. PhD thesis, Universität Kaiserslautern, 2003. DISKI 262, infix-Verlag.
31. B. Smyth and E. McKenna. Modelling the competence of case-bases. In B. Smyth and P. Cunningham, editors, *Advances in Case-Based Reasoning, 4th European Workshop, EWCBR-98, Dublin, Ireland, September 1998, Proceedings*, LNAI 1488, pages 208 – 220. Springer-Verlag, 1998.
32. A. Stahl. Learning similarity measures: A formal view based on a generalized cbr model. In H. Muñoz-Avila and F. Ricci, editors, *Case-Based Reasoning, Research and Development, 6th International Conference, on Case-Based Reasoning, ICCBR 2005, Chicago, IL, USA, August 23-26, 2005, Proceedings*, LNCS 3620, pages 507 – 521. Springer-Verlag, 2005.
33. Y. Sure, A. Maedche, and S. Staab. Leveraging Corporate Skill Knowledge - From ProPer to OntoProPer. In U. Reimer, editor, *Proceedings of the Third International Conference on Practical Aspect s of Knowledge Management (PAKM 2000)*, volume 34 of *CEUR Workshop Proceedings*, Basel, Switzerland, 2000. CEUR-WS.org.
34. R. Weber, D. W. Aha, and I. Becerra-Fernandez. Categorizing intelligent lessons learned systems. In D.W.Aha and R. Weber, editors, *Intelligent Lessons Learned Systems: Papers from the AAAI 2000 Workshop*, pages 63 – 67, Menlo Park, 2000. CA:AAAI Press.
35. D. C. Wilson. *Case-Based Maintenance: the Husbandry of Experience*. PhD thesis, Indiana University, 2001.
36. T. Wolf, S. Decker, and A. Abecker. Unterstützung des Wissensmanagements durch Informations- und Kommunikationstechnologie. In A.-W. Scheer and M. Nüttgens, editors, *Electronic Business Engineering, 4. Internationale Tagung Wirtschaftsinformatik*, pages 745 – 766, Heidelberg, 1999. Physica-Verlag.

The Needs of the Many: A Case-Based Group Recommender System*

Kevin McCarthy, Lorraine McGinty, Barry Smyth, and Maria Salamó

Adaptive Information Cluster, School of Computer Science & Informatics,
University College Dublin, Belfield, Dublin 4, Ireland
{kevin.mccarthy, lorraine.mcginty, barry.smyth, maria}@ucd.ie

Abstract. While much of the research in the area of recommender systems has focused on making recommendations to the individual, many recommendation scenarios involve groups of inter-related users. In this paper we consider the challenges presented by the latter scenario. We introduce a (case-based) group recommender designed to meet these challenges through a variety of recommendation features, including the generation of reactive and proactive suggestions based on user feedback in the form of critiques, and demonstrate its effectiveness through a live-user case-study.

1 Introduction

Recently one of the authors of this paper was trying to book a skiing holiday for a group of 4 friends. This turned out to be far more complex than first imagined, despite the prevalence of many sophisticated search and recommender systems in this domain (e.g., TripMatcher, provided by Triplehop Technologies [3], vacation-coach.com and TripAdvisor.com and also DieToRecs [13]). To begin with it was difficult to capture the many and varied preferences of the group participants. For example, most people only revealed a few of their more salient preferences at the outset and then further requirements were disclosed in the face of certain holiday suggestions later on. In addition, all of the available recommender systems in this domain really were designed for single-user usage. While they obviously provided facilities for a user to search for a package that would accommodate a group of people, it was not possible to introduce the individual sets of preferences of those involved. Instead the responsibility of combining these (often competing) preferences into a single coherent query, fell to the lead searcher [13]. All of this led to a very unnatural, not to mention extremely inefficient, search process. For example, early recommendations were passed on to the group to get individual feedback, and then this feedback needed to be integrated into a new query by our lead searcher in order to generate another batch of suggestions. This process continued for many cycles and the lead searcher had to regularly justify to others why particular options were appropriate, explaining them in the light of the preferences of others. Eventually a holiday was booked, and everyone

---

* This material is based on works supported by Science Foundation Ireland under Grant No. 03/IN.3/I361.

T.R. Roth-Berghofer et al. (Eds.): ECCBR 2006, LNAI 4106, pp. 196–210, 2006.

had a great time, but surely better recommendation support could have been provided.

In this paper we consider a group recommendation scenario just like the one outlined above and we describe a conversational recommendation framework that has been implemented to provide the type of support that we feel is critical. Briefly, the recommender system implements an asynchronous model of group recommendation, allowing a group of users to engage in a collaborative recommendation session via a Web-based interface[1]. This framework provides for a variety of recommendation features including the generation of reactive and proactive suggestions based on user feedback in the form of critiques. One of the critical challenges of group-based recommendation scenarios involves the development of a reliable group-preference model. We will describe how such a model is constructed by analyzing individual user feedback, and how the model works to complement the individual preference models that are maintained for each user during the selection of recommendations. In addition, it is also critically important for a group recommender to help individual users to understand the evolving preferences of the group such that they can better appreciate the compromises that may be required if a satisfactory conclusion is to be reached [6]. To this end we describe a number of innovative interfacing features that are designed to act as *consensus barometers* in order to help the group develop a shared mutual awareness of each others' preferences.

2   Background

One of the key issues that has guided the development of our group recommender concerns the type of feedback that can be solicited from individual users. In our work we are especially interested in *critiquing* (see, [2,4,8,9,14]) as a form of feedback as it strikes a useful balance between the information content of the feedback and the level of user effort or domain expertise that is required. For example, in a travel vacation recommender, a user might indicate that they are interested in a vacation that is *longer* than the one week offered by the currently recommended option; in this instance, *[duration, >, 1wk]* is a critique over the *duration* feature that can be used to filter out certain cases from consideration (i.e., those that have shorter durations) in the next recommendation cycle. Thus, the key advantage of critiquing is that it is a relatively low-cost form of feedback, in the sense that the user does not need to provide specific feature values.

Recently there has been renewed interest in critiquing, especially in product recommendation scenarios, where users have limited domain knowledge, but where they can readily provide feedback on some product features. As a result, the basic approach has been enhanced in a number of ways [1,10,11,12]. In this work we use the *incremental critiquing* technique [12] as a way to effectively leverage a user's critiquing history during recommendation. Incremental

---

[1] Our recommendation framework has been designed to operate with different types of interaction modalities and later we will discuss an alternative interface that is based on the Mitsubishi DiamondTouch interactive tabletop.

critiquing uses a preference model for user U that is made up of the set of critiques $\{I_1, .., I_n\}$ that have been applied by a user in a given session. As new critiques are made by the user, their preference model is updated. This may involve removing past critiques if they conflict with, or are subsumed by the most recent critique. For example, if a user had previously indicated a *Price* < *$600* critique and a new *Price* < *$500* critique is later applied then the earlier critique will be removed to reflect the users refined *Price* preference. Similarly, if a user had previously indicated a *Price* < *$600* critique but the new critique is for *Price* > *$650*, then the earlier conflicting critique is deleted. In this way the user's preference model remains a consistent reflection of their most recent preferences.

This model is then used to influence future recommendations so that they are not only compatible with the current critique (and preference case) but so that they are also compatible with past critiques so far as is possible. In the standard approach to critiquing, the most recent critique is used to *temporarily* filter out incompatible cases and a new recommendation is selected from the remaining cases on the basis of its similarity to the critiqued case (i.e., the preference case). The problem with this approach is that no account is taken of how compatible the remaining cases are with past critiques that have been applied; since the critiques only act as temporary filters over the case-base, cases which are incompatible with past critiques may be reconsidered in the future. One of the advantages of the incremental critiquing approach is that it allows candidate recommendations to be ranked not only because they are similar to the preference case but also on the basis of their compatibility with prior critiques in the form of the user's current preference model. To do this, each candidate recommendation, c', is scored according to its compatibility to the user's current preference model as shown in Equation 1. Essentially, this compatibility score is equal to the percentage of critiques in the user's model that are satisfied by the case; for example, if c_r is a $1000 vacation case then it will satisfy a *price* critique for less than $1200 ($I_i$) and so $satisfies(I_i, c_r)$ will return 1.

$$compatibility(c_r, U) = \frac{\sum_{\forall i} satisfies(I_i, c_r)}{|U|} \qquad (1)$$

The *quality* of a case c_r with respect to a preference case c_p, is a weighted sum of preference similarity and critique compatibility. When a user U critiques c_p the next case recommended will be the one with the highest quality score; see Equation 2. By default, for incremental critiquing $\alpha = 0.5$ to give equal weight to preference similarity and critique compatibility.

$$quality(c_p, c_r, U) = \alpha * compatibility(c_r, U) + (1 - \alpha) * similarity(c_p, c_r) \quad (2)$$

2.1   Group Recommendation Challenges

Perhaps the most critical challenge for a group recommender system is how to develop of a comprehensive account of the evolving preferences of the group with a view to using their combined preferences to influence group recommendations. In this work we adapt the incremental critiquing approach for group recommendation. We will describe how critique histories can be combined to produce a group preference model and how future recommendations can be influenced by their compatibility with this group model. In this way we can bias recommendations towards those cases that are likely to be acceptable to the group as a whole as well as the individual participants; see Section 3 for further details.

Ultimately, for this type of recommendation to work effectively we must ensure that individual users come to appreciate their role within the group. It is natural for many users to want to maximise their own preferences, and so if left unchecked, we might expect users to proceed in ignorance of the evolving group preferences as a whole; this is especially true if users are collaborating remotely, thorough a Web interface for example. Hence one of the key challenges in this work has been to look at effective ways for the recommender system to communicate group preferences to all users, in an effort to help individuals develop a mutual awareness of their friends' preferences [5,6], with a view to encouraging compromises across the group as a whole. If users are not willing to compromise then it is unlikely that they will be satisfied with the recommendations they receive, and the only way that we can encourage compromise is by making sure that users come to appreciate the features that are important to others.

In our work this "mutual awareness" goal [6] has translated into a number of interactivity and interface features that are designed to highlight the opinions of other users and the preferences of the group as a whole. These include interactive features such as: (1) the proactive recommendation of cases (separate from the reactive recommendation in response to user critiques) that exceed a certain threshold of acceptability for the group; and (2) a facility that allows users to set aside certain cases that they feel strongly positive about so that these cases may be promoted to other group members. In addition, there are a range of visual interface elements that help each user to see the opinions and preferences of the others so that preferred cases are annotated accordingly.

3   The Collaborative Advisory Travel System (CATS)

In this section we describe how the CATS group recommender, helps a group of users to plan a skiing vacation. The CATS system described here is implemented as a Web-based client-server system with each user interacting with the system through a standard Web browser interface. In Section 5 we will briefly touch on another implementation of the system that uses a very different type of interaction technology with a view to facilitating a more natural form of collaboration between group of up to four members. In both cases, however, the core interface components remain broadly similar. To begin with we will summarize the key components of the CATS interface before describing its core user modeling and recommendation generation techniques.

Before proceeding it is worth highlighting one important point: we are not proposing the CATS system as the optimal way to offer group recommendations per se, but rather as a framework for experimenting with, and evaluating, different types of feedback, preference communication and recommendation strategies. It is important to bear this in mind when reading the following sections because many design decisions have been made in order to evaluate particular design features and recommendation strategies, rather than on the basis of a strong commitment to one particular design or strategy.

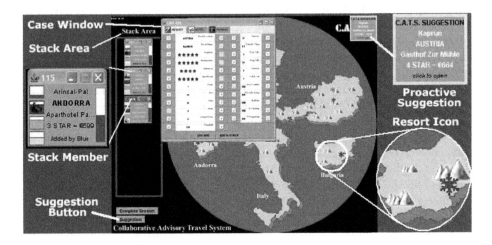

Fig. 1. The main CATS interface

3.1   The CATS Interface

Ultimately a recommender system is a way to translate the preferences of a user (or, in this case, a group of users) into a set of product suggestions. With this in mind, the CATS interface is the primary tool for capturing the preferences of individual users, communicating these preferences to the group as a whole, and then presenting the recommendations that are derived from these preferences to group members. It does this through a combination of interface elements (see Fig. 1) and recommendation techniques. In the remainder of this section we describe each of these elements in detail.

The Case Window. The most familiar element of the CATS interface, the *case window*, presents the user with a case description and some possible critiques. In CATS, each case relates to a ski package, and consists of more than 40 features (attribute-value pairs) describing various aspects of the resort and accommodation. For example, Fig. 2 shows resort information for *case 834*, describing features about the its location, ski runs/lift system, and its appropriateness for different levels of skier. The *hotel* features can be viewed from the *hotel tab* and resort photographs are also available. From this window the user has three basic options—she can *discard* the case; she can add it to the *stack area*, or she can *critique* one of its features to initiate a new recommendation—as follows:

1. Critiquing allows the user to request cases that are like the one displayed but different in terms of at least one feature. For example, our user might request a new recommendation that is *"like the one shown but with more green runs"*. The user can perform such a critique, by clicking on the relevant critique icon beside the feature, see Fig. 2. We will describe how the next recommendation is generated in more detail later.

2. Alternatively our user can decide to add the case to the stack area to indicate that she is interested in this vacation and wants to draw it to the attention of the other group members. The stack area is visible to all group members and is an important way to communicate emerging group preferences to users. We will return to this feature below.

3. Finally, the user can chose to discard the case if she is confident that she would not be at all satisfied with this vacation. Discarding the case means that this particular case will not be used as a suggestion to any of the users for the remainder of the recommendation session.

Fig. 2. The *case window* presents the user with a complete description of a case and is used as the starting point for collecting critiquing-based feedback from each user

The Map Window: The map window displays a graphical representation of the resorts covered by the cases in the case-base and is the initial screen users see when they begin a session. This window provides a way for users to browse through the various resort cases. Each resort is marked by a *mountain range* icon and by selecting a resort icon the user will receive a summary of the resort and a list of its cases. The user can view any case and interact with it in the normal way as described above. The map window also displays important information about the activity of group members and how well particular resorts match evolving group preferences. For instance, if a user is currently accessing a case from a particular resort, then the resort is annotated with a colour-coded *snowflake* icon; in Fig. 1 we see that a user in our group is currently accessing one of the Bulgarian resorts, for example. In addition, the size of the resort icon reflects the compatibility rating of its most group-compatible case; that is, the resort case that satisfies the most critiques contained in the group model appears larger. Thus, the map window is a vital tool for communicating the focus of group activity and preferences.

The Stack Area: Every so often a user will come across a case that they really like or that they imagine may be of interest to other group members. The user can communicate this to the group by adding the case to the stack area where it can be evaluated by other users. In a sense, this allows an individual user to play the role of *recommender* and the stack area serves as a user-based recommendation list. When a case is added to the stack it becomes a *stack member* and is displayed in summary form as shown in Fig. 1. In addition, each stack member is annotated on its left-hand side with a set of colour-coded *compatibility barometers*, each reflecting how compatible the case in question is with respect to the critiques contained in each user's individual model. For example, the stack member highlighted in Fig. 1 for 3-star accommodation in Andorra is annotated to indicate that it is very compatible with the preferences of the blue and green users, but not so compatible with the yellow user, and only marginally compatible with the red user; note that we also indicate which user added the case to the stack with the *thumbs-up* icon overlayed on their compatibility barometer. An overall group-level compatibility barometer is displayed to the right of the stack member to indicate overall compatibility with the group preference model; in this case we see that the stack member is about 50% compatible with the overall group model. These compatibility barometers are dynamically updated during the session to reflect current compatibility levels and provide another important source of preference feedback for the users. At any time any user can view and critique a stack member that has been added by someone else, but currently only the user who originally added the case can remove it from the stack. Finally, the stack area is important when it comes to delivering the final recommendation to the group at the end of the session since this recommendation will be drawn from the current stack members.

Proactive Suggestions: So far we have described two types of recommendations: those that are generated in response to user critiques and, those that are generated by the users themselves as they add cases to the stack for others to evaluate. There is a third type of recommendation: *proactive recommendation*. The CATS system is constantly comparing the group preference model to the remaining cases available for consideration; that is, cases that have not been previously viewed or discarded by any of the group members. Occasionally, one or more of these cases exceeds a certain critical *compatibility threshold* with respect to the group preference model and when this happens the most compatible case is proactively recommended by CATS to all users. For example, one such case (for a 4-star hotel in Austria) has been proactively recommended in Fig. 1 and will appear on the map window for all users where they can interact with it in the usual way. Once again this provides users with direct feedback on the evolving group preference model in an attempt to draw their collective attention towards cases that appear to maximally satisfy their preferences; we will revisit this form of recommendation in the following sections.

Completing the Session: At any time a user can request CATS to recommend another case by selecting the *Suggestion* button; we will discuss the precise mechanism for this form of recommendation below. Also, a user can terminate their session at any time by selecting the *Session Complete* button and once all users have completed their sessions the system reverts with final ranking of the stack cases according to their compatibility with the group preference model and returns the most compatible case.

3.2   Modeling Group and User Preferences

The maintenance of preference models is critical to the operation of the CATS recommender system. As discussed earlier these models are critique-based: a preference model is made up of a set of unit critiques provided by a user. CATS maintains two types of preference model. An *individual model* is maintained for each user and is equivalent to the preference models maintained in the standard form of incremental critiquing as proposed by [12]. Thus each user U is associated with an individual preference model, IM^U, that is made up of the critiques that they have submitted (see Equation 3) with conflicting and redundant critiques removed as summarized in Section 2.

$$IM^U = \{I_1, ..., I_n\} \qquad (3)$$

In addition, a group preference model, $GM(U_1, ..., U_k)$, is also maintained by combining the individual user models and associating each unit critique with the user who contributed it as shown in Equation 4 such that G_i^U refers to the ith critique in the preference model for user U.

$$GM^{U_1, ..., U_k} = \{I_1^{U_1}, ..., I_n^{U_1}, ..., I_1^{U_k}, ..., I_m^{U_k}\} \qquad (4)$$

During recommendation it will sometimes be necessary (as we will see in the next section) to leverage part of the group preference model, usually the model less some individual user's critiques. Thus we will often refer to the *partial group model* or the *members model*, MM^U, to be the group model without the critiques of user U as shown in Equation 5.

$$MM^U = GM^{U_1, ..., U_k} - IM^U \qquad (5)$$

This means that the group preference model is based on the preference models for individual users after they have been processed to remove inconsistent or redundant critiques. We have chosen not to repeat this processing over the group preference model and therefore it is possible, indeed likely, that the group preference model will contain conflicting preferences, for example. Of course, during recommendation these inconsistencies will have to be minimised by preferring cases that are maximally compatible with the overall group model.

3.3   Recommendation Generation

In Section 3.1 we highlighted how CATS is capable of making a number of different types of recommendations:

1. *Critiquing-based recommendations* are generated when a user critiques a case through the case window.
2. *User-requested suggestions* are generated when the user selects the *suggestion* button.
3. *Proactive recommendations* are generated when CATS locates a case that exceeds a preset compatibility threshold with the group preference model.
4. A *final recommendation* is drawn from the stack when all of the users complete their session.

Each of these recommendations is generated differently by combining individual and group preference models in different ways. This was largely an attempt to experiment with a variety of combination strategies as opposed to making a strong commitment to these specialized strategies. They may work well in practice but we are not proposing them as *best* practice.

Critiquing-Based Recommendations. This is arguably the most important source of recommendations in CATS and involves a two-step procedure. As in the standard model of critiquing [2], the first step is to temporarily filter-out cases that are not compatible with the current critique. This leads to a set of *recommendation candidates*. The standard approach to critiquing ranks these candidates according to their similarity to the critiqued case (c_p), whereas incremental critiquing uses a quality metric that combines similarity to the critiqued case and compatibility with past critiques (IM^U). Our group recommender is based on the latter but adapted to include the preferences of the other group members (MM^U) in the quality metric, as well as the preferences of the user applying the critique, to select a recommendation according to Equation 6.

$$c_{rec} = argmax_{c_r}(quality(c_p, c_r, IM^U, MM^U)) \qquad (6)$$

Thus, we compute a new compatibility score, for a recommendation candidate c_r, as shown in Equation 7 and combine this with similarity to the preference case (c_p) as in Equation 8. The β parameter controls how much emphasis is placed on individual versus group compatibility while α controls the emphasis that is placed on compatibility versus preference similarity; by default we set both parameters to 0.5. In this way, the case that is recommended after critiquing c_p will be chosen because it is compatible with the critique, similar to c_p, and compatible with both the user's own past critiques and the critiques of other users. Thus we are implicitly treating past critiques as *soft constraints* for future recommendation cycles [15]. It is not essential for recommendation candidates to satisfy all of the previous critiques (individual or group), but the more they satisfy, the better they are regarded as recommendation candidates. As an aside, the binary features of a case are only considered during the similarity calculation when a user has shown a preference for that feature.

$$GCompatibility(c_r, IM^U, MM^U) = \beta * compatibility(c_r, IM^U) + \\ (1 - \beta) * compatibility(c_r, MM^U) \quad (7)$$

$$quality(c_p, c_r, IM^U, MM^U) = \alpha * GCompatibility(c_r, IM^U, MM^U) + \\ (1 - \alpha) * similarity(c_p, c_r) \quad (8)$$

User-Requested Suggestions. This type of recommendation is generated in the same way as critiquing-based recommendation in the sense that the next highest quality case is chosen. Thus the suggestion button allows the user to move down through the list of ranked cases after a critique has been chosen.

Proactive Recommendations. The idea behind this type of recommendation is as a mechanism to bring certain cases to the attention of all users if they satisfy an unusually high proportion of the group preferences. As mentioned earlier, these cases are drawn from the set of cases that have not yet been critiqued by any user or discarded and a given case is selected according to the following rule:

$$argmax_c(compatibility(c, GM^U)) \text{ iff } compatibility(c, GM^U) > 0.65 \quad (9)$$

The use of the compatibility threshold is important. It limits the frequency of proactive recommendations; after all it is unwise to interrupt users too often during the course of their session. More importantly perhaps is that the threshold also ensures that, when cases are proactively suggested, they are likely to be acceptable to all users.

Final Recommendation. Once all of the users have completed their session the CATS system recommends the case in the stack area that has the highest compatibility with the group preference model; see Equation 10. The stack area is provided for users to share their favourite cases during the session and at the end of the session the final recommendation is the one that satisfies the greatest proportion of group preferences.

$$c_{final} = argmax_{c_{stack}}(compatibility(c_{stack}, GM^{U_1, \ldots, U_n})) \quad (10)$$

4   Experimental Analysis

With CATS as very much a "work in progress" our core evaluation objective was to understand how users would respond in a group recommendation setting to the particular combination of feedback, communication, and recommendation that CATS provided. Given this objective it was clear that there would be little value in performing an off-line or artificial user study. Instead we carried out a small-scale live-user trial, the results of which are summarized in this section.

4.1 Trial Setup

As mentioned in the previous section the CATS system operates over a comprehensive case base of European skiing holidays consisting of 5700 cases, each made up of 43 different features related to the *resort* (25 features such as *country, transfer time, lift system, etc.*) and the accommodation (18 features such as *accommodation rating, price, ski room facilities, restaurant facilities, etc.*). The trialists were 3 groups of 4 computer science graduate students with varying degrees of interest and experience when it came to skiing.[2] Prior to the start of the trial we gathered some preliminary information about the preferences of each user, in order to judge the quality of the cases ultimately recommended by the group recommender. By comparing the cases selected by the members of a given group we were also able to understand the extent to which each group agreed/disagreed on various case features.

Each group of users was provided with a short demonstration of the operation of the system paying particular attention to the core features such as critiquing, the stack area and its compatibility indicators, the map and its activity icons, and proactive recommendations. They were instructed to behave as if they were really trying to plan and book a skiing holiday to go on together. As such, they were reminded that some compromises would likely be required from each user. In each trial user interactions and recommender activity was recorded. At the end of each session the users were asked to complete an extensive questionnaire covering issues such as: their satisfaction with the final case; their evaluation of the recommendations provided; the ease-of-use of the interface etc.

4.2 Behaviour Results

Overall the average session length, measured in terms of the total number of cases each user interacted with, across all three trials was just under 18. Almost two thirds (63%) of case accesses were the result of users critiquing cases (see Fig. 3(a)) with the remainder of accesses arising out of the users interacting directly with the map (14%), accessing a stack member (12%), and opening one of the occasional proactive suggestions that are made by CATS (8%). These results are encouraging in that they demonstrate that users at least made regular use of CATS' secondary case access mechanisms, although the 'suggest' button was rarely used (2% of accesses). In particular, we see that users are frequently attracted to the stack area which plays a vital role in communicating strong group preferences and also provides the source of cases for the final group recommendation. The trial data indicates that the average user places between 3 and 4

---

[2] All trials were conducted in the computer laboratories at the School of Computer Science & Informatics at University College Dublin, Ireland.

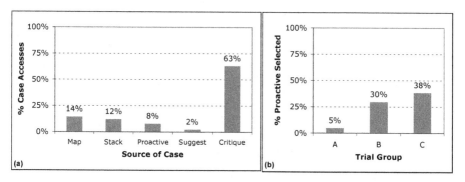

Fig. 3. (a) Source of case accesses; (b) Proactive recommendations selected

cases on the stack which corresponds to about 18% of the cases that they view. In other words, users are presented with cases that satisfy their needs about 18% of the time with other users accessing these cases about 14% of the time; thus there is a strong correlation between stack additions and selections.

It is also worth commenting on the quality of the proactive recommendations. These recommendations contributed only 8% of the cases to the average user session, but this is more a reflection of the rarity of these suggestions than their quality. Remember that by definition these suggestions are only made once a case has been found that satisfies 65% of the group's current preferences. However, when this condition is met and a proactive suggestion is made, we see that users respond to these suggestions approximately 26% of the time on average; see Fig. 3(b). Groups B and C respond positively to these suggestions 30% and 38% of the time respectively, with group A users responding only 4% of the time; in fact 3 of the 4 group A users completely ignored the proactive suggestions and on the basis of the post-trial questionnaire this seems to have been due a lack of awareness of the feature, as opposed to any negative comment on recommendation quality. Finally, it is worth supporting the above statistics with information from the post-trial questionnaire regarding the perceived quality of the recommendation received during group sessions. In particular, only 2 of the 12 users indicated they were not happy with the general quality of recommendations.

4.3   Group Compromise and User Satisfaction

Ultimately the success of any group recommender system will depend critically on its ability to identify cases that achieve reasonable compromise between the potentially competing requirements of different users. At the start of the trial we asked users to pick an example case that they would be interested in booking. They were also asked to highlight up to 5 features from this case that viewed as especially attractive. We refer to these features as the user's *initial preferences*; remember these features were not explicitly used during the trial, although it seems reasonable to assume that users may have started by looking for cases that satisfied these. During the course of the trial each user's critiques contributed to another set of preferences, which we will call their *trial preferences*.

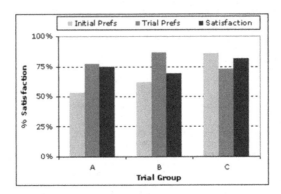

Fig. 4. The level of critique compatibility and user satisfaction with the case that is ultimately recommended to the group

We can use these preferences to evaluate the quality of the final case recommended to each group of users by measuring how many of these preferences are satisfied or contradicted by the the final case. The results (see Fig. 4) show that the final case satisfied just over 66% of the initial preferences across the 3 groups and almost 79% of the trial preferences. During the post-trial questionnaire users we asked how happy they were with the final case by rating it on a scale of 1 ("not happy at all") to 5 ("really happy"). On average the 12 users rated the final case as a 4 ("fairly happy") with 10 out of the 12 users providing a rating of at least 3 ("happy"); we have expressed these results as a percentage value in Fig. 4. These results suggest that the CATS system effectively translates the often competing preferences of a group of individual users into a recommendation that broadly satisfies the whole group.

5   Concluding Remarks

While traditional research has focused on making recommendations to the individual, many recommendation scenarios involve groups of inter-related users. Here the most critical challenge for a group recommender system is how to develop of a comprehensive account of the evolving preferences of the group with a view to using their combined preferences to influence group recommendations.

In this paper we have described an approach to asynchronous, cooperative group recommendation that: (1) uses a variety of interface cues to communicate group, as well as individual, preferences and activity, and (2) constructs a reliable group-preference model by combing critique histories in order to generate recommendations on a proactive and reactive basis. Preliminary evaluation results suggest that our approach to group recommendation effectively generates recommendations that satisfy group needs. Furthermore users responded positively to the various interface elements and recommendation strategies implemented by the CATS prototype group recommendation system.

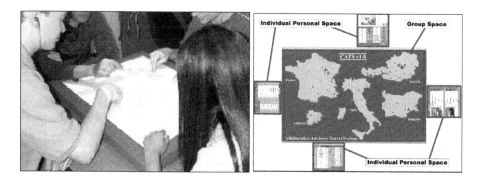

Fig. 5. Illustrating the CATS interaction with the DiamondTouch

Our future work will focus on exploring a range of different strategies for combining individual preferences with a view to generating improved recommendations. This will of course include extended live-user evaluations. In addition is it worth highlighting recent work [7] that we have carried out that looks at alternative interfacing modalities for this group recommendation approach. While in this paper we have concentrated on our Web-base interface, CATS has also been implemented Mitsubishi DiamondTouch interactive tabletop. The DiamondTouch (see Fig. 5) consists of a touch sensitive tabletop display and supports the interaction of multiple simultaneous users. Its 'coffee table' form factor is ideal for supporting collaborative tasks. The CATS system interface has been adapted to offer users personal interaction spaces and a shared group space as shown in Fig. 5.

References

1. R. Burke. Interactive Critiquing for Catalog Navigation in E-Commerce. *Artificial Intelligence Review*, 18(3-4):245–267, 2002.
2. R. Burke, K. Hammond, and B.C. Young. The FindMe Approach to Assisted Browsing. *Journal of IEEE Expert*, 12(4):32–40, 1997.
3. J. Delgado and R. Davidson. Knowledge Bases and User Profiling in Travel and Hospitality Recommender Systems. In *Proceedings of the ENTER 2002 Conference*, pages 1–16. Springer Verlag, 2002. Innsbruck, Austria.
4. B. Faltings, P. Pu, M. Torrens, and P. Viappiani. Design Example-Critiquing Interaction. In *Proceedings of the International Conference on Intelligent User Interface(IUI-2004)*, pages 22–29. ACM Press, 2004. Funchal, Madeira, Portugal.
5. A. Jameson. More than the sum of its members: Challenges for group recommender systems. In *Proceedings of the International Working Conference on Advanced Visual Interfaces*, pages 48–54, Gallipoli, Italy, 2004.
6. A. Jameson, S. Baldes, and T. Kleinbauer. Enhancing mutual awareness in group recommender systems. In B. Mobasher and S.S. Anand, editors, *Proceedings of the IJCAI 2003 Workshop on Intelligent Techniques for Web Personalization*. AAAI, Menlo Park, CA, 2003.

7. K. McCarthy, M. Salamó, L. Coyle, L. McGinty, and B. Smyth & P. Nixon. CATS: A Synchronous Approach to Collaborative Group Recommendation. In *Proceedings of the FLAIRS 2006 Conference*, pages 1–16. Springer Verlag, 2006. Florida, USA.

8. L. McGinty and B. Smyth. Tweaking Critiquing. In *Proceedings of the Workshop on Personalization and Web Techniques at the International Joint Conference on Artificial Intelligence*. Morgan-Kaufmann, 2003.

9. Q.N. Nguyen, F. Ricci, and D. Cavada. User Preferences Initialization and Integration in Critique-Based Mobile Recommender Systems. In *Proceedings of Artificial Intelligence in Mobile Systems 2004, in conjunction with UbiComp 2004*, pages 71–78. Iniversitat des Saarlandes Press., 2004. Nottingham, UK.

10. P. Pu and B. Faltings. Decision Tradeoff Using Example Critiquing and Constraint Programming. *Special Issue on User-Interaction in Constraint Satisfaction. CONSTRAINTS: an International Journal.*, 9(4), 2004.

11. J. Reilly, K. McCarthy, L. McGinty, and B. Smyth. Dynamic Critiquing. In P.A. Gonzalez Calero and P. Funk, editors, *Proceedings of the European Conference on Case-Based Reasoning (ECCBR-04)*, pages 763–777. Springer, 2004. Spain.

12. J. Reilly, K. McCarthy, L. McGinty, and B. Smyth. Incremental Critiquing. In M. Bramer, F. Coenen, and T. Allen, editors, *Research and Development in Intelligent Systems XXI. Proceedings of AI-2004*, pages 101–114. Springer, 2004. UK.

13. F. Ricci, K. Woeber, and A. Zins. Recommendations by Collaborative Browsing. In *Proceedings of the 12th International Conference on Information and Communication Technologies in Travel & Tourism (ENTER 2005)*, pages 172–182. Springer Verlag, 2005. Innsbruck, Austria.

14. S. Sherin and H. Lieberman. Intelligent Profiling by Example. In *Proceedings of the International Conference on Intelligent User Interfaces (IUI 2001)*, pages 145–152. ACM Press, 2001. Santa Fe, NM,US.

15. M. Stolze. Soft Navigation in Electronic Product Catalogs. *International Journal on Digital Libraries*, 3(1):60–66, 2000.

Contextualised Ambient Intelligence Through Case-Based Reasoning

Anders Kofod-Petersen and Agnar Aamodt

Department of Computer and Information Science,
Norwegian University of Science and Technology,
7491 Trondheim, Norway
{anderpe, agnar}@idi.ntnu.no
http://www.idi.ntnu.no

Abstract. Ambient Intelligence is a research area that has gained a lot of attention in recent years. One of the most important issues for ambient intelligent systems is to perceive the environment and assess occurring situations, thus allowing systems to behave intelligently. As the ambient intelligence area has been largely technology driven, the abilities of systems to understand their surroundings have largely been ignored. This work demonstrates the first steps towards an ambient intelligent system, which is able to appreciate the environment and reason about occurring situations. This situation awareness is achieved through knowledge intensive case-based reasoning.

1 Background and Motivation

Mark Weiser coined the term ubiquitous computing to describe the way computers would "... weave themselves into the fabric of everyday life until they are indistinguishable from it" [1, p. 1]. Since then this area of research has gained considerable impetus, as well as many names. Although there are subtle differences, the term pervasive computing is also frequently used to refer to these kind systems. Methods that aim to give this type of highly distributed systems intelligent properties, are often referred to by the label *ambient intelligence*.

The visions and scenarios described within the wide area of pervasive computing have grown from the original and simple, describing augmented artefacts assisting users in their day to day living, into full grown systems that assume responsibility from the user, and display a large degree of common sense reasoning as well as elaborate problem-solving. Examples of these ambient intelligent systems can be seen in the way Fred receives help from the omnipresent system Aura [2, p. 3], or in the way Maria is helped through her business trip [3, p. 4].

To display these kinds of complicated behaviours, an entity must be able to interpret the environment in which it is situated, i.e. possess a sufficient level of *context-awareness*. So far, most of the work on context-aware computing have been largely technology driven, leading to, for example, a large number of ways to identify the location of individuals or artefacts using various kinds of position detectors. Hence, many of the pervasive computing systems around today

T.R. Roth-Berghofer et al. (Eds.): ECCBR 2006, LNAI 4106, pp. 211–225, 2006.

are rarely more than stimuli-response systems, which regard context merely as location, as earlier pointed out in [4]. Over the last few years, however, there has been a growing interest, within pervasive computing in general and ambient intelligence in particular, in issues surrounding the modelling and representation of context in a wider sense [5,6].

A broader view on context, and an active role for context in situation assessment, calls for an explicit model of context that is an integral part of the overall knowledge model. Our hypothesis is that case-based reasoning (CBR), supported by a rich model of general domain knowledge, is a promising way to achieve ambient intelligent systems. The very nature of CBR lends itself easily to reasoning about context and situation assessment. The use of context to guide the case-based reasoning process has been demonstrated in [7], where *relevance* and *focus* are regarded as the essential properties of context. The goal of an agent becomes part of the context used to focus the attention, and thereby to identify the knowledge needed to execute the actions associated with the goal.

Zimmermann demonstrates the feasibility of CBR for identifying the correct combination of parameters required to display situation understanding [8]. He proposes to initially cluster similar cases, and consecutively generalise cases prior to the reasoning process. The work presents an instance-based approach to the underlying problem of all context aware pervasive computing applications; namely to identify similarities between contextual parameters, using a general reasoning mechanism.

In the work by Ma et al. [9] case-based reasoning is used to adapt the behaviour of smart homes to users' preferences. A multi-user smart home can, even with a very limited number of connected devices, present itself with a large number of interdependent processes. CBR is used to identify these interdependencies, due to its ability to reason in ill-defined and poorly structured domains. Cases are represented as frames, where the findings are: the user, the environment, the time, and the values from active devices. When new cases are instantiated, the similarities between the new and existing cases are calculated using 1- or k-nearest neighbour.

Kwon and Sadeh [10] applies CBR to a multi-agent environment in order to estimate a best purchase in comparative shopping. In comparative shopping consumers who wish to purchase a product can compare prices, warranties, and other aspects between suppliers of a product. Correspondingly, suppliers can tailor their products to specific customers or customer groups. Since it is difficult to estimate the buyers' exact utility function, a negotiation agent employs case-based reasoning to match a current state to possible outcomes. The findings of a case are the product in question, the price, the level of quality, together with contextual information consisting of location, weather and calendar info.

The above methods have clearly shown the potential of CBR for ambient intelligence. However, they are all characterised by a k-NN, or knowledge-poor, approach to similarity assessment, and no explicit or elaborated model of context exists. Hence, reasoning about context and the role of context in situation assessment, at different levels of abstraction, is problematic.

We are studying how knowledge intensive CBR can be a suitable method for achieving situation awareness. To obtain this, careful considerations must be made when defining the knowledge. We argue that our particular approach to CBR, in which cases are submerged within a general knowledge model, allows for elaborate reasoning about context beyond what is obtainable in other approaches. In our work we lean on results from within the pervasive computing community, combined with insight from Activity Theory [11]. Our approach also draws on results from work on cooperative CBR [12] as well as ontology modelling of CBR processes [13].

The work described here started within the EU project called AmbieSense, aimed at providing focused guidance and targeted information pushing for people on travel [14,15]. Rather than travelers, our current example application is for support of health workers cooperating in patient diagnosis and treatment. Individual PDA-based assistants will provide information based on their assessment of the current situation, which also includes being able to agree on a common interpretation of the current situation. Our results so far do not demonstrate a final solution for achieving ambient intelligence; rather they show how the combination of our particular knowledge model, the description of cases, and the system architecture, is a promising approach to achieving ambient intelligence.

The paper is structured as follows: First, a short overview of the system architecture is given. Secondly, the knowledge model used to describe the environment, situations and cases is explained. Thirdly, the case model is described. This is followed by an example in our domain of situation assessment within a hospital ward. A conclusion and pointers to future work ends the paper.

2   System Architecture

The system is designed as a three layered architecture (see Figure 1). Each of the three layers has its own specific responsibility. This three layered division is comparable to the three levels required to achieve *situation awareness* proposed

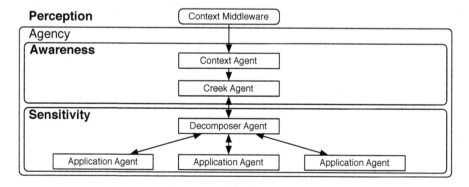

Fig. 1. Structured System Architecture

by Endsley et al. [16, p. 14], where there is a *perception* layer, corresponding to our Perception layer; a *comprehension* layer, comparable to our Awareness layer; and a *projection* layer, which roughly corresponds to our Sensitivity layer.

The *Context Middleware* layer in Figure 1 provides a generic context management infrastructure that collects and maintains data from the environment, in a coherent and structured way [15]. This layer communicates with the agency through the *Context Agent*, which receives notifications of changes in the context. This notification is translated into the ontology used inside the agency, and relayed to the *CREEK Agent*.

The CREEK agent is the agent responsible for assessing the context and classifying the situation. This agent uses and extends the CREEK CBR system [17]. Once a classification of the situation has been achieved, the goal associated with the specific type of situation, and the context describing the part of the world available for satisfying the goal are transmitted to the *Decomposer Agent*.

The decomposer agent is responsible for selecting the correct sequence of tasks for execution, as well as drafting the correct *Application Agents* necessary. The latter is done by querying a matchmaker agent for agents having the correct post- and pre-conditions for execution of the sub-tasks. UPML [18] is used to describe the components of plans, corresponding to task sequences. Once a suitable collection of agents has been gathered, the sequence of actions is executed and the result is returned to the CREEK agent.

Application agents are autonomous agents that are capable of executing one or more actions. An action may range from the mundane to services requiring complicated reasoning. Each application agent corresponds to an artefact in the specific domain, which offers one or more services.

A more thorough description of the overall architecture can be found in [14,19], the overall agency is described in detail in [20], and the decomposition of tasks and execution of actions are described in [21].

3   Context as Lenses

Context is used in two distinct ways, as illustrated in Figure 2. It is initially used as a focus lens on the part of the world that can be perceived. In this sense, context is the part of the world that is available to the awareness part for identifying the situation. The part of the world depicted as Perceived in the *Perception* part of Figure 2, and as Situations Context in the *Awareness* part, are the parameters CREEK uses in the retrieval part of the CBR cycle. These parameters can be the location where the situation is occurring, the people present, and the time of day. A more elaborate example is given in Section 7.

The other use of context is for solving the particular problem associated with a situation. Once CREEK has identified the situation, the corresponding goal is also identified. For example, when a *pre-ward round* situation has been identified, it is also known that the goal of the situation is to *evaluate treatment* of the patient. Along with the goal, is a sequence of tasks that will achieve the goal. The different artefacts or persons that can contribute by executing the actions that

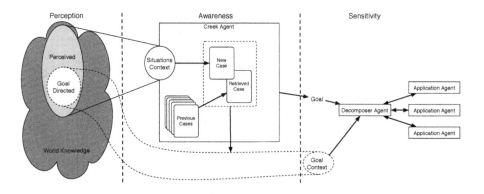

Fig. 2. Functional System Architecture

correspond to the tasks in the sequence, may differ depending on the context. Thus, the context, as depicted in the *Sensitivity* part of Figure 2, is viewed as a focus lens on the world given by the goal in question. This represent a further constraint on the information available. If, for instance, the initial task in a sequence is to acquire the name of the patient, and this information can be obtained from several sources, it is important to know what information sources are available in the given situation. In this example the name of the patient might be obtained from the patient chart, the nurse, or the electronic patient record; however, if context contains only the patient chart and the nurse, then the electronic patient record can't appear in the sequence of actions.

4   Knowledge Model

The CREEK system follows a knowledge intensive approach to Case-based Reasoning. There is a strong coupling between the case specific knowledge and the general domain knowledge, as the cases share the same multi-relational semantic network as the domain knowledge [22]. This integration of specific and general knowledge requires a strong focus on knowledge acquisition and modelling [23].

Our knowledge model has been constructed partly top-down and partly bottom-up. As Figure 3 illustrates, all knowledge types are integrated into a single semantic network. Each node is a concept described in a frame structure. The three parts generic to any CREEK application are the top-level ontology (called ISOPOD), the domain-specific model of general and factual knowledge, and the case base. The two subparts developed for the ambient intelligence system are the Basic Context Model and the Activity Theory model.

As one of the most important aspects of situations are the activities occurring, Activity Theory was used to capture these aspects of the world and integrate them into the knowledge model. This part is concerned with notions such as roles, artefacts, and communities, and their relationships. For a thorough discussion on the use of Activity Theory for context modelling see [24,25].

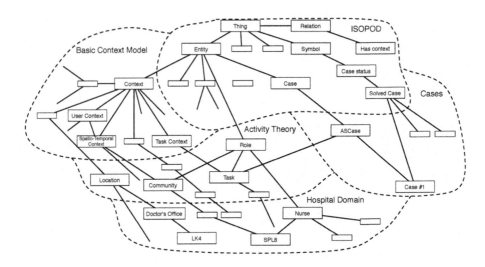

Fig. 3. The Integrated Knowledge Model

This Basic Context Model is structured around a taxonomy inherited from the context-aware pervasive computing tradition [26]. The model is divided into five main aspects describing a situation: *i*) Personal Context, describing information about the user of the system; *ii*) Task Context, which is concerned with describing the task performed by the user, and other entities to achieve the goal; *iii*) Social Context, detailing the roles of the user; *iv*) Spatio-Temporal Context, which holds information on location, time and the community shared by the user; *v*) Environmental Context, describing the entities present, such as other persons and artefacts.

The model was populated through observations done at the St. Olav Hospital in Trondheim through the summer of 2005. Some of the data gathered were used in a bottom-up approach to enrich the model. The enrichment included: the different locations at the wards; the roles that employees, patients, and visitors assumes; the classes of persons encountered in the wards; artefacts and services they offer and consume.

5   Case Model

A case has two main parts: the *findings* of the situation, which consists of the perceived context; and the *solution*, which consists of the goal to be achieved and the corresponding task to be accomplished. Note that, in this application, to interpret a situation involves identifying its goal, i.e. to determine what is to be done in the situation. A situation is a meeting between health personnel, and these meetings always have a purpose, or a goal, which may be to agree on a diagnosis for a patient, to decide whether a particular examination should be made, or evaluate what treatment to give. An example of a situation instantiated, but not yet classified, in CREEK, is shown in Figure 4.

```
(UnsolvedCase001 (
  has-case-status: Unsolved
  has-context: Context:UserContextSituation001 (
    context-of: Person:User:AL7
    has-part: SpatioTemporalContext:SpatioTemporalContextSituation001 (
      has-part: Location:DoctorsOffice:LK4
      has-part: Time:0915
      has-part: Community:Situation001Community (
        has-part: Role:PatientResponsibleRole
        has-part: Role:GroupLeaderRole))
    has-part: SocialContext:SocialContextSituation001 (
      has-part: Role:PatientResponsibleRole)
    has-part: EnvironmentalContext:EnvironmetalContextSituation001 (
      has-part: Person:HealthWorker:Nurse:SPL8
      is-present: Artefact:PatientList
      is-present: Artefact:PatientChart
      is-present: Artefact:PAS)
  has-goal:
  has-task: ))
```

Fig. 4. Unknown situation

This case describes a situation where several things are known. All of the findings of the case are described as the *has-context* part. It describes a context for *AL7*, who is the user of this system. It is known that the situation is occurring in *LK4*. If we look at the knowledge model, we will discover that LK4 is a specific *Doctor's office*, which again is a type of location. The situation is occurring at 09:10, and the *community* consists of two roles, the *PatientResponsibleRole* and the *GroupLeaderRole*, which are played by AL7 (the user) and SLP8 (a nurse).

The example above is taken from our data set (see Section 6), thus all possible parameters are not included. A case is a specific view on the knowledge contained in the system. This is a key feature of the system. The Awareness layer (see Figure 1) constrains the part of the knowledge base that the Sensitivity layer should rely on to solve the problem in particular situations.

Once a situation has been classified, or in other words, a matching case has been retrieved, the solution is acquired from the matching case. This solution contains the goal of the situation and the main task which achieves this goal.

The exact sequences of tasks used to accomplish the goals are not stored directly in the cases. They are stored and maintained in the decomposer agent. Since the nature of a goal does not vary significantly within situations of the same type, it was not deemed necessary to adapt the task sequence itself as part of the reasoning cycle. Rather, we assume that instead of the tasks varying, the artefacts and communities required to execute the actions vary across situations of the same type. Thus, as a rule, the task sequence does not need to be redefined for each situation, rather a generic sequence can be populated with willing and able agents for each situation (for more on the execution of plans see: [21]). Along with the goal and the main task, the artefacts and communities available can now be transmitted as context to the decomposer agent, i.e. the second use of context, as described in Section 3.

6 Data Set

The applicability of the overall architecture has been demonstrated in [15], where a test of a stimuli-response type behaviour was conducted. For various reasons this test did not include the full case-based reasoning cycle. One of the most important reasons was a lack of suitable situation data. The lack of data has now been remedied, as a large amount of data on situations has been gathered.

Table 1. Context parameter describing situations

Location	The room where the situation occurred
User	The user of the system
Role	The role of the user
Present	Other persons present
Role	The role of each of the persons present
Patient ID	The ID of the patient in question
Time	The time of day

The data was collected through a period of one month at the St. Olav Hospital in Trondheim. A medical student followed several employees and recorded the situations that occurred throughout the days. Two wards were studied: the cardiology and gastroenterology ward. The data set contains 197 situations for cardiology and 163 for gastroenterology. Approximately two-thirds of the situations from cardiology concerning the consultant physician (OL9) were transferred into the system, and classified, manually. This set of situations gives the system a set of initial cases to reason about. The last third are used to test if the system can classify the situations, identify the sequence of actions, and execute them.

The data gathered was structured into two main types: the type that is primarily related to comprehending the situation (Table 1), and the type primarily related to achieving the goal and constructing the task structure (Table 2).

Table 2. Context parameters for problem-solving

Source	Information sources and targets
I/O	The direction of the information flow
Information	Type of information

The data describing the context of situations (Table 1) include some information which could easily be sensed though available hardware. These are the location where the situation is occurring; the user whose perspective we are adopting; other persons present; and the time of the situation occurring. It is debatable if the role of the persons present, and the ID of the patient in question (whom is not necessarily present), are readily available for automatic sensing. However, we have regarded this issue as problems of engineering, and not critical for testing the applicability of our method.

The context parameters describing the situation are modelled as part of the case-base, as exemplified in Figure 4. These data are primarily used during the *retrieve* phase of the cycle. However, being part of the general knowledge model, they are also available to the decomposer agent for problem-solving.

The problem-solving data (Table 2) is used for two purposes. They are first used to populate the knowledge model with information on the artefacts (sources) present and the services (information) they offer and consumes. Secondly, they are used in the decomposer agent for constructing action sequences. Initially they are constructed and generalised manually.

Currently, the data for the consultant physician OL9 at the cardiology ward has been incorporated into the system. The 197 situations, including all the physicians, are distributed as described in Table 3

Table 3. Distribution of observed data for cardiology

Situation	AL7	AL9	AL14	OL9	Sum
Pre-pre-ward-round	5				5
Pre-ward-round	7	22	11	26	66
Ward-round	7	21	11	26	65
Examination		8	2	9	19
Post-work		8	9	13	30
Pre-discharge			2	4	6
Heart meeting		1		1	2
Discharge meeting				4	4

Eight different types of situations have been identified in the data set. Four different physicians were observed, where three were assistant physicians (AL7, AL9, AL14) and one was a consultant physician (OL9). Beside these, several nurses, patients, and relatives are present in different situations.

7   Example

To clarify how this system is used to identify situations and solve the problem associated with a situation, this example will demonstrate the chain of events occurring when an unknown situation is presented to the system. First, we exemplify a stored case, then we show how the case is utilized after having been retrieved by CREEK's two-step similarity assessment method [22].

As described in Section 6, a sub-set of the observed situations are used to populate the knowledge model with initial cases. In this example a case describing a pre-ward round situation is used. Figure 5 describes its findings and solution.

A pre-ward round is a type of meeting that occurs every morning between the physician on duty and the nurse in charge. In this meeting the patients on the ward are discussed and the treatment is evaluated to define the further treatment for the day in question. These types of meetings typically include all the patients in the ward. However, we have chosen to divide the meeting

```
(ASSolvedCase01 (
  has-case-status: Solved
  has-context: Context:UserContextAL7Previsit001 (
    context-of: Person:User:AL7
    has-part: SpatioTemporalContext:SpatioTemporalContextAL7Previsit001 (
      has-part: Location:DoctorsOffice:LK4
      has-part: Time:0910
      has-part: Community:PrevisitCommunityAL7001 (
        has-part: Role:PatientResponsibleRole
        has-part: Role:GroupLeaderRole))
    has-part: SocialContext:SocialContextAL7Previsit001 (
      has-part: Role:PatientResponsibleRole)
    has-part: EnvironmentalContext:EnvironmentalContextPrevisit001 (
      has-part: Person:HealthWorker:Nurse:SPL8
      is-present:Artefact:PatientList
      is-present:Artefact:PatientChart
      is-present:Artefact:ElectronicPatientRecord)
  has-goal: EvaluateTreatment
  has-task: EvaluateTreatmentTask))
```

Fig. 5. Pre-ward-round initial case

into distinct situations, each containing the evaluation of one patient. In other words, the system perceives the evaluation of each patient as one situation, so each meeting may consist of several situations.

Along with these findings, the goal of the situation is stored in the case. In the example of the pre-ward round, the goal of *evaluate treatment* has been manually identified in the observed data. From the examination of the observed data, we have also identified the typical sequence of tasks corresponding to the evaluation of the patient's treatment:

1. Acquire name of patient
2. Acquire changes in patient's conditions since yesterday
3. Examine, and possible change, medication scheme
4. Acquire any new results from tests
5. Note changes in treatment

Initially, the identification of the patient in question is acquired. Based on this identification, any changes in the patient's condition is mapped out. Now, the medication scheme and any new test results are examined. Finally, any changes in the treatment, such as changes in medication or scheduling of new tests, are noted. Once the case based has been populated with a set of cases, a new and unknown situation – shown in Figure 4 – is presented. The case in Figure 5 is returned as the best match.

Comparing these two situations, it is evident that they have a strong resemblance. The only significant difference is the time when the situations occur. Hence, it is no big surprise that CREEK infers that these two situations are highly similar; actually it concludes that the matching strength is 88% (see Figure 6, in which the explanation structure supporting the match is also shown).

CREEK has now determined that the most likely candidate for identifying the situation is a pre-ward round. Knowing this, CREEK can also tell the sensitivity part of the system that the goal of this situation is to *evaluate treatment*. However, as noted earlier, even though the sequence of tasks are the same, the

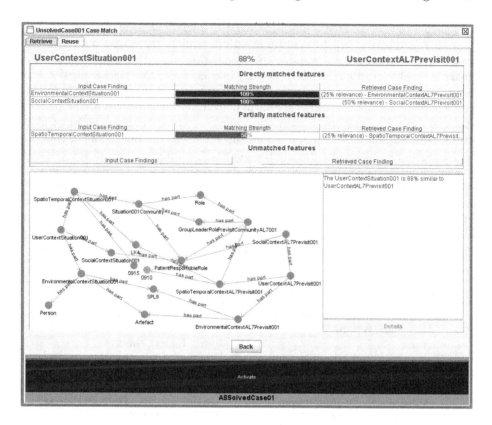

Fig. 6. Matching Cases

exact actions required can differ from the original situation. So to achieve the best possible execution of the sequence of actions, the context in which the tasks occur is transmitted along with the goal. In this case, this context is the observed parameters, as well as the artefacts present in this situation. In the case of this newly classified pre-ward round situation, these artefacts are: the list of patients, able to supply the name of the patient; the patient chart, able to supply the medication plan, the PAS system (a patient administration system), and of course the nurse.

This context guides the task decomposition process in the sensitivity part. In this example there is no reason to enquire the electronic patient record for any results of a blood sample, as only the patient chart and the nurse are present. The decomposer can now select the plan for evaluating the patient's treatment, and draft the application agents that are able and willing to execute the actions corresponding to the tasks in the plan.

In this example the task was to initially acquire the name of the patient in question. Looking at the artefacts present, as described in the knowledge model, the only one capable of supplying this information is the *patient list*, so the corresponding agent is drafted. Following the identification of the patient, any changes in the patient's condition must be identified. Only two entities are capable of supplying this type of information, namely the *nurse* or the *patient chart*. The next step is to examine the medication plan. Here, only the *patient chart* is capable of supplying the necessary information. Once the medication has been examined, the next step is to acquire any new test results. Looking at the context there are two artefacts capable of delivering this information: the *patient chart* and the *PAS* system. Finally, any changes to the patient's treatment plan must be noted, and both the *nurse* and the *PAS* system are capable of this.

The left side of Figure 7 depicts the observed chain of actions in the original known situation. The right side depicts the possible artefacts that can supply the information required in this context. When we compare the two different instances of a pre-ward round situation, the main difference is that we do not know who will actually supply any changes in the patient's condition (point 2 in Fig. 7), and the fact that any new results can only be acquired from the patient chart, and not the electronic patient record (point 4 in Fig. 7).

1. Acquire name of patient Patient list	1. Acquire name of patient Patient list
2. Acquire changes in patient's conditions since yesterday Nurse	2. Acquire changes in patient's conditions since yesterday Nurse, Patient chart,
3. Examine, and possibly change, medication scheme Patient chart	3. Examine, and possibly change, medication scheme Patient chart
4. Acquire any new results from tests Patient chart, electronic patient record	4. Acquire any new results from tests Patient chart, PAS
5. Note changes in treatment Nurse	5. Note changes in treatment Nurse, PAS

Fig. 7. Two sequences of actions

This combination of the goal received from the CREEK agent, along with the context, allows the decomposer agent to generate the sequence of actions depicted on the right side of Figure 7, as well as executing it using the agents drafted. To verify that the identification of the situations, as well as the generated tasks, are sensible we can look at the observed data, to figure out what really happened. In the observed data the situation that we just classified had the following sequence of actions:

1. The *patient list* supplied the patient's name
2. The *nurse* informs about the changes to the patient's condition
3. The *patient chart* supplied the medication scheme, which was changed
4. The *nurse* informs about the result of a blood sample
5. The *PAS* system was informed about result of this pre-ward round

When we compare this real world sequence with the possible sequence proposed by the decomposer, we can observe that it easily encompasses the one that actually happened.

8   Conclusion and Future Work

This paper outlines how a knowledge intensive Case-Based Reasoning system can be constructed to facilitate ambient intelligence. It has been shown how a combination of generic concepts for reasoning and modelling, a context taxonomy, and elements from Activity Theory, can influence the way a knowledge model for situation awareness can be implemented. A case model has exemplified how cases should be structured with context as the problem defining part, and the general goal and task as the solution to the implicit problem in situations.

There are clear indications that ambient intelligent systems can benefit from the socio-technical analysis made by applying Activity Theory. This is beneficial when defining the knowledge model, as well as when constructing guidelines for observations.

It has been demonstrated how all the above parts can be combined into a coherent architecture, which allows for the perception of the environment, reasoning about context to identify situations, and problem-solving based on this understanding.

Based on the data we collected for the cardiology ward, we are currently populating the case based with more cases; as well as constructing the generic task sequences corresponding to the eight different situations discovered. The next step is to do an initial verification of the system's integrity, and test CREEK's ability to correctly identify new cases; before executing a full fledge simulation of the system.

Some issues have intentionally been left out of this description. Most importantly the question of how CREEK may learn when it is run on-line. Several approaches have been discussed, such as simply asking the user, or trying to perceive the user's behaviour based on the recommendations given by the system. Each has its benefits and drawbacks. Asking the user directly is likely to be the technical easiest approach, however, this can very easily be quite intrusive for the user. Attempting to perceive the behaviour by looking at the situations perceived is most likely the most complicated, but also the least intrusive. However, recent studies on conversational CBR in our group show promising results for optimising user querying strategies [27] by combining observation and conversation.

Acknowledgements

Part of this work was carried out in the AmbieSense project, which was supported by the EU commission (IST-2001-34244). We would like to thank several of our colleagues for the cooperation on the observations used; in particular Inger Dybdahl Sørby for facilitating the data collection at St. Olav Hospital and Siri Haug Strømmen for collecting the data.

References

1. Weiser, M.: The computer for the 21st century. Scientific American (1991) 94–104
2. Satyanarayanan, M.: Pervasive computing: Vision and challenges. IEEE Personal Communications **8** (2001) 10–17
3. Ducatel, K., Bogdanowicz, M., Scapolo, F., Leijten, J., Burgelman, J.C.: Scenarios for Ambient Intelligence in 2010. Technical report, IST Advisory Group (2001)
4. Schmidt, A., Beigl, M., Gellersen, H.W.: There is more to Context than Location. Computers & Graphics Journal **23** (1999) 893–902
5. Liu, H., Maes, P.: What would they think? In: Proceedings of the 2004 International Conference on Intelligent User Interfaces, ACM Press (2004) 38–45
6. Brézillon, P.: Task-realization models in contextual graphs. In Dey, A.K., Kokinov, B., Leake, D., Turner, R., eds.: Modeling and Using Context: 5th International and Interdisciplinary Conference CONTEXT 2005. Volume 3554 of Lecture Notes in Computer Science., Springer Verlag (2005) 55–68
7. Öztürk, P., Aamodt, A.: A context model for knowledge-intensive case-based reasoning. International Journal of Human Computer Studies **48** (1998) 331–355
8. Zimmermann, A.: Context-awareness in user modelling: Requirements analysis for a case-based reasoning application. In Ashley, K.D., Bridge, D.G., eds.: ICCBR 2003, Case-Based Reasoning Research and Development. Number 2689 in Lecture Notes in Artificial Intelligence, Springer Verlag (2003) 718–732
9. Ma, T., Kim, Y.D., Ma, Q., Tang, M., Zhou, W.: Context-aware implementation based on cbr for smart home. In: Wireless And Mobile Computing, Networking And Communications, 2005. (WiMob'2005), IEEE, IEEE Computer Society (2005) 112–115
10. Kwon, O.B., Sadeh, N.: Applying case-based reasoning and multi-agent intelligent system to context-aware comparative shopping. Decision Support Systems **37** (2004) 199–213
11. Vygotsky, L.S.: Mind in Society. Harvard University Press, Cambridge, MA (1978)
12. Plaza, E., Arcos, J.L., Martín, F.J.: Cooperative case-based reasoning. In Weiss, G., ed.: Lecture Notes in Artificial Intelligence. Volume 1221 of Lecture Notes in Computer Science. Springer Verlag (1997) 180–201
13. Díaz-Agudo, B., González-Calero, P.A.: An architecture for knowledge intensive cbr systems. In Blanzieri, E., Portinale, L., eds.: Advances in Case-Based Reasoning: 5th European Workshop, EWCBR 2000. Volume 1898 of Lecture Notes in Computer Science., Springer Verlag (2000) 37–48
14. Myrhaug, H.I., Whitehead, N., Göker, A., Fægri, T.E., Lech, T.C.: AmbieSense – A System and Reference Architecture for Personalised Context-Sensitive Information Services for Mobile Users. In Markopoulos, P., Eggen, B., Aarts, E., Crowley, J.L., eds.: Ambient Intelligence: Second European Symposium on Ambient Intelligence, EUSAI 2004. Volume 3295 of Lecture Notes in Computer Science., Springer Verlag (2004) 327–338
15. Kofod-Petersen, A., Mikalsen, M.: Context: Representation and Reasoning – Representing and Reasoning about Context in a Mobile Environment. Revue d'Intelligence Artificielle **19** (2005) 479–498
16. Endsley, M.R., Bolté, B., Jones, D.G.: Designing for Situation Awareness: An Approach to User-Centered Design. Taylor & Francis (2003)
17. Aamodt, A.: A knowledge-intensive, integrated approach to problem solving and sustained learning. PhD thesis, University of Trondheim, Norwegian Institute of Technology, Department of Computer Science (1991) University Microfilms PUB 92-08460.

18. Fensel, D., Motta, E., Benjamins, V.R., Crubezy, M., Decker, S., Gaspari, M., Groenboom, R., Grosso, W., van Harmelen, F., Musen, M., Plaza, E., Schreiber, G., Studer, R., Wielinga, B.: The unified problem-solving method development language upml. Knowledge and Information Systems **5** (2003)

19. Kofod-Petersen, A., Mikalsen, M.: An Architecture Supporting implementation of Context-Aware Services. In Floréen, P., Lindén, G., Niklander, T., Raatikainen, K., eds.: Workshop on Context Awareness for Proactive Systems (CAPS 2005), Helsinki, Finland, HIIT Publications (2005) 31–42

20. Lech, T.C., Wienhofen, L.W.M.: AmbieAgents: A Scalable Infrastructure for Mobile and Context-Aware Information Services. In: AAMAS '05: Proceedings of the fourth international joint conference on Autonomous agents and multiagent systems, New York, NY, USA, ACM Press (2005) 625–631

21. Gundersen, O.E., Kofod-Petersen, A.: Multiagent Based Problem-solving in a Mobile Environment. In Coward, E., ed.: Norsk Informatikkonferance 2005, NIK 2005, Institutt for Informatikk, Universitetet i Bergen (2005) 7–18

22. Aamodt, A.: Knowledge-intensive case-based reasoning in creek. In Funk, P., Calero, P.A.G., eds.: Advances in case-based reasoning, 7th European Conference, ECCBR 2004, Proceedings. (2004) 1–15

23. Aamodt, A.: Modeling the knowledge contents of CBR systems. In: Proceedings of the Workshop Program at the Fourth International Conference on Case-Based Reasoning, Vancouver. Naval Research Laboratory Technical Note AIC-01-003 (2001) 32–37

24. Kofod-Petersen, A., Cassens, J.: Activity Theory and Context-Awareness. In Schulza, S., Leake, D.B., Roth-Berghofer, T.R., eds.: Proceedings of the IJCAI-05 Workshop on Modeling and Retrieval of Context (MRC 2005). Volume 146., CEUR Workshop Proceedings (2005) 1–12

25. Cassens, J., Kofod-Petersen, A.: Using activity theory to model context awareness: a qualitative case study. In: Proceedings of the 19th International Florida Artificial Intelligence Research Society Conference, Florida, USA, AAAI Press (2006)

26. Göker, A., Myrhaug, H.I.: User context and personalisation. In: Workshop proceedings for the 6th European Conference on Case Based Reasoning. (2002)

27. Gu, M., Aamodt, A.: Dialog learning in conversational cbr. In: Proceedings of the 19th International Florida Artificial Intelligence Research Society Conference, Florida, USA, AAAI Press (2006)

Improving Annotation in the Semantic Web and Case Authoring in Textual CBR*

Juan A. Recio-García, Marco A. Gómez-Martín,
Belén Díaz-Agudo, and Pedro A. González-Calero

Dep. Sistemas Informáticos y Programación
Universidad Complutense de Madrid, Spain
{jareciog, marcoa}@fdi.ucm.es, {belend, pedro}@sip.ucm.es

Abstract. This paper describes our work in textual Case-Based Reasoning within the context of Semantic Web. Semantic Annotation of plain texts is one of the core challenges for building the Semantic Web. We have used different techniques to annotate web pages with domain ontologies to facilitate semantic retrieval over the web. Typical similarity matching techniques borrowed from CBR can be applied to retrieve these annotated pages as cases. We compare different approaches to do such annotation process: manually, automatically based on Information Extraction (IE) rules, and completing the IE rules within the rules that result from the application of Formal Concept Analysis over a set of manually annotated cases. We have made our experiments using the textual CBR extension of the jCOLIBRI framework.

1 Introduction

Textual CBR is an increasingly important CBR sub-discipline. Textual CBR techniques can facilitate rapid construction of CBR systems by reducing or eliminating the task of feature-design in domains in which raw cases consist of free or semi-structured text [2]. There are approaches where retaining a textual case representation may be more effective than engineering an intermediate feature representation. However, reasoning with text cases either requires considerable efforts to elicit meaningful features –beyond single words– or remains restricted to weak text retrieval based on information retrieval (IR) methods [14].

Ideally, we would like to find an inexpensive way to automatically, efficiently, and accurately represent textual documents as structured feature-based case representations. One of the challenges, however, is that current automated methods that manipulate text are not always useful because they are either expensive (based on natural language processing, NLP) or they do not take into account word order and negation (based on statistics) when interpreting textual sources. Information Extraction (IE) methods have been typically used for automatically extracting relevant factual information for the process of transforming texts into structured cases [3]. Other approaches have also been proposed aiming to take

---

* Supported by the Spanish Committee of Education & Science (TIN2005-09382-C02-01).

T.R. Roth-Berghofer et al. (Eds.): ECCBR 2006, LNAI 4106, pp. 226–240, 2006.

the domain knowledge into consideration, as the use of Generative Ontologies proposed in [10] or the use of graphs that conserve and convey the order and structure of the source text [5].

"*The Semantic Web is an extension of the current web in which information is given well-defined meaning, better enabling computers and people to work in cooperation*" [1]. The Semantic Web aims at machine agents that search and filter the knowledge in the web pages based on explicitly specified semantics of contents. A core technology for making the Semantic Web happen is the field of *Semantic Annotation*, which turns human-understandable content into a machine understandable form [11]. There has been many literature about ontology-based semantic annotation of web pages [7], and there are different tools to help in this purpose [17].

In our ongoing work, we are considering the problem of semantic annotation of web pages (Section 2), and relating this problem to the feature elicitation problem in textual CBR (Section 3). The semantic web provides with such a set of plain Web Pages and Ontologies but is looking for automatic techniques to do such a labeling process. We begin with an initial set of web pages that have been manually annotated according to a certain ontology. Manual annotation is a tedious process that lacks from thoroughness and can not guarantee the uniformity of the tagged texts. So, we propose a semi-automatic process based on manually defined IE rules that results in an uniform labeling process but misses the inherent relationships between the labels that are not explicitly in the texts but exist in the domain and are available in the domain ontology. To solve the problem of connecting sparse information (e.g. a telephone number and an address in the contact information) we use Formal Concept Analysis, a data analysis technique that helps to find dependencies between the tags. Section 4 details the whole process. To show the goodness of our method, we have done an experiment annotating a set of web pages representing restaurants. Section 5 describes the experiment in detail while Section 6 compare the set of labels obtained by the different methods. The annotation process is used in a restaurant recommender system that improves the one presented in [16].

2   Annotation for the Semantic Web

Tim Berners-Lee's great dream of the Semantic Web may be visualized as computers that are able to *understand* what data is available on the Web. However, in a foreseeable future, machines will still be too dumb to understand what people have put on the Web. Therefore, to make this dream come true people must provide computer-understandable data. The building blocks have been elaborated in recent writings [8]: we need standardized languages to describe semantic self describing data and programs to exchange and understand semantic data. However, we are missing the key point here: where and how can we obtain semantic data?

The process of providing semantic data is often referred to as *semantic annotation* [11] because it typically involves the annotation of existing plain text, that is only understandable by people, with semantic metadata available in ontologies.

The process of semantic annotation of these texts is a hard process. There have been different approaches, tools and annotation frameworks to help in this annotation process. Most of the current technology is based on human centered annotation. Typically they comprise methods for completely manual annotation and authoring of documents, where documents and contents are described at the same time. The large majority of annotation tools address the problem of single document annotation. This approach presents visualization and scalability problems, because the tagging knowledge in the ontologies can be huge and distributed and cannot be managed as a whole. The manual approach makes using very large ontologies very difficult. This is the main problem in tools like SMORE, OntoMat Annotizer, COHSE, Ontomat and MnM [17].

There are also semi-automatic annotation approaches based on IE that are trained to handle structurally and/or linguistically similar documents. Examples are KIM, Semantic World and Melita. A problem with this approach is that the process requires writing a large number of wrappers for information sources, and that extraction is limited to highly regular and structured pages. Besides, maintenance becomes a complex problem because when pages change their format, it is necessary to re-program the wrapper [12]. The approach is not applicable to irregular pages or free text documents. Also there is a problem of completeness because there is sparse information that is difficult to connect and there is also subjective information that is impossible to capture within IE rules. In the restaurants example, the *atmosphere* of a restaurant is a tag that reflects the general flavor of the place. Although sometimes we find words in the texts reflecting this feature, this is not the typical case, and the tag depends on the general and knowledge intensive impression of the skilled reader.

3   Textual CBR and Annotation

Textual CBR methods described in the CBR literature often focus on transforming textual data in semi-structured cases that can be used by the usual CBR methods. This process is analogous to the annotation of Semantic Web documents because both processes share the same goals: obtain a structure that allows indexing, retrieval and manipulation of the web documents/cases. The Semantic Web applications will use this structured information to let agents to search and manipulate web pages whereas CBR community will use this data for the CBR systems that work with structured cases.

We have continued our work in the jCOLIBRI framework and its Textual CBR extension presented in [16]. As jCOLIBRI is organized as a Task/Method decomposition system we developed several Problem-Solving Methods (PSMs) that process plain text files and obtain structured cases. Our framework divides CBR applications in three main tasks: precycle, cycle and postcycle. The textual extension implements PSMs that can be used in the precycle to transform plain text cases into structured ones. This way, these structured cases will be

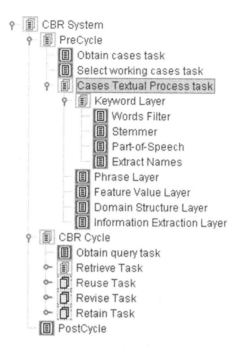

Fig. 1. jCOLIBRI Textual Tasks

manipulated by our library of PSMs that implement the CBR cycle (retrieve, reuse, revise, retain and all their subtasks). Figure 1 shows the task subdivision of the Textual process in jCOLIBRI. Each of these tasks must be solved by a method from our PSMs library.

The implementation of the Textual Extension is based in the theoretic Lenz layers for TCBR [13]. The developed methods described in [16] apply Natural Language Processing algorithms and Regular Expressions to perform the Information Retrieval and Information Extraction processes defined in each layer. After executing these methods jCOLIBRI obtains several syntactic features of the text that can be used as attributes in a structured case.

This paper presents one more step (see Figure 2): the use of ontologies to provide a semantic structure to the extracted features that improve the performance of the CBR cycle. For example, the retrieval task will use the semantic tags to recover semantically similar cases and the reuse phase will use this semantic information to manipulate the cases better. To achieve this goal we have looked at the Semantic Web community because it gives us the two features that we need to enhance the representation of our cases: semantic languages (like OWL) to represent data and repositories of ontologies. This new stage starts with the final structure returned by the set of subtasks shown in Figure 1. This structure contains description features that have been elicited through IE rules. We have slightly adapted the original IE rules to commit a certain domain ontology. With this transformation, the IE process returns pieces of data that correspond

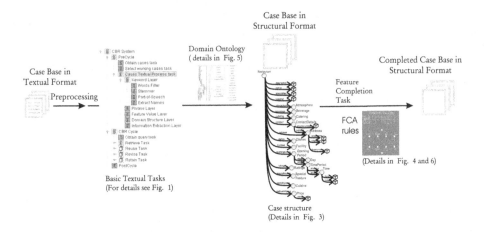

Fig. 2. Case Base refinement process

to concepts of an ontology. But the IE rules by themselves are unable to extract the whole structure of concepts imposed by the ontologies. For example, in the description of a *restaurant* there are *contact details* with *phone numbers* and an *address*; this address will be composed by the description of an *street* that has its *type*, *name* and *door number*. All these names in italics are concepts of the ontology but only some of them (usually the leaves of the grouping structure) can be obtained by the IE rules. In this example, the composite concepts: restaurant, contact details, address and street could not be extracted using simple IE rules.

To solve this problem of connecting sparse information we have applied Formal Concept Analysis (FCA) for completing the representation of the cases. With this new process we can accurately accomplish the transformation of plain text documents into semantically structured cases. These new cases will be based in an ontology that allows us to improve their manipulation in the CBR cycle. Our feature completion method begins with a set of manually tagged texts. We apply FCA as it is describe in Section 4 to extract dependencies between tags. Finally, we use these dependencies to complete the tags inferred by the IE process.

This method is used by our restaurant recommender presented in [16]. This CBR system developed using jCOLIBRI utilizes a case base composed by several texts describing restaurants. Then the IR and IE methods extract the attributes of the cases. The FCA annotation method described in this paper enhances the representation of the cases adding the semantics of the restaurant ontology. This added information improves the indexing, retrieval, and adaptation of the cases obtaining better qualitative results.

4   Annotation Enhancement Based on FCA

Previous sections make clear that both Semantic Web and Textual CBR lack automatic techniques to content annotation (web pages and plain texts).

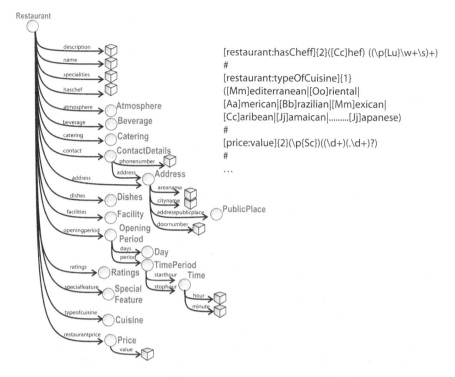

Fig. 3. Case Structure

In this section, we describe our semiautomatic annotation method, useful for both type of contents, and Section 5 and 6 show an experiment and its results.

Our annotation method combines an automatic annotator using Information Extraction rules and Formal Concept Analysis as a mean of obtaining dependencies (association rules) between tags, to provide hints to an expert human in order to facilitate his task of annotating contents.

Formal Concept Analysis is a mathematical approach to data analysis. It was first introduced in [18], and has been extensively used in many areas. See [19] for a gentle introduction.

FCA distinguishes between *formal objects* (or entities) and *formal attributes* (or features). We consider every text (or case) manually tagged as an object, and every possible tag as an attribute. The input of FCA is a binary relation called *formal context* that relates formal objects and formal attributes. The context is usually represented as an incidence table, with rows representing objects and columns representing attributes. Cells contain a cross when the object of that row has the attribute of that column.

In our case, we consider texts (or web pages) as *formal objets*, and tags as *formal attributes*. The formal context created has as many objects as texts, and as many attributes as distinct tags on them. A text (*formal objet*) is related with those tags (*formal attributes*) that appear in the manually annotated text.

Alegria
3510 Sunset Blvd.
Silver Lake
(323) 913-1422
The best food here re-
volves around ...

(a) Plain restaurant
description

```
...
<restaurant:contact>
<contact:ContactDetails>
<contact:phoneNumber
  rdf:datatype="string">
(323) 913-1442
</contact:phoneNumber>
<contact:address>
<address:Address>
<address:areaName
  rdf:datatype="string">
Silver Lake
</address:areaName>
<address:addressPublicPlace>
<address:Boulevard
```

```
rdf:ID="Sunset_Blvd."/>
</address:addressPublicPlace>
<address:cityName
  rdf:datatype="string">
Silver Lake
</address:cityName>
<address:doorNumber
  rdf:datatype="string">
3510
</address:doorNumber>
</address:Address>
</contact:address>
</contact:ContactDetails>
</restaurant:contact>
...
```

(b) Tagged restaurant

	contact	contactDetails	phoneNumber	addressPublicPlace	Boulevard	cityName	doorNumber	price	startHour	TakeAwayFacility	atmospheres	...
Alegria	■	■	■	■	■	■	■	■	■	■		...
Alex	■	■	■	■		■	■	■			■	...
Antique	■	■	■	■		■	■				■	...
Beverly	■	■	■			■						...
⋮	⋮	⋮	⋮	⋮	⋮	⋮	⋮	⋮	⋮	⋮	⋮	⋱

(c) Formal context(tags' prefixes have been omitted for clarity)

Fig. 4. FCA example in restaurant context

Figure 4 shows an excerpt of the plain description of a restaurant, its annotated version and a section of the formal context where that restaurant appears.

With the formal context, FCA is able to build a set of *formal concepts* (or briefly *concepts*). Formally speaking, a concept is a pair (A, B), where A is a set of objects (known as *extent*) and B the set of the common attributes of these objects (*intent*). Formal concepts represent maximal groups of texts (or cases) with shared properties. The concepts of a given context can be ordered using the subconcept–superconcept relation and can be represented as a lattice, like the one showed in Figure 6a.

Though the formal concepts and lattice structure could be useful on their own [6], we use the capacity of mining association rules from it. An association rule is an expression $A \rightarrow B$ where both A and B are sets of attributes. They means that objects having all the attributes in A will probably have those attributes in B.

Association rules are characterized by two parameters: confidence and support. Confidence express the *probability* of that rule to hold, or in other words, the percentage of objects that, having all the attributes in A also have those in B. On the other hand, support indicates the number of objects where the rule is applicable, formally speaking, the number of objects with attributes in A and B divided by the total number of objects.

Rule extraction algorithms based on FCA are able to efficiently extract all the association rules that have a confidence above a threshold. There are several algorithms, though we have used Duquenne–Guigues [9] to extract exact association rules (100% of confidence) and Luxenburguer [15] for non-exact ones.

Our annotation method starts with a set of texts or cases (C_1) that we annotate manually. Now ahead, we call the set of tags (labels) created manually for every text from C_1 as $L_M(C_1)$ (that stands for *l*abels *m*anually extracted) and it is composed of every text and its set of tags. With them, we then construct the formal context as described above (see Figure 4). Next, we apply FCA to extract the association rules between attributes (or tags). The set of rules, $R = fca(L_M(C_1))$, will be used later on the annotation process.

As an example, R can include a rule like

```
address:Address -> restaurant:contact
```

because all texts in C_1 that have `address:Address` tag also have the annotation `restaurant:contact`.

When our method receives a new text T to be annotated, it first uses Information Extraction rules to obtain a first version of its tags, $L_{IE}(T)$. IE is not expected to extract all the tags because of the limitations stated in Section 3. To enhance the results, we apply the rules R to the tags. Association rules will discover those tags that have not been discovered by the IE process, and we get our final set of tags, $L_{FCA} = Apply(R, L_{IE}(T))$.

Following the previous example, if $L_{IE}(T)$ has `address:Address` but lacks `restaurant:contact`, the application of R to the set of tags will discover that this tags has to be added.

To probe the enhancement of our annotation method, we have run it through a set of restaurant texts. We have compared the set of tags of the manual version (L_M) with the tags extracted by the information extraction rules (L_{IE}) and the final set of tags after the application of association rules (L_{FCA}). Section 5 details the experiment, and Section 6 shows the results.

5   Experiment Description

To run an experiment, we need an ontology and a set of web pages (or texts) to be annotated with it. Section 5.1 describes the ontology and Section 5.2 describes the set of texts we have used.

5.1   Ontology

Text annotation is made using a domain ontology. We have reused external ontologies created by the Agentcities Project[1]. These resources where originally

---

[1] http://www.agentcities.org

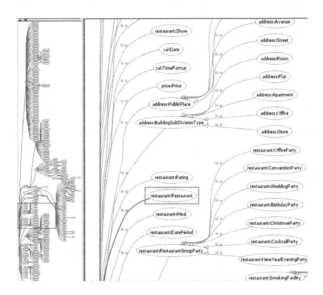

Fig. 5. Restaurant ontology

written in DAML+OIL [4]. We firstly translated them to OWL and then composed them properly.

Our final restaurant ontology combines several sub-ontologies (address, price, calendar and food), and it has more than 1000 concepts, though only a few of them are used in the tagging process. Figure 5 shows a partial view of it. The complete version is available at http://gaia.fdi.ucm.es/ontologies/restaurants.owl.

5.2   Test Case Bases

We originally started from a case base of 268 textual cases with information about restaurants extracted from http://www.laweekly.com/eat-drink. To manage these textual cases we removed all the html tags of the original web pages obtaining only the plain text descriptions about restaurants.

Our goal was to compare our annotation method with the completely manual one. This way we had to manually annotate the texts describing restaurants with the ontology tags. But, this manual method is really complex and time consuming, so finally we did our experiment with a subset of 30 restaurants. On the other hand, the development of the IE rules adapted to the ontology cost about 4 times less that the manual process. So, we realized that if our annotation method had similar results to the manual one it would improve greatly the annotation process. Now ahead we will refer this set of 30 texts as C and its manually tagged version as $L_M(C)$.

We have duplicated the experiment, performing the annotation method and studying its accuracy twice in experiments A and B. In both of them, we split the set of restaurants C in two different sets, $C_{1\{A,B\}}$ and $C_{2\{A,B\}}$, having 20

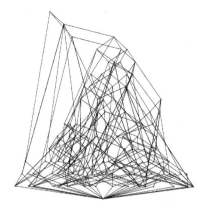

Confidence	Set A	Set B
100%	137	117
95%	138	121
90%	168	166
85%	183	176
80%	192	180

(a) Lattice of training set A   (b) Number of association rules

Fig. 6. FCA results

and 10 restaurants respectively. We have applied FCA to C_1 and applied the association rules extracted together with Information Extraction to C_2. Finally we compare the resulting tags ($L_{FCA}(C_2)$) with the manually annotated versions of C_2 ($L_M(C_2)$).

Both training sets A and B have been selected on purpose to reflect the best and the worst scenario. Set C contains several irregular descriptions that don't contain the same information that the other ones because some data and therefore tags like the address, price or type of food has been skipped. We have chosen sets A and B to contain these descriptions in C_1 or C_2. This way, experiment A contains the irregular descriptions in the set where we apply FCA: C_{1A}. On the other side, experiment B has these irregularities in the set of manually annotated restaurants that are extended with the FCA rules: C_{2B}. With this split we have intended to check how the noisy training examples can affect the accuracy of our method.

We have performed each experiment in four steps:

- The first one consists on the analysis of both training sets, C_{1A} and C_{1B} using FCA. As we have explained previously, association rules extraction has the minimum confidence as a parameter. Instead of just fixing it at 100% (exact association rules) we have used different levels of it to be able to infer how this parameter affects to the final results. Concretely, we extract the set of association rules from 100% (R_{A100} and R_{B100}) to 80% (R_{A80} and R_{B80}) of confidence using a decrement of 5%. Just to show the complexity of the case base, Figure 6 shows the lattice associated with training set A (C_{1A}) that has 135 formal concepts and the number of association rules we got.
- The second step takes the other 10 restaurants in their plain version (without manual annotation) and uses the IE rules to annotate them. These rules are a slight adaptation of the original rules to commit the restaurant ontology

used in [16]. Thereby, most of this task has been done reusing previous work in the jCOLIBRI textual methods.

Using the same notation as in Section 4, we call $L_{IE}(C_{2A})$ the set of tags we get in this step for experiment A and $L_{IE}(C_{2B})$ for B. We will write $L_{IE}(C_2)$ meaning the tags extracted applying IE to the plain texts. As we will see in Section 6, the number of tags in $L_{IE}(C_2)$ was about 40% of the number tags in the manual version, $L_M(C_2)$.

- In the third step, we apply the FCA rules of the first step in the restaurant annotated with IE. Obviously, we use R_{Ax} to enhance $L_{IE}(C_{2A})$ and R_{Bx} against $L_{IE}(C_{2B})$.
- The last step of our experiment compares the number of suggested annotations using FCA rules against the number of tags contained in M_1. Section 6.2 details this comparison.

Though it has only a theoretical value, we have perform an extra experiment, just to compare it with the other ones. It is what we will call in the next section "Complete Set". We have applied the association rules extractor to the complete set of manually annotated restaurants (C). Then we have applied IE to the same set of restaurants and enhance the results with the rules. Briefly speaking, we have applied our annotation method to the same set of cases that we used to train it. This experiment has no meaning in practice but in theory tells us the upper limit of the recall of the method. If our process was perfect this experiment should give us a perfect recall and precision because it checks the results with the same set used to train the system.

6   Experimental Results

We have performed several experiments to compare the accuracy of the Information Extraction and its improvement with the FCA rules. To measure the experiment we have used the two typical quality values:

- *Precision = Correctly extracted tags / total extracted tags*
  Tells if the extracted tags are correct (belong to the training set).
- *Recall = Correctly extracted tags / total correct tags*
  Represents the amount of correct tags that have been extracted.

6.1   Comparison Between L_M and L_{IE}

We have compared the tag set obtained using Information Extraction and the manual annotated set. The IE rules can only extract the tags corresponding with the leaves or final attributes of each restaurant annotation. The reason is that the upper concepts of the annotation tree are abstract concepts that cannot be extracted directly from the text. This problem of connecting sparse information was explained in Section 3.

Thereby, if the representation of a restaurant utilizes about 40 concepts and properties we have created IE rules for 20 of them. With these rules our IE

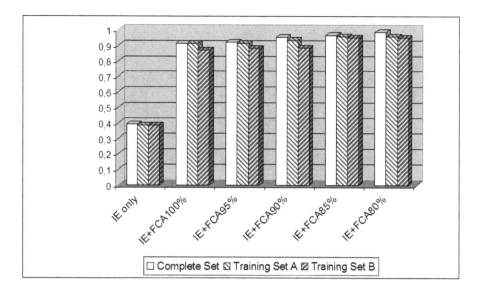

Fig. 7. Recall

process could obtain at most 50% of the total tags used in a restaurant annotation. The experimental results show that we extract 40% (in average) of the total tags. This value is represented in the first group of columns (IE only) of Figure 7 that shows the recall values obtained in our experiment. This value could be interpreted as a low value because other IE systems have a better performance, but in our approach we have not focused on the generation of high-quality IE rules. Our idea consists on developing the IE rules quickly and complete them with the FCA rules, saving time and effort in the whole annotation process. The precision of this comparison (tags extracted by the IE process that are also in the manual annotation) remained above the 98% of the total tags (see first group of columns of Figure 8). The rest of the tags (less than 2%) are the so called "false positives" returned by our IE module.

6.2 Comparison Between L_M and L_{FCA} Rules

Our experiments show that the FCA rules that complete the tags obtained by the IE module increase the recall from 40% to 90%. These results are shown in Figure 7 where recall increases as we decrease the confidence of the rules. Each group of columns in this figure represents the same experiment with different levels of confidence (IE+FCA100%, IE+FCA90%, ...).

On the other hand, as we increase the confidence we obtain a lower precision. Obviously, this is a direct effect of the confidence because it means more general rules that are more prone to generate "false positives". As Figure 8 shows, a confidence below 90% decreases too much the precision so the best configuration for our method in this experiment should use a value above 90%.

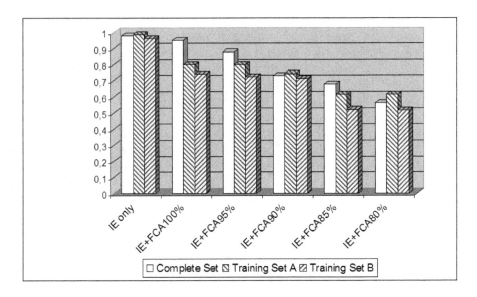

Fig. 8. Precision

In both Figures 7 and 8 the "Complete Set" column shows the value with the complete training set. The "Training Set A" and "Training Set B" columns represent the values when using the C_{1A} and C_{1B} training sets.

As we explained in Section 5.2 the "Complete Set" is a theoretic indication of the accuracy of our method and the results show that it is always higher than the practical experiments. It is important to note that the recall values are really close although the precision has significant differences. This result means that the main advantage of our method is that it retrieves nearly all the tags in the training set. Contrary, the main drawback of our method consists on retrieving too many incorrect tags besides the correct ones. This is specially meaningful in the experiments using confidence below 90%.

Using the division of the training examples in A and B we can obtain one more conclusion. Experiment A contains the noisy examples in the set used to extract the FCA rules C_{1A} whereas experiment B has these examples in the set enhanced with the FCA rules C_{2B}. As the results in A are better than in B we can conclude that the generation of FCA rules hides the errors produced by the irregular descriptions. Experiment B has worse results because its FCA rules are similar to A and C_{2B} has the noisy descriptions that, even enhanced with the rules, return a worse accuracy.

The global conclusion of the experiment is that FCA rules improve greatly the accuracy of the IE process. In theory, our scenario restricts the Information Extraction performance to obtain only 50% of the tags. In practique we obtain a value of 40% using simple and quickly developed IE rules. Completing the tagging with the FCA rules we increase automatically this value to 90% (loosing only 15% of the precision).

The recall increase indicates that our system extracts most of the concepts in the ontology that can not be obtained using Information Extraction. This way the system could automatically propose the concepts of the ontolgy inferred from the text that might be used during the semantical tagging process.

7   Conclusions

The aim of the research conducted is to investigate the relation between the problem of semantic annotation of web pages and the feature elicitation problem in textual CBR. Both processes share the same goals: obtain a structure that allows indexing, retrieval and manipulation of the web documents/cases.

The semantic web provides the CBR community with a very good field of experimentation. It provides with a lot of Web Pages (texts) that can be annotated with the knowledge on Ontologies. The underlying goal is to let machine agents to search and filter the knowledge in the web pages based on explicitly specified semantics of contents. From our point of view, this process can be understood and solved using CBR techniques where the cases are the annotated Web Pages.

We propose an annotation method that is based on three components: a set of IE rules, a domain ontology and a set of rules automatically extracted by the application of FCA to an initial set of manually annotated pages.

In this paper we have compared the accuracy of the annotation process. We have concluded that FCA allows finding dependency rules to solve the problem of connecting sparse information in the texts, and to find additional tags that depends on previously assigned tags. We have shown the results of comparing the set of labels obtained by the different methods. The annotation process is used in a restaurant recommender system that improves the one presented in [16].

References

1. T. Berners-Lee, J. Hendler, and O. Lassila. The semantic web, 2001.
2. L. K. Branting and R. Weber, editors. *Textual Case-Based Reasoning Workshop, at the 6th International Conference on Case-Based Reasoning*, Chicago, IL, USA, August 2005.
3. S. Brüninghaus and K. D. Ashley. The role of information extraction for textual CBR. In *Proceedings of the 4th International Conference on Case-Based Reasoning, ICCBR '01*, pages 74–89. Springer, 2001.
4. D. Connolly, F. v. Harmelen, I. Horrocks, D. L. McGuinness, P. F. Patel-Schneider, and L. A. Stein. *DAML+OIL Reference Description*. World Wide Web Consortium, March 2001.
5. C. Cunningham, R. Weber, J. M. Proctor, C. Fowler, and M. Murphy. Investigating graphs in textual case-based reasoning. In P. Funk and P. A. González-Calero, editors, *Proceedings of Advanced in Case-Based Reasoning, 7th European Conference on Case-Based Reasoning, ECCBR 2004*, volume 3155 of *Lecture Notes in Computer Science*, pages 573–587. Springer, 2004.
6. B. Díaz-Agudo and P. A. González-Calero. Formal Concept Analysis as a Support Technique for CBR. In *Knowledge-Based Systems, 14 (3-4)*, pages 163–172. Elsevier, June 2001.

7. M. Erdmann, A. Maedche, H. P. Schnurr, and S. Staab. From manual to semi-automatic semantic annotation: About ontology-based text annotation tools. *ETAI Journal - Section on Semantic Web (Linköping Electronic Articles in Computer and Information Science)*, 6(2), 2001.

8. Y. Gil, E. Motta, V. R. Benjamins, and M. A. Musen, editors. *The SemanticWeb, 4th International SemanticWeb Conference, ISWC 2005*, volume 3729 of *Lecture Notes in Computer Science*, Galway, Ireland, November 2005. Springer.

9. J.-L. Guigues and V. Duquenne. Familles minimales d'implications informatives resultant d'un tableau de données binaires. *Math. Sci. Humanies 95, 1986, 5-18.*

10. K. M. Gupta. The role of generative ontologies in textual CBR. In *Invited Talk in the Textual CBR Workshop at the 6th International Conference on Case-Based Reasoning, Chicago, IL*, 2005.

11. S. Handschuh and S. Staab, editors. *Annotation for the semantic Web*. IOS Press, 2003.

12. N. Kushmerick, D. Weld, and R. Doorenbos. Wrapper induction for information extraction. In *Fifteenth International Joint Conference on Artificial Intelligence, IJCAI'97*, pages 729–737, Nagoya, Japan, 1997. Morgan Kaufmann.

13. M. Lenz. Defining knowledge layers for textual case-based reasoning. In *Proceedings of the 4th European Workshop on Advances in Case-Based Reasoning, EWCBR-98*, pages 298–309. Springer, 1998.

14. M. Lenz. Knowledge sources for textual CBR applications. In M. Lenz and K. Ashley, editors, *AAAI-98 Workshop on Textual Case-Based Reasoning*, pages 24–29, Menlo Park, CA, 1998. AAAI Press.

15. M. Luxenburguer. Implications partielles dans un contexte. *Mathématiques, Informatique et Sciences Humaines*, 113(29):35–55, 1991.

16. J. A. Recio, B. Díaz-Agudo, M. A. Gómez-Martín, and N. Wiratunga. Extending jCOLIBRI for textual CBR. In H. Muñoz-Avila and F. Ricci, editors, *Proceedings of the 6th International Conference on Case-Based Reasoning, ICCBR 2005*, volume 3620 of *Lecture Notes in Artificial Intelligence, subseries of LNCS*, pages 421–435, Chicago, IL, US, August 2005. Springer.

17. Semantic web annotation and authoring.
http://annotation.semanticweb.org/tools/.

18. R. Wille. *Restructuring Lattice Theory: an approach based on hierarchies of concepts*. Ordered Sets, 1982.

19. K. E. Wolff. A first course in formal concept analysis. How to understand line diagrams. In F. Faulbaum, editor, *SoftStat, Advanced in Statistical Software*, pages 429–438. Gustav Fischer Verlag, 1993.

Unsupervised Case Memory Organization: Analysing Computational Time and Soft Computing Capabilities

A. Fornells, E. Golobardes, D. Vernet, and G. Corral

Research Group in Intelligent Systems
Enginyeria i Arquitectura La Salle, Ramon Llull University
Quatre Camins 2, 08022 Barcelona, Spain
{afornells, elisabet, dave, guiomar}@salle.url.edu
http://www.salle.url.edu/GRSI

Abstract. There are problems that present a huge volume of information or/and complex data as imprecision and approximated knowledge. Consequently, a Case-Based Reasoning system requires two main characteristics. The first one consists of offering a good computational time without reducing the accuracy rate of the system, specially when the response time is critical. On the other hand, the system needs soft computing capabilities in order to construct CBR systems more tractable, robust and tolerant to noise. The goal of this paper is centred on achieving a compromise between computational time and complex data management by focusing on the case memory organization (or clustering) through unsupervised techniques. In this sense, we have adapted two approaches: 1) neural networks (Kohonen Maps); and 2) inductive learning (X-means). The results presented in this work are based on datasets acquired from medical and telematics domains, and also from UCI repository.

Keywords: Data Intensive, Maintenance and management for CBR, Case Memory, Soft Case-Based Reasoning, Clustering, Kohonen Maps.

1 Introduction

There are different problems that present a huge volume of information or very complex data. Therefore, they may present imprecision, uncertainty, partial truth, and approximated knowledge. Case-Based Reasoning (CBR) [1] tries to solve new problems using others previously solved. Nevertheless, CBR systems often have to face two main problems when they have to manage a huge dataset. The first problem is a reduction of system accuracy when the cases are composed by a large set of features. In this case, the system may not be able to detect the most relevant features. The second problem is an increase in CPU time because the retrieval phase depends of the number of features and cases. In this sense, the organization of the case memory may be crucial in order to reduce the computational cost of the retrieval phase (i.e. minimize the CPU time), and, if it is possible, improve system accuracy. On the other hand, soft computing techniques (e.g. neural networks) can be used for building CBR systems that

T.R. Roth-Berghofer et al. (Eds.): ECCBR 2006, LNAI 4106, pp. 241–255, 2006.

can exploit a tolerance for imprecision, uncertainty, approximate reasoning, and partial truth in order to achieving more tractable, robustness, low solution cost and closer to the human making process [7].

Nowadays, there are lots of real domains with these characteristics. Our work in some of these areas has been the motivation of this paper. The first domain is related to applications on medical field. In fact, we mainly work on breast cancer diagnosis using mammographic images. A mammographic image is processed in order to identify the microcalcifications (μCa) that appear. After characterizing the μCa through a set of features, we diagnose each image using machine learning techniques. Previous studies applying machine learning techniques have found that these techniques improve the accuracy rate (in terms of correct classifications) but decrease the reliability rate (in terms of robustness and stability) compared to human experts [17]. The second domain, in which we are working, is related to security applications on computer networks. Comprehensive network security analysis must coordinate diverse sources of information to support large scale visualization and intelligent response [10]. Security applications require of some intelligence to recognize malicious data, unauthorized traffic, identify intrusion data patterns, learn from previous decisions and also provide a proactive security policy implementation [8,32].

We propose a data intensive approach based on a soft computing technique such as neural networks [4], Kohonen Maps [28], in order to organise the CBR case memory. The main goals of this approach are to manage complex data such as the explained domains, and improve the computational time spent on retrieving the information. Furthermore, these goals have to be defined to avoid decreasing the accuracy rate. We previously organized the CBR case memory using an inductive approach based on the adaptation of the X-means algorithm [38] in order to reduce the computational time [45]. For this reason, we compare both approaches to measure the benefit of our new proposal. The experiments presented in this work are based on datasets acquired from medical and telematics domains, and also from UCI repository [5].

The paper is organized as follows. Section 2 surveys related work using clustering techniques to organize the CBR case memory. Section 3 resumes the main ideas of Kohonen Maps and the adaptation of the X-means algorithm in order to explain later their roles in the case memory. Section 4 explains the approaches proposed to organize the case memory based on inductive learning and neural networks. Section 5 summarizes the experiments and a comparative study of the two approaches. Finally, we present the conclusions and further work.

2   Related Work

This section summarises related work found in the literature on the subject of clustering methods and regarding different approaches used to organise the case memory in Case-Based Reasoning systems.

First of all, most of the clustering methods are described in Hartigan's book [22]. There exist a large number of clustering algorithms. Thus, the choice of a clustering algorithm depends on the type of available data and on the particular purpose and application [19]. In general, clustering methods can be classified in the following approaches.

The first approach is the *partitioning method*. It consists of clustering training data into K clusters where $K < M$ and M is the number of objects in the data set. One of the most representative examples of this approach is the K-means algorithm [21]. There are special variations to improve some aspects of the algorithm. One variation is the K-medoids algorithm or PAM (Partition Around Medoids) [26], whose objective is to reduce the sensibility of the K-means algorithm when some extremely large values that distort data distribution are found. A variation of the K-medoids algorithm is the CLARA algorithm (Clustering LARge Applications) [27]. In this case, the algorithm extends the capabilities of the last algorithm in order to perform results when large data sets are explored. The automatic definition of the number of clusters was proposed in the X-means [38] algorithm. Finally, another widely used algorithm is the Self Organizing Maps (SOM) or Kohonen Maps [28], which is based on neural network theory [4].

The second approach is called *hierarchical method*, which works by grouping data objects into a tree of clusters. The hierarchical decomposition can be formed as a bottom-up or top-down procedure.

Another considered approach is based on the *density-based method*. The main objective of this method is to discover clusters with an arbitrary shape. This typically regards clusters as dense regions of objects in the data space that are separated by regions of low density (representing noise). The most popular algorithms in this category are the following: DBSCAN (Density-Based Spatial Clustering of Applications with Noise) [14], OPTICS (Ordering Points to Identify Clustering Structure) [3] and DENCLUE (DENsity-based CLUstEring) [24].

Grid-based method uses a multiresolution grid data structure that divides the space into a finite number of cells that form a grid structure on which all clustering operations are performed. This method has a constant processing time as an advantage, independently of the number of data objects. In this group we can identify algorithms such as CLIQUE (Clustering High-Dimensional Space) [2], STING (STatistical INformation Grid) [47], and WaveCluster [42] (an algorithm that clusters using the wavelet transformation).

Finally, *model-based method* uses mathematical and probability models. This method can be focused on two ways: firstly, as a statistical approach, and secondly, as a neural network approach. Some examples of these methods are AU-TOCLASS [6] and COBWEB [15].

Hanson and Bauer stated that clustering of objects or events without a context, goal or information concerning the function of the derived clusters (as in [33]) is not likely to be useful for real-world problems [20]. Therefore, they proposed a different point of view and approach real-world problems by means of the WITT algorithm [20].

Regarding to the case memory organization in CBR systems, the most important approaches are the following: RISE [13] treats each instance as a rule that can be generalised. EACH [40] introduced the Nested Generalized Exemplars (NGE) theory, in which hyperrectangles are used to replace one or more instances, thus reducing the original training set. And finally, a method that avoids building sophisticated structures around a case memory or complex operations is presented by Yang and Wu [49]. Their method partitions cases into clusters where the cases in the same cluster are more similar than cases in other clusters. Clusters can be converted to new smaller case-bases. However, not all the approaches are focused on the organisation of the case memory in order to improve the case memory and, at the same time, the computational time.

3   Clustering Methods

Case-Based Reasoning (CBR) systems solve problems by reusing the solutions to similar problems stored as cases in a case memory [39] (also known as case-base). However, these systems are sensitive to the cases present in the case memory and often their good accuracy rate depends on the stored significant cases. Also, CBR systems have problems when a huge number of cases exist in the case memory, specially when the response time is critical (e.g. real time systems). Therefore, a compromise between computational time and soft computing capabilities will be pursued. Clustering the case memory tries to obtain different clusters of cases. Each cluster represents a generic case which corresponds to a region of the domain. Thus, the retrieval phase [1] only has to find a similar cluster to the new case. Consequently, the system improves its computational time. The key is: *Which is the better way to cluster the case memory?*

Previously to explain the integration of our new approach based on Kohonen [28], and the other approach based on the adaptation of X-Means [38] used to make the evaluation, we will make a short review of both algorithms. Although CBR [1,29,31] is used in a wide variety of fields and applications (e.g. diagnosis, planning, language understanding), we focus on CBR as an automatic classifier.

3.1   Kohonen Maps Algorithm

Kohonen Maps or Self-Organizing Maps (SOM) [28] are one of the major unsupervised learning paradigms in the family of artificial neural networks. The most important features of a SOM neural network are the following: (1) It preserves the original topology; (2) It works well even though the original space has a high number of dimensions; (3) It incorporates the selection feature approach; (4) Although one class has few examples they are not lost; (5) It provides an easy way to show data; (6) It is organized in an autonomous way to be adjusted better to data. On the other hand, the drawbacks of this technique are that it is influenced by the order of the training samples, and it is not trivial to define how many clusters are needed. They have successfully been used in a variety of clustering applications such as systems for Content-Based Image Retrieval (CBIR) [30] or documents retrieval [25]. Also, they have been used in a large variety of domains such as medical [46], chemical [44] or financial [11] data.

The SOM network is composed by two layers. First, there is the input layer, which is represented by a set of n-dimensional inputs that define the example to evaluate. The other is the output layer, which is a m-dimensional (although it is usually bidimensional) grid where neurons are placed. Each one of these neurons represents a cluster or model with certain properties. Also, each neuron is connected with all the n-inputs.

Figure 1 details the SOM training process algorithm. The models, which are represented by a set of properties using a n-dimensional vector, are iteratively fitted in order to create clusters with different properties. This process is achieved by means of updating the models using the training samples. For each training sample, a model is selected using a similarity measure shown in the Equation 1. Then, the model vector selected and the neighbours models are updated to better fit to this example by means of the Equation 2. This updating process is performed in two steps: (1) First, it affects the great majority of the models with a high influence value; (2) Second, it only affects the selected model and its immediately neighbours with a low influence. The training ends when the lowest error value is achieved, or the configured iteration ends.

---

input : *CM* is the case memory; I_s is the new example; *Total* is the number of iterations; T_1 is the number of iterations of the first phase; E_{min} is the lower error accepted; *Map* is the Kohonen map of size $K \times K$; $\alpha(0)$ - $\alpha(F)$ and $\nu(0)$ - $\nu(F)$ are the initial and final values of the learning and neighbour factors respectively

output : *Map* is the built Kohonen Map

1 **Function** *trainingSOM* **is**
2   The $N_{i,j}$ models of *Map* are randomly initialized between $[0..1]$
3   **for** $(t=0;\ ((t < Total)\&(E_{min} < error));\ t++)$ **do**
4   error=0
5   **forall** $I_s \in CM$ **do**
6   Let N_{best} be the most similar model to I_s using the Eq. 1
7   All the neighbour models of N_{best} are updated using the Eq. 2
8        $error=error+ \|\overline{I_s} - \overline{N_{best}}\|$
9      $error=error/\ K \times K$
10      $\alpha(t)$ and $\nu(t)$ are updated by the Eq. 3, if $t < T_1$
11   **return** *Map*

Fig. 1. Cluster creation through the SOM algorithm

$$\forall i,j : 1 \leq i,j \leq K : \|\overline{I_s} - \overline{N_{best}}\| \leq \|\overline{I_s} - \overline{N_{i,j}}\| \tag{1}$$

$$\overline{N_{i,j}}(t+1) = \overline{N_{i,j}}(t) + \alpha(t) \cdot (\overline{I_s} - \overline{N_{i,j}}(t)) \tag{2}$$

$$X(t+1) = X(0) + (X(F) - X(0)) \cdot \frac{t}{T_1} \tag{3}$$

3.2 SX-Means Algorithm

The adaptation of the X-means algorithm [38] in order to cluster the CBR case memory was proposed in [45]. This variation finds spherical data groups through moving the location of the centre of these spheres, called centroids. The centroid is the mean value for all the objects in the cluster. It also uses splitting to determine the right number of centroids and, consequently, the number of clusters. It restricts the search of the best cluster distribution by setting a lower and an upper threshold of the number of clusters. The algorithm starts allocating the centroids with K-means [21] using the lower value of K. It continues adding centroids until the upper threshold of K is reached. At each step only one centroid is inserted by splitting the original in two; then, a sub-cluster from the original cluster is detected. Thus, centroids relocation is achieved regarding to the same elements of the original cluster. The centroid set that achieves the best score is selected, based on a BIC (Bayesian Information Criterion) function. This is a recursive process that finishes when K reaches the upper bound and the local sub-K-means has run for all centroids. Figure 2 resumes the main steps of the X-means algorithm. We will call this adaptation using spheres as SX-means (Sphere X-means) algorithm.

K-means and X-means algorithms have been applied in a variety of clustering applications including systems for 3D objects modeling [12], computer architecture research [18], network security [8] or text summarization [35].

---

input   : CM is the case memory; *lowerbound* and *upperbound* are the minimal and maximum value of K;

output : The K clusters defined

1 **Function** X-*means* **is**
2   Let $k[i]$ be the actual number of clusters by class
3   Let $kbest[i]$ be the best number of clusters by class
4   Let *accuracy* be the rate of examples correctly classified
5     $maxaccuracy=0$
6   **for** *(i=0; (i < NumberOfClasses); i++)* **do**
7       $k[i]=kbest[i]=lowerbound$ class i
8   initialize $k[i]$ clusters ramdomly in class i
9   **for** *(i=0; (i < NumberOfClasses); i++)* **do**
10   **for** *(j=k[i]; (j < upperbound class i); j++)* **do**
11   cluster class i in j partitions
12   verify system accuracy
13   **if** *(accuracy >maxaccuracy)* **then**
14           $maxaccuracy=accuracy$
15   save configuration in $kbest$
16   **return** $kbest$

Fig. 2. Cluster creation through the SX-means algorithm (X-means adaptation)

4   Organizing the Case Memory

This section presents our new approach based on Kohonen Maps, and it also describes the previous approach based on SX-Means.

4.1   Kohonen Maps into CBR: The Neural Network Approach

Kohonen Maps [28] are a soft computing technique that allows the management of uncertain, approximate, partial truth and complex knowledge.

We propose a case memory organized such as a map of size $K \times K$ as we can see in the left part of the Figure 3, where each neuron is represented by a vector that models the behaviour and the properties of the samples that it represents. We propose a Kohonen Map training based on the X-means strategy to automatically define the number of clusters: execute several map configurations using different sizes of K, and select the one which has the lowest error. This is a critical decision because we want to improve the retrieval time through the separation of data in several clusters, and the lowest error value will be achieved with few clusters. Thus, a minimal value of clusters needs to be forced. This way of organizing the case memory affects the retrieval and retain phase as CBR function (see Figure 4) describes. The difference is that this approach only compares the cases of the most similar cluster instead of comparing all the elements. Thus, CPU time is reduced. On the other hand, clusters are built at the beginning of the process. The SOM network can not be readjusted and it needs to be rebuilt. Therefore, the optimal environment is the one where the memory is not modified.

This strategy has been implemented over a framework called SOM-CBR (*Self-Organizing Maps inside a Case-Based Reasoning*). Other authors have adapted SOM approach to work as the CBR [34], but they do not integrate SOM inside the CBR in order to manage complex data and to improve the retrieval time, that are our main goals. Also, we propose an automatic definition of the map size in this work.

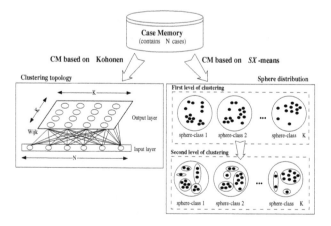

Fig. 3. Case memory representation through the Kohonen and SX-Means approaches

4.2 SX-Means into CBR: The Inductive Approach

This approach proposes a case memory organization based on two levels of clustering as we can see in the right part of the Figure 3 by means of the SX-means algorithm [45]. Firstly, a construction of the spheres is done based on the class distribution of the cases present in the case memory. The concept of sphere was introduced in the CaB-CS and exploited with success in preliminary work such as [17]. The success of this type of Case Memory representation is based on two aspects: first of all this representation greatly improves the speed of the CBR system, and secondly the spheres offer high reliability in the selection of the candidate cases. Each case from the original case memory is distributed to one sphere depending on the class associated with the case. All the cases that belong to the same sphere represent the same class. The union of all spheres is the whole set of cases in the original case memory. Later, a second level of clustering is applied using the results of the previous one. Consequently, each sphere contains a set of clusters obtained using the SX-means algorithm. This strategy is implemented in ULIC (*Unsupervised Learning in CBR*)[45].

As in the SOM-CBR approach, the organization of the case memory affects the retrieval and retain phase as Figure 4 describes. The retrieval phase is only applied over the cases of the selected cluster, and it allows CBR to reduce the CPU time. Adding a new example into the case memory implies updating the centroids of clusters. If a lot of examples are added the case memory performance can be drastically reduced. For this reason, rebuilding the clusters is the only way to assure a good performance. Anyway, the update process could be done in background mode.

---

input   : CM is the case memory; I_s is the example to classify; $K - NN$ is the
              number (odd) of cases to retrieve
output : C is the classification predicted
1 **Function** CBR **is**
2 $\quad$ //Retrieve phase
3 $\quad$ **if** *method configured is Kohonen* **then**
4 $\quad\quad$ Let S be the most similar cluster of the I_s example
5 $\quad\quad$ Select the most $K - NN$ similar samples from S in comparison with I_s
6 $\quad$ **if** *method configured is SX-means* **then**
7 $\quad\quad$ Select the most $K - NN$ similar centroids
8 $\quad$ //Reuse phase
9 $\quad$ Propose a classification C for I_s using the retrieved cases
10 $\quad$ //Revise phase
11 $\quad$ Evaluate if class C is correct
12 $\quad$ //Retain phase
13 $\quad$ Add I_s in case memory if it is 'useful' by means of an updating (SX-means)
   $\quad$ or rebuilding (Kohonen) task
14 $\quad$ **return** C

Fig. 4. CBR cycle [1] adapted to apply the Kohonen and the SX-means clustering strategies

5   Experiments and Results

In this section we shall describe the data sets for testing the proposed techniques and the obtained results.

5.1   Testbed

The performance rate is evaluated using the datasets described in Table 1. *Breast Cancer Wisconsin, Glass, Ionosphere, Iris, Sonar and Vehicle* come from UCI repository [5]. The rest of them are from medical and telematics domains. The medical datasets deal with *breast cancer diagnosis*. These are mammographic images digitalized by the Computer Vision and Robotics Group from the University of Girona. The *Biopsy* [16] and *Mammogram* [17] datasets contain samples of mammographies previously diagnosed by surgical biopsy in Trueta Hospital (in Girona), which can be benign or malign. DDSM [23] and MIAS [43] are public mammographic image datasets, which have been studied and preprocessed in [37,36] respectively. DDSM and MIAS classify mammography densities, which was found relevant for the automatic diagnosis of breast cancer. Experts classify them either in four classes (according to BIRADS [41] classifications) or three classes (classification used in Trueta Hospital).

Regarding to telematics domain, datasets are focused on network security. There are no standard datasets that contain all the information obtained after a thorough security test is performed, so there are no class labels for the data and so no obvious criteria to guide the search. On the other hand, security experts have noticed that collecting logs, capturing network traffic and identifying potential threats is becoming difficult to handle when managing large data sets. A corporate network can handle many devices, thus a thorough test can result in a great amount of data [8]. Therefore, trying to manually find a behaviour pattern or certain vulnerabilities becomes a difficult task.

In order to perform our evaluation of Kohonen Maps and SX-means in a completely unsupervised environment such as data from security tests, we have applied these clustering algorithms to three datasets obtained from Consensus system [9]. These datasets differ in the number and detail of the attributes that describe a case (see Table 1). As explained before, this domain is completely unsupervised; therefore the number of classes is unknown. This is why techniques such as Kohonen Maps and SX-means can help discovering 'natural' grouping in a set of patterns without knowledge of any class labels.

All the proposed datasets aim to be a representative benchmark of the different characteristics of the type of problems to solve. These datasets have been tested using CBR, Kohonen and SX-means . All the approaches have been tuned with 1-Nearest Neighbour algorithm and Euclidean distance without weighting methods as retrieval strategy. We have chosen this configuration because our goal is focused on the evaluation of the retrieval time.

5.2   Results and Discussion

This section presents a discussion over the clustering methods explained before. First, we analyse the accuracy rate and the computational time needed to retrieve

Table 1. Description of the datasets used in this work

Code	Dataset	Cases	Features	Classes	Uncertainty
BC	Breast-cancer (Wisconsin)	699	9	2	Yes
GL	Glass	214	9	6	No
IO	Ionosphere	351	34	2	No
IR	Iris	150	4	3	No
SO	Sonar	208	60	2	No
VE	Vehicle	846	18	4	No
BI	Biopsy	1027	24	2	Yes
MA	Mammogram	216	23	2	Yes
DD	DDSM	501	143	4	Yes
M3	Mias-3C	320	153	3	Yes
MB	Mias-Birads	320	153	4	Yes
NS1	Network Security (Consensus) 1	45	60	-	Yes
NS2	Network Security (Consensus) 2	45	57	-	Yes
NS3	Network Security (Consensus) 3	45	165	-	Yes

a case using both approaches over the UCI Repository and medical datasets. Second, we perform a qualitative study of the case memory organization obtained using the evaluated clustering methods in telematics domain.

Table 2 summarizes the results of SOM-CBR (Kohonen) and ULIC (SX-means) approaches. In SX-means approach we have clustered cases in several spheres in order to detect different behaviours of the data contained in them. On the other hand, in Kohonen approach we have mapped data patterns onto a n-dimensional grid of neurons or units. For each technique, we present the average percentage of accuracy resulting of a 10-fold stratified cross-validation, their corresponding standard deviations, and the average computational time (i.e. CPU time) in milliseconds of one case resolution. In addition, the results shown in Table 2 are the mean of ten executions using several random seeds in a P4-3Ghz computer with 1 GRAM. All the experiments have been done without retaining any case in the case memory because this paper does not focus on Retain phase.

As we can observe, results in general improve both the mean accuracy and the CPU time of classifying one case. Clustering the case memory is the result of grouping similar data, which possibly have the same classification. When the Retrieve phase is applied, CBR only compares with potentially 'good' examples and not with redundant data. We consider 'good' examples these examples which are similar in comparison with the new example to classify.

The accuracy rate has been analysed by means of the t-test student (at 95% confidence level). In SX-means CM approach the accuracy rate is usually maintained or improved (not significantly) in comparison with Linear CM in UCI problems. However, the accuracy rate is significantly reduced in some problems (SO, VE, BI, MB and M3) which present more uncertainty. On the other hand, SOM CM approach is more stable and it provides results like the Linear CM. Also, it improves the results in MA dataset in comparison with Linear CM, and

Table 2. Summary of the mean percentage of accuracy rate (%AR), the standard deviation (std) and the mean retrieval time of one case (in milliseconds) of a CBR with three case memory organization approaches: linear, SOM and SX-means. The best accuracy rates are marked in **Bold**. The ↑ and ↓ indicate if the cluster method significantly improves or decreases the accuracy rate in comparison with Linear CM when a t-test student (at 95% of confidence level) is applied . The √ indicates that SOM CM significatively improves SX-means CM.

Code	Linear CM		SOM CM		SX-Means CM	
	%AR (std.)	Time	%AR (std.)	Time	%AR (std.)	Time
BC	96.14 (2.1)	1.8000	96.42 (2.6)	0.7000	**96.71 (1.9)**	1.0200
GL	69.16 (7.3)	0.6000	70.66 (7.8)	0.2100	**70.79 (8.7)**	0.5500
IO	**90.32 (4.2)**	0.3600	89.12 (4.8)	0.0800	90.31 (5.3)	0.0060
IR	96.32 (3.1)	0.3000	96.00 (3.2)	0.0150	**97.33 (3.2)**	0.0015
SO	**87.02 (6.9)**	0.3600	85.58 (7.2) √	0.1400	82.93 (7.7)	↓ 0.1600
VE	69.05 (6.1)	0.4800	**69.15 (5.7)** √	0.2200	65.60 (3.7)	↓ 0.0080
BI	**83.15 (3.5)**	0.7200	82.08 (3.7)	0.4300	81.40 (3.7)	↓ 0.3100
MA	62.50 (13.7)	0.1200	**68.06 (8.3)** √ ↑ 0.0400		63.89 (9.8)	0.0900
DD	46.51 (5.4)	1.9800	**46.41 (4.1)**	1.2000	46.17 (5.2)	1.1000
$M3$	**70.81 (6.9)**	1.5000	69.57 (6.09) √	0.7000	65.34 (6.2)	↓ 0.5400
MB	**70.31 (5.5)**	1.5000	**70.31 (5.4)** √	0.7000	60.16 (9.2)	↓ 0.5400

it significatively improves the results in SO, VE, MA, M3 and MB datasets in relation with SX-means CM.

Concerning to the the CPU time, the two approaches always drastically reduce computational time requirements. This is directly related to the number of clusters defined by each approach. Table 3 summarizes the clusters defined for each configuration explained in Table 2. In both approaches, the ideal number of clusters has been tuned in order to minimize the minimal square error. SX-means tends to build more clusters than SOM because SX-means defines several 'patterns' for each class, whereas SOM defines patterns that work as 'index' to compare only with the most potentially similar cases. Thus, SX-means only compares with the 'patterns', and SOM compares with the patterns and its cases. This situation produces that the computational time in SOM is higher than in SX-means approach because it has to use more information. Eq. 4, 5 and 6 model the cost (time) needed to retrieve one case by Linear, SOM and SX-means approaches respectively, where Tr represents the number of cases in the case memory and K the number of clusters used. Depending on the number of clusters (K), the size of case memory (Tr), and the cases distribution in the clusters the difference of performance between SOM CM and SX-means CM could vary.

$$time(Linear) = O(Tr) \tag{4}$$

$$time(SOM) = O(K + \frac{Tr}{K}) \tag{5}$$

$$time(SX - means) = O(K) \tag{6}$$

Table 3. Summary of the number of the case memory clusters for each dataset and method. Also, SOM approach includes the map size $(K \times K)$, and SX-means includes the number of clusters by class.

Code	Classes	Clusters in SOM CM	Clusters in SX-means CM
BC	2	30 (K=8)	42 (27-15)
GL	7	7 (K=6)	78 (20-15-10-0-20-3-10)
IO	2	44 (K=8)	30 (24-6)
IR	3	10 (K=6)	34 (20-4-10)
SO	2	37 (K=8)	52 (25-27)
VE	4	62 (K=10)	115 (25-20-35-35)
BI	2	4 (K=4)	44 (28-16)
MA	2	8 (K=16)	90 (50-40)
DD	4	3 (K=8)	10 (1-4-2-3)
M3	3	6 (K=10)	8 (2-3-3)
MB	4	6 (K=10)	8 (2-3-3)
NS1	-	3 (K=8)	3 (3)
NS2	-	8 (K=8)	8 (8)
NS3	-	8 (K=8)	8 (8)

Therefore, we can conclude that CPU time is improved and the accuracy rate is maintained for all the problems when the SOM approach is applied, because it seems to be more suitable to tackle general or uncertain problems due to its soft computing capabilities. On the other hand, SX-means improves the CPU time but the accuracy rate decreases in problems with uncertainty.

Regarding to network security and clustering, not only SX-means [8] but also Kohonen Maps have revealed very good results when using port scanning and operative system fingerprinting information as main features. We must highlight that this domain was completely unsupervised; thus, the number of classes was unknown. However, both techniques have found 8 different clusters for the used datasets. They have identified groups of similar computers, but have also found devices that unexpectedly appear separated from what it seamed like similar devices. Therefore, these techniques can help analysts handling information obtained from security tests in order to detect abnormal groups of devices or atypical system behaviours.

6   Conclusions and Further Research

This paper has proposed a case memory organization based on Kohonen Maps in order to manage complex and uncertain problems, and also reduce the retrieval time. Furthermore, we have analysed this approach in comparison with a Linear CM organization and a SX-means CM organization previously proposed in [45] over datasets from UCI Repository and from medical and telematics domains.

The results have shown that the soft computing capabilities of Kohonen Maps allow CBR to better retrieve the information in comparison with a SX-means CM organization when the problems present uncertainty, and faster in comparison with the Linear CM organization. However, the SX-means CM needs less operations to retrieve one case because only needs to compare with 'pattern' (centroids) and not with the cases of the 'patterns'. Therefore, the solution with best accuracy is the Linear CM, the faster is the SX-means CM, and the more balanced is SOM CM. Anyway, SOM case memory organization is more suitable for managing uncertain domains.

One weak point of both approaches, and more concretely in SOM-CBR, is the Retain phase. The case memory is clustered at the beginning of the process and the clusters are built to promote the groups between similar data. If we add knowledge in the case memory in form of new cases, these relations can be altered and the performance is reduced. One issue of further work would be focused on the Retain phase in order to add new cases without reducing the system performance (accuracy rate and computational time).

All the studied datasets are composed by numeric attributes because the metric used in SX-means and Kohonen Maps do not support discrete data with reliability. Thus, it would be interesting to study the application of other metrics such as the Heterogeneous distance [48].

Acknowledgements

We would like to thank the Spanish Government for their support under grants TIC 2002-04160-C/02-02, TIN 2005-08386-C05-04 and CIT-390000-2005-27, and *Generalitat de Catalunya* (DURSI) for its support under grants 2005SGR-302 and 2006FIC-0043. Also, we would like to thank *Enginyeria i Arquitectura La Salle* of Ramon Llull University for their support to our research group.

References

1. A. Aamodt and E. Plaza. Case-based reasoning: Foundations issues, methodological variations, and system approaches. *IA Communications*, 7:39–59, 1994.
2. R. Agrawal, J. Gehrke, Dimitrios Gunopulos, and Prabhakar Raghavan. Automatic subspace clustering of high dimensional data for data mining applications. In *Proceedings of ACM SIGMOD International Conference on Management of Data*, pages 94–105, 1998.
3. M. Ankerst, M.M. Breunig, H. Kriegel, and J. Sander. OPTICS: ordering points to identify the clustering structure. In *Proceedings ACM SIGMOD International Conference on Management of Data*, pages 49–60. ACM Press, 1999.
4. Christopher M. Bishop. *Neural Networks for Pattern Recognition*. Oxford University Press, 1995.
5. C.L. Blake and C.J. Merz. UCI repository of machine learning databases, 1998.
6. P. Cheeseman and J. Stutz. Bayesian classification (autoclass): Theory and results. In *Advances in Knowledge Discovery and Data Mining*, pages 153–180, 1996.
7. W. Cheetham, Simon Shiu, and R. Weber. Soft case-based reasoning. *The Knowledge Engineering*, 0:1–4, 2005.
8. G. Corral, E. Golobardes, O. Andreu, I. Serra, E. Maluquer, and A. Martínez. Application of clustering techniques in a network security testing system. *Artificial Intelligence Research and Devolopment*, 131:157–164, 2005.

9. G. Corral, A. Zaballos, X. Cadenas, and A. Grane. A distributed vulnerability detection system for an intranet. In *Proceedings of the 39th IEEE International Carnahan Conference on Security Technology*, pages 291–295, 2005.

10. J. Dawkins and J. Hale. A systematic approach to multi-stage network attack analysis. *Second IEEE Int. Inf. Assurance Workshop*, 2004.

11. G. Deboeck and T. Kohonen. *Visual Explorations in Finance using self-organizing maps*. Springer-Verlag, 1998.

12. A. Domingo and M.A. Garcia. Hierachical clustering of 3d objects and its application to minimum distance computation. In *Proceedings of IEEE International Conference on Robotics and Automation*, pages 5287–5292, 2004.

13. F. Domingos. Control-sensitive feature selection for lazy learners. *Artificial Intelligence Review*, 11(1-5):227–253, 1997.

14. M. Ester, H.P. Kriegel, and X. Xu. A database interface for clustering in large spatial databases. In *Knowledge Discovery and Data Mining*, pages 94–99, 1995.

15. D.H. Fisher. Knowledge acquisition via incremental conceptual clustering. In *Machine Learning*, pages 2:139–172, 1987.

16. J.M. Garrell, E. Golobardes, E. Bernadó, and X. Llorà. Automatic diagnosis with genetic algorithms and case-based reasoning. *AI in Engineering*, 13(4):362–367, 1999.

17. E. Golobardes, X. Llorà, M. Salamó, and J. Martí. Computer aided diagnosis with case-based reasoning and genetic algorithms. *Journal of Knowledge Based Systems*, 15:45–52, 2002.

18. G. Hamerly, E. Perelman, , and B. Calder. Comparing multinomial and k-means clustering for simpoint. In *Proceedings of the International Symposium on Performance Analysis of Systems and Software*, 2006.

19. J. Han and M. Kamber. Data mining: Concepts and techniques, 2000.

20. S. J. Hanson. *Conceptual Clustering and Categorization: Bridging the Gap Between Induction and Causal Models*, volume 3. Kaufmann, 1990.

21. J. Hartigan and M. Wong. A k-means clustering algorithm. In *Applied Statistics*, pages 28:100–108, 1979.

22. J.A. Hartigan. *Clustering Algorithms*. John Wiley and Sons, New York, 1975.

23. M. Heath, K. Bowyer, D. Kopans, R. Moore, and P.J. Kegelmeyer. The digital database for screening mammography. *International Workshop on Dig. Mammography*, 2000.

24. A. Hinneburg and D.A. Keim. An efficient approach to clustering in large multimedia databases with noise. In *Knowledge Discovery and Data Mining*, pages 58–65, 1998.

25. S. Kaski, T. Honkela, K. Lagus, and T. Kohonen. Websom—self-organizing maps of document collections. *Neurocomputing*, 21(1):101–117, 1998.

26. L. Kaufman and P.J. Rousseeuw. Clustering by means of medoids. In *Statistical Data Analysis Based on the L1-Norm and Related Methods*, pages 405–416. Y. Dodge, 1987.

27. L. Kaufman and P.J. Rousseeuw. Finding groups in data: An introduction to cluster analysis. *John Wiley & Sons*, 1990.

28. T. Kohonen. The self-organizing map. *In Proc. of the IEEE*, 78:1464–1480, 1990.

29. J. Kolodner. Reconstructive memory, a computer model. *Cognitive Science*, 7:281–328, 1983.

30. J. Laaksonen, M. Koskela, and E. Oja. Picsom: Self-organization maps for content-based image retrieval. *Proceedings of International Joint Conference on NN*, 1999.

31. R. López de Mántaras and E. Plaza. Case-based reasoning : An overview. *AI Communications, IOS Press*, 10(1):21–29, 1997.

32. F. Martin. *Case-Based Sequence Analysis in Dynamic, Imprecise, and Adversarial Domains*. PhD thesis, Universitat Politècnica de Catalunya, 2004.

33. R.S. Michalski. Knowledge acquisition through conceptual clustering: A theoretical framework and an algorithm for partitioning data into conjunctive concepts. Technical Report 1026, LIIA, Ensais/Univ. Louis-Pasteur, Urbana, Illinois, 1980.

34. L. E. Mujica, J. Vehí, and J. Rodellar. A hybrid system combining self organizing maps with case based reasoning in structural assessment. In *Artificial Intelligence Research and Development*, volume 131, pages 173–180. IOS Press, 2005.

35. T. Nomoto and Y. Matsumoto. An experimental comparison of supervised and unsupervised approaches to text summarization. In *First IEEE International Conference on Data Mining*, page 630, 2001.

36. A. Oliver, J. Freixenet, A. Bosch, D. Raba, and R. Zwiggelaar. Automatic classification of breast tissue. *Iberian Conference on Pattern Recognition and Image Analysis*, pages 431–438, 2005.

37. A. Oliver, J. Freixenet, and R. Zwiggelaar. Automatic classification of breast density. In *International Conference on Image Processing*, 2005.

38. D. Pelleg and A. Moore. X-means: Extending K-means with efficient estimation of the number of clusters. In *Proceedings of the 17th International Conference of Machine Learning*, pages 727–734. Morgan Kaufmann, 2000.

39. C. K. Riesbeck and R. C. Schank. *Inside Case-Based Reasoning*. Lawrence Erlbaum Associates, Cambridge, MA, 1989.

40. S. Salzberg. A nearest hyperrectangle learning method. *Machine Learning*, 6:277–309, 1991.

41. T. H. Samuels. *Illustrated Breast Imaging Reporting and Data System BIRADS*. American College of Radiology Publications, 3rd edition, 1998.

42. G. Sheikholeslami, S. Chatterjee, and A. Zhang. WaveCluster: A multi-resolution clustering approach for very large spatial databases. In *Proceedings of 24th International Conference Very Large Data Bases, VLDB*, pages 428–439, 24–27 1998.

43. J. Suckling, J. Parker, and D.R. Dance. The mammographic image analysis society digital mammogram database. In A.G. Gale, editor, *Proceedings of 2nd Internat. Workshop on Digital Mammography*, pages 211–221, 1994.

44. A. Ultsch. Self organized feature maps for monitoring and knowledge acquisition of a chemical process. *International Conference on Artificial Neural Networks*, pages 864–867, 1993.

45. D. Vernet and E. Golobardes. An unsupervised learning approach for case-based classifier systems. *Expert Update. The Specialist Group on Artificial Intelligence*, 6(2):37–42, 2003.

46. T. Villmann. Neural networks approaches in medicine - a review of actual developments. *Proceedings of European Symposium on Artificial Neural Networks*, pages 165–176, 2000.

47. W. Wang, J. Yang, and R.R. Muntz. STING: A statistical information grid approach to spatial data mining. In *The VLDB Journal*, pages 186–195, 1997.

48. D.R. Wilson and T.R. Martinez. Improved heterogeneus distance functions. *Journal of Artificial Intelligence Research*, 6:1–34, 1997.

49. Q. Yang and J. Wu. Keep it simple: A case-base maintenance policy based on clustering and information theory. In *Proceedings of the Canadian AI Conference*, pages 102–114, 2000.

Further Experiments in Case-Based Collaborative Web Search*

Jill Freyne and Barry Smyth

School of Computer Science and Informatics,
University College Dublin, Belfield, Dublin 4, Ireland
{Jill.Freyne, Barry.Smyth}@ucd.ie

Abstract. Collaborative Web Search (CWS) proposes a case-based approach to personalizing search results for the needs of a community of like-minded searchers. The search activities of users are captured as a case base of search cases, each corresponding to community search behaviour (the results selected) for a given query. When responding to a new query, CWS selects a set of similar cases and promotes their selected results within the final result-list. In this paper we describe how this case-based view can be broadened to accommodate suggestions from multiple case bases, reflecting the expertise and preferences of complementary search communities. In this way it is possible to supplement the recommendations of the host community with complementary recommendations from related communities. We describe the results of a new live-user trial that speaks to the performance benefits that are available by using multiple case bases in this way compared to the use of a single case base.

1 Introduction

Improving the quality of Web search results is a challenging problem—the sheer scale and heterogeneity of the Internet is exacerbated by vague and ambiguous queries [4,8]—but if improvements can be made they will have a significant impact on this very important application area. In our work we have looked at the application of case-based techniques to Web search by looking for query repetition and selection regularity amongst user search patterns. Our key insight has been that, although repetition and regularity is often absent from generic search, it is present in the search patterns of like-minded communities of users that naturally exist [16]. Our collaborative Web search (CWS) approach is designed to operate as a form of meta-search. It relies on some underlying search engine(s) to provide a basic result-list for a user query, but then uses a case base of past search patterns from the user's community to identify key results for promotion.

CWS contemplates a society of community-based search engines, each with their own case base of search cases corresponding to some distinct community of searchers. Ordinarily the searches of a specific (*host*) community are answered

---

* The support of the Informatics Research Initiative of Enterprise Ireland is gratefully acknowledged.

T.R. Roth-Berghofer et al. (Eds.): ECCBR 2006, LNAI 4106, pp. 256–270, 2006.

with reference to their local case base: the traditional single case base model of CBR. Recently a number of researchers have investigated the benefits available from combining multiple case bases, each providing access to a different set of problem-solving experiences [9,11,12,13]. We adopt a similar strategy in CWS by leveraging the search experience of search communities related to the host (multiple case bases) when responding to queries originating from the host. In doing so we build on work reported in [3], which considered this multiple case base approach in the context of a simple notion of community relatedness, and which provided evaluation results based on an artificial user evaluation. We propose a more sophisticated model of community relatedness and demonstrate the value of the new approach in terms of a new extended live-user trial.

The work presented in this paper touches on a number of areas of related research by combining ideas from Web information retrieval and case-based reasoning. Of particular importance is the idea that Web search experience can be usefully captured as a case base of reusable cases and that this experience can be distributed across multiple case bases which correspond to the different needs of different communities of searchers. There is a long history of the use of case-based methods in a variety of information retrieval tasks. For example, the work of Rissland [14] looks at the application of CBR to legal information retrieval (see also [1]), and Burke et al. [2] describe a case-based approach to question-answering tasks. However these approaches have all tended to focus on particular application domains rather than the broader area of Web search. That said there is some CBR work in the broader context of Web search. For example, the *Broadway* recommender system [7] is notable for its use of case-based techniques to recommend search query refinements, based on refinements that have worked well in the past. Perhaps more related to the core work in this paper is the *PersonalSearcher* [5] which combines user profiling and textual case-based reasoning to dynamically filter Web documents according to a user's learned preferences.

The idea that experience can be distributed across multiple case bases is not new, and in recent years many researchers have considered the use of multiple case bases during problem solving. For example, Leake et al. [9] consider the benefits and challenges when reusing the experience of multiple case bases that reflect different tasks and environments. They consider how a local case base can usefully determine when to look to external case bases as a source of knowledge, and how external cases might be adapted in line with the local task and environment; see McGinty & Smyth [11] for similar work in the route planning domain. Nagendra Prasad & Plaza [13] investigate cooperative problem solving among agents possessing either the same or different capabilities and incorporate potentially different knowledge and problem solving behaviors. Nagendra Prasad et al. [12] present a different situation where no single source of information may contain sufficient information to give a complete solution. They envisage the piecing together of mutually related partial responses from several distributed sources of queries in order to create a complete solution.

2   A Review of Collaborative Web Search

The CWS technique is conceived of as a form of meta-search; see Figure 1.

Each user query, q_T, is submitted to base-level search engines (S_1 - S_n) after adapting q_T for each S_i using the appropriate adapter, A_i. Similarly, the result set, R_i, returned by a particular S_i is adapted for use by I-SPY to produce R'_i, which can then be combined and re-ranked by I-SPY, just like a traditional meta-search engine. The key novelty stems from how a second ranked result-list, R_T, is produced which reflects the learned preferences of a community of like-minded searchers. This involves reusing selection results from past search cases for similar queries, promoting those results that were reliably selected in the past.

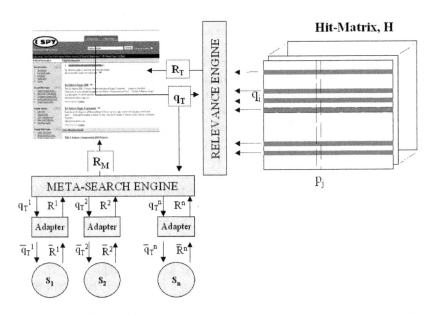

Fig. 1. Collaborative Web search as implemented in I-SPY (*ispy.ucd.ie*)

2.1   The Community Search Case Base

The *hit-matrix* associated with community C, H^C, is a key data structure for CWS, which relates page selections to past queries for a community of users. Specifically, H^C_{ij} (the *hit value* of page p_j for query q_i in community C) is the number of times that page p_j has been selected for query q_i by members of community C; H^C_{ij} is incremented each time p_j is selected for q_i. The hit-matrix forms the basis of a case base. Each row corresponds to a search case (see Equation 1) or, equivalently, a $k + 1$-tuple made up of the query component (a set of query terms) plus k result-pairs, each with a page id, p_j, and an associated percentage relevance value, r_j, computed from the hit value for this page and query combination; we will explain how this relevance value is computed below in Equation 6. The *problem specification* part of the case (see Equation 2) corresponds to the query terms. The *solution* part of the case (see Equation 3) corresponds to the result-pairs; that is, the set of page selections that have been accumulated as a result of past uses of the corresponding query. The *target problem* is, of course, represented by the target query terms.

$$c_i = (q_i, (p_1, r_1), ..., (p_k, r_k)) \tag{1}$$

$$Spec(c_i) = q_i \tag{2}$$

$$Sol(c_i) = ((p_1, r_1), ..., (p_k, r_k)) \tag{3}$$

$$Rel(p_j, c_i) = r_j \text{ if } (p_j, r_j) \in Sol(c_i); = 0, otherwise. \tag{4}$$

2.2   Retrieving Similar Search Cases

For each new target query q_T we retrieve a set of similar search cases to serve as a source of relevant results. Case similarity can be measured using a simple term-overlap metric (Equation 5); evaluating alternative metrics is a matter of ongoing research. During the retrieval stage, this allows CWS to rank-order past search cases according to their similarity to the target query so that all, or a subset of, these similar cases might be reused during result ranking.

$$Sim(q_T, c_i) = \frac{|q_T \cap Spec(c_i)|}{|q_T \cup Spec(c_i)|} \tag{5}$$

2.3   Reusing Result Selections

Consider a page, p_j, that is part of the solution of a case, c_i, with query, q_i. The relevance of p_j to this case is given by the relative number of times that p_j has been selected for q_i; see Equation 6. And the relevance of p_j to the current target query q_T is the combination of $Relevance^C(p_j, q_i)$'s for all pages that are part of the solutions to cases $(c_1, ..., c_n)$ deemed to be similar to q_T, as shown in Equation 7. Essentially each $Relevance^C(p_j, q_i)$ is weighted by $Sim(q_T, c_i)$ to discount the relevance of results from less similar queries; $Exists(p_j, c_i) = 1$ if $H_{ij} <> 0$ and 0 otherwise.

$$Relevance^C(p_j, q_i) = \frac{H_{ij}^C}{\sum_{\forall j} H_{ij}^C} \tag{6}$$

$$WRel^C(p_j, q_T, c_1, ..., c_n) = \frac{\sum_{i=1,...,n} Relelevance^C(p_j, c_i) \bullet Sim(q_T, c_i))}{\sum_{i=1,...,n} Exists(p_j, c_i) \bullet Sim(q_T, c_i)} \tag{7}$$

This weighted relevance metric is used to rank-order the promotion candidates. These ranked pages are then recommended ahead of the remaining meta-search results, which are themselves ranked (according to a standard meta-search scoring metric), to give R_T. Of course, alternative promotion models can also be envisaged but are omitted here due to space constraints.

3   Reusing Multiple Case Bases

There are a number of reasons why we might want to look beyond the host community for a complementary source of search experience. A host community might be immature and, as such, may not have accumulated sufficient experience to respond effectively to a target query. However, other similar, more mature, communities may be available and perhaps they could provide relevant results for the host query. Even a mature host community may not contain sufficient information on a target query; perhaps the query relates to a very specialised information request within the community context. For example, in a community of automobile enthusiasts a specialised query related to the specialised task of restoring a classic s-type Jaguar might be better answered by a related community that is more focused on car restoration.

The main focus of this paper is to explore the various ways that we might exploit the complementary search expertise of related communities by allowing their search cases to contribute to searches by members of the host community using a community cooperation (CC) model. To do this we need to solve two core issues: 1) how to evaluate the relatedness of two communities so that related communities may be identified; 2) how to present the results of a related community to the searchers.

3.1   Evaluating Community Relatedness

When is one community related to another? For the purposes of helping to respond to the search results of our host community, C_h, we can consider two important factors—community similarity and community experience—and we use these measures to evaluate the relatedness of C_h to some other community C_r as shown in Equation 8. *CommunitySimilarity* and *CommunityExperience* are defined in the following paragraphs.

$$RelatedCommunity(C_h, C_r, q_T) =$$
$$CommunitySimilarity(C_h, C_r) * CommunityExperience(q_T, C_r) \quad (8)$$

Community Similarity. It makes sense to look to the recommendations of communities that are demonstrably similar to the host community. But how might community similarity be measured? There are potentially many ways to look at the concept of community similarity. For example we might start by supposing that if two communities have similar query term distributions then they might reflect the interests of two similar communities of users. However this is not necessarily the case, and not sufficient for our needs. For instance, a motoring community might share many queries with a community about wild cats (e.g., 'jaguar', 'puma', 'cougar' are all common car names) but very different result selections will have been made by each community's searchers. Instead we propose to look at the shared results that have been selected in response to searches as an estimate of community similarity (see Equation 9 for the similarity between some host community, C_h, and another community, C_r).

$$CommunitySimilarity(C_h, C_r) = \frac{|ResultSelection(C_h) \cap ResultSelection(C_r)|}{|ResultSelection(C_h)|} \tag{9}$$

Community Experience. As a measure of relatedness, community similarity only tells part of the story. We wish to exploit communities which are similar to the host community and also have a rich store of search information pertaining to a target query. Thus, community experience measures the amount of search history a hit-matrix has for a query. That is, community C is considered to be experienced for a target query, q_T, if its hit-matrix, H^C, contains lots of similar queries and if these similar queries have been successful (users have selected their results frequently) in the past. To measure this, we compare q_T to each of the queries stored in H^C to look for related queries; that is queries with a non-zero similarity to q_T; see Equation 5. For each of these related queries, q_r, we can compute a success score. The *success score* for a query in a hit-matrix is the relative number of hits (selections) that it has contained within its matrix entry, compared to the total number of hits in that hit-matrix; see Equation 10. This metric will deliver high success scores to queries that have resulted in lots of page selections. The degree to which q_T is related to H^C can be computed as the sum of the success scores for each similar query weighted by the degree of similarity; see Equation 11.

$$Success(q_r, H^C) = \frac{\sum_{\forall i} H_{ri}^C}{\sum_{\forall ij} H_{ij}^C} \tag{10}$$

$$Related(q_T, H^C) = \sum_{\forall q_r : Sim(q_T, q_r) > 0} Sim(q_T, q_r) * Success(q_r, H^C) \tag{11}$$

$$CommunityExperience(q_T, C) = \frac{Related(q_T, H^C)}{\sum_{\forall C} Related(q_T, H^C)} \tag{12}$$

Community C's experience score reflects the percentage of total query experience contained in its hit-matrix for a target query as shown in Equation 12. This technique allows us to identify a set of communities which all have a rich information history on a target query.

3.2   Result Ranking

Once a set of related communities has been identified (by their similarity to the host community) they can each be used to produce a set of results in response to the target query, q_T, from the host. In this case, for each related community we only seek to retrieve the set of result recommendations coming from their respective hit-matrix (search case base). Thus, each related community, C_i, produces a set of recommended results, R_i. These result-lists complement the result-list R_T that is produced for the host community;

3.3   Result Presentation

In this paper, we propose keeping recommendations in their original result-lists and presenting the searcher with a selection of recommendation lists, each from a related community, rather than combining all of the promoted results, into a single promoted result-list for presentation. Each list is labeled with its community name and context and, we argue, that allows the searcher to better understand the nature of the promoted results. In effect this provides for a unique approach to result clustering [6,10,17]. Instead of clustering search results by some analysis of their overlapping terms, we are clustering results based on their selection frequencies in different communities of searchers.

An example of this approach is presented in Figure 2 for a collection of search communities related to skiing; these examples use the I-SPY system (ispy.ucd.ie) which is a robust, fully deployed version of CWS. The target query, 'late deals', is provided by a member of the host community, *European Skiing*, and this community's recommendations are shown in the main result page. The section of the result-list shown presents the recommendations from the host community; those results that have been selected and ranked from previous similar cases for this community.

Notice that along the top of the recommended results there is a set of tabs containing the title of a related community. In this example, there are 3 related communities shown, in order of their similarity to the host community. Inset into the figure is the recommendation list from the *American Skiing* community. These recommendations offer late deals in American resorts complement those of the host community. They are however still clearly relevant to the target query.

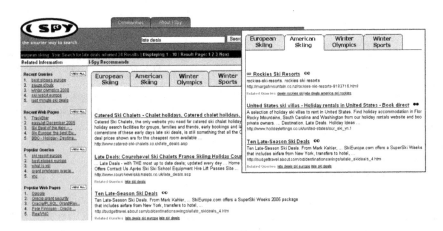

Fig. 2. The recommended results from a selection of skiing communities including the host community (European skiing) and one of the related communities (American skiing)

4   Evaluation

In previous work we have demonstrated the benefits of the standard single case base version of CWS, through a range of live-user trials. For example, in [15,16] we present the results of two different user trials that show how CWS can significantly improve the precision and recall of an underlying search engine (Google in this case) with respect to the needs of a community of like-minded searchers.

In this paper we have speculated about the value of including recommendations from other search communities when responding to a query submitted in a specific host community. In particular, we have claimed that similar communities will recommend results that are related to the target query and the searcher's needs. Indeed we believe that, in general, communities that are more related to the host will be a more reliable source of relevant results. We also suspect that communities which are less closely aligned to the host may still have a role to play in suggesting results that are partially relevant and that might not otherwise be promoted by the host community. In this section we will describe the results of an experiment designed to test these hypotheses.

4.1   Methodology

The evaluation is carried out in the IT domain with search information collected from a Dublin based software company. The search data was collected over a 9 week period in 2004 and is made up of 1986 search sessions, each containing an internet protocol addresses, a query and at least one result selection, (ip, q, r_1-r_n). This data was used to populate a set of search communities, each made up of the employees of a different division within the company. We tested our hypothesis by querying the resulting case bases with separate sets of real-user queries and judged the recommendations in terms of coverage and precision.

Community Creation. In order to test our community cooperation theory, we needed to create a series of separate communities from the collection of data available. The simplest and most effective way of separating the information was to split the data into standard company departments, each department having its own search community. In total, 7 communities were created, varying in department topic and size, from the *Development B* community containing 749

Table 1. Pairwise community similarities

Community (sessions)	Web Devel	Marketing	Proj Man.	Devel A	QA	Finance	Devel B
Web Devel(58)		0%	15%	19%	22%	3%	33%
Marketing (52)	0%		9%	25%	13%	11%	20%
Proj Man (204)	3%	2%		17%	20%	4%	29%
Devel A (370)	3%	3%	12%		21%	3%	29%
Quality A (486)	3%	1%	11%	17%		3%	28%
Finance (53)	3%	8%	17%	18%	22%		24%
Devel B (749)	2%	1%	10%	15%	18%	2%	

sessions to the *Marketing* community with 52 sessions; see Table 1. We acknowledge that in a small company one large search community would probably best serve the employees. However we wish to use the departmental communities created to explore the possible benefits gained through the use of our community cooperation technique.

Hit-Matrix Population. Populating the hit-matrices for this experiment was a straightforward task. Each community's search data (i.e. query result pairs) was arranged in chronological order. The first 80% of the data - the training data - was used to populate the hit-matrix for that community. The result was a hit-matrix populated as it would have been had a CWS engine been used by searchers at the time the searches were conducted.

Relevance Testing. When training was complete we had 7 communities of various sizes, all in some way related to the business of the company. The remaining 20% of search sessions for each community were combined to form a global test set containing 403 queries, each tagged with its host community. The queries contained an average of 2.66 terms and were a mix of general and computing queries; e.g. *"public holidays Ireland"* and *"profiler 3.0 linux installation"*.

Our hypothesis is that more experienced, similar communities are better candidates for cooperation than less experienced, less similar communities. Table 1 shows the community similarity figures for all 7 communities. Figure 3 shows the average experience (see Equation 12) of each related community for the test queries of a selection of hosts and the relatedness scores (see Equation 8) for each related community for the same hosts. The performance of each host community for their own test queries (those that they actually contributed to the test set) is compared to the performance of the other six communities, their related communities. Thus for each host community, its test queries are submitted to I-SPY in the traditional manner, generating a host result-list, R_h from the host's hit-matrix. In parallel, each of the six related communities also receive the test query and produce recommendation lists based on the information in their hit-matrices, $R_1,..,R_k$. We should point out here that no meta-results were contained in the result-lists just promoted results from the relevance engine.

Although we have access to the results that the original searchers selected, it does not follow that we can assume that unselected results are irrelevant. For our evaluation we needed some way of identifying other results as potentially relevant. Our solution was to use Google's "similar pages" feature as a means to generate lists of results that are similar to those selected by the original searchers (the *seed pages*). This allowed us to generate a list (on average 15.15 results) of *relevant candidates* for each search session from its seed pages. Finally, to determine if some recommended page was relevant for a given query we used Lucene's page similarity function to evaluate the similarity between the page and each of the seed pages and relevant candidates for the test session in question. If the page exceeded a given similarity threshold then it was deemed relevant; a threshold of 0.3 was used for seed pages and 0.5 for the relevant candidates.

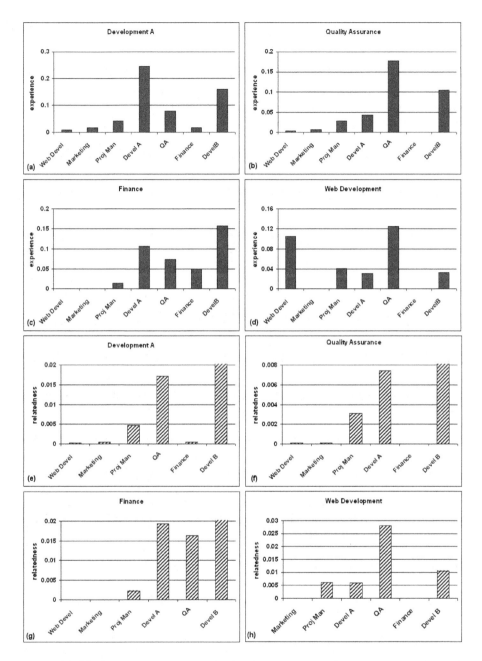

Fig. 3. (a)-(d) Average experience of related communities for host queries from the Finance, Development A, Quality Assurance and Web Development communities. (e)-(h) Relatedness of related communities for host queries from the Finance, Development A, Quality Assurance and Web Development communities.

4.2   Query Coverage

In our first test we looked at the number of queries for which recommendations could be generated by CWS in comparison to the CC approach. It is important to realise that when we talk about a *recommendation* being generated, we are referring to the promotion of a specific search result based on its previous selection history. Table 2 shows that the CC approach enjoys a clear advantage over the standard CWS approach. Only 82 (20%) of the 403 queries submitted to the standard CWS system resulted in recommendations being generated compared to 130 queries for the CC approach, representing a relative increase in recommendation coverage of more than 58% for the CC approach.

Table 2. Technique performance

	CWS	CC
Recommendations	82	130
Successful Queries	54	69

Table 3. Percentage of queries to receive recommendations

Recommendations	Web Devel	Marketing	Proj Man.	Devel A	QA	Finance	Devel B
Host	50%	83%	67%	75%	70%	15%	47%
Related	45%	33%	67%	78%	52%	86%	92%

In Table 3 we break down these figures and examine how each community performed for its own test queries. The table shows for each community the percentage of their queries that received promotions from their own case base and the percentage that received recommendations from the 6 related communities combined. It shows, for example, that 15% of the *Finance* queries received recommendations from the immature *Finance* community, but 86% of the *Finance* queries received recommendations from a related community. Examination of the *Finance* experience graph in Figure 3(c) shows that a number of related communities have more experience relating to the Finance queries than the *Finance* community itself and thus produce more recommendations. However even the larger, more established *Development A & B* communities see an increase in recommendation numbers, when cooperation is in place. Overall a 13% increase in number of queries to receive recommendations is observed.

4.3   Result Relevance

Of course query coverage is not a revealing measure as it says nothing about recommendation relevance. Thus, we look at the quality of the recommendations generated by each approach. Specifically, we look at the number of queries for which at least one *relevant* recommendation was generated—*successful queries*. The results presented in Table 2 again speak to the benefits of the CC approach, which delivers 69 successful queries against CWS's 54; a relative increase of 27% for the CC approach over standard CWS.

166 relevant results were generated by the traditional CWS technique across its 54 successful queries. When we look at the similar-community recommendations generated for these queries we find 45 relevant results. However crucially, we see that 38 of these 45 relevant recommendations are unique. In other words, over 84% of the relevant recommendations that originate from similar communities are different from the recommendations generated by the host community. It is worth noting that the community with the greatest similarity to the host in most cases, the *Development B* community, did not contribute any unique results to this set, thus showing that communities that are very similar to a host often do not contribute as many unique results as less similar communities.

4.4   Result Precision

403 queries were submitted to each of the 7 communities in turn, noting the performance of the host community in comparison to the other related communities. Figure 4 shows the precision scores for different result-list sizes, $k = 5...100$ for each of the communities and compares the host's result-list precision scores to the result-lists provided by related communities. It is worth noting that only 33% of the test queries received recommendations, which immediately reduces the average precision scores across the test queries. Taking this into consideration, we look at the precision scores in order to compare the traditional CWS technique and the community cooperation model.

As expected, precision values are highest at low values of k and fall as k increases. An immediate trend appears; in four out of seven graphs (Figure 4 (a - d) the *Development B* community's recommendations outperform the host community's recommendations in terms of accuracy. In these cases a related community has returned more relevant results than the host community, a trend not observed in the previous simulated evaluation [3]. That is, a related community exists, that is better equipped to answer queries than the host. It is worth noting that, even when the *Development B* community does not outperform the host community, it is the best performing related community. The next best performing communities are the *Quality Assurance* and *Development A* communities, which also often equal or outperform host communities.

We proposed that considering a candidate community's experience for a target query and its similarity to a host community informs us of its relatedness to a search scenario. In this evaluation we see the proof of this concept. On average the three largest and thus most experienced communities for the test queries are the *Development B*, *Quality Assurance* and *Development A* communities; see Figure 3 (a-d). These three communities also have the highest average similarity to the other communities; see Table 1. It follows that these community's suitability to cooperation be reflected in their precision scores. The encouraging finding is that the correlation between precision at k=5 and relatedness is 0.82, supporting our hypothesis that *related* communities, i.e. those that are similar and posses the search knowledge required for the task, are the best candidates for community cooperation where highly similar result-lists are favoured.

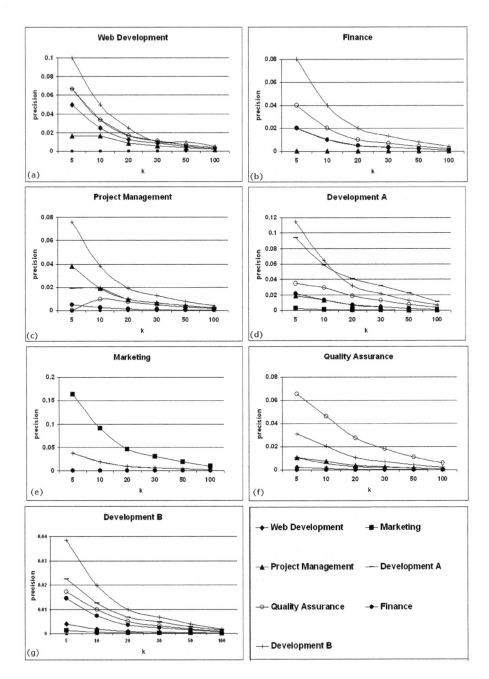

Fig. 4. Precision scores for the (a) Web Development, (b) Finance, (c) Project Management, (d) Development A, (e) Quality Assurance, (f) Marketing and (g) Development B communities

4.5   Conclusion

In this work we have shown how Web search experience can be captured as a case base of search cases, and how this experience can be distributed across multiple case bases. Our community collaboration technique aims to supplement a host community's recommendations with complementary recommendations from the search cases contained within the case bases of related communities. We have seen its potential to improve query coverage in terms of increasing the instances where recommendations can be made, increasing the number of queries to receive relevant recommendations and also increasing the number of relevant results returned per query. It has also shown us that, when a group of relevant communities exist the level of accuracy from partner communities can exceed the level of accuracy from the host recommendations, depending on experience and similarity. We have shown that the experience of communities of searchers can be usefully leveraged to help searchers from other communities. These related communities can serve as a source of recommendations that are both relevant and distinctive.

References

1. Kevin D. Ashley. Modeling Legal Argument: Reasoning with Cases and Hypotheticals. Technical 88–01, Department of Computer and Information Science, University of Massachusetts., Amherst, MA, 1990.
2. Jay Budzik and Kristian J. Hammond. User Interactions with Everyday Applications as Context for Just-In-Time Information Access. In *IUI '00: Proceedings of the 5th International Conference on Intelligent User Interfaces*, pages 44–51, New York, NY, USA, 2000. ACM Press.
3. Jill Freyne and Barry Smyth. Communities, Collaboration and Cooperation in Personalized Web Search. In *Proceedings of the 3rd Workshop on Intelligent Techniques for Web Personalization (ITWP'05) in conjunction with the 19th International Joint Conference on Artificial Intelligence (IJCAI '05)*, pages 73–80, Edinburgh, Scotland, 2005.
4. George W. Furnas, Thomas K. Landauer, Louis M. Gomez, and Susan T. Dumais. The Vocabulary Problem in Human-System Communication. *Communications of the ACM*, 30(11):964–971, 1987.
5. Daniela Godoy and Anala Amandi. PersonalSearcher: An Intelligent Agent for Searching Web Pages. In *IBERAMIA-SBIA '00: Proceedings of the International Joint Conference, 7th Ibero-American Conference on AI*, volume 1952, pages 43–52. Springer-Verlag, 2000.
6. Nigel Hamilton. The mechanics of a Deep Net Metasearch Engine. In *Proceedings of the 12th International World Wide Web Conference (Posters)*, Budapest, Hungary, April 2003.
7. Rushed Kanawati, Michel Jaczynski, Brigitte Trousse, and Jean-Marc Andreoli. Applying the Broadway Recommendation Computation Approach for Implementing a Query Refinement Service in the CBKB Meta-search Engine. In *Coinference Fraicaise sur le Raisonnement a Partir de Cas (RaPC'99)*, 1999.
8. Steve Lawrence and C. Lee Giles. Context and Page Analysis for Improved Web Search. *IEEE Internet Computing*, July-August:38–46, 1998.

9. David B. Leake and Raja Sooriamurthi. When Two Case-Bases Are Better than One: Exploiting Multiple Case Bases. In David W. Aha and Ian Watson, editors, *Proceedings of the 4th International Conference on Case-Based Reasoning (ICCBR '01)*, volume 2080 of *Lecture Notes in Computer Science*, pages 321–335. Springer, 2001.

10. Anton Leuski. Evaluating document clustering for interactive information retrieval. In Ling Liu Henrique Paques and David Grossman, editors, *Proceedings of 10th International Conference on Information and Knowledge Management (CIKM'01)*, pages 41–48, Atlanta, Georgia, USA, 2001. ACM Press.

11. Lorraine McGinty and Barry Smyth. Collaborative Case-Based Reasoning: Applications in Personalised Route Planning. In David W. Aha and Ian Watson, editors, *Proceedings of the 4th International Conference on Case-Based Reasoning (ICCBR '01)*, volume 2080 of *Lecture Notes in Computer Science*, pages 362–376. Springer, 2001.

12. M.V. Nagendra Prasad, Victor R. Lesser, and Susan E. Lander. Retrieval and Reasoning in Distributed Case Bases. *Journal of Visual Communication and Image Representation, Special Issue on Digital Libraries*, 7(1):74–87, January 1996.

13. M.V. Nagendra Prasad and Enric Plaza. Corporate Memories as Distributed Case Libraries. In *Proceedings of the Corporate Memory and Enterprise Modeling Track in the 10th Knowledge Acquisition Workshop*, 1996.

14. Edwina L. Rissland and Jody J. Daniels. A Hybrid CBR-IR Approach to Legal Information Retrieval. In *ICAIL '95: Proceedings of the 5th International Conference on Artificial Intelligence and Law*, pages 52–61. ACM Press, 1995.

15. Barry Smyth, Evelyn Balfe, Oisín Boydell, Keith Bradley, Peter Briggs, Maurice Coyle, and Jill Freyne. A Live-User Evaluation of Collaborative Web Search. In *Proceedings of the 19th International Joint Conference on Artificial Intelligence (IJCAI '05)*, pages 1419–1424, Edinburgh, Scotland, 2005.

16. Barry Smyth, Evelyn Balfe, Jill Freyne, Peter Briggs, Maurice Coyle, and Oisín Boydell. Exploiting Query Repetition and Regularity in an Adaptive Community-Based Web Search Engine. *User Modeling and User-Adapted Interaction*, 14(5):383–423, 2004.

17. Dell Zhang and Yisheng Dong. Semantic, Hierarchical, Online Clustering of Web Search Results. In *Proceedings of the 6th Asia Pacific Web Conference (APWEB)*, pages 69–78, Hangzhou, China, April 2004.

Finding Similar Deductive Consequences – A New Search-Based Framework for Unified Reasoning from Cases and General Knowledge

Ralph Bergmann and Babak Mougouie

University of Trier
Department of Business Information Systems II
54294 Trier, Germany
{bergmann, mougouie}@wi2.uni-trier.de

Abstract. While reasoning with cases is usually done in a similarity-based manner, additional general knowledge is often represented in rules, constraints, or ontology definitions and is applied in a deductive reasoning process. This paper presents a new view on the combination of deductive and similarity-based reasoning, which is embedded in the CBR context. The basic idea is to view general knowledge and cases as a logical theory of a domain. Similarity-based reasoning is introduced as search for the most similar element in the deductive closure of the domain theory. We elaborate this approach and introduce several related search algorithms, which are analyzed in an experimental study. Further, we show how several previous approaches for using general knowledge in CBR can be mapped to our new view.

1 Introduction

Although the primary source of knowledge in a case-based reasoning (CBR) system is the specific knowledge in the cases, it has always been recognized that additional general knowledge is often required for problem solving [1,6,9,7,12,2]. This general knowledge complements the knowledge in the cases, for example for the purpose of describing appropriate ways of adapting cases. While reasoning with cases is usually done in a similarity-based manner, general knowledge is often represented in rules, constraints, or ontology definitions and is usually applied in a deductive reasoning process. Therefore, the question of combining specific and general knowledge is strongly connected with the question of combining logic-oriented (deductive) and approximate reasoning [14].

This paper presents a new way of combining deductive and approximate reasoning in a unified manner, which is significantly different from previous approaches such as the theory proposed by Michalski [10]. Our basic idea is to view general knowledge and cases as a logical theory of a domain. In this theory, cases are usually encoded as facts. General knowledge is added to this theory in form of general logical sentences and possibly additional facts. The theory must be constructed such that the deductive closure represents the knowledge we know with certainty to be true in that domain. Similarity-based reasoning is

T.R. Roth-Berghofer et al. (Eds.): ECCBR 2006, LNAI 4106, pp. 271–285, 2006.

then introduced as follows: for a given query (together with a similarity measure) we search for the k most similar elements in the deductive closure and thus find the most similar deductive consequences.

This paper explores this new view in detail (Sect. 3) and positions it in the context of previous CBR research (Sect. 2, 3.4, and 6). Thereby it provides a generalized view on several earlier approaches, particularly:

- using rules for case completion [6]
- using rules or operators for transformational adaptation [6,5,8]
- using constraints to restrict admissible combinations of components for configuration or design [17,13]
- using constraints to define a generalized case [4,11,19]

It also can be regarded as a general framework for integrating structural CBR with ontology-based knowledge management as envisioned in [3].

Further the paper presents several new algorithms that integrate the similarity-based search with the search process performed during deduction (see Sect. 4). These algorithms show a different and unified way of performing the case-based reasoning tasks from the above mentioned original approaches. The developed algorithms differ in the heuristics used for pruning the huge overall search space. Hence, an empirical evaluation is presented in Sect. 5. Finally, we discuss the potential impact of our work.

2   Combining Cases and General Knowledge

We now review selected previous work that combines general knowledge and cases.

2.1   Completion Rules

The formulation of completion rules is a very straightforward use of general knowledge [6], which is widely used in practical CBR applications. Rules are applied for inferring additional properties not explicitly represented in the cases or the query, but which are necessary for the similarity assessment. They are usually used to define functionally dependent virtual attributes [15]. Here, deductive and similarity-based reasoning are strictly separated. Completion rules are applied to the cases when they are inserted into the case base. They are also applied prior to the retrieval process to compute the completion of the query. The similarity search is a separate step that is based on results of these deductions.

2.2   Transformational Adaptation with Rules or Operators

When using transformational adaptation, the most similar case is first retrieved from the case base using some notion of similarity. Then, in a separate adaptation step, appropriate case adaptations are determined by deductively applying adaptation knowledge, for example in the form of rules or operators. Bergmann and Wilke [5] propose a formal model of transformational adaptation that views adaptation as a search process in the space spawned by adaptation operators. An adaptation operator is a partial function that transforms a case into a successor case. The aim is to find an optimal solution with respect to some quality function encoding an overall similarity measure.

When applying transformational adaptation, the two steps namely the similarity-based retrieval and the deductive application of adaptation knowledge are separated in the first place, but additional measures are usually applied in order to ensure that adaptable cases are retrieved [16]. Despite those measures, it is usually not assured that the best solution is found, because not every case with every adaptation sequence is considered. Hence, this approach is a heuristic.

2.3   Case-Based Configuration with Constraints

Case-based approaches for solving configuration or design problems have to take into consideration the knowledge about relationships among design parameters as well as relations (for example technical constraints) among design objects. The difficulties in solving such problems are caused to some extent by the size and structure of the space of acceptable configurations. CBR is used in this context either for guiding the search to improve the problem solving speed, for replacing general knowledge by cases to reduce the knowledge engineering effort, or to find approximate solutions to problems that cannot be solved exactly because an exact solution that is inside the design space does not exist [17]. In the context of this paper, approaches of the two last kinds are of interest. Cases describe components (e.g. available hard disks, mainboards, etc.) as well as predefined sub-configuration (e.g. available barebone PCs, memory sub-systems, etc.) and constraints are used to describe technically required relationships (e.g. bus compatibility of components). Stahl and Bergmann [17] describe a case-based configuration approach that adapts retrieved components through search in the space of component replacements that is guided by a similarity measure used as target function. As with transformational adaptation, the involved search is not complete and hence it is not guaranteed that the best solution is found.

2.4   Generalized Cases

Generalized cases are cases that cover a subspace rather than a point in the problem-solution space [4]. A single generalized case immediately provides solutions to a set of closely related problems rather than to a single problem only. Generalized cases naturally occur in certain CBR applications, such as for the recommendation of parameterized products within electronic commerce or brokerage services. The selection of reusable electronic designs [19] or the selection of insurance policies [18] are concrete example applications.

Generalized cases can be represented by a set of constraints over the case attributes. For such representations, the similarity assessment between a query and generalized cases is a difficult problem, addressed e.g. in [11,19]. The task is to find the distance between the point query and the closest point of the area covered by the generalized cases. This task can either be addressed by converting it into an optimization problem [11,19] or by sampling the generalized case, which results in a set of point cases. Again the latter approach is based on a strict separation of deductive reasoning (sampling of the constraints) and approximate reasoning (finding the most similar sampled point), while the first approach performs approximate reasoning by considering the constraints defining the feasible region for optimization. Due to the large search space involved, both approaches typically don't guarantee that they find the best solution.

3   Finding Similar Deductive Consequences

The approaches described in the previous section have shown that similarity-based and deductive reasoning are used in CBR in combined form in various ways. However, there is no general formal framework that covers these ways of integrated reasoning. We think that such a framework is quite useful, much beyond its use for analyzing former research work. Particularly, it can be the starting point for the development of new ways to integrate both reasoning forms. This is in particular what we want to propose.

3.1   General Formalization

First, we need as basis a logical system with an inference calculus in which all knowledge, including cases, are represented. We can think of using predicate logic, Horn-logic, frame logic, or description logic. The latter appears to be very promising due to its use in ontology languages. However, for our current investigation and in order to serve the readability of this paper we now restrict ourselves to Horn logic. To define similar deductive consequences we assume that the following is given[1]:

- a domain theory Σ consisting of formulas of the logic (in Horn logic it consists of a set of facts and rules).
- a query $q \equiv p(t_1, ..., t_n)$ where p is an n-ary predicate symbol and t_i are terms (this is also what is called query in Horn logic / Prolog)
- a similarity measure $sim_p : AF_p \times AF_p \mapsto [0,1]$ where AF_p is the set of all atomic formulas starting with the n-ary predicate symbol p.

In this paper we restrict our consideration of similarity to the comparison of atomic formulas starting with the same predicate and hence having the same arity. If one further restricts the use of the terms t_i to constants, one ends up with a traditional similarity measure for a case representation with n attributes. Please note that the use of an (unbounded) variable is similar to specifying an unknown value for an attribute. We further formalize similarity measures following the local-global principle as follows: For $q' = p(t'_1, \ldots, t'_n)$:

$$sim_p(q, q') = \Omega(sim_1(t_1, t'_1), \ldots, sim_n(t_n, t'_n))$$

---

[1] When possible we will use the Prolog-style notation for formulas, i.e. predicate symbols, function symbols and constants are written in small first letters; variables start with a capital letter.

where Ω is an aggregate function that is monotonous in every argument and $0 \leq sim_i(t_i, t'_i) \leq 1$ for $i = 1, \ldots, n$ are local similarites. For the sake of simplicity, we write sim instead of sim_p.

Definition 1. (Most Similar Deductive Consequences, MSDC, k-MSDC)
The most similar deductive consequence is defined as follows:

$$MSDC(q) = \arg\max_{q' \in closure_p(\Sigma)} sim(q, q')$$

where $closure_p(\Sigma) = \{p(t_1, \ldots, t_n) \mid \Sigma \vdash p(t_1, \ldots, t_n)\}$ is the deductive closure of Σ restricted to atomic formulas starting with the n-ary predicate symbol p.
  This can be easily extended to k-$MSDC(q)$ which delivers the k-most similar deductive consequences:

$$k\text{-}MSDC(q) = \{q_1, \ldots, q_k\} \subseteq closure_p(\Sigma) \ s.t.$$
$$sim(q, q') \leq \min\{sim(q, q_i) | i = 1, \ldots, k\} \quad \forall q' \in closure_p(\Sigma) - \{q_1, ..., q_k\}.$$

3.2   A Simple Example

We now provide a first simple example to clarify this definition. Assume the following domain theory Σ denoted in traditional notation for Prolog:

```
q(X,Y) :- c(X,Y).
q(X,Y) :- c(X1,Y1), a(X,Y,X1,Y1).
c(2,5).
c(8,9).
a(X,Y,X1,Y1) :- D is X-X1, D>0, D<3, Y is Y1+X-X1.
```

In this example we make use of typical built-in predicates (such as `is`) available in most Prolog environments. Further assume the following similarity measure $sim_q((q(X,Y), q(X1,Y1)) = 1 - (|X - X1|/10)$, with values for the variables X and X_1 being bounded to $[0, 10]$. In this example the deductive closure is:

$$closure_q(\Sigma) = \{q(2,5), q(3,6), q(4,7), q(8,9), q(9,10), q(10,11)\}$$

The most similar deductive consequence for various queries are:

MSDC(q(1,Z)) = { q(2,5) }   MSDC(q(2,Z)) = { q(2,5) }
MSDC(q(3,Z)) = { q(3,6) }   MSDC(q(4,Z)) = { q(4,7) }
MSDC(q(5,Z)) = { q(4,7) }   MSDC(q(6,Z)) = { q(4,7), q(8,9)}
MSDC(q(7,Z)) = { q(8,9) }   MSDC(q(8,Z)) = { q(8,9) }

3.3   Discussion of the Example

We now give a CBR interpretation for this example. Consider the facts with the predicate c to be cases with the first argument representing the problem and the second argument representing the solution. As usual, the similarity measure assesses the similarity of the problem attribute. The first clause in the domain theory represents the fact that a query can be answered directly by a case (without adaptation) while the second clause describes that a case `c(X1,Y1)` is selected and then an adaptation operator is applied such as in transformational adaptation. The last clause represents the adaptation operator: if the difference in the problem is less than 3 then the solution is linearly adapted by the formula mentioned. Given this interpretation, it becomes obvious that the MSDC represents the result of a CBR system. Of course, a traditional Prolog interpreter, does not compute MSDCs but it is able to enumerate elements of the deductive closure if it is finite and if variables are appropriately instantiated. Computing the MSDC requires two kinds of searches: the search in the space to find a resolution-based proof-tree for an element in the deductive closure (which is naturally done by Prolog) and second, the search for the most similar element in the closure. Hence a simple but computationally inefficient solution even for finite deductive closures would do this sequentially: first, let Prolog enumerate the deductive closure and then, linearly search for the most similar element in it. More efficient solutions merging both searches will be presented in Sect. 4.

3.4   MSDC View of CBR Approaches

We now review the approaches from Sect. 2 in the light of MSDC.

Completion Rules. We consider completion rules that consist of a precondition and an action that computes a (new) value for an attribute. As shown in the previous example, all cases from the case base are encoded as facts (one term per attribute) in the domain theory. Then each completion rule is transferred into a Horn clause of the following schema:

$$c(X_1, ..., X_{k-1}, XNew_k, X_{k+1}, ...X_n) : - c(X_1, ..., X_n), pre(X_1, ..., X_n),$$
$$XNew_k \text{ is } action(X_1, ..., X_n).$$

The head of the clause represents the case that results by the completion; the variable $XNew_k$ gets a new value. *pre* is a Horn clause representation of the rule's precondition defined over the values $X_1, ..., X_n$ of the attribute of the selected case. If the precondition is fulfilled the expression *action* computes the new value. Of course in the regular deduction process, several completion rules can be chained. Completion rules are usually applied to a case-base when it is loaded into the CBR system. This is equivalent to pre-computing the deductive closure and storing it.

Transformational Adaptation. The example given in Sect. 3.2 can be generalized to a scheme for adaptation operators, which extends the representation of completion rules. It is as follows:

$$c(X_1, ..., X_n) : - c(Y_1, ..., Y_n), pre(Y_1, ..., Y_n),$$
$$X_1 \text{ is } action_1(Y_1, ..., Y_n), ...,$$
$$X_n \text{ is } action_n(Y_1, ..., Y_n).$$

Again, the head of the clause represents the result of the adaptation and *pre* is the operator's precondition based upon the selected case. Then the value of each attribute X_i is adapted by a separate $action_i$. Of course, adaptation rules can be chained and can be combined with completion rules. Computing MSDCs thus corresponds in a traditional CBR approach to selecting the best possible case and adapting it. However, unlike a traditional CBR approach the search covers the full set of adapted solutions. Here, pre-computing the deductive closure is getting computationally intractable and sophisticated search approaches are required (see Sect. 4).

Case-Based Configuration with Constraints. We restrict the discussion of how to encode case-based configuration in the MSDC view to a simple approach in which a system should be configured from several components while configuration constraints must be taken into account. The query represents the desired properties; the result will be a configuration being as similar as possible to the query. Cases represent components of the system to be configured. They are included as facts in the domain the ory; for each component type we use a different predicate (e.g. `mainboard`, `cpu`, `ram`, `harddisk` in the example below).

```
mainboard(asus,soa,ddr,ata,120). mainboard(kt,so478,ddr,sata,140).
cpu(Athlon,soa,2600,180). cpu(Celeron,so478,2800,sata,80).  ...
ram(infineon,ddr333,1024,132). ram(kingston,ddr400,256,42).  ...
harddisk(samsung,ata100,250,98). harddisk(ibm,sata,320,140).  ...
```

Several components are then combined to form a system or sub-system while taking the constraints into account. These combinations of components with related constraints are encoded in a Horn clause and inserted into the domain theory as well. Here is an example:

```
computer(CPUSpeed, RamSize, DiskSize, Price,
    BoardType, CPUType, RamType, DiskType) :-
    mainboard(BoardType,SocketType,RamBusNeeded,DiskBus,Price1),
    cpu(CPUType,CPUSocket,CPUSpeed,Price2),
    ram(RamType,RamBus,RamSize,Price3),
    harddisk(DiskType,DiskBusType,DiskSize,Price4),
    constraintCompatibleCpu(SocketType,CPUSocket),
    constraintCompatibleRam(RamBusNeeded,RamBus),
    constraintCompatibleDisk(DiskBusType,DiskBus),
    Price is Price1+Price2+Price3+Price4.
```

This clause specifies that the computer system is described by 8 attributes (arguments of the `computer` predicate); the first four contain the properties of the computer also specified in the query, the last four contain the configuration ifself. The last four literals in the body of this clause are examples of compatibility constraints among the components and compute a system property (price) from the components properties, respectively. Of course the compatibility constraints must be specified by additional Horn clauses.

When computing the MSDCs for a `computer` query with the first four attributes specified, the most similar overall configuration from the available components is determined.

Generalized Cases. Also generalized cases can be easily encoded in a domain theory used for the MSDC approach. A generalized case can be represented by a set of constraints that specify the subspace the case consists of. It is converted into a rule whose body contains those constraints:

$$c(X_1, ..., X_n) : - cons_1(X_1, ..., X_n, X_{n+1}, ..., X_{n+m}), ...,$$
$$cons_k(X_1, ..., X_n, X_{n+1}, ..., X_{n+m}).$$

In this schema $cons_i$ are the constraints which relate the variables in the case and possibly local variables to one another. Of course the used constraints must be specified in Horn logic by additional clauses. When computing the MSDC for a query, the most similar generalized case is determined with respect to the original definition provided in [4].

4   Formalizing and Solving the Search Problem

We now develop several standard AI search methods and some of their varieties and combinations to compute $k\text{-}MSDC(q)$ or to deliver an approximation of it. In the following we assume that the query q is of the form $q \equiv p(t_1, \ldots, t_n)$ for some arbitrary terms t_i. We start with a formalization of the state space for search.

4.1   The State-Space

Our search space to find the elements of $closure_p(\Sigma)$ is a state space in which each state differs from its successor in one resolution step. The complete state space $\mathcal{T}$ can be constructed as follows:

1. Set $(\langle q^* \rangle, q^*)$ with $q^* = p(X_1, \ldots, X_n)$ be the starting state of $\mathcal{T}$
   /* X_i are some new variables */
2. Let $\mathcal{S} = (\langle q_1, ..., q_d \rangle, \bar{q})$ be a state of $\mathcal{T}$;
   For all q_i $(i = 1, ..., d)$ do
   {
      2.1. For each substitution σ such that $\sigma(q_i) \in \Sigma$
        (**trim** $(\langle \sigma(q_1), \ldots, \sigma(q_{i-1}), \sigma(q_{i+1}), \ldots, \sigma(q_d) \rangle), \sigma(\bar{q}))$
        is a direct successor state of $\mathcal{S}$;   /* Resolution with a fact*/
      2.2. For each substitution σ such that $\sigma(q_i) = \sigma(r)$ for $r :\text{-} r_1, ..., r_m \in \Sigma$
        (**trim** $(\langle \sigma(q_1), \ldots, \sigma(q_{i-1}), \sigma(r_1), \ldots, \sigma(r_m), \sigma(q_{i+1}), \ldots, \sigma(q_d) \rangle), \sigma(\bar{q}))$
        is a direct successor state of $\mathcal{S}$;   /* Resolution with a rule*/
   }.

list **trim**($list$)
{ For all $q_i \in list$ do
    If q_i is a true built-in predicate then remove q_i from $list$;
  return $list$;
}.

By iteratively applying step 2 of this procedure, the tree of the state space $\mathcal{T}$ is constructed. Final states of the form $(\langle\rangle, q')$ are elements of the deductive closure $closure_p(\Sigma)$ and it holds $\exists \sigma$ s.t. $\sigma(q^*) = q'$. Final states that are not of this form are search branches not leading to a logical consequence of Σ.

Although $closure_p(\Sigma)$ might have a finite number of elements, $\mathcal{T}$ might have a huge (or even infinite) number of states. Since there is usually not enough time or memory available to search the entire state space, it is necessary to carefully explore a subspace T of the state-space $\mathcal{T}$. This subspace T is the search space of the heuristic search methods described below. In many cases it cannot be guaranteed that T includes k-MSDC completely, hence the optimal solution may get lost. However, as mentioned in Sect. 2, CBR involving adaptation also only computes heuristic solutions in many cases. Therefore, this cannot be considered a drawback, but obviously the deviation from the optimum should be considered.

4.2   Depth First Search Methods (dfs, dfs_MAS)

For this and the following search methods we assume that the state space is finite, which ensures the termination of the algorithms. The first complete search method which delivers the exact solutions of k-$MSDC$ is depth first search (dfs). We run dfs($q, \mathcal{S}, k$-$MSDC, k$) such that $\mathcal{S}$ is initiated to $(\langle q^*\rangle, q^*)$ with $q^* = p(X_1, \ldots, X_n)$ and k-$MSDC$ is an empty list:

dfs(query q, state $\mathcal{S}$, list k-$MSDC$, int k)
{
  If $\mathcal{S} = (\langle\ \rangle, q')$ then **insert**(q, q', k-$MSDC, k$);   (*)
    else for all direct successors $\mathcal{S}'$ of $\mathcal{S}$ do
        { **dfs**($q, \mathcal{S}', k$-$MSDC, k$); } }.
insert(query q, object o, list $\mathcal{L}$, int $list\_length$)
{
  If **length**($\mathcal{L}$) $= list\_length$ then
  {
    Let $\bar{o} = arg \min\limits_{o' \in \mathcal{L}} sim(q, o')$;
    If $sim(q, \bar{o}) < sim(q, o)$ then { **remove**($\bar{o}$, $\mathcal{L}$); **append**(o , $\mathcal{L}$) }
  }
  otherwise **append**(o , $\mathcal{L}$); }.

The above dfs algorithm is an exhaustive algorithm. It explores the entire $\mathcal{T}$ to deliver the optimal k-$MSDC$. However, it is possible to reduce the size of the explored search space by introducing a *minimum acceptable similarity* and *prune* the solutions whose similarities to q are less than this value. We define **dfs_MAS**($q, \mathcal{S}, k$-$MSDC, k, Min\_Acc\_Sim$) as follows:

First, replace line (*) of the dfs algorithm by the following line:

If $\mathcal{S} = (\langle\rangle, q')$ and $sim(q, q') \geq Min\_Acc\_Sim$ then **insert**$(q, q', k\text{-}MSDC, k)$;

And second, terminate search whenever $k\text{-}MSDC$ contains k elements.

This algorithm cuts the search space at the cost of not assuring to finding the optimal solution to the k-MSDC problem. It only finds up to k solutions with a similarity higher than Min_Acc_Sim. To use this approach it is of course required to know in advance a good value for Min_Acc_Sim. One could use a fixed value if it is possible to extract one from application requirements (e.g. a user might never be interested in results less similar than 0.5). Alternatively one could develop methods that compute good approximations for this value based on the domain theory and the query. This aspect is further discussed in Sect. 5.

4.3   Breadth First Search (bfs)

Breadth first search (bfs) is also a standard search method that can be applied to compute a solution to the k-MSDC problem. It maintains a list of open states, which causes the well-known problem of high memory complexity. However, bfs is clearly complete and therefore results in an exact solution to the k-MSDC problem. We run bfs$(q, [(\langle q^*\rangle, q^*)], k\text{-}MSDC, k)$ with $q^* = p(X_1, \ldots, X_n)$. Initially $k\text{-}MSDC$ is an empty list.

bfs(query q, list $open\_states$, list $k\text{-}MSDC$, int k)
{
   $next\_open\_states := \emptyset$;
   For all $\mathcal{S} \in open\_states$ do
   {
     For all successors $\mathcal{S}'$ of $\mathcal{S}$ do
       If $\mathcal{S}' = (\langle\ \rangle, q')$ then
         insert$(q, q', k\text{-}MSDC, k)$
       else
         append$(\mathcal{S}', next\_open\_states)$;   (**)
   }
   If $(next\_open\_states \neq \emptyset)$ then **bfs**$(q, next\_open\_states, k\text{-}MSDC, k)$; }.

4.4   Beam Search (beam)

Beam search is a middle course between bfs and dfs. It can prune a substantial fraction of the entire state space. A beam search **beam**$(q, [(\langle q^*\rangle, q^*)], k\text{-}MSDC, k, Max\_Num\_Sol)$ is the same as bfs except for the line (**) which is replaced by:

$$\text{**insert**}(q, \mathcal{S}', next\_open\_states, Max\_Num\_Sol);$$

where Max_Num_Sol is the *maximum number of solutions*, i.e. the beam width[2]. Of course, it is wise to choose Max_Num_Sol significantly greater than k in order

---

[2] For the definition of the *insert* function see the dfs algorithm.

to guarantee that the final k-$MSDC$ contains at least k solutions. Beam search significantly reduces the search space at the cost of not being able to guarantee that the best k solutions are found. Hence, only an approximation of k-MSDC is determined.

4.5   Look-Ahead Pruning (lap, lap_beam)

In order to improve the pruning approaches described before, we now introduce a more elaborate branch-and-bound technique. The idea is to determine for each open state a lower and an upper bound for its similarity to the query. The lower bound can be the similarity between the query and an arbitrary solution element in the subtree below that state. In this work, this is determined by a look-ahead computation by calling a dfs_MAS search with $k = 1$, starting at the current state. The upper bound is obtained by simply assigning all local similarities related to variables to their maximum possible value 1. We can then use this information to prune states whose upper bound similarities are lower than any lower bound similarity determined by the look-ahead computation for other states. Pruned states are called *renegade* states. With this strategy, the optimal solution is never lost. We formally define this as follows:

Definition 2. *Given a similarity measure $sim(q, q')$, a query $q = p(t_1, \ldots, t_n)$, and a state $\mathcal{S} = (\langle q'_1, \ldots, q'_d \rangle, q')$ such that without loss of generality $q' = p(X'_1, \ldots, X'_l, t'_{l+1}, \ldots, t'_n)$ and $X'_1, \ldots, X'_l$ are some variables. $sim_{min}(q, \mathcal{S})$ and $sim_{max}(q, \mathcal{S})$ are now defined as follows:*

$$sim_{max}(q, \mathcal{S}) = \Omega(1, \ldots, 1, sim_{l+1}(t_{l+1}, t'_{l+1}), \ldots, sim_n(t_n, t'_n))$$

$$sim_{min}(q, \mathcal{S}) = \begin{cases} sim(q, \bar{q}) & \textit{iff} \quad dfs\_MAS(q, \mathcal{S}, \langle \rangle, 1, 0) = \{\bar{q}\} \\ 0 & \textit{iff} \quad dfs\_MAS(q, \mathcal{S}, \langle \rangle, 1, 0) = \{\} \end{cases}$$

Definition 3. (Renegade State) *Let $\mathcal{S}_1$ and $\mathcal{S}_2$ be two states of $\mathcal{T}$. $\mathcal{S}_1$ is renegade if*

$$sim_{max}(q, \mathcal{S}_1) < sim_{min}(q, \mathcal{S}_2).$$

The resulting algorithm, which we call **lap**, is the same as bfs except for line (**) which is replaced by the following:

If $\mathcal{S}'$ is not renegade then **append**($\mathcal{S}'$,*next_open_states*);

To test the renegade condition, we maintain the value $sim_{minmax} = max$ $sim_{min}(q, \mathcal{S})$ for any known $\mathcal{S}$ and update it whenever a new state is added to *open_list*. Then, $\mathcal{S}'$ is renegade if $sim_{max}(q, \mathcal{S}') < sim_{minmax}$. This algorithm finds the most similar solution, but does not guarantee to include the second best solution in the final k-MSDC.

To further cut the search space this method can also be combined with beam search by changing line (**) of the bfs algorithm as follows:

If $\mathcal{S}'$ is not renegade then **insert**($q, \mathcal{S}'$, *next_open_states*, Max_Num_Sol);

We call the resulting algorithm **lap_beam**. Obviously, it does not guarantee any more that the best solution is delivered.

5   Experimental Evaluation

To evaluate the performance of the algorithms with respect to their computation
time and similarity error caused by the pruning heuristics, they are implemented
in SWI-Prolog. As test domain we employ the case-based configuration scenario
described in Sect. 2.3 that deals with the configuration of PCs. The formalization
of the domain theory Σ is similar to the one described in Sect. 3.4, except that
it is much more complex and realistic. It contains 93 rules and facts, the closure
$closure_q(\Sigma)$ for a fixed q, contains 287280 elements.

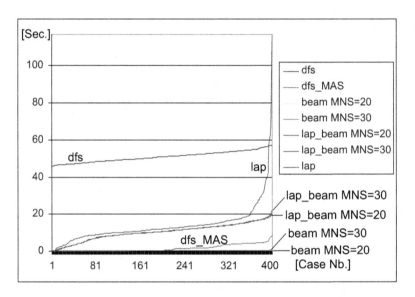

Fig. 1. The computation times per seconds of the algorithms with $K=10$ for 400 queries

Experimental Setting and Measured Results. All experiments were executed on the same Intel Pentium 4 computer (1.8 GHz, 480 MB Ram). Each
algorithm was executed with the parameter $k = 10$ for the same 400 randomly
generated queries, each of which describes a demand for a PC. The plot in Fig. 1
shows the computation time in CPU seconds for various algorithms plotted over
the 400 individual queries. The different algorithms together with the parameter
Max_Num_Sol (abbreviated with MNS) are shown together with the results of
a detailed evaluation in Table 1.

For each query we measured the computation time for the search (CTime)
as well as the average number of solutions found (NbSol). The set of test algorithms includes the complete dfs algorithm, which computes k-MSDC exactly.
The computation time can be considered as a base line which we aimed to improve with the various algorithms. The dfs algorithm also serves as a base line
for the similarity of the k-best solutions, which allows to determine the error
caused by the heuristic pruning. Therefore, we determined the similarity error,

Table 1. Comparison of the algorithms

Algorithm	MNS	CTime	NbSol	MinEr1	MaxEr1	AveEr1	MinEk	MaxEk	AveEk
dfs	–	50.94	10	0	0	0	0	0	0
dfs_MAS	10	1.52	10	0	0.087	0.047	0	0.103	0.050
beam	20	0.29	10	0	0.233	0.044	0	0.240	0.059
beam	30	0.48	10	0	0.208	0.037	0	0.215	0.050
lap_beam	20	10.34	7.65	0	0.157	0.014	0	0.166	0.028
lap_beam	30	10.42	7.65	0	0.050	0.001	0	0.158	0.021
lap	–	13.84	7.65	0	0	0	0	0.120	0.012

i.e. the difference in similarity of the retrieved ith-best solution found with some algorithm and the similarity of the ith-best solution found by dfs. The following measures were introduced: MinEr1 is the minimal similarity error for the best solution over all 400 queries. Correspondingly, MaxEr1 is the maximum error and AveEr1 is the average error for the best solution. Further MinEk, MaxEk, and AveEk denote the minimum, maximum, and average similarity error averaged over all k solutions retrieved for each query.

Discussion of Results. Clearly, dfs is the slowest algorithm and beam the fastest, but at the cost of producing a much higher similarity error. lap_beam clearly produces a lower error, but is significantly slower than beam. However it is sill about five times faster than dfs. The results of dfs_MAS are surprising: it is fast and produces only a small maximum error. The reason for this is the particular choice of the parameter Min_Acc_Sim. For testing the potential of this algorithm it is set very close to the real similarity for the k-best solution. For testing purposes it could be easily extracted from the results of the dfs algorithm. For this approach to be useful in general, a good and fast approximation algorithm for the similarity of the kth-best solution is required, because dfs is too slow. We are currently making significant progress on this problem and once it is solved, dfs_MAS will probably be the best choice.

6   Conclusion, Related and Future Work

The proposed new view of finding similar deductive consequences unifies previous approaches for integrating cases with general knowledge. It even allows to merge these approaches if the domain theory is constructed accordingly and also provides a perspective for thinking about new ways of integrating cases with general knowledge. The proposed algorithms demonstrate a unified way of reasoning, which is radically different than what was performed before in CBR. Due to its generality one cannot expect that the exact solution of the k-MSDC problem is as efficient as the specific reasoning processes used traditionally in CBR. Hence we proposed the idea of approximating the solutions of k-MSDC, which is again in the tradition of CBR.

Plaza and Arcos proposed constructive adaptation [12] as a search-based framework that integrates cases and general knowledge in the context of adaptation.

What is different is that their framework is located at a higher level of granularity and does not integrate per se deductive inference and similarity.

Case Retrieval Nets (CRN) have also been extended to flexibly integrate similarity and rule-based reasoning [9]. Rules are inserted as a special kinds of nodes in the CRN. However this approach is restricted to propositional logic and requires to explicitly model the derivation tree as part of the CRN.

Michalski's inferential theory of learning [10] might be considered related to our approach as it also integrates various forms of reasoning including deduction and analogy. However, our framework is significantly different and not an instance of it. Michalski's approach introduces similarity (with a threshold) as binary inference step with the consequence that it does not allow to rank different solutions with respect to their similarity, which is essential in the context of CBR.

Future research should focus on a detailed comparison k-MSDC and traditional approaches. It should also investigate methods for further speeding-up the search, e.g. by new heuristics, knowledge compilation techniques, or by integrating search control knowledge. The investigation of techniques that allow an a-priori estimation of the similarity error would also be quite useful.

Acknowledgment. The authors want to thank Alexander Tartakovski, Michael Richter and the anonymous reviewers for helpful comments on this paper. This work is partially funded by the research fund of the University of Trier.

References

1. A. Aamodt. *A Knowledge-Intensive, Integrated Approach to Problem Solving and Sustained Learning*. PhD thesis, University of Trondheim, 1991.
2. A. Aamodt. Knowledge-intensive case-based reasoning in creek. In P. Funk and P.A. Gonzlez Calero, editors, *Proceedings of the 7th European Conference on Case-Based Reasoning*, pages 1–15. Springer, 2004.
3. R. Bergmann and M. Schaaf. Structural Case-Based Reasoning and Ontology-based Knowledge Managemenet: A Perfect Match? *Journal of Universal Computer Science*, 9(7), 2003.
4. R. Bergmann and I. Vollrath. Generalized cases: Representation and steps towards efficient similarity assessment. In W. Burgard, Th. Christaller, and A. B. Cremers, editors, *KI-99: Advances in Artificial Intelligence.*, LNAI 1701. Springer, 1999.
5. R. Bergmann and W. Wilke. Towards a new formal model of transformational adaptation in case-based reasoning. In *European Conference on Artificial Intelligence (ECAI'98)*, 1998.
6. R. Bergmann, W. Wilke, I. Vollrath, and S. Wess. Integrating general knowledge with object-oriented case representation and reasoning. In H. D. Burkhard and M. Lenz, editors, *4th German Workshop on CBR*, pages 120–127, HU Berlin, 1996.
7. B. Diaz-Agudo and P.A. Gonzalez-Calero. An architecture for knowledge intensive cbr systems. In E. Blanzieri and L. Portinale, editors, *Advances in Case-Based Reasoning (EWCBR'2000)*, pages 37 – 48. Springer, 2000.
8. B. Fuchs, J. Lieber, A. Mille, and A. Napoli. Towards a unified theory of adaptation in case-based reasoning. In K.-D. Althoff, R. Bergmann, and L.-K. Branting, editors, *Case-Based Reasoning Research and Development (ICCBR'99)*, pages 104 – 117. Springer Verlag, 1999.

9. M. Lenz and H.D. Burkhard. Case Retrieval Nets: Foundations, properties, implementation, and results. Technical report, Humboldt University, Berlin, 1996.
10. R. Michalski. Inferential theory of learning. In R. Michalski and G. Tecuci, editors, *Machine Learning – A Multistrategy Approach*. Morgan Kaufmann, 1994.
11. B. Mougouie and R. Bergmann. Similarity assessment for generalized cases by optimization methods. In S. Craw and A. Preece, editors, *Advances in Case-Based Reasoning, Proc. ECCBR2002*, pages 249 – 263. Springer, 2002.
12. E. Plaza and J.-L. Arcos. Constructive adaptation. In S. Craw and A. Preece, editors, *Advances in Case-Based Reasoning (ECCBR'2002)*, pages 306 – 320. Springer, 2002.
13. L. Purvis and P. Pu. Adaptation using constraint satisfaction techniques. In A. Aamodt and M. Veloso, editors, *Case-Based Reasoning Research and Development (ICCBR'95)*, pages 289–300. Springer Verlag, 1995.
14. M. M. Richter. Logic and approximation in knowledge based systems. In W. Lenski, editor, *Logic vs. Approximation – Essays Dedicated to Michael M. Richter on the Occasion of his 65th Birthday*, pages 184 – 203. Springer, 2004.
15. M.M. Richter. Fallbasiertes Schliessen. *Informatik Spektrum*, 3(26):180–190, 2003.
16. B. Smyth and M. Keane. Retrieving adaptable cases. In S. Wess, K.-D. Althoff, and M.M. Richter, editors, *Topics in Case-Based Reasoning (EWCBR-93)*, Lecture Notes in Artificial Intelligence, pages 209–220. Springer, Berlin, 1994.
17. A. Stahl and R. Bergmann. Applying recursive CBR for the customization of structured products in an electronic shop. In E. Blanzieri and L. Portinale, editors, *Advances in Case-Based Reasoning (EWCBR'2000)*. Springer, 2000.
18. A. Tartakovski, M. Schaaf, and R. Bergmann. Retrieval and configuration of life insurance policies. In H. Munoz-Avila and F. Ricci, editors, *Advances in Case-Based Reasoning (ICCBR'2005)*, pages 552 – 565. Springer, 2005.
19. A. Tartakovski, M. Schaaf, R. Maximini, and R. Bergmann. Minlp based retrieval of generalized cases. In P. Funk and P.A. Gonzlez Calero, editors, *Advances in Case-Based Reasoning (ECCBR'2004)*, pages 404 – 418. Springer, 2004.

Case-Based Sequential Ordering of Songs for Playlist Recommendation[*]

Claudio Baccigalupo and Enric Plaza

IIIA - Artificial Intelligence Research Institute
CSIC - Spanish Council for Scientific Research
Campus UAB, 08193 Bellaterra, Catalonia, Spain
Vox: +34-93-5809570; Fax: +34-93-5809661
{claudio, enric}@iiia.csic.es

Abstract. We present a CBR approach to musical playlist recommendation. A good playlist is not merely a bunch of songs, but a selected collection of songs, arranged in a meaningful sequence, e.g. a good DJ creates good playlists. Our CBR approach focuses on recommending new and meaningful playlists, i.e. selecting a collection of songs that are arranged in a meaningful sequence. In the proposed approach, the Case Base is formed by a large collection of playlists, previously compiled by human listeners. The CBR system first retrieves from the Case Base the most relevant playlists, then combines them to generate a new playlist, both relevant to the input song and meaningfully ordered. Some experiments with different trade-offs between the diversity and the popularity of songs in playlists are analysed and discussed.

1 Introduction

A typical music recommender considers songs the user likes, has listened to, or has bought, and proposes similar songs that the user will probably like, be interested in listening, or buying. Only a few recommenders are addressed to suggest *playlists of similar songs* with an inherent *sequential structure*.

Creating a playlist is a common manual operation in audio user experience. Imagine a user wants to assemble a playlist, on the basis of a specific song he likes, has listened to or has bought. He could either choose each song manually, or follow the advice of a recommender, adding one proposed song after the other. In both cases, the process would be slow; besides, the user would also have to *order* the songs, for a playlist is expected to contain songs in a specific sequence.

In this paper, we describe a case-based approach to playlist recommendation. Given a song chosen by the user, we don't focus on finding isolated *similar songs*; instead we put the emphasis on recommending *good playlists*. A playlist is a sequence—not a set—of songs; thus its quality is given both by the songs it contains, and by their ordering (their relative positions).

---

[*] This research is supported in part by a MusicStrands scholarship and by CBR-ProMusic under the project TIC2003-07776-C02-02.

T.R. Roth-Berghofer et al. (Eds.): ECCBR 2006, LNAI 4106, pp. 286–300, 2006.

This paper presents a CBR system that takes a song as the input and returns a recommended playlist as the output. The possible applications include: personalised radio programs, playlist generators, digital music organisers, and in general any scenario where the user desires a good sequence of songs, related to a chosen one, without the burden of compiling it manually.

In this paper, after reviewing related works (Sect. 2), we present the problem of recommending a playlist from a song (Sect. 3). Then we describe the CBR process: in Sect. 4, we illustrate the structure of the Case Base; in Sect. 5, we explain the Retrieve process, and introduce the basic concepts of pattern and relevance; in Sect. 6, we describe how the retrieved playlists are combined in the Reuse process. In Sect. 7 we report about the tests with an actual Case Base of playlists. Section 8 ends the paper with a brief conclusion and future works.

2   Related Work

Several approaches have been investigated to develop an Automatic Playlist Generator [2,7,17,3,20,16]. Some of them require a large pre-existent *music-related* knowledge, either in form of music metadata [18] or acoustic-based measures [12]. In this paper we introduce a 'knowledge-light' approach to recommendation, based only on *user-related* knowledge. In this sense, our approach is comparable with SmartRadio and CoCoA Radio, two systems with which we share the vision that the work involved in compiling a playlist of music can be distributed to other listeners [10]. SmartRadio [8] is an Automatic Collaborative Filtering recommender that generates personalised playlists on the basis of playlists of users whose profiles are similar. Similarly, CoCoA Radio [4] recommends new playlists, but it also assumes that the knowledge of a playlist is encoded in the order of its songs. Our system is, in a sense, *lighter* than SmartRadio and CoCoA Radio. We also do assume that, in any well chosen collection of music, there is some great *implicit* value in the order of its songs, but we use this and only this knowledge to generate new playlists, without, for instance, collecting users' profiles or managing *explicit* ratings.

Some common points can be found between our system and the approach presented by Ragno et Al. [21]. In their work, similarity is inferred analysing the occurrences of songs in broadcasted streams of music, and new playlists are generated using a *graph-search process* (where the songs are the nodes of the graph and the similarities between them represent the weights of the arcs).

In our approach, the recommender is implemented as a *Case-Based Reasoning* (CBR) process [1,14]. Every playlist is seen as a case whose relevance is inferred measuring the *co-occurrences* of its songs in a large collection of past playlists. Co-occurrences analysis [11] has been proved effective in many domains where information is available as large sets of sequential data. Applications range from semantical similarity recognition [13] to weather forecast [22]. Pachet et al. [15] have originally proposed co-occurrences analysis as a method to evaluate similarity between songs. In this paper, we combine this method with an explicit notion of sequentiality, in order to infer similarity between songs and playlists.

3   Playlist Recommendation

In our approach, the user chooses an input song s and a desired length λ; the goal of the recommender is to return a playlist p (with λ songs) such that: **(G1)** p contains s; **(G2)** p is varied; **(G3)** p is coherently ordered. A playlist is *varied* if it does not repeat the same track or artist in the sequence, or at least if repetitions are not close. We say a playlist is *coherently ordered* if its songs make sense in the proposed sequence. The problem we have to solve is then to determine *which sequences of songs are coherently ordered*.

In order to answer this issue, we analyse a large repository of playlists, previously compiled by human listeners. In this analysis, we seek for those sequences (of two or more songs) that occur more often, with the same order, in these playlists. The idea is that the higher the number of playlists where a sequence occurs, the stronger the evidence that sequence is coherently ordered. This idea takes inspiration from studies of *co-occurrences analysis*. Basically, these studies argue that when two items appear frequently in the same context, this proves the existence of some similarity between them. For instance, linguists regularly use co-occurrences analysis to extract clusters of semantically related words from large collections of texts. We adapt this approach to a musical context: if some songs occur frequently, in the same order, in a collection of past playlists, then we assume that the order in which they appear is meaningful. We call such sequences of songs *relevant patterns*.

Relevant patterns are the starting point for the recommender we present; to fulfil the aforementioned goals we employ a Case-Based Reasoning approach that comprises four subsequent steps:

1. Assemble a Case Base from a repository of playlists *(Case Base Setup)*.
2. Prompt the user for an input song s and the desired length λ of the recommendation *(Problem Description)*.
3. Retrieve from the Case Base a subset of playlists that satisfy most of the goals. Specifically, the retrieved playlists are varied **(G2)** and include relevant patterns that contain s **(G1)** *(Retrieve Process)*.
4. Combine the songs of the retrieved playlists to generate a coherently ordered playlist **(G3)** with length λ *(Reuse Process)*.

Notice that the knowledge that guides the CBR process comes from the same content of the Case Base, in the form of relevant patterns. Hence the quality of the recommendation depends mostly on the quality of past playlists: the more accurately they have been compiled by the users with a meaningful order, the more this order will be reflected in the output. Clearly, different repositories may lead to different recommendations.

4   The Case Base

Let $\mathcal{P}$ be the repository of past playlists. $\mathcal{P}$ may include, for example, tracklists from radio programs, web streams, music compilations, DJ sessions, and

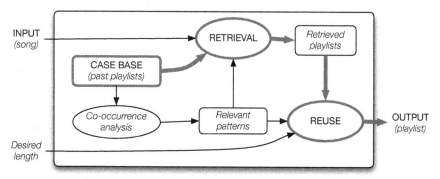

Fig. 1. General view of the CBR process

in general lists of songs that have been compiled with a meaningful order. By the way, the repository could include some *noisy* playlists, that is, playlists that have not been compiled with a great accuracy, and that would lower the quality of the Case Base if used. Examples of noisy playlists are: very long sequences of songs (that are probably only large *sets* of songs, with no meaningful order), very short sequences (from which we cannot extract any relevant pattern), and sequences in alphabetical order (that is hardly a meaningful order). Before using the repository, we filter $\mathcal{P}$ to remove such playlists; the result $\mathcal{C}$ is the Case Base.

Every playlist of $\mathcal{C}$ is a sequence of songs: $p = (s_1, s_2, .., s_n)$. Let $\Lambda(p) = n$ be the length of p. A song s is contained in a playlist p if the following condition holds: $In(s, p) \equiv \exists i, 1 \leqslant i \leqslant n : s = s_i$

Every song is characterised by a set $\mathcal{A}$ of attributes (e.g.: an identifier of the track, an identifier of the album it belongs to, the artist that performs it, etc.). We assume that the user will disapprove of recommendations where close songs repeat the same attributes: for example playlists where many songs belong to the same album or artist. Such playlists lack necessary variety, and our approach intends to avoid these cases, in order to boost diversity. For every attribute $a \in \mathcal{A}$, we introduce a parameter γ_a, called *safe distance for a*, as the minimum number of songs that must occur before we allow a value of a to be repeated. For instance, if $\gamma_a = 10$, the same value of a can be repeated without restriction only after 10 songs. To quantify how many, and how close, are the potential repetitions of an attribute in a playlist, we introduce a function called *attribute variety*:

Definition 1. (Attribute variety) *Let $p \in \mathcal{C}$ be a playlist, $p = (s_1, s_2, .., s_n)$, and $a \in \mathcal{A}$ be a song attribute; the variety of a in p is a function $V_a : \mathcal{C} \rightarrow (0, 1]$ such that:*

$$V_a(p) = \prod_{i=1}^{n} \begin{cases} \frac{j-i}{\gamma_a} & \text{if } \exists j, i < j \leqslant \min(n, i + \gamma_a) : a(s_i) = a(s_j) \\ & \wedge \forall k, i < k < j, a(s_i) \neq a(s_k) \\ 1 & \text{otherwise} \end{cases}$$

In other words, a playlist has an attribute variety $V_a(p) = 1$ only if no value of a is repeated within the safe distance γ_a; otherwise the more and the closer the repeated values, the smaller $V_a(p)$. Combining the values of $V_a(p)$ for all the song attributes with a t-norm (e.g. product), we obtain a global measure of *variety of a playlist* $p \in \mathcal{C}$:

$$Var(p) = \prod_{a \in \mathcal{A}} V_a(p)$$

The variety of a playlist p equals 1 only if no attribute is repeated in p within its safe distance. According to **(G2)**, we are interested in recommending this kind of playlists. We will see in Sect. 5 how $Var(p)$ will be used, inside the Retrieve process, to prefer varied playlists over repetitive ones.

5   Retrieve

In a classic CBR approach, the goal of the retrieval task is to return a subset of cases that contain the *solutions* for *problems* similar to the proposed one. In our approach, we do not intend to characterise the cases in terms of problem and solution parts: our Retrieve process is not focused on finding which songs in the Case Base are the most *similar* to the input song. Instead, we look for useful cases [6], that is, previous users' playlists that are useful to achieve the requested goals. The idea is to retrieve a subset of those playlists that include s **(G1)**, are varied **(G2)**, and contain relevant patterns, or else are coherently ordered **(G3)**.

Before presenting the Retrieve process, we introduce the *Relevance function* and the *Rating function*. The Relevance function $Rel(q, t)$, defined in Sect. 5.1, takes as input a sequence of songs q, and a song t contained in q, and returns the degree in which q is a *relevant pattern* for t. The Rating function $\rho(p, s)$, defined in Sect. 5.2, takes in input a playlist $p \in \mathcal{C}$ and the chosen song s, and returns a combined measure of the variety of p and the relevant patterns in p that contain s. At the end of the section, we present the Retrieve process that, given all the playlists of $\mathcal{C}$, returns only the k playlists that are more useful to fulfil our goals.

5.1   Patterns and Relevance

Let q be a sequence of songs. We say q a *pattern* if q is sub-sequence of at least one playlist of $\mathcal{C}$, where $q = (t_1, t_2, ..., t_m)$ is *sub-sequence* of $p = (s_1, s_2, ..., s_n)$ when the following condition holds: $Sub(q, p) = \exists i : \forall j, 1 \leqslant j \leqslant m, t_j = s_{i+j}$. The *pattern count* $\phi(q) = |\{p \in \mathcal{C} : Sub(q, p)\}|$ is the number of playlists of $\mathcal{C}$ that q is sub-sequence of.

Let t be a song, $Q(t) = \{q : \Lambda(q) \leqslant \theta \wedge In(t, q) \wedge \exists p \in \mathcal{C} : Sub(q, p)\}$ be the set of patterns, with at most θ songs, that contain t, and $q \in Q(t)$ be one of these patterns. To assess whether q is a relevant pattern for t, we can consider how many times t occurs in the playlists of $\mathcal{C}$ together with the other songs of q. According to co-occurrences analysis, in fact, the higher this number, the higher the evidence that q is a relevant pattern for t. Thus, it makes sense to use the pattern count $\phi(q)$ as a measure of the relevance of q

for t. Nevertheless, the actual value of $\phi(q)$ can be biased by two properties of q: its length and the popularity of its songs. In general, short patterns or patterns made of very popular songs have a higher probability of occurring in many playlists, independently from their relevance for a specific song.

Example 1. To understand why shorter patterns are likely to have a higher pattern count, consider the patterns $(S2, S3)$ and $(S2, S3, S4)$ in Table 1. Notice that $(S2, S3)$ is shorter than $(S2, S3, S4)$, and $\phi((S2, S3)) > \phi((S2, S3, S4))$. This is not surprising, for $(S2, S3)$ is contained in $(S2, S3, S4)$, so it occurs at least every time that $(S2, S3, S4)$ occurs in some playlist. To understand why patterns made of popular songs are likely to have a higher pattern count, consider the patterns $(S2, S3)$ and $(S9, S2)$, both containing $S2$. In the first case, $S2$ is followed by a "popular" song ($S3$ occurs 6 times in Table 1); in the second case, $S2$ is preceded by a less popular song ($S9$ occurs only 3 times). Notice that $\phi((S2, S3)) > \phi((S9, S2))$; this is not surprising, for $S3$ has a higher probability than $S9$ to co-occur with $S2$, due to its high popularity.

Table 1. A sample repository and the list of patterns with $\phi > 1$

Playlists	Patterns	
$A = (S1, S2, S4)$	$(S1, S2)$	$(\phi = 2)$
$B = (S1, S2, S3, S4, S5, S7, S1, S8)$	$(S2, S3, S4)$	$(\phi = 3)$
$C = (S4, S6, S9, S2, S2, S3)$	$(S2, S3)$	$(\phi = 6)$
$D = (S2, S3, S2, S3, S4)$	$(S3, S4)$	$(\phi = 3)$
$E = (S2, S3, S4, S6, S5)$	$(S4, S6)$	$(\phi = 2)$
$F = (S9, S2, S3, S5, S9, S1)$	$(S9, S2)$	$(\phi = 2)$

In a nutshell, short patterns and patterns made of popular songs are likely to have a high pattern count, independently from being relevant to a particular song. Therefore, to estimate the relevance of a pattern q to a song t, we combine $\phi(q)$ with two factors that balance the effect of the length of q, and of the popularity of its songs. We define the *Relevance* of a pattern q for a song t as follows:

$$Rel(q, t) = \phi(q) \cdot \frac{\alpha^{\theta - \Lambda(q)}}{\psi^\beta(q, t)}$$

where $\alpha^{\theta - \Lambda(q)}$ and $\psi^\beta(q, s)$ are the two factors intended to reduce the bias of the length of q, and of the popularity of its songs, on the relevance value. Hereafter, we explain in detail these two factors.

Length factor. Let $q_1 \in Q(t)$ and $q_2 \in Q(t)$ be two patterns, with same pattern count and different length (e.g. $\Lambda(q_1) > \Lambda(q_2)$). In this case, we consider q_1 more relevant for t than q_2, because q_1 occurs the same number of times than the (more probable) shorter pattern q_2. Moreover, since q_1 is longer, it contains more songs co-occurrent with t than q_2. For this reason, we introduce a *length factor* $\alpha^{\theta - \Lambda(q)}$ that we multiply $\phi(q)$ for, in order to substantially decrease the relevance of shorter patterns. The shorter q (that is, the more distant is $\Lambda(q)$ to the maximum pattern length θ), the smaller this factor, the smaller the relevance value. The parameter α can be tuned inside $(0, 1]$, to control if the length of q should affect more (small α) or less (high α) the relevance value.

Popularity factor. Let $q_1 = (t, u)$ and $q_2 = (t, v)$ be two patterns of two songs with the same pattern count (e.g. $\phi(q_1) = \phi(q_2) = 5$), and let u be more popular than v (e.g. u occurs in 600 playlists of $\mathcal{C}$, while v only in 6). Notice that u occurs relatively few times in $\mathcal{C}$ preceded by t (5 out of 600), while v occurs relatively many times preceded by t (5 out of 6). In the whole, q_2 appears in $\mathcal{C}$ more frequently *in relation to the popularity of its songs*; in this sense it is more relevant for t. For this reason, we introduce a *popularity factor* $\psi^\beta(q, t)$ that we divide $\phi(q)$ by, in order to decrease the relevance of patterns made of popular songs. This factor acts as a measure of inverse songs' frequency of q; precisely, $\psi(q, t)$ is the number of times that the sequence q occurs in $\mathcal{C}$ "independently from t": $\psi(q, t) = |\{p \in \mathcal{C} : \exists i : \forall j, 1 \leqslant j \leqslant m, q_j = p_{i+j} \vee q_j = t\}|$. The parameter β can be tuned inside $[0, 1]$ to control if the popularity of the songs should affect more (high β) or less (small β) the relevance value.

Example 2. To understand the effects of α and β on the relevance value, consider the patterns in Table 1, ranked according to how *relevant* they are to a specific song, $S3$. Table 2 shows the relevance values, using different values of α and β.

Notice that $(S2, S3)$ has the highest pattern count, and indeed is the most relevant pattern when $\alpha = 1$ and $\beta = 0.5$. However, if we decrease the relevance of *short patterns* ($\alpha = 0.5$), then the most relevant pattern becomes $(S2, S3, S4)$, that occurs less times but is longer. Similarly, if we decrease the effect of popular songs ($\beta = 1$), then the most relevant pattern is $(S2, S3, S4)$, for it occurs 3 out of the 3 times that $S2$ and $S4$ occur in some playlist of Table 1 separated by one song.

Table 2. Relevance to $S3$ of the patterns from Table 1

Patterns $q_i \in Q(S3)$	$\Lambda(q_i)$	$\phi(q_i)$	$\psi(q_i, S3)$	$Rel(q_i, S3)$ ($\alpha = 1\ \beta = 0.5$)	$Rel(q_i, S3)$ ($\alpha = 0.5\ \beta = 0.5$)	$Rel(q_i, S3)$ ($\alpha = 1, \beta = 1$)
$(S2, \underline{S3}, S4)$	3	3	3	1.73	**1.73**	1
$(S2, \underline{S3})$	2	6	8	**2.12**	1.06	0.75
$(\underline{S3}, S4)$	2	3	4	1.50	0.75	0.75

5.2   Coherence and Retrieval

We are now able to define the Rating function $\rho(p, s)$, that assigns a high value to playlists that are varied and coherent with the input song s. This function is a combination of $Var(p)$ (the variety of the playlist) and $Coh(p, s)$ (the coherence of the playlist to the input song), where $Coh(p, s)$ is defined as the sum of the relevance values of the patterns, present in p, that contain s:

$$Coh(p, s) = \sum_{q \in \Omega(s,p)} Rel(q, s)$$

where $\Omega(s,p) = \{q : \Lambda(q) \leqslant \theta \wedge In(s,q) \wedge Sub(q,p)\}$. The more the relevant patterns that contain s in p, and the higher their relevance to s, the higher $Coh(p, s)$. The Rating function $\rho(p, s)$ is defined as a combination of variety and coherence:

$$\rho(p, s) = Var(p) \cdot Coh(p, s), \quad \forall p \in \mathcal{C}$$

As a result, a playlist $p \in \mathcal{C}$ has a high value of $\rho(p, s)$ if it contains s, is varied, and is coherently ordered. Actually, this is the kind of playlist that we intend to retrieve from $\mathcal{C}$. Let k be the number of playlists to retrieve, the Retrieve process returns the first k playlists of $\mathcal{C}$, every playlist $p \in \mathcal{C}$ ranked according to $\rho(p, s)$.

6   Reuse

The goal of the Reuse process is to transform the k retrieved playlists into a single, recommended playlist of a specific length λ. Notice that the retrieved playlists can have any length, so they cannot be directly returned as recommendations. The approach we take for Reuse is that of Constructive Adaptation [19]. Following this approach, we use the elements of the retrieved cases (i.e. the songs from the retrieved playlists) to build a new combination of elements (i.e. a new playlist), that is a solution for the current problem. Building this playlist is seen as a search process, guided by the information contained in the Case Base (in the form of relevant patterns).

Basically, Constructive Adaptation [19] is composed of two processes: *Hypotheses Generation* and *Hypotheses Ordering*. Hypotheses Generation determines how partial solutions are extended in the search process (i.e. which songs from the retrieved playlists can be combined and how). Hypotheses Ordering uses the knowledge from the Case Base to rank the nodes visited during the search (i.e. the sequences of songs generated so far) in order for the search process to follow the best paths to the solution. Thus, the Reuse process is a search process where:

- the goal is to find a playlist of λ songs, that includes the input song s;
- every node in the search is a sequence made of songs from the retrieved playlists;
- the singleton sequence (s) is taken as the initial node;
- the successors of every node contain the same sequence of songs of that node, plus another song, either at the beginning or at the end of the sequence.

The fastest method to reach a sequence of length λ starting from (s) (a sequence of length 1) is to always explore the search tree "as deep as possible", that is, to always visit first the nodes with the longest sequences of songs found so far. For this reason, the system uses a Depth-First Search process: at first, it expands the initial node (s) by generating all its successors; at each subsequent step, it considers one of the most recently generated nodes, generates its successors, and ranks them according to a heuristic; if at any moment it finds a node with λ songs, returns it as the solution; if otherwise it finds a node with no successors, it backtracks to expand another of the most recently generated nodes.

6.1   Hypotheses Generation

The nodes of the search are sequences made of elements from the retrieved cases, that is, of songs from the retrieved playlists. Let $T = (t_1, t_2, .., t_n)$ be a node, and let T' be a successor of T. T' contains the same songs of T, and another song u from the retrieved playlists, either at the beginning or at the end of T'. We distinguish these two cases with the notations $\langle u + T \rangle$ and $\langle T + u \rangle$. Let, for instance, be $T' = \langle u + T \rangle$. Notice that in T', u occurs before t_1. In order for T' to be coherently ordered, u should occur before t_1 at least in one retrieved playlist; basically we consider T' a valid successor of T if $\exists p \in Ret(s) : Sub((u, t_1), p)$, where $Ret(s)$ is the set of k retrieved playlists. Similarly, a sequence $\langle T + u \rangle$ is a valid successor of T if $\exists p \in Ret(s) : Sub((t_n, u), p)$. The set of all the valid successors of a node T is defined as $Succ(T) = \{\langle u + T \rangle, \forall u \in Pre(T) \vee \langle T + u \rangle, \forall u \in Post(T)\}$, where $Pre(T) = \{u : \exists p \in Ret(s) : Sub((u, t_1), p)\}$ and $Post(T) = \{u : \exists p \in Ret(s) : Sub((t_n, u), p)\}$.

In the next subsection, we will describe how such sets of successors are sorted in the search process in order to finally reach a sequence of λ songs that is varied, coherently ordered, and relevant to s.

6.2   Hypotheses Ordering

In ordering the successors of a node, we promote those sequences that are varied and include relevant patterns. In other words, given any successor T' of T (where u is the added song), we determine if T' is a *good successor* of T using the heuristic function $H(T') = Rel(T', u) \cdot Var(T')$. Using H, we are able to rank highly a node T' that contains a varied and coherently ordered sequence of songs. However we cannot determine whether the successors of T' will be varied and coherently ordered sequences as well. To solve this issue, we introduce in the heuristic a parameter L, called look-ahead factor, such that:

- If $L = 0$, we evaluate H on T', as above;
- If $L = 1$, we evaluate H on *all the successors* of T'; then we return the maximum value found as the heuristic value for T';
- If $L = 2$, we evaluate H on *all the successors at depth 2* of T', that is, the successors of the successors of T'; then we return the maximum value found as the heuristic value for T'; and so on.

The higher is L, the more reliable is the heuristic; on the other hand, the number of requested evaluations of H grows steeply with L. The value of L is usually a compromise between a good heuristic and a reasonable performance. Finally, we define the heuristic function as follows:

Definition 2. *(Look-ahead heuristic) Let T be a node of the search tree; any successor T' of T is ranked using the heuristic function:*

$$H'(T', L) = \begin{cases} H(T') & \text{if } L = 0 \\ \max_{T'' \in Succ(T')} H'(T'', L - 1) & \text{if } L > 0 \end{cases}$$

Summing up, the Reuse process follows a Constructive Adaptation approach in which a) Hypotheses Generation explores the possible combinations of the songs of the retrieved playlists and b) Hypothesis Ordering ranks the partial sequences according to a heuristic based on relevance and variety. At the end, the result is a playlist of length λ that combines the best sub-sequences in the retrieved playlists into a varied and coherent recommendation.

Example 3. Let $S3$ be the input song, and $\lambda = 5$ the desired length. Let the repository of Table 1 be the Case Base, and $Ret(S3) = \{B, C, E, F\}$ be the subset of $k = 4$ playlists retrieved. Consider how, in the Reuse process, these playlists are combined using a search process (for brevity, the computation of H' is omitted):

1) Generate the successors of $(S3)$ and sort them using H': $(\underline{S3}, S4)$, $(S2, \underline{S3})$, $(\underline{S3}, S5)$. Next node to visit: $(S3, S4)$.

2) Generate the successors of $(S3, S4)$ and sort them using H': $(S3, S4, S6)$, $(S2, \underline{S3, S4})$, $(\underline{S3, S4}, S5)$. Next node to visit: $(S3, S4, S6)$.

3) Generate the successors of $(S3, S4, S6)$ and sort them using H': $(S2, \underline{S3, S4, S6})$, $(\underline{S3, S4, S6}, S9)$, $(\underline{S3, S4, S6}, S5)$. Next node to visit: $(S2, S3, S4, S6)$.

4) Generate the successors of $(S2, S3, S4, S6)$ and sort them using H': $(S9, \underline{S2, S3, S4, S6})$, $(S1, \underline{S2, S3, S4, S6})$, $(\underline{S2, S3, S4, S6}, S9)$, $(\underline{S2, S3, S4, S6}, S5)$. Next node to visit: $(S9, S2, S3, S4, S6)$.

5) The node $(S9, S2, S3, S4, S6)$ has $\lambda = 5$ songs, hence is returned as the solution.

Notice that the solution is a varied and coherent combination of sub-sequences from the retrieved playlists: $(S2, S3, S4)$ from B, $(S4, S6)$ and $(S2, S3)$ from C, $(S2, S3, S4, S6)$ from E and $(S9, S2, S3)$ from F.

7   Experimental Results

We have tested the described CBR recommending system using a collection of playlists from MusicStrands[1]. In the Case Base, we have represented playlists as pairs $(track, artist)$, being *track* and *artist* two integers that allow us to univocally identify every track and every artist in the MusicStrands database. We have pre-processed the collection of playlists, discarding those with less than 5 songs, with more than 50 songs, and those alphabetically ordered (backwards and forwards) along the names of the track and/or of the artist. Eventually, we have assembled the Case Base using a subset (about 300,000) of playlists from MusicStrands.

---

[1] For more information visit: http://www.musicstrands.com.

Table 3. Sample of recommended playlists

Test 1. Input song: **Only Shallow** (*My Bloody Valentine*)	Test 2. Input song: **American Pie** (*Don McLean*)
Kool Thing *Sonic Youth*	We're An American Band *VV.AA.*
Stupid Preoccupations *Vic Chesnutt*	Sweet Home Alabama *Lynyrd Skynyrd*
Seed Toss *Superchunk*	More Than a Feeling *Boston*
Flyin' The Flannel *Firehose*	Bad Moon Rising
Only Shallow *My Bloody Valentine*	*Creedence Clearwater Revival*
Exhibit A *The Features*	**American Pie** *Don McLean*
Lover's Spit *Broken Social Scene*	Mr. Blue Sky *Electric Light Orchestra*
Gigantic *The Pixies*	Switch *Will Smith*
Kamera *Wilco*	This Love *Maroon 5*
From Blown Speakers	Walkie Talkie Man *Steriogram*
The New Pornographers	Walkin' On The Sun *Smash Mouth*

Test 3. Input song: **Mrs. Robinson** (*Simon & Garfunkel*)	Test 4. Input song: **Soldier** (*Destiny's Child*)
Unchained Melody	Let Me Love You *Mario*
The Righteous Brothers	Hush *LL Cool J*
Kicks *Paul Revere & The Raiders*	Red Carpet (Pause, Flash)
Cherry Hill Park *Billy Joe Royal*	*R. Kelly*
Windy *The Association*	Hot 2 Nite *New Edition*
Sunshine Superman *Donovan*	Wonderful *Ja Rule*
Mrs. Robinson *Simon & Garfunkel*	My Prerogative *Britney Spears*
Nights In White Satin *The Moody Blues*	Two Step *Ciara*
Only One *Yellowcard*	**Soldier** *Destiny's Child*
Pain *Jimmy Eat World*	Only U *Ashanti*
Quiet Ones *Tears For Fears*	Pass Out *Ludacris*

Test 5. Input song: **Roots Bloody Roots** (*Sepultura*)	Test 6. Input song: **Strangers In The Night** (*F. Sinatra*)
Satan Spawn, The Caco-Daemon	It Had To Be You *Steve Tyrell*
Deicide	Jamaica Farewell *Desmond Dekker*
Rapture *Morbid Angel*	Just The Way You Are *Diana Krall*
Serenity In Fire *Kataklysm*	Let's Fall In Love *Diana Krall*
Roots Bloody Roots *Sepultura*	Nunca Es Para Siempre
Plague Rages *Napalm Death*	*Presuntos Implicados*
Blend As Well *Coalesce*	**Strangers In The Night** *F. Sinatra*
God Send Death *Slayer*	Candy Man, The *Sammy Davis Jr.*
Token *Damad*	Unforgettable *Nat King Cole*
Heaven In Her Arms *Converge*	What A Wonderful World
Fear Of Napalm	*Louis Armstrong*
Terrorizer	Falling In Love Again *Billie Holiday*

Table 4. Sample of recommended playlists, without dampening popular songs

Test 2b. Input song: **American Pie** (*Don McLean*)	Test 4b. Input song: **Soldier** (*Destiny's Child*)
Behind These Hazel Eyes *Kelly Clarkson*	Disco Inferno *50 Cent*
Beverly Hills *Weezer*	Mockingbird *Eminem*
I Just Wanna Live *Good Charlotte*	Obsession *Frankie J*
American Idiot *Green Day*	I Just Wanna Live *Good Charlotte*
American Pie *Don McLean*	Boulevard Of Broken Dreams *Green Day*
Hotel California *The Eagles*	Since U Been Gone *Kelly Clarkson*
Cocaine *Eric Clapton*	Two Step *Ciara*
Emerald Eyes *Fleetwood Mac*	**Soldier** *Destiny's Child*
Carry On Wayward Son *Kansas*	Drop It Like It's Hot *Snoop Dogg*
Sweet Home Alabama *Lynyrd Skynyrd*	Get Back *Ludacris*

Concerning parameters, we were interested in recommending playlists where tracks were mostly never repeated ($\gamma_{track} = 200$) and artists were hardly repeated ($\gamma_{artist} = 50$). We have chosen $\theta = 5$ as the maximum pattern length (longer patterns very rarely appeared more than once), $k = 50$ as the number of retrieved playlists, $\alpha = 0.5$ and $\beta = 1$ as the length factor and popularity factor for the relevance, and $L = 1$ as the look-ahead factor.

Table 3 shows six sample recommendations, where the desired length is $\lambda = 10$, and the input songs have been chosen from different genres and periods. Notice that the suggested songs are similar (both acoustically and in terms of metadata) to the input songs, especially those that appear closely before or after them in the proposed sequences[2]. On the whole, the songs in the playlists sound well in the presented order, and their genres are never too distant from the one of the input song.

It is also worth noticing that many of the proposed songs are not very popular, yet they form a coherently ordered playlist with the input songs. This is due to effect of the popularity factor in the relevance function ($\beta = 1$), by which we dampen playlists made of popular songs. In this way, we enable the user to *discover new music*, because we are suggesting songs the user has probably never listened to, and yet will appreciate, since they are correlated with the input song. Should users long for recommendations with more popular songs, they would just have to lower this value. For instance, in Table 4 we present two recommendations, obtained with the same input songs of Test 2 and Test 4, but generated with $\beta = 0$, that is, *without* dampening popular songs. Consider, for instance, the song *American Idiot*, recommended in Test 2b ($\beta = 0$) before the input song *American Pie*. These two songs co-occur in sequence 7 times in the Case Base, which is, in general, a relevant pattern count. However, this pattern count becomes irrelevant when compared to the popularity of *American Idiot*,

---

[2] A 30" excerpt of every song, along with detailed metadata, is available on Music-Strands web-site.

which is a very popular song (it appears in 8,479 playlists) and *only 7 out of 8,479 times* it is followed by *American Pie*. As a result, the system does not recommend this sequence in Test 2 ($\beta = 1$), where pattern counts are dampened for sequences made of popular songs.

As a matter of fact, by proposing different recommendations from the same input, the parameter β allows to improve the *diversity* of the solutions. This is indeed an important feature for a recommending system, and a key issue for CBR systems [5].

8   Conclusions and Future Work

We have presented a CBR system for recommending playlists made of meaningful sequences of songs. The Case Base is a collection of playlists of different quality, provided by different people. While most recommendation systems are concerned with suggesting an unorganised set of songs, "similar" to those selected by the user, our work focuses on recommending meaningful sequences of songs (playlists). The proposed recommendations are not deeply "personalised", since the model we have of the user requesting a playlist is given only by the selected (input) song. Future works will explore how to further constrain the playlist to recommend by acquiring a larger input from the user.

This paper contributes to develop Case-based Reasoning in a variety of ways. First, we address the important issue of reasoning about sequential cases (here, in the form of coherently ordered playlists). Both the Case Base and the solution provided by the CBR system are based on the sequential ordering of songs; the problem-solving process of the CBR system exploits the informational content of the Case Base to provide a solution with a coherent order.

A second issue of interest is that our Case Base contains only *solutions* and not *problems*. In the usual CBR approach, the Case Base contains pairs (p, s) (p is a problem, s is a solution); to find the solution for a new problem p', the system retrieves from the Case Base a set of *similar problems*, takes into account their solutions, and returns one of them, or a combination of them, as the solution for p'. In our approach, instead, the Case Base contains only *solutions* (playlists), and no explicit *problems*: we know that the playlists in the Case Base are meaningful, but we ignore for which input songs they are good recommendations. In this context, we have designed the simplest CBR approach that can exploit the information contained in a large Case Base of meaningful sequences. We have explicitly avoided complex user models, which are a common feature of Collaborative Filtering systems. User models are not helpful in relation to our goal: they seek relations between people and preferred songs or playlists, but disregard any sequential information *contained* in the playlists.

A third issue of interest is the Reuse process: rather than recommending an existing playlist, we combine the retrieved playlists using the same criteria (variety and coherence) that we used in the Retrieve process. In this way we recommend a playlist that has the desired length λ and higher variety and coherence values than those of the retrieved playlists.

Further, we have investigated the issue of applying co-occurrences analysis in a musical context. In this approach, we have opted for a minimal *Problem Description* (only one song and the length of the desired recommendation) in order to generate meaningful playlists by exploiting the co-occurrences present in the Case Base. We have avoided more constrained inputs (e.g. two songs, such that the recommendation starts with the first one and ends with the other, and is coherently ordered). The problem with over-constrained input is that the system returns low quality solutions when the constraints are too strong (e.g. a user requests a playlist to start with a rap song and to end with a requiem). In the future, however, we plan to enlarge the input capabilities of the user, to partially constrain the recommended playlist. For instance, the user could provide a short sequence of songs, and the system could recommend a playlist with *most* of them; or else the user could indicate a specific genre, or tag, to consider or to avoid in the recommended playlist.

We have tested the system using a collection of manually-generated playlists, but in the future we plan to work with other forms of sequential music data. For instance, MusicStrands provides MyStrands, an iTunes plug-in that recommends new songs to the user, on the basis of the last songs effectively played in iTunes. We plan to improve this tool with the introduction of an explicit notion of sequentiality, in order to recommend *on-line, meaningful, personalised playlists*, on the basis of previous sequences of songs effectively played by the user.

The evaluation of the *quality* of the recommendation is an open issue for recommender systems. We agree with Hayes et al. [9] that user satisfaction can only be measured in an on-line context. Although the proposed system has not yet been evaluated by a significant number of users, we have deployed it on the Internet[3]. Users can select an input song, the desired length, and other parameters, and can compare the (meaningfully ordered) recommendation generated with the presented approach with the playlist proposed by the MusicStrands recommender. We plan to employ the users' feedback as an evaluation for our work and, once recommendations have been positively *revised* by the users, to *retain* in the MusicStrands repository those that have been approved as good playlists, to use them as new cases for future recommendations.

References

1. A. Aamodt and E. Plaza. Case-based reasoning: Foundational issues, methodological variations, and system approaches. *Artificial Intelligence Communications*, 7(1):39–59, 1994.
2. M. Alghoniemy and A.H. Tewfik. User-defined music sequence retrieval. In *Proc. ACM Multimedia*, 356–358, 2000.
3. J.-J. Aucouturier and F. Pachet. Scaling up Music Playlist Generation. In *Proc. of the 3rd IEEE Intl. Conf. on Multimedia and Expo*, 2002.
4. P. Avesani, P. Massa, M. Nori, and A. Susi. Collaborative radio community. In *Proc. of Adaptive Hypermedia*, 2002.

---

[3] http://labs.musicstrands.com

5. K. Bradley and B. Smyth. Improving recommendation diversity. In *Proc. of the 12th Irish Conference on Artificial Intelligence and Cognitive Science*, 2001.

6. H.-D. Burkhard. Extending some Concepts of CBR – Foundations of Case Retrieval Nets. In *Case-Based Reasoning Technology – From Foundations to Applications*, 9:17–50, 1998.

7. D. B. Hauver and J. C. French. Flycasting: Using Collaborative Filtering to Generate a Playlist for Online Radio. In *Proc. of the Intl. Conf. on Web Delivering of Music*, 2001.

8. C. Hayes and P. Cunningham. Smart radio: Building music radio on the fly. In *Expert Systems*, 2000.

9. C. Hayes, P. Massa, P. Avesani and P. Cunningham. An online evaluation framework for recommender systems. In *Proc. of the RPEC Conference*, 2002.

10. C. Hayes and P. Cunningham. Context-boosting collaborative recommendations. *Knowledge-Based Systems*, 17:131-138, 2004.

11. T. Hofmann and J. Puzicha. Statistical models for co-occurrence data. *Memorandum, MIT Artificial Intelligence Laboratory*, 1998.

12. B. Logan. Music recommendation from song sets. In *Proc. of the 5th ISMIR Conference*, 2004.

13. C. Manning and H. Schütze. Foundations of Natural Language Processing. 1999.

14. R. López de Mántaras, D. McSherry, D. Bridge, D. Leake, B. Smyth, S. Craw, B. Faltings, M-L. Maher, M.T. Cox, K. Forbus, M. Keane, A. Aamodt, I. Watson. Retrieval, reuse, revision, and retention in case-based reasoning. *Knowledge Engineering Review*. In press, 2006.

15. F. Pachet, G. Westerman, and D. Laigre. Musical data mining for electronic music distribution. In *Proc. of the Intl. Conf. on Web Delivering of Music*, 2001.

16. E. Pampalk, T. Pohle, and G. Widmer. Dynamic Playlist Generation Based on Skipping Behaviour. *Proc. of the 6th ISMIR Conference*, 2005.

17. S. Pauws and B. Eggen. PATS: Realization and User Evaluation of an Automatic Playlist Generator. In *Proc. of the Intl. Conf. on Music Information Retrieval*, 2002.

18. J. Platt, C. Burges, S. Swenson, C. Weare, and A. Zheng. Learning a gaussian process prior for automatically generating music playlists. In *Advances in Neural Information Processing Systems*, 14:1425-1432, 2002.

19. E. Plaza and J.-L. Arcos. Constructive adaptation. *Lecture Notes in Artificial Intelligence*, 2416:306–320, 2002.

20. T. Pohle, E. Pampalk, and G. Widmer. Generating similarity-based playlists using traveling salesman algorithms. In *Proc. of the Intl. Conf. on Digital Audio Effects*, 2005.

21. R. Ragno, C. J. C. Burges, and C. Herley. Inferring Similarity Between Music Objects with Application to Playlist Generation. *ACM Multimedia Information Retrieval*, 2005.

22. K. Wang. Discovering Patterns from Large and Dynamic Sequential Data. *Journal of Intelligent Information System*, 8–33, 1995.

A Comparative Study of Catalogue-Based Classification

Petra Perner

Institute of Computer Vision and Applied Computer Sciences
Körnerstr. 10, 04107 Leipzig
pperner@ibai-institut.de
www.ibai-institut.de

Abstract. In this paper we study the performance of a catalogue-based image classifier after applying different methods for performance improvement, such as feature-subset selection and feature weighting. The performance of the image catalogues is assessed by studying the reduction of the prototypes after applying Chang`s prototype-selection algorithm. We describe the results that could be achieved and give an outlook for further developments on a catalogue-based classifier.

1 Introduction

Although digital image scanners and cameras are quite common in many applications, it is still not standard to have a large enough image database as basis for the development of an image-interpretation system. People rather like to store image catalogues comprised of one prototypical image for each class instead of constantly collecting images into a database. This is especially true for medical and biological applications. Therefore it seems to be natural to use case-based reasoning as problem-solving method.

The use of case-based reasoning in applications with prototypical cases has been successfully studied for medical applications by Schmidt and Gierl [1] and Nilsson and Funk [2] on time-series data. The simple nearest-neighbor approach [4] as well as hierarchical indexing and retrieval methods [1] have been applied to the problem. It has been shown that an initial reasoning system could be built up based on these cases. The systems are useful in practice and can acquire new cases for further reasoning [3] during utilization of the system. A deep evaluation was often not possible, since the broad variation of the problem could not be captured by the few initial prototypes. Due to the sparse data-set problems such topics as case editing and condensing have not been studied in these application areas. There are comparative studies of case editing for other applications, such as SPAM filtering by Delany and Cunnigham [5] and Ontañón and Plaza for symbolic data [6].

The problem of feature-subset selection [8] and feature weighting [9] are empirically studied on standard machine-learning data bases, as well as on real-world data.

We have developed case-based reasoning methods for all the different stages of an image-interpretation system [10]. Usually the methods were evaluated by a case-base

T.R. Roth-Berghofer et al. (Eds.): ECCBR 2006, LNAI 4106, pp. 301–308, 2006.

that has been collected by the domain expert, but the cases were not considered as prototypical cases.

In this paper we are studying the following question: is it possible to build an image-interpretation system based on a prototypical image for each class and if so, what necessary features should such a system have? The basis for our study were four different image <u>catalogues</u> of HEp-2 cell images collected by different manufacturers of HEp-2 cell diagnostica and by a diagnostic laboratory. HEp-2 cell stands for human epithelial cell line type 2. The catalogues are comprised of one prototypical image for each class.

In Section 2 we shortly describe the image catalogues. The image analysis and the features extracted for the objects in the image are described in Section 3. The resulting databases are described in Section 4. The nearest-neighbor classifier and the feature selection and feature-weighting algorithm are described in Section 5. Likewise we describe in Section 5 the prototype-selection method that allows us to find out the quality of the image catalogues. Finally, we give results in Section 6 and an outlook for further work in Section 7.

2   Image Catalogues

Image Catalogues usually show one prototypical image for one class. These catalogues represent the visual knowledge of an image inspection domain. They are available as hardcopies or as a collection of digital images. They are usually used to train novices for the specific image-inspection task. Together with the prototypical images a verbal description of the appearance of the pattern is represented. Unlike in other tasks such as industrial inspection, these verbal descriptions are not standardized visual image descriptions allowing a human to build up conceptual knowledge.

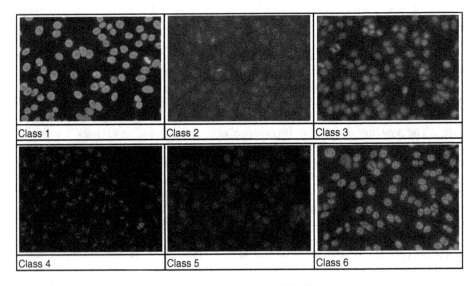

Fig. 1. Prototypical Images of Six Classes

Therefore, as long as no automatic image-interpretation system is available, a lot of work is invested in order to build up ontologies to improve the overall quality of image-inspection tasks.

Prototypical images of HEp-2 cell patterns for six classes are shown in Fig. 1. We should note that for each class we have only one prototypical image comprised of a small number of cells showing the appearance of the pattern. Therefore we do have an unknown number of single cells in each image showing the pattern of interest for each class. Each cell could be considered as a prototype itself. That will result in a data base of prototypes with an unequal number of samples for each class.

3 Creation of the Database

Each image was processed by the image-analysis procedure described in [11]. The color image has been transformed into a gray-level image. The image is normalized to the mean and standard gray level calculated from all images to avoid invariance caused by the inter-slice staining variations.

Automatic thresholding has been performed by the algorithm of Otsu. The algorithm can localize the cells with their cytoplasmatic structure very well, but not the nuclear envelope itself. We then applied morphological filters like dilation and erosion to the image, in order to get a binary mask for cutting out the cells from the image.

The gray levels ranging from 0 to 255 are quantized into 16 intervals t. Each subimage $f(x,y)$ containing only a cell gets classified according to the gray level into t slices, with $t=\{0,1,2,..,15\}$. For each slice a binary image is calculated, containing the value "1" for pixels with a gray level value falling into the gray level interval of slice t and value "0" for all other pixels. We call the image $f(x,y,t)$ in the following slice image. Object labeling is done in the slice images with the contour-following method. Then features from these objects are calculated for classification.

For the objects in each slice features are calculated for classification. The first one is a simple Boolean feature which expresses the occurrence or non-occurrence of objects in the slice image. Then the number of objects in the slice image is calculated. From the objects the area, a shape factor, and the length of the contour are calculated. However, not a single feature of each object is taken for classification, but a mean value for each feature is calculated over all the objects in the slice image. This is done in order to reduce the dimension of the feature vector. Since the quantization of the gray level was done in equal steps and without considering the real nature, we also calculated for each class the mean value of the gray level and the variance of the gray level. A total of 178 features are calculated that make up a very intelligent structure and texture descriptor for cells. It has been shown in [11] that not all features of the complex structure and texture descriptor are relevant for a particular texture description. The feature selection procedure of the decision tree induction process used in the study described in [11] for building the classifier selects only a subset of features from the whole set of features. However, using decision-tree induction requires a sufficiently large sample set which is not the assumption in this study and when producing as many features as possible for an object without being informed about the relevance of the features, a good feature-subset selection strategy is required, no matter which classifier is used.

4   The Databases

For our investigation we used four different image catalogues that came from four different manufacturers of Hep-2 cells. The databases differ in the number of classes and the number of samples per class, see Table 1. It cannot be expected that the distribution of the samples or the classes, respectively is the same in any database. More likely than this any situation can happen. Although most of the databases were obtained from the manufacturers, they could not provide samples for all classes.

Table 1. Name of Database and Number of Classes and Samples per Class

Name	\multicolumn{26}{c}{Class Number}																										Number of Classes	Number of Cases
	1	2	3	4	5	6	7	8	9	10	11	12	13	14	15	16	17	18	19	20	21	22	23	24	25	26		
DB_1	105	96	63	83																							4	347
DB_2	8	2	2	14	7	5	15	9	5	4	14	9	8	10	48	23	17	31	3	3	3	7	5	2	13	5	26	298
DB_3	7	30	29	28	11	7	13	5	13	13																	10	156
DB_4	25	12	18	21	5	16	22	24	21	20	5	14															12	203

5   The Classification Method

Our assumption for this study is that we have only a prototypical image for each class which is comprised of a number of cells and which represents the general appearance of the pattern of each class. Therefore, a prototype-based classification based on the nearest-neighbour rule is the appropriate choice for the classification method. However, since we have created complex structure and texture features comprised of several low-level features for the description of the pattern of each class, we need a feature-subset selection and feature weighting procedure to specify the importance of each low-level feature.

Prototypical images are created or selected by humans and thus they show variability because of the subjective influence of a human. Besides that they are comprised of a number of cells in the images in this kind of applications. In other applications a number of different prototypes might be selected. Therefore, we also use a prototype- selection strategy to come up with the right number of prototypes that reflect the right variance within the class and describe the class borders well. The most popular prototype-selection strategy is Chang´s algorithm which seems to be appropriate for our first study [11].

5.1   Nearest-Neighbour Rule

This nearest-neighbour rule [4] classifies x in the category of its nearest neighbour. More precisely, we call $x_n \in \{x_1, x_2, ..., x_n\}$ a nearest-neighbor x to if $\min d(x_i, x) = d(x_n´, x)$ where $i = 1, 2, ..., n$.

The nearest-neighbor rule chooses to classify x into category C_n, where x_n is the nearest neighbor to x and x_n belongs to class C_n.

In the case of the k-nearest neighbour we require k-samples of the same class to fulfil the decision rule. As distance measure we use the Euclidean distance.

5.2 Prototype Selection by Chang`s Algorithm

For the selection of the right number of prototypes we used Chang´s algorithm [11]. The outline of the algorithm can be described as follows: Suppose a training set T is given as $T = \left\{ t^1, ..., t^i, ..., t^m \right\}$ with t^i the *i-th* initial prototype. The idea of the algorithm is as follows: We start with every point in T as a prototype. We then successively merge any two closest prototypes p^1 and p^2 of the same class by a new prototype p, if the merging will not downgrade the classification of the patterns in T. The new prototype p may be simply the average vector of p^1 and p^2. We continue the merging process until the number of incorrect classifications of the pattern in T starts to increase.

Roughly, the algorithm can be stated as follows: Given a training set T, the initial prototypes are just the points of T. At any stage the prototypes belong to one of two sets – set A or set B. Initially, A is empty and B is equal to T. We start with an arbitrary point in B and initially assign it to A. Find a point p in A and a point q in B, such that the distance between p and q is the shortest among all distances between points of A and B. Try to merge p and q. That is, if p and q are of the same class, compute a vector p^* in terms of p and q. If replacing p and q by p^* does not decrease the recognition rate for T, merging is successful. In this case, delete p and q from A and B, respectively, and put p^* into A, and the procedure is repeated once again. In the case that p and q cannot be merged, i.e. if either p and q are not of the same class or merging is unsuccessful, move q from B to A, and the procedure is repeated. When B becomes empty, recycle the whole procedure by letting B be the final A obtained from the previous cycle, and by resetting A to be the empty set. This process stopps when no new merged prototypes are obtained. The final prototypes in A are then used in a nearest-neighbour classifier.

5.3 Feature Subset Selection and Feature Weighting

The wrapper approach [12] is used for selecting a feature subset from the whole set of features. This approach conducts a search for a good feature subset by using the k-NN classifier itself as an evaluation function. By doing so it takes into account the specific behaviour of the classification methods. The 1-fold crossvalidation method is used for estimating the classification accuracy and the best-first search strategy is used for the search over the state space of possible feature combination. The algorithm terminates if we have not found an improved accuracy over the last k search states.

The feature combination that gave the best classification accuracy is the remaining feature subset. After we have found the best feature subset for our problem, we try to further improve our classifier by applying a feature-weighting technique.

The weights of each feature w_i are changed by a constant value δ: $w_i := w_i \pm \delta$. If the new weight causes an improvement of the classification accuracy, then the weight will be updated accordingly; otherwise, the weight will remain as it is. After the last weight has been tested, the constant δ will be divided into half and the procedure repeats. The procedure terminates if the difference between the classification accuracy of two iterations is less than a predefined threshold.

6   Results

We calculated the classification accuracy for the simple nearest-neighbour classifier and the k-nearest neighbour with $k = 3$ based on 1-fold crossvalidation. The results for the different databases are shown in Table 2. The experiments differ in the feature-weight setting (all weights are one or learnt based on the procedure described in Section 5.3) and the setting for the number of neighbours k, see Table 3. For the experiment P1K1 (feature weights are for all features one, $k=1$), the best results could be achieved for the database DB_1. This is not surprising, since this data base has enough prototypes for each class and a low number of classes. The result for the k-nearest-neighbour classifier was slightly better for the database DB_1. A poor result was achieved for the database DB_2, i.e. the database with the highest number of classes and the smallest number of prototypes per class. Contrary to our expectation, the result for the database DB_4 was the poorest , although the number of samples in each class seems to be moderate.

It is clear that we cannot achieve a significant improvement of the accuracy for the database DB_2 when applying the k-NN classifier, since there are often only two prototypes of the same class.

If we use the feature-weighting procedure described in Section 5.3, we can improve the classification accuracy for DB_1 and DB_2 in the case of the simple nearest-neighbour classifier and for DB_4 for the k-nearest-neighbour classifier. The highest improvement (5%) can be achieved for the database DB_2. In [13] we have shown that different feature-subset selection strategies select different feature subsets from a set of features and that there is often only a small intersection between the selected subsets. Therefore, we were not concerned about the kind of selected features, rather we looked for the improvement in accuracy. We could show by our results that feature-subset selection is an essential feature of a catalogue-based classifier.

In an early experiment [12] we achieved an accuracy of 75% for six classes and based on decision trees. For each of the six classes we had 53 images. If we set our actual results into this context, we can conclude that every result that is higher than 60% accuracy is a good result.

Table 2. Classification Accuracy for the different Databases

DataBase	TestID			
	P1K1	P1K3	P3k1	P3K3
DB_1	80,12	80,20	80,71	78,04
DB_2	48,31	45,69	50,94	45,32
DB_3	69,44	69,44	69,87	69,78
DB_4	44,22	44,22	45,99	46,28

Table 3. Experiment Set-up

Experiment	Feature Weights	K-NN
P1K1	1	1
P1K3	1	3
P3K1	learnt	1
P3K3	learnt	3

If we apply Chang´s prototype-selection strategy to our data base DB_1, we can reduce the number of protoypes by 75,5 % for the simple nearest-neighbour approach while preserving the accuracy, see Table 4. It is interesting to note that for this data base only 15 samples are adopted; whereas 70 samples are generated. There is enough redundancy among the samples.

In the case of the database DB_2, that is the database with the largest number of classes, but only a few samples per class, the reduction of samples is only 21.32%. The majority of samples are adopted, whereas only a few new prototypes are generated. The prototype generation is mostly performed for the classes with more than two samples. As a result we have to conclude that the only two samples in some of the classes do not cover well the solution space for these classes.

We observe the same situation for the database DB_4, whereas for the database DB_3 we see a reduction by 42.31%. That implies that the database DB_4 has much class overlap in the samples and it is not a true gold standard. It is the only database that comes from a diagnostic lab and not from a manufacturer.

Table 4. Reduction of Samples after Application of Chang`s Algorithm

Name	Number of Classes	Number of Cases	Generated	Overtaken	Total Number	Number of Loops	Reduction in %
DB_1	4	347	70	15	85	192	75,50
DB_2	26	272	43	171	214	15	21,32
DB_3	10	156	33	57	90	33	42,31
DB_4	12	203	39	110	149	15	26,60

7 Conclusions

We have studied the use of prototypical images for the development of an automatic image-interpretation system based on nearest-neighbour classification. The results are promising. They show that it is possible to build an image-interpretation system with sufficient classification accuracy based on a small number of prototypical images. Feature-subset selection and feature weighting are essential functions of such a system. These functions can significantly improve the classification accuracy, especially in the case of small samples. Prototype generation has been applied in the sense that samples are generalized to one prototype. This function can be used in order to judge the quality of the prototypical case-base. The higher the reduction rate, the higher is the redundancy of the prototypes. The new function that is necessary is prototype enrichment for that case where only a small number of prototypes is available. A method of Bayesian Case Reconstruction has been developed by Hennessy et. al [7] to broaden the coverage of a case library by sampling and recombining pieces of existing cases to construct a large set of "plausible" cases. However, this method is not applicable in our case. We need to develop a method for our problem. This is left to further work.

References

1. R. Schmidt and L. Gierl, Temporal Abstractions and Case-Based Reasoning for Medical Course Data: Two Prognostic Applications. MLDM 2001: 23-34
2. M. Nilsson and P. Funk, A Case-Based Classification of Respiratory Sinus Arrhythmia, In: ECCBR 2004 673-685
3. I. Bichindaritz, E. Kansu, K. M. Sullivan: Case-Based Reasoning in CARE-PARTNER: Gathering Evidence for Evidence-Based Medical Practice. EWCBR 1998: 334-345
4. D.W. Aha, D. Kibler, and M.K. Albert, Instance-based Learning Algorithm, Machine Learning, 6(1):37-66, 1991.
5. S.J. Delany, P. Cunningham, An Analysis of Case-Base Editing in a Spam Filtering System. ECCBR 2004 128-141
6. S. Ontañón, E. Plaza: Justification-Based Selection of Training Examples for Case Base Reduction. ECML 2004: 310-321
7. Daniel N. Hennessy, Bruce G. Buchanan, John M. Rosenberg, Bayesian Case Reconstruction. ECCBR 2002 148-158
8. D. Wettschereck, D. W. Aha, Weighting Features, In: M. M. Veloso, A. Aamodt (Eds.): Case-Based Reasoning Research and Development, lncs 1010, Springer 1995, p. 347-358
9. P. Perner: CBR-Based Ultra Sonic Image Interpretation. In: E. Blanzieri, L. Portinale (Eds.): Advances in Case-Based Reasoning, lnai 1898, Springer 2000, p. 479-490
10. P. Perner, H. Perner, and B. Müller, Mining Knowledge for Hep-3 Cell Image Classification, Artificial Intelligence in Medicine, 26(2002), p. 161-173.
11. C.-L. Chang, Finding Prototypes for Nearest Neighbor Classifiers, IEEE Trans. on Computers, vol C-23, No. 11, p. 1179-1184.
12. P. Perner, Data Mining on Multimedia Data, Springer Verlag, lncs 2558, 2002
13. P. Perner, Improving the Accuracy of Decision Tree Induction by Feature Pre-Selection, Applied Artificial Intelligence, Vol. 15, No. 8, p. 747-760

Ontology-Driven Development of Conversational CBR Systems*

Hector Gómez-Gauchía, Belén Díaz-Agudo, and Pedro González-Calero

Dep. Sistemas Informáticos y Programación
Universidad Complutense de Madrid, Spain
{hector, belend, pedro}@sip.ucm.es

Abstract. Conversational CBR has been used successfully for several years but building a new system demands a great cognitive effort of knowledge engineers and using it demands a similar effort of users. In this paper we use ontologies as the *driving force* to structure a development methodology where previous design efforts may be reused. We review the main issues of current CCBR models and their specific solutions. We describe afterwards how these solutions may be integrated in a common methodology to be reused in other similar CCBR systems. We particularly focus on the authoring issues to represent the knowledge.

1 Introduction

Conversational Case-Based Reasoning (CCBR) has been proposed to bridge the knowledge gap between the users and the case bases in CBR systems. It means that if users are not able to give a well-defined problem description (query), the CBR system will not be able to find a similar and appropriate case. CCBR approaches are appropriate when users have vague ideas about their problems at the beginning of the retrieval process. The system guides the user to a better understanding of his problem and what aspects he should describe. CCBR provides the means to dialog and guide users to refine their problem descriptions incrementally through a question-answer sequence.

Conversational CBR has been used successfully for several years but to build a new system demands a great cognitive effort on knowledge engineers and to use it demands a similar effort on users. While a lot of effort is being devoted to identify the problems related to building a new CCBR system from scratch, work on tool support and development methodologies for CCBR applications is still in its infancy. Different kinds of CCBR systems have proposed different approaches, issues and solutions. Our approach proposes defining ontologies that can be exploited by different CCBR applications.

Many works share our goal:[16] to minimize the cognitive effort demanded on users to use the system successfully and on the knowledge engineers to build the system. In [18] it is pointed how the design and development of CCBR systems would greatly benefit from the existence of generic inference methods. These

---

* Supported by the Spanish Committee of Education (TIN2005-09382-C02-01).

T.R. Roth-Berghofer et al. (Eds.): ECCBR 2006, LNAI 4106, pp. 309–324, 2006.

methods can be used to anticipate user needs and to reduce the amount of information that the user must provide (e.g., number of answered questions) prior to successful case retrieval [4,9,17]. There are approaches based on the definition of special relations among questions, such as causal or taxonomical relations [18]. Other approaches are based on the creation of inferencing rules used to control the conversation and to infer new answers from answers to other related questions [9,3]. In the line of defining reusable and generic methods, Gu & Aadmodt [16] propose to decompose the selection of the most discriminative questions through several subtasks: feature inferencing, question ranking, consistent question clustering, and coherent question sequencing.

Apart from the query formulation process there are works regarding other more specific aspects. We emphasize the study of user variability: to deal with user preferences [9]; to adapt to the level of expertise [10]; to consider the user temperament and current mood [11]; to introduce different conversation styles [28] and conversation strategies [13]; and to improve the *case authoring* bottleneck, i.e.: building case bases, by new tools and specific techniques [21].

The knowledge representation issue has an important role in most of the previous solutions. Most of the recent CCBR works tend to use a knowledge rich approach which includes general knowledge of the domain in ad-hoc representations [16]. In general, the diversity of applications generates many types of conversational systems with specific characteristics. Regarding to the domain task, we distinguish between diagnosis systems [16,22], decision support systems [10,3,24], recommenders [9] and systems which justify their recommendations [27], generation systems that are capable of generating expressive musical performances with user interaction [5], design systems [20], interactive teaching of didactic methods [17], textual CCBR [26], and planning [24].

In order to deal with so different issues, our proposal is based on the idea that if we can formalize each issue separately and find a solution for each issue, we are able to find partial solutions incrementally until we cover the main issues. This way we keep very few inter-relations among different issues. To represent all these different issues and their inter-relations we use an ontology-driven approach to help designing different types of CCBR systems. Our framework COBBER [11] formalizes different aspects of conversational systems. We have defined CCBRonto, an ontology which has two layers: a meta-model and a content-model. The meta-model is where most of the reuse takes place. The meta-model includes the skeleton where we can define additional characteristics of CCBR systems, like tasks, methods, domain knowledge issues, representation formalisms (textual, graphics, multimedia), conversation issues (strategies, conceptualization), and user's issues. We describe how we solve the user's issues in [14] where we describe a model dealing with temperaments and emotions.

In this article we have three goals: to propose the ontology-driven approach as a common methodology to integrate the diversity of CCBR types (Section 3), to present the CCBRonto ontology as a knowledge model to support the methodology (Section 4). And to show the model at work in a classic CCBR domain: a diagnosis/help-desk system (Section 5). In the same section we describe the conversation reasoning tasks which CCBRonto supports. They belong to COB-BER [13], which includes other tasks not relevant to this article.

2   The Scenario

To illustrate this article we use a domain example, which is to design and develop a conversational help-desk system to solve problems about company management software. We have several sources of knowledge, such as documents and experts. In Figure 1 we depict the conversation with the ideal characteristics we want in our scenario.

We want to reduce the Knowledge Engineering and cognitive efforts reusing other CCBR models, their static domain knowledge, tasks and problem solving methods. There are many CCBR systems but they are difficult to reuse because they have ad-hoc solutions for a particular domain. We look for a common knowledge representation model, which supports different CCBR types and domains with text, images and multimedia materials. This model should support different levels of abstraction and case sizes. The language we use should be formal and support the implementation at the same time.

We need an incremental methodology to define CCBR systems and a knowledge model which supports the methodology. We want to design the system in a structured and incremental way, with no scalability problems for large domains. The model should have elements which guide us in the development process of the CCBR system, such as conversation basic structures –or skeletons–, task and method decompositions in hierarchies –or skeletons–. The system should keep a conversation which guides the user to formulate the query in an incremental way. In Figure 1 we see how the system asks questions to complete the query and to obtain the data to solve it. The user may answer only some questions and the system does the completion task. The system should decide which are the relevant questions to ask in the next cycle, e.g.: in the figure the sentence "deduces what information to show" indicates it. The system should avoid the repetition of questions and answers. Besides asking questions, the completion task should include several aspects: deductions, calculations and function executions. The system should deduce and calculate answers from previous answers, as depicted in Figure 1: the system deduces that the company type is "AA" because it corresponds to companies considered *small*, i.e.: 15 is the maximum number of employees and 1300 is the maximum benefit per employee in a year. If the system needs the "benefit by year", the system should be able to calculate it, e.g.: in the figure the calculated answer is 12000. The system should be able to execute actions outside the CCBR system, such as displaying images or the execution of functions, e.g.: in the figure the `IncomeTaxFormulaAA`.

The system should adapt the conversation to the user, i.e.: his domain expertise level, his preferences, his temperament and his mood. In Figure 1 there are two different paths of the conversation: *example A* for a novice user, where the indications (suggestions) are very basic and *example B* for an advanced user, where the indications are more conceptual, assuming that he knows better the

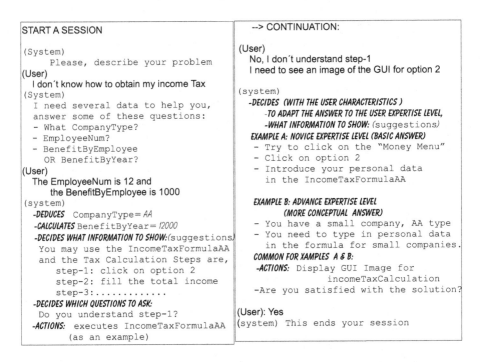

Fig. 1. The conversation example for our scenario: a help-desk domain

domain concepts. The temperament and mood adaptation consists in treating the user in different way according to his current mood and temperament (this is described in [14].)

In next sections we describe our approach which improve the issues described in the scenario.

3   The Ontology-Driven Development

Ontology Engineering [15] has similar difficulties to the Knowledge Acquisition and Representation fields of Knowledge Engineering. There are several methodologies to build ontologies [8], but we find limitations dealing simultaneously with diverse sources of knowledge, such as texts and experts, and to have a structured cycle of the development process. To overcome these limitations we developed a conceptualization methodology which includes, in a refinement cycle manner, the main guidelines of the current methodologies, Information Retrieval techniques and interviews techniques with experts. For details see a complete description in [12]. We focus this article on the application of the methodology to Conversational CBR systems.

This is an overview of the proposed ontology-driven approach applied to develop a CCBR system. We perform several tasks:

1. To *describe* in a text format the domain and the problem to be solved. To *decompose* the description into a set of –prototypical– situations, each of them has a description of a problem and its solution. We need a vocabulary which represents each situation: to *define* relevant concepts (classes) and relations (properties) among them. See [12] for a description of techniques.

2. To *define* the questions which are relevant to the situation and all their possible answers. To *build* a question hierarchy to help organizing the question sequence, which is the path to find the solution.

3. To *build* the cases: each situation may need a set of related cases, which are defined at different level of abstraction, going from abstract general cases to their specific versions. Cases are independent, only related semantically by the questions and answers which describe the situation represented by each case. They can be represented graphically as a hierarchy or a network, but they do not have hardwire links among them. This design gives a lot of flexibility and creates several different possible conversation sequences driven by the answers of the user. This description is specific for our model explained in next sections. The designer performs three tasks for each case:
   - To *assign* which set of questions and answers define the specific situation represented by the case.
   - To *define* the solutions for that case (suggestions and actions.)
   - To *link* the questions to be asked in the next cycle (intentional questions.)

4. To *select* one of the available case similarity methods from our model library of reusable problem solving methods (PSMs) or to *build* your domain specific method.

5. To *build* or *select* from the reusable PSMs library the set of appropriated tasks and methods for the system type in development. To *adapt* the chosen tasks and methods to the domain.

6. To *define* the queries to test the cases. To *refine* the cases. Experts supervise these tasks.

We claim that this approach reduces the cognitive effort in several aspects. We use a common vocabulary for the domain in a formal representation that supports the implementation. The ontology presents a global picture of the domain: concept taxonomies, explicit relationships or properties, tasks and methods. The ontology building process drives the analysis of the domain and its functionality. Ontologies based on Description Logics (DLs) have inference capabilities [6], which we describe in section 3.1. This feature simplifies the implementation of relations among questions, the inference and calculation of new answers. The definitions of relations and conditions are declarative and independent to the software (we use a standard reasoner), this simplifies an incremental development, re-engineering, prototyping and testing.

Other works use ontologies in CCBR as well: they use in [23] the SERVO ontology, written in RDF language, as representation of the domain or metadata. Other use an ad-hoc representation similar to an ontology, e.g.: in [16], Gu and Aamodt use an Object-Level Knowledge Representation Model, part of the model reuse from CREEK [1]. The main differences between these approaches and our approach is that a Description Logics based ontology has built-in reasoning mechanisms and declarative conditions, which are easily updatable with a standard ontology editor such as Protégé [19]. Both, the reasoning mechanisms and the declarative conditions are independent of the CCBR system. In the next section we introduce Description Logics.

3.1 Description Logics

Description Logics are considered one of the most important knowledge representation formalism unifying and giving a logical basis to the well known traditional approaches: Frame-based systems, Semantic Networks and KL-ONE-like languages; Object-Oriented representations; Semantic data models; and Type systems. In a DL, there are three types of formal objects: *concepts* and *relations*, and *individuals*. The first two types are descriptions with a potentially complex structure. It is formed by composing a limited set of description-forming operators. *Individuals* are simple formal constructs intended to directly represent objects in the domain of interest. Individuals may be recognized as concept instances, and related to other individuals through relation instances.

DL's reasoning mechanisms are based on: *subsumption*, which determines whether a description –concept or relation– is more general than another; and *instance recognition*, which determines if a individual belongs to a concept. This is performed by checking if the individual satisfies the asserted conditions of the concept definition. The instance recognition may be applied to check if a tuple of individuals satisfy some relations as well. Subsumption supports classification, i.e., the ability of automatically classifying a new description within a –semi– lattice of previously classified descriptions. We use this in our model for case description similarity. Instance recognition supports completion, which is the ability of drawing logical consequences of assertions about individuals. We use this to infer new answers from previous answers. *Contradiction detection* is used for descriptions and assertions about individuals. It completes the basic set of reasoning mechanisms provided by DL systems. We use these mechanisms in the retrieve phase as well. In the next section we describe how we use DLs based ontologies in our model.

4   CCBRonto: An Ontology for CCBR Systems

We define a knowledge representation model, CCBRonto, to support the methodology. CCBRonto is a DLs based ontology, which extends CBRonto [7]. CBRonto is our ontology to develop CBR systems. It has two main aspects: task-method decomposition and concepts which define the structure of domain knowledge. In this article we focus on extending the second aspect: the concept structure which supports the main functionality of the conversation mechanism.

Figure 2 outlines our layered architecture where we integrate different types of knowledge: CBROnto provides CBR vocabulary for describing terms involved in the CBR problem-solving processes, while CCBROnto provides a conceptualization of the knowledge needed in a conversational CBR system. The use of this

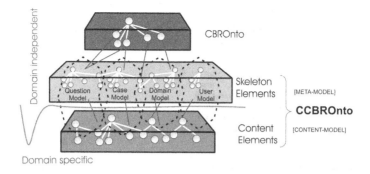

Fig. 2. The specialization layers in our ontology approach

organizing knowledge allows the CBR processes to have semantic information about the domain. CCBROnto helps to organize the domain knowledge within the cases. It has four interrelated models: the domain model, the case model, the question model, and the extended user model. We define cases using these models.

In our models we have elements which are concepts and relations. The two bottom layers in Figure 2 are two different levels of our models: a meta-model with *skeleton elements* defines domain independent elements –written with squared thick font in next figures– and a content-model with *content elements* defines domain dependent concepts –written with round thin font in next figures– and extends the skeleton elements. Content elements include the individuals created for a domain –a diamond shape in next figures–. The skeleton elements give a structure to the domain elements. It is important to mention that our models are domain independent, but we describe them in the next sections using a the help-desk domain, presented in Section 2, for clarity purposes. For each model we describe only what seems more relevant to understand the whole approach.

4.1   The Question Model

In Figure 3 we describe the question model applied to the help-desk domain. There is a taxonomy of question types defined at different levels of abstraction. Questions have three roles: questions in the user query describe the problem to be solved; questions inside cases, as input slots –see `hasActivatingQuestions` and their expected answers `hasConceptAnswerValuePairs` in Figure 4–, describe the case itself for explanatory purposes in the case authoring phase; and questions inside cases, as output slots, guide the conversation in the next reasoning cycle. A question may belong to one or more cases. Once a question has an answer, all the cases associated to the question see the answer. The system only asks a question if the system retrieves the case and there is no answer yet. The system stores the answers in the user model to perform this process.

Each question has semantic relations (properties) with other questions. We can declare explicitly any kind of relation among questions. Some are predefined, such

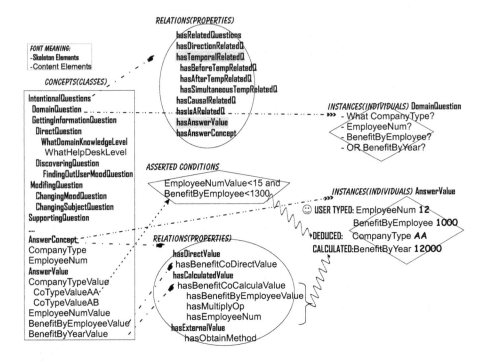

Fig. 3. Question model and some of the possible relations among questions

as taxonomical, causal, temporal (before, after, simultaneous, mutually exclusive) questions. Each question is designed to obtain a set of values **hasAnswerValue** of a set of concepts **hasAnswerConcept**. Normally there is one concept for each question. Some questions are standard, e.g.: confirmation questions "are you satisfied with the solution?". There are several types of descriptions to formulate the question: text in natural language, diagrams, multiple-choice, yes-no.

In Figure 3 we illustrate the answers as individuals of **AnswerValue**. There are four ways to get the answer: the user writes the **AnswerValue** of questions (DirectValue). The second way, DeducedValue, is to deduce **AnswerValue** from the asserted conditions of a concept, such as the **CompanyTypeValue** (AA) using the **EmployeeNum** (12) and **BenefitByEmployee** (1000). The third way, CalculatedValue, is calculating **AnswerValue** by a specific method declared explicitly, such as **hasBenefitCoCalculaValue**, which defines the value multiplying the **BenefitByEmployeeValue** by **EmployeeNum**. The last way is to obtain **AnswerValue** from an external source, such as a database, by the execution of a method. We define conditions in a logic-based declarations to deduce **AnswerValue**. A DLs oriented reasoning engine, such as Pellet, can infer conclusions using these conditions. An example is the deduced **AnswerValue** for the CompanyType(AA) mentioned before.

Other works use the question model as well. A similar one is in [16] which follows a knowledge-intensive approach. [18] uses taxonomic and causal relations

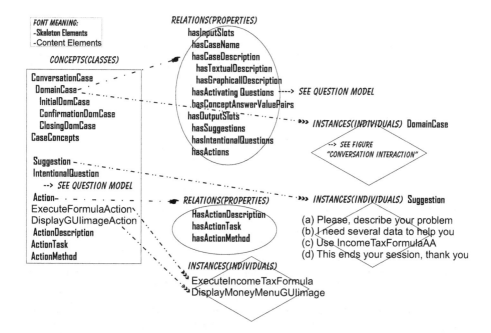

Fig. 4. Case model: main components and their links with other models

among questions and deduces rules from questions. Our conditions are similar to rules among questions in other models [4]. The difference with our approach is the characteristics of DLs mentioned before.

4.2 The Case Model

We define a *case skeleton* with a set of domain independent concepts to simplify case authoring. In Figure 4 we show the most relevant elements of the case model. There are specialized case types for specific moments in the conversation, with fix values, such as `InitialDomCase`. It is used to start a conversation session with a welcome message. And there are other general types to use throughout the conversation. The input slots represent the description of the case. They include concepts to retrieve the case: if the system asks the `ActivatingQuestions` and obtains similar `ConceptAnswerValuePairs` of a case, the system retrieves the case. Cases have a set of output slots:

- *IntentionalQuestions*: One important difference of our model in respect of the other systems is that we include references to the questions inside the cases. This mechanism discriminates which questions to ask in the next cycle and simplifies case authoring.
- *Suggestions* are the solution to the problem. If the case is abstract, the solution is only partial. It needs to continue the conversation to get to the specific solution. Suggestions may have any kind of format to be displayed: text, graphics, multimedia.

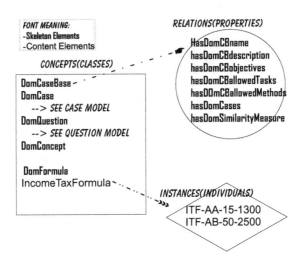

Fig. 5. Domain model main components and their links with other models

– *Actions* are operations to execute outside the CCBR system, e.g.: in our domain we have ExecuteFormula or DisplayGUIImage.

4.3   The Domain Model

The domain model defines all the knowledge about the domain and includes the question and case models described in sections 4.1 and 4.2. The most relevant *skeleton elements* of the domain model are: DomainDescription, DomCaseBase, DomCase and a generic concept DomConcept – for auxiliary concepts, such as DomFormula–. The main element is the DomCaseBase concept. Besides its description and cases, it has the objectives of the case base and the possible tasks and methods which can be performed with it. The *content elements* are domain specific: cases, questions, tasks, methods, and other auxiliary concepts, such as the IncomeTaxFormula. Our domain model example is the composition of Figures 3, 4 and 5.

4.4   The Extended User Model

We define an extended user model to support some of the previously described tasks, those related to question-answer optimization and system adaptation to the user. The two main concepts for those tasks are UserExpertiseLevel and the SessionData which are depicted in Figure 6. We use UserExpertiseLevel for the task to adapt the conversation to the user domain expertise level, e.g.: level 1 is novice, level 2 is knowledgeable, level 3 is expert. Figure 7 and Section 5 describe the role of this concept, which is to select cases according to the complexity level. We use SessionData to optimize the question-answer process. If the user has already answered a question in the current or a previous session, the system does not ask again the same question. To support this task, the model

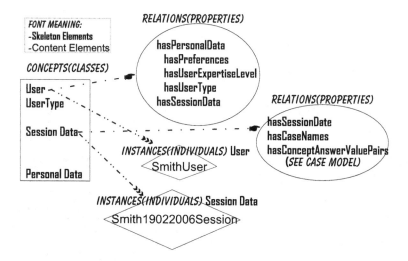

Fig. 6. User model main components

stores the names of the visited domain cases and their questions and obtained answers –`ConceptAnswerValuePairs` of the case model in Figure 4–. Another task of the extended user model is to be able to anticipate user behaviors and answers. To support this task we use a temperament ontology. We can retrieve similar users to the current user and their answers from previous sessions. For more details of this temperament ontology see the article [14].

5   The Model at Work

We extend the standard CBR cycle [2] to include the conversational issues but keeping all the original tasks. In a CCBR, the query definition and the retrieval tasks keep a short subcycle until the user agrees with the description and the retrieved answer. Then, he may need to continue with the next tasks: reuse, repair and retain. We define a control task to support the interactions among tasks and ontologies. This control task is in charge of calling the next task with the right knowledge. This is implemented in our prototype with an agenda, where each task, at the end of its execution, modifies the agenda according to its conclusions. In the prototype we use a blackboard implementation to transfer the correct knowledge –cases, questions and answers– among tasks.

To perform the knowledge authoring task of the help-desk domain we have as domain sources: a set of manuals about the software to be supported with the help-desk system, and an expert with limited time for us. We follow the steps of section 3. The first step is to create a domain model with an ontology, which includes a question model with all kinds of relations and several levels of abstraction. We reuse the *skeleton elements* and specialize new *content elements* of our domain. In the next step we define the case base where each case is

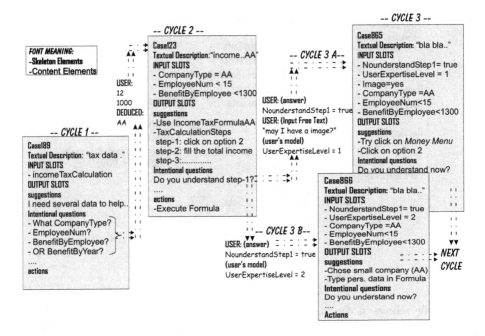

Fig. 7. Conversation interaction: questions, user's or inferred answers and domain cases

defined by a set of answers to some questions. And the third step is to get the tasks and methods. We create them or reuse them from a library, if there already are adequate tasks and methods available. Finally, after several refinements, we came up with the set of models described in previous sections.

Figure 7 depicts the reasoning process of the system. We show three cycles. Previous to them there is a standard *initial case* to start the conversation: "Describe your problem" –not in the figure–. The user answers: "I do not know how to obtain my income Tax". The system retrieves case *case189* and shows the suggestion and the questions of the case. The important aspect is the way this is performed. The user may answer the `hasEmployeeNum` and the `hasBenefitbyEmployee` only, because the company type may be deduced with the assertions `hasEmployeeNum < 15` and `hasBenefitbyEmployee < 1300`. In the next cycle, the system retrieves case *case123* using as query the user answers and shows the suggestions and intentional questions again.

The system does not ask for those concepts which already have explicit or deductible values. In the *cycle 3 A* of the figure, when the `UserExpertiseLevel=1` the proposed suggestion is very basic: "try to click in the Money menu" – *Case865*–. But, in the *cycle 3 B* of the figure, for the `UserExpertiseLevel=2`, the retrieved case is different and the solution is more technical : "option2 is for small companies(AA)" –*Case866*–. This is because the system assumes that the expert has more deep and comprehensive knowledge about the domain. In the first situation –*cycle 3 A*–, the user, besides answering the questions, asks in a free text format for an explanatory image. The system processes this text with a NLP module and includes the concepts from the text in the query to retrieve the case. The retrieved case *Case865* has the `image=yes` condition and has an *action* to display a GUI image to help to understand the "step-1" of the suggestions in *Case123* of *cycle 2*.

6   Conclusions

To reduce the cognitive effort of the CCBR systems development we propose to find a common methodology and a model where we can include the many different CCBR types and approaches. The main feature of the methodology is to use DLs based ontologies as the driving force of the development. The supporting model reuses interchangeable knowledge, tasks and methods within an intensive knowledge approach. To support those characteristics we need to include general domain, user and conversation knowledge. The representation of this knowledge is a set of DLs based ontologies. We use ontologies for two purposes: to represent the concepts and to support the decomposition task-method. In this article we focus on the first purpose.

We claim that this approach reduces the cognitive effort in several aspects by using: a common domain vocabulary, a domain independent formal representation which supports the implementation, the standard inference capabilities and standard engines of the Description Logics based ontologies. The improved aspects are: to communicate with the same language among experts, users and knowledge engineers; to have a global picture of the domain: concept taxonomies with explicit relationships, case bases, tasks and methods; the implementation of relations among questions, the inference and calculation of new answers.

We tested this approach in two different projects. The first one is the personalization of the linux environment based on temperaments and other user variations [14]. The second one is COBBER, a prototype of affective computing framework for CCBR systems [11]. Both projects reuse ontologies. COBBER has several tasks, which are CBR systems. All of them reuse the meta-model – skeleton elements– of CCBRonto and some content-models for common domains. They reuse too some methods and tasks. We have no numeric measurements of the benefits. The qualitative benefits were very significative:

- The conceptualization phase is more fluent because the methodology [12] structures the process in several phases with clear results and uses conceptual maps, a graphical technique for discussing the representation of the ontology elements. This obtains a common vocabulary of the domain.
- The analysis phase is simplified because it reuses the meta-model. The different elements of new tasks are easily included in the content-models by extensions of the meta-model or content-models of other similar tasks. The ontologies are enough formal to act as specifications. Ontologies are self-documented, they have the documentation embedded within the elements.
- The implementation phase reuses directly the ontologies because they maybe loaded in a reasoning engine or generate automatically the class structure

code in a programming language such as java. Projects may reuse tasks and methods if the domain is similar. If the domain differs in few tasks or methods, it is simple to exchange one task or method.

- Reuse includes the powerful reasoning method embedded in the ontology language based on description logics (OWL). There are standard reasoning engines (Pellet). We can implement and reuse other reasoning methods without interfere with the standard one.
- The test phase is easy too because we use content-models with different regression tests. This allows to repeat and to include new tests.
- These phases are easily repeated in a refinement cycle because is simple to create the meta-model and content-model in an incremental manner.

As further work we are developing a taxonomy of CCBR system types in order to determined frequent tasks and methods. They will be included in the CCBRonto and reuse when building new CCBR systems. We are interested in implement, using our approach, some of the other approaches to test the viability and scalability of the proposed integration in our CCBR ontology and COBBER framework. We are working to include the COBBER model in jCOLIBRI as a conversational extension.

References

1. A. Aamodt. Knowledge-intensive case-based reasoning in creek. In P. Funk and P. A. González-Calero, editors, *ECCBR*, volume 3155 of *Lecture Notes in Computer Science*, pages 1–15. Springer, 2004.
2. A. Aamodt and E. Plaza. Case-based reasoning: Foundational issues, methodological variations, and system approaches. *AI Communications*, 7(i), 1994.
3. D. W. Aha, L. A. Breslow, and H. Muñoz-Avila. Conversational case-based reasoning. *Applied Intelligence*, 14(1):9–32, 2001.
4. D. W. Aha, T. Maney, and L. Breslow. Supporting dialogue inferencing in conversational case-based reasoning. In B. Smyth and P. Cunningham, editors, *EWCBR*, volume 1488 of *Lecture Notes in Computer Science*, pages 262–273. Springer, 1998.
5. J. L. Arcos and R. L. D. Mántaras. An interactive case-based reasoning approach for generating expressive music. *Applied Intelligence*, 14(1):115–129, 2001.
6. F. Baader, D. Calvanese, D. L. McGuinness, D. Nardi, and P. F. Patel-Schneider, editors. *The description logic handbook: theory, implementation, and applications.* Cambridge University Press, New York, NY, USA, 2003.
7. B. Díaz-Agudo and P. A. González-Calero. CBROnto: a task/method ontology for CBR. In S. Haller and G. Simmons, editors, *Procs. of the 15th International FLAIRS'02 Conference (Special Track on CBR*, pages 101–106. AAAI Press, 2002.
8. M. Fernández-López and A. Gómez-Pérez. Overview and analysis of methodologies for building ontologies. *Knowl. Eng. Rev.*, 17(2):129–156, 2002.
9. M. Göker and C. Thompson. Personalized conversational case-based recommendation. In L. P. E. Blanzieri, editor, *Advances in Case-Based Reasoning. Proceedings of the 8th European Workshop on Case-Based Reasoning,(EWCBR '2000) LNAI 1898.* Springer, 2000.

10. M. H. Göker. Adapting to the level of experience of the user in mixed-initiative web self-service applications. In *Aha, D. (ed.), Proceedings, Workshop on Mixed Initiative Case-Based Reasoning, at the 5th International Conference on Case Based Reasoning, ICCBR, Trondheim, Norway, June 23-26*, 2003.

11. H. Gómez-Gauchía, B. Díaz-Agudo, P. P. Gómez-Martín, and P. A. González-Calero. Supporting conversation variability in cobber using causal loops. In Muñoz-Avila and Ricci [25], pages 252–266.

12. H. Gómez-Gauchía, B. Díaz-Agudo, and P. A. González-Calero. A pragmatic methodology for conceptualization with two layered knowledge representation: a case study. In *Pfeiffer, H., Wolf, K., Delugach, H., (Eds.): Contributions to ICCS 2004. 12th International Conference on Conceptual Structures, ICCS 2004*, Shaker. Verlag, December, 20-22 2004.

13. H. Gómez-Gauchía, B. Díaz-Agudo, and P. A. González-Calero. Cobber, toward an affective conversational ki-cbr framework. In B. Prasad, editor, *B. Prasad(Ed.) Procs of the 2nd Indian International Conference on Artificial Intelligence IICAI-05*, pages 1804–1820, Pune, India, December, 20-22 2005. IICAI.

14. H. Gómez-Gauchía, B. Díaz-Agudo, and P. A. González-Calero. Automatic personalization of the human computer interaction using temperaments. In *Proceedings of the Fifteenth International Florida Artificial Intelligence Research Society Conference, FLAIRS06, Melbourne Beach, Florida, USA*. AAAI Press, May 11-13 2006.

15. A. Gomez-Perez, O. Corcho-Garcia, and M. Fernandez-Lopez. *Ontological Engineering*. Springer-Verlag New York, Inc., Secaucus, NJ, USA, 2003.

16. M. Gu and A. Aamodt. A knowledge-intensive method for conversational cbr. In Muñoz-Avila and Ricci [25], pages 296–311.

17. N. Guin-Duclosson, S. Jean-Daubias, and S. Nogry. The ambre ile: How to use case-based reasoning to teach methods. In *ITS '02: Proceedings of the 6th International Conference on Intelligent Tutoring Systems*, pages 782–791, London, UK, 2002. Springer-Verlag.

18. K. M. Gupta and D. W. Aha. A framework for incremental query formulation in mixed-initiative case-based reasoning. In K. D. Ashley and D. G. Bridge, editors, *Workshops in Case-Based Reasoning*, volume 2689 of *Lecture Notes in Computer Science*. Springer, 2003.

19. H. Knublauch. User-defined datatypes in protege-owl. http://protege.stanford.edu/plugins/owl/xsp.html, 2005.

20. D. B. Leake and D. C. Wilson. A case-based framework for interactive capture and reuse of design knowledge. *Applied Intelligence*, 14(1):77–94, 2001.

21. E. Mckenna and B. Smyth. An interactive visualisation tool for case-based reasoners. *Applied Intelligence*, 14(1):95–114, 2001.

22. D. McSherry. Interactive case-based reasoning in sequential diagnosis. *Applied Intelligence*, 14(1):65–76, 2001.

23. G. C. F. Mehmet S. Aktas, Marlon Pierce and D. Leake. A web based conversational case-based recommender system for ontology aided metadata discovery. In *Fifth IEEE/ACM International Workshop on Grid Computing (GRID'04)*, pages 69–75, 2004.

24. H. Muñoz-Avila, D. W. Aha, L. Breslow, and D. Nau. HICAP: an interactive case-based planning architecture and its application to noncombat evacuation operations. In *AAAI '99/IAAI '99: Procs of the sixteenth national conference on Artificial Intelligence*, pages 870–875, Menlo Park, CA, USA, 1999. AAAI.

25. H. Muñoz-Avila and F. Ricci, editors. *Case-Based Reasoning, Research and Development, 6th International Conference, on Case-Based Reasoning, ICCBR 2005, Chicago, IL, USA, August 23-26, 2005, Proceedings*, volume 3620 of *Lecture Notes in Computer Science*. Springer, 2005.

26. J. A. Recio, B. Díaz-Agudo, M. A. Gómez-Martín, and N. Wiratunga. Extending jCOLIBRI for textual CBR. In Muñoz-Avila and Ricci [25], pages 421–435.

27. J. Reilly, K. McCarthy, L. McGinty, and B. Smyth. Explaining compound critiques. *Artif. Intell. Rev.*, 24(2):199–220, 2005.

28. H. Simazu, A. Shibata, and K. Nihei. Expertguide: A conversational case-based reasoning tool for developing mentors in knowledge spaces. *Applied Intelligence*, 14(1):33–48, 2001.

Complexity Profiling for Informed Case-Base Editing

Stewart Massie, Susan Craw, and Nirmalie Wiratunga

School of Computing,
The Robert Gordon University,
Aberdeen AB25 1HG, Scotland, UK
{sm, smc, nw}@comp.rgu.ac.uk

Abstract. The contents of the case knowledge container is critical to the performance of case-based classification systems. However the knowledge engineer is given little support in the selection of suitable techniques to maintain and monitor the case-base. In this paper we present a novel technique that provides an insight into the structure of a case-base by means of a complexity profile that can assist maintenance decision-making and provide a benchmark to assess future changes to the case-base. We also introduce a complexity-guided redundancy reduction algorithm which uses a local complexity measure to actively retain cases close to boundaries. The algorithm offers control over the balance between maintaining competence and reducing case-base size. The ability of the algorithm to maintain accuracy in a compacted case-base is demonstrated on seven public domain classification datasets.

1 Introduction

Case-Based Reasoning (CBR) is an experience based problem-solving approach that uses a case-base of previously solved problems as a knowledge source to help solve new problems. The case-base is a key knowledge container [13] and, as such, the CBR process draws heavily on case knowledge. This is particularly true in case-based classification systems for which retrieval is the key stage.

The CBR paradigm typically employs a lazy learning approach, such as k-nearest neighbour [5], for the retrieval stage of the process which delays generalisation until problem-solving time. This is attractive because training is not necessary, learning is fast and incremental, algorithms are simple and intuitive, and advance knowledge of the problems to be faced is not required. However, with large case-bases, the drawbacks of lazy learning are high memory requirements since all examples are stored, slow retrieval times, and the possible inclusion of harmful cases.

At the initial case authoring stage, the case-base can consist of all available examples. Alternatively, the knowledge engineer can create a hand-crafted case-base by storing only selected examples in the case-base giving rise to a need for algorithms that control the size of the case-base. In addition, the case-base gets larger over time, often as a result of indiscriminate storage of cases during the retain stage of the CBR cycle. The cases may be redundant and provide no improvement in competence or may even be harmful, noisy cases that result in a reduction in competence. In either case the inclusion of additional cases will increase storage requirements and retrieval times. The cost of retrieval can grow to the extent that it outweighs the benefit of additional cases. This

T.R. Roth-Berghofer et al. (Eds.): ECCBR 2006, LNAI 4106, pp. 325–339, 2006.
© Springer-Verlag Berlin Heidelberg 2006

is called the *utility problem* [7,14] and results in an ongoing requirement to control case-base growth.

Understandably, there has been considerable research on the case-base editing problem giving the knowledge engineer a choice of potential approaches. However, most contemporary editing algorithms give no control over the size of the edited case-base or the impact on competence, and provide no explanation of their decisions. We argue that the knowledge engineer should have more control over the balance between the reduction in the size of the case-base and maintaining competence.

It is often assumed that any of the numerous maintenance approaches available will work well on all domains. However, research has identified that no one algorithm is *best* in all situations [4,6]. The knowledge engineer must make a choice between alternative techniques based on knowledge of the case-base and the system's competence, retrieval and storage space requirements. What technique to choose is not obvious because it requires knowledge about the structure of the case-base that is often hidden. Given a dataset it is not clear what level of redundancy or noise it contains. Low accuracy may be the result of a lack of case knowledge due to a sparse case-base, a difficult problem with long, complex decision boundaries or noisy data. The knowledge engineer does not know whether to apply a noise reduction algorithm, a case creation algorithm or a redundancy reduction algorithm. Methods that improve the comprehension of the case-base structure would aid this decision-making process.

In this paper, we present a novel case-base profiling technique that provides an insight into the structure of the case-base, assisting informed maintenance decisions. In addition, we introduce a new case-base editing algorithm that gives the knowledge engineer more control of the balance between case-base size and competence and also provides some explanation of its editing decisions. Both techniques are evaluated experimentally and shown to have benefit.

The remainder of this paper describes our approach and evaluates it on several public domain case-bases. In Section 2 we review existing research on case-based editing techniques. Section 3 discusses complexity profiling of a case-base and how it can aid the knowledge engineer make maintenance choices. An evaluation of our profiling technique is presented in Section 4. Our new case-base editing technique is then introduced in Section 5 with experimental results being reported on seven datasets in Section 6. Finally, we provide conclusions and recommendation for future work in Section 7.

2   Related Work on Case-Base Editing in CBR

Considerable research effort has been aimed at case-base maintenance and much of the research has focused on control of the case-base by case deletion or case selection policies. Two distinct areas have been investigated: the control of noise; and the reduction of redundancy.

Noise reduction algorithms aim to improve competence by removing cases that are thought to have a detrimental effect on accuracy. These may be corrupt cases with incorrect solutions or, alternately, they may be cases whose inclusion in the case-base results in other cases being incorrectly solved. These algorithms usually remove only a few cases. Wilson Editing [20], also called ENN, is the best known algorithm and attempts to remove noise by removing cases that are incorrectly classified by their nearest neighbours. ENN removes noisy cases but also deletes cases lying on boundaries between classes leaving smoother decision boundaries. Tomek extends ENN with the Repeated Wilson Editing method (RENN) and the All k-NN method [18]. RENN extends ENN by repeating the deletion cycle until no more cases are removed. The All k-NN is similar, except that after each iteration the value of k is increased. The Blame-Based Noise Reduction (BBNR) algorithm [6] is a noise reduction algorithm that takes a slightly different approach in attempting to identify cases that cause misclassification and removing them if they cause more *harm* than *good*. Noise reduction can reduce competence, hence careful consideration should be given to the domain and structure of the case-base before applying these algorithms to ensure there is a need for noise reduction. Our work does not advance research on noise reduction but rather identifies datasets where noise reduction is required.

Redundancy reduction algorithms can be either incremental, starting with an empty edited set and selecting cases, or decremental where cases are deleted from an initially complete set. Hart's [8] Condensed Nearest Neighbour rule (CNN) was an early incremental approach in which only cases not solved by the edited set are added to it. CNN is sensitive to the case presentation order and numerous extensions or modifications have suggested improvements [1,19]. McKenna and Smyth's [11,17] competence-guided editing techniques use local case information from their competence model [16] to rank cases prior to case selection, so that redundant cases are presented later in the editing process. Several ranking measures are proposed based on a case's *coverage* and *reachability* sets including *relative cover* ranking (RC), which is shown to give a large reduction in case-base size while retaining competence. McKenna and Smyth also developed the CASCADE authoring system [12] in which the case-base developer, guided by a model of case competence, could interact with an interface to manage the selection of which cases to add or remove from the case-base.

Several contemporary decremental approaches use similar local case competence knowledge to guide their editing decisions. Wilson and Martinez's Reduction Technique range of algorithms (RT1-3) [21] is guided by a case's *associates*. The associates of a case is the set of cases which have that case as one of their nearest neighbours and is analogous to Smyth & Keane's [15] coverage set. The algorithms remove a case if at least as many of its associates would be correctly classified after deletion. Brighton and Mellish [3] adopt a similar approach with their Iterative Case Filtering algorithm (ICF). A case is deleted if its reachable set is larger than its coverage set, i.e., more cases can solve the case than it can solve itself. The process is repeated until no more cases are removed. This results in boundary cases being retained and central cases being removed. Delaney and Cunningham [6] employ a similar approach in their Conservative Redundancy Reduction algorithm (CRR) in which a case with smallest coverage set is selected first and any cases that it solves are deleted from the training set. This algorithm was tested on email classification where it is shown that conservative redundancy reduction achieves a higher accuracy than comparable but more aggressive algorithms.

Redundancy reduction algorithms require a trade off between the level of compaction and competence preservation. The more modern algorithms (RC, RT3, ICF and CRR) all provide a good but different balance between these conflicting objectives. Our approach gives the knowledge engineer control of this balance. The contemporary redundancy editing approaches all rely on models [10,15,16] of the case-base to supply local information about the relationship between cases. These relationships are used to *indirectly* retain cases on decision boundaries. In our approach we also calculate local case information but the information identifies the position of a case in relation to a decision boundary. We aim to *directly* identify and retain cases on or near decision boundaries.

3   Case-Base Complexity Profiling

Our objective is to help the knowledge engineer make decisions on maintenance strategies by providing a global case-base measure of accuracy, noise and redundancy plus local information on the structure of the case-base. Our approach is to provide a profile of a local case metric. We use a case complexity measure to provide the local measure and a ranked profile of this measure to provide a view of the overall effect within the case-base. The complexity profile identifies the mix of local complexities. In the rest of this section we first define the local case complexity measure used and then look at our profiling approach to providing a global picture of the case-base.

3.1   Complexity Measure

The foundation of our approach is to measure the local complexity based on the spatial distribution of cases within the case-base. Complexity is calculated using a metric based on the composition of its neighbours while incrementally increasing the size of its neighbourhood.

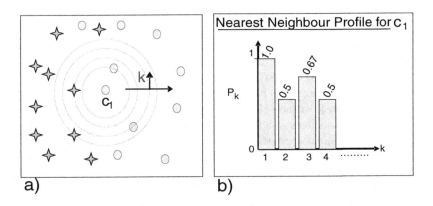

Fig. 1. Calculation of the complexity metric

The complexity measure is calculated for each case by looking at the class distribution of cases within its local neighbourhood. P_k is the proportion of cases within a case's k nearest neighbours that belong to the same class as itself. In Figure 1(a) a case is represented by a symbol on the plot with the class of the case distinguished by the shape, star or circle. If we consider case c_1, then as the value of k increases, the sequence of P_k starts 1, 0.5, 0.67, 0.5. A nearest neighbour profile can now be plotted for c_1 using P_k as k increases. The complexity metric is based on the area of the graph under the profile, the shaded area in Figure 1(b). Case complexity is calculated by

$$\text{complexity} = 1 - \frac{1}{K} \sum_{k=1}^{K} P_k$$

for some chosen K. With K=4 the complexity of c_1 is 0.33. A large value for K has little impact on the results because the metric is biased towards a case's nearest neighbours. We have used K=10 in our calculations for all but the smallest case-base sizes.

Cases with high complexity are close to classification boundaries and identify areas of uncertainty within the problem space. Cases with complexity greater than 0.5 are closer to cases of a different class than those of their own class, and are potentially noisy. Cases with low complexity are surrounded mainly by cases with the same class as themselves, and are located in areas of the problem space in which the system would be more confident in making a decision on the class of a new problem. Cases with a zero complexity value are surrounded by a sizeable group of cases with the same class as itself, and may be considered redundant because other cases in the group would be able to solve new problems in this region of the problem space.

3.2   Profile Approach

The complexity measure provides a local indicator of uncertainty within the problem space and has been shown to be useful in informing a case discovery algorithm [9]. However, it is difficult for the knowledge engineer to use this local information directly to gain an insight into the structure of a case-base from a global perspective. Our approach to providing the knowledge engineer with meaningful access to this pool of local information is to present the data as a ranked profile of case complexities. In this approach the mix of complexities within the case-base can be viewed as a profile allowing comparisons to be made between case-bases.

The ranked complexity profile is created by first calculating the case complexity of each case, as described in Section 3.1. The cases are then ranked in ascending order of complexity. Then, starting with cases with the lowest complexity, case complexities are plotted against the proportion of cases used. Thus the x-axis shows the proportion of the case-base and the y-axis gives the complexity value for a particular case. A typical profile plot, for a case-base containing redundancy, is shown in Figure 2. An exponentially shaped curve is positioned to the right of the graph after the redundant cases with zero complexity.

Three key global indicators can be taken from this plot to give a measure of accuracy, redundancy and noise respectively, as follows:-

- **Error Rate:** The area under the curve, shown as the shaded area on the plot, gives the overall complexity of the problem being faced and provides a measure of expected error rate.
- **Redundancy:** The position at which the plot breaks away from the x-axis, shown on the profile as x_1, gives a measure of the level of redundancy within the case-base. This is a measure of the proportion of cases located in single class clusters.

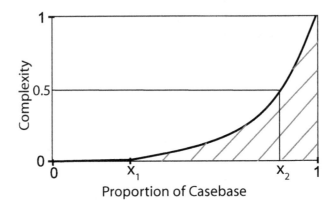

Fig. 2. Typical graph of local complexity profile

- **Noise:** A case with a complexity greater than 0.5 has the majority of its neighbours belonging to a different class. These cases can be considered noisy. The proportion of noisy cases can now be portrayed as the distance from x_2 to 1; i.e., $1-x_2$.

It is expected that these three indicators will correlate well with typical measures of error rate, redundancy and noise. This will be investigated in the evaluation that follows. However, it is the graph itself that provides the best insight into the structure of the case-base, and allows informed decisions to be made by the knowledge engineer in relation to whether the number of cases in the case-base is appropriate to the domain and its level of complexity.

4   Experimental Evaluation of Profiling

We evaluate complexity profiles on two levels in this section. First we examine whether complexity profiling can provide useful comparisons of case-bases from different domains. Then we investigate our hypothesis that the complexity profile indicators accurately predict global error rates and levels of noise and redundancy.

4.1   Cross Domain Comparisons

In the previous section we looked at a *typical* complexity profile and claimed that this profiling provided a good approach at making comparisons across different domains. To examine this claim we look at example complexity profiles from four domains. Figure 3(a)-(c) show the complexity profiles for three public domain classification datasets from the UCI ML repository [2], together with the complexity profile for an artificial dataset in Figure 3(d).

Wine (Figure 3(a)) is a simple three class problem with 14 numeric attributes and 178 instances. It can be seen from the profile that a high level of classification accuracy is expected due to the small area under the complexity curve (0.05). The expected level of noise is very low with an estimate of 4% and a maximum complexity value for an instance being well below 1. A high level of redundancy is also evident with 75% of the

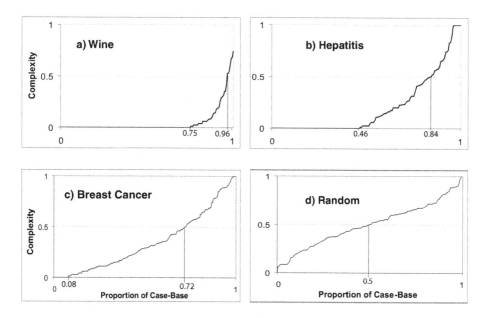

Fig. 3. Complexity profiles for sample datasets

instances having a zero complexity value. A case-base created from this dataset, containing less redundancy, could form part of an excellent CBR problem-solver because the similarity measure forms the instances into clusters with the same solutions - similar problems have similar solutions.

Hepatitis (Figure 3(b)) is a smaller dataset of 155 instances represented by 20, mostly nominal, features containing some missing values. This is a more complex problem with an overall complexity of 20% and a gentler slope to the curve than for Wine, suggesting more complex decision boundaries. There is a moderate predicted level of noise (16%) with several instances completely surrounded by instances of an opposing class resulting in a peak complexity value of 1. Although there is less redundancy than for wine, the level is still high with 46% of the instances surrounded by at least 10 instances with the same class. Applying noise reduction algorithms would probably improve the level of accuracy achieved and redundancy reduction algorithms could be applied to reduce storage requirments without affecting accuracy levels.

Breast Cancer (Figure 3(c)) is a binary classification domain with 9 multi-valued features containing missing data. This is a complex problem, with the low slope on the graph indicating most instances lie close to decision boundaries. There is a high estimated level of noise (28%) and little redundancy (8%). This profile would suggest a dataset that is not suitable for a CBR application as it stands. Applying noise reduction algorithms may improve accuracy levels. In addition, improvements in the similarity measure or case representation could be investigated to create a design in which problems with similar solutions are better recognised as being similar.

The final profile, Figure 3(d), is for an artificial dataset with 100 instances. This is a binary classification problem with 2 numerical features where the class of an instance is randomly selected. This is a problem that has been created so that similar problems will not form into a cluster of instances with similar solutions. The dataset would not make a suitable case-base for a case-based problem-solver and this is confirmed by the complexity profile. As expected, the predicted error rate is 50% and the predicted noise level is also 50% because instances are as likely to be surrounded by instances of an opposing class as the same class. There is no redundancy because the instances do not form into large same class clusters.

4.2 Accuracy and Noise Predictions

The evaluation of complexity profiles from different domains, and the insight the profile provides, assumes that the error rate, noise level and redundancy level indicators are good predictors of the real values contained within the data. While conceptually the use of these indicators appears reasonable, we want to investigate the relationships empirically.

Table 1. Results summary of complexity profile indicators compared to alternative measures

	ERROR RATE		NOISE		REDUNDANCY
Case-Base	TEST SET	PROFILE	ENN	PROFILE	PROFILE
Wine	0.037	0.050	0.033	0.04	0.75
Iris	0.059	0.058	0.048	0.05	0.79
Hepatitis	0.189	0.203	0.176	0.16	0.46
Lymphography	0.187	0.242	0.155	0.14	0.23
Breast Cancer	0.339	0.344	0.306	0.28	0.08
House Votes	0.079	0.083	0.071	0.07	0.77
Zoo	0.038	0.085	0.061	0.06	0.70

Accuracy or error rate is the easiest indicator to compare. We calculate error rate experimentally using ten fold cross-validation. Nine folds are retained as the training set with the remaining fold being the unseen test set. The average error rates for seven UCI datasets, calculated using 1-NN, are shown in column 2 of Table 1 with the corresponding error rate indicator from the complexity profiles shown in column 3. There is a strong correlation between the results as can be seen by the close fit to the straight line in Figure 4, which plots the complexity profile prediction against test set error rate.

There is not an obvious measure of noise with which to make a comparison. However, ENN is the best known noise reduction algorithm. Hence, we use the reduction in the size of a dataset after applying ENN as a benchmark measure of noise with which to compare our predicted indicator from the complexity profile. The average edited set size after applying ENN as a proportion of the original dataset size is shown in column 4 of Table 1. This is compared with the average complexity profile noise indicator, as shown in column 5. Again there is a strong correlation between the results, as shown by the fit to a straight line in Figure 5, which plots the complexity profile noise prediction with the proportional reduction in the size of the dataset from applying ENN.

These results confirm that the complexity profile is a good predictor of accuracy and noise. The ability of the complexity profile to predict redundancy is difficult to measure directly but is investigated in more detail in Section 5.

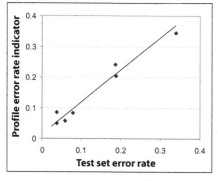 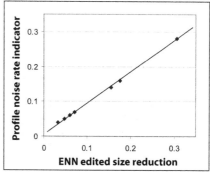

Fig. 4. Error rate correlation   **Fig. 5.** Noise level correlation

5   Complexity Threshold Editing

The case-base complexity profile provides a tool that can be used for informed redundancy editing in which the knowledge engineer has control over the level of redundancy reduction. As with most redundancy editing algorithms, our approach aims to give a high classification accuracy and to provide significant storage space reduction. However, these objectives can be contradictory. Aggressive case editing can achieve large reductions in case-base size but at the expense of classification accuracy [6]. The complexity profile provides a measure of the proportion of redundant cases compared to cases near decision boundaries giving an explanation of the effect of different levels of redundancy reduction on competence.

In classification problems redundant cases are found in clusters with the same classification preferably far from decision boundaries. Our approach to case-base editing is to identify and delete redundant cases while at the same time retaining boundary cases. The complexity measure, described in Section 3.1, is a good identifier of boundary cases, with a high complexity value, and redundant cases with a low complexity. We use the local case complexity to guide our editing algorithm.

The benefits of this approach over existing techniques are two-fold. Firstly, the knowledge engineer is in control of the maintenance process and is able to make an informed decision on a suitable level of case-base compaction dependent on a system's performance requirements. This decision is not made by selecting an arbitrary case-base size. Rather, through a review of the complexity profile, a judgement can be made on the impact of different complexity thresholds. If storage space or retrieval time requirements are crucial to the design a higher threshold can be chosen in the understanding that it will reduce competence. Secondly, the complexity profile provides an explanation of the editing process by providing a transparency to the process and a justification for deleting the selected cases.

The basic approach is to set a complexity threshold and delete cases with a complexity below the threshold. The threshold is set on the y-axis, and the resulting size of the case-base can be noted on the x-axis. Our expectation is that setting a zero threshold will remove only cases that are likely to be redundant and not result in a fall in competence. Competence is expected to decline gradually as the complexity threshold is increased. The basic approach gave promising results but also highlighted several problems.

- Noisy cases are by their very nature boundary cases and hence will be retained by this algorithm. Adopting the approach of most other contemporary editing algorithms, we add a pre-processing noise editing algorithm (RENN).
- Clusters of cases all with zero complexity can form. Setting a simple threshold can delete the complete cluster. It would be better to retain at least one case to represent the cluster. To overcome this problem an iterative approach is employed with case complexities being recalculated after each case deletion and the cases being re-ranked in ascending order of complexity.
- A further problem with clusters of cases with zero complexity is the choice of order of deletion. If a random selection is made cases nearer decision boundaries may be selected for deletion first. This would harm the performance of the algorithm so we introduce a *friend* to *enemy* distance ratio as a secondary ranking. The friend distance is the average distance to the case's nearest like neighbours whereas the enemy distance is the average distance to the case's nearest unlike neighbours. A high ratio indicates a case closer to a decision boundary and farther from cases of the same class, whereas a low ratio indicates a case farther from a decision boundary and in a cluster of cases of same class.

The Complexity Threshold Editing algorithm (CTE), incorporating the changes introduced above, is described in Figure 6.

```
T,          Dataset of n cases (c₁ ....cₙ)
COM(S),     Calculate case complexity, distance
            ratio and order cases in set S
RENN(S),    Apply noise removal to set S
Count=0

COM(T)
For each c in T
   if ( complexity(c)<threshold) count++
End-For
E-Set ← RENN(T)
For 0 to count
   COM(E-Set)
   c ← First case in E-Set
   E-Set ← E-Set - c
End-For
Return (E-Set)
```

Fig. 6. Complexity threshold editing algorithm

6   Experimental Evaluation of Complexity Threshold Editing

In this evaluation we compare the performance of Complexity Threshold Editing with several existing redundancy reduction algorithms. The algorithms being compared can be split into three categories.

- Complexity Threshold Editing (CTE) is our new redundancy reduction algorithm and directly comparable with existing redundancy reduction algorithms. It is evaluated with four different complexity thresholds (0, 0.1, 0.2 and 0.3)
- Existing redundancy reduction algorithms (CRR, ICF and RC). These are modern redundancy reduction algorithms that aim to reduce the size of the case-base while maintaining competence. They have been shown to perform well in previous comparisons but each provides a different balance between compaction and competence: CRR provides a conservative approach to redundancy editing, RC is an aggressive algorithm deleting the highest number of cases, whereas, ICF falls in the middle giving a moderate level of case-base compaction.
- Noise reduction algorithms (ENN and RENN). These algorithm aim to improve competence but remove only a few cases and are not comparable with redundancy reduction algorithms. They are included in the evaluation because RENN has been used as the pre-processing algorithm for all the redundancy reduction algorithms including CTE. RENN provides a benchmark for accuracy that the redundancy reduction algorithms aim to maintain.

6.1   Experimental Setup

A ten times 10-fold cross validation experimental set-up is used giving one hundred case-base/test set combinations per experiment. The editing algorithms were applied to each case-base and the resulting edited set size is recorded. Test set accuracy, using 1-NN retrieval, was measured for the original case-base and for each of the edited sets created by the editing algorithms.

Comparisons have been made on seven UCI datasets and the averaged results are shown in Tables 2 and 3. Table 2 contains the average test set accuracy for each algorithm on each domain. The highest accuracy result achieved by the redundancy reduction algorithms in each domain is highlighted in bold. Table 3 gives the unedited dataset size in column 2 together with the edited dataset size as a proportion of the original in the other columns. The values in bold are the size reduction achieved by the redundancy algorithm with the highest accuracy. Both tables include an *average* row but this should be used with care as it is calculated across different domains.

6.2   Results of Evaluation

The results of the evaluation can be summarised in each of the categories as follows:

- The CTE algorithm provides the highest accuracy of the redundancy reduction algorithms in six of the seven domains. At zero complexity threshold, CTE has the highest average accuracy of 87.5% compared to 86.5% for CRR. This is achieved with smaller case-base sizes, 32.8% of original size on average compared to 39.4%,

Table 2. Comparison of average test set accuracy for alternative editing algorithms

Case-Base	ORIG	REDUNDANCY			CTE				NOISE	
		CRR	ICF	RC	0	0.1	0.2	0.3	RENN	ENN
Breast Cancer	0.661	**0.740**	0.736	0.688	0.738	0.734	0.728	0.709	0.753	0.736
Hepatitis	0.808	0.839	0.833	0.821	**0.859**	0.853	0.847	0.822	0.834	0.862
House Votes	0.922	0.905	0.901	0.904	**0.922**	0.916	0.898	0.854	0.911	0.920
Iris	0.940	0.947	0.931	0.943	**0.949**	0.933	0.882	0.878	0.952	0.952
Lymphography	0.812	0.759	0.749	0.757	0.775	0.775	**0.776**	0.758	0.772	0.781
Wine	0.963	0.957	0.934	0.923	**0.959**	0.924	0.884	0.822	0.948	0.953
Zoo	0.957	0.906	0.902	0.904	**0.921**	0.901	0.876	0.778	0.904	0.926
Average	0.866	0.865	0.855	0.850	**0.875**	0.862	0.842	0.803	0.868	0.876

Table 3. Comparison of edited case-base size for alternative editing algorithms

Case-Base	ORIG	REDUNDANCY			CTE				NOISE	
		CRR	ICF	RC	0	0.1	0.2	0.3	RENN	ENN
Breast Cancer	258	**0.248**	0.160	0.071	0.604	0.450	0.292	0.163	0.674	0.694
Hepatitis	140	0.403	0.082	0.061	**0.355**	0.265	0.186	0.102	0.796	0.824
House Votes	392	0.471	0.035	0.038	**0.155**	0.093	0.061	0.038	0.908	0.928
Iris	135	0.389	0.296	0.065	**0.177**	0.078	0.038	0.037	0.952	0.952
Lymphography	134	0.415	0.180	0.152	0.625	0.460	**0.322**	0.189	0.815	0.846
Wine	161	0.439	0.159	0.099	**0.208**	0.098	0.056	0.033	0.965	0.967
Zoo	91	0.355	0.486	0.110	**0.241**	0.138	0.096	0.075	0.927	0.938
Average	187	0.394	0.153	0.074	**0.328**	0.221	0.146	0.087	0.853	0.870

showing that CTE is an excellent algorithm for conservative redundancy reduction. At moderate levels of redundancy reduction, with a threshold of 0.1, CTE achieves slightly better accuracies than ICF but retains slightly more cases. Overall the performance is comparable with ICF. With higher complexity thresholds, for agressive redundancy reduction, CTE does not perform so well and is outperformed by RC.

- The three existing redundancy reduction algorithms all provide a different compromise on the trade-off between case-base compaction and maintaining competence. CRR, designed to take a conservative approach to redundancy reduction, has the highest accuracy on each domain and the highest average accuracy of 86.5% compared to 85.5% for ICF and 85.0% for RC. However, CRR obtains the improved accuracy by retaining, on average, 39% of the cases, more than twice that of ICF (15%) and five times RC (7%). Very aggressive redundancy reduction is achieved by RC but the results confirm that this is at the expense of loss of accuracy. The performance of ICF lies between the others on both competence retention and case-base size reduction.

- There is little to choose between the performance of the noise reduction algorithms. In these datasets ENN gives the highest average accuracy but that is probably because many of these datasets are not noisy and ENN gives the best results on data with low levels of noise. RENN removes slightly more cases and generally performs better on noisy data but worse on low noise datasets. It is worth noting that on four of the datasets all the noise reduction algorithms harm accuracy but on Breast Cancer and Hepatitis substantial accuracy gains are achieved by noise reduction.

CTE provides the best performance for conservative redundancy reduction, providing superior accuracy on six out of the seven domains. We checked the significance of these differences using a 2-tailed t-test with 95% confidence level. The superiority of CTE was found to be significant in 4 domains; Hepatitis, House Votes, Lymphography and Zoo.

As expected, setting a zero level threshold maintained accuracy at a similar level to that achieved after RENN noise reduction in all the domains and overall there was actually a slight increase in accuracy from 86.8% to 87.5%. This confirms that at the local level the case complexity measure identifies redundant cases and at a global level the redundancy indicator estimated from the complexity profile is a good predictor of the level of redundancy within a case-base. When the complexity threshold is increased above zero, accuracy initially falls away gradually at first, as non-redundant cases start to be deleted and then more quickly as cases nearer to decision boundaries are deleted.

The performance of CTE for aggressive levels of redundancy reduction with the higher complexity thresholds was disappointing. This suggests that while case complexity provides a good measure for identifying redundant cases away from boundaries, it is not so good at selecting between boundary cases.

The expectation that accuracy would fall as the size of the edited case-base falls is corroborated both for the existing redundancy reduction algorithms and for varying complexity thresholds with CTE. This confirms previous research results that there is a trade-off between the conflicting objectives of compaction of the case-base and maintaining competence.

The inconsistent performance of the noise removal algorithms across the different datasets highlights the need to apply different maintenance strategies for different domains. Complexity profiling of the case-base can play a role in identifying appropriate maintenance strategies for a case-base.

7   Conclusions and Future Work

The novel contribution of this work is the use of a local case complexity measure, together with a case-base profile to guide the case editing process. The complexity measure identifies redundant cases for deletion and cases on class decision boundaries for retention. Complexity profiling gives a measure of the level of complexity, redundancy and noise inherent in the data. This knowledge provides an element of control over the compromise required between the contradictory objectives of the reduction in case-base size and the retention of competence.

Complexity profiling can play a further role in assisting the knowledge engineer to make choices between alternative maintenance techniques depending on the structure of the data and a system's performance requirements. Profiling also provides the opportunity to create a benchmark for comparison with future versions of the case-base to monitor the impact of changes over time.

We have introduced the Complexity Threshold Editing algorithm and demonstrated its effectiveness on seven public domain datasets. The algorithm was shown to provide superior performance characteristics when compared to existing techniques for conservative levels of editing and comparable performance at moderate levels of editing. One limitation of the approach is an average performance for aggressive editing because the complexity measure does not make a balanced selection between alternative boundary cases. Enhancements are being investigated to improve this selection on boundaries.

Complexity profiling has also been introduced and evaluated on public domain datasets. The interpretation of several profiles has been discussed to show how they can help the knowledge engineer develop a suitable case-base maintenance policy. The global indicators on accuracy, redundancy and noise, extracted from the profiles, are shown to correlate well with alternative measures.

In this paper we have concentrated on providing support for the knowledge engineer in the redundancy editing problem. However we are keen to see how the use of profiling might be used more generally to provide support in other case-base maintenance areas, such as noise reduction.

References

1. Aha, D., Kibler, D., Albert, M.: Instance-based learning algorithms. *Machine Learning* 6(1) (1991) 37–66
2. Blake, C., Keogh, E., Merz, C.: UCI repository of machine learning databases. (1998)
3. Brighton, H., Mellish, C.: Identifying competence-critical instances for instance-based learners. In *Instance Selection and Construction for Data Mining* (2001) 77–94
4. Brighton, H., Mellish, C.: Advances in instance selection for instance-based learning algorithms. *Data Mining and Knowledge Discovery* 6(2) (2002) 153–172
5. Cover, T., Hart, P.: Nearest neighbor pattern classification. *IEEE Transactions on Information Theory*, 13(1) (1967) 21–27
6. Delany, S.J., Cunningham, P.: An analysis of case-base editing in a spam filtering system. In *Proceedings of the 7th European Conference on Case-Based Reasoning* (2004) 128–141
7. Francis, A., Ram, A.: Computational models of the utility problem and their application to a utility analysis of case-based reasoning. In *Proceedings of the Workshop on Knowledge Compilation and Speed-Up Learning* (1993)
8. Hart, P.: The condensed nearest neighbour rule. *IEEE Transactions on Information Theory*, 14 (1968) 515–516
9. Massie, S., Craw, S., Wiratunga, N.: Complexity-guided case discovery for case based reasoning. In *Proceedings of the 20th National Conference on Artificial Intelligence* (2005) 216–221
10. McKenna, E., Smyth, B.: A competence model for case-based reasoning. In *9th Irish Conference on Artificial Intelligence and Cognitive Science* (1998)
11. McKenna, E., Smyth, B.: Competence-guided case-base editing techniques. In *Proceedings of the 5th European Workshop on Case-Based Reasoning* (2000) 186–197

12. McKenna, E., Smyth, B.: An interactive visualisation tool for case-based reasoners. *Applied Intelligence*, 14(1) (2001) 95–114

13. Richter, M.: Introduction. In *Case-Based Reasoning Technology: From Foundations to Applications* (1998) 1–15

14. Smyth, B., Cunningham, P.: The utility problem analysed: A case-based reasoning perspective. In *Proceedings of the 3rd European Workshop on Case-Based Reasoning* (1996) 392–399

15. Smyth, B., Keane, M.T.: Remembering to forget. In *Proceedings of the 14th International Joint Conference on Artificial Intelligence* (1995) 377–382

16. Smyth, B., McKenna, E.: Modelling the competence of case-bases. In *Proceedings of the 4th European Workshop on Case-Based Reasoning* (1998) 208–220

17. Smyth, B., McKenna, E.: Building compact competent case-bases. In *Proceedings of the 3rd International Conference on Case-Based Reasoning* (1999) 329–342

18. Tomek, I.: An experiment with the edited nearest-neighbour rule. *IEEE Transactions on Systems, Man, and Cybernetics*, 6(6) (1976) 448–452

19. Tomek, I.: Two modifications of CNN. *IEEE Transactions on Systems, Man, and Cybernetics*, 7(2) (1976) 679–772

20. Wilson, D.: Asymptotic properties of nearest neighbour rules using edited data. *IEEE Transactions on Systems, Man, and Cybernetics*, 2(3) (1972) 408–421

21. Wilson, D.R., Martinez, T.R.: Reduction techniques for instance-based learning algorithms. *Machine Learning*, 38(3) (2000) 257–286

Unsupervised Feature Selection for Text Data

Nirmalie Wiratunga, Rob Lothian, and Stewart Massie

School of Computing,
The Robert Gordon University,
Aberdeen AB25 1HG, Scotland, UK
{nw, rml, sm}@comp.rgu.ac.uk

Abstract. Feature selection for unsupervised tasks is particularly challenging, especially when dealing with text data. The increase in online documents and email communication creates a need for tools that can operate without the supervision of the user. In this paper we look at novel feature selection techniques that address this need. A distributional similarity measure from information theory is applied to measure feature utility. This utility informs the search for both representative and diverse features in two complementary ways: CLUSTER divides the entire feature space, before then selecting one feature to represent each cluster; and GREEDY increments the feature subset size by a greedily selected feature. In particular we found that GREEDY's local search is suited to learning smaller feature subset sizes while CLUSTER is able to improve the global quality of larger feature sets. Experiments with four email data sets show significant improvement in retrieval accuracy with nearest neighbour based search methods compared to an existing frequency-based method. Importantly both GREEDY and CLUSTER make significant progress towards the upper bound performance set by a standard supervised feature selection method.

1 Introduction

The volume of text content on the Internet and the widespread use of email-based communication have created a need for text classification, clustering and retrieval tools. There is also growing research interest in email applications, both within the Case-Based Reasoning (CBR) community [6,12] and more generally in Machine Learning [15]. Fundamental to this interest is the challenge posed by unstructured content, large vocabularies and changing concepts. Understandably, much of the research effort is directed towards mapping text into structured case representations, so as to facilitate meaningful abstraction, comparison, retrieval and reuse.

Feature selection plays an important role for the indexing vocabulary acquisition task. Often this initial selection can be either directly or indirectly applied to identify representative dimensions with which structured cases can be formed from unstructured text data. Applied directly, each selected feature corresponds to a dimension in the case representation. When applied indirectly, selected features are first combined to identify new features in a process referred to as feature extraction before they can be used as dimensions for case representation [4,25]. Although feature extraction is undoubtedly more effective than feature selection at capturing context, our experiences with supervised tasks suggests that feature selection is an important complementary precursor to

T.R. Roth-Berghofer et al. (Eds.): ECCBR 2006, LNAI 4106, pp. 340–354, 2006.

the extraction phase [24]. In this paper we are interested in feature selection applied directly to derive case representations for unsupervised tasks involving text data.

Feature selection reduces dimensionality by removing non-discriminatory and sometimes detrimental features, and has been successful in improving accuracy, efficiency and comprehension of learned models for supervised tasks in both structured [8,10] and unstructured domains [26]. Feature selection in an unsupervised setting is far more challenging, especially when dealing with text data. Typical applications (e.g. email, helpdesk, online reports) involve clustering of text for retrieval and maintenance purposes. The exponential increase in on-line text content creates a need for tools that can operate without the supervision of the user. However, in spite of this need, current research in feature selection is mainly concerned with supervised tasks only.

The aim of this paper is to apply unsupervised feature selection to text data. We introduce feature selection methods that are applicable to free text content as in emails and to texts that are sub-parts of semi-structured problem descriptions. The latter form is typical of reports such as anomaly detection or medical reports. Analysis of similar words and their neighbourhoods provide insight into vocabulary usage in the text collection. This knowledge is then exploited in the search for representative yet diverse features. In a GREEDY search, the next best feature to select is one that is a good representative of some unselected words, but also unlike previously selected words. This procedure maintains representativeness while ensuring diversity by discouraging redundant selections. Greedy search can of course result in locally optimal, yet globally non-optimal feature subsets. Therefore, a globally informed search, CLUSTER selects representative features from word clusters.

Central to feature selection methods introduced in this papers is the notion of similarity between words. Word co-occurrence behaviour is a good indicator of word similarity, however co-occurrence data derived from textual sources is typically sparse. Hence, distance measures must assign a distance to all word pairs, whether or not they co-occur in the data. Distributional similarity measures (obtained from information theory) achieve this by comparing co-occurrence behaviour on a separate disjoint set of target events [18]. In this paper events are all other words. Intuitively, if a group of words are distributed similarly with respect to other words then selecting a single representative from a neighbourhood of words will mainly eliminate redundant information. Consequently, this selection process will not hurt case representation, but will significantly reduce dimensionality. A further advantage of exploiting co-occurrence patterns is that it provides contextual information to resolve ambiguities in text such as similar meaning words that are used interchangeably (synonyms) and the same word being used with different meaning (polysemies). In both situations similar cases can be overlooked during retrieval if these semantic relationships are ignored.

Section 2 presents existing work in unsupervised feature selection and work related to distributional distance measures and clustering based indexing schemes. Next we establish our terminology before presenting the baseline method in Section 3. Details of distributional distance measures and the role of similarity for unsupervised feature selection is discussed in Section 4. Section 5 introduces the two similarity-based selection methods, GREEDY and CLUSTER. Experimental results are reported on four email datasets in Section 6, followed by conclusions in Section 7.

2   Related Work

Feature selection for structured data can be categorised into filter and wrapper methods. Filters are seen as data pre-processors and generally, unlike wrapper approaches, do not require feedback from the final learner. As a result they tend to be faster, scaling better to large datasets with thousands of dimensions, as typically encountered in text applications. Comparative studies in supervised feature selection for text have shown heuristics based on Information Gain (IG) and the Chi-squared statistic to consistently outperform less informative heuristics that rely only on word frequency counts [26].

Unlike with supervised methods, comparative studies into unsupervised feature selection are very rare. In fact, to our knowledge there has only been one publication explicitly dealing with unsupervised feature selection for text data [16]. Generally, existing unsupervised methods tend to rely on heuristics that are informed by word frequency counts over the text collection. Although frequency can be a fair indicator of feature utility it does not consider contextual information. Ignoring context can be detrimental for text processing tasks because ambiguities in text can often result in poor retrieval performance. A good example is when dealing with polysemous relationships such as "financial bank" and "river bank", where the word frequency for "bank" is clearly insufficient to establish its context and hence its suitability for indexing or case comparison.

In Textual Case-Based Reasoning (TCBR) research [22] the reasoning process can be seen to generally incorporate contextual information in two ways: as part of an elaborate indexing mechanism [2]; or as part of the case representation [24]. The latter requires simpler retrieval mechanisms, hence is a good choice for generic retrieval frameworks; while the former, although better at capturing domain-specific information, is more demanding of the retrieval process. A further distinguishing characteristic of TCBR systems is the different levels of knowledge sources employed to capture context [14]. These levels vary from deep syntactic parsing tools and manually acquired generative lexicons in the FACIT framework [7]; to semi-automated acquisition of domain-specific thesauri with the SMILE system; to automated clause extraction exploiting keyword co-occurrence patterns in PSI [25]. Of particular interest to this paper is the capture of co-occurrence based, contextual information within the case representation. Current research in this area is focused on feature extraction, which unlike feature selection aims to construct new features from existing features. Interest in this area has resulted in extraction techniques for both supervised (e.g. [25,27]) and unsupervised settings (e.g. [4,11]).

In text classification and applied linguistic research the problem of determining context is commonly handled by employing distributional clustering approaches. Introduced in the early nineties for automated thesaurus creation [18], distributional clustering has since been widely adopted for feature extraction with supervised tasks, such as text classification [1,20]. Word clusters are particularly useful because contextual information is made explicit by grouping together words that are suggestive of similar context. Additionally, word clusters also provide insight into vocabulary usage across the problem domain. Such information is essential if representative features are to be selected. Of particular importance for word clustering are distributional distance measures. These measures ascertain distance by comparison of word distributions conditioned over a disjoint target set. Typically, class labels are the set of targets and so cannot be applied to unsupervised tasks.

The textual case retrieval system SOPHIA introduced a novel approach to combining distributional word clustering with textual case base indexing [17]. Here feature distance is measured by comparing word distributions conditioned on other co-occurring words (instead of class labels). Indexing is enabled by identifying seed features that act as case attractors. They argue that seed features are those that have non-uniform distributions having low entropy, referred to as specific word contexts. However the entropy based measure cannot distinguish between representative and diverse features even if they have specific contexts.

In structured CBR, clustering is commonly employed as a means to identify representative and diverse cases for casebase indexing. A good example is the footprint-driven approach [21] where a footprint case is: representative of its neighbourhood because of its influence; and diverse because its area of competence cannot be matched by any other case. This notion of identifying diverse yet representative cases has also been exploited in casebase maintenance [6,23].

In summary, the representativeness and diversity of an entity can be measured by analysing its neighbourhood. In this paper the entity is the feature and representativeness and diversity are also important for feature selection. Central to feature neighbourhood analysis is a good distance metric. When features are words, the distance metric must take context into account. Distributional distance measures do this by exploiting word co-occurrence behaviour.

3   Frequency Based Unsupervised Feature Selection

We first introduce the notation used in this paper to assist presentation of the different feature selection techniques. Let $\mathcal{D}$ be the set of documents and $\mathcal{W}$ the set of features, which are essentially words. A document d is represented by a feature vector, $\mathbf{x} = (x_1, \ldots, x_{|\mathcal{W}|})$, of frequencies in d of words from $\mathcal{W}$ [19]. In some applications, the frequency information is suppressed, in which case the x_i are binary values indicating the presence or absence of words in d. The main aim of unsupervised feature selection is to reduce $|\mathcal{W}|$ to a smaller feature subset size m by selecting features ranked according to some utility criterion. The selected m features then form a reduced word vocabulary set $\mathcal{W}'$, where $\mathcal{W}' \subset \mathcal{W}$ and $|\mathcal{W}'| \ll |\mathcal{W}|$. The new representation of document d is the reduced word vector $\mathbf{x}'$, which has length m.

Frequency counts are often used to gauge feature utility particularly in an unsupervised setting. The Term Contribution (Tc) is one such measure, showing promising results in [16]:

$$Tc(w) = \sum_{\substack{i,j \\ i \neq j}} F(w, d_i) * F(w, d_j)$$

$$F(w, d) = f(w, d) * log_2 \frac{|\mathcal{D}|}{n}$$

Here F computes the tf*idf score which is a measure of the discriminatory power of a word given a document. Term frequency f is the within document frequency count of a feature and n is the number of documents containing feature w. Tc's frequency based ranking and selection of features is the base line feature selection method used in this paper and we will refer to it as BASE (Figure 1).

m = feature subset size
BASE
    Foreach $w_i \in \mathcal{W}$
        calculate Tc score using $\mathcal{D}$
        sort $\mathcal{W}$ in decreasing order of Tc scores
    $\mathcal{W}' = \{w_1, \ldots, w_m\}$
    Return $\mathcal{W}'$

Fig. 1. Feature selection with Tc based ranking

Tc will typically rank frequent words appearing in fewer documents above those appearing in a majority of documents. In this way the BASE method will attempt to ignore overly frequent (or rare) features. Its main drawback is its inability to address the need for both representative and diverse features. This leads to selection of non-optimal dimensions that fail to sufficiently capture the underlying document content.

4   Role of Similarity for Unsupervised Feature Selection

A representative feature subset is one that can discriminate between distinct groups of problem-solving situations. In a classification setting, these groups are identified by their class labels and are typically exploited by the feature selection process. However in the absence of class knowledge, we need to identify and incorporate other implicit sources of knowledge to guide the search for features.

Similar problem situations are typically described by a similar set of features forming an operational vocabulary subset. When these subsets are discovered the search for features can be guided by similarity in problem descriptions. In particular knowledge about feature similarity enables the search process to address both the need for representative and diverse features. The question then is how do we define similarity between features. A good starting point is to analyse feature co-occurrence patterns because features that are used together to describe problems are more likely to suggest the same operational vocabulary subset than features that rarely co-occur. In the rest of this section we look at how feature utility can be inferred from similarity knowledge extracted from feature co-occurrence patterns.

4.1   Feature Utility Measures

For a given word $w \in \mathcal{W}$, our first metric estimates the average pair-wise distance $\overline{Dist}$ between w and its neighbourhood of k nearest word neighbours.

$$\overline{Dist}(w, \mathcal{A}, k) = \frac{1}{k} \sum_{w_N \in N_k(w, \mathcal{A})} Dist(w, w_N)$$

where N_k returns the k nearest neighbours of w chosen from $\mathcal{A} \subseteq \mathcal{W}$, and $Dist$ is the distance of w from its neighbour w_N. Lower values for $\overline{Dist}$ suggests representative words that are centrally placed within dense neighbourhoods.

An obvious distance measure for words is to consider the number of times they co-occur in documents [19]. However the problem with such a straight forward co-occurrence count is that similar words can be mistaken as being dissimilar because they may not necessarily co-occur in the available document set $\mathcal{D}$. This is typical with text due to problems with sparseness [4].

4.2 Distributional Distance Measures

Often, related words do not co-occur in any document in a given collection, due to sparsity and synonymy. This limits the usefulness of similarity measures based purely on simple co-occurrence. Distributional distance measures circumvent this problem by carrying out a comparison based on co-occurrence with members of a separate disjoint target set [18]. Applied to text, the idea measures distances between word pairs by comparing their distributions conditioned over the set of other words. Since the conditioning is undertaken over a separate disjoint set, distances between non co-occurring word pairs need no longer remain unspecified.

Let us first demonstrate the intuition behind distributional distance measures by considering three words, a, b and c, and their fictitious word distribution profiles (see Figure 2). The x-axis contains a set of target events w_i, while the y-axis plots the conditional probabilities $p(w_i|w)$, for $w = a, b, c$. Comparison of the three conditional probability distributions suggests a higher similarity between a and b (compared to profiles of a and c). When target events on the x-axis are words, then a comparison between conditional probability distributions provides a similarity estimate based on word co-occurrence patterns. The next question then is how can we measure distance between feature distributions.

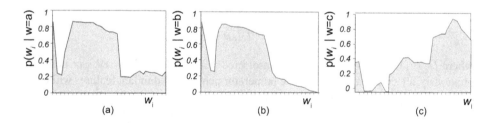

(a)   (b)   (c)

Fig. 2. Conditional probability distribution profiles

Let q and r be two features from $\mathcal{W}$ whose similarity is to be determined. For notational simplicity we write $q(w_i)$ for $p(w_i|w = q)$ and $r(w_i)$ for $p(w_i|w = r)$, where $w_i \in \mathcal{W} \setminus \{q, r\}$ and p denotes probabilities calculated from the training data $\mathcal{D}$. Research in linguistics has shown that the α-Skew metric is a useful measure of the distance between word distributions, when applied to the task of identifying similar noun pairs [13]. It is argued that the asymmetric nature of this distance measure is appropriate for word comparisons, since one word (e.g. 'fruit') may be a better substitute for another (e.g. 'apple') than vice-versa. Here we adopt this metric to compare word distributions and thereby determine the distance from word $q \in \mathcal{W}$ to word $r \in \mathcal{W}$.

$$Dist(q, r) = \sum_i r(w_i) log \frac{r(w_i)}{q(w_i)}$$

is the Kullback-Leibler (KL) divergence, which is derived from information theory. It measures the average inefficiency in using $r(w_i)$ to code for $q(w_i)$ [3].

In our context, a large value of $Dist(q, r)$ would suggest that the word q is a poor representative of the word r, but not necessarily vice-versa. However, the $Dist$ is undefined if there are any words for which $q(w_i) = 0$, but $r(w_i) \neq 0$. The α-Skew metric avoids this problem by replacing q with $\alpha q + (1 - \alpha)r$, where the parameter α is less than one. In practice, our $Dist$ is the α-Skew metric with $\alpha = 0.99$, as suggested in [13].

5   Similarity Based Unsupervised Feature Selection Methods

$\overline{Dist}$ is the simplest measure that can be employed to rank features. However, we wish to use it so that a diverse yet representative set of features is discovered. This can be achieved in two alternatively ways: a GREEDY search that is locally informed; or a more globally informed CLUSTER-based search.

5.1   Greedy Search for Features

What we propose here is a greedy local search for the best feature subset. At each stage, the next feature is selected to be both representative of unselected features and distant from previously selected features. The feature utility score FUS_k, combines the average neighbourhood distance $\overline{Dist}$ from both the selected and unselected feature neighbourhoods as follows:

$$FUS_k(w) = \frac{\overline{Dist}(w, \mathcal{S}, k)}{\overline{Dist}(w, \mathcal{U}, k)}$$

where $\mathcal{U} \subseteq \mathcal{W}$ contains previously unselected features, and $\mathcal{S} = \mathcal{W} \setminus \mathcal{U}$ contains previously selected features. Here the numerator penalises redundant features while the denominator rewards representative features.

The FUS_k based ranking and selection of features is the first unsupervised feature selection method introduced in this paper and we will refer to it as GREEDY (Figure 3). Unlike Tc, FUS_k's reliance on distributional distances to capture co-occurrence behaviour undoubtedly makes it far more computationally demanding. However this cost is justified by FUS_k's attempt to address the need for both representative and diverse features. One problem though is that GREEDY is a hill-climbing search where the decision to select the next best feature is informed by local information, hence it can select feature subsets that, although locally optimal, can nevertheless be globally non-optimal.

m = feature subset size
$S = \emptyset; \mathcal{U} = \mathcal{W}$
GREEDY
   Repeat
      Foreach $w_i \in \mathcal{U}$
         calculate FUS_k score
      sort $\mathcal{U}$ in decreasing order of FUS_k scores
      w_j = top ranked feature in $\mathcal{U}$
      $S = S \cup \{w_j\}$
      $\mathcal{U} = \mathcal{U} \setminus \{w_j\}$
   Until $(|S| = m)$
   $\mathcal{W}' = S$
   Return $\mathcal{W}'$

Fig. 3. GREEDY method using FUS_k based ranking

5.2   Clustered Search for Features

Clustering of words provides a global view of word vocabulary usage in the problem description space. Each cluster contains words that are contextually more similar to each other than to words outwith their own cluster. Partitioning the feature space in this way facilitates the discovery of representative features because each cluster can now be treated as a distinct sub-part of the problem description space.

We use a hierarchical agglomerative (bottom-up) clustering technique, where at the beginning every feature forms a cluster of its own. The algorithm then unites features with greatest similarity in small clusters and these clusters are iteratively merged until m number of clusters are formed. The decision to merge clusters is based on the furthest neighbour principle, where those two clusters with least distance between their most dissimilar cluster members are merged. Typically, this form of cluster merging leads to tightly bound and balanced word clusters.

Merging of clusters requires that a distance metric is in place. For this purpose we use the *Dist* metric from Section 4. However, we must first address the question of how to deal with the asymmetrical nature of this metric when comparing distances between members of separate clusters. There are essentially three ways in which the two distances can be consolidated: use the maximum; the minimum or the average. We advocate the maximum distance, which combines with the furthest neighbour principle to form clusters in which there are no large distances.

Figures 4 and 5 illustrates how the choice of distances can affect the final cluster structure. In this example, clusters are formed with keywords extracted from a PC-Mac hardware FAQs mailing list. A closer look at the five word clusters formed using the maximum of the assymetrical distance between a feature-pair suggests that the resulting groups are not only semantically meaningful (e.g. cluster membership of "dos") but are also more balanced (e.g. number of words in a cluster).

Once clusters are formed we need a mechanism to uniformly select one representative feature from each cluster. In Figures 4 and 5 underlined words indicate such representatives (often referred to as cluster centroids or seeds). Previously, we stated that a

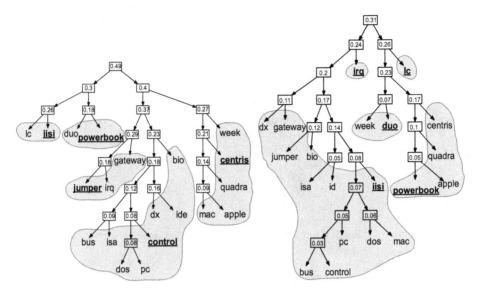

Fig. 4. Maximum distance   **Fig. 5.** Minimum distance

m = feature subset size
$\mathcal{W}' = \emptyset$
generate set of word clusters $\{\mathcal{C}_1, \ldots, \mathcal{C}_m\}$
CLUSTER
    Foreach $\mathcal{C}_i \subset \mathcal{W}$
        w_j = feature with max $\text{FUS}_\mathcal{C}$ in $\mathcal{C}_i$
        $\mathcal{W}' = \mathcal{W}' \cup w_j$
Return $\mathcal{W}'$

Fig. 6. CLUSTER method using $\text{FUS}_\mathcal{C}$ based ranking

representative feature is identified by its placement within dense neighbourhoods. Using this same idea and the $\overline{Dist}$ metric in Section 4 we estimate the representativeness of feature w within a cluster $\mathcal{C}$ as a function of the average pair-wise distance between itself and its cluster members:

$$\text{FUS}_\mathcal{C}(w) = \bigl(1 - \overline{Dist}(w, \mathcal{C}, |\mathcal{C}|)\bigr)$$

The second unsupervised feature selection method introduced in this paper is CLUSTER. It uses the $\text{FUS}_\mathcal{C}$ score to rank features in a cluster, choosing w with highest $\text{FUS}_\mathcal{C}$ from each cluster. The main steps appear in Figure 6. Here the number of clusters formed is equal to the desired feature subset size, m. This determines the stopping criterion for clustering. Like GREEDY, CLUSTER also addresses the need for representativeness and diversity, however, we expect CLUSTER to have an edge over GREEDY because its selection is influenced more globally.

6   Evaluation

We wish to determine the effectiveness of the two similarity-based searches for features, compared to the frequency-based search:

- GREEDY, introduced in this paper with ranking using FUS_k [1] (Figure 3);
- CLUSTER, also introduced in this paper, exploits clustering and ranking using FUS_C (Figure 6); and
- BASE, the baseline with ranking on Tc (Figure 1).

The Tc-based ranking used by BASE is the only unsupervised method that has up to now been shown to perform better than the basic document frequency and the term strength methods [16]. We would hope to significantly improve upon the performance of BASE. Now the upper-bound for any unsupervised technique is its supervised counterpart, therefore, we also compare all our unsupervised methods with the standard IG-based SUPERVISED feature ranking and selection method.

It is generally harder to carry out empirical testing within a truly unsupervised setting compared to a supervised one. This is because, the absence of supervised labels calls for alternative sophisticated evaluation criteria, such as comparison of retrieval rankings or establishing measures of cluster quality. Instead, we applied our unsupervised methods on labelled data ignoring labels until the testing phase. Essentially we are exploiting class labels only as a means to evaluate retrieval performance which indirectly measures the effectiveness of the case representation. Note that we are not interested in producing a supervised classifier.

Experiments were conducted on 4 datasets; all involving email messages. Each email message belongs to one mail folder. Here folders are the class labels. As in previous experiments we used the 20Newsgroups corpus of 20 Usenet groups [9], with 1000 postings (of discussions, queries, comments etc.) per group, to create 3 sub-corpuses [24]: SCIENCE (4 science related groups); REC (4 recreation related groups) and HW (2 hardware problem discussion groups, one on Mac, the other on PC). With each sub-corpus the groups were equally distributed. A further set of 1000 personal emails, used for Spam filtering research forms the final dataset, USREMAIL, of which 50% are Spam [5].

We created 15 equal-sized disjoint train-test splits. Each split contains 20% of the full dataset, selected randomly, but constrained to preserve the original class distribution. All text was pre-processed by removing stop words (common words) and punctuation and the remaining words were stemmed. In the interest of reducing time taken for repeated trials, the initial vocabulary size was cut down to a subset composed of the 500 most and 500 least discriminating words (using IG). These 1000 words then form $\mathcal{W}$. An effective feature selection method should eliminate the non-discriminating words and assemble a representative and non-redundant combination of the discriminating ones.

The effectiveness of feature selection is directly reflected by the usefulness of the case representation obtained. Therefore, case representations derived by GREEDY, CLUSTER, BASE and SUPERVISED are compared on test set accuracy from a retrieve-only system, where the weighted majority vote from the 3 best matching cases are used to

---

[1] In our experiments k=15 is used as FUS_k's neighbourhood size.

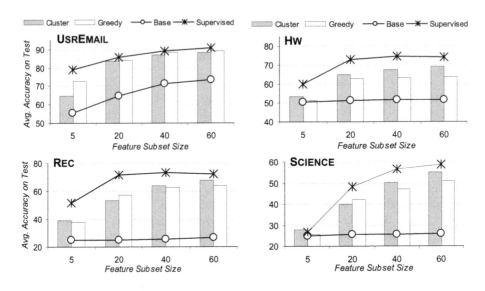

Fig. 7. kNN accuracy results for 4 datasets

classify the test case. For each test corpus and each method the graphs show the test set accuracy (averaged over 15 trials) computed for representations with 5, 20, 40 and 60 feature subset sizes (Figure 7).

6.1   Results

Analysis of overall performance of SUPERVISED on the 4 datasets indicates that the classification of emails from USREMAIL as Spam or legitimate presents the easiest task. Here, SUPERVISED obtained 80% accuracy with just 5 features, compared with only 60% accuracy on the SCIENCE dataset. In all datasets except SCIENCE, we observe a steep rise in accuracy up to about 20 features, followed by a levelling-off as more features are added. This indicates that SCIENCE is the most difficult problem. Unlike USREMAIL, the other binary-classed HW dataset is harder, because similar terminology (e.g. monitor, hard drive) can be used in reference to both classes (i.e. PC and Apple Mac). Additionally, the same hardware problem can be relevant to both mailing lists, resulting in cross-posting of the same message.

We note that BASE performs very poorly on all datasets compared to GREEDY, CLUSTER and SUPERVISED. With the exception of the easiest problem (USREMAIL), it barely outperforms random allocation of classes and does not improve its performance as more features are added. Both GREEDY and CLUSTER clearly outperform BASE on all four datasets and improve their performance as the number of features increase. BASE's poor performance is explained by the fact that it selects features purely on the basis of term frequency information. Although frequent words will co-occur with many other words these co-occurrences will not necessarily be with similar words. Since similar words are indicative of similar areas in the problem space, BASE is not able to identify words that are representative of the problem space.

As expected, the SUPERVISED method achieves highest accuracy. Although both GREEDY and CLUSTER never match the performance of the supervised method, they make good progress towards the upper bound which it is expected to provide. Interestingly, CLUSTER improves relative to GREEDY as feature subset size increases and by 60 features, it is clearly better on the three more difficult datasets and only slightly worse on USREMAIL.

The fact that GREEDY is competitive with CLUSTER at lower feature subset sizes, but falls behind at higher subset sizes, suggests that GREEDY is more susceptible to overfitting. This effect can be seen in Figure 8, which plots training and test set accuracy for GREEDY and CLUSTER on the HW dataset. In these plots, data points lying significantly above the line $x = y$ are indicative of overfitting. Comparison of the scatter-plots confirms that GREEDY is more likely to overfit the selected feature subset to the training set.

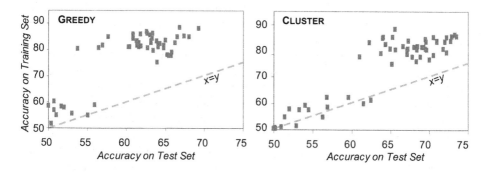

Fig. 8. Comparison of overfitting behaviour with GREEDY and CLUSTER on HW

6.2 Evaluation Summary

We checked the significance of observed differences between GREEDY and CLUSTER, using a 2-tailed t-test with a 95% confidence level for feature subset size, m equal to 60 (see Table 1). This test indicated that the superiority of CLUSTER over GREEDY was significant in all three datasets (bold font), but that of GREEDY on USREMAIL was not shown to be significant at this level. The superior scaling of CLUSTER can be explained by the fact that small optimal feature subsets need not be subsets of larger ones. GREEDY can be expected to suffer from overfitting at larger feature subset sizes, since the greedily chosen early features are locked in and cannot be altered to improve

Table 1. Results summary for feature subset size 60 according to significance

60 features	USREMAIL	HW	REC	SCIENCE
GREEDY	89.3	63.7	64.0	51.0
CLUSTER	88.3	**69.1**	**67.7**	**54.9**
BASE	73.5	51.7	26.5	26.2
SUPERVISED	90.8	74.0	72.0	58.7

the global quality of a larger feature set. CLUSTER avoids this problem by dividing the entire feature set into as many clusters as required, before then selecting one keyword to represent each cluster.

7   Conclusions

The methods introduced in this paper are particularly suited to generating case representations from free text data for unsupervised tasks. The novelty of these methods lies in their exploitation of distributional similarity knowledge to assess the utility of candidate features.

We introduce two unsupervised feature selection methods: GREEDY and CLUSTER. Key to both these methods is the selection of representative yet diverse features using similarity knowledge. Distributional distance measures are able to adequately capture feature similarity by addressing sparseness in co-occurrence data [18]. Evaluation results show significant retrieval gains with case representations derived by GREEDY and CLUSTER, over an existing proven method (BASE) from a previous comparative study [16]. It is also encouraging to report that both GREEDY and CLUSTER make good progress towards the upper bound which is provided by a standard supervised feature selection method. Generally GREEDY is able to generate good feature subsets early on in the search for features while CLUSTER's global search approach consistently outperforms the GREEDY search with increasing feature subset sizes. This is due to the locally informed GREEDY search identifying locally optimal, yet globally sub-optimal, subsets. Results also indicate that GREEDY is more susceptible to overfitting. We intend studying the influence of representativeness and diversity on overfitting, using a weighted form of FUS_C to control the balance between representativeness and diversity.

Previously we have shown that feature selection is a useful integral part of feature extraction when applied to text classification [24]. One difficulty that we have encountered since then, is that a majority of applications involving text are not necessarily supervised. This work is a first step towards resolving this shortcoming in existing feature discovery tools. Future work will look at combining feature selection with more powerful feature extraction methods to create comprehensive tools for text representation, indexing and retrieval for both supervised and unsupervised tasks.

References

1. Baker, L., McCallum, A.: Distributional clustering of words for text classification. In *Proceedings of the 21st ACM International Conference on Research and Development in Information Retrieval* ACM Press (1998) 96–103
2. Bruninghaus, S., Ashley, K.: The role of information extraction for textual CBR. In *Case-Based Reasoning Research and Development: Proceedings of the 4th International Conference on CBR* Springer (2001) 74–89
3. Cover, T., Thomas, J.: *Elements of Information Theory*. John Wiley (1991)
4. Deerwester, S., Dumais, S., Landauer, T., Furnas, G., Harshman, R.: Indexing by latent semantic analysis. *Journal of the American Society of Information Science* 41(6) (1990) 391–407

5. Delany, S., Cunningham, P.: An analysis of case-base editing in a spam filtering system. In *Proceedings of the 7th European Conference on Case-Based Reasoning* Springer (2004) 128–141

6. Delany, S., Cunningham, P., Doyle, D., Zamolotskikh, A.: Generating estimates of classification confidence for a case-based spam filter. In *Case-Based Reasoning Research and Development: Proceedings of the 6th International Conference on CBR* Springer (2005) 177–189

7. Gupta, K., Aha, D.: Towards acquiring case indexing taxonomies from text. In *Proceedings of the Seventeenth International FLAIRS Conference* AAAI Press (2004) 307–315

8. Jarmulak, J., Craw, S., Rowe, R.: Genetic algorithms to optimise CBR retrieval. In Enrico Blanzieri and Luigi Portinale, editors, *Proceedings of the 5th European Workshop on CBR* Springer (2000) 137–149

9. Joachims, T.: A probabilistic analysis of the Rocchio algorithm with TFIDF for text categorisation. In *Proceedings of the Fourteenth International Conference on Machine Learning* (1997)

10. John, G., Kohavi, R., Pfleger, K.: Irrelevant features and the subset selection problem. In *Proceedings of the Eleventh International Conference on Machine Learning* (1994) 121–129

11. Kang, N., Domeniconi, C., Barbara, D.: Categorization and Keyword identification of Unlabelled Documents. In *Proceedings of the 5th IEEE International Conference on Data Mining* (2005)

12. Lamontagne, L., Lapalme, G.: Textual reuse for email response. In *Proceedings of the 7th European Conference on Case-Based Reasoning* Springer (2004) 242–256

13. Lee, L.: On the effectiveness of the skew divergence for statistical language analysis. In *Artificial Intelligence and Statistics 2001* (2001) 65–72

14. Lenz, M.: Defining knowledge layers for textual CBR. In *Proceedings of the 4th European Workshop on CBR* Springer (1998) 298–309

15. David D. Lewis and Kimberly A. Knowles. Threading electronic mail: A preliminary study. *Information Processing and Management* 33(2) (1997) 209–217

16. Liu, T., Liu, S., Chen, Z., Ma, W.: An evaluation on feature selection for text clustering. In *Proceedings of the Twentieth International Conference on Machine Learning* (2003) 488–495

17. Patterson, D., Rooney, N., Dobrynin, V., Galushka, M.: Sophia: A novel approach for textual case-based reasoning. In *Proceedings of the Nineteenth IJCAI Conference* (2005) 1146–1153

18. Pereira, F., Tishby, N., Lee, L.: Distributional clustering of english words. In *Proceedings of the 30th Annual Meeting of the Association for Computational Linguistics* (1993) 183–190

19. Salton, G., McGill, M.: *An introduction to modern information retrieval.* McGraw-Hill (1983)

20. Slonim, N., Tishby, N.: The power of word clusters for text classification. In *Proceedings of the 23rd European Colloquium on Information Retrieval Research* (2001)

21. Smyth, B., McKenna, E.: Building compact competent case-bases. In Klaus-Dieter Althoff, Ralph Bergmann, and L. Karl Branting, editors, *Proceedings of the Second International Conference on Case-Based Reasoning* Springer (1999) 329–342

22. Weber, R., Ashley, K., Bruninghaus, S.: Textual case-based reasoning. *To appear in The Knowledge Engineering Review* (2006)

23. Wiratunga, N., Craw, S., Massie, S.: Index driven selective sampling for case-based reasoning. In *Case-Based Reasoning Research and Development: Proceedings of the 5th International Conference on CBR* Springer (2003) 637–651

24. Wiratunga, N., Koychev, I., Massie, S.: Feature selection and generalisation for textual retrieval. In *Proceedings of the 7th European Conference on Case-Based Reasoning* Springer (2004) 806–820

25. Wiratunga, N., Lothian, R., Chakraborty, S., Koychev, I.: Propositional approach to textual case indexing. In *Proceedings of the 9th European Conference on Principles and Practice of Knowledge Discovery in Databases* (2005) 380–391

26. Yang, Y., Pedersen, J.: A comparative study on feature selection in text categorisation. In *Proceedings of the Fourteenth International Conference on Machine Learning* (1997) 412–420

27. Zelikovitz, S.: Mining for features to improve classification. In *Proceedings of Machine Learning, Models, Technologies and Applications* (2003)

Combining Case-Based and Similarity-Based Product Recommendation

Armin Stahl

German Research Center for Artificial Intelligence (DFKI) GmbH
Research Group Image Understanding and Pattern Recognition (IUPR)
Technical University of Kaiserslautern
Erwin-Schrödinger-Str. 57, 67663 Kaiserslautern, Germany
Armin.Stahl@dfki.de

Abstract. Product recommender systems are a popular application and research field of CBR for several years now. However, almost all CBR-based recommender systems are not case-based in the original view of CBR, but just perform a similarity-based retrieval of product descriptions. Here, a predefined similarity measure is used as a heuristic for estimating the customers' product preferences. In this paper we propose an extension of these systems, which enables case-based learning of customer preferences. Further, we show how this approach can be combined with existing approaches for learning the similarity measure directly. The presented results of a first experimental evaluation demonstrate the feasibility of our novel approach in an example test domain.

1   Introduction

With the increasing success of e-Commerce web-sites, the development of intelligent *recommender systems* has become a popular field of research. Today, many e-Commerce sites are already deploying recommender systems to support their customers during the selection of a product that best matches their requirements and preferences. Depending on the type of offered products, the desire for such support can be explained by different issues:

- When being confronted with huge product databases, the search for a suitable product can become very time consuming.
- When purchasing complex products (e.g. technical products like PCs, travels [1], insurance products [2]) customers often do not possess the expertise to select the optimal product with respect to their requirements.
- Some products cannot be described sufficiently by explicit and objective properties (e.g. books, music [3], videos [4]) but are selected on the basis of subtle aspects like personal taste. Without a recommendation a customer cannot estimate the personal value of such a product until purchasing it.

Since the requirements on the actual recommendation process are varying between different business scenarios, many different recommendation techniques

T.R. Roth-Berghofer et al. (Eds.): ECCBR 2006, LNAI 4106, pp. 355–369, 2006.

have been developed during the last few years (for an overview see [5,6]). In principle, two major approaches can be distinguished: *content-based recommendation* and *collaborative filtering (CF)*.

Content-based recommendation can deal with the first two issues, i.e. finding suitable products in large databases or advising customers when purchasing complex products. The customer has to define his product requirements, e.g. by filling out a predefined query form. This information is then compared with the descriptions of the available products in order to identify a set of potential product candidates. If the comparison is based on exact match (e.g. by performing a simple SQL query), this is called *filter-based recommendation (FBR)*. FBR often leads to unsatisfactory results. An alternative is *similarity-based recommendation (SBR)*. Here, the comparison between the query and the product descriptions is based on a specific similarity measure which also allows to rank retrieved products. As *Case-Based Reasoning (CBR)* provides powerful techniques for realizing similarity-based retrieval it has become a popular technique for building SBR systems [7].

Collaborative filtering [8], on the other hand, is typically used to deal with the third issue, i.e. to provide recommendations for products that cannot be described sufficiently by explicit properties. The basic idea of CF is to collect user ratings about seen or bought products and to use rating correlations between different users and products in order to recommend products. Hence, CF relies on a vast amount of user feedback before producing satisfactory recommendations.

In recent years several hybrid recommendation techniques which incorporate content-based and collaborative approaches have been developed [6], and some of them apply also CBR techniques [9,10,1,11].

In principle, a recommender system must possess knowledge about the customers' requirements and preferences and their relationship to the offered products. Generally, the following types of user needs can be distinguished [1]:

- hard requirements vs. preferences
- explicit vs. implicit preferences, i.e. is the preference explicitly expressed in the query or not
- general vs. individual preferences, i.e. is it a general preference of almost all customers or is it customer specific
- short-term vs. long-term preferences, i.e. is the preference only valid for the actual recommendation process or durable

FBR can only treat the hard, explicit, individual and short-term preferences encoded in the query. SBR allows a much wider consideration of customer preferences. Similarity-measures (which may be customer specific) can be used to model almost all kind of preferences. Only implicit subtle preferences, that are difficult to express formally, can be treated exclusively by CF techniques.

The most challenging task when building a recommender system is the acquisition of knowledge about the different kinds of preferences. While CF strictly relies on user feedback, SBR is applicable without any feedback by using a predefined similarity measure as a heuristic. However, the quality of this heuristic influences the recommendation quality dramatically.

In this paper we propose a novel approach for learning customer preferences in content-based recommender systems. The approach combines SBR with the original idea of CBR, i.e. the reuse of collected experience knowledge. Therefore, it incorporates knowledge about successful recommendations of the past into the similarity-based product retrieval. We show that an additional optimization of the underlying similarity measure results in further improvements to the recommendation quality.

The advantage of our approach is its easy integration into state-of-the-art SBR systems. At the beginning the system can be applied with a standard similarity measure without relying on any user feedback. If feedback becomes available during usage it will enable the system to learn its users' preferences automatically over time leading to improved recommendation results. Moreover, our approach also provides the possibility to consider more subtle product properties which are not explicitly described by existing product descriptions.

Section 2 starts with a short review of the functionality of SBR systems and existing approaches towards learning customer preferences. Section 3 then describes our novel approach which combines case-based learning with existing techniques for learning similarity measures. The results of an experimental evaluation presented in Section 4 demonstrate the feasibility of our approach. After discussing related work in Section 5, we conclude with a summary and an outlook on future work.

2   Similarity-Based Product Recommendation Systems

Similarity-based recommendation systems have become a very popular CBR research area and numerous successful commercial applications are in use today. Surprisingly, on a closer look, most of these systems are not at all CBR systems in the traditional view of CBR since the used "cases" do not represent problem-solution pairs of the past but are typically just product descriptions.

2.1   Utility-Oriented Matching

The basic functionality of a SBR system is illustrated in Figure 1. Given a customer *query* which describes the desired product properties, a CBR system applies a predefined similarity measure for comparing the query with the descriptions of all available products which are stored in a *product database (PB)*. Finally, a ranked set of the s most similar products (a typical value of s is 10) is presented as the *result set (RS)* to the customer[1].

If we look at this scenario, it becomes obvious that the system does not compare two problem descriptions as assumed by the traditional idea of CBR. Instead, it compares a problem—the query—directly with potential solutions—the products. This works well for product recommendation because here problems and solutions can be described by using the same vocabulary. However, it also

---

[1] In this paper we do not consider adaptation.

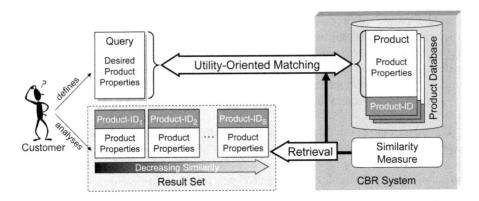

Fig. 1. Product Recommendation by Utility-Oriented Matching

restricts the features that can be used during the recommendation process to the information contained in existing product descriptions.

Traditional cases consisting of problem-solution pairs are not used at all in this scenario. Some authors have characterized this approach as *utility-oriented matching* because the similarity measure is directly used to approximate the utility of known solutions—here product descriptions—for a given problem [12].

In principle, the utility of a product description p_i with respect to a given query q can be characterized as the conditional probability that the product will be accepted by the customer—we denote this event as ω_i—given q, i.e. we may define a *utility function* u as follows by applying Bayes rule:

$$u(q, p_i) = P(\omega_i|q) = \frac{P(q|\omega_i) \cdot P(\omega_i)}{P(q)} \tag{1}$$

In a SBR system, a predefined similarity measure *sim* is used to approximate this unknown utility function u. Since it does not possess any other knowledge about the customers' preferences, the recommendation quality of such a system depends completely on the accuracy of this approximation.

2.2   Dealing with Customer Preferences

However, because of the complexity of customer preferences, in practice standard similarity measures such as the Euclidean Distance will result in a poor approximation of u. In principle, u will be determined by different kinds of preferences with different locality in the problem space:

1. the different importance of general product properties, e.g. "the price is usually much more important than the color"
2. preferences concerning different values of product properties
   (a) independent from q and other properties, e.g. "black cars are generally preferred over white cars"
   (b) depending on q but independent from other properties, e.g. "if a black car is desired, a dark blue car will likely be preferred over a yellow car"

(c) depending on other properties, e.g. "black BMWs are mostly preferred over red BMWs"
3. product specific preferences that are independent from q (in the probabilistic view this is the prior probability $P(\omega_i)$ of class ω_i in formula (1)), e.g. "the silver BMW 320i is a very popular car and is generally preferred over many other similar cars"

With similarity measures commonly supported by CBR tools [13], influence 1 can be modeled with global *feature weights* and influences 2a) and 2b) can be modeled with *local similarity measures*. However, in particular the definition of accurate local similarity measures is a very time consuming task.

The consideration of influences 2c) and 3) would require more sophisticated measures requiring a modeling effort that is usually not tolerable in practice. But the more serious problem of defining an accurate similarity measure is the fact that knowledge about the customers' preferences is a priori completely missing or only partially known.

In our previous work we have proposed to apply a machine learning approach which allows automatically learning of feature weights and local similarity measures based on user feedback [14,15,13]. We have shown that this approach also allows the incorporation of partially known background knowledge into the learning process [16]. However, in particular the learning of local similarity measures is generally susceptible to overfitting if not enough user feedback is available. Moreover, the approach does not provide a solution for the consideration of all above enumerated kinds of preferences.

3   Case-Based Learning of Customer Preferences

In this section we present an alternative approach for learning customer preferences which avoids some of the problems of the previously described approaches.

The basic idea of this approach is illustrated in Figure 2. At the beginning of its life cycle, the extended recommender system will behave like a standard SBR system, i.e. it will perform utility-oriented matching on the given PB. However, any time a customer has selected a product that is acceptable for him (e.g. if he orders the product), his query (optionally together with additional information, see Section 3.2) will be stored in the case base CB together with the product-ID of the selected product. These records now represent actual cases in the traditional view of CBR; the combination of a problem description—the query—and a corresponding solution—the accepted product. Such cases do not necessarily represent optimal cases, because in general it cannot be guaranteed that the customer orders the optimal product regarding to his query. Nevertheless, such cases contain some implicit knowledge about the customers' preferences, i.e. the relationship between certain queries and products that are at least acceptable for the customer.

During subsequent recommendation sessions, this knowledge can be used to estimate u more accurately than possible with a predefined similarity measure sim alone. Therefore, the current query q is not only matched against PB,

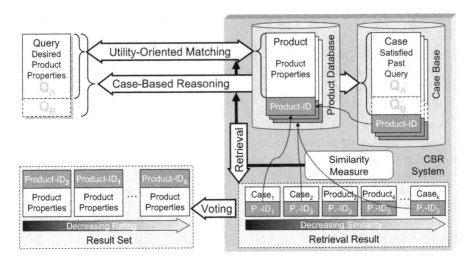

Fig. 2. Case-Based Learning of Customer Preferences

but also against CB by using sim. This is possible because both PB and CB contain product descriptions (Q_A in Figure 2). This procedure results in the corresponding *retrieval result* $RR := (r_1, \ldots, r_k)$ where $r_i \in PB \cup CB$ with $sim(q, r_i) \geq sim(q, r_j)$ for all $i < j$. RR cannot be used directly as result set because different r_i may refer to the same product p_i. In order to generate a unique result set, some post-processing of RR, e.g. by applying a voting strategy, is required.

3.1 Voting Strategy

Because in the recommendation scenario one is not only interested in the probably most useful product, but in a set of the s most useful products, the definition of a fixed size k of RR is not suited for our approach. If RR contains only r_i that correspond to $t < s$ different products, the system will not be able to recommend s different products. Hence, k has to be determined dynamically after each retrieval process. It will be set to the smallest possible value k, so that RR includes exactly s different products.

Now RR can be used to generate the required result set RS consisting of s different product proposals. The ranking of these products within RS will be determined by some voting strategy. Different voting strategies are commonly used in k-NN classification, e.g. simple majority voting, weighted voting [17] or advanced and adaptive approaches [18,19]. In our experiments (see Section 4) product p_x is ranked over product p_y (written as $p_x \succ p_y$) according to the following weighted majority voting rule, where all $r_i^{p_x}$ correspond to the same product p_x:

$$p_x \succ p_y \Leftrightarrow \sum_{r_i^{p_x} \in RR} sim(q, r_i^{p_x}) > \sum_{r_i^{p_y} \in RR} sim(q, r_i^{p_y}) \tag{2}$$

This means, that r_i which are very similar to q will have a higher impact on the majority voting. Such a simple weighted voting strategy may lead to overfitting problems as long as only a few cases have been collected because the corresponding products will then have a much higher probability to be recommended compared with still unbought products. More adaptive strategies which take the cases' distribution into account might outperform the proposed strategy.

Finally, the actual product descriptions have to be retrieved from the product database in order to generate the final result set to be presented to the customer. This is necessary because the retrieval result might contain only cases from CB which do not contain the product description itself but only the product-ID.

3.2   Learning Additional Case Indexes

Up to now, we have assumed that queries consist of the same attributes that are used in the original product descriptions (denoted as Q_A in Figure 2). As already described, this is a precondition for applying utility-oriented matching. However, by learning cases of successful recommendation sessions, this is no longer strictly necessary. One may enable the customer to ask also for additional product properties that are not contained at all in the original product descriptions (part Q_B of the query). Typical examples of such additional query items are more subtle (e.g. "I want a very sporty car") or functional requirements (e.g. "I want to use my PC mainly for gaming"). In principle, a fixed set of such additional features may be considered explicitly in the query interface or the interface may provide the option to enter some free text to be processed by textual CBR techniques. In order to handle this additional information during the retrieval step, the used similarity measure sim has to be extended appropriately. This extension will only influence the retrieval of cases in CB but not the retrieval of product descriptions in PB.

The additional desires of the customer cannot improve the recommendations if the case base is still empty. However, the more cases that contain such information are stored in the case base, the higher will be the influence of this information on the recommendation results. In principle, the queries of the customers are then used to implicitly index the products automatically by using additional features which would be too expensive to be done manually by domain experts. At some point, the collected information could also be extracted automatically from the case base by applying statistical techniques in order to explicitly extend the product descriptions stored in the product database. Another possibility is the incorporation of collaborative features (e.g. user profiles) [1] in part Q_B of the query.

3.3   Acquisition of Training Data

As typical for a supervised learning approach, the acquisition of accurate training data is crucial. In our approach, we assume that the customer states some query (this query might also be the result of a sales dialog [20]) and in the case that he accepts one of the proposed products (e.g. because he orders it), this data is used to create a new training example, i.e. a new case. To control the learning process, one may choose one of the CBL algorithms [21]. For example, when applying the CBL2 algorithm, one would store a new case only if the ordered product was not recommended as the optimal product.

However, in general it cannot be guaranteed, that the resulting case represents an optimal query-product pair. Maybe there are other products in PB that the customer has not seen, for example, because they were not included in the result set, but that he would definitely prefer. Moreover, changes in PB may also influence the quality of the collected cases. Maybe a customer would now prefer a newer product which was not available at the time the case was created.

This means, we will only get *relative utility feedback* [22] about the utility of the products included in the original result sets[2] of past recommendation sessions. If the system proposes s different products $p_1, \ldots, p_s$ and the customer orders p_3 we only get evidence that $u(q, p_3) \geq u(q, p_i)$ for all $i \leq s$, but we do not obtain reliable information about the absolute value of $u(q, p_3)$. However, this information would be necessary in order to ensure that the learned case alone represents accurate knowledge about u.

This situation is less problematic if the retrieval set contains the optimal case with high probability, even if it is not ranked correctly. Hence, the quality of the predefined similarity measure which determines the initial result sets is crucial in order to restrict the noise in the training data required for case-based learning. However, learning of extremely noisy training examples is generally unlikely because then the customer would not have ordered the product.

To guarantee a minimal quality of the used similarity measure it is possible to apply machine learning, too. In [14,15,13] we have presented an algorithm for learning similarity measures which can handle the kind of relative utility feedback that we obtain in the recommendation scenario. Hence, this feedback can also be used to optimize the similarity measure in parallel or a priori to learning new cases in order to reduce the noise in the training data.

4   Experimental Evaluation

In order to evaluate our novel approach we have performed some first experiments in a simulated product recommendation scenario.

4.1   Test Domain

As test scenario we have chosen a used cars domain consisting of 100 descriptions of different used cars which we have extracted from a real world online used cars market. Each car is described by 4 numeric and 4 symbolic attributes, such as price, power, color, year of construction, etc. For a more detailed description of the used test domain see [13]. In the described evaluation we have not investigated the possibility to learn additional product features during the recommendation process (cf. Section 3.2), i.e. the 8 mentioned features solely correspond to part Q_A of the query illustrated in Figure 2.

---

[2] Here we assume that the customer analyzes each product contained in the result set.

Since we were not able to perform an experiment with real world customers, we have simulated imaginable average customer preferences with a manually defined similarity measure sim_U consisting of specific feature weights and specific local similarity measures for each attribute. Of course, such a model is not sufficient for simulating the actual behaviour of real world customers. On the one hand, it does not simulate the inconsistencies between the individual preferences of different customers that would occur in the real world. On the other hand, it also does not model all the kinds of preferences discussed in Section 2.2 (2c and 3 cannot be modeled with such a kind of similarity measure). However, it is sufficient for a first proof of concept of our approach.

4.2   Experiments

In order to evaluate the capability to learn the simulated customer preferences in the described test domain, we have performed several experiments where we have applied the proposed case-based learning approach and/or our previous algorithm for learning feature weights [14]. In principle, each experiment consisted of the following steps:

1. create empty case base CB, empty feedback set FB, and initialize standard similarity measure sim with uniform weights
2. select a set of training queries $Q_{train} := (q_1, \ldots, q_{10000})$
3. for each $q_i \in Q_{train}$ do
   (a) generate result set $RS_i := (p_1, \ldots, p_{10})$ consisting of 10 product descriptions p_j by following the procedure described in Section 3 and by using q_i, sim, CB and the static product database PB
   (b) determine *preferred product* $pp_i := \arg\max_{p_j \in RS_i} sim_U(q_i, p_j)$
   (c) generate feedback $FB_i := (pp_i, (\bar{p}_1, \ldots, \bar{p}_9))$ where $\bar{p}_l \in RS_i \setminus pp_i$
   (d) store feedback, i.e $FB := FB \cup FB_i$
   (e) optional: learn feature weights from FB and update sim accordingly
   (f) create a new case c_i from q_i and the product-ID of pp_i
   (g) optional: insert c_i into CB by applying CBL1 or CBL2
   (h) if $i \in \{5, 10, 25, 50, 100, 250, 500, 1000, 2500, 5000, 10000\}$ then evaluate the recommendation accuracy on query test set Q_{test} using sim_U

By different combinations of the optional learning steps 3(e) and 3(g) we have generated the following five experiments:

SIM: Exclusively learning of feature weights by using the relative utility feedback FB which only expresses that the pp_i are more useful than all other p_j contained in the respective result sets RS_i.

CBL1/2: Exclusively applying case-based learning algorithms CBL1 (each c_i is stored) or CBL2 (c_i is stored only if $pp_i \neq p_1$ holds) (cf. [21]).

SIM-CBL1/2: A-priori learning of feature weights using the feedback of the first 5/10/25/50 queries and activation of CBL1/2 starting from query 51.

Each experiment was repeated with 5 different, a priori randomly generated training query sets where each attribute value of the individual queries was selected randomly. For the evaluation of the achieved recommendation accuracy a static set of 250 independent randomly generated test queries Q_{test} was used to compute 4 different quality measures:

mpp-**in**-*x*: The average percentage of recommendation sessions, where the theoretically *most preferred product* $mpp = \arg\max_{p_i \in PB} sim_U(q, p_i)$ was contained in the first $x \in \{1, 3, 10\}$ recommended products.

avg-*mpp*: The average position of *mpp* in the result sets.

4.3   Results

Figure 3 summarizes the results of the experiments SIM and CBL1/2. The left chart shows the achieved improvements concerning the *mpp*-in-*x* measures. For the exclusive optimization of *sim* one observes a rapid ascent of all learning curves where about 10 training queries are sufficient to achieve the maximal improvements, e.g. for the *mpp*-in-10 measure an increase from 52% to 81%.

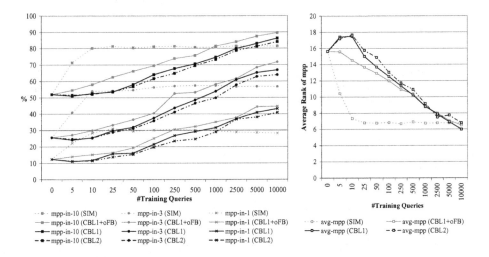

Fig. 3. Results of Experiments SIM and CBL1/2

In contrast, the learning curves of the CBL experiments show much slower improvements of the recommendation quality. However, after 1000-2500 training queries case-based learning starts to outperform similarity measure learning and achieves significantly better results after 10000 queries, e.g. for the *mpp*-in-1 measure over 40% (compared to about 29%). This is not surprising since the case-based learning approach is able to learn the preferences encoded in the local similarity measures of sim_U which cannot be modeled with feature weights. However, surprisingly the differences between the CBL1 and CBL2 are very small, even though the average number of stored cases is significantly lower in the CBL2 experiment (6032 compared to 10000 in CBL1).

In order to be able to evaluate the impact of noisy feedback, we have performed an additional CBL1 experiment with optimal feedback (CBL1+oFB) by using *mpp* instead of *pp* in step 3(b). The CBL1+oFB learning curve shows continuous recommendation improvements from the beginning. In the more realistic experiments CBL1/2 the improvements achieved with less then 50 training queries are quite small or even negative. This can be explained by overfitting which will be amplified by the noisy training data in CBL1/2 and becomes more obvious in the avg-*mpp* measure (right chart of Figure 3).

Figure 4 shows the results of the experiments SIM-CBL1/2. Here, the first 50 queries[3] were used to exclusively optimize the similarity measure in order to improve the feedback quality for the subsequent case-based learning process.

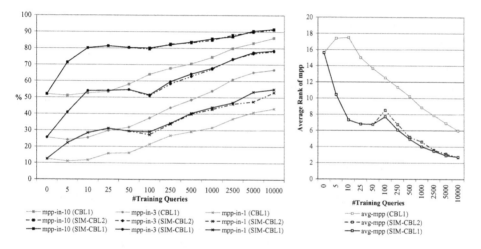

Fig. 4. Results of Experiments SIM-CBL1/2

The achieved results clearly show the advantage of the combination of both learning techniques. On the one hand, a priori optimization of *sim* ensures much faster performance gains compared with applying case-based learning alone. Now only 250 training queries are sufficient to outperform the results of SIM. This also leads to increased robustness against overfitting, since the negative impact of a too small case base is compensated by the preliminary improvements achieved by optimizing *sim*. However, the avg-*mpp* curves clearly show that the overfitting effect is still present (see peak at 100 training queries) as long as the case base contains less than 50 cases[4]. Although overfitting is more prominent in SIM-CBL2, in general the differences between SIM-CBL1 and SIM-CBL2 are almost not recognizable. This is all the more surprising because the average number of learned cases is further reduced (4930) compared to experiment CBL2.

---

[3] According to the results of SIM even 25 queries would be sufficient.

[4] Note, that the first 50 queries were not used for learning cases.

On the other hand, the finally achieved recommendation accuracy is significantly higher compared with the results that can be achieved with each learning technique alone. This becomes particularly obvious in the avg-mpp quality measure. While each learning technique alone was able to decrease the average rank of mpp from about 16 to 6, the combination of both approaches finally achieves an average rank smaller than 3. This would allow to decrease the size of the returned result sets significantly, e.g. if displayed on mobile devices [23].

5   Related Work

The work that is most related to the approach presented in this paper are the results of the DIETORECS project [1,24]. In this project, an advanced travel recommendation system which combines case-based and CF-based techniques has been developed. This system also uses the combination of a raw product database and a case base containing so-called *session-cases*. These cases describe recommendation sessions of the past, containing stated queries, selected travel components, and also collaborative features.

The major difference compared to our work is the way the two databases are used. In the DieToRecs system, on the one hand, the product database is used for an initial filter-based retrieval which requires conversational techniques in order to obtain useful result sets. On the other hand, the case base is used only to determine the ranking of the previously selected cases by using collaborative techniques. Moreover, the system does not optimize the similarity measure required to retrieve session-cases.

An early algorithm which integrates case-based learning with optimization of the required similarity measure is the CBL4 algorithm [21]. However, this algorithm is designed for simple classification tasks and requires absolute utility feedback [22] about the correctness of the solution proposed by the CBR system. Hence, it is not applicable in the product recommendation scenario.

Other work which deals with learning of user preferences is described in [25,26,27]. However, none of these approaches applies a combination of case-based and similarity measure learning as proposed in this paper.

6   Conclusion and Future Work

In this paper we have presented a novel approach for learning customer preferences in content-based recommender systems. This approach extends the functionality of existing similarity-based recommender systems by applying case-based learning in combination with similarity measure learning. On the one hand, optimizing the similarity measure directly improves the accuracy of the approximation of the unknown utility function. On the other hand, it also improves the quality of the absolute utility feedback required by the case-based learner.

The best suited target applications for our approach are product recommendation systems which deal with relatively static product databases. Very dynamic product databases will lead to problems because then the risk that stored cases become obsolete is very high. In this paper we have only considered learning of general or average preferences of all or at least a certain class of customers. In principle, our approach can also be used to support personalized recommendation. However, in practice this will only be feasible in domains where individual customers frequently buy the same type of products.

Although in this paper we have focused on product recommendation, the approach is not restricted to this application scenario. It is also suited to learn other types of user preferences, e.g. like those occurring in knowledge management domains where users are interested in getting advice about available knowledge resources (e.g., documents, web sites, pictures) with respect to their individual information needs [28].

The advantage of our approach is its broad applicability and its compatibility with already successfully applied SBR systems. Moreover it allows an automatic extension of the set of features used to characterize products or information resources. The results of the presented experimental evaluation show the principal ability of our approach to learn customer preferences from easy to acquire customer feedback.

For future work we are planning to perform a more realistic evaluation by using a more sophisticated model of the customers' preferences including all kinds of preferences discussed in Section 2.2 and also nondeterministic behavior. In such a scenario the learning task is generally more challenging. However, here the case-based approach should also outperform solely learning of the similarity measure more clearly due to its less restricted hypotheses space. In such an extended evaluation it would also be interesting to investigate the impact of learning additional product features (cf. Section 3.2).

We also plan to further improve our approach. On the one hand, advanced voting strategies which incorporate statistical information about the learned cases might allow to model the prior probabilities $P(\omega_i)$ explicitly in order to improve the recommendation accuracy. Moreover, this might also help to reduce the risk of overfitting for small case bases. Generally, we plan to investigate the potential of the generation and incorporation of statistical models into the recommendation process with the increasing number of collected cases. On the other hand, smarter learning policies than CBL2 (e.g. such as CBL3 [21]) can help to reduce the size of the case base while maintaining or even improving the recommendation accuracy. This is important in order to minimize retrieval times. Another interesting issue would be the application of our advanced similarity measure learning algorithm which allows an optimization of local similarity measures [15,13,16].

Last but not least, we want to investigate whether our approach is also suited to be used in domains where products can customized [29,30].

Acknowledgements

This work was partially funded by the German Federal Ministry of Education and Research (BMBF) under the IPeT (01 IW D03) project and by the federal state Rhineland-Palatinate under the project ADIB (Adaptive Provision of Information).

References

1. Ricci, F., Venturini, A., Cavada, D., Mirzadeh, N., Blaas, D., Nones, M.: Product Recommendation with Interactive Query Management and Twofold Similarity. In: Proceedings of the 5th International Conference on CBR, Springer (2003)
2. Tartakovski, A., Schaaf, M., Bergmann, R.: Retrieval and Configuration of Life Insurance Policies. In: Proceedings of the 6th International Conference on CBR, Springer (2005)
3. Hayes, C., Avesani, P., Baldo, E., Cunningham, P.: Re-using Implicit Knowledge in Short-Term Information Profiles for Context-Sensitive Tasks. In: Proceedings of the 6th International Conference on CBR, Springer (2005)
4. Miller, B.N., Albert, I., Lam, S.K., Konstan, J.A., Riedl, J.: MovieLens Unplugged: Experiences with an Occasionally Connected Recommender System. In: Intelligent User Interfaces. (2003)
5. Schafer, J.B., Konstan, J., Riedi, J.: Recommender systems in e-commerce. In: Proceedings of the 1st ACM Conference on Electronic commerce, ACM Press (1999)
6. Burke, R.D.: Hybrid Recommender Systems: Survey and Experiments. User Modeling and User-Adapted Interaction **12**(4) (2002)
7. Bergmann, R., Schmitt, S., Stahl, A.: Intelligent Customer Support for Product Selection with Case-Based Reasoning. In: E-Commerce and Intelligent Methods. Physica-Verlag (2002)
8. Breese, J.S., Heckerman, D., Kadie, C.M.: Empirical Analysis of Predictive Algorithms for Collaborative Filtering. In: Proceedings of the 14th Conference on Uncertainty in Artificial Intelligence. (1998) 43–52
9. Hayes, C., Cunningham, P., Smyth, B.: A Case-Based Reasoning View of Automated Collaborative Filterning. In: Proceedings of the 4th International Conference on Case-Based Reasoning (ICCBR'2001), Springer (2001)
10. O'Sullivan, D., Wilson, D., Smyth, B.: Improving Case-Based Recommendation: A Collaborative Filtering Approach. In: Proceedings of the 6th European Conference on Case-Based Reasoning (ECCBR'2002), Springer (2002)
11. Burke, R.D.: Hybrid Recommender Systems with Case-Based Components. In: Proceedings of the 7th European Conference on CBR. (2004) 91–105
12. Bergmann, R., Richter, M.M., Schmitt, S., Stahl, A., Vollrath, I.: Utility-Oriented Matching: A New Research Direction for Case-Based Reasoning. In: Professionelles Wissensmanagement: Erfahrungen und Visionen. Proceedings of the 1st Conference on Professional Knowledge Management, Shaker (2001)
13. Stahl, A.: Learning of Knowledge-Intensive Similarity Measures in Case-Based Reasoning. Volume 986. dissertation.de (2004)
14. Stahl, A.: Learning Feature Weights from Case Order Feedback. In: Proceedings of the 4th International Conference on Case-Based Reasoning (ICCBR'2001), Springer (2001)
15. Stahl, A., Gabel, T.: Using Evolution Programs to Learn Local Similarity Measures. In: Proceedings of the 5th International Conference on Case-Based Reasoning (ICCBR'2003), Springer (2003)
16. Gabel, T., Stahl, A.: Exploiting background knowledge when learning similarity measures. In: Proceedings of the 7th European Conference on Case-Based Reasoning (ECCBR'2004), Springer (2004)
17. Dudani, S.A.: The Distance-Weighted k-Nearest Neighbor Rule. IEEE Transactions on Systems **6** (1981)

18. Rovatti, R., Tagazzoni, R., Kovcs, Z.M., Guerrieri, R.: Adaptive Voting Rules for k-NN Classifiers. Neural Computation **7**(3) (1995)
19. Wang, H., Bell, D.: Extended k-Nearest Neighbours based on Evidence Theory. The Computer Journal **47**(6) (2004)
20. Schmitt, S.: Dialog Tailoring for Similarity-Based Electronic Commerce Systems. Ph.D. Thesis, Kaiserslautern University of Technology (2003)
21. Aha, D.: Case-Based Learning Algorithms. In: Proceedings of the DARPA Case-Based Reasoning Workshop, Morgan Kaufmann (1991) 147–158
22. Stahl, A.: Learning Similarity Measures: A Formal View Based on a Generalized CBR Model. In: Proceedings of the 6th International Conference on Case-Based Reasoning, Springer (2005)
23. Smyth, B., McClave P.: Similarity vs. Diversity. In: Proceedings of the 4th International Conference on Case-Based Reasoning, Springer (2001)
24. Ricci, F., Arslan, B., Mirzadeh, N., Venturini, A.: Itr: A case-based travel advisory system. In: Proceedings of the 6th European Conference on CBR, Springer (2002)
25. Coyle, L., Cunningham, P.: Exploiting Re-ranking Information in a Case-Based Personal Travel Assistent. In: Workshop on Mixed-Initiative Case-Based Reasoning at the 5th International Conference on Case-Based Reasoning (ICCBR'2003), Springer (2003)
26. Branting, K.: Acquiring Customer Preferences from Return-Set Selections. In: Proceedings of the 4th International Conference on Case-Based Reasoning (ICCBR'2001), Springer (2001)
27. Gomes, P., Bento, C.: Learning User Preferences in Case-Based Software Reuse. In: Proceedings of the 5th European Workshop on Case-Based Reasoning (EWCBR'2000), Springer (2000)
28. Holz, H.: An Incremental Approach to Task-Specific Information Delivery in SE Processe. In: 18th IEEE International Conference on Automated Software Engineering. (2003)
29. Stahl, A., Bergmann, R.: Applying Recursive CBR for the Customization of Structured Products in an Electronic Shop. In: Proceedings of the 5th European Workshop on Case-Based Reasoning (EWCBR'2000), Springer (2000)
30. Schmitt, S., Bergmann, R.: Product Customization in an Electronic Commerce Environment Using Adaptation Operators. In: Proceedings of the 7th German Workshop on Case-Based Reasoning (GWCBR'99). (1999)

On the Use of Selective Ensembles for Relevance Classification in Case-Based Web Search*

Maurice Coyle and Barry Smyth

Smart Media Institute, School of Computer Science and Informatics, University
College Dublin, Belfield,
Dublin 4, Ireland
{maurice.coyle, barry.smyth}@ucd.ie
http://ispy.ucd.ie

Abstract. Collaborative Web Search (CWS) is a technique used to re-
rank the results of Web search engines to reflect the collective preferences
of a community of online searchers. It applies a case-based reasoning
perspective to Web search. In simple terms, past search sessions (queries
and result selections) are stored as search cases and reused in response to
similar queries; previously selected results, which have been regularly selected for similar queries in the past, are promoted in response to the new
query. One of the limitations of CWS is that it only facilitates the promotion of previously selected results. In this paper we propose a solution by
adopting a different type of case representation in which a search session
is represented by a relevance model (e.g., a decision tree) learned from
the selections made during the session. Each new target query results in
the retrieval of a set of similar search cases and their component decision
trees are dynamically combined to produce an ensemble classifier that is
then used to re-rank the result-list to promote community-relevant results. We present the results of an evaluation based on live-user searching
histories and show that this ensemble-based approach can outperform a
standard CWS system.

1 Introduction

Collaborative Web Search (CWS) [1] is a form of meta-search which seeks to personalize the results returned by a traditional search engine(s) according to the
preferences of a community of like-minded searchers. It is a case-based approach
to Web search in the sense that each community is represented by a case-base
of past search experiences or *search cases*. Each search case is composed of a
query and the result pages that have been selected by community members in
response to the query plus selection frequency information. When faced with
a new target query submitted by a community member, a set of search cases
with similar queries is retrieved and their most frequently selected results are
promoted within the result-list that is returned by the underlying search en-
gine(s). Search communities can be defined in a variety of different ways but

---

* The support of the Informatics Initiative of Enterprise Ireland is gratefully accepted.

T.R. Roth-Berghofer et al. (Eds.): ECCBR 2006, LNAI 4106, pp. 370–384, 2006.

one example includes the use of general purpose search boxes as part of topic specific Web sites. For example, consider the query "jordan pictures" submitted through a Google search box. Ordinarily, there is not enough information here to tell Google about whether the searcher is looking for pictures of the Arab state, the Formula One (F1) racing team, the basketball player, or the British glamour model. With CWS, however, if the query originates from an F1 Web site, for example, then it is likely that other similar queries will have occurred in the past and that these queries will have led to F1-related selections. CWS will respond to this query by retrieving cases for these similar queries and promoting the most selected F1 results from these cases. Previous work has demonstrated how CWS can significantly improve the quality of search results in many realistic search scenarios [2,3].

CWS suffers from certain limitations, which ultimately limit the occasions where it can contribute relevant promotions to user searches. Perhaps the most significant limitation is that it can only accommodate the promotion of results that have been previously selected by community members. Frequently, the underlying search engines used by CWS to provide an initial result-list may return results that are highly relevant to the community but if they have not been selected previously then they cannot be promoted. This is a missed opportunity.

In this paper we describe one potential solution to this problem that involves a key change of case representation to facilitate a more flexible approach to relevance judgement. Instead of storing the results that have been selected for some query, we propose to use these selected results as positive examples with which to train a relevance classifier (in this case a decision tree). We also use certain unselected results as negative training examples. Instead of using the document terms contained within these positive and negative examples we look at the terms contained in their title and snippet texts; each search engine result is accompanied by a human-generated title and a query-focused summary snippet that allows for a more efficient analysis of relevance. Our new cases are then composed of a query and a decision tree and when faced with a new target query, as before we retrieve a set of similar cases, but this time use their decision trees to produce an ensemble classifier that can be used to classify the results in the initial result-list, with a view to promoting the most relevant ones. When taken individually the decision trees learned for individual queries constitute very weak classifiers, but when combined as an ensemble we will demonstrate that they are capable of identifying relevant results in order to improve the result-list quality offered by the standard approach to CWS.

We would like to highlight two important contributions of this work. First and foremost, we are helping to address an important limitation of an already successful approached to case-based Web search; our live-user trial results point to an overall improvement in result precision above and beyond that offered by CWS. Secondly, our approach contributes to work in the area of machine learning and ensemble-based classifiers. We believe that our technique of selecting ensemble members at run-time, according to the target problem (query), is novel in this context. Essentially we are advocating a lazy approach to ensemble construction by choosing ensemble members according to their similarity to the current problem (target query). In the remainder of this paper we first look at related work on Web search and ensemble learning (Section 2), before describing our new selective ensemble-based approach to relevance classification in Web search (Section 3), and then go on to provide some preliminary experimental evidence in support of this approach (Section 4), before concluding.

2   Related Work

Improving the quality of Web search results is the substantive problem motivating our research, especially when it comes to dealing with the type of vague queries [4,5] that are commonplace in Web search. Like others, we believe that the adaptation of search results, so that they better reflect the context of the search or the preferences of the searcher [6], is an important element of any overall solution to this problem. Lawrence [7] provides an excellent summary of early work in the area of context sensitive search and distinguishes between two different approaches to deriving context; *explicit* context declaration ([8,9,10]) and *implicit* context inference ([11,12]. Attempts to provide searchers with results that better reflect their current search needs have involved the use of *relevance feedback* [13]: feedback provided by the user on an initial set of results (e.g., their initial selections) can be used as the basis for a follow-up search. Indeed [14] provide evidence that implicit relevance feedback in Web search can be just as effective as the availability of explicit feedback.

More recently, both academic ([15,16]) and commercial[1,2] research has begun to look at leveraging *search history* information as a way to personalize search results in line with the observed preferences of users. Our own research on collaborative Web search (see Section 1) is similarly focused on personalizing search results based on historical searches but instead of focusing on the individual we have chosen to focus at the level of a community of like-minded searchers [2,3]. CWS is conceived of as a post-processing layer that works in tandem with an underlying (non-personalized) search engine and works to tailor the results returned by this underlying search engine so that they better reflect the preferences of a target community. As described in [1], CWS is fundamentally a case-based approach to Web search, with each community's search experiences represented as a case-base of search cases, and each case corresponding to a query (the case specification) and a set of selected results (the case solution). CWS promotes the results associated with search cases that are similar to the target query on the basis that since these results have been selected for similar queries in the past, there is a high chance they will also be relevant to the target query; this assumption has been largely borne out in practice. It should be noted for completeness here, that the now-defunct (with some of the core technology possibly still in some use at Ask.com, via technology acquired from Teoma) DirectHit[3]

---

[1] http://myweb2.search.yahoo.com
[2] http://www.google.com/psearch
[3] http://www.searchengines.com/directhit.html

search engine used search histories to re-rank search results, though a universal notion of page popularity was leveraged, so that no personalization occurred whereby a user received results different from those presented to a different user who submitted the same query.

The primary goal of this work is to propose an alternative approach to result promotion in CWS based on the use of an ensemble of weak classifiers trained from search histories. The quest for increased accuracy and stability in machine learning classifiers has led to the advent of *ensemble* or *committee* based techniques, which seek to create multiple classifiers from training data and *aggregate* the predictions of those classifiers to generate more accurate target classifications ([17,18,19,20]). In many cases ensemble classifiers have been shown to out-perform their individual members since the instability of individual classifiers in the presence of noisy data or other changes to the training data is counteracted by other ensemble members; this is true as long as the ensemble members are sufficiently diverse ([21]). Normally an ensemble classifier is made up of a static collection of ensemble members that are then used as the basis for the final classification. However, recently researchers have begun to investigate more selective approaches to ensemble construction involving the selection of a subset of possible members; see for example the work of [22,23]. For instance, [23] describe an approach for selecting ensemble members using a genetic algorithm. An original training set S is sampled t times and a set of t decision trees is learned over each sample to generate an ensemble, E; thus $E = \{e_1, ..., e_t\}$. A genetic algorithm is used to evolve a population of ensembles, each represented by a set of binary weights, $\{w_1, ..., w_t\}$, such that w_i indicates the probability of the ith component learner being a member of the ensemble or not. The *fitness* of a population member is the inverse of its classification error over a validation set. The resulting ensemble will typically contain a subset of the possible members, $E^* \subset E$, with E^* being a function of the training data S (i.e., $E^* = f(S)$) and E^* has been shown to outperform non-selective ensembles in terms of generalization accuracy; see also related work on the generation of selective ensembles of neural networks [22].

In this work we too propose an approach to ensemble classification in which the individual ensemble members are decision trees learned from the selection patterns of a searcher in response to some query. The result is a large collection of weak classifiers for a given community of searchers. We use these weak classifiers as an ensemble when it comes to judging the relevance of new search results, but instead of using the complete set of classifiers we also produce a selective ensemble. However, our ensemble members are chosen at classification time with reference to the current target problem, T; in other words E^* is a function of the training data, S, and the target problem, T, that is, $E^* = f(S, T)$.

3   Selective Ensembles for Relevance Assessment

As mentioned in Section 1, one of the main drawbacks of Collaborative Web Search (CWS) is that result promotions are limited to results that have been selected in the past. At best this limits the promotion prospects available to CWS, passing over certain relevant results when it comes to promotion. But at worst it introduces a tendency for CWS to promote old or even out-of-date results, which may serve to degrade result-list quality in the long run. Our ensemble-based solution involves a number of stages that will be discussed in this section in detail: the generation of ensemble members; the representation of ensemble members as reusable cases; and, the construction of a suitable ensemble at search-time for use in classifying a new result-list.

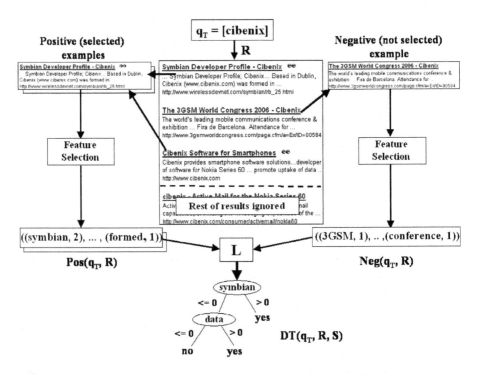

Fig. 1. Each ensemble member is a decision tree generated for the target query q_T from a set of positive and negative examples based on the terms contained in the titles and snippets of selected results and certain unselected results in the final result-list. A machine learning algorithm L combines both sets of training examples to generate a decision tree.

3.1   Generating Ensemble Members

An overview of the ensemble member generation process is shown in Figure 1. In what follows we will use the phrase *search session* to refer to a user initiating a new search (with some target query, q_T) and then reviewing the ordered result-list, $R = r_1, ..., r_n$ to make an ordered sequence of selections, $S = s_1, ..., s_m$. We refer to the *rank* of a selection, denoted by $rank(s_i)$ to be the position of the selection in the result list; thus, $rank(s_i) = k$ iff $s_i = r_k$ and the top result has a rank of 1.

Identifying Positive Training Examples. In any given search session we can treat S as a (noisy) set of positive training examples with respect to q_T in the sense that S refers to the set of result pages that the searcher deemed to be at least partially relevant to their query; see Equation 1.

$$Pos(q_T, R) = S \qquad (1)$$

Identifying Negative Training Examples. By the same token we could view the set $R\backslash S$ (the complete set of results that were not selected) to be a set of negative training examples: since our searcher chose to ignore these results we can assume that she did not find them at all relevant. This reasoning is surely flawed however. We cannot be sure that the searcher even considered all of these unselected results; for example, she may have found a suitable result early on in the result-list, thus obviating the need to look further. For this reason, it seems to be more sensible to treat a subset of $R - S$ as negative examples, namely only those unselected results that occurred before the last selected result (the selected result with the largest rank); see Equation 2. This makes sense because we can be confident that the searcher at least looked through the result-list up to and including the selected result with the largest rank.

$$Neg(q_T, R) = \{n_i : n_i \epsilon (R\backslash Pos(q_T, R)) \wedge rank(n_i) < rank(s_{|S|})\} \qquad (2)$$

Term-Based Example Representation. Each positive and negative example is made up of a *title* and a *snippet* but must be converted into a suitable term-based representation prior to training. We use a standard *bag-of-words* representation after first removing stop words from the example text and applying Porter's stemming algorithm [24] to the remaining words. The feature selection method used is a simple one, with features corresponding to terms, with the selection criterion that a term must occur in the title or snippet text of at least 2 results to be considered. All such terms in the entire result list are identified, leading to the generation of a k-dimensional feature vector. Thus, we can create a term-based representation of the result list in which each example, corresponding to some search result r, is represented as a k-dimensional vector, $e_r = \{v_1, ..., v_k\}$ such that v_i refers to the number of times that the ith term occurs in result r.

Decision Tree Learning. Once we have a set of positive and negative training examples we can of course rely on a wide range of instance-based classification techniques to produce a classifier for a given set of training examples. In this paper we focus on producing decision trees and rely on the Weka ([25]) machine learning toolkit to produce two types of decision trees using the J48 algorithm (a variation of the popular C4.5 algorithm described in [26]) and alternating decision trees (ADTrees) [27][4]. We use $DT(q_T, R, S)$ to denote a decision tree

---

[4] ADTrees use a measure of confidence (the *classification margin*) with different nodes of the decision tree to generate a final classification (see [27]) and are generated using a number of *boosting* iterations [18,20] to the decision tree generation process in an attempt to strengthen any weak hypotheses by the underlying classification algorithm by combining them - a type of ensemble generation in itself.

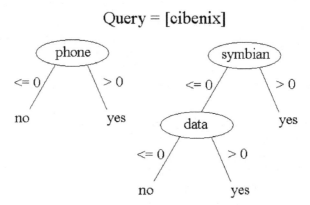

Query = [cibenix]

Fig. 2. Two decision trees generated from two search sessions for the query "cibenix" (a well-known company in the mobile domain)

constructed by the learner L for the query q_T with a result-list R and a set of result selections S. Two sample decision trees, learned after two search sessions for the query *"cibenix"*, are shown in Figure 2. Notice how weak the decision trees are: the sessions that led to these trees contained only one or two positive (i.e. result selections) and a similar number of negative training examples. On their own, these trees would not be expected to perform well when it comes to classifying new results as relevant or not. However, we will see how even small ensembles of these classifiers can deliver reasonably accurate predictions.

3.2   Case Representation and Reuse

Now that we can use information contained in each search session (the query and selection information) as training data for a decision tree, we can convert each session into a new search case, c_i. In the standard approach to CWS each case is composed of a query and a set of result selections. In our new version (CWS^E), which uses an ensemble of decision trees for result promotion, cases are composed of a query and a decision tree (DT) learned from the session data. In turn the specification part of a case refers to the query and the solution part is the decision tree; see Equations 3-5.

$$c_i = (q, DT(q, R, S)) \qquad (3)$$
$$Spec(c_i) = q \qquad (4)$$
$$Sol(c_i) = DT(q, R, S) \qquad (5)$$

When a new target query, q_T is submitted by a community member, CWS^E submits the query to the underlying search engine(s) to retrieve an initial result-list, R. In addition the query is compared to the search cases in the community's case-base to identify a set of related cases, $c_1, ..., c_r$ - cases whose specifications (queries) share terms with the target query; see Equation 6. These cases provide the ensemble members needed to reclassify the result-list R. To do this each

$r_i \epsilon R$ is first converted into a term-based example representation as described above. Next, we compute a *relevance* score for each converted result from the classification decisions of the individual ensemble members; that is, the decision trees stored as the solutions of each related case. The relevance score is computed from the average of the weighted sum of the individual classifications from each ensemble member. Ensemble members that come from more similar queries to the target are given more weight than those associated with less similar queries, as shown in Equation 7, where $Classify(r_i, Sol(c_k))$ is a binary decision made about the relevance of result r_i by the decision tree represented by $Sol(c_k)$.

$$Sim(q_T, c_i) = \frac{|q_T \cap Spec(c_i)|}{|q_T \cup Spec(c_i)|} \tag{6}$$

$$Relevance(r_i, q_T, c_1, ..., c_r) = \tag{7}$$
$$\frac{\sum_{\forall k=1...r} Classify(r_i, Sol(c_k)) * Sim(q_T, Spec(c_k))}{r}$$

4   Evaluation

In this work we set out to solve a limitation of the existing CWS technique by facilitating the promotion of novel search results that have not been previously selected by a community member. In this section we assess the precision performance of our ensemble-based approach against the standard CWS technique, which has already been shown to offer significant improvements over its underlying search engines [2,3].

4.1   Test Data

To evaluate our ensemble-based approach we use search data collected during a live-user trial of the I-SPY CWS system conducted over a period of 45 weeks among the employees of a Dublin-based software company, which operates in the mobile domain; this group constitutes a single search community. During this time employees were asked to use I-SPY as their primary search engine and the resulting search logs include information about the queries submitted, the result-lists returned, and the results ultimately selected plus their ranks. The trial search data covers a total of 6831 search sessions, 4005 (58%) of which include at least one selected result. Unfortunately not all of this information could be used in the current evaluation because the original trial logging system did not guarantee the logging of all result title and snippet information. Nevertheless, title and snippet information was available for 1933 search sessions. In our evaluation we are only interested in sessions that will lead to at least two positive training examples and 1 negative example during decision tree learning and so we further eliminated all of those sessions with fewer than 2 selections or those with no unselected results appearing above a selected result. This left 946 search sessions for the evaluation. We found an average of 2.43 selections per session, which led to 2.43 positive and 5.56 negative training examples on average per decision tree training session; the resulting decision trees had an average of 5.286 and 1.466 nodes for the ADTree and J48 decision trees, respectively[5].

4.2   Methodology

During the trial the test sessions were replayed in sequence through different variations of the I-SPY CWS system in order to develop different search case-bases[6]. Each variation re-ranked each result list according to its own internal measure of relevance so that different results could be promoted from their original position by each variation. These variations included:

- *I-SPY.* The standard version of I-SPY [2,3] which only promotes results that have been previously selected.
- *J48.* A version of I-SPY designed to use our ensemble-based approach, building the decision trees for its search cases using Weka's J48 algorithm.
- *ADTree.* A second ensemble-based version of I-SPY that uses Weka's ADTree algorithm to learn its search result decision trees.

During the session replay process the different test systems built their own search case-bases. In addition, each search was responded to by each system with reference to this case-base. For example, consider what happens at the kth session in the search logs. At this point each system will have developed a case-base from the k-1 sessions that have gone before. When responding to the query contained in this k^{th} session, q_k, each system will use its available cases to produce its own promotion list. In fact, at this stage we actually consider two more system variations in addition to the above. The *I-SPY+J48* variation refers to a version of CWS that produces a new promotion list that includes the standard I-SPY promotions first, followed by the J48 ensemble-based promotions, and similarly for the *I-SPY+ADTree* variation, which combines standard and ADTree promotions. In each of the 5 systems the final result-list (returned to the user) is made up of the appropriate promoted results, followed by the remaining results from the original result-list of the underlying search engines.

For this evaluation we focused on the top 8 results contained in these final result-lists; we found that users rarely selected results beyond the top 8. We measured their quality with reference to the results that were actually selected during a given session. Thus, to test the quality of a result-list produced by system variation V for the query of the kth session (call this promotion list P_k^V) we simply calculate the *precision* of P_k^V as relative overlap between P_k^V and the results that were logged as selected for the searcher during this k^{th} session. For example, consider the J48 variation producing a result-list with 5 promotions for the kth search session; remember we are focusing on the top 8 results so the first 5 of these are ensemble promotions followed by 3 original results. If we find

---

[5] the ADTree produces trees with larger numbers of nodes depending on how many boosting iterations are applied. The default of 10 iterations was found to be superior to both larger and smaller numbers of iterations.

[6] In all experiments, a case similarity threshold of 0.5 was used.

that 4 of the 8 results were originally selected by the searcher for q_k, then the precision of the list is 0.5. Note that, according to this methodology, the upper bound for the precision of a result list is governed by the number of selections the user made from that list, which is generally quite small (2.43 on average in these tests). That is, if 3 selections were made during the original trial from within a given result list, measuring the precision of any re-ranking mechanism over the top 8 results can have a maximum score of 0.375.

4.3   Results

To begin with we computed a mean precision value, for the final result-list (top 8 results) produced by each of the 5 system variations, averaged over all sessions that contained promotions. Note that because of the relatively high query similarity threshold used for retrieving cases (0.5) this limited the total number of sessions with promotions to just under 150 test sessions.

The initial results were disappointing. They showed an average precision of 29.5% for I-SPY but a lower average precision for all other techniques; for example, J48 presented with an average precision of just under 28%; these results are presented in Figure 3 as the bars for ensembles with ≥ 1 decision trees.

Why do the ensemble based methods perform poorly on average across the test sessions? Our focus turned to the type of decision trees retrieved, and in particular the number of decision trees in the ensembles used in each session. There is no doubt that, taken individually, the decision trees in the J48 or ADTree case-bases are unlikely to be good classifiers. After all each decision tree is learned from the minimal set of training examples that can be extracted from a given search session. Moreover the quality of an ensemble constructed at search-time will likely depend significantly on the number of decision trees available as its members (hence the number of related cases that can be retrieved); ensemble quality will also depend on member diversity, a point we will return to later.

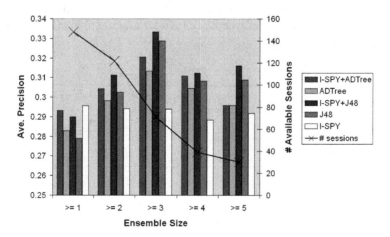

Fig. 3. Final result-list precision for test sessions with ensembles of given sizes

If ensemble size is likely to have an impact on search performance then it makes sense to analyse the results by looking at sessions involving increasingly large ensembles. Hence, Figure 3 presents the average precision results for each technique calculated over groups of test sessions that involve ensembles of a minimum size, from ≥ 1 to ≥ 5. The results suggest that the ensemble-based techniques are capable of outperforming the standard I-SPY CWS approach as the size of the ensembles grows. For example, for search sessions with ensembles containing ≥ 3 decision trees, the I-SPY+J48 result-lists have an average precision of about 33%, a 10% relative improvement over the precision offered by standard I-SPY. Figure 3 also shows the number of sessions in each group; for example, there were 70 sessions with ensembles containing ≥ 3 classifiers.

In general we find that, for sessions whose ensembles contain at least two decision trees, there is a benefit accruing to the ensemble-based methods. Interestingly the J48-based methods (J48 and I-SPY+J48) consistently outperform the ADTree-based method (ADTree and I-SPY+ADTree) probably because the ADTrees are over-fitting to the minimal (and possibly noisy) training data available in each training session. We also see a consistent benefit for the combination of I-SPY and ensemble-based promotions suggesting that these types of promotions identify complementary results for promotion. Looking at the results in Figure 3 for the larger ensembles, we see an apparent decline in the relative benefits associated with the ensemble-based methods. However, we suggest that this is largely a consequence of the availability of a much smaller number of test sessions containing ensembles of these sizes. For example, there are only about 30 test sessions with ensembles made up of at least 5 decision trees.

Let us consider the issue of the apparent superiority of the J48 ensembles compared to the ADTree ensembles. It is well known that an ensemble's accuracy depends critically on the disagreement between ensemble members [28]. In turn [29] demonstrated how the diversity of ensemble members can be similarly important in terms of accuracy. As a crude measure of diversity we can calculate the overlap that exists in the terms used between pairs of decision trees within the ensemble. For example, a diversity of 0.75 for an ensemble of 5 decision trees

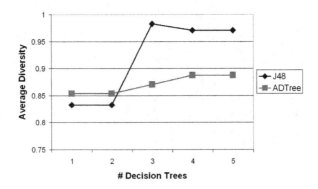

Fig. 4. Average diversity of decision trees produced by J48 and ADTree classifiers

means that on average pairs of decision trees drawn from the ensemble share 25% of their terms. Figure 4 shows the average diversity of the ensembles used during the evaluation; again we look at sessions with ensembles of a given minimum size. The results indicate that the J48 ensembles contain a more diverse set of decision terms than their ADTree counterparts. For example, for ensembles of 3 or more members, the J48 ensembles on average share only about 3% of their terms compared to the ADTree ensembles that share about 13% of their terms.

5   Discussion

The results provided here present a preliminary evaluation of our ensemble-based promotion technique. On the positive side they are based on real rather than artificial user data. However, they are limited in scope: a relatively modest number of search sessions were suitable for the evaluation and the ensembles generated at search time were generally small (containing an average of 2.207 decision trees). Nevertheless, we feel that the positive results that were noted constitute a compelling proof of concept of our ensemble-based technique; even small ensembles were seen to provide a precision benefit. And although the precision improvements found are relatively modest, these represent an incremental improvement over the standard version of I-SPY, which was previously shown to be capable of offering significant improvements over standard Web search engines.

Perhaps it is surprising that this technique has worked at all. After all the training examples that are available during a typical search session are extremely limited and thus the individual decision trees are likely to be very weak relevance classifiers. Of course the use of ensemble techniques is one way to boost classification accuracy. However, it should also be remembered that the relevance classification task is constrained by virtue of the results that are retrieved by the underlying search engine at search-time. In this sense we do not expect a limited ensemble of weak classifiers to perform well on arbitrary search results. The ensembles are only ever used to classify search results that have already been filtered for relevance by the underlying search engine.

Obviously there is a need for a large-scale evaluation, involving an order of magnitude more search data. Such an evaluation will allow for the development of richer search case-bases that are likely to lead to greater query overlap and hence the construction of much larger ensembles, made up of tens of decision trees. Unfortunately, this data is difficult to come by. For example, the standard information retrieval (IR) test datasets such as TREC (see http://es.csiro.au/TRECWeb) do not provide the type of comprehensive search data that we need (queries, result-lists, snippets, and selection information), and so we must continue to work to identify alternative evaluation scenarios.

We have also identified a number of opportunities for improving the core technique as part of our future research programme. For instance, we chose a very simple feature extraction technique for turning session data into positive and negative training examples, scoring individual terms based on a simple frequency count. A wide range of alternative techniques are available and certainly the application of standard IR weighting schemes (such as the TF*IDF measure, for example) seems appropriate so that special attention can be given to terms that are especially predictive of a positive or negative example.

Finally, it is worth highlighting some ideas for how our search cases might be used to support search tasks other than result promotion. One such task concerns the elaboration of vague queries or the recommendation of new queries to a searcher. We are interested in exploring how a decision tree, or an ensemble of decision trees, might be converted into an elaborated query or a new query. For example, in the evaluation search data one of the vague queries noticed was *"four courts dublin"* (referring to the landmark on Dublin's northside - the popular Four Courts Hostel is also nearby) and the ensemble constructed for this query suggested that snippet terms such as *"hostel"* were indicative of non-relevance. It seems unlikely that search results for accommodation in Dublin would be of interest to our Dublin-based trialists, and the search cases learned during the evaluation reflected this. We believe that it may be possible to convert decision trees into sophisticated queries that can be recommended directly to searchers as a form of community-based recommendation.

6 Conclusions

Collaborative Web search is a case-based approach to Web search that involves the reuse of search cases learned from the search patterns of a community of like-minded searchers. We set out in this work to solve a known limitation in collaborative Web search regarding its inability to promote results that have not been previously selected. Our solution involves a new type of case representation: each search session is represented as a search case that contains the session query and a decision tree learned from the snippet texts of results that were selected (positive examples) or ignored (negative examples). Then, at search-time the decision trees contained in cases that are similar to the target query are used to produce an ensemble that can be applied to classify the results returned by an underlying search engine to identify relevant results for promotion. We have presented the results of an evaluation based on real users' searching histories to show that this technique is capable of producing result-lists that contain more relevant promotions than the original CWS result-lists produced by I-SPY.

References

1. Balfe, E., Smyth, B.: Case-based collaborative web search. In: Proceedings of the European Conference on Case-Based Reasoning (ECCBR '04). (2004) 489–503
2. Smyth, B., Balfe, E., Boydell, O., Bradley, K., Briggs, P., Coyle, M., Freyne, J.: A Live-user Evaluation of Collaborative Web Search. In: Proceedings of the 19th International Joint Conference on Artificial Intelligence (IJCAI '05), Morgan Kaufmann (2005) 1419–1424 Ediburgh, Scotland.

3. Smyth, B., Balfe, E., Freyne, J., Briggs, P., Coyle, M., Boydell, O.: Exploiting query repetition and regularity in an adaptive community-based web search engine. User Modeling and User-Adapted Interaction: The Journal of Personalization Research **14**(5) (2004) 383–423
4. Silverstein, C., Henzinger, M., Marais, H., Moricz, M.:   Analysis of a Very Large AltaVista Query Log.   Technical Report 1998-014, Digital SRC (1998) http://gatekeeper.dec.com/pub/DEC/SRC/technical-notes/abstracts/src-tn-1998-014.html.
5. Spink, A., Bateman, J., Jansen, B.J.: Searching heterogeneous collections on the web: behaviour of excite users. Information Research: An Electronic Journal **4**(2) (1998)
6. Pitkow, J., Schütze, H., Cass, T., Cooley, R., Turnbull, D., Edmonds, A., Adar, E., Breuel, T.: Personalized search. Communications of the ACM **45**(9) (2002) 50–55
7. Lawrence, S.:   Context in Web Search.   IEEE Data Engineering Bulletin **23(3)** (2000) 25–32
8. Glover, E., Lawrence, S., Gordon, M.D., Birmingham, W.P., Giles, C.L.: Web Search - Your Way. Communications of the ACM **44**(12) (2000) 97–102
9. Glover, E.J., Flake, G.W., Lawrence, S., Birmingham, W.P., Kruger, A., Giles, C.L., Pennock, D.M.: Improving Category Specific Web Search by Learning Query Modifications. In: Proceedings of the Symposium on Applications and the Internet (SAINT), IEEE Computer Society (2001) 23–31
10. Baeza-Yates, R.A., Hurtado, C.A., Mendoza, M.:   Query recommendation using query logs in search engines. In: Current Trends in Database Technology - EDBT 2004 Workshops, EDBT 2004 Workshops PhD, DataX, PIM, P2P&DB, and Clust-Web. (2004) 588–596
11. Lieberman, H.:   Letizia: An Agent That Assists Web Browsing. In Mellish, C., ed.: Proceedings of the International Joint Conference on Artificial Intelligence, IJCAI'95, Morgan Kaufman Publishers (1995) 924–929 Montreal, Canada.
12. Budzik, J., Hammond, K.: User Interactions with Everyday Applications as Context for Just-In-Time Information Access. In: Proceedings of the International Conference on Intelligent User Interfaces., ACM Press (2000) 44–51
13. J. J. Rocchio, J.: Chapter 14: Relevance Feedback in Information Retrieval. In: The Smart Retrieval System: Experiments in Automatic Document Processing. Prentice Hall (1971) 313–323
14. White, R.W., Ruthven, I., Jose, J.M.: The use of implicit evidence for relevance feedback in web retrieval. In: Proceedings of the 24th BSC-IRSG European Colloquium on IR Research (ECIR 2002). (2002)
15. Teevan, J., Dumais, S.T., Horvitz, E.: Personalizing search via automated analysis of interests and activities. In: Proceedings of the 28th annual international ACM SIGIR conference on Research and development in information retrieval (SIGIR '05), New York, NY, USA, ACM Press (2005) 449–456
16. Liu, F., Yu, C., Meng, W.: Personalized Web Search for Improving Retrieval Effectiveness. IEEE Transactions on Knowledge and Data Engineering **16(1)** (2004) 28–40
17. Breiman, L.: Bagging predictors. Machine Learning **24**(2) (1996) 123–140
18. Freund, Y., Schapire, R.E.: A decision-theoretic generalization of on-line learning and an application to boosting. In: European Conference on Computational Learning Theory. (1995) 23–37
19. Quinlan, J.R.: Bagging, boosting, and c4.5. In: AAAI/IAAI, Vol. 1. (1996) 725–730
20. Drucker, H., Cortes, C.: Boosting decision trees. In: Advances in Neural Information Processing Systems. (1996) 479–485

21. Cunningham, P., Zenobi, G.: Case representation issues for case-based reasoning from ensemble research. In: ICCBR. (2001) 146–157

22. Z.-H. Zhou, J.W., Tang, W.: Ensembling neural networks: Many could be better than all. Artificial Intelligence **137**(1-2) (2002) 239–263

23. Zhou, Z., Tang, W.: Selective ensemble of decision trees. In: Lecture Notes in Artificial Intelligence 2639, 2003, pp.476-483, Berlin: Springer (2003)

24. Porter, M.F.: An algorithm for suffix stripping. (1997) 313–316

25. Witten, I.H., Frank, E.: Data Mining: Practical Machine Learning Tools and Techniques (Second Edition). Morgan Kauffman (2005)

26. Quinlan, J.R.: C4.5: programs for machine learning. Morgan Kaufmann Publishers Inc., San Francisco, CA, USA (1993)

27. Freund, Y., Mason, L.: The alternating decision tree learning algorithm,. In: Proceedings of the 16th International Conference on Machine Learning, Morgan Kaufmann, San Francisco, CA (1999) 124–133

28. Krogh, A., Vedelsby, J.: Neural network ensembles, cross validation, and active learning. In: Advances in Neural Information Processing Systems. (1994) 231–238

29. Zenobi, G., Cunningham, P.: Using diversity in preparing ensembles of classifiers based on different feature subsets to minimize generalization error. In: EMCL '01: Proceedings of the 12th European Conference on Machine Learning, London, UK, Springer-Verlag (2001) 576–587

What Evaluation Criteria Are Right for CCBR?
Considering Rank Quality

Steven Bogaerts and David Leake

Computer Science Department, Indiana University, Lindley Hall 215
150 S. Woodlawn Avenue, Bloomington, IN 47405, U.S.A.
{sbogaert, leake}@cs.indiana.edu

Abstract. Evaluation criteria for conversational CBR (CCBR) systems are important to guide development and tuning of new methods, and to enable practitioners to make informed decisions about which methods to use. Traditional criteria for evaluating CCBR performance by *precision* and *efficiency* provide useful information, but are limited by their focus on the single point at which a case is selected at the end of the system dialogue, and by their dependence on a model of the user's case selection criteria. This paper begins by revisiting issues in the evaluation of CCBR systems, arguing for the value of assessing the quality of the intermediate dialogue before case selection. It then proposes an evaluation approach based on *rank quality* to provide a fuller picture of system performance, and illustrates with an empirical study the use of rank quality to illuminate characteristics of similarity assessment strategies for partially-specified cases.

1 Introduction

Conversational case-based reasoning (CCBR) is an interactive paradigm in which situation assessment is done incrementally in a dialogue with the user. Because CCBR is extensively used in CBR applications (e.g., [1]), having the right criteria for evaluating the CCBR process is crucial, both scientifically and practically, for guiding developers and practitioners in system tuning. At each step of the basic CCBR cycle, the system presents the user with a set of potentially relevant cases and questions; the user may either select a question to answer or terminate the dialogue by selecting a case. Each time the user answers a question, the answer adds to the system's problem description, and the system generates a new candidate list. Because CCBR can be seen as aiming to rapidly drill down to a relevant case, influential work by Aha and Breslow [2] proposed evaluating CCBR systems based on *precision*, which measures whether the solution of the selected case adequately resolves the target problem, and *efficiency*, which measures the number of questions that are asked before a candidate case is selected.

Precision and efficiency criteria focus on a snapshot at the time of case selection, and do not reflect properties of the intermediate dialogue such as how consistently the system's suggested cases converge towards the final ranking. Such information may be especially important to assess as CCBR expands beyond traditional diagnostic tasks into new areas such as product recommendation, in which the initial dialogue may affect final user preferences. In addition, assessing precision and efficiency requires having a model of which cases the user will select, which—as results in this paper demonstrate—may strongly influence evaluation results. To address these issues, this paper proposes

T.R. Roth-Berghofer et al. (Eds.): ECCBR 2006, LNAI 4106, pp. 385–399, 2006.

an alternative approach to CCBR system evaluation, *rank quality*, which assesses how well the list of system-proposed cases at each step approximates the list of cases that would be generated if a complete problem description were available. This is meaningful at any point in the dialogue, and can be evaluated independent of the user's case selection criteria.

Despite the intuitive appeal of the rank quality approach, formalizing rank quality involves surprisingly subtle issues. This paper briefly illustrates some of these issues, presents a rank quality criterion designed to address them, and defines a property of case bases, *distance granularity*, which can help determine the suitability of the defined rank quality metric for a particular case base.

The paper then presents an experimental examination of characteristics of precision and efficiency compared to rank quality in practice, for CCBR systems using five different similarity assessment strategies for partially-specified cases from Bogaerts and Leake [3], applied to three datasets from the UCI archive [4]. The experiments demonstrate the sensitivity of precision–efficiency approaches to the case selection model and illustrate how the rank quality approach can provide useful information about characteristics of the overall dialogue, illuminating differences in candidate similarity assessment strategies. This makes rank quality a promising tool for guiding the choice of similarity assessment strategies during system development. The paper closes by placing the results in context of other approaches to evaluating CCBR systems.

2 Precision, Efficiency, and Rank Quality Measures

Precision and efficiency are useful because they address two central concerns for CCBR: to identify a case which solves the current problem (as measured by precision), and to do so rapidly (as measured by efficiency). These measures are normally calculated by simulation experiments, based on a model of user behavior. The new approach proposed here, rank quality, quantifies the degree to which the list of candidate cases provided by the CCBR system at the current point in the dialogue matches the list that would be retrieved if all information about the current problem were known.

More precisely, let t be a full description of a target problem (i.e., a description in which all attribute values that will be revealed in the dialogue are already known). Let $\hat{t}$ represent the current incomplete state of that problem description, under development in a CCBR dialogue. Let L be the set of possible ordered lists of cases presented by the CCBR system to the user, and let L_d be the ordered list of cases presented by the CCBR system to the user when the currently-known problem attributes correspond to description d.[1] The rank quality value is $c(L_t, L_{\hat{t}})$, for L_t the ideal list, $L_{\hat{t}}$ the current candidate list, and $c : L \times L \rightarrow [0, 1]$ a list order comparison function. We note that this formulation of the rank quality calculation depends on having access to a fully known target problem; it is intended to be applied in experimental settings in which such information is available, e.g., when testing alternative similarity assessment strategies during system development. A topic for future research is how rank quality might be

---

[1] Here we assume that retrieval will depend only on the attributes in d, not on the order in which those attributes were revealed to the system. Adjusting the definition to allow for order-dependent case selection would not affect the substance of the definition of rank quality.

applied to measure system performance up to the current point in an actual dialogue, e.g., by assuming the current problem description is "fully known".

To capture intuitions concerning rank quality, the value of c should increase monotonically with the "similarity" of the ordering of cases in the lists, with $c(l, l) = 1$ for any $l \in L$. However, to actually define an appropriate function is surprisingly subtle. Section 3 discusses general motivations for rank quality, while assuming that a function with intuitive behavior is available, and Section 4 proposes a formal definition.

3   Motivations for a Rank Quality Approach

Compared to precision and efficiency, rank quality approaches bring two primary benefits: (1) Providing a fuller picture of system behavior, because they can be applied at any point in a CCBR dialogue and because they assess the entire candidate list, and (2) not requiring assumptions about the user's criteria for final case selection.

Removing the Need for Selection Criteria Assumptions: Because precision and efficiency can only be determined at case selection time, automated evaluations of these properties typically gather performance statistics for a simulated user. These statistics are often gathered in either *leave-one-out* trials, in which a given case from the case base provides the target problem and the correct solution, and is removed from the case base for the duration of the trial, or *leave-one-in*, in which the target case remains in the case base [2]. At each step in the dialogue, the simulated user either selects a question to answer according to the target problem, or terminates the dialogue by selecting a suggested case. Case selection may be triggered, for example, when the similarity of a candidate case exceeds a threshold, or when no unasked questions remain. As we show in Section 5, precision and efficiency results can depend strongly on the specific user (case selection) model chosen. This dependence is problematic for assessing CCBR systems, because there are no obvious criteria for settings to use in such tests. McSherry [5] has shown that it is sometimes possible for a system itself to automatically terminate the dialogue without loss of solution quality, but a user might still choose to terminate the dialogue early, or might choose a suboptimal case. Consequently, the user model plays an important role in evaluation. To our knowledge, no human-subjects studies have systematically evaluated the case selection process for different subject populations. Even if such studies were done, a developer might lack information on the likely user population for a specific system. Because rank quality is based on a comparison of alternative system outputs, independent of the user, it removes the need for a case selection model.

Ability to Assess the Dialogue Instead of the Single Selected Case: Another benefit of the rank quality approach is the ability to provide information about how the system performed at each point during the CCBR dialogue. We expect the ability of rank quality to assess the quality of a set of intermediate suggestions to be useful to system designers because of how case ordering in intermediate steps may affect user confidence, the user's ability to make the right decisions about when to terminate a dialogue, and the user's ability to internally clarify his or her own needs and to choose between competing alternatives:

– **Effects on user confidence:** A classic issue for expert systems, identified early in expert systems research, is the decrease in user confidence in a system—regardless of the quality of its conclusions—if the system appears to "lose focus" during its interaction with the user [6]. Thus given two systems with equal efficiency and precision, we expect user confidence to be higher if the system presents cases which converge consistently towards the final candidate list. As a result, although rank quality does not directly measure confidence, rank quality considerations may be a useful supplement to confidence approaches which focus on assessing the quality of the final result (e.g., [7]).
– **Effects on choosing between alternatives:** Research on expert systems for medical diagnosis showed that diagnostic decision-making may consider not only which diagnosis appears most likely, but also the competition between alternative diagnoses. If the top and next diagnoses are similarly ranked, additional *differential diagnosis* may be needed [8]. Consequently, it may be valuable not only to find a highly-ranked case, but to find a set of best cases to be available for comparison—i.e., for the system to provide a list of top cases early, in order to initiate extra tests to find the values of distinguishing attributes.
– **Effects on the user's ability to identify needs:** Precision and efficiency focus on the ability to drill down to a single case relevant to a fixed problem description. This conception is apt for traditional CCBR troubleshooting tasks. However, as observed in work by McSherry [9] and by McCarthy et al. [10], for newer CCBR areas such as shopping recommenders, the user may initially provide information that is inaccurate or needs to be revised in order to retrieve the right case—the dialogue itself may change the target of the retrieval. Providing the user with a case list with high rank quality early on gives the user an early idea of alternatives consistent with early attribute choices, enabling changing parameters for a new search if those alternatives are not satisfactory.

When comparing rank quality to precision and efficiency, a natural question is whether variants of precision and efficiency could be measured incrementally, by using simulated dialogues in which the best case is "selected" at each step, and precision and efficiency calculated accordingly. However, efficiency calculated in this way would be uninformative, for the incremental efficiency measure would merely be a count of the number of questions asked. Incremental precision values could be more meaningful, but ultimately, a user model is still required to select a case at each step, and we will show that this user model can have a strong impact on experimental results. Thus considering rank quality has benefits even compared to incremental precision criteria.

4   Rank Quality Considerations and Formal Definition

Although rank quality is intuitively easy to grasp, to develop a suitable comparison function is surprisingly subtle. Due to space limitations, we cannot discuss this fully here, but we illustrate a few issues. Recall that the basic task is to compare the k top-ranked cases in the candidate and ideal lists. Issues include:

– **Handling ties between cases on the lists:** When multiple cases are equally similar to the target (as may be more likely when not all information is available, blurring distinctions), the comparison function must break ties to obtain a linear ordering of candidate cases. This process can have a strong effect on rank quality.

- **Handling boundary splits:** The set of tied cases may extend past the boundary of the list of k top cases presented to the user. The placement of some tied cases outside the boundary could distort results. This requires methods that are not unduly influenced by sequences of ties extending beyond the boundary.
- **Avoiding undue influence from list length:** One possible approach to handling the boundary split problem would be to use a threshold-based retrieval criterion instead of kNN. However, for the measures we considered, longer lists tended to be scored better than short ones, suggesting that it is desirable to avoid comparison of lists with dramatically different lengths.

Our list comparison function calculates the difference in the weighted sum of distances for both lists, with distances weighted by rank. Ties in the candidate list are handled by applying, to all cases in the tied sequence, the average of the weights w_m through w_n of the cases in that sequence. In this way, the arbitrary ordering of the tied cases is irrelevant in the weighted sum, as the same weight is applied to all. Thus all cases in the sequence have the same effect. Splits across the k-boundary in the candidate list are handled by a slight *expansion* or *contraction* of the candidate list from length k to length $\hat{k}$, to either include or exclude the entire sequence which was originally split. The decision of expansion or contraction depends on which would result in the smaller change in list length. More formally, for weights w_j set as explained below, we define:

$$c(L_t, L_{\hat{t}}) = \begin{cases} 0 & \text{if } \hat{k} = 0 \\ 1 - \frac{\sum_{i=0}^{\hat{k}-1} \hat{w}_i \; distance(t, L_{\hat{t}}[i]) - \sum_{i=0}^{k-1} w_i \; distance(t, L_t[i])}{\sum_{i=0}^{k-1} w_i} & \text{otherwise} \end{cases}$$

$$\hat{w}_i = \begin{cases} w_i & L_{\hat{t}}[i] \text{ is not involved in a tie} \\ \frac{\sum_{j=m}^{n} w_j}{(n-m+1)} & \text{otherwise} \end{cases}$$

$$\hat{k} = \begin{cases} k & startIndex = endIndex & \text{; no splitting} \\ startIndex & k - startIndex < (endIndex - startIndex + 1)/2 \\ endIndex + 1 & \text{otherwise} \end{cases}$$

where $startIndex$ and $endIndex$ are the 0-based indices marking the start and end of the sequence of tied cases splitting across the boundary. Note that the contraction process assures that the denominator of the previous weight formula is always nonzero.

Weight Assignment: Exponentially decreasing weights emphasize higher-ranked cases:

$$w_i = minV + (maxV - minV) \left(\frac{i - (k-1)}{k-1} \right)^{2\lambda}$$

λ is a positive integer representing the rate of decrease in the weights, and $minV$ and $maxV$ are the desired minimum and maximum weights, respectively. For the experiments of this paper, $minV = 0$, $maxV = 1$, and $\lambda = 2$. The weights could also be set based on characteristics of how the user examines the case list, if that information were available (e.g., if some user examined all cases in the list equally without regard for their ranking, equal weights would be more appropriate).

Contraction to 0 and Distance Granularity: According to the above formula, when $\hat{k} = 0$, $c(L_t, L_{\hat{i}}) = 0$ as well. This situation occurs when all cases in the candidate list, plus a proportionately large number beyond the list, are equally similar to the target problem. For example, if $k = 10$ and the top 25 retrieved cases are tied, then this list is contracted to exclude the tied cases (reflecting that the majority of tied cases were excluded even before the list contraction). This results in $\hat{k} = 0$, for a rank quality of 0. We call this *contraction to 0*. This process is consistent with the intuition that rank quality should be low when the system's ordering of candidate cases is arbitrary, with no grounds for distinguishing any candidate cases from many non-candidates.

We note, however, that the result may be counterintuitive in a special case. For example, if 10 cases are presented and the *ideal* list has the top 25 cases tied, and the candidate list presents 10 of these cases, its rank quality would still be 0, even though intuitively no alternative list would be better. Thus in this case, the function reflects not only objective case suggestion quality but the system's ability to select which cases to present. Although we are exploring alternatives to reflect objective rank quality alone, fully capturing intuitions in such a function has proven surprisingly difficult, with "natural" alternatives having more severe problems. From our own observations, contraction to 0 appears very unlikely to happen in standard domains with non-categorical attributes, though it may occur in domains with few attributes (proportional to case base size), if all of them are categorical. To quantify the extent to which this might cause difficulties for a leave-one-out test, we can determine the likelihood of tests avoiding contraction to 0 by calculating the *distance granularity*—the average proportion, over the cases, of unique distances in the case base. For each case c_j, define $uniqueDCount(c_j)$ as the number of unique values of $distance(c_j, c_i)$, for all c_i in case base CB. Then:

$$caseGranularity(c_j, CB) = uniqueDCount(c_j)/|CB|$$

$$distanceGranularity(CB) = \frac{\sum_i caseGranularity(c_i, CB)}{|CB|}$$

5   Experimental Comparisons of the Measures

We conducted experiments to explore the sensitivity of precision–efficiency approaches to the case selection strategy (the simulated user), and to examine the information provided by the different measures. All experiments were conducted using the Indiana University Case-Based Reasoning Framework (IUCBRF), a freely-available open-source Java framework for rapid and modular CBR system development [11]. All datasets are from the University of California-Irvine (UCI) repository [4], for classification. These experiments use the Pima dataset with entirely numerical attributes, and the Spect and Zoo datasets with entirely categorical attributes.

We apply the measures to evaluating CCBR performance for systems using different similarity assessment strategies for partially-specified cases [3]. Under a representativeness assumption, the case base is used to predict information about as-yet-unasked attributes in a problem. These strategies are selected here not to be evaluated per se, but to illustrate the measures of this paper. The strategies behave as follows when comparing corresponding attribute values for which at least one is unknown:[2]

- **DefaultDifference(0)** (DD) - Assume a difference of 0 between the attribute values.
- **FullAggregate** (FA) - Assume the unknown value is the aggregate (e.g. mean for numeric attributes, majority vote for categorical) value of that attribute in the entire case base.
- **NNAggregate(DefaultDifference(0))** (ND) - Assume the unknown value is the aggregate attribute value of the nearest cases. "Nearest" is defined by a similarity measure using DefaultDifference(0) to handle missing attributes.
- **NNAggregate(FullAggregate)** (NF) - Similar to above, except "nearest" is defined by a similarity measure using FullAggregate to handle missing attributes.
- **RegionAggregate(DefaultDifference(0))** (RA) - Assume the unknown value is the aggregate attribute value of cases in the corresponding region. The regions are predetermined offline by a similarity measure using DefaultDifference(0) to handle missing attributes.

5.1 Experimental Setup

This experiment generally follows the template laid out in [2]. Five systems were constructed, one for each of the five missing attribute strategies above. A case is chosen and its attributes are gradually "revealed" as answers to system questions. (Note that we have done leave-one-out rather than leave-one-in; for the datasets used here, which are not irreducible, we expect comparable conclusions with either approach).

Questions are selected randomly by the system, in order to remove the effects of particular question selection strategies. Each target is tested multiple times, for different random question patterns, with the results averaged. Each time a question is answered, the system calculates the rank quality of the candidate list obtained according to its missing attribute strategy. This process continues until every question is answered, regardless of when a final case is selected for the purpose of precision and efficiency calculations.

Simulated user design: To calculate precision and efficiency first requires tracing the dialogue until it reaches a stopping point — when the user selects a case. We informally describe a *restrictive* simulated user as one with criteria for case selection that are more difficult for a candidate list to meet. Four types of simulated users were examined:

- **T5** (top 5) - Select a case when it is among the top 5 candidate cases and is below a distance threshold h. If multiple cases fall below the threshold at the same time, the highest ranking one is selected.
- **T1** (top 1) - Select a case when it is the top-ranked candidate case and is below a distance threshold h.
- **A5** (average 5) - When the average distance of the top 5 candidate cases is below a distance threshold h, randomly select a case with a distance less than the average (that is, one of the better cases of the candidate list).

---

[2] The 2004 paper uses slightly different names, as follows: FullMean instead of FullAggregate; NNMean instead of NNAggregate; and RegionMean instead of RegionAggregate.

- **DL** (dialogue length) - Select a case when it is the top-ranked candidate case and it contains the target solution. The efficiency for this user is the *dialogue length*. The precision will always be 1.0 except for rare circumstances where no case is selected and the top case at the end of a dialogue does not contain the target solution.

Precision and Efficiency Calculation: Efficiency is $1 - \frac{revealed}{total}$ for $revealed$ the number of attributes revealed and $total$ the total number of attributes in the domain (thus efficiency is between 0 and 1). Precision is 1 if the selected case solution is identical to the target case solution, 0 otherwise. Note that only one precision and efficiency measurement is taken per dialogue, upon case selection.

Threshold calculation: Each of these users depends on a distance threshold h. We chose to form a "level playing field" for comparison by calculating thresholds for each domain as follows. A leave-one-out process is used to calculate a set of thresholds for a range of restrictiveness, controlled by the choice of a parameter $b \in (0, 1)$ reflecting the proportion of the case base to contain in a given neighborhood. For $|CB|$ the size of the case base, we set $i = round(b \cdot |CB|)$. For each case, cases are retrieved using the problem of the selected case as the query. The distance between the target and the ith-ranked case for each retrieval is averaged across the case base (that is, throughout the leave-one-out process), and is set as the fixed distance threshold for case selection for the corresponding domain. In this way, domain-specific influences are accounted for, and the threshold is chosen based on its effect in relation to the domain properties. Four thresholds were computed for each domain, from fairly restrictive to very unrestrictive thresholds, corresponding to b values of $0.05, 0.10, 0.15$, and 0.30.

Distance granularities: Distance granularities are computed for the three domains of this experiment. Pima is an entirely non-categorical domain, and so it is not surprising that its distance granularity is 0.999. Zoo, with all categorical attributes, has a much lower distance granularity of 0.116, though no contractions to 0 occurred in our experiments. Spect, also with all categorical attributes, has a distance granularity of 0.064. This proved low enough for some inappropriate contractions to 0 to occur, but the general patterns and conclusions as seen in the other domains remain, showing that even in this situation, the comparison function provided useful information.

5.2   Results and Discussion

Preliminary Notes: Fig. 1 shows precision and efficiency results for various users, and Fig. 2 shows selected rank quality results. The Pima rank quality results (not shown due to space limitations) are similar to the Spect and Zoo results in overall suggestions of missing attribute strategies, although the strategies were not as distinguished in Pima as in the other domains, and their order did not change for different numbers of attributes. Note that the strategies vary in performance across domains, both in magnitude, and occasionally in overall ranking. This is not interpreted as evidence of problems with precision and efficiency, and we note that similar domain differences are evident for rank quality.

We also caution the reader not to expect an exact connection between rank quality and precision–efficiency. Precision and efficiency are performance snapshots at the *end of the dialogue*, which changes depending on when a case is selected. Consequently,

Domain	A5, 0.05	T1, 0.05	T5, 0.05	T5, 0.10	T5, 0.15	T5, 0.30	DL
Zoo	RA 0.401	RA 0.394	DD 0.415	DD 0.431	DD 0.425	FA 0.456	RA 0.413
	ND 0.386	ND 0.375	ND 0.400	ND 0.418	ND 0.415	NF 0.453	ND 0.409
	DD 0.315	DD 0.315	RA 0.396	RA 0.412	RA 0.412	DD 0.447	DD 0.393
	NF 0.277	NF 0.305	NF 0.370	NF 0.386	NF 0.380	RA 0.440	NF 0.339
	FA 0.199	FA 0.273	FA 0.341	FA 0.363	FA 0.367	ND 0.444	FA 0.293
	rng 0.202	rng 0.121	rng 0.074	rng 0.068	rng 0.058	rng 0.012	rng 0.120
Spect	NF 0.475	FA 0.470	DD 0.422	DD 0.491	DD 0.496	DD 0.498	RA 0.503
	FA 0.474	NF 0.469	ND 0.412	ND 0.484	ND 0.491	ND 0.495	ND 0.486
	DD 0.459	DD 0.467	RA 0.411	RA 0.483	RA 0.490	FA 0.493	DD 0.446
	RA 0.458	RA 0.458	FA 0.380	NF 0.482	FA 0.490	RA 0.493	FA 0.399
	ND 0.458	ND 0.452	NF 0.379	FA 0.481	NF 0.490	NF 0.493	NF 0.397
	rng 0.017	rng 0.018	rng 0.043	rng 0.010	rng 0.006	rng 0.005	rng 0.106
Pima	RA 0.301	RA 0.309	FA 0.422	DD 0.406	DD 0.419	DD 0.435	DD 0.485
	ND 0.274	ND 0.286	NF 0.421	FA 0.358	FA 0.389	FA 0.423	ND 0.485
	NF 0.246	NF 0.266	ND 0.415	NF 0.358	NF 0.373	NF 0.416	RA 0.482
	FA 0.223	DD 0.249	DD 0.387	RA 0.352	RA 0.362	ND 0.392	NF 0.452
	DD 0.201	FA 0.243	RA 0.358	ND 0.344	ND 0.360	RA 0.378	FA 0.441
	rng 0.100	rng 0.066	rng 0.064	rng 0.062	rng 0.059	rng 0.057	rng 0.044

(a) Efficiency

Domain	A5, 0.05	T1, 0.05	T5, 0.05	T5, 0.10	T5, 0.15	T5, 0.30	DL
Zoo	RA 0.997	RA 0.995	RA 0.996	RA 0.989	RA 0.987	RA 0.881	ND 1.000
	ND 0.997	ND 0.995	DD 0.992	ND 0.981	ND 0.982	ND 0.879	FA 0.999
	DD 0.996	DD 0.991	ND 0.991	DD 0.971	DD 0.968	DD 0.852	DD 0.999
	NF 0.996	NF 0.975	FA 0.981	FA 0.956	FA 0.954	NF 0.753	RA 0.999
	FA 0.995	FA 0.973	NF 0.980	NF 0.956	NF 0.946	FA 0.700	NF 0.999
	rng 0.002	rng 0.022	rng 0.016	rng 0.033	rng 0.041	rng 0.181	rng 0.001
Spect	RA 0.674	ND 0.637	DD 0.673	RA 0.598	RA 0.629	RA 0.602	RA 0.999
	ND 0.665	FA 0.632	RA 0.660	ND 0.597	ND 0.601	ND 0.595	ND 0.999
	FA 0.641	NF 0.631	ND 0.659	DD 0.579	DD 0.581	DD 0.586	DD 0.994
	NF 0.641	RA 0.627	NF 0.628	FA 0.576	FA 0.569	NF 0.549	FA 0.986
	DD 0.633	DD 0.596	FA 0.617	NF 0.560	NF 0.559	FA 0.544	NF 0.986
	rng 0.041	rng 0.042	rng 0.056	rng 0.038	rng 0.070	rng 0.058	rng 0.013
Pima	RA 0.666	RA 0.660	ND 0.706	RA 0.648	RA 0.648	RA 0.644	FA 0.998
	DD 0.634	DD 0.591	RA 0.706	DD 0.592	DD 0.591	DD 0.580	NF 0.998
	ND 0.632	ND 0.581	DD 0.693	ND 0.565	ND 0.575	ND 0.562	DD 0.996
	FA 0.629	NF 0.576	NF 0.650	NF 0.554	NF 0.553	NF 0.551	RA 0.995
	NF 0.629	FA 0.561	FA 0.606	FA 0.531	FA 0.522	FA 0.530	ND 0.994
	rng 0.037	rng 0.099	rng 0.100	rng 0.117	rng 0.126	rng 0.114	rng 0.004

(b) Precision

Fig. 1. a) Efficiency and b) precision results for various users and domains. Each column represents a case selection strategy, with column heading showing user type and b value with which to compute the threshold. Columns are organized from most restrictive user on the far left, to least restrictive on the far right, except for DL, which has varying restrictiveness dependent upon the number of cases in the case base containing a given target solution. Each cell lists the five missing attribute strategies in order of decreasing performance. The final number in each cell ("rng") indicates the range of values in that cell.

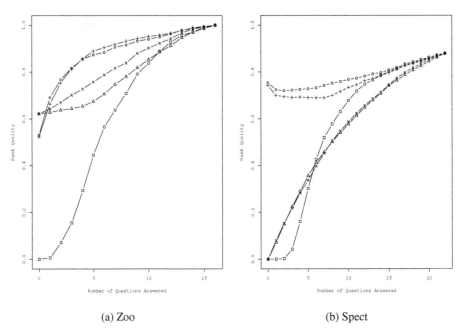

(a) Zoo   (b) Spect

Fig. 2. Rank quality results for the a) Zoo, and b) Spect, domains. The lines correspond to the strategies as follows: RA ∘, ND +, DD □, NF x, and FA △.

these measures are not easily comparable to any single portion of a rank quality graph, although to some extent ranges can be compared, as shall be demonstrated below.

Also note that precision measures solution applicability, and efficiency measures speed of case selection, while rank quality is a measure of similarity. Clearly there is a connection, in that a similar case is assumed to have an applicable solution, and a candidate list with high similarity will likely be selected from sooner. Nevertheless, these are different measures, with solution applicability depending not only on the similarity but also on less definable domain properties, and with case selection also depending on user properties. Thus, efficiency and precision measures are not directly comparable to rank quality, though there are connections in the general trends shown by both.

Effects of Different User Models on Precision and Efficiency. The first experiment explores the potential sensitivity of precision–efficiency approaches to the chosen user model. Fig. 1 presents efficiency and precision results, organized to place more restrictive case selection criteria towards the left, with restrictiveness decreasing towards the right. (The one exception is DL, with varying restrictiveness dependent upon the number of cases in the case base containing a given target solution.) Each cell orders the performance of each strategy according to the measure of the table. The bottom number in each cell represents the range of values in that cell.

In some cases, performance is quite similar across similarity assessment strategies. When there are clear distinctions between the strategies' performance, RA, ND, and DD tend to be the best by both measures, with NF and FA tending to be the worst. This supports a reasonable regularity of conclusions across user types. This is a good result for the utility of precision and efficiency, for if they were totally dependent on user type, then generally applicable conclusions would be very difficult to make.

However, the regularity of conclusions is far from absolute. For example, consider the efficiency results for the Zoo and Spect domains in Fig. 1(a). The range of values decreases given decreasing restrictiveness. With Spect, for T5 with higher thresholds, the range of values is very low. If only these users were examined, a researcher might erroneously conclude that there is no significant distinction in missing attribute strategy performance. Another example is Pima's precision results, which, surprisingly, were higher for $(T5, b = 0.05)$ than for more restrictive users. The reasons for this are unclear. Nevertheless, these examples demonstrate that the user model affects conclusions about system performance.

Other efficiency examples demonstrate this same point. Considering the efficiency performance of RA and DD for the Zoo and Pima domains, we note that comparatively, RA is favored for the most restrictive users, but is closer to the middle or even the bottom for the less restrictive users. On the other hand, the ranking of DD increases for less restrictive users. Thus the researcher's choice of RA and DD may depend on the type of user examined. This difference in performance for different users is an important result, but is captured in efficiency measures only by careful and broad user modeling.

The precison results in Fig. 1(b) reflect this issue as well. It is interesting to note the relationship between restrictiveness and range of precision values. All three domains demonstrate the opposite relationship to that observed for efficiency: Although the range of efficiency values for a given strategy decreases given *decreasing* user restrictiveness, range of precision decreases given *increasing* user restrictiveness.

Another interesting result is that in some domains, results appear to be fairly independent of the user model. For the Zoo domain, for almost every user, the precision results are quite close, and extremely high. It appears that in this domain, the relationship between problem similarity and solution applicability is very strong. Only for a very unrestrictive user model can clear distinctions be seen.

As discussed previously, if it is possible to select a user model known to capture specific user characteristics, the sensitivity of precision-efficiency judgments to the user model is not an issue, and is in fact desirable. However, we are unaware of human-subjects studies in the literature evaluating such models. For many domains, it may be unclear which models fit, and developing the right models may be impractical, or even impossible. In that case, the measures' sensitivity to possibly arbitrary characteristics of simulated users is problematic. This supports the appeal of approaches such as rank quality, which do not depend on case selection criteria in a user model.

Revealing Trends in the Three Measures: As discussed above, there are limits to the comparability of the measures, but this section shows that the rank quality results are comparable to precision–efficiency in a broad sense, and the ability to apply rank quality at any point in the dialogue can reveal performance trends crucial to system analysis.

The most obvious way to compare precision and efficiency to rank quality is to examine the final conclusions which can be drawn from each. According to the efficiency and precision results in Fig. 1, the best strategies are typically RA and ND, and often (but not always) DD. The worst strategies are generally NF and FA. Similar results for rank quality are reflected in Fig. 2. In these graphs, RA and ND are generally the best whenever there is a clear winner, with NF and FA among the worst.

One of the most interesting comparisons comes from the DD results in the Spect domain. Here DD efficiency is approximately 0.5 for less-restrictive users (T5, $b = 0.30$, 0.15, 0.10), corresponding to an average of 11 questions answered in a dialogue. For the same users, precision for DD is approaching that of ND and RA, with the overall ordering being RA, ND, DD, FA/NF (roughly tied). This corresponds to the same ordering in the rank quality graph, for 11 questions answered: RA, ND, DD, FA/NF.

The efficiency of DD for T5, $b = 0.05$, a model of a more restrictive user, decreases to 0.422, corresponding to an average of 12.1 questions answered. The precision measure for this user for DD is 0.673, slightly better than RA and ND. Although rank quality results for 12.1 questions answered still show DD lower than RA and ND, DD is in fact rising at a more rapid pace, and is closer to them than for 11 questions answered.

This trend for DD continues for the T1 and A5 users in the Spect domain. Why these users' efficiency results differ from those of more restrictive users is a subject for future study. The efficiency results for DD are higher than the T5, $b = 0.05$ efficiency results, but lower than the other T5 efficiency results. Specifically, the average efficiency between the two users T1 and A5, 0.463, corresponds to approximately 11.8 questions answered. Upon examination of the rank quality graph, we would therefore expect the corresponding DD precision results to be lower than the T5, $b = 0.05$ results, and higher than the other T5 results, as observed. Thus again we see a general correspondence between the rank quality and precision and efficiency measures.

Again, we do not expect an exact correspondence between efficiency and precision and rank quality, given the clear differences in their design. However, the correspondence among general conclusions is reassuring in that rank quality captures the broad outlines of the more traditional measures, while providing much more information. Although precision and efficiency provide a single snapshot of performance of a single case upon selection, rank quality can be used to show the development of the candidate list across the entire dialogue. The rank quality graphs illustrate that DD starts out very poorly, but rises quickly until, when most questions have been asked, it performs nearly as well as the other strategies. In fact it can be seen in the rank quality graphs that nearly all strategies perform approximately equally when most questions have been asked. This is intuitive, for missing attribute strategies have less opportunity to distinguish themselves when there are fewer missing attributes. On the other hand, when very few questions have been asked in the dialogue, rank quality shows that RA and ND still consistently perform fairly well. FA and NF fare well in the Zoo domain at this stage, but not in Spect. DD, on the other hand, is consistently bad at this stage. Such conclusions are readily apparent in viewing rank quality graphs, but would be much more difficult to make by examining precision and efficiency results, hoping to select the right set of users to get a useful range of data.

6   Related Work

Many existing CCBR evaluation efforts use forms of efficiency or precision for performance evaluation, with some approaches relating to rank quality.

Variations of Efficiency, Precision, and Rank Quality: Evaluation criteria related to efficiency are widely used. For example, McCarthy et al. [10] examine the process of *dynamic critiquing*, in which the user refines the problem description in reaction to the presented candidate list. The number of "tweaks" performed by the user is measured, similar to efficiency. Precision does not apply in the same manner, because presumably the user does not stop critiquing until a satisfactory result is obtained. McSherry [12] uses the leave-one-in process in the context of *irreducible* case bases, in which each case has a unique solution, and there is at most one applicable case for any given problem. McSherry suggests a *recall* and slightly modified precision measure for evaluation of CCBR systems of this nature. Recall is the percentage of queries in which the single perfect case is among the retrieved cases. His precision measure captures the probability that the single applicable case could be selected at random from the candidate list. In [13], the target case of leave-one-in serves as the single applicable case, the goal to be ultimately selected. *Conversational efficiency* is then defined as the number of questions required to get a 100% similarity rating with this target. This is similar to an efficiency measure with a case selection threshold of 100%.

The *retrieval accuracy* measure of Gupta et al. [13] is reminiscent of both precision and rank quality, although with key differences. Retrieval accuracy measures the average rank of the applicable case. It is similar to precision in that it considers applicability of a single case, and to rank quality in that it examines the rank of a case throughout the dialogue. However, this measure does not consider the ranks of the other cases, which may be important for the reasons discussed in Section 3.

In [14], the frequency of successful retrievals is measured, where a successful retrieval has the top three cases of the ideal list in the top five of the candidate list. Thus, similar to rank quality, it compares the candidate list to the ideal, though less information about the full list is gathered.

Measures for Other CCBR Properties: There are a number of measures used in evaluation of CCBR systems that fall outside the scope of the three measures considered here. For example, McSherry [9] measures the length of explanations of retrieval failures, and how many compromises to the original query are required for recovery from these failures. Gupta et al. [13] present three measures related to question ranking: conversational accuracy (how suitable the question rankings are), the number of questions presented to the user at a time, and conversational adaptiveness (the ability of the system to adapt the dialogue to the user's ability level). The same paper also presents two measurements aimed at knowledge engineering: the effort required to insert a case or a new attribute type into the case base.

Connections beyond CBR: The broad question of how to evaluate the quality of a list of provided information resources is also of great importance outside of CBR, for tasks such as ranking Web search results. Although we are not aware of any directly-applicable results from that literature, steps taken there have some bearing on rank quality research for CCBR. It is a common practice in Web search research to use humans as judges of the relevance of a retrieved site. However, in [15] it is argued that human relevance judgments do not lead to stable measures, and that disagreements about even the single most relevant result are frequent. If this holds true for CCBR, it would be an additional impediment to relying on human ranking judgments. If users are presented with search results with detailed summaries, and followed links are automatically marked "relevant," it is possible to use this information to estimate relevance during search engine use [16], a method which might be usable for CCBR. Various approaches exist for aggregating relevance ratings to obtain a rating of a list of search results, including the *ranked half life* measure, which calculates the degree to which relevant documents are located at the top of the list [17], and a measure of the expected number of irrelevant documents to be searched through before relevant documents are found [18].

7   Conclusion

This paper has examined issues in CCBR system evaluation and has proposed rank quality for CCBR system evaluation. This approach enables evaluation at any point in the dialogue, and removes the requirement, needed by precision and efficiency methods, of modeling the user's case selection decision. The paper has presented experimental results illustrating the value of decreasing dependence on a case selection model, by demonstrating that—although the case selection model must often be selected somewhat arbitrarily in practice—it may strongly influence evaluation results. Rank quality can provide useful information during the CCBR conversation, to help select strategies which provide the user with useful cases early on. This may be valuable for increasing user confidence, helping the user to choose between alternatives, and identifying needs for CCBR tasks such as supporting product recommendation. Due to the surprisingly subtle issues involved in rank quality calculation, and the fundamental importance of CCBR to CBR applications, we see further exploration of such criteria and their relationship to user satisfaction as a promising area for future research.

Acknowledgments

We thank the anonymous ECCBR reviewers for their very valuable comments.

References

1. Watson, I.: Applying Case-Based Reasoning: Techniques for Enterprise Systems. Morgan Kaufmann, San Mateo, CA (1997)
2. Aha, D., Breslow, L.: Refining conversational case libraries. In: Proceedings of the Second International Conference on Case-Based Reasoning, Berlin, Springer Verlag (1997) 267–278
3. Bogaerts, S., Leake, D.: Facilitating CBR for incompletely-described cases: Distance metrics for partial problem descriptions. In Funk, P., Calero, P.A.G., eds.: Proceedings of the Seventh European Conference On Case-Based Reasoning, Berlin, Springer (2004) 62–76
4. Newman, D., Hettich, S., Blake, C., Merz, C.: UCI repository of machine learning databases (1998)
5. McSherry, D.: Minimizing dialog length in interactive case-based reasoning. In: Proceedings of the seventeenth International Joint Conference on Artificial Intelligence (IJCAI-01), San Mateo, Morgan Kaufmann (2001) 993–998
6. Buchanan, B., Shortliffe, E.: Rule-Based Expert Systems: The MYCIN Experiments of the Stanford Heuristic Programming Project. Addison-Wesley, Reading, MA (1984)

7. Cheetham, W., Price, J.: Measures of solution accuracy in case-based reasoning systems. In: Proceedings of the Seventh European Conference On Case-Based Reasoning. (2004) 106–118

8. Miller, R., Pople, H., Meyers, J.: Internist-i, an experimental computer-based diagnostic consultant for general internal medicine. New England Journal of Medicine **307**(8) (1982) 468–476

9. McSherry, D.: Incremental relaxation of unsuccessful queries. In Funk, P., Calero, P.G., eds.: Proceedings of the Seventh European Conference on Case-Based Reasoning. Volume 3155., Berlin, Springer-Verlag (2004) 331–345

10. McCarthy, K., Reilly, J., McGinty, L., Smyth, B.: Experiments in dynamic critiquing. In: IUI '05: Proceedings of the 10th international conference on Intelligent user interfaces, New York, NY, USA, ACM Press (2005) 175–182

11. Bogaerts, S., Leake, D.: IUCBRF: A framework for rapid and modular CBR system development. Technical Report TR 617, Computer Science Department, Indiana University, Bloomington, IN (2005)

12. McSherry, D.: Precision and recall in interactive case-based reasoning. In: ICCBR '01: Proceedings of the 4th International Conference on Case-Based Reasoning, London, UK, Springer-Verlag (2001) 392–406

13. Gupta, K.M., Aha, D.W., Sandhu, N.: Exploiting taxonomic and causal relations in conversational case retrieval. In: ECCBR '02: Proceedings of the 6th European Conference on Advances in Case-Based Reasoning, London, UK, Springer-Verlag (2002) 133–147

14. Kohlmaier, A., Schmitt, S., Bergmann, R.: Evaluation of a similarity-based approach to customer-adaptive elect ronic sales dialogs (2001)

15. Voorhees, E.M.: Evaluation by highly relevant documents. In: SIGIR '01: Proceedings of the 24th annual international ACM SIGIR conference on Research and development in information retrieval, New York, NY, USA, ACM Press (2001) 74–82

16. Boyan, J., Freitag, D., Joachims, T.: A machine learning architecture for optimizing web search engines. In: Proceedings of the AAAI Workshop on Internet-Based Information Systems, Portland, Oregon (1996)

17. Borlund, P., Ingwersen, P.: Measures of relative relevance and ranked half-life: performance indicators for interactive ir. In: SIGIR '98: Proceedings of the 21st annual international ACM SIGIR conference on Research and development in information retrieval, New York, NY, USA, ACM Press (1998) 324–331

18. Cooper, W.S.: Expected search length: A single measure of retrieval effectiveness based on the weak ordering action of retrieval systems. American Documentation **19**(1) (1968) 30–42

Fast Case Retrieval Nets for Textual Data

Sutanu Chakraborti, Robert Lothian, Nirmalie Wiratunga,
Amandine Orecchioni, and Stuart Watt

School of Computing,
The Robert Gordon University
Aberdeen AB25 1HG, Scotland, UK
{sc, rml, nw, ao, sw}@comp.rgu.ac.uk

Abstract. Case Retrieval Networks (CRNs) facilitate flexible and efficient retrieval in Case-Based Reasoning (CBR) systems. While CRNs scale up well to handle large numbers of cases in the case-base, the retrieval efficiency is still critically determined by the number of feature values (referred to as Information Entities) and by the nature of similarity relations defined over the feature space. In textual domains it is typical to perform retrieval over large vocabularies with many similarity interconnections between words. This can have adverse effects on retrieval efficiency for CRNs. This paper proposes an extension to CRN, called the Fast Case Retrieval Network (FCRN) that eliminates redundant computations at run time. Using artificial and real-world datasets, it is demonstrated that FCRNs can achieve significant retrieval speedups over CRNs, while maintaining retrieval effectiveness.

1 Introduction

A prominent theme in current text mining research is to build tools to facilitate retrieval and reuse of knowledge implicit within growing volumes of textual documents over the web and corporate repositories. Case-Based Reasoning (CBR), with its advantages of supporting lazy learning, incremental and local updates to knowledge and availability of rich competence models, has emerged as a viable paradigm in this context [15]. When dealing with text, documents are usually mapped directly to cases [4]. Thus, a textual case is composed of terms or keywords; the set of distinct terms or keywords in the collection is treated as the feature set [15]. In practical usage scenarios, the feature set size and the number of cases can both be extremely large, posing challenges to retrieval strategies and memory requirements.

The Case Retrieval Network (CRN) formalism proposed in [1] offers significant speedups in retrieval compared to a linear search over a case-base. Lenz *et al.* [6, 7] have successfully deployed CRNs over large case-bases containing as many as 200,000 cases. The applicability of CRNs to real world text retrieval problems has been demonstrated by the FALLQ project [10]. Balaraman and Chakraborti [5] have also employed them to search over large volumes of directory records (upwards of 4 million). More recently spam filtering has benefited from CRN efficiency gains [9].

While CRN scales up well with increasing case-base size, its retrieval efficiency is critically determined by the size of the feature set and nature of similarity relations

T.R. Roth-Berghofer et al. (Eds.): ECCBR 2006, LNAI 4106, pp. 400–414, 2006.

defined on these features. In text retrieval applications, it is not unusual to have thousands of terms, each treated as a feature [10]. The aim of this paper is to improve the retrieval efficiency of CRNs. We achieve this by introducing a pre-computation phase that eliminates redundant similarity computations at run time. This new retrieval mechanism is referred to as Fast CRN (FCRN). Our experiments reveal that the proposed architecture can result in significant improvement over CRNs in retrieval time without compromising retrieval effectiveness. The architecture also reduces memory requirements associated with representing large case-bases.

Section 2 presents an overview of CRNs in the context of retrieval over texts. We introduce FCRNs in Section 3 followed by an analysis of computational complexity and memory requirements. Section 4 presents experimental results. Section 5 discusses additional issues, such as maintenance overheads that need to be considered while deploying real world applications using FCRNs. Related work appear in Section 6, followed by conclusions in Section 7.

2   Case Retrieval Networks for Text

The CRN has been proposed as a representation formalism for CBR in [1]. To illustrate the basic idea we consider the example case-base in Fig. 1(a) which has nine cases comprising keywords, drawn from three domains: CBR, Chemistry and Linear Algebra. The keywords are along the columns of the matrix. Each case is represented as a row of binary values; a value 1 indicates that a keyword is present and 0 that it is absent. Cases 1, 2 and 3 relate to the CBR topic, cases 4, 5 and 6 to Chemistry and cases 7, 8 and 9 to Linear Algebra.

Fig. 1(b) shows this case-base mapped onto a CRN. The keywords are treated as feature values, which are referred to as Information Entities (IEs). The rectangles

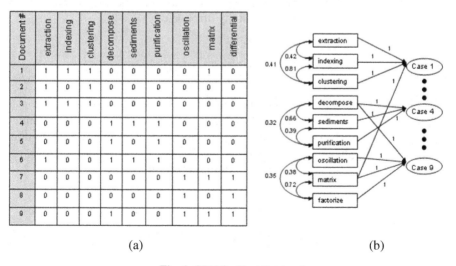

Document #	extraction	indexing	clustering	decompose	sediments	purification	oscillation	matrix	differential
1	1	1	1	0	0	0	0	1	0
2	1	0	1	0	0	0	0	0	0
3	1	1	1	0	0	0	0	0	0
4	0	0	0	1	1	1	0	0	0
5	0	0	0	1	0	1	0	0	0
6	1	0	0	1	1	1	0	0	0
7	0	0	0	0	0	0	1	1	1
8	0	0	0	0	0	0	1	0	1
9	0	0	0	1	0	0	1	1	1

(a)   (b)

Fig. 1. CRN for Text Retrieval

denote IEs and the ovals represent cases. IE nodes are linked to case nodes by relevance arcs which are weighted according to the degree of association between terms and cases. In our example, relevance is 1 if the IE occurs in a case, 0 otherwise. The relevances are directly obtained from the matrix values in Fig. 1(a). IE nodes are related to each other by similarity arcs (circular arrows), which have numeric strengths denoting semantic similarity between two terms. For instance, the word "indexing" is more similar to "clustering" (similarity: 0.81) than to "extraction" (similarity: 0.42). While thesauri like WordNet can be used to estimate similarities between domain-independent terms [2], statistical co-occurrence analysis supplemented by manual intervention is typically needed to acquire domain-specific similarities.

To perform retrieval, the query is parsed and IEs that appear in the query are activated. A similarity propagation is initiated through similarity arcs, to identify relevant IEs. The next step is relevance propagation, where the IEs in the query as well as those similar to the ones in the query spread activations to the case nodes via relevance arcs. These incoming activations are aggregated to form an activation score for each case node. Cases are accordingly ranked and the top k cases are retrieved.

A CRN facilitates efficient retrieval compared with a linear search through a case-base. While detailed time complexity estimates are available in [3], intuitively the speedup is because computation for establishing similarity between any distinct pair of IEs happens only once. Moreover, only cases with non-zero similarity to the query are taken into account in the retrieval process.

3   Speeding Up Retrieval in Case Retrieval Networks

In this section we present the FCRN. To facilitate further analysis, we formalize the CRN retrieval mechanism described in Section 2. A CRN is defined over a finite set of s IE nodes E, and a finite set of m case nodes C. Following the conventions used by Lenz and Burkhard [1], we define a similarity function σ:

$$\sigma: E \times E \rightarrow \Re$$

and a relevance function

$$\rho: E \times C \rightarrow \Re$$

We also have a set of propagation functions $\Pi_n: \Re^n \rightarrow \Re$ defined for each node in $E \cup C$. The role of the propagation function is to aggregate the effects of incoming activations at any given node. For simplicity, we assume that a summation is used for this purpose, although our analysis applies to any choice of propagation function.

The CRN uses the following steps to retrieve nearest cases:

Step 1: Given a query, initial IE node activations α_0 are determined.

Step 2: *Similarity Propagation*: The activation is propagated to all similar IE nodes.

$$\alpha_1(e) = \sum_{i=1}^{s} \sigma(e_i, e).\alpha_0(e_i) \tag{1}$$

Step 3: *Relevance Propagation*: The resulting IE node activations are propagated to all case nodes

$$\alpha_2(c) = \sum_{i=1}^{s} \rho(e_i,c).\alpha_1(e_i) \tag{2}$$

The cases are then ranked in descending order of $\alpha_2(c)$ and the top k cases retrieved.

We observe that in the face of a large number of IEs, Step 2 accounts for most of the retrieval time. The idea of FCRN stems from the need to identify and eliminate redundant computations during this similarity propagation step.

3.1 Fast Case Retrieval Network (FCRN)

We now present an adaptation to CRN to facilitate more efficient retrieval. We substitute the expansion of the term $\alpha_1(e)$ from (1) into the expression for final case activation in (2). This yields:

$$\alpha_2(c) = \sum_{j=1}^{s} \rho(e_j,c). \sum_{i=1}^{s} \sigma(e_i,e_j).\alpha_0(e_i) \tag{3}$$

Let us consider the influence of a single IE node e_i on a single case node c. For this, we need to consider all distinct paths through which an activation can reach case node c, starting at node e_i. Fig.2 illustrates three different paths through bold dashed arrows from e_i to c, along with activations propagating through each path.

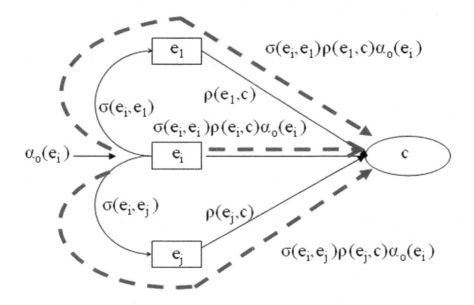

Fig. 2. Different paths through which an activation can reach case c from an IE e_i

We observe that the influence of node e_i on node c can be computed as the aggregation of effects due to all nodes e_j that e_i is similar to, and is given by:

$$inf\ (e_i, c) = \sum_{j=1}^{s} \rho(e_j, c)\sigma(e_i, e_j)\alpha_0(e_i). \tag{4}$$

The last term can be extracted out of the summation as follows:

$$inf\ (e_i, c) = \left\{ \sum_{j=1}^{s} \rho(e_j, c)\sigma(e_i, e_j). \right\} \alpha_0(e_i) \tag{5}$$

We refer to the term within parenthesis as the "effective relevance" of the term e_i to case c and denote it by $\Lambda\ (e_i,\ c)$. It can be verified that (3) can be alternatively rewritten as:

$$\alpha_2(c) = \sum_{i=1}^{s} \Lambda(e_i, c).\alpha_0(e_i) \tag{6}$$

The significance of this redefinition stems from the observation that given an effective relevance function $\Lambda : E \times C \rightarrow \Re$, we can do away with Step 2 in the CRN retrieval process above. We can now construct a CRN that does not use any similarity arcs in the retrieval phase. Instead, a pre-computation phase makes use of similarity as well as relevance knowledge to arrive at effective relevances Λ. The resulting CRN is called FCRN (for Fast CRN) and its operation is shown in Fig. 3. The equivalence of the expressions for final case activations in (2) and (6) above leads us to the following result.

Theorem 1. For any query with initial IE node activations α_0, such that $\alpha_0(e_i) \in \Re$ for all i, the case activations (and hence the rankings) produced by the FCRN are identical to those produced by the CRN. Thus the CRN and the FCRN are equivalent with respect to retrieved results.

Precomputation Phase
The similarity and relevance values are used to pre-compute the effective relevance values

$$\Lambda(e_i, c) = \left\{ \sum_{j=1}^{s} \rho(e_j, c)\sigma(e_i, e_j). \right\}$$

Retrieval Phase
Step 1: Given a query, initial IE node activations α_0 are determined.

Step 2: The resulting IE node activations are propagated directly to all case nodes

$$\alpha_2(c) = \sum_{i=1}^{s} \Lambda(e_i, c).\alpha_0(e_i)$$

The cases are then ranked according to their activations, and the top k retrieved

---

Fig. 3. Precomputation and Retrieval in FCRN

Fig. 4 shows an example CRN depicting a trivial setup with 4 IEs and 4 cases, and the corresponding equivalent FCRN. It is observed that while the relevance values in the original CRN were sparse, the effective relevance values in the FCRN are relatively dense. This is because in the FCRN an IE is connected to all cases that contain similar IEs. In the example shown, the effective relevance between case C_1 and Information Entity IE_1 is computed as follows:

$$\Lambda(IE_1,C_1)= \rho(IE_1,C_1)\sigma(IE_1,IE_1) + \rho(IE_2,C_1)\sigma(IE_1,IE_2) + \rho(IE_3,C_1)\sigma(IE_1,IE_3) + \rho(IE_4,C_1)\sigma(IE_1,IE_4)$$
$$= (1\times1) + (0\times0) + (0\times0.5) + (1\times0.7) =1.7$$

Other elements of the effective relevance table can be similarly computed. It is interesting to note that the effective relevance of the ith IE with the jth case is given by the dot product of the ith row of the similarity table (σ) with the jth row of the relevance table (ρ).

Relevance function ρ

	IE_1	IE_2	IE_3	IE_4
C_1	1	0	0	1
C_2	0	1	1	0
C_3	1	0	1	0

Similarity function σ

	IE_1	IE_2	IE_3	IE_4
IE_1	1	0.0	0.5	0.7
IE_2	0.0	1	0.5	0.0
IE_3	0.5	0.5	1	0.3
IE_4	0.7	0	0.3	1

Effective Relevance function Λ

	IE_1	IE_2	IE_3	IE_4
C_1	1.7	0	0.8	1.7
C_2	0.5	1.5	1.5	0.3
C_3	1.5	0.5	1.5	1.0

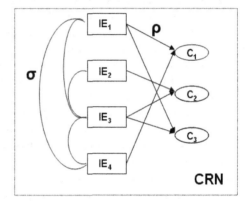

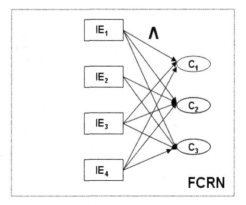

Fig. 4. A CRN over 3 cases and 4 IEs, and an operationally equivalent FCRN

3.2 Time Complexity Analysis

In this section we briefly compare the retrieval time complexity of FCRNs with CRNs. Fig. 5 illustrates the pseudo-codes for retrieval using the CRN and FCRN.

The retrieval complexity is a function of loops /* A */ and /* B */ in the pseudo-codes:

$$complexity(CRNRetrieval) \propto O(A \times B)$$

and

$$complexity(FCRNRetrieval) \propto O(B)$$

The following two reasons contribute to the speedup in FCRN retrieval:

(a) Step A in the CRNRetrieval pseudo-code involves spreading activation to IE nodes similar to the query IEs based on similarity values. This step is eliminated in FCRN retrieval since the similarity knowledge is transferred to the effective relevance values during the pre-computation step. Thus, FCRN retrieval amounts to a simple table lookup for all cases "effectively" relevant to the query IEs and aggregating the scores received by each case from the individual query IEs. Using FCRNs, we can obtain efficiency very similar to inverted files typically used in Information Retrieval applications [8]. However unlike inverted files, FCRNs also integrate similarity knowledge in the retrieval process.
(b) Step B in FCRNRetrieval involves a loop over IE nodes activated by the query. In contrast, Step B of the CRN retrieval loops over all IEs similar to IE nodes activated by the query. In a situation where most IEs are connected to many others by non-zero similarities, Step B in FCRN would involve much fewer iterations compared to step B of a CRN.

CRNRetrieval
FOR each activated query IE (attribute A, value V_q in query)   /* A */
    Determine all related IEs using similarity function σ
    FOR each IE that is found relevant   /* B */
        Determine all cases relevant to that IE using relevance function ρ
        Increment scores of relevant cases
    END FOR
END FOR
Rank and display related cases

FCRNRetrieval
FOR each activated query IE (attribute A, value V_q in query)   /* B */
        Determine all cases relevant to that IE using effective relevance function Λ
        Increment scores of relevant cases
END FOR
Rank and display related cases

Fig. 5. Pseudo-codes for retrieval using CRN and FCRN

3.3 Memory Requirements

Typically CRNs consume more memory when compared to a flat case-base, which has a linear listing of cases along with their constituent attribute values. This difference can be largely attributed to the following two factors: CRNs explicitly record $|E|$ number of values corresponding to IEs, and $|E|^2$ values are required to model similarities between IEs. In addition we have $|Casebase| \times |E|$ relevance values between the IEs and the cases.

A flat case-base that models the case memory as a linked list of all cases will need to store $|Casebase|$ number of cases and $|Casebase| \times |E|$ number of relevance values.

$$
\begin{aligned}
\textit{memory (flat case-base)} \;\propto\;& |Casebase| \times |E| + |Casebase| \\
\propto\;& |Casebase| \times (|E| + 1)
\end{aligned}
$$

The memory requirement of a CRN is approximately given by:

$$
\begin{aligned}
\textit{memory (CRN)} \;\propto\;& |E| + |CaseBase| + |E|^2 + |Casebase| \times |E| \\
\propto\;& |E| + |E|^2 + |CaseBase| \times (|E|+1) \\
\propto\;& |E| + |E|^2 + \textit{memory(flat case-base)}
\end{aligned}
$$

In FCRN we do not need to explicitly record the similarities between IEs, since this knowledge is contained within effective relevance values. The memory requirement of FCRN is given by:

$$
\begin{aligned}
\textit{memory (FCRN)} \;\propto\;& |E| + |CaseBase| \times (|E|+1) \\
\propto\;& |E| + \textit{memory(flat case-base)}
\end{aligned}
$$

In textual applications, the number of IEs could be extremely large, and the saving of $|E|^2$ could mean substantial gains in terms of memory requirements.

It is worth noting that while the in-memory requirement for FCRN retrieval is considerably less than in CRN, we would still need to store the $|E|^2$ similarity values for off-line maintenance. In a situation where a particular IE is deleted, we would need to re-evaluate the effective relevance values to reflect this change. This is possible only when the similarity information is available.

4 Experimental Results

In this section, we present empirical results to illustrate FCRN efficiency in practical applications. The objective of our first set of experiments is to observe how CRNs and FCRN scale up with increasing number of IEs, and with varying nature of similarity interconnections between these IEs. Towards this end, it is sufficient to simulate a large number of IEs and cases with randomly generated similarity and relevance values. The synthetic nature of the datasets is not a major concern, since we are not really concerned with the actual cases retrieved. Sparseness of similarity values can be simulated by forcing a fraction of these values to 0. In any real world application, the actual non-zero similarity and relevance values used would be different from the randomly generated values used in our evaluation, but the time complexity of the retrieval process is independent of the actual values used, since neither the CRN nor FCRN exploit the distributions of values to alter retrieval process.   So our experiments are expected to provide fair estimates of efficiency over realistic datasets. An experimental strategy similar to ours was also used in [14].

Table 1 shows the impact of the increase in number of IE nodes on the retrieval time. For this experiment, the query was randomly generated and IE nodes activated accordingly. The case-base has 1000 cases. The similarity matrix is optimally dense in that each IE node is connected to each other by a non-zero similarity value. Thus this result may be viewed as a worst-case comparison of the CRN performance against FCRN. It may be noted that the CRN retrieval time increases almost linearly as the number of IE nodes increases from 1000 to 6000. As the number of IEs goes beyond 6000, CRN performance degrades steeply. In contrast, the FCRN shows stable behaviour with increasing number of IEs. This is attributed to the savings in similarity computation, and corresponds closely to our theoretical analysis in Section 3.2.

Table 1. Retrieval time as a function of number of IE nodes

No. of IE Nodes	CRN Retrieval Time (secs.)	FCRN Retrieval Time (secs.)
1000	0.04	$<10^{-3}$
2000	0.12	$<10^{-3}$
3000	0.22	$<10^{-3}$
4000	0.35	$<10^{-3}$
5000	0.49	$<10^{-3}$
6000	0.66	$<10^{-3}$
7000	1.42	0.01
8000	3.40	0.01
9000	3.86	0.01
10000	4.98	0.02

The objective of our next experiment is to empirically evaluate the impact of the nature of similarity interconnections on the relative performance of the CRN and the FCRN. We recall that a bulk of the savings in retrieval time with FCRNs can be accounted for by the fact that FCRN does away with the similarity propagation step. The time consumed in similarity propagation is critically dependent on the density of the similarity matrix, which is defined as the proportion of non-zero similarity values in the similarity matrix. We conducted an experiment to study the FCRN performance against CRN, as a function of the similarity matrix density. Our experimental setup is similar to that in the first experiment. We simulate 8000 IEs and 1000 cases with randomly generated similarity and relevance values. We now relax the density of similarity matrix, by deliberately setting a value of 0 to a fraction of the similarity values, and compare FCRN performance against the CRN, for different settings of similarity matrix density. The results are shown in Table 2. As the density increases from 0 (when no IE node is similar to any other node) to 1 (when all IE nodes are related to all others), the CRN retrieval time increases considerably from a sub-millisecond to about 3.38 seconds. Since FCRN does away with the step of similarity propagation across IEs, its performance is not critically impeded by growth in similarity matrix density. The very small increment in the FCRN retrieval time when the density increases from 0.8 to 1.0 is not surprising, given the fact that the effective relevance values are influenced by the density of the similarity matrix. Hence an increase in number of similarity interconnections can have an adverse effect on the sparseness of the effective relevance values, leading to a consequent slowdown in retrieval. It may be noted that retrieval times recorded in all tables in this section are rounded to two significant decimal places.

Table 2. Retrieval time as a function of the density of similarity matrix

Density of the Similarity Matrix	CRN Retrieval Time (secs.)	FCRN Retrieval Time (secs.)
0	$<10^{-3}$	$<10^{-3}$
0.2	0.92	$<10^{-3}$
0.4	1.71	$<10^{-3}$
0.6	2.43	$<10^{-3}$
0.8	2.81	$<10^{-3}$
1.0	3.38	0.01

In addition to empirical evaluation on synthetic data, we also carried out experiments on a real world classification task over a textual dataset comprising 2189 personal emails organized into 76 folders (classes). Each class corresponds to one of the folders (like "sports", "hobbies" or "meetings") into which the emails are organized. The total number of features in this dataset is 32,699. Since many of these features have very poor discriminatory power, the feature set size was pruned to 6000 using chi-square based feature selection [16]. A CRN was constructed to classify incoming emails into one of the 76 classes. Instead of modeling the emails as textual cases as is usually done, we treated the classes as cases. Thus the CRN had 6000 IE nodes and 76 case nodes.

In deploying a CRN architecture for a real world domain, we need to address the issue of acquiring similarity and relevance knowledge. Several knowledge light strategies for acquiring knowledge in CRNs for classification domains have been explored in literature [11]. Traditional techniques for modelling relevance do not directly apply in our case, since relevance values in our architecture relate IEs to classes, instead of relating IEs to cases. In our classifier, we use the chi-square metric [16] as a measure of the relevance of an IE to a particular class. The chi-square metric measures the lack of independence between an IE and a class. Thus the relevance value is 0 when an IE is independent of the class, and high when it is strongly dependent.

The similarity between IEs is computed using Latent Semantic Indexing (LSI), using the method described in [11]. While LSI-based metrics recover well from noise due to word choice variability, one other significant consequence is that the matrix of similarity values between IEs is no longer sparse. As the number of IEs increase, this can lead to considerable slowdown in retrieval or classification.

In Table 3, we report experimental results comparing the time performances of the FCRN against a CRN in this domain. As the number of IEs increase from 1000 to 6000, the CRN slows down considerably. The slowdown is especially conspicuous when the number of IEs exceeds 4000. In contrast, the FCRN scales up well.

Table 3. Time performance as a function of the number of IEs in the email dataset

No. of IE Nodes	CRN Retrieval Time (secs.)	FCRN Retrieval Time (secs.)
1000	0.02	$<10^{-3}$
2000	0.22	$<10^{-3}$
3000	0.34	$<10^{-3}$
4000	1.01	$<10^{-3}$
5000	1.87	0.01
6000	2.82	0.01

5   Discussion

In this section we consider some additional issues that need to be taken into account when building CBR systems using FCRNs.

5.1 Computation Node

One obvious limitation of the CRN mechanism is its inability to handle query values (in the textual case, terms) that are not present in the predefined set of IEs used to build the CRN. To address this issue, Lenz and Burkhard [3] present the concept of a computation node which is created at run time. A computation node represents an IE corresponding to the new query value. The similarity of the computation node to existing IE nodes is computed at run-time using a similarity function that needs to be defined over the attribute space. Once the new similarity arcs are constructed, the retrieval can proceed in the usual manner. With FCRNs, a similar computation node creation step is involved. However, it only plays a role in activating the IE nodes via the newly constructed similarity arcs. If one or more of these IE nodes were already activated, the new activations are added to the existing values. Once the IE node activations (α_0 values) are evaluated, the case nodes are activated directly using the effective relevance values.

5.2 Maintenance Overheads with FCRNs

The downside of FCRNs is that incremental and batch maintenance of the case-base involves extra pre-computations. The effective relevance values need to be recomputed each time new cases or IEs are inserted or existing cases/IEs deleted or edited. However, the recomputations can be limited to only those effective relevance values that could potentially be affected. We consider two specific update scenarios below:

(a) *Insertion of new cases or deletion of existing cases*: Deletion of an existing case is straightforward and only involves setting all effective relevance values connecting IEs to that case, to zero. This does not influence the effective relevances of the other cases. However, when a new case is added, the effective relevances of IEs present in the case to the case needs to be pre-computed, based on the similarity and relevance knowledge. Existing effective relevance values of IEs to the remaining cases are not affected, since effective relevance of an IE to a case is independent of the relevance of the IE to any other case in the case-base.

(b) *Insertion of new IEs or deletion of existing IEs:* When an existing IE is deleted, effective relevances of all IEs having non-zero similarity to the deleted IE, need to be updated. This can prove to be computationally expensive, especially in the face of large numbers of IEs and cases. We present an efficient update strategy (we have not empirically evaluated this claim) that is based on two key ideas. Firstly, we make incremental changes to existing effective relevance values, rather than recomputing these values from scratch. Secondly, we eliminate redundant computations by restricting incremental changes to only those effective relevance values that can get affected. When an IE node e_d is deleted, the effective relevance of a node $\Lambda(e_i, c)$ is decremented by an amount $\Delta\Lambda(e_i, c)$ to yield the revised relevance value $\Lambda*(e_i, c)$ which is given by:

$$\Lambda^*(e_i, c) = \begin{cases} 0 \ when \ i = d \\ \Lambda(e_i, c) - \Delta\Lambda(e_i, c) \ where \ \Delta\Lambda(e_i, c) = \sigma(e_i, e_d)\rho(e_d, c) \ otherwise \end{cases}$$

These operations can be speeded up by maintaining an *update table*, which is constructed from the similarity and relevance tables and plays the role of an inverted index. A lookup on the table shows the incremental change that must be made on each of the affected effective relevance values and saves the overhead of computing the values from scratch

It may be noted that no updates are needed in situations where $\Delta\Lambda(e_i, c)$ evaluates to zero. This happens when either $\sigma(e_i, e_d)$ is 0 or when $\rho(e_d, c)$ is 0. The update table eliminates such redundant computations by restricting incremental changes to only those effective relevance values that get affected.

As in the case of IE deletion, when a new IE is added, the effective relevances of all IEs bearing non-zero similarity to the new IE need to be re-evaluated. When a new IE node e_n is added, the revised relevance values are given by:

$$\Lambda^*(e_i, c) = \begin{cases} \sum_{j=1}^{s} \rho(e_j, c)\sigma(e_i, e_j). \ when \ i = n \\ \Lambda(e_i, c) + \Delta\Lambda(e_i, c) \ where \ \Delta\Lambda(e_i, c) = \sigma(e_i, e_n)\rho(e_n, c) \ otherwise \end{cases}$$

Again, we can restrict incremental updates to only those effective relevance values that get affected by the IE insertion.

We note that it may be restrictive to suppose that the update operations can always be localized to those similarity and relevance values that are immediately affected by the nodes inserted or deleted. The approaches outlined above for speeding up updates work well when the similarity and relevance knowledge are externally obtained (as from background knowledge like WordNet [2]) or are derived from local properties of the collection (the relevance of an IE to a case is not dependent on other IEs or cases). However they may result in incorrect updates when similarity or relevance knowledge is introspectively derived from global properties of the collection. In textual datasets, the relevance knowledge is often derived using a combination of local measures like term frequency and global measures like inverse document frequency [8]. A single case deletion will necessitate the recomputation of inverse document frequencies pertaining to all relevance values. As with relevance values, similarity knowledge can also be introspectively inferred from the text collection [11] and may need revision each time an update is made. In realistic situations, such bulk updates will be computationally expensive. A practical approach would be to perform incremental local updates as outlined above whenever a node is inserted or deleted, and relegate bulk recomputations to a later time, when enough updates would have happened to make significant impact on the global measures. It is important to note that this recomputation overhead when using introspective techniques to acquire similarity and relevance knowledge is not specific to the FCRN, but is a concern shared by CRN and the flat case-base representation as well.

6   Related Work

Several techniques have been proposed in literature to speed up retrieval in CBR systems. Unlike FCRNs, Discrimination Networks [17] are hierarchical. They are limited by their assumption that the underlying domain can be neatly partitioned, and their inability to recover from missing values. The Fish and Sink Algorithm [18] also aims at speeding up retrieval but needs the triangle inequality to be satisfied by the distance metric. Also, unlike Fish and Sink, FCRNs do not need similarities between cases in the case-base to be pre-computed. K-d trees [19] are efficient data structures that decompose the case-base iteratively into smaller parts, and use a top-down search with backtracking for retrieval. One serious limitation is that the construction of memory structures used in k-d trees becomes computationally expensive with increasing numbers of features and cases. Also, like Discrimination Networks, k-d trees cannot handle missing values. While the applicability of k-d trees is restricted to ordered domains, FCRNs can be used over unordered domains as well.

Spreading-activation techniques have been used for retrieval in domains outside CBR. Most Neural Network [20] formalisms operate over distributed subsymbolic representations of data, organized as a network of nodes and weighted connections. However, while nodes and weights in FCRNs have meaning with respect to the domain being modeled, Neural Networks are typically black-boxes and no domain-specific meaning can be attributed to either the nodes or the inter-connections. Marker passing algorithms [21] also operate over a network structure, but have a different objective compared to focused query-driven retrieval in FCRNs; hence the search over the network is much more undirected compared to FCRNs, with a significant number of search paths terminating in a dead end. Other approaches have also been reported in the context of analogical retrieval [22], where the objective is to retrieve cross-domain analogies. FCRNs differ from these implementations in that FCRNs are specifically designed to retrieve cases within a single domain.

7 Conclusion

We have presented a Fast Case Retrieval Network formalism that remodels the retrieval mechanism in CRNs to eliminate redundant computations. This has significant implications in reducing retrieval time and memory requirements when operating over case-bases indexed over large numbers of IEs and cases. A theoretical analysis of computational complexity and memory requirements comparing FCRNs against CRNs is presented. Experimental results over large case-bases demonstrate significant speedup in retrieval with FCRN. While we have used text as the running theme for presenting our work, FCRN could, in principle, be applied to any large scale CBR application.   As part of future work, we plan to extend the FCRN formalism to model widely used similarity measures in textual and non-textual CBR domains.

References

1. Lenz, M., Burkhard, H.-D.: Case Retrieval Nets: Basic Ideas and Extensions. KI (1996) 227-239
2. Chakraborti, S., Ambati, S., Balaraman, V., Khemani, D.: Integrating Knowledge Sources and Acquiring Vocabulary for Textual CBR. Proc. of the 8th UK CBR Workshop (2003) 74-84
3. Lenz, M., Burkhard, H.: Case Retrieval Nets: Foundations, Properties, Implementation, and Results, Technical Report, Humboldt-Universität zu Berlin (1996)
4. Lenz, M.: Knowledge Sources for Textual CBR Applications, Textual CBR: Papers from the 1998 Workshop Technical Report WS-98-12 AAAI Press (1998) 24-29
5. Balaraman, V., Chakraborti, S.: Satisfying Varying Retrieval Requirements in Case-Based Intelligent Directory Assistance. Proc. of the FLAIRS Conference (2004)
6. Lenz,M.: Case Retrieval Nets Applied to Large Case-Bases. Proc. 4th German Workshop on CBR, Informatik Preprints, Humboldt-Universität zu Berlin (1996)
7. Lenz, M., Auriol, E., Manago, M. : Diagnosis and Decision Support (Chapter 3) Case-Based Reasoning Technology, Lecture Notes in Artificial Intelligence 1400, (1998) 51–90
8. Rijsbergen, C. J.: Information Retrieval. 2nd edition, London, Butterworths (1979)
9. Delany, S.J., Cunningham, P., Tsymbal, A., Coyle, L.: A Case-based Technique for Tracking Concept Drift in Spam Filtering, Applications and Innovations in Intelligent Systems XII, Procs. of AI 2004, Springer (2004) 3-16
10. Lenz,M., Burkhard, H.-D.: CBR for Document Retrieval - *The FAllQ Project.* Case-Based Reasoning Research and Development, (Proc. Of International Conference on CBR, 1997) Springer Verlag, LNAI 1266 (1997)
11. Chakraborti, S., Watt, S.,Wiratunga, N: Introspective Knowledge Acquisition in Case Retrieval Networks for Textual CBR. Proc. of the 9th UK CBR Workshop (2004) 51-61
12. Wilson,D., Bradshaw,S.: CBR Textuality. Proc. of the Fourth UK Case-Based Reasoning Workshop (1999) 67-80
13. Lytinen, S.L., Tomuro,N. : The Use of Question Types to Match Questions in FAQFinder, Mining Answers From Texts and Knowledge Bases, AAAI Technical Report SS-02-06, AAAI Press (2002) 46-53
14. Lenz, M.: Case Retrieval Nets as a Model for Building Flexible Information Systems, PhD dissertation, Humboldt Uni. Berlin. Faculty of Mathematics and Natural Sciences (1999)

15. Lenz, M., Hubner A, Kunje M.: Textual CBR (Chapter 5) Case-Based Reasoning Technology, Lecture Notes in Artificial Intelligence 1400, (1998) 115-137
16. Yang,Y., Pederson,J.O. : A Comparative Study on Feature Selection in Text Categorization, Proc. of the International Conference on Machine Learning (1997) 412-420
17. Kolodner, J.L. : Case-Based Reasoning, Morgan Kaufmann, San Mateo (1993)
18. Schaaf, J.W., "Fish and Sink": An Anytime Algorithm to Retrieve Adequate Cases, Case-Based Reasoning Research and Development (Proc. of International Conference on CBR 1995), Springer, LNAI 1010 (1995) 371-380
19. Weβ, S., Althoff, K.-D., Derwand, G.: Using k-d trees to Improve the Retrieval Step in Case-Based Reasoning, Topics in Case-Based Reasoning, Proc. of European Workshop on CBR-93, Springer (1994) 167-181
20. Rumelhart, D.E., McClelland, J.L., PDP Research Group (1986). Parallel distributed Processing: Explorations in the Microstructure of Cognition. Volume 1: Foundations. MIT Press, Cambridge (1986)
21. Wolverton, M.: An Investigation of Marker Passing Algorithms for Analogue Retrieval, Case-Based Reasoning Research and Development (Proc. of International Conference on CBR 1995), Springer, LNAI 1010 (1995) 359-370
22. Wolverton, M., Hayes-Roth, B.: Retrieving Semantically Distant Analogies with Knowledge-Directed Spreading Activation, Proc. AAAI -94 (1994)

Combining Multiple Similarity Metrics Using a Multicriteria Approach

Luc Lamontagne[1] and Irène Abi-Zeid[2]

[1] Department of Computer Science and Software Engineering,
Laval University, Québec, Canada, G1K 7P4
Luc.Lamontagne@ift.ulaval.ca
[2] Department of Operations and Decision Systems
Laval University, Québec, Canada, G1K 7P4
Irene.Abi-Zeid@osd.ulaval.ca

Abstract. The design of a CBR system involves the use of similarity metrics. For many applications, various functions can be adopted to compare case features and to aggregate them into a global similarity measure. Given the availability of multiple similarity metrics, the designer is hence left with two options in order to come up with a working system: Either select one similarity metric or try to combine multiple metrics in a super-metric. In this paper, we study how techniques borrowed from multicriteria decision aid can be applied to CBR for combining the results of multiple similarity metrics. The problem of multi-metrics retrieval is presented as an instance of the problem of ranking alternatives based on multiple attributes. Discrete methods such as ELECTRE II have been proposed by the multicriteria decision aid community to address such situations. We conducted our experiments for ranking cases with ELECTRE II, a procedure based on pairwise comparisons. We used textual cases and multiple metrics. Our results indicate that the use of a combination of metrics with a multicriteria decision aid method can increase retrieval precision and provide an advantage over weighted sum combinations especially when similarity is measured on scales that are different in nature.

1 Introduction

When building a CBR system, similarity metrics have to be defined in order to support case retrieval functionalities. This process involves determining a mechanism to compare the different values of each case feature (local similarity) and to aggregate these evaluations to measure the closeness of a target problem to the cases in the system's case base (global similarity). Many options at each of these steps are available and, to come up with a working CBR system, the designer must make a decision regarding the combination of metrics that will be incorporated in the retrieval component.

The motivation behind this work stems from previous results pertaining to Textual CBR [1, 2]. Lamontagne *et al.* [3] studied and compared three (3) approaches based on statistical language processing techniques for estimating the similarity of fully textual cases (*i.e.* cases where both problems and solutions are textual in nature). It was observed that the three metrics had dissimilar behaviour and that their relevance

T.R. Roth-Berghofer et al. (Eds.): ECCBR 2006, LNAI 4106, pp. 415–428, 2006.

varied as a function of the textual CBR systems properties such as the size of the case base, the number of neighbours in the case base, the length of the case descriptions, etc. It is therefore interesting to verify whether these metrics can be combined in order to take advantage of their individual strengths. We deem this issue worthwhile investigating for retrieval within a CBR system.

In this paper, we describe how a multicriteria aggregation approach developed within the decision aid community can contribute to combining global similarity results. Our main research question is to determine whether using multiple metrics can potentially improve performance in the retrieval phase of CBR systems. We chose the ELECTRE II method to conduct our experimentation and to verify whether it allows obtaining higher precision for case retrieval. To highlight the advantages and limitations of our multicriteria approach, we compared these experimental results with results obtained based on a weighted sum of the same metrics.

Section 2 of this paper presents information on the textual CBR background pertaining to this work and introduces the metrics used for our experimentation. In section 3, we propose a short introduction to multicriteria decision aid and present a detailed description of the ELECTRE II aggregation procedure. We explain in section 4 how the multicriteria setting is applied to CBR. We describe and discuss in section 5 our experimental results and conclude with perspectives for future work.

2 Multiple Perspectives on the Similarity of Textual Cases

The motivation behind this work stems from an investigation of textual case retrieval [3] where three (3) similarity metrics based on statistical natural language processing (NLP) methods were compared. The metrics were the following:

Cosine measure: As is frequently the case with information retrieval systems, a cosine metric (scalar product) can be applied to measure the relatedness of the cases. Case descriptions are represented as vectors with elements corresponding to individual words present in both the case problems and solutions. Words are assigned a tf*idf weight that quantifies their relative importance. For two given cases, this measures the mutual coverage of the two bags of words that define their content.

Case expansion measure: This measure relies on the expansion of case descriptions using lists of word co-occurrences. Word co-occurrences, denoting some associations between different words, are usually selected using a mutual information estimator. Case expansion is then applied on the solutions descriptions by adding words from these lists. For instance, a case containing the phrase *conference call* in its problem description could find words such as *phone number* or *dial* added to its solution. This measure tries to overcome the lexical shortcomings proper to short case descriptions by inserting additional words that might help find implicit similarities between cases.

Translation measure: This measure makes use of a statistical translation model to evaluate the probability that an existing solution was likely generated from an existing problem description. The translation model, obtained from an alignment algorithm [4, 5], computes the probability that a problem word suggests the use of another word in the solution (this corresponds to a local similarity measure). The resulting global similarity measure is the cumulative probability that a case solution could be associated to a given target problem.

As can be seen from the preceding descriptions, these metrics are based on totally different principles. Experimental results have revealed that they had different properties and unequal performances. A cosine measure performs well for routine cases, *i.e.* problems that are frequently submitted to a system. These routine cases tend to be described using a limited number of words, which facilitates lexical comparisons. On the other hand, the two other metrics make it possible to infer associations between different words, a property that may reveal interesting for more complex case formulations. A case expansion measure is more predictive in nature but less precise for handling frequent and longer case descriptions. The translation approach has a greater potential for discriminating among word associations and is more accurate when used for providing a small number of recommended similar cases. However, this approach requires a substantial corpus in order to build a model capable of covering a large variety of problems.

Considering that the three measures can be more or less appropriate in different contexts, it is reasonable to expect an improvement in the retrieval performance of a CBR system when these three measures are combined. However, a problem may arise when the metrics are measured on very different scales. For example, in our test case base, cosine similarity values belong to a normalized scale of $[0,1]$ and have a mean similarity value of 0.08 with a standard deviation of 0.12; whereas case expansion is measured on a non normalized scale yielding an average similarity value of 0.26 and a standard deviation of 0.11; finally the biggest challenge is to take into account the translation measure, a probability estimate of the words comprised in the case description, which very small values range from 10^{-4} to 10^{-800}. This last measure is obviously non commensurable with the cosine and case expansion measures. Although a logarithmic conversion can somehow help to exploit the translation measure, it remains difficult to combine it with the other metrics because of scale disparities.

A discrete multicriteria aggregation procedure seemed a promising direction for tackling this combination problem. This field of research has been studied for many years by the decision aid community and a multitude of techniques exist to address the problem of ranking alternatives based on multiple conflicting and non commensurable criteria. We introduce this approach in the next section.

3   Discrete Multicriteria Decision Aid

Discrete multicriteria decision Aid (MCDA) [6] provides a framework for supporting a decision maker or a group of decision makers in their decision process where a set of discrete options is considered, a set of often conflicting and non commensurable criteria is used to evaluate these options, and where the expected outcome of the process is: A recommendation of a set of good options (choice problem); a ranking of the options considered (ranking problem); or the assignment of the options considered to predefined categories (classification problem). The preferences of the decision maker(s) are modeled through a set of parameters reflecting the importance of the criteria, as well as indifference, preference and veto thresholds. A variety of aggregation procedures exist to aggregate the local preferences (based on each criterion) into a global preference (based on all the criteria).

The decision problem is represented as a set of m options $A= (a_1, a_2, ...a_m)$, a set of n criteria $G= (g_1, g_2, ...g_n)$, and the $m \times n$ evaluations $g_j(a_i)$ of option i on criterion j expressed in a decision table $\mathbf{E}$, $i=1..m$, $j=1..n$ (Fig. 1). An interesting feature of some of the multicriteria aggregation procedure is that evaluations do not have to be on similar scales. Moreover they do not even have to be numerical in nature. For instance, one criterion can be measured on a cardinal scale with real numbers while another can be evaluated on an ordinal scale of linguistic echelons such as *weak, average, strong*.

$$\mathbf{E} = \begin{bmatrix} e_{11} = g_1(a_1) & ... & e_{i1} = g_1(a_i) & ... & e_{mn} = g_1(a_m) \\ \vdots & & \vdots & \vdots & \vdots \\ e_{1j} = g_j(a_1) & ... & e_{ij} = g_j(a_i) & ... & e_{mj} = g_j(a_m) \\ \vdots & & \vdots & \vdots & \vdots \\ e_{1n} = g_n(a_1) & ... & e_{in} = g_n(a_i) & .... & e_{mn} = g_n(a_m) \end{bmatrix}$$

Fig. 1. An example of multicriteria decision table

Each criterion must be assigned a weight that indicates the relative importance of the criteria to the decision maker(s). The set of weights $\{\omega_j\}$ does not depend on the scales or values used for the corresponding evaluations. However, it is often assumed that the sum of weights is equal to 1.

Outranking methods are a family of multicriteria aggregation procedures based on pairwise comparisons of the options. In the following paragraphs, we describe one such popular method for ranking options, ELECTRE II.

3.1 ELECTRE II – An Multicriteria Aggregation Procedure

The multicriteria aggregation procedure we chose for our project is ELECTRE II [7, 8]. This was the first multicriteria ranking method developed based on the outranking relation principle. Given two options A and B, A outranks B means that A is *at least as good as B*. There are two major phases in ELECTRE II: The construction and the exploitation of the outranking relation. The construction of the outranking relation allows us to aggregate, for each pair of options, the local preferences evaluated on each criterion into a global preference structure. This means that we move from a pairwise comparison of the options based on individual criteria, to a global comparison of the pairs of options based on all the criteria. This translates into the existence or non-existence of the two following binary relations:

- AP_sB: A strongly outranks B.
- AP_wB: A weakly outranks B.

Once we have constructed the outranking relations between all pairs of options, we proceed to establish a direct ranking, an inverse ranking, and a final ranking. This is the exploitation phase of the outranking relation. The final ranking reflects the decision maker(s) preferences, subject to the method, the evaluations, the preferences model, and the method's parameters.

Construction of the outranking relation. From a numerical point of view, we first need to compute concordance and discordance indices. The concordance index of a pair of options (A,B) denoted by $C(A,B)$ corresponds to the degree to which the criteria support the assertion that A is *at least as good as* B (majority rule). It is the sum of the weights of the criteria where A is evaluated equally or better than B. This is defined below where $g_j(A)$ is the evaluation of option A on criterion j and ω_j is the weight of criterion j. C is therefore a concordance matrix of $m \times m$.

$$C(A,B) = \sum_{j:g_j(A) \geq g_j(B)} \omega_j \tag{1}$$

We next compute for each criterion and each pair of options, the discordance index, $d_j(A,B)$. This denotes the degree to which criterion j does not agree with the assertion that A is *at least as good as* B. It can be interpreted as the possibility for criterion j to apply its veto (respect of minority rule) and is defined below. We must compute n discordance matrices of $m \times m$.

$$d_j(A,B) = \begin{cases} 0 & \text{if } g_j(A) \geq g_j(B) \\ g_j(B) - g_j(A) & \text{if } g_j(A) < g_j(B) \end{cases} \tag{2}$$

Once we have computed concordance and discordance indices, we apply concordance and non discordance tests in order to verify, for each pair of options (A, B) whether we have AP_sB, AP_wB, or no outranking relation. These tests use concordance and discordance thresholds, parameters that reflect the decision maker(s) values and preferences. There are three (3) global concordance thresholds, $0.5 < c_1 < c_2 < c_3 \leq 1$ and two (2) discordance or veto thresholds per criterion $0 < v_1(j) < v_2(j) < E(j)$, where $E(j)$ is the scale width of criterion j. When the concordance thresholds are large, we require that many criteria support the assertion that A outranks B; and for small values of the discordance (veto) thresholds, we require that none of the criteria strongly disagrees with the assertion that A outranks B. Denote by condition 1 the following:

$$\frac{\sum_{j:g_j(A)>g_j(B)} \omega_j}{\sum_{j:g_j(A)<g_j(B)} \omega_j} > 1 \qquad \textbf{condition 1} \tag{3}$$

Strong outranking test. For each pair of options (A, B): $AP_sB \Leftrightarrow$ **condition 1** is met and

$$\begin{aligned} C(A,B) \geq \mathbf{c_1} \text{ and } d_j(A,B) \leq \mathbf{v_2}(j) \, \forall j \ \underline{\textbf{or}} \\ C(A,B) \geq \mathbf{c_2} \text{ and } d_j(A,B) \leq \mathbf{v_1}(j) \, \forall j \end{aligned} \tag{4}$$

If the pair of options (A, B) does not pass the strong outranking test, we go on to apply the weak outranking test.

Weak outranking test. For each pair of options (A, B) that do not pass the strong outranking test: $AP_wB \Leftrightarrow$ **condition 1** is met **and**

$$C(A, B) \geq \mathbf{c_3} \text{ and } d_j(A, B) \leq \mathbf{v_2}(j) \, \forall j \tag{5}$$

As an illustration, consider the situation where $C(A,B)$ is high, implying that A is evaluated better than B on a set of criteria that have an important total weight, and suppose that $d_j(A,B)$ is high, meaning that B is better than A on criterion j by an important difference, larger than the veto values $\mathbf{v_1}(j)$ and $\mathbf{v_2}(j)$ for criterion j. This means that the data does not support the assertion that A outranks B, which does not automatically imply that B outranks A.

Exploitation of the outranking relation and construction of the final ranking. Based on the strong and weak outranking relations, we proceed to construct a direct ranking and an inverse ranking (total pre-orders). In a total pre-order, each pair of options A, B either A is ranked better than B, or B is ranked better than A, or they have the same rank. In the direct ranking, the first rank is occupied by the options that are not strongly outranked by any other options. The options in the next rank are those that are not outranked by any non-ranked options, they may be outranked by options from previous ranks, and so on. The weak outranking relation is used to differentiate between options occupying the same rank. The inverse ranking is obtained in a similar fashion. The last rank is obtained by the options that do not strongly outrank any other options. The previous rank is obtained by the options that do not outrank any non-ranked options; they may outrank options from the rank below, and so on. It is possible that some options have different ranks in the direct and inverse ranking while others end up with the same ranks.

A final ranking is obtained by combining the direct and inverse rankings through either a computation of a median rank or by intersection. In a final ranking by intersection, an option A outranks option B, if it has a higher rank in at least one of the two direct or inverse rankings, and if it has a higher or equal rank to it in the other ranking. Two options are equivalent, have the same rank, if and only if they have the same rank in both direct and inverse rankings. Two options are incomparable if and only if one has a higher rank in one of the direct or inverse rankings and a lower rank in the other ranking. Although more recent algorithms such as ELECTRE III were later developed for ranking alternatives (see [6] for specific examples), we chose ELECTRE II because it is much simpler and easier to use. Furthermore, it requires less parameters and thresholds that are somewhat arbitrary.

4   Application to CBR Retrieval

It is possible to envisage various ways to apply a multicriteria approach to CBR retrieval. Multicriteria methods could be used to aggregate local similarity values obtained at the attribute level (as in [9]). They could also be used to select the most appropriate metric as a function of case and problem characteristics. Furthermore, they can be applied, as we have done in this paper, to conduct cases retrieval based on multiple global similarity evaluations.

Given a target problem t, a case base C and a set of metrics M, we applied the ELECTRE II aggregation procedure to CBR retrieval as follows:

- Each candidate case c_i is considered an option. The decision problem consists of ranking the cases in the case base in a decreasing order of relatedness to a new problem. This leads to deciding which case(s) from the case base will be recommended as potential solutions.
- Each similarity metric m_j is a criterion of the decision process. It is assumed that the set of similarity metrics M evaluate different facets of the ability of the cases to solve a target problem t.
- The evaluations contained in the decision table correspond to the similarity measures of the target problem t with each candidate case c_i according to a specific metric m_j. Hence the evaluation $g_j(c_i) = sim_{mj} (t,c_i)$.
- The decision process consists of establishing the final ranking of the cases in the case base and of selecting the first k candidates with the highest ranks.

We present in Fig. 2 a general scheme for a multicriteria combination of the results obtained from multiple similarity metrics. *MCDADecide* is the ELECTRE II decision function described in section 3 of this paper, W is the set of weights assigned to the metrics and w_m is the relative weight of metric m.

```
MCDASelection(t, C, k, M, W) {
   // Build the decision table
   for each metric m_j of M {
      for each case c_i of C {
         DecisionTable[c_i][m_j] = sim_mj (t,c_i)
   }}
   // Conduct the decision process and return the first k actions
   R = MCDADecide_ElectreII(DecisionTable, W)        // a ranking of C
   S = the first k elements of R
   return S
}
```

Fig. 2. Algorithm for selecting the k most similar cases using multiple metrics and a MCDA aggregation procedure (ELECTRE II)

This strategy corresponds to a brute force application of ELECTRE II to CBR retrieval. In practice, this approach might reveal impractical for large case bases as its complexity is $O(|C|^2)$ with a significant constant. Therefore, for large scale applications, we considered two variations of this approach for limiting the number of pairwise comparisons: The bounded approach and the lexicographical approach.

In the bounded approach, the ranking results provided by the individual metrics are used to filter the cases that will be retained as options in the multicriteria aggregation process. The set of retained candidates is the union of the sets of the nearest cases based on individual metrics. The corresponding algorithm is described in Fig 3.

```
BoundedMCDASelection(t, C, k, M, W, b) {
    // Filter the candidate cases for the multicriteria process
    for each metric mⱼ of M {
        Cⱼ = the first b cases cᵢ ranked according to simₘⱼ(t,cᵢ)
        C' = C + Cⱼ
    }
    S = MCDASelection(t, C', k, M, W)
    return S
}
```

Fig. 3. Algorithm for a bounded selection of the *k* most similar cases using multiple metrics and a MCDA aggregation procedure (ELECTRE II)

The lexicographical approach is a hierarchical approach: Cases are first filtered based on the lead metric, the one with the highest weight. Subsequently, the remaining candidate cases are ranked based on all the metrics using the multicriteria aggregation procedure. Hence the lead metric determines the candidate cases used as options while the other metrics help discriminate among them. This scheme is illustrated in Fig. 4.

```
LexicographicalMCDASelection(t, C, k, M, W, b) {
    // Filter the candidate cases to be part of the decision process
    mₗₑₐ𝒹 = the metric of M with the largest weight w
    C' = the first b cases ranked according to sim ₘₗₑₐ𝒹 (t,cᵢ)
    S = MCDASelection(t, C', k, M, W)
    return S
}
```

Fig. 4. Algorithm using a lead metric to filter candidate cases before selecting the *k* most similar ones

5 Experimental Analysis

Tests were conducted using 73 cases from an Email Response application, where a case consists of a request message (the problem) and its corresponding response (the solution). Since these cases are textual in nature, we used the three metrics described in Section 2 of this paper to measure similarity. The results presented in this section were obtained from a leave-one-out evaluation of the retrieval component. In order to evaluate the performance of various combinations of metrics, we assessed the best k cases according to the following indicators:

- *Precision*: The proportion of relevant cases in the first *k* nearest-neighbours (*k*=5, for this experiment); Cases are considered relevant when case solutions share common themes, which indicates that a response can be reused.
- *Relevant First*: The proportion of trials for which the nearest neighbour is relevant.

5.1 Individual vs. Combined Metrics

The first issue was to determine whether a multicriteria combination of metrics can provide a better performance than using one metric at a time. As presented in Table 1, experimental results indicate that a combination of the three metrics can improve the performance of the system by approximately 5 to 7 % (in terms of precision and relevance of the first recommendation). These results were obtained by assigning a weight distribution of W = {0.25, 0.5, 0.25} to the Cosine, Case Expansion and Translation measures respectively. We observed throughout our experimentations that similar results could be obtained if higher weights were assigned to the Case Expansion measure. However, this improvement in performance was not significant when higher weights were assigned to the Cosine and Translation measures, in which case the precision obtained was 0.6.

Table 1. Performance using individual and a combination of similarity metrics with ELECTRE II.

Similarity metric	Precision	Relevant First
Cosine measure	0.57	0.58
Case Expansion measure	0.61	0.68
Translation measure	0.56	0.63
Multicriteria combination of the three metrics	0.64	0.73

To better understand the influence of each metric on system performance, we used combinations of pairs of metrics with equal weights of 50%. The results, presented in Table 2, indicate that all the MCDA pairs outperformed the precision of their constituents when used individually. One intriguing observation is that the combination of Cosine and Case Expansion measures provides the same performance as a MCDA combination of the three metrics.

Table 2. Performance of MCDA combination of pairs of similarity metrics

Similarity metric	Precision	Relevant First
Cosine + Case Expansion	0.64	0.73
Cosine + Translation	0.60	0.62
Case Expansion + Translation	0.63	0.62

Fig. 5 clearly shows that when the majority of weight is assigned to the Case Expansion metric, then using the other metric helps increase the global precision of the MCDA retrieval combination. Otherwise, the precision either remains constant or degrades. For instance, in Fig. 5a, we observe some improvement of performance when weight values inferior to 0.5 are allocated to the Cosine metric. An abrupt decrease in precision occurs when more weight is assigned to this metric. Therefore, we can draw the conclusion that improvement can be expected from MCDA combinations of metrics when the best performing metric (Case expansion) has a higher weight coefficient.

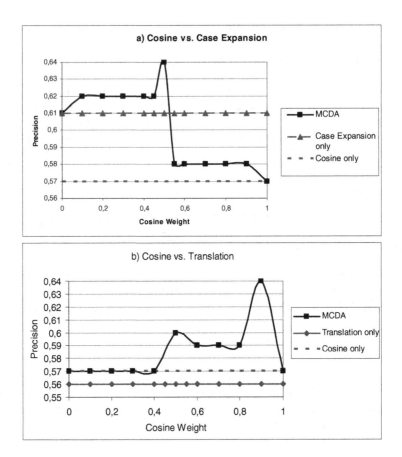

Fig. 5. Effect of weight variation on the performance of MCDA pairs of metrics

5.2   Bounding the Number of Cases Before Applying the MCDA Combination

The results we obtained are presented in Fig. 6. The bounded version of MCDA combinations (algorithm described in Fig. 3) has a slight degradation of performance of approximately 1.5% in precision when the number of cases used in the aggregation procedure is between 5 and 10. However, when more than 13 cases are used as options, it offers a precision either equal or higher than a brute force MCDA combination. Also, the relevance of the first case (not shown on this figure) is on average as good as the Brute Force MCDA approach when the case limit is above 5.

The lexicographical version is less stable and presents a slower performance improvement than the preceding approach. We note that a higher case limit (> 20) is required to reach performances equal or superior to the basic MCDA combination. On the other hand, our experiments indicate that the relevance of the first case is not influenced when using more than 6 cases.

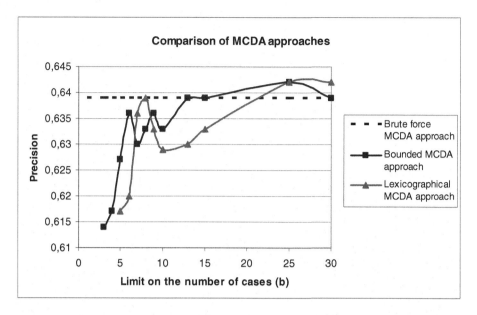

Fig. 6. Effect of limiting the number of cases on the performance of MCDA approaches

5.3 MCDA Combination vs. Weighted Sum Combination

A question may arise regarding the pertinence of using MCDA combinations as op-posed to a weighted sum of the metrics. To help answer this question, we present in Table 3 comparison results where the same set of weights is used in order to ensure comparisons on the same basis.

Table 3. Comparison of the performance of a MCDA combination of the three metrics and the weighted sum (W = {0.2, 0.5, 0.3})

Similarity metric	Precision	Relevant First
MCDA combination	0.64	0.73
Weighted Sum	0.57	0.62

This table seems to indicate that the MCDA combination is a better choice than the weighted sum. However, if we perform an ablation study of the metrics (Fig. 7), we observe the following: Fig. 7a) shows that, for Cosine and Case Expansion metrics, MCDA and Weighted Sum combinations behaved similarly.

This is explained by the fact that the scales for both metrics are similar. The Weighted Sum can provide higher precision if a weight assignment for the Cosine metric is carefully chosen (weight interval ranging from 0.3 to 0.45); however it per-formance is degraded when the Cosine weight is in the 0.1-0.3 interval. Fig. 7b) pre-sents a different picture. The weighted sum combination fails to outperform the other approach for the large majority of the weight assignments. Moreover, almost no

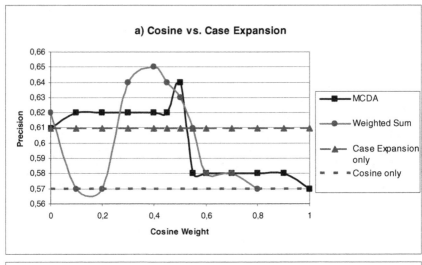

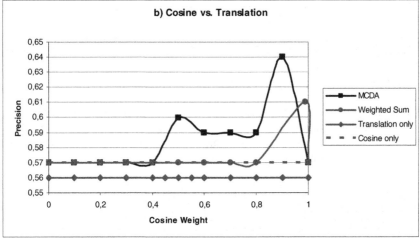

Fig. 7. Effect of weight variation on MCDA and Weighted sum combinations

improvement can be attained except when weight of the Cosine metric in the 0.8-0.9 interval. Therefore, the scale difference between the two Cosine and Translation metrics seems to affect significantly the performance of the weighted sum approach.

This behaviour can be explained by the difference in the magnitudes of the metrics and the weights. In the weighted sum approach, the weights are used to establish a compromise between the scales of the various metrics, hence making both components strongly dependent on each other. The weighted sum is a completely compensatory method where a small evaluation on one metric is cancelled by a high evaluation on another metric. In the MCDA approach, evaluations are used for pairwise comparisons of actions with respect to a single metric. Evaluations from different metrics are not explicitly aggregated. Furthermore, the weights are used for the concordance and discordance computations. Therefore, the MCDA approach is not dependent on the closeness of the weights magnitudes and the metrics scales.

6 Conclusion

In this paper, we have explored how a discrete multicriteria aggregation procedure can be used to combine metrics for case ranking in a case retrieval process. The motivation behind this work was to investigate whether CBR systems could benefit from using multiple metrics simultaneously.

Our results indicate that multicriteria combinations can improve the performance of individual metrics. This approach revealed particularly advantageous when metrics are evaluated on different non commensurable scales. One interesting finding is that the output quality of the multicriteria procedure depends on the relative importance of the most performing metrics.

In order to reduce the computational burden, we proposed filtering strategies that allowed reducing the number of cases used as options in the MCDA ranking process, without sacrificing performance.

As future work, the engineering of multi-metrics CBR systems will require techniques, based on machine learning, to assist the designer in the assignment of relative weights to criteria in the ranking process. Sensitivity analysis will also help evaluate the impact on the ranking process of the various parameters used by the aggregation method. Experiments with aggregation procedures other than ELECTRE II, will help understand if the outranking approach is viable for CBR retrieval. We foresee even greater potential for applications where the similarity computations exploit non numerical syntactic and semantics properties of the cases. Multi-metric combinations can then take into account various perspectives for evaluating textual similarity. Finally, MCDA pairwise comparisons of cases should be investigated to assist other phases of the CBR cycle such as maintenance and case authoring.

References

1. Lamontagne, L. ; Lapalme, G. ; (2002) "Raisonnement à base de cas textuels – état de l'art et perspectives", Revue d'Intelligence Artificielle, Hermes, Paris, vol. 16, no. 3, pp. 339-366.
2. Lenz, M.; Hübner, A.; Kunze, M.; (1998) "Textual CBR", in Lenz, M.; Bartsch-Spörl, B.; Burkhard, H.-D.; Wess, S. (Editors), *Case-Based Reasoning Technology: From Foundations to Applications*, Lecture Notes in Computer Science 1400, Springer, pp. 115-138.
3. Lamontagne, L. ; Langlais, P. ; Lapalme, G. ; (2003) "Using Statistical Models for the Retrieval of Fully-Textual Cases", in Russell, I.; Haller, S. (Editors), Proceedings of FLAIRS '03, AAAI Press, Ste-Augustine, Florida, pp.124-128.
4. Knight, K. (1999), A Statistical Machine Translation (MT) Tutorial Workbook, unpublished document, *http://www.isi.edu/natural-language/mt/wkbk.rtf.*
5. Brown, P., Cocke, J., Della Pietra, S., Della Pietra, V., Jelinek, F., Mercer, R., Roossin, P., (1990), "A Statistical Approach to Machine Translation", *Computational Linguistics*, 16(2), pp. 79-85.

6. Vincke, Ph.; (1992) *Multicriteria decision aid*, J. Wiley, New York.
7. Roy, B. and Bertier, P. (1973), La méthode ELECTRE II : une application au média-planning, *Proceedings of the sixth IFORS'72*, Ross (ed.), North-Holland Pub.
8. Simpson, L, (1996), "Do decision makers know what they prefer?: MAVT and ELECTRE II", *Journal of the Operational Research Society*, 47(7): pp. 919-929.
9. San Pedro, J., Burstein, F. (2003) "A Framework for Case-Based Fuzzy Multicriteria Decision Support for Tropical Cyclone Forecasting", Proceedings of HICSS 2003, ACM Press, pp. 85-92.

Case Factory – Maintaining Experience to Learn

Klaus-Dieter Althoff, Alexandre Hanft, and Martin Schaaf

University of Hildesheim
Institute of Computer Science
Intelligent Information Systems Lab
Marienburger Platz 22, 31141 Hildesheim, Germany
{althoff, hanft, schaaf}@iis.uni-hildesheim.de

Abstract. In this paper, we outline our vision of a case factory that deals with developing (future) knowledge-based systems. The functionality of such a system is provided by different kinds of agents. We focus especially on case-based-reasoning agents, which play an important part within our vision and the corresponding architecture. Our method of constructing a case-based reasoning system using agents is based on integration with the experience factory approach. We define a single architecture adopting ideas from the concept of software product-lines with a focus on combining technical and organizational knowledge. Finally, the paper closes with a brief overview of the current state of our work and a conceptual evaluation of its components with respect to related work.

1 Introduction

Our society needs and expects sophisticated services, which are typically "knowledge-intensive" and can only be delivered if necessary organizational and technical requirements are fulfilled. In addition, cost-benefit analysis from the service provider point of view needs to be positive. Continuous improvement and goal-directed (partial) automation of such services is therefore of crucial importance. As a contribution to this we describe our current research vision of *case factory* and knowledge-line for (partially) automated support of knowledge work(ers) using knowledge-based systems with a specific focus on case-specific knowledge.

By *case factory* we mean the adoption of the experience factory approach known from software engineering to case-based reasoning. A *knowledge-line* denotes the use of the software product-line method, also known from software engineering, with a focus on aspects applicable to knowledge-based systems. As a consequence, we consider a knowledge-based system as a multi-agent system where a general task is decomposed into subtasks and distributed to particular software agents[1]. As a first step – and only this is presented, here – we consider these agents to be case-based reasoning agents. In subsequent steps we will extend this narrow view and integrate other kinds of agents as well.

---

[1] Please note that we use software agents primarily as a means for configuring our software architecture.

T.R. Roth-Berghofer et al. (Eds.): ECCBR 2006, LNAI 4106, pp. 429–442, 2006.

As a specific feature of our *case factory* approach, we assign roles from the experience factory concept to software agents. The former human role owners take over the task of coaching these agents by providing their experience to these software agents and taking over difficult decisions.

In section 2 we describe our vision in more detail including the integration of case-based reasoning, experience factory, software product-lines, and multi-agent systems. Section 3 focuses on the software architecture from a conceptual perspective. Section 4 presents the current state of our work, reports on the evaluation of its basic components, motivates and compares our approach to related work. Finally we briefly summarize the paper and provide an outlook on future work.

2   Vision on Knowledge-Based Systems for Knowledge Work(ers)

The vision presented in this paper reflects experiences from research projects of the past ten years. Before going into detail, this section will give a brief motivation addressing the particular technologies and methodologies in general.

2.1   Motivation of Our Research Vision

The shift of relative importance from more traditional product factors to the new, increasingly important product factor "knowledge" characterizes the development of new economical structures [11]. The incorporation of external knowledge is becoming more and more strategically important for companies for adapting to structural changes (decentralization, more flexibility). For instance, up-to-date knowledge is required not only for intended innovations but also for organization-internal changes, production, and sales of products. However, often such knowledge cannot be elicited organization-internally.

Knowledge-intensive services and especially knowledge work [21, 22] represent a quickly increasing part of the service sector. "Knowledge-intensive work" includes activities that require an intensive education and experience on a specific subject that has been accumulated over many years [53, 33]. "Knowledge-intensive services" need the resource knowledge as their most important input factor when delivered [26]. "Knowledge work" denotes activities where the problem solving process is based not only on once acquired but on constantly revised, improved and updated knowledge [53, 33]. Experience represents the success-critical knowledge for knowledge-intensive services and knowledge work [24].

Within this paper we describe our research vision of how to develop knowledge-based systems for supporting knowledge work and knowledge-intensive services with a specific focus on the use of experience (case-specific knowledge) [27, 7]. Our vision especially includes computer-based, fully and/or partially automated knowledge work. Besides the known application possibilities within service economics (for a lot of success stories see [20]), our research also contributes to ambitious goals being formulated by the European Union, for instance the ambient intelligence initiative [28] and scenarios described in the report on "converging technologies" [23, 42]. Fully or partially automating knowledge work has the additional advantage of providing knowledge to users and computers as well. This enables automated processing of knowledge and offers a unique additional value if compared with more traditional approaches.

Many requirements have to be considered during development of such knowledge-based systems. In addition, the service expectation of our society is increasing and this is not going to change in the near future. Then, users expect information systems to support them smartly, to behave "intelligently", and to learn from experience thereby improving their behavior. As a consequence, such knowledge-based systems should be flexible, modular, and easy to adapt and maintain. These systems should contain a lot of valuable knowledge understandable for both the user and the computer.

Implementing such knowledge-based systems comprises numerous problems. Some of them have already been solved in principle or exemplarily for selected tasks. However, corresponding solutions are mostly developed by different research communities with very limited exchange/communication in between although past experience has shown that achieving major progress for fields like the implementation of knowledge-based systems requires integrating methods and techniques from different (sub-) disciplines. We present a research vision that has been developed while the authors were working in the computer science sub-disciplines software engineering (SE), artificial intelligence (AI), and business information systems. As a consequence, our vision is based on an integration of approaches from these fields.

In particular, this includes the SE experience factory, software product-line approaches as well as case-based reasoning, intelligent agents, and machine learning from AI. Furthermore, there are a lot of relationships to knowledge management and business processes, which may be considered as part of business information systems.

2.2 Integration of Case-Based Reasoning, Experience Factory, Software Product-Lines, and Agent Technology

Experience factory (EF) is a logical and/or physical infrastructure for continuous learning from experience (Fig. 1). It includes an experience base for storage and reuse of knowledge. The experience factory concept was introduced in the mid 1980s to support the central process of SE, the software development process [19, 18]. Basili and Rombach consider software development running in projects separate from the learning organization experience factory because these two sub-organizations have different goals. Projects have to achieve their project goals, that is, developing software according to the given requirements. Experience factory, however, supports learning across projects. From a project perspective this can be viewed as additional effort and might lead to a goal conflict. Such a separation of learning and project organization is a characteristic feature of an experience factory [16] and has been validated in practice.

The experience factory concept follows the quality improvement paradigm, a goal-oriented learning cycle for the experience based improvement of project planning, project execution, and project learning. Goal-oriented measurement and evaluation is used as a systematic procedure for evaluation [17]. Fig. 1 shows the separation between learning and project organization, the main interfaces between projects and experience factory as well as various roles within the experience factory. While the experience factory manager has the overall responsibility, the experience manager has associated the task of deciding about content development and structuring. The experience engineer is responsible for packaging and analyzing the experience base.

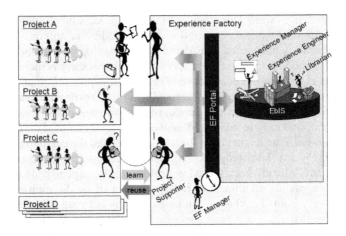

Fig. 1. Experience factory

While the librarian cares about the technical and administrative tasks, the project supporter finally is the main contact to the respective projects.

Basili, Rombach et al. [16] identified important problems in the mid 1990s. In particular, how to implement an experience base, how the necessary processes for developing an experience factory/base should look like in detail, as well as how experiments about implementation issues could be carried out.

Case-based reasoning caused a focus within AI on knowledge-based systems dedicated to experience management [14, 2, 13, 5] in the late 1980s and the 1990s. Utilizing the dynamic-memory-idea of Schank [46], the CBR approach makes use of situation knowledge usually resulting in good user acceptance. Accordingly, a number of commercial tools and many real-life applications were developed (e.g. [12, 20, 49]). Important problems tackled in the mid 1990s were the systematic development of CBR systems, their operation, integration into an industrial environment, and their evaluation.

The following integration of the experience factory and the case-based reasoning concepts [48] led to numerous advantages. Because CBR makes use of experiences captured as cases immediately, it fits very well as technology supporting the experience factory concept. A lot of detailed knowledge about the case-based reasoning processes was already available in the corresponding community and could be used as a very good starting point for describing experience factory processes. On the other hand, the experience factory provided a methodology when applying case-based reasoning systems to commercial organizations. In addition, it contributed an approach for evaluating case-based reasoning systems: goal-oriented measurement and evaluation [6].

We denote the integration of experience factory and case-based reasoning as *case factory*. Enhancing this integration also led to the integration of systematic reuse into the software development process. Hence, the implementation of the case base was based on the software product-line approach [38, 44, 37] and introduced a so-called "experience based information system" (EbIS). Thus, a case base was no more realized as a single system but as an entire system family. The underlying system

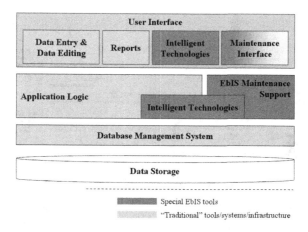

Fig. 2. Product-line architecture for experience based information systems [38]

architecture is shown in Fig. 2. As several of the presented components have different implementations, the architecture describes a family of systems that is defined with respect to a number of carefully designed common features [45].

2.3 Vision

The significance of knowledge as production factor was already pointed out in the beginning of this section. We emphasized our vision on developing knowledge-based systems supporting knowledge work and knowledge-intensive services, focusing on creating added-value through increasingly automated use of available knowledge. This resulted in the idea of a "knowledge product-line" (or short *knowledge-line*). A *knowledge-line* denotes adoption of the software product-line approach to knowledge-based systems.

Knowledge-lines enable the necessary "knowledge level modularization" for building potential variants in the sense of software product-lines. This could be achieved by making use of multi-agent systems [24, 51] as basic approach for knowledge-based systems. An intelligent agent is implemented as a case-based reasoning system, which, besides case-specific knowledge, can also include other kinds of knowledge. Each case-based reasoning system agent is embedded in a *case factory* that is responsible for all necessary knowledge processes like knowledge inflow, knowledge outflow as well as knowledge analysis. Such a *case factory* is potentially fully automated, because software agents are available for each role known from experience factory, and perform these roles in an increasingly automated way. For example, machine learning techniques are used for analyzing, evaluating, and maintaining the case base. As part of the vision both, the case-based reasoning system agents and the *case factory* agents, can learn from experience. As a consequence, the vision considers distributed learning systems as a model for future (intelligent) software systems.

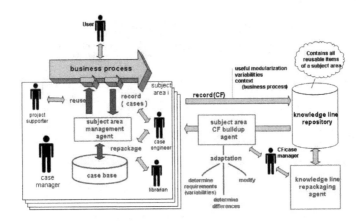

Fig. 3. Knowledge-line based on a (partially) agent-operated case factory

Fig. 3 presents an overview of the case factory approach structured according to the knowledge-line. The left part shows the case-based-reasoning-enabled operation of a *case factory* for different subject areas. The right part of Fig. 3 describes the knowledge-line part of a *case factory* responsible for the systematic development of a case-based reasoning system.

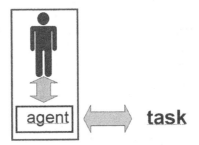

Fig. 4. Case factory role owner as a coach for the respectively associated software agent

For each role within a *case factory* there is at least one software agent. However, each software agent has associated a human coach being responsible for the role, which is assigned to both in a collaborative sense (see Fig. 4). The human role owner "introduces the agent to his job" by taking over difficult decisions and providing his case-specific knowledge. Based on case-based reasoning and machine learning techniques, the corresponding software agent should learn while interacting with its human coach taking over more and more tasks (if accepted by its coach). This enables a gradual transition from purely human based processes to processes where routine tasks are increasingly carried out by software agents, and humans can spend more time on creative tasks.

Using the software product-line approach enables a modularization already on the knowledge level. The modules have associated the variability and requirements that they satisfy. As a consequence, such knowledge-line modules can be selected using a catalogue of requirements. By doing so, the development of further case factories is simplified and speeded up. Nick [38] has identified an efficiency improvement by a factor greater than 4 for developing the design of an experience based information system. Further efficiency improvement for the buildup of case factories will be expected from increasing automation of a *case factory buildup agent*.

3   Software Architecture for Knowledge-Based Systems

In this section, a software architecture for knowledge-based systems as motivated above is described. Thus, it was designed with the aim of building knowledge-based systems as knowledge-lines as mentioned before.

According to our vision, future knowledge-based systems should support reusing already captured knowledge as much as possible and provide their services within a generic architecture. The idea behind this is (if we have built a similar system before) to more or less configure a knowledge-based system instead of developing it from scratch. Of course, such issues are not specific to knowledge-based systems but important research topics in adjacent areas, for instance patterns [29] and frameworks (e.g., JADE [34]). However, we believe that adopting the software product-line concept and focusing on knowledge is a promising alternative to already existing methodologies for developing AI systems.

Beside the aspects of product lines, newer development processes for knowledge-based systems should be prepared for the following questions:

- Which kind of knowledge is available? Is it more general knowledge like rules, (e.g., best practices), more case-specific knowledge (e.g., lessons learned), or only simple documentation of past events (textual documentation of "raw experience")?
- What are the characteristics of the available case-specific and general knowledge?
- What requirements are given for the solution?
- Could the provided solution contain (small) errors or must it be correct and proven?
- What are the environmental conditions and the context?

When introducing a knowledge-based system, such knowledge is typically not available and must be collected in advance. Therefore, we have to build up a case base with the aim of reusing the contained case-specific (and at this time also general) knowledge.

3.1   Using the Multi-agent Paradigm for Structuring Knowledge-Based Systems

As shown in [43] or in [1], maintenance is a long-running process during the lifecycle of such a system, which should be done beneath the usual processes (like *retrieve* in case-based reasoning). This could be done partially or completely offline and has, in this case, to capture different versions and states of elements of knowledge as, for example, shown in the special domain of textual case-based reasoning [30]. Because buildup and maintenance are such different tasks compared with usual working tasks, we put them into completely separate active software components such as agents. Here, we use the agent-oriented programming paradigm to decompose and organize inherently different tasks.

3.2 Four-Tier Architecture

The general architecture is decomposed into four tiers. On the first system tier called system tier is at least one knowledge-based system. The second one, the knowledge worker tier contains some knowledge-based agents, each specialized on different problem solving techniques, for example, case-based reasoning. Whereas the third tier, also known as maintenance tier, contains agents maintaining the used knowledge and the knowledge itself is stored in the fourth tier. Each tier should not be confused with tiers from related SE-multi-tiered models as those are more technically motivated containing business logic only on the middle tier. In contrast, the first, second and third tier of a knowledge-based system performs business logic. Additionally, all of the four tiers can be distinguished by the kind of service they provide. Each element of a tier provides some (knowledge-based-) services and makes use of some underlying ones. Fig. 5 gives an overview. In this figure a knowledge-based system KBS_1 uses two *knowledge-worker agents*: CBR $Agent_1$ and Search $Agent_3$. The (case-) knowledge situated in case-base 1 is maintained by a *case factory* represented by CF $Agent_1$.

The term service instead of classes or components was chosen according to the idea of web services [50]. Using services achieves independency between a consumer of a service (which only knows the URL and description of a service) and the implementation of a service. Additionally, the architecture allows systems running locally or physically dispersed.

The motivation behind distinguishing four tiers is the following: We describe the requirements of each tier on different levels of abstraction. Afterwards we can exchange elements of each tier without changing the other ones. In other words: we want to enable changing problem solving techniques, maintaining models, and GUI independently from one another to separate used knowledge as much as possible.

3.2.1 System Tier: Knowledge-Based System

The first is the most general tier and exposes services provided by the entire knowledge-based system. This is the interface as a normal user would recognize and interact with it. Different kinds of interfaces like rich clients running on local machines, web-based interfaces (thin clients), or simply web services are feasible. Inside a knowledge-based system the service is decomposed into several sub-services. In a first step only one knowledge-based system is considered. Of course, following the product-line approach in the next step(s) different knowledge-based systems should be configurable from the lower tiers.

3.2.2 Knowledge Worker Tier: Knowledge-Worker Agents

The service of an arbitrary knowledge-based system has to be executed by (at least one) agent capable to fulfill the sub-services according to the business processes of the respective knowledge-based system. Therefore, different kinds of so-called *knowledge worker agents* should be available, according to the categories of problems to be solved. The knowledge-worker agents are, in our work, case-based reasoning agents but, in principle, deductive problem solving agents, theorem proving agents, planning agents, or internet-search agents are also possible. In the best or optimal case we have at least one kind of agent for each possible sub-service. In real world scenarios, we can expect only a subset of agents.

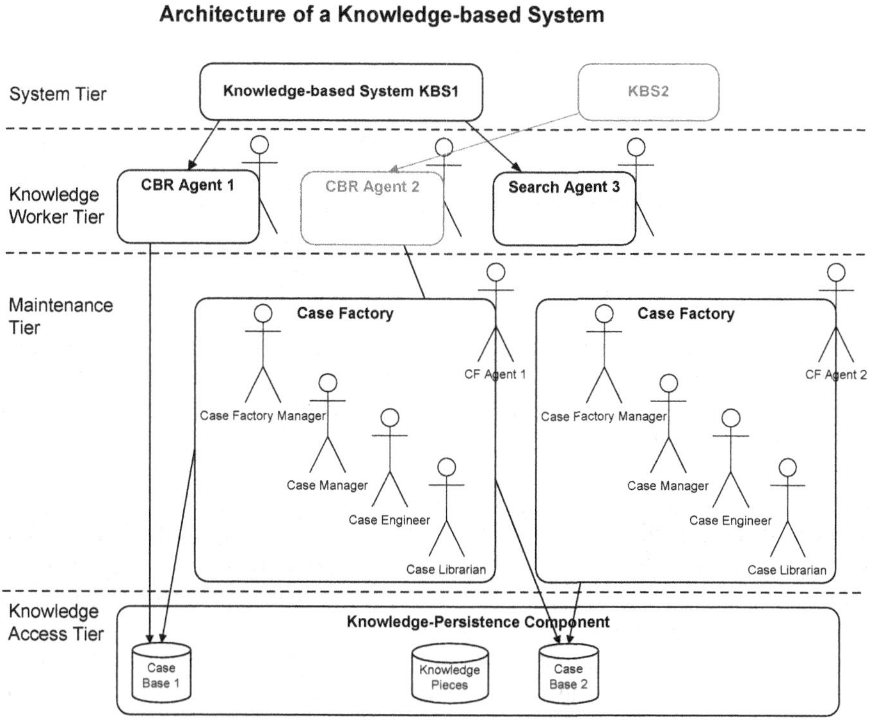

Architecture of a Knowledge-based System

Fig. 5. Overview of the system architecture with four tiers

3.2.3 Maintenance Tier: Case-Factory Agents

This tier contains active maintenance agents responsible for the knowledge or experience used by the *knowledge worker agents* on the second tier. Each agent maintains (some part of) the knowledge, keeps it up to date, repackages, and extends it. According to different conceivable models, various agents could exist. Although each maintenance agent corresponds to a certain kind of *knowledge worker agent,* we separate both from each other. By this we integrate two different aspects of improving knowledge: Firstly each *knowledge worker agent* learns individually from its own experience and secondly each *knowledge worker agent* can also learn from the experience of other *knowledge worker agent* through a relationship between the respective *case factories* managed by the respective *case factory manager agent.*

For this paper, we describe the introduced *case factory* as a concept of maintaining the case-specific (and general) knowledge used by a *case-based reasoning agent.*

3.2.4 Knowledge Access Tier

On this tier we foster all the knowledge utilized by agents from tiers above. It is outsourced from the *knowledge worker agents* to give the *case factory agents* access to all the knowledge independently from the respective *knowledge worker agents.* In addition, also the knowledge of all the *case factory agents* is outsourced. Thus, these agents also can learn. However, these learning processes are supported via the case manager and the *case factory manager agents*.

3.2.5 Communication Interfaces Between Tiers

There exists an interface defining a minimal set of services all knowledge agents have to provide. It bases on basic class interfaces that are used for all tiers, hence the communication between agents of the same tier and different tiers can achieved as well..

3.3 A Case-Based Reasoning Agent (as an Example of the Second Tier)

A case-based reasoning agent provides services that are typical for a case-based reasoning system: retrieve cases, reuse and revise solutions, retain new cases. In addition more than one cbr-agent implementing different case-based reasoning approaches could exist side by side.

3.3.1 Case Factory

This section describes *case factory* as the notion of an experience factory approach for building-up and maintaining case-based reasoning systems. Despite the whole *case factory* is represented by one agent, the tasks inside the *case factory* (closely related to the tasks of an experience factory) done are executed by other (subordinated) agents as well. This could be (in a first iteration) human (as shown in Fig. 4) but also software agents. Following agents are involved: *case factory manager*, *case manager*, *case engineer*, *case librarian*, subject area management agent, knowledge-line repackaging agent, and *buildup agent*.

Based on the low-effort collaborative maintenance model we described in [30], we want to briefly sketch the ideas behind. The *case factory manager* has the overall responsibility for the whole *case factory* and decides about strategic goals using this case-based reasoning system. Obviously, it is the most appropriate candidate having a human coach because its task is difficult to automate and the final decision should be delegated to a human. Although the low-effort model has no official administrator, developers and administrators feel responsible for this project and keep it alive.

The *case manager* is associated with the task of deciding about development and improvement of the case base and the other knowledge containers. An example of managing improvement is setting the score levels and maintenance intervals.

The *case engineer* has (in cooperation) the task of packaging and structuring existing experience into a case-based reasoning system, for example, modeling the case format. The *case librarian* is responsible for technical aspects like maintaining the case base, storing, and publishing new cases. The *subject area management agent* is responsible for collecting the domain knowledge that is specific for the current subject area. The knowledge-line *repackaging agent* (both not shown Fig. 5) is responsible for restructuring and repacking the available case-specific and general knowledge. The *buildup agent* is responsible for building up a new case-based reasoning system. This could be a human administrator installing the software and/or a database administrator setting up a new database for storing a case base.

4   Evaluation and Related Work

While the work presented here is mainly on a conceptual level, it covers research being done from the mid 1990 until now. It deals with the integration of four different approaches from AI and SE leading to a promising development methodology for knowledge-based systems that has, to our knowledge, not reported yet. The goal of this paper is not only to summarize previous work but also to actively predict the scientific future of the fields described.

For a deeper analysis of case-based reasoning principles used here see [3, 11, 10]. With respect to the integration of case-based reasoning and experience factory we incorporate the results described in [48, 47, 9]. From a maintenance perspective we actively use the results described in [38, 39, 31]. Regarding software product-lines we start from the software product-line described in [38]. Our work, however, is also influenced by earlier work on a software product-line on technical diagnosis [52, 10] and follow-up work [20, 6]. In spirit our work is also related to integrated learning (and problem solving) architectures [40], especially to work done in the groups around Agnar Aamodt [4], Enric Plaza [3], and Josep Lluis Arcos [15]. As we already mentioned, our research goal has some similarities to goals of work on expert system shells or tool boxes, for example, work done in the group around Frank Puppe [41].

Though there are many relationships to other work we are convinced that the work described and proposed in this paper will lead to some new research directions. One reason for this is the – to a high extend – deep integration of SE and AI approaches which, to our knowledge, is missing within other work.

5   Conclusion and Outlook

In this paper we introduced *case factory* as the integration of the case-based reasoning and experience factory approaches and *knowledge-line* as the systematic application of the software product-line approach to the knowledge in knowledge-based systems. The goal of this paper is to have a résumé of previous work *and* to actively predict the scientific future for the development of knowledge-based systems for supporting knowledge work and knowledge-intensive services as described above. In a first step we focused on case-specific knowledge and case-based reasoning for its processing. We presented a four-tier software architecture for developing knowledge-lines using different knowledge worker as well as *case factory agents*.

We try to integrate research work that started already in the beginning 1990s of both ourselves and others with more recent work. Our next goals include the implementation (of parts) of the described software architecture and its validation for selected applications. We try to integrate also other interested research groups into this process.

References

1. Aamodt, A.: Invited Talk at ECCBR 2004 in Madrid.
2. Aamodt, A.: Robust expert systems that learn from experience - An architectural framework. EKAW-89, Third European Knowledge Acquisition for Knowledge-based Systems Workshop, Paris, July 1989. pp. 311-326.

3. Aamodt, A. & Plaza, E.: Case-based reasoning: Foundational issues, methodological variations, and system approaches. *AI Communications 7(1)*, 1994, 39-59.
4. Aamodt, A.: A knowledge-intensive, integrated approach to problem solving and sustained learning, Ph.D (Dr.Ing.) dissertation, University of Trondheim, Norwegian Institute of Technology, Department of Computer Science, May 1991. University Microfilms PUB92-08460, 1992.
5. Aha, D.W.: The AAAI-99 KM/CBR Workshop: Summary of Contributions. Proc. ICCBR '99 Workshops, II-37–II-44. Technical Report, LSA-99-03E, TU Kaiserslautern, 1999.
6. Althoff, K.-D. & Nick, M.: How to Support Experience Management with Evaluation – Foundations, Evaluation Methods, and Examples for Case-Based Reasoning and Experience Factory. Accepted for publication by Springer Verlag, Lecture Notes of Computer Science/Artificial Intelligence, Berlin, 2006 (in progress).
7. Althoff, K.-D., Mänz, J. & Nick, M.: Maintaining Experience to Learn: Case Studies on Case-Based Reasoning and Experience Factory. In Proc. 6th Workshop Days of the German Computer Science Society (GI) on Learning, Knowledge, and Adaptivity (LWA 2005) Workshop on Machine Learning, Knowledge Discovery, and Data Mining, Saarland University, Germany, Oct. 2005.
8. Althoff, K.-D.: Case-Based Reasoning. In: S.K. Chang (Ed.), Handbook on Software Engineering and Knowledge Engineering. Vol.1, World Scientific, 2001; pp. 549-587.
9. Althoff, K.-D., Birk, A., Gresse von Wangenheim, C. & Tautz, C.: Case-Based Reasoning for Experimental Software Engineering. In [36], 1998, pp. 235-254.
10. Althoff, K.-D.: Evaluating Case-Based Reasoning Systems: The INRECA Case Study. habilitation treatise, Department of Computer Science, University of Kaiserslautern, 1997.
11. Althoff, K.-D. & Aamodt, A.: Relating case-based problem solving and learning methods to task and domain characteristics: towards an analytic framework. AI Communications, 9 (3), 1996, pp.1-8.
12. Althoff, K.-D., Auriol, E., Barletta, R. & Manago, M.: A Review of Industrial Case-Based Reasoning Tools. AI Perspectives Report, Oxford, UK: AI Intelligence, 1995.
13. Althoff, K.-D., Kockskämper, S., Maurer, F., Stadler, M. and Wess, S.: Ein System zur fallbasierten Wissensverarbeitung in technischen Diagnosesituationen. In: Retti, J. and Leidlmeier, K. (eds.), 5th Austrian AI-Conference, Springer Verlag, 1989; 65-70.
14. Bartsch-Spörl, B.: Ansätze zur Behandlung von fallorientiertem Erfahrungswissen in Expertensystemen. KI 4, 1987, 32-36.
15. Arcos, J. L., Plaza E.; Noos: an integrated framework for problem solving and learning. Proceedings of the KEML'97. 7th Workshop on Knowledge Engineering: Methods and Languages. England. (IIIA-RR-97-02), 1997.
16. Basili, V.R., Caldiera, G. & Rombach, H.D.: Experience Factory. In Marciniak, J.J. (ed.), Encyclopedia of SE, vol 1, John Wiley & Sons; 1994; 469–476.
17. Basili, V.R., Caldiera, G. & Rombach, H.D.: Goal Question Metric Paradigm. In Marciniak, J.J. (ed.), Encyclopedia of SE, vol 1, Wiley & Sons, 1994; 528-532.
18. Basili, V.R. & Rombach, H.D.: The TAME Project: Towards improvement-oriented software environments. IEEE Transactions on SE, SE-14(6), 1988; 758-773.
19. Basili, V.R.: Quantitative evaluation of software methodology. In Proceedings of the First Pan-Pacific Computer Conference, Melbourne, Australia, September 1985.
20. Bergmann, R., Althoff, K.-D., Breen, S., Göker, M., Manago, M., Traphöner, R. & Wess, S.: Developing Industrial Case-Based Reasoning Applications. LNAI 1612, Springer Verlag, Berlin, 2003.

21. Bullinger, H.-J. & Ilg, R.: Leben und Arbeiten in einer vernetzten, mobilen Welt. In Uhr, W., Esswein, W. & Schoop, E. (Hrsg.), Wirtschaftsinformatik 2003 Band I, Physica Verlag, 2003, 1-8.

22. Bundesministerium für Forschung und Technologie, Bekanntmachung über die Förderung von Forschungsvorhaben auf dem Gebiet „Wissensintensive Dienstleistungen", 14.1.2000.

23. Bibel, W., Andler, D., Da Costa, O., Küppers, G. & Pearson, I. D.: Converging Technologies and the Natural, Social and Cultural World. Report of the EU High Level Expert Group on "Forsighting the New Technology Wave" (FoNTWave), 30.6.2004.

24. Brasse, C. & Uhlmann, M.: Integration von Erfahrungswissen. In [32], S. 121-132.

25. Burkhard, H.-D.: Software-Agenten. In Görz, G., Rollinger, C.-R. & Schneeberger, J., Handbuch der Künstlichen Intelligenz, 4. Auflage, 2003, S. 943-1020.

26. Cramer, J.: Management wissensintensiver Dienstleistungen. In [32], S. 179-203.

27. Decker, B. & Althoff, K.-D.: Prozesslernen und Erfahrungsmanagement: Ergebnisse aus dem indiGo-Projekt. In: Proc. Lernen - Wissen – Adaptivität 2004 (LWA 2004), 138-145.

28. Ducatel, K., Bogdanowicz, M., Scapolo, F., Lejten, J. & Burgelman, J.-C.: Scenarios of Ambient Intelligence in 2010. IST Advisory Group (ISTAG), European Commission Community Research, 2001.

29. Gamma, Erich etal, Design Patterns: Elements of Reusable Object-Oriented Software, Addison-Wesley Professional Computing Series, 1997.

30. Hanft, A. & Minor, M.: A Low-Effort, Collaborative Maintenance Model for Textual CBR, Textual CBR Workshop on ICCBR 2005, Chicago, 2005.

31. Hanft, A.: Collaborative Maintenance in einem FBS System, diploma thesis, Humboldt University of Berlin, Berlin, 2004.

32. Hermann, S. (Hrsg.): Integrierter Schlussbericht - Verbundprojekt SIAM „Strategien, Instrumente und arbeitsorganisatorische Gestaltungsmodelle zur Förderung der Dienstleistungskompetenz in Unternehmen, 2003. http://www.siam.iao.fraunhofer.de/intern/intern-berichte/siam-schlussbericht-final.doc (Accessed on Oct. 20, 2005).

33. Hermann, S.: Produktive Wissensarbeit – Eine Herausforderung. In [32], S. 204-224.

34. JADE: Java Agent Development Framework, http://jade.tilab.com/, visited on 2006-02-06

35. Kiehl, M. Arbeitsmarktentwicklung und wissensintensive Dienstleistungen im östlichen Ruhrgebiet. Universität Dortmund, LS VWL, insb. Raumwirtschaftspolitik, Arbeitskreis Strukturpolitik, 12.6.2003.

36. Lenz, M., Burkhard, H.-D., Bartsch-Spörl, B., Wess, S. (eds.): In Case-Based Reasoning Technology - From Foundations to Applications, LNAI 1400, Springer-Verlag, Berlin 1998.

37. Muthig, D.: Systematischer Aufbau und Einsatz von Wissen zur effizienten Entwicklung von Software-Varianten. KI (2)2005, 5-11.

38. Nick, M.: Experience Maintenance through Closed-Loop Feedback. PhD Thesis, Department of Computer Science, University of Kaiserslautern, 2005.

39. Nick, M., Althoff, K.-D., Tautz, C.: Systematic Maintenance of Corporate Experince Repositories. Computational Intelligence 17(2), 2001, pp364-386.

40. Plaza, E., Aamodt, A., Ram, A., van de Velde, W., van Someren, M.: Integrated learning architectures. In: Machine Learning: ECML-93, European Conference on Machine Learning, Vienna, Austria, April 5-7 1993. Springer Verlag, 1993, pp.429-441 . http://www.iiia.csic.es/People/enric/ila.html.

41. Puppe, F.: Knowledge reuse among diagnostic problem-solving methods in the Shell-Kit D3. Int. Journal of Human Computer Studies, Volume 49, No 4, 1998, pp 627-649l

42. Rech, J. &, Althoff, K.-D.: Artificial Intelligence and Software Engineering - Status and Future Trends.Special Issue on Artificial Intelligence and Software Engineering, KI (3) 2004, 5-11.

43. Roth-Berghofer Thomas R.: Knowledge Maintenance of Case-Based Reasoning Systems – The SIAM Methodology, dissertation at University of Kaiserslautern, available as DISKI 262, Akademische Verlagsgesellschaft GmbH, Berlin 2003.

44. Schmid, K.: Systematische Wiederverwendung im Produktlinienumfeld – Ein Enscheidungsproblem. Special Issue on Artificial Intelligence & Software Engineering, KI (3) 2004, 33-35.

45. Schmid, K.: Planning Software Reuse — A Disciplined Scoping Approach for Software Product Lines. PhD thesis, University of Kaiserslautern, IRB Verlag, 2002.

46. Schank, R. C.: Dynamic Memory: A Theory of Learning in Computers and People. Cambridge University Press, 1982.

47. Tautz, C. & Althoff, K.-D.: A Case Study on Engineering Ontologies and Related Processes for Sharing Software Engineering Experience. In: Proc. 12th International Conference on Software Engineering and Knowledge Engineering (SEKE'00).

48. Tautz, C.: Customizing Software Engineering Experience Management Systems to OrganizationalOrganizational Needs. PhD Thesis, Department of Computer Science, University of Kaiserslautern; Fraunhofer IRB Verlag, 2000.

49. Watson, I. (ed.): Applying Knowledge Management: techniques for building corporate memories. Morgan Kaufmann Publishers Inc. San Francisco CA, 2003.

50. Web Service Standardization: http://www.w3.org/, visited on 2006-02-06.

51. Weiß, G. (Ed.): Multiagent systems. A modern approach to distributed artificial intelligence. The MIT Press, 1999.

52. Wess, S.: Fallbasiertes Problemlösen in wissensbasierten Systemen zur Entscheidungsunterstützung und Diagnostik, Dissertation, Department of Computer Science, University of Kaiserslautern, available as DISKI 126, infix Verlag, 1995.

53. Willke, H.: Organisierte Wissensarbeit. In: Zeitschrift für Soziologie, Vol 3, 1998, 161-177.

Retrieval over Conceptual Structures*

Pablo Beltrán-Ferruz, Belén Díaz-Agudo, and Oscar Lagerquist

Dep. Sistemas Informáticos y Programación
Universidad Complutense de Madrid, Spain
belend@sip.ucm.es

Abstract. The aim of the research conducted is to investigate how the knowledge in Ontologies can be used to acquire and refine the weights required in Case Retrieval Networks (CRNs). CRNs are designed to perform efficient retrieval processes even in large case bases but they lack from the flexibility and over restrict the circumstances under which the cases are retrieved. We investigate how ontologies can be used to relax these restrictions. We propose a retrieval method where the cases are embedded in a CRN but the weights are dynamically computed using the knowledge from the domain ontology and from the query description.

1 Introduction

Case Based Reasoning (CBR) is a technique within the field of machine learning that aims on solving problems using past experience. A case typically contains a problem description and a solution to the problem and is stored in a *case base*. The query describes the current problem that is compared with the cases in the case base. The most similar case or cases are then retrieved and their solutions presented to the user.

In the CBR literature there are many different approaches to case retrieval. We have taken into account what CBR researchers have considered to be requirements for a case retrieval method. The following three conditions should be met: [12]

Efficiency concerns with the time and resources used to retrieve cases similar to the query. Resource expensive approaches should be avoided.

Completeness guarantees that all cases with sufficient similarity is considered in the retrieval.

Flexibility expresses that there are no inherent restrictions concerning the circumstances under which a particular piece of knowledge can be recalled.

Note that these conditions have contradicting goals. When structuring the memory to reach efficiency it is most often to the cost of flexibility. This is the case of Case Retrieval Nets (CRNs), a well-known technique to retrieve cases efficiently from a large case base that is based on a structured memory model[11].

---

* Supported by the Spanish Committee of Education & Science (TIN05-09382-C02-01).

T.R. Roth-Berghofer et al. (Eds.): ECCBR 2006, LNAI 4106, pp. 443–457, 2006.

CRN technology is designed to perform efficient retrieval but it lacks from flexibility and restricts very much the circumstances under which the cases are retrieved. As we described in Section 3 the designer of a CRN provides a set of weights to adjust the relevance and similarity functions. If weight adjustment is made manually it becomes a tedious process that lacks of thoroughness, and can be incomplete or incorrect when the creator is not skilled enough. The problem with automatic processes is that they typically miss many of the inherent relationships between the entities. We claim that these relations are available and can be extracted from domain ontologies that include generic and reusable knowledge. Note that we use existing ontologies that are not created ad-hoc for each system.

We investigate how ontologies can be used to relax the restrictions that are inherent to CRNs. The aim of the research conducted is to integrate the use of CRNs with the knowledge in domain ontologies. Our previous work on knowledge intensive CBR [4,5] describes the benefits of building integrated systems that combine case specific knowledge with models of general domain knowledge. We have learnt that even though the main source of knowledge is a set of previous specific experiences, the system reasoning power can be improved through the use of general knowledge about the domain. For example, retrieval benefits from the similarity implicitly defined by the distance of two individuals using the subsumption links in the domain taxonomy. Different approaches to case retrieval based on instance recognition and concept classification have been proposed in the literature [9,18,2] but they are not usually applied to real size case bases due to efficiency problems.

We claim that the use of ontologies together with CRNs improves flexibility without losing efficiency. We propose a retrieval method where the cases are embedded in a CRN but weights are dynamically computed using the ontology knowledge and the query description. We keep the best of both worlds: the flexibility of ontology driven retrieval and the efficiency of CRNs.

We have performed our experiments within the jCOLIBRI framework. jCOLIBRI[1] is an object-oriented framework in Java for building different types of CBR systems [16]. The ontologies we are using for our experiments are mainly borrowed from the Semantic Web, are formalized in the OWL language [15] and are available from our web page[2].

The rest of the paper is structured as follows. Section 2 briefly introduces the example domain we are using in the paper. Section 3 and 4 describe, respectively, Case Retrieval Nets and Classification Based Retrieval. Section 5 describes our approach to enrich the CRN structure within the knowledge in the domain ontology. We use the ontology to compute the weights of the relevance and similarity functions in CRNs. Section 6 compares the three approaches: retrieval with CRNs, classification based retrieval and CRNs enriched with ontologies. Section 7 summarizes the results and concludes the paper.

---

[1] http://sourceforge.net/projects/jcolibri-cbr/
[2] http://gaia.fdi.ucm.es/ontologies/index.html

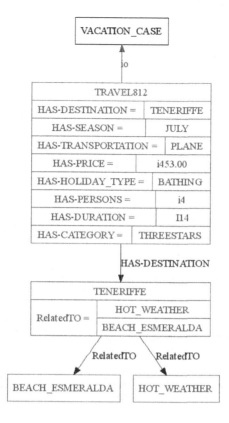

Fig. 1. Travel example case

2   Travel Domain

Imagine an online catalog of a travel agency. Every single travel is represented by a case in the travel case base. A recommender CBR system retrieves the vacation that best matches a client request. The values that represent a vacation case are instances and concepts ordered in a conceptual taxonomy. We use the *vacations ontology* that is formalized in the OWL language [15] and is available through our web page[3].

The case base and the ontology are both quite simple, easy to understand and adequate for our experiment. On the top of the taxonomy we have the node CBR_INDEX and it is the parent node for all the concepts. We have concepts for each one of the case attributes. The attributes can be of different types; namely of infinitive nature like price and duration, or of finite nature like holiday type and destination.

We are using a case base of 1024 cases[4] each with 11 attributes describing different holiday/hotel destinations. A typical case within the case base might

---

[3] http://gaia.fdi.ucm.es/ontologies/index.html
[4] www.ai-cbr.org/cases.html

look like the one in Figure 1. The case describes a vacation to the Spanish island *Tenerife*. It offers a two weeks vacation on a three stars hotel for four people. The season for this vacation is July and you will get there with a plane for 453 Euros.

Consider a customer that wants to go with his family to *Gran Canaria* for vacation. He wants to go to a warm and relaxing destination but does not want to spend more than 500 euros.

Ideally, he would use some kind of form to place his query. The input from the user would be interpreted by the system as a problem description and a set of suitable solutions should be presented. The case of Figure 1 is a case that might be retrieved and presented to the user, although the destination is *Tenerife*. The system will realize that *Gran Canaria* and *Tenerife* are both two Canary islands with similar properties.

3   Case Retrieval Nets

Executing a query in a large Case Base is an expensive and time-consuming task. Several sophisticated techniques to deal with this problem have been presented by many researchers. Mario Lenz at the Dept. of Computer Science, Humboldt University Berlin presents a memory model called Case Retrieval Nets [11] that takes ideas from Artificial Neural Networks (ANN). The key idea of the network is to apply a spreading activation to find the most similar case to a given query. While more traditional techniques use a top-down approach, CRN use a bottom-up process that propagates, in an efficient and flexible manner, the query values towards the cases.

3.1   Brief Explanation of the Net Structure

The nodes in the CRN are built up by Information Entities (IEs), which are attribute-value pairs. Each case holds a set of IE nodes that describes its features. All nodes are placed in the network and they are the most essential part of the CRN. If two cases have an identical attribute-value-pair they will share the same IE node. IE nodes that are similar to each other will have a weighted connection beltwren them describing the similarity. When a query is executed in the network, the IE nodes similar to the query values will be activated. These activated IE nodes will propagate the activation to similar IE nodes using the weighted connection, in a manner similar to ANN. All activated IE nodes will then propagate their value to the connected cases.

The main idea of CRNs is illustrated with a travel agency example. The system will return vacations that are similar to a given query. In the example a user has told the system that he would like to go to *Gran Canaria* on vacation and the IE node representing *Gran Canaria* will be activated (Figure 2). The IE node is also connected to other destinations like *Mallorca* and *Cyprus* since they share similar features; they are all islands with a warm climate. However,

Query: Destination: Gran Canaria
       Season: June
       Holiday type: Bathing
       ...

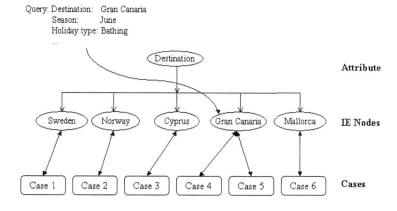

Fig. 2. Example of a CRN showing the Destination Attribute with connected IE nodes and cases

the destinations Sweden and Norway will not be activated since they are rather different to the query destination. Note that both the vacation cases four and five have the same destination and therefore share the same IE node.

3.2   A Formal Mathematical Model of Basic Case Retrieval Nets

Here follows a formal mathematical definition of the Basic CRN (BCRN). A set of different extensions to BCRNs exist, but they are all based on this mathematical model. For more information, see [12,11].

Definition 1. An Information Unit or Entity (IE) is an atomic knowledge item in the domain, i.e. an IE represents the smallest part of knowledge representation, such as a particular attribute-value-pair.

Definition 2. A *case* consists of a unique case descriptor and a set of IEs.

Definition 3. A *Basic Case Retrieval Net* (BCRN) is defined as a structure $N = [E, C, \sigma, \rho, \Pi]$ where
E is the finite set of IE nodes;
C is the finite set of case nodes;
σ is the *similarity function*

$$\sigma : E \times E \to R$$

which describes the similarity $\sigma(e', e'')$ between IEs e', e'';

ρ is the *relevance function*

$$\rho : E \times C \to R$$

which describes the relevance $\rho(e, c)$ of the IE e to the case c;

Π is the set of *propagation functions*

$$\pi_n : R^E \to R.$$

for each node $n \in E \cup C$.

The relevance between a case and each IE node is given by the relevance function $\rho(e, c)$. If there is no arc between the IE node and the case the function will return zero. The similarity function indicates how similar two IE nodes are to each other. Likewise, if there is no arc between them the similarity will be zero. When the relevance and the similarity have been calculated, the propagation function $\pi_n : R^E \to R$ calculates the propagation value. These values will be used to calculate a nodes activation value using the activation function α.

Definition 4. An *activation* of a BCRN $N = [E, C, \sigma, \rho, \Pi]$ is a function $\alpha : E \cup C \to R$

Considering the BCRN, the activation at a given time $t + 1$ is:

$$\alpha_{t+1}(e) = \pi_e(\sigma(e_1, e) \cdot \alpha_t(e_1), \dots, \sigma(e_s, e) \cdot \alpha_t(e_s))$$

for IE nodes and

$$\alpha_{t+1}(c) = \pi_c(\rho(e_1, c) \cdot \alpha_t(e_1), \dots, \rho(e_s, c) \cdot \alpha_t(e_s))$$

for cases.

The activation of a case c or an IE node e is determined by the activation function. The value computed by the function tells the importance of the current node with respect to the given query. Also, negative values can be used to express rejections of cases that contain a certain IE node. To place a query in the system, all IE nodes in the system that are described in the query will be activated at time zero: $\alpha_0(e)$ is 1 for the IE nodes e in the query, and 0 otherwise.

4   Classification Based Retrieval

When rich domain models are available, we can use a representational approach to solve the case retrieval task. This method assigns similarity meaning to the path joining two individuals in the domain model. With this approach A is more similar to B than C to B iff A is closer to B than C. When this approach uses the subsumption links in the domain taxonomy to define the distance between two individuals, it is called Knowledge intensive Classification Based Retrieval. It has been described in the literature [10,20,9,14,18,7,3].

Our specific method [7] is based on a formal representation of the domain knowledge using Description Logics (DLs)[1], so that we can rely on its reasoning capabilities to automatically organize the cases according to their descriptors.

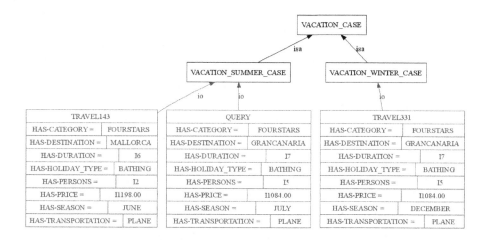

Fig. 3. Classification Based Retrieval

4.1   Brief Explanation of Classification Based Retrieval

Knowledge Intensive Classification Based Retrieval strongly depends on the knowledge structure where cases are located. We begin with an ontology of primitive domain concepts representing the basic domain vocabulary (or terminology) and complete the domain model with other *defined concepts*. Each explicitly included defined concept represents a meaningful abstraction, and, therefore, the very existence of that concept should affect the similarity function. Defined concepts are described by the necessary and sufficient restrictions to be satisfied for their instances (see [1] for a detailed introduction to DLs).

These concept definitions can be included manually or extracted from the case base using inductive techniques. In [3] we have proposed the use of Formal Concept Analysis as an inductive technique that elicits knowledge embedded in a concrete case library and enriches the domain conceptual taxonomy.

All cases in the *casebase* are classified as instances of defined concepts verifying if they fulfil their necessary and sufficient conditions [1].

For example, Figure 4 includes the definition of the VACATION_RELAX _CASE concept. A travel case c_i is recognized as an instance of this concept if the travel properties of c_i agree with the restrictions within the concept definition, in this case, a relax travel is a travel where the destination country has a beach and the season of the travel is summer.

Once the case base is classified below a set of concepts –we call them index concepts– each new query is treated as a case and classified in the hierarchy. Classification based retrieval filters the case base and selects cases sharing the same classification than the query.

This retrieval method chooses those cases having more and more specific common index concepts with the query. For example in Figure 3 we should obtain case TRAVEL143 instead of TRAVEL331. Query and TRAVEL143 shares

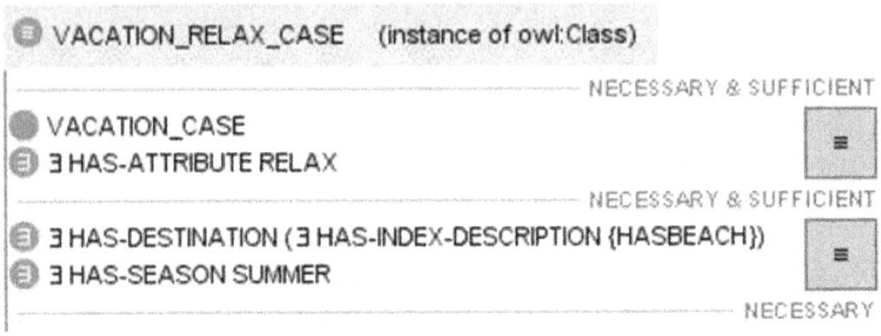

Fig. 4. Defined Concept: Vacation type Relax

the index concepts VACATION_SUMMER_CASE and VACATION_CASE, and TRAVEL331 and query only shares the root concept VACATION_CASE.

Next subsection formalizes the classification based approach.

4.2   A Formal Model of Classification Based Retrieval

We are interested in computing the similarity between a given pair of individuals: one representing the query, and another representing the candidate case description. An individual is defined in terms of the concepts of which is an instance and the roles explicitly asserted for it or entailed by the contents of the Knowledge Base ($\mathcal{KB}$). In DLs, the roles of an individual are represented as relations connecting the individual to other individuals or primitive values (*fillers*).

The concept-based similarity between two individuals will be given by the similarity between the two sets of concepts of which those individuals are instances. We can simplify the problem by selecting only the most specific concepts from both sets, since a concept carries all the information contained in its superconcepts. A further simplification is to consider, as the most on point concept for describing an individual, the one obtained as the conjunction of the most specific concepts of which that individual is an instance, which may or may not exist in the concept taxonomy. This way we reduce the problem of comparing two sets of concepts to that of comparing two single concepts.

Evaluating relatedness using network representations is a problem with a long history in Artificial Intelligence. A natural way to evaluate semantic similarity in a taxonomy is to evaluate the distance between the nodes corresponding to the items being compared: the shorter the path from one node to another is, the more similar they are. A problem with this *intensional approach*, however, is that it relies on the notion that links in the taxonomy represent uniform distances.

An alternative *extensional approach* can be applied when nodes in the taxonomy represent classes of individuals, which are also available in the system, as is the case in DLs with concepts and its instances. In this case, the similarity between two concepts can be obtained, basically, by the number of its common instances. This is the approach described in [17], extended with ideas from information theory. The problem with the extensional approach is that it relies on a basic assumption, which may or may not apply for a given $\mathcal{KB}$, namely, that concepts are evenly populated with instances. A non-homogeneous distribution of individuals among concepts will bias the similarity measure, since the number of instances determines the information content.

Notice that both (intensional and extensional) approaches present a non-monotonic behavior; different results will be obtained for the similarity between two given concepts as concepts and/or individuals are added or removed from the $\mathcal{KB}$.

For concept-based similarity we adopt an intensional approach where we have applied the *vector space model* used in Information Retrieval [19]. In this model, every indexable item is represented by an attribute vector, and the similarity between two items is obtained by some kind of algebraic manipulation of the vectors associated with them.

We consider as attributes the concepts defined in the $\mathcal{KB}$. Formally, given the set $C = \{c_1, \ldots, c_N\}$ of concepts defined in a $\mathcal{KB}$, for each concept $c_i \in C$ we define a vector v_i such that its component k equals 1 if c_k subsumes c_i, and 0 otherwise.

Once the vectors have been built, the *conceptual similarity* between two concepts is computed as the cosine of the angle formed by the vectors representing them, a similarity function usually applied in the vector space model:

$$\text{sim}(c_i, c_j) = \frac{v_i \cdot v_j}{\|v_i\| \cdot \|v_j\|}$$

In [6] it is proved that this expression is equivalent to the following one, the one that we really use to compute the similarity among concepts:

$$\text{sim}(c_i, c_j) = \frac{|\bigcap \text{super}(c_i, C)\text{super}(c_j, C)|}{\sqrt{|\text{super}(c_i, C)|} \cdot \sqrt{|\text{super}(c_j, C)|}}$$

where $\text{super}(c, C)$ computes the set of concepts in C which are superconcepts of c. So, the similarity between two concepts is given by the number of their common superconcepts and their total number of superconcepts, which can be dynamically computed, making unnecessary the explicit representation of attribute vectors.

Although this retrieval method is very powerful and flexible it lacks from good efficiency behavior. Next section describes our approach to enrich CRNs with the knowledge of the conceptual taxonomy.

5   CRNs Enriched with Ontologies

CRNs based retrieval is based on the weights of the functions of similarity σ and relevance ρ. In order to construct these two functions we can decide on two solutions: let an expert include the weights manually, so that she has to label each one of the relations between the IE nodes; or use of an automatic method.

Our work belongs the second group. The problem typically associated to these automatic methods it that they lose the inherent relations that exist between the

IE nodes [13,8]. To solve this problem, we propose using conceptual taxonomies to automatically calculate the weights needed for the σ and ρ functions. As we describe in next section we propose using the classification of the concepts of the ontology to obtain the values of the similarity function (σ) and to use the relations that occur between these concepts to obtain the relevance function (ρ).

5.1   Formalization of the Weight Computation Based on Classification

For the calculation of the weights of the functions of similarity and relevance we use querying and reasoning capabilities of DLs over the ontology.

We state that two concepts are more similar when they are closer in the taxonomy. In this way we can use the same expression as we used in clasification based retrieval to compute σ :

$$\sigma\left(c_{i}, c_{j}\right)=\frac{\left|\bigcap \operatorname{super}(c_{i}, C) \operatorname{super}(c_{j}, C)\right|}{\sqrt{\left|\operatorname{super}(c_{i}, C)\right|} \cdot \sqrt{\left|\operatorname{super}(c_{j}, C)\right|}}$$

Besides, the relevance function we are calculating is based on the relations that are common to the query. Then we estimate that cases that contain more relations with other instances similar to the query are preferred before cases where properties have not been specified or are different from the query.

We consider that an instance is defined by its relations given by the set

$$\left\{R_{1}\left(I_{R_{1}, 1}, I_{R_{1}, 2}\right), \ldots, R_{N}\left(I_{R_{N}, 1}, I_{R_{N}, 2}\right)\right\}$$

and the query Q by

$$\left\{R_{1}\left(Q_{R_{1}, 1}, Q_{R_{1}, 2}\right), \ldots, R_{N}\left(Q_{R_{N}, 1}, Q_{R_{N}, 2}\right)\right\}$$

The calculation of the relevance function is:

$$\rho\left(I, C\right)=_{i=1}^{n} \sum \sigma\left(C_{I_{i, 2}}, C_{Q_{j, 2}}\right)\Big|_{I_{j} \in C, Q_{j, 2} \in C_{Q_{j, 2}}, R_{j}(I_{j}, Q_{j, 2}) \in I, R_{i}=R_{j}}^{I_{i} \in C, I_{i, 2} \in C_{I_{i, 2}}, R_{i}(I_{i}, I_{i, 2}) \in I}$$

Figure 5 allows observing the operation of these functions for the calculation of similarity for the IE nodes.

$\sigma(Hotel\text{-}A, Hotel\text{-}B) = 1/4 \longrightarrow$ They have a common parent at level two (Middle-class-hotel).

$\sigma(Restaurant\text{-}R, Restaurant\text{-}S) = 1/2 \longrightarrow$ They have a common parent at level one (Restaurant).

$\rho(I, Middle\text{-}class\text{-}hotel) = \sigma(Restaurant\text{-}R, Restaurant\text{-}S) = 1/2 \longrightarrow$ Instance I has a relation with an instance (Hotel-A) of Middle-class-hotel. Hotel-A has the relation "has-attribute" in common with the query. Fillers of these common relations are used to compute ρ function. In this example, has-attribute(Hotel-A,Restaurant-R) and has-attribute (Hotel-B,Restaurant-S).

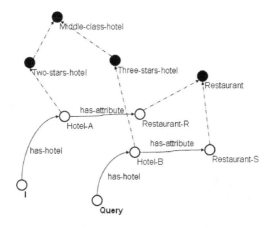

Fig. 5. Example of CRN enriched with ontologies

Retrieval works like in a CRN system but we use this approach to calculate the value of the σ and ρ functions in execution time. Note that the key point here is that the functions are dynamically calculated depending on the specific query and the inferences and the new knowledge we can obtain from the query and the ontology.

6   Retrieval Methods Comparison

The retrieval methods described in previous sections have been implemented and included in the method library of the jCOLIBRI framework. We have tested these methods with the travel case base. Next subsections summarize the results.

6.1   Advantages and Drawbacks of CRNs

The major advantage of retrieval using CRNs is that it provides efficient retrieval even with large case bases. During the spreading activation the similarity between IE nodes is computed. Several extensions and approaches exist [12].

However, retrieval with CRNs presents limitations as far as flexibility concerns. The reason is that having fixed values for weights does is not flexible in the sense that the same property could have a different importance (weight) depending on the specific query. For example, if the query is about a business travel the proximity of the destination is, generally, much more important than in a leisure travel. Holiday travels usually require to keep the type of holidays restrictions (like "I want to go to the beach") but not the specific destination. Thus if we have assigned weights to make the system retrieve leisure travels the configured CRN will not be able to adapt to different types of queries.

Besides, even if CRNs is a very efficient retrieval method used with simple cases, CRNs might not be the best choice in domains where structural similarity plays an important role; and they can not be applied in domains where the

▼ ● VACATION_NO_RELAX_CASE
   ▼ ● VACATION_BUSINESS_CASE
      ► ● VACATION_EUROPE_BUSINESS_CASE
      ► ● VACATION_AMERICA_BUSSINESS_CASE
   ► ● VACATION_FAMILY_CASE
▼ ● VACATION_RELAX_CASE
   ► ● VACATION_SPRING_CASE
   ► ● VACATION_SUMMER_CASE
   ► ● VACATION_WINTER_CASE
   ► ● VACATION_AUTUM_CASE

Fig. 6. Part of defined concept hierarchy

internal structure of cases is crucial [11]. Another drawback of this technique is that is very retrieval specialized, i.e., it does not allow to cover other processes of the CBR cycle. For instance, it does not cover aspects such as how the retrieved cases can be reused, or how learning could be integrated into the system. In this sense other techniques have to be integrated into the system to make it complete.

6.2   Advantages and Drawbacks of Classification Based Retrieval

We have made queries with different types of travels using classification based retrieval. Our method works well and it is able to flexibly adapt to different types of queries and to the knowledge variations in the ontology concepts. Depending on the hierarchy of defined concepts we can vary the importance of the attributes (see Figure 6).

The main disadvantage we have pointed out with the experiment is retrieval efficiency. The problem is due to the query classification into the concept taxonomy in runtime.

As an advantage –even if it has not been exemplified in the experiment– case representation based on DLs is specially well suited in domains where cases are internally structured. In the simple example used in this paper we have oversimplified the representation capabilities of DLs, because we have used simple cases – the one used by CRNs – that ignore the relationships among IEs.

There are other advantages regarding the explicit representation of the domain knowledge. For example, the same knowledge base can be used during adaptation to find substitutes for a certain item, and to check dependencies and consistency of the adapted case. Besides, case learning is extremely easy to implement, as we only have to write the new case and rely on the automatic classification capabilities.

6.3   Advantages and Drawbacks of CRN Enriched with Ontologies

Retrieval over CRNs enriched with ontologies keeps the best of both worlds: the flexibility of ontology driven retrieval and the efficiency of CRNs.

Efficiency: Problems about efficiency in classification based retrieval are due mainly to classification tasks. Classifying the original ontology provided by ex-

	Time
Case Retrieval Nets	8 ms
Classification Based Retrieval	38200 ms
CRNs enriched with ontologies	10 ms

Fig. 7. Time Comparison

perts could be done as a pre-execution task and its time is not taken into account. The problem arises if each time we have a new query, we need to re-classify the ontology to calculate similarity measures.

In this approach classifying the query is not required because we compute similarity using CRN methods. Calculations needed in similarity and relevance function do not need to make any classification task. So, this method is nearly as efficient as conventional CRNs, see figure 7.

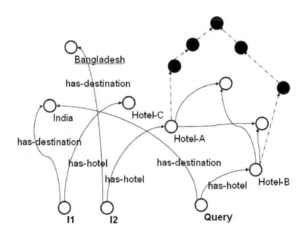

Fig. 8. Retrieval example

Flexibility: Flexibility advantages are due to the fact that similarity is dynamically defined using the relations established between the cases and the query.

The calculation of the weights of the similarity and relevance functions using the ontology causes that these weights can vary according to the relations between instances of the ontology.

As an additional advantage, system designers can define similarity among cases using a descriptive approach by creating relations in the ontology rather than establishing numerical measures. They could also benefit from DLs inferred knowledge.

Final users also benefit from flexibility. The more details are given about one specific characteristic, the more information is taken into account and more accuracy results achieved.

For example, in Figure 8, I1 and Query has the same destination. Although I2 and Query have different destinations, detailed information about the hotel is given in the query and it is taken into account. In this case relevance function makes that I2 is retrieved as the more similar case.

7   Conclusions

In the CBR literature there are many different approaches to case retrieval making a tradeoff between efficiency, completeness and flexibility properties. There are techniques like Case Retrieval Nets, that prioritize the efficiency at flexibility expenses because they over restrict the circumstances under which the cases are retrieved. Other knowledge intensive techniques rely on domain models that allow different similarity criteria on the same query and case base. However they lack from good results regarding efficiency.

The aim of the research conducted is to investigate how the knowledge in Ontologies can be used to acquire and refine the weights required in Case Retrieval Networks.

We propose a retrieval method where the cases are embedded in a CRN but the weights are dynamic computed using the knowledge from the domain ontology and from the query description.

CRNs retrieval is based on the weights of the similarity and relevance functions. If weight adjustment is made manually it becomes a tedious process that lacks from thoroughness, and can be incomplete or incorrect when the creator is not skilled enough. The problem with automatic processes is that they typically miss many of the inherent relationships between the entities. We claim that these relations are available and can be extracted from previously existing domain ontologies. The main idea consists of using the classification of the concepts of the ontology to obtain the values of the similarity function and to use the relations that occur between these concepts to obtain the relevance function.

We have shown that our method shares advantages but lacks from the main disadvantage of CRNs. It is practically as efficient as conventional CRNs but it is much more flexible, as it is possible to define the similarity between the concepts dynamically depending on the domain relations existing among them. We have tested our method using the well known travel example domain We have developed the prototype using jCOLIBRI: an open source framework to develop CBR systems.

References

1. F. Baader, D. Calvanese, D. McGuinness, D. Nardi, and P. Patel-Scheneider, editors. *The Description Logic Handbook*, 2005.
2. B. Díaz-Agudo and P. A. González-Calero. Classification based retrieval using formal concept analysis. In *Case-Based Reasoning Research and Development, 4th International Conference on Case-Based Reasoning, ICCBR 2001*, pages 173–188.
3. B. Díaz-Agudo and P. A. González-Calero. A declarative similarity framework for knowledge intensive CBR. In *Case-Based Reasoning Research and Development, 4th International Conference on CBR, ICCBR 2001*, pages 158–172.

4. B. Díaz-Agudo and P. A. González-Calero. An architecture for knowledge intensive cbr systems. In *Advances in Case-Based Reasoning, 5th European Workshop,
   EWCBR 2000*, pages 37–48, 2000.
5. B. Díaz-Agudo and P. A. Gonz'alez-Calero. Knowledge intensive CBR through
   ontologies, 2001.
6. P. González-Calero. *Aplicación de técnicas basadas en conocimiento como soporte
   a la reutilización en bibliotecas orientadas a objetos. PhD Dissertation*. Departamento de Informática y Automática, Universidad Complutense de Madrid, 1997.
7. P. Gonzalez-Calero, B. Diaz-Agudo, and M. Gomez. Applying DLs for retrieval
   in case-based reasoning. *Procs of the Description Logics International Workshop
   (DL'99)*, 1999.
8. R. Hervás and P. Gervás. Case retrieval nets for heuristic lexicalization in natural
   language generation. In C. Bento, A. Cardoso, and G. Dias, editors, *EPIA*, volume
   3808 of *Lecture Notes in Computer Science*, pages 55–66. Springer, 2005.
9. G. Kamp. Using description logics for knowledge intensive case-based reasoning.
   In *Advances in Case-Based Reasoning, Third European Workshop, EWCBR-96*,
   pages 204–218, 1996.
10. J. Koehler. An application of terminological logics to case-based reasoning. *Pro-
    cedings of Knowledge Representation KR'94*, 1994.
11. M. Lenz. Case retrieval nets as a model for building flexible information sys-
    tems. phd thesis, mathematisch-naturwissenschaftliche fakultat ii der humboldt-
    universitat zu berlin, 1999. 1999.
12. M. Lenz and H.-D. Burkhard. Case retrieval nets: Basic ideas and extensions. In
    KI - Kunstliche Intelligenz, pages 227–239, 1996.
13. M. Lenz, H.-D. Burkhard, and S. Brückner. Applying case retrieval nets to diagnos-
    tic tasks in technical domains. In I. F. C. Smith and B. Faltings, editors, *EWCBR*,
    volume 1168 of *Lecture Notes in Computer Science*, pages 219–233. Springer, 1996.
14. A. Napoli, J. Lieber, and A. Simon. A classification-based approach to case-based
    reasoning, 1997.
15. Web ontology language. `http://www.w3.org/2004/OWL/`.
16. J. A. Recio, A. Sánchez, B. Díaz-Agudo, and P. González-Calero, editors.
    jCOLIBRI 1.0 in a nutshell. A software tool for designing CBR systems,
    http://ukcbr.org.uk/. Cambridge, UK, 2005.
17. P. Resnik. Using information content to evaluate semantic similarity in a taxonomy.
    In *Procs. IJCAI'95*, 1995.
18. S. Salotti and V. Ventos. Study and formalization of a case-based reasoning system
    using a description logic. In *Advances in Case-Based Reasoning, 4th European
    Workshop, EWCBR-98*, pages 286–297, 1998.
19. G. Salton and M. J. McGill. *Introduction to Modern Information Retrieval*. 1983.
20. J. Yen, H. Teh, and X. Liu. Using description logics for software reuse and case-
    based reasoning. *Procdings of Description Logics Workshop DL'94*, 1994.

An Analysis on Transformational Analogy: General Framework and Complexity

Vithal Kuchibatla and Héctor Muñoz-Avila

Department of Computer Science & Engineering;
Lehigh University; Bethlehem, PA 18015

Abstract. In this paper we present TransUCP, a general framework for transformational analogy. Using our framework we demonstrate that transformational analogy does not meet a crucial condition for a well-known worst-case complexity scenario, and therefore the results about plan adaptation being computationally harder than planning from the scratch does not apply to transformational analogy. We prove this by constructing a counter-example that does not meet this condition. Furthermore, we perform experiments that demonstrate that this counter-example is not an exception. Rather, our experiments show that it is unlikely that this condition will be met when performing plan adaptation with transformational analogy.

1 Introduction

Transformational analogy is a problem-solving technique in which a pre-selected plan, defined as a sequence of actions, is modified to solve a new problem (Carbonell, 1983). Possible modifications to the plan include removing actions, adding new actions, and changing the parameters from actions. Interest on transformational analogy started from early case-based reasoning systems (Cox et al., 2006). In particular, the CHEF system constructs cooking recipes, which are plans because recipes are sequences of cooking steps such as boiling a certain amount of water (Hammond, 1990). These recipes are modified depending on factors such as the ingredients currently available.

Over the years, derivational analogy, an alternative problem-solving technique that advocates reusing the sequence of derivations that led to a solution plan rather than the plan itself, gained prominence among the case-based planning community. Part of the reason for this prominence is the interest in problem solving by combining first-principles planners and case-based reasoning. If the first-principles planner is used to generate plans, then it is straightforward to annotate the derivations that these planners followed to obtain the plans (Veloso, 1994). Thus, derivational analogy is a good fit for this line of research. There has been recent work on developing DerUCP, a framework using derivational analogy (Au et al., 2002). It enhances the universal classical planning (UCP) framework to build a generic, domain-independent plan adaptation algorithm. An analysis of DerUCP demonstrates that it does not fall under the worst-case complexity scenario by Nebel and Koehler (1995), and therefore, their results about plan adaptation been computationally harder than plan adaptation does not apply to it.

T.R. Roth-Berghofer et al. (Eds.): ECCBR 2006, LNAI 4106, pp. 458–473, 2006.

Despite some well-documented applications of derivational analogy, a major difficulty of using this technique is the requirement about the availability of the derivational trace that led to a solution. Even when a domain theory is available, we might not know how a particular plan was created. For example, the rules for playing chess are known but we might not know the reasoning behind a player making a sequence of moves. This knowledge engineering requirement of derivational analogy is well known (Cunningham *et al.*, 1996). Perhaps for this reason, application-oriented papers in case-based reasoning conferences that use some form of adaptation frequently use transformational analogy. Yet, despite this interest no general framework for analyzing transformational analogy exists to date.

In this paper, we present TransUCP, a general framework for transformational analogy built on top of UCP. Using our framework we demonstrate that transformational analogy does not meet the worst-case complexity results of Nebel and Koehler (1995), and therefore, their results about plan adaptation been computationally harder than plan adaptation does not apply to it. We prove this by constructing a counter-example in which a crucial condition is not met. Furthermore, we perform experiments that demonstrate that this counter-example is not en exception. Rather, our experiments show that it is very unlikely that transformational analogy falls under the scenario described in Nebel and Koehler (1995).

The paper continues as follows. The next section describes the Universal Classical Framework, on which TransUCP is based. Section 3 presents TransUCP. The next two sections describe an example of problem-solving with TransUCP and analyze the search space followed by TransUCP. Section 6 proves that TransUCP does not fall under the scenario of Nebel and Koehler (1995). The next section describes the experimental results. We conclude this paper with some final remarks.

2 Background

The SPA system (Hanks and Weld, 1995) is a general purpose algorithm for transformational analogy. SPA takes advantage of the partial-order plan representation of partial-order planners to modify an existing plan. Our general framework enhances SPA to other forms of planning by taking advantage of the UCP framework, which we describe below.

2.1 Partial Plan

The algorithm proposed in this paper uses to a large extent similar representation format and data structures as of that used in the UCP algorithm as proposed by Kambhampati and Srivastava, (1995). A partial plan is represented by the 4-tuple $<T, O, B, L>$ where:

- T is the set of all the steps in the partial plan,
- O is the set of ordering constraints between the steps of T,
- B is the set of binding (co-designation constraints, which require variables to take the same value) and prohibitive bindings (non co-designation constraints, which requires variables not to take the same value) in the preconditions and post-conditions of the operators, and,

- L is the set of auxiliary constraints, which are of 3 types:
  - ○ Ordering constraints are of the form ($t_i \rightarrow t_j$) indicating that step t_i precedes step t_j, though not necessarily immediately.
  - ○ Interval Preservation Constraints which are the form ($t_i \rightarrow^Q t_j$) which means that the condition Q has to be true between the steps t_i and t_j of T. This is a "causal link" used in partial-order planners such as SNLP. If ($t_i \rightarrow^Q t_j$) holds, it implies that ($t_i \rightarrow t_j$) also holds.
  - ○ Contiguity constraints, which are the form ($t_i * t_j$) which means that the step t_i has to be immediately followed by step t_j.

We illustrate these concepts with an example in the logistics transportation domain. In this domain, there are different packages located at various locations and some or all of these packages have to be re-located to specific locations. There are also means of transportation such as trucks located at various cities and these are used to move the packages. The instance of the problem used here is the same as that used by Au *et al.* (2002). The problem shown in Figure 1 requires package P1 in location A, and package P2 in location D, to be relocated in location C. The figure also shows two trucks V1 and V2 at locations A and D respectively.

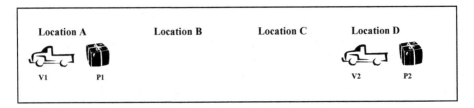

Fig. 1. Planning problem in the logistics transportation domain

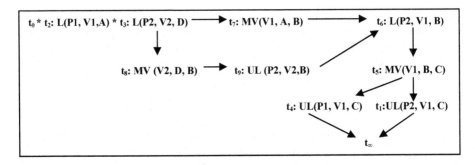

Fig. 2. Partial plan solving the problem in Figure 1

Figure 2 shows a partial plan solving the problem depicted in Figure 1. Arrows denote either ordering or interval preservation constraints. The plan consists of 11 steps, denoted by t_k. Steps t_0 and t_∞ are special steps that we will explain momentarily. The other steps are labeled according to the following conventions:

- The action L (P,V,Lc) indicates that the vehicle V is *loading* the package P from location Lc.
- UL (P,V,Lc) indicates that P is *unloaded* from V onto location Lc.
- MV (V, L1, L2) indicates that V is *moved* from L1 to L2.

Under these conventions P1 is loaded in V1 and P2 into V2. P2 is relocated in B using V2, where it is picked by V1, which has moved from A to B. V1 continues to C, where both packages are unloaded. Besides these steps, other primary attributes of a partial plan are its open conditions and threats. A *condition* has the form ($\rightarrow^Q t_k$) indicating that the condition Q has to be satisfied for step t_j. Each step t_j in the plan can produce effects ($t_j \rightarrow^Q$) which can be used to satisfy conditions. A condition $\rightarrow^Q t_k$ *is satisfied* by adding an interval preservation constraints $t_m \rightarrow^Q t_k$, such that $t_m \rightarrow^Q$ holds. If a condition has not been satisfied, it is said to be an *open condition*. A *threat* is a 3-tuple ($t_k, t_i \rightarrow^Q t_j$) where t_k can be inserted between t_i and t_j and the post condition of t_k can negate or add Q. Threats occur as a result of the partial ordering between steps. So for example, the condition Q might use a truck to satisfy a condition in t_j, but another step t_k might use the same truck. Threats are solved by adding constraints to the plan such as ordering relations between steps. For instance, one might reorder the steps to make sure that the truck is used only once at any point of time.

Operators have a set of preconditions which must be satisfied before the step can be applied and a set of post-conditions which are true after the step has been applied. When an operator is applied it is added to a plan as a step. This is how steps t_1 to t_9 where added to the plan in Figure 2. When planning starts a so-called initial *null plan* is created. This plan consists of two steps: t_0 and t_∞. The step t_0, called the initial state, has no preconditions and has as effects the conditions that are true in the opening state. The step t_∞, called the *final state*, has no effects and has as the conditions the goals to be achieved. The null plan has also an ordering constraint, $t_0 \rightarrow t_\infty$, and no bindings. The objective of the planning problem is to refine the initial plan into a *solution plan*, a partial plan with no open conditions and no threats. Open conditions and threats in a partial plan are referred to as *flaws* of the plan.

2.2 Universal Classical Planning

The Universal Classical Planner (UCP) takes a partial plan and performs refinements to it in an iterative manner until a solution plan is generated. During each pass of the iteration, the refinement done to the plan can be addition of steps or constraints to the existing partial plan. The possible types of refinements that a UCP planner can choose to perform on the partial plan on each iterative pass are:

i.   **Forward state space plan refinement:** A head step of a partial plan is defined as a step t_j of the plan where $t_0 * t_1 * \ldots * t_j$ and there is no step $t`$ such that $t_j * t`$. The sequence of steps $t_0 * t_1 * \ldots * t_j$ is called the header of the plan. The set of all states t_i that can immediately follow the head step t_j is called the head fringe. Forward state space plan refinement involves selecting a new step or a step from the head fringe of a plan and appending it to its header.

ii. **Backward state space plan refinement:** A tail step of a partial plan is defined as the step of t_j of the plan where $t_j * t_{j-1} * \ldots * t_\infty$ and there is no step $t`$ such that $t` * t_j$. The sequence of steps $t_j * t_{j-1} * \ldots * t_\infty$ is called the trailer of the plan. The set of all states t_i that can immediately precede the tail step t_j is called the tail fringe. Backward state space plan refinement involves selecting a new step or a step from the tail fringe of a plan and putting it immediately before its trailer.

iii. **Partial plan space refinement:** During plan space refinement, a flaw is selected at random from the current plan. This flaw could be either an open condition or a threat. If it is an open condition, it is resolved by adding or changing ordering constraints to the plan or by adding a new step such that it satisfies the required open condition. There can be more than one way to reorder the steps and, similarly, there can be more than one step that can be added to satisfy the open condition. Therefore, resolving the open condition can result in multiple partial plans. If the selected flaw is a threat, it is handled by a "Resolve Threat" function. Given a threat of the form $(t_k, t_i \rightarrow^Q t_j)$, this function resolves it by either

- Ordering t_k before t_i consistently, or,
- Ordering t_k after1 t_j consistently, or,
- Adding the appropriate binding constraints to the plan so as to negate the threat

Figure 3 illustrates the working of a universal classical planner. During each iteration, it can choose one of the above three refinements and modify the partial plan according to the selected refinement strategy.

2.3 Definitions

In this paper, we introduce the TransUCP framework and prove that it does not fall under the category of a conservative planner, as per definitions below, taken directly from (Nebel & Koehler, 1995).

1. **PLANSAT** is the following decision problem: given an instance of the planning problem Π, does there exist a plan Δ that solves Π?
2. A **conservative approach** to plan modification is one that solves the following *plan modification problem*: given a planning-problem instance Π_l and a plan Δ that solves another instance Π, produce a plan Δ_l that solves Π_l by minimally modifying Δ
3. **MODSAT** is the following decision problem: Given a planning-problem instance Π_l, a plan Δ that solves another instance Π, and an integer k, does there exist a plan Δ_1 that solves Π_1 and contains a sub plan of Δ of at least length k?

3 The TransUCP Planning Algorithm

The main idea behind the TransUCP algorithm is to solve the planning problem by using transformational analogy over UCP. The inputs to the algorithm are: the initial state, the goal state and the case library. TransUCP returns the solution plan or a failure message if it could not generate one.

Progressive refinements are defined as those modifications made to the plan which increase its possible number of ground linearisations or increase the total number of steps in the plan. In terms of searching in a plan space graph, all those refinements that take a node to its parent nodes can be looked upon as non-progressive refinements and the ones that take the current node to one of its children would be progressive refinements. The three kinds of refinements used in the universal classical planning algorithm (Section 2.2) constitute the progressive refinements. All refinements made to a plan that are not progressive refinements can be termed as *non-progressive*.

Purpose Tags. The TransUCP algorithm generates and modifies a partial plan in an iterative manner doing one refinement (progressive or non-progressive) in each pass. During each pass, a step and/or a set of constraints are added/deleted to/from the plan. We associate each set modifications done to the plan in each pass is with a data structure called the *purpose tag* which indicates the purpose of these modifications. These tags are primarily used when we retract the plan backwards i.e. when we delete steps or constraints from a plan. The different types of tags used in TransUCP are:

i.   Purpose (Step Added, t_j, forward state): This tag is added to a step which is added to the plan during forward state space refinement.
ii. Purpose (Step Added, t_j, backward state): This tag is added to a step which is added to the plan during backward state space refinement.
iii. Purpose (protect $((t_k, ti \rightarrow^Q t_j)))$: This tag is added to an ordering/binding constraint which has been added to the plan to resolve the threat $((t_k, ti \rightarrow^Q t_j))$.
iv. Purpose (establish link, $t_i \rightarrow^Q t_j$): This tag is added to an ordering constraint which has been added to the plan to satisfy the open condition $(\rightarrow^Q t_j)$.

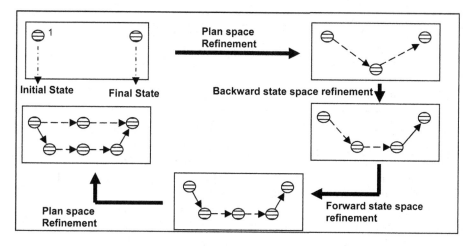

Fig. 3. Universal Classical Planning

3.1 The Algorithm

TransUCP first retrieves a case from the case library that is the best match for the current problem in terms of most similar initial and goal states. Though this suggests a probable heuristic for case retrieval from the case library, the actual logic to be used for this is not discussed in this paper as it is not the primary focus.

The plan returned from the case library, LibraryPlan, is adjusted so as to make its initial and goal states the same as Initial and Goal. This process includes adding sub-goals of Initial and Goal that are not present in the initial and goal states of the LibraryPlan and deleting those sub-goals that are not present in Initial and Goal and are present in their counterparts of LibraryPlan. During this process of addition and deletion, some steps of the partial plan along with their ordering, binding and auxiliary constraints might have to be deleted. As a result, there might be open conditions and threats in the adjusted plan. The TransUCP algorithm tries to remove these open conditions and threats to make the plan a solution plan.

The plan returned by the AdjustExactly function, AdjustedPlan, is then checked to see if it is a solution to the current problem. If it is not, we add the plans, <AdjustedPlan, UP> and <AdjustedPlan, DOWN> to the PlanPool. The purpose of the direction indicators, UP and DOWN is discussed in detail in later sections. This collection of plans PlanPool is passed to the function TransformPlan, which returns the solution plan.

TransUCP (Initial, Goal, Library) Returns: Final Plan P or Failure

LibraryPlan = select the plan from the Library with the most similar initial and
                 goal   states
AdjustedPlan = AdjustExactly (LibraryPlan, Initial, Goal)
IF AdjustedPlan is a solution
        THEN return AdjustedPlan
PlanPool = {<AdjustedPlan, UP>, <AdjustedPlan, DOWN>}
FinalPlan = TransformPlan (Initial, Goal, PlanPool)
IF FinalPlan == *failure*
        THEN return *failure*
Return FinalPlan

The TransformPlan function is called recursively until a solution plan is arrived at or a failure is returned, which happens when the PlanPool is extinguished. Given the PlanPool, which is passed as an argument to the function, it chooses a plan from it non-deterministically and checks if it is a solution, and if so, returns it. If not, it checks for the direction pointer of the selected plan P.

If the direction pointer of the chosen plan is DOWN, it performs progressive refinements and if not, it performs non-progressive refinements. If the direction pointer is DOWN, the algorithm chooses non-deterministically which of the three possible refinements is to be applied. All the plans returned by the progressive refinement chosen are added to the PlanPool and the TransUCP is recursively called until a solution plan or a failure is encountered.

If the direction pointer is UP, one of the decisions made in the current plan is retracted back through non-progressive refinements, by the call to RetractRefinement, and the resulting plans are added to the PlanPool followed by the recursive call to TransUCP. Basically, the RetractRefinement function selects a step from the current partial plan and removes it from the plan. The RetractRefinement function takes as argument the plan P and selects a purpose tag from it. Having chosen the tag to retract, it undoes the progressive refinement associated with this tag. The exact criteria to be followed in choosing the purpose tag to be retracted are not dealt in this paper. A good heuristic to be followed for this selection process can be found in Hanks and Weld (1996). The progressive refinement to undo can be any of the three kinds of refinements used in the universal classical planning algorithm (Section 2.2).In all of the three cases, the function removes the steps, constraints or bindings which were associated with this tag and added to the plan. If the tag selected was associated with forward state space refinement, then the step added is removed, through a call to RemoveStep, and all other ways of performing forward state space refinement to the plan are returned to be added to the plan pool. Before adding the plan P_1 to PlanPool, it is made sure that it does not map onto the original retracted plan P. This is to ensure that we do not add the same plan back to the pool again. By saying that one plans *maps* onto another plan, we mean that there is a 1:1 mapping between their steps, links, binding constraints and purpose tags.

Similar processing is done for backward and partial plan space refinement tags. When the refinement to be retracted is a partial plan space refinement, the step associated with the purpose tag selected is retracted and the flaw that originally caused this refinement to be made to the plan is also returned to RefinePlanSpace. This is done to ensure that only those partial plans formed by resolving this particular flaw through RefinePlanSpace are added to the plan pool. In essence, we are constricting RefinePlanSpace from selecting a flaw to be resolved at random. This completes the explanation of the TransUCP algorithm. In the subsequent sections, the working of the algorithm and its properties are elucidated with examples.

TransformPlan (Initial, Goal, PlanPool) Returns: Final Plan P or Failure

    If PlanPool is empty THEN return failure.
    <P, D> = select an element from PlanPool.
    Delete <P, D> from PlanPool
    If P is a solution THEN return P
    If D == DOWN THEN //Progressive Refinements
        Non-deterministically, select any one of
        1. P' = RefinePlanForwardStateSpace (P)
            Add <P', DOWN> and <P', UP> to PlanPool
        2. P' = RefinePlanBackwardStateSpace (P)
            Add <P', DOWN> and <P', UP> to PlanPool
        3. RefinePlanSpace (P)
            For each plan P_i returned by RefinePlan (P, *null*) do
            Add <P_i, DOWN> to PlanPool
    ELSE IF (D == UP) // Non-progressive Refinements
        Add all elements of RetractRefinement (P) to PlanPool
    Recursive Invocation:
        TransUCP (Initial, Goal, PlanPool)

4   Example

In this section, we take a planning problem and the solution plan returned when the UCP algorithm (Kambhampati & Srivastava; 1996) solves it. For this example, we use the problem and plan described in Figures 1 and 2 respectively as the input case. In the new problem to be solved, we have the same goals, to relocate package p1 and p2 into location C. The difference is that this time there is no truck in location D as illustrated in Figure 4. The AdjustExactly function takes this plan and modifies it so as to match the initial and goal states of the new problem and of the case. In our example, the goals happen to be the same but the initial states are different. Since the truck V2 is not available in the new problem, we remove V2 from the initial state and all those steps and constraints that involve V2. In doing so, we get the partial incomplete plan as shown in Figure 5. It can be seen that steps t_3, t_7, t_8 and t_9 have been deleted. The open threats and conditions that result from this modification and that need to be resolved are also shown in the figure.

Let us denote this plan by P_1. Since this is not a solution plan, we add the direction pointer pairs $<P_1, UP>$ and $<P_1, DOWN>$ to the PlanPool and this pool is passed to TransformPlan. Let us assume that TransformPlan chooses the pair $<P_1, DOWN>$ from the plan pool to refine. Since the direction pointer is DOWN, it performs progressive refinement on the plan P_1. Assuming without the loss of generality that the refinement strategy chosen is forward state space refinement, the current head step is t_2 and we can append a new step t_8 MV(V1, A, D) to the head step with the constraint $t_2 * t_8$ as the preconditions of t_8 are satisfied at t_2. The resulting plan, labeled as P_2 is shown in Figure 6 and the 2-tuple $<P_2, DOWN>$ is added to the PlanPool.

RetractRefinement (Plan P): Returns: List of (Plan, Direction) pairs

Define L: a local list of plans
R = select a purpose
(F, P_0) = RemoveStep(R, P)
Add the tuple (P_0, UP) to local list L
IF purpose in R was forward state space refinement THEN
      For each plan P_1 returned by RefinePlanForwardStateSpace (P_0)
      Do   If P_1 does not map onto P, add $<P_1, DOWN>$ to list L.
Else IF purpose in R was forward state space refinement THEN
      For each plan P_1 returned by RefinePlanBackwardStateSpace (P_0)
      Do   If P_1 does not map onto P, add $<P_1, DOWN>$ to list L.
Else IF purpose in R was partial plan space refinement THEN
      For each plan P_1 returned by RefinePlanSpace (P_0, F)
      Do   If P_1 does not map onto P, add $<P_1, DOWN>$ to list L.
Return all plans, direction pairs collected in list L.

During the second pass of TransUCP, the PlanPool contains the pairs ($<P1, UP>$, $<P_2, DOWN>$, $<P_2, UP>$). If the pair chosen by TransUCP was $<P_2, DOWN>$ and the progressive refinement chosen was partial plan space refinement, let us assume that the open condition selected to resolve is $(\rightarrow^Q t_6)$, where $Q = $ at $(B, truck)$. This flaw is resolved by adding a new step $t_9 : MV (V1, A, B)$ and ordering it before t_6 with the ordering constraint $t_8 < t_9 < t_6$. This resolves the flaw and results in the plan P_3 shown in Figure 7. By adding the step t_9, the open condition $(\rightarrow^Q t_9)$, where $Q = $ at $(A, truck)$, is introduced and is added to the set of flaws of the plan. Continuing in this manner TransUCP continuously keeps refining the partial plan and searches for the first solution node. Figure 8 shows one of the possible solution plans returned by TransUCP.

5   How TransUCP Traverses the Search Space

Plan adaptation as done by TransUCP to find a solution plan is carried out in a similar fashion as searching through a partial plan space. The entire process is comparable to searching for a solution plan node in a graph, in which, each node represents a partial plan. Edges between the nodes represent refinements between the plans represented by the nodes – progressive or non-progressive.

The nodes resulting from performing non-progressive refinements on a node are referred to, in this paper, as the parents of the node and similarly, the nodes resulting from performing progressive refinements are referred as the children of the node. The graph being searched is not necessarily a tree because, given a node, non-progressive refinements on it can be performed in more than one way, thus producing multiple

---

RemoveStep (Purpose R, Plan P): Returns: List of (Flaw, Plan) pair

IF purpose in R was forward or backward state space refinement THEN
        Remove the step tagged with R and all links and constraints associated with it to get the resulting plan P_0.
        Return $(null, P_0)$.
ELSE //partial plan space refinement
        IF R is of the form (protect $((t_k, t_i \rightarrow t_j))$ THEN
                $F = (ti \rightarrow^Q t_j, t_k)$
                $P_0 = $ a copy of P
                Delete from P_0 all constraints tagged with R
                Return (F, P0)
        ELSE IF R is of the form (establish link, $t_i \rightarrow t_j$) THEN
                $F = (\rightarrow^Q t_j)$
                $P_0 = $ a copy of P
                Delete link $(t_i \rightarrow t_j)$ from P_0
                Delete from P_0 all constraints tagged with R
                IF P_0 contains no link of the form $t_i \rightarrow t_j$ for any step t_k and condition Q THEN
                        Delete t_i from P_0 along with all constraints tagged with (Step Added, t_i, plan space)
                Return (F, P_0)

parents for a given node. Given a plan from the case library and a planning problem (initial and goal states), TransUCP first modifies the case plan so as to match its initial and goal states to those of the given problem. Once this has been done, it starts the process of searching for the solution plan in the plan space. The modified input plan would be the starting point of the search (see Figure 9). This node would be an inner node in the graph. In the TransUCP function, when the direction pointer chosen is UP, the planner browses upwards into the parents of the current node by performing non-progressive refinements, i.e. by deleting some steps or constraints from the current plan.

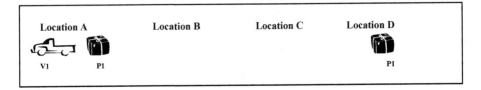

Fig. 4. Planning problem in the transportation domain to be solved

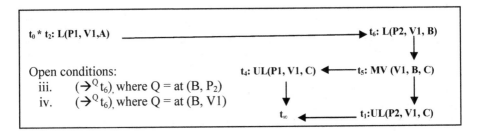

Fig. 5. Partial plan P_1 after initial adjusting

When the direction pointer chosen is DOWN, it scales the graph "downward", into the children nodes of the node by performing progressive refinements, i.e. by adding steps or constraints. It performs this process of traversing the graph until it hits the first node that satisfies the conditions of being a solution plan for the given problem. It is to be noted that the planner takes care never to visit a node more than once during its execution.

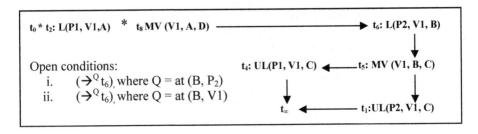

Fig. 6. Partial plan P_2

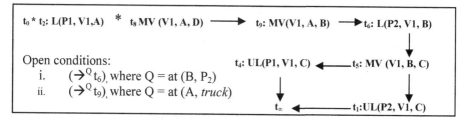

Fig. 7. Partial plan P_3

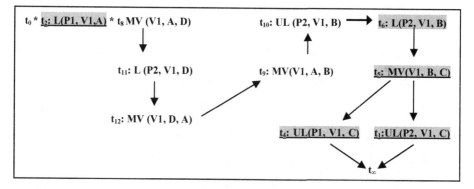

Fig. 8. Solution plan generated by TransUCP

6 Properties

In this section, we show that TransUCP does not use a conservative plan modification approach, as per the definitions in Section 2.3, to find the solution plan for a given planning problem. We also discuss completeness and the issue of non-determinism in TransUCP. The three possible ways in which TransUCP traverses the search space and finds the solution plan node are:

i.   The planner finds the solution plan node without having to retract beyond the starting node (input plan node in Figure 9). That is, it never visits the parents of the input plan node. This is the case when Node A in Figure 9 is returned as the solution node by the planner.
ii. The planner, in search of the solution plan node, retracts all the way back to the null plan node and starts planning from first principles thereon.
iii. The planner retracts, but not all the way until the null plan node. This is the case when Node B in Figure 9 is returned as the solution node by the planner.

Theorem. In each of the three cases mentioned above, TransUCP does not necessarily produce minimal modifications of the given case plan Δ.

Proof: The proof is by contradiction. Let us consider the first case above where the planner does not retract beyond the starting node (input plan node in Figure 9). Let us assume that TransUCP always produces solution plans that are minimal modifications of the given case plans. We shall provide a counter example to show that this is not true.

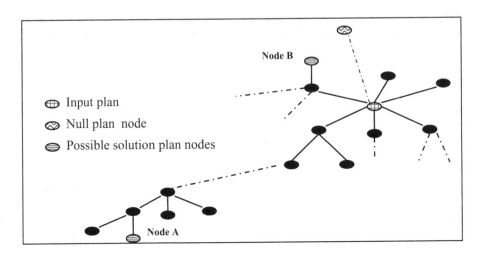

Fig. 9. Graph Traversal by TransUCP

Consider the planning problem instance (Figure 4) and its solution generated by TransUCP (Figure 8). The solution plan generated by TransUCP certainly comes under the first case because the planner does not retract beyond the input plan node at any point during the execution of the algorithm. If TransUCP were to always produce solution plans that are minimally modified, then no other plan which solves the same instance of the planning problem should contain a sub plan of the original case plan which is greater in size (number of steps) than the sub plan of solution produced by TransUCP.

But the plan shown in Figure 10 solves the planning problem in Figure 4 and is minimally modified from the case plan shown in Figure 2. The highlighted steps show those that have been reused from the original plan. It is to be noted that only those steps that have been directly taken from the original plan are taken into account as reused steps and those that have been derived from first principles are not. If this plan is compared to the solution plan generated by TransUCP (Figure 8), also in which the reused steps have been highlighted, it can be seen that it is not minimally modified from the original case plan. This is a contradiction to our initial assumption. We can similarly produce counter examples for the remaining two cases and show that TransUCP does not necessarily always generate solution plans that are minimally modified from the original case plans. Hence we can conclude and prove that TransUCP is not a conservative planner in the sense of as per the definitions of Nebel and Koehler (1995).   ☐

Therefore, TransUCP does not fall under the category of MODSAT as defined in Section 2.3. It has been proved by Nebel and Koehler that answering the MODSAT decision problem can be computationally harder than PLANSAT. Since TransUCP does not satisfy the requirement for being a MODSAT problem, as it does not guarantee to generate a minimally modified plan, its complexity would not fall in this worst case scenario, i.e. problem solving with TransUCP will be computationally harder than problem solving from scratch.

Non-determinism of TransUCP. There are "decision points" at various stages of the implementation where choices are made non-deterministically, without any heuristic being used. The selection of a plan from the plan pool and the choice of progressive or non-progressive refinements to be made to the plan constitute some of these decision points. Forward state space and backward state space planning further contains points where random choices are made. The TransUCP framework, as proposed in this paper, is meant as a generic domain-independent framework for a planner. Hence there is non-determinism at various decision points. It is expected that, when the planner is used in a particular domain, appropriate domain dependent heuristics would be added and used at these decision points to improve the performance and efficiency of the planner. One of the most likely places where heuristics could help the most are when selecting a plan from the PlanPool, where by assigning weights based on heuristics to each plan, the choice of the next plan to be chosen for refined can be altered. This would ensure that the search of the plan space is carried out in a more guided and efficient fashion. Therefore, it is quite logical that non-determinism is replaced by heuristics in the actual implementation of this planner.

Completeness of TransUCP. Completeness of a planner, as defined by Hanks and Weld (1995), says that a planner will eventually find the solution plan for a particular planning problem, if there exists one. It has been proven (Kuchibatla, 2006) that TransUCP is complete, under the assumption that the given planning problem has a solution and that the partial plan search space has finite boundaries.

7 Empirical Results

In this section, we describe the details of the implementation of TransUCP and elucidate its results. The purpose of these experiments was to show that the counter-example shown in the previous section was not an exception and that that TransUCP very rarely behaves like a conservative planner.

The TransUCP algorithm was implemented to generate solutions in the logistics transportation domain. In the experiments performed, the problems were randomly generated, meaning each of them contains an arbitrary number of the elements in the domain such as trucks and locations. Since the search space can be very large we added pruning techniques reducing the chances that plans that clearly contain redundant steps (e.g., move form A to B, followed by move from B to A) are further refined. The case plan to be reused is the one from Figure 2. After running TransUCP giving as input 10 randomly generated problems and the case plan, non-minimal solution plans were generated in every run. Figure 11 shows the average number of nodes in the plan space graph that were traversed before the solution node was found versus the number of elements (trucks, cities and packages) in the problem.

For example, 6 elements mean that there were 4 locations and 2 trucks in the problem. From the figure we can see that even for a small problem with just 6 elements, the size of the search space is very large, which is why it is very unlikely that a minimal plan modification is generated.

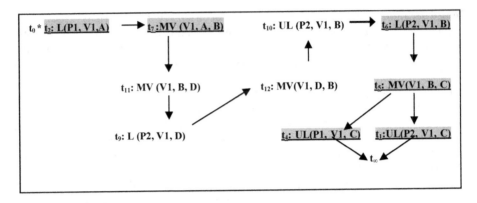

Fig. 10. Minimally modified solution plan

8 Final Remarks

In this paper we introduced TransUCP, a general framework for transformational analogy. Using our framework we demonstrate that transformational analogy does not always perform a conservative plan adaptation by carefully constructing an example where conservative plan adaptation does not occur. Therefore, transformational analogy does not fall under the worse case scenario of Nebel & Koehler (1995). Furthermore, we perform experiments that demonstrate that it is unlikely that any plan adaptation with transformational analogy will be conservative.

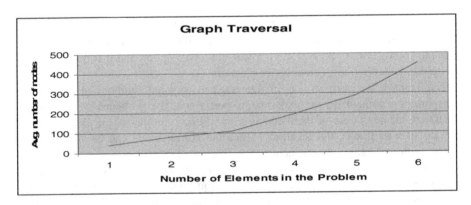

Fig. 11. Number of nodes traversed in the graph

Acknowledgements

This research is sponsored by DARPA and managed by NRL under grant N00173-05-1-G034. The views and conclusions contained here are those of the authors and should not be interpreted as necessarily representing the official policies, either expressed or implied, of DARPA, NRL, or the US Government.

References

Au, T.C., Muñoz-Avila, H., & Nau, D.S. (2002) On the Complexity of Plan Adaptation by Derivational Analogy in a Universal Classical Planning Framework. In proceedings of the Sixth European Conference on Case-Based Reasoning (ECCBR-02). Springer.

Carbonell, J.G. (1983) Learning by analogy: formulating and generalizing plans from past experience. Machine Learning: An Artificial Intelligence Approach. R.S. Michalski, J. G. Carbonell, and T. M. Mitchell (Eds.). Tioga, Palo Alto, California.

Carbonell, J.G. (1986) Derivational analogy: A theory of reconstructive problem solving and expertise acquisition. Machine Learning.

Cunningham, P., Finn, D., & Slattery, S. (1996) Knowledge Engineering Requirements in Derivational Analogy. In Proceedings of the European Workshop on Case-Based reasoning (ECCBR-96). Springer.

Kambhampati, S. and Srivastava B. (1995) Universal Classical Planner: An algorithm for unifying state-space and plan-space planning. In: Proeedings of the. Third European Workshop on Planning (EWSP-95).

Hammond, K. (1990). Explaining and repairing plans that fail. Artificial Intelligence, 45: 173-228.

Hanks, S. and Weld, D. (1995). A domain-independent algorithm for plan adaptation. Journal of Artificial Intelligence Research, 2.

Ihrig, L. & Kambhampati, S. Design and implementation of a replay framework based on a partial order planner. In Weld, D., editor, In: Proceedings of AAAI-96. IOS Press, 1996.

Nebel, N. and Koehler, J (1995). Plan reuse versus plan generation: a theoretical and empirical analysis, Artificial Intelligence, 76, p427–454.

Veloso, M. Planning and learning by analogical reasoning. Berlin: Springer-Verlag, 1994.

Cox, M. T., Munoz-Avila, H., & Bergmann, R. (2006). Case-based planning. To appear in Knowledge Engineering Review.

Weld D. (1994) An Introduction to Least Commitment Planning. AI Magazine, 15(4), pages 27-61. AAAI Press.

Kuchibatla, V. (2006) TransUCP: An Analysis on Transformational Analogy. MS Thesis. Computer Science and Engineering. Department. Lehigh University.

Discovering Knowledge About Key Sequences for Indexing Time Series Cases in Medical Applications

Peter Funk and Ning Xiong

Department of Computer Science and Electronics
SE-72123 Västerås, Sweden
{peter.funk, ning.xiong}@mdh.se

Abstract. Coping with time series cases is becoming an important issue in case based reasoning. This paper develops a knowledge discovery approach to discovering significant sequences for depicting symbolic time series cases. The input is a case library containing time series cases consisting of consecutive discrete patterns. The proposed approach is able to find from the given case library all qualified sequences that are non-redundant and indicative. A sequence as such is termed as a key sequence. It is shown that the key sequences discovered are highly usable in case characterization to capture important properties while ignoring random trivialities. The main idea is to transform an original (lengthy) time series into a more concise representation in terms of the detected occurrences of key sequences. Three alternate ways to develop case indexes based on key sequences are suggested. These indexes are simply vectors of numbers that are easily usable when matching two time series cases for case retrieval.

1 Introduction

Coping with time series cases has become increasingly important in applying case based reasoning in many domains with dynamic properties. Unlike static case bases where objects are described by attributes which are time independent, a time series case base contains profiles of time-varying variables wherein pieces of data are associated with a timestamp and are meaningful only for a specific segment in the case duration. Temporal aspect of time series cases has to be taken into account in the tasks of case indexing and case retrieval. Abstraction and representation of temporal knowledge in CBR systems were discussed in [4, 7, 16].

Signal analysis techniques have been applied to extract relevant features from time series signals such as sensor readings. The most common methods used in applications are Discrete Fourier Transform and Wavelet Analysis, see [5, 12, 13, 20]. Both have the merit of capturing significant characteristics of the original signal with a compact representation, and the features extracted are directly usable in building similarity measures for case matching and retrieval. However the available signal processing techniques are inherently restricted to dealing with numerical values, they are not applicable to time series consisting of non-ordered discrete symbols.

This paper aims to extract useful sequences for depicting symbolic time series cases. As behaviors in dynamic processes are usually reflected from transitional

T.R. Roth-Berghofer et al. (Eds.): ECCBR 2006, LNAI 4106, pp. 474–488, 2006.

patterns over time, occurrences of certain sequences are believed to be significant evidences to identify properties existing in historical sequential records. Deciding which sequences as characteristic while others as trivial in characterization of time series cases is largely domain dependent. Knowledge acquisition and discovery thus becomes imperative in circumstances when no prior knowledge is available.

This study presented would be relevant to many medical applications where physicians have to investigate sequences of symptoms of patients before making clinical diagnoses, and frequently conditional changes with patients are more important than their static states within single time segments. In particular this work is motivated by our ongoing AI project in stress medicine in which stress levels have to be estimated according to a given series of breathing dysfunctional patterns detected for consecutive respiration cycles. Related medical research has revealed that certain transitions of breathing patterns over time may have high co-occurrence with stress levels of interest [17]. An outline of this application scenario and the problem to be addressed will be formulated in the next section.

We developed a knowledge discovery approach to sequence extraction employing a case base as the information source. The utilized case base is assumed to be symbolic and contains a collection of time series cases consisting of consecutive discrete patterns. The proposed approach is able to find from the given case library all those sequences that are non-redundant and indicative in having strong occurrences with a certain class. A sequence as such is termed as a key sequence. We show that the knowledge about key sequences is highly valuable in case characterization to capture important properties while ignoring randomly occurred trivialities in a dynamic process. Three ways to index time series cases according to the set of discovered key sequences are suggested. The results of case indexing based on key sequences can then be used directly in construction of similarity measures for case retrieval.

It is worthy noting that the knowledge discovery treated here distinguishes itself from traditional learning included in a CBR cycle. The retain step in CBR typically stores a new case in the library or modifies some existing cases and may contain a number of sub-steps [1]. Learning therein is therefore case specific with knowledge stemming directly from newly solved cases. Contrarily, in our approach, learning is treated as a background task separated from the retain step and the whole case library is the input to the knowledge discovery process. Some relevant works combining knowledge discovery and CBR systems include: genetic-based knowledge acquisition for case indexing and matching [8], incremental learning to organize a case base [14], exploitation of background knowledge in text classification [21], and analysis of pros and cons for explanations in CBR systems [9].

The remainder of the paper is organized as follows. Section 2 briefly outlines a medical scenario motivating our research followed by formulation of the problem to be addressed. In section 3 criteria to evaluate sequences are established. Section 4 presents a sequence search algorithm and the simulation results. Then, in section 5, we explain how to index time series cases using key sequences discovered. Related works are outlined in section 6 and finally we conclude the paper in section 7.

2 A Medical Scenario and Problem Statements

In this section we first briefly outline a typical medical scenario in which patients' stress levels are to be determined based on a series of respiratory sinus arrhythmia (RSA) breathing patterns. Then the problem to be addressed in this context shall be formulated.

2.1 Classification Via Respiratory Sinus Arrhythmia

In stress medicine, RSA signals obtained from patients are typically employed to classify their stress levels. A patient is usually tested through a series of 40-80 breathing cycles (including inhalation and exhalation). Every respiration cycle lasts on average 5-15 seconds and corresponds to either a normal breathing pattern or one of the dysfunctional patterns. The patterns of breathing (also called RSA patterns) are identified from RSA measurements in the respective respiration periods. Further patterns from consecutive breathing cycles constitute a symbolic time series, which is to be investigated to find information reflecting stress levels of patients.

An overview of the stress medicine project is depicted in Fig. 1. First the RSA signal measured during the whole test period is decomposed into a collection of sub-signals. By sub-signal in Fig. 1 we denote the portion of the signal recorded for the *ith* cycle. Each sub-signal *i* is delivered to the block "signal classifier" to decide upon pattern *i* corresponding to it. The identified patterns are then composed into a symbolic series in terms of their appearance order in time. So far the part of signal classifier has been implemented in the previous work using wavelet analysis and case based reasoning [12]. The next step of the project is further to estimate the level of stress given a time series of respiration patterns. For applying CBR again in the second step we feel it necessary to acquire knowledge about key sequences to characterize and index time series cases.

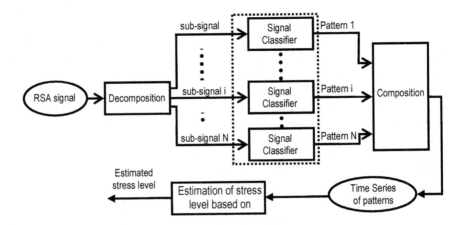

Fig. 1. An overview of the stress medicine project

2.2 Problem Statements

To clearly present our work fitting into the scenario, we now give descriptions of the various terms and concepts that are related. We begin with the definitions about time series, sequences, and time series case bases, and then we precisely formulate the problem to tackle.

Definition 1. A time series is a series of elements occurred sequentially over time, $X = \langle x(1), x(2), \cdots x(i), \cdots, x(n) \rangle$, where i indexes the time segment corresponding to a recorded element and n can be very large.

The elements x in time series can be numerical or symbolic values. But in the discussions of this paper we restrict our attention to symbolic time series consisting of discrete patterns.

Moreover, every time series has an inherent class. The previous time series data are supposed to have been classified and they are stored in a case base together with their associated classes. A formal definition of time series case bases for purpose of classification is given as follows:

Definition 2. A time series case base is a set of pairs $\{(X_i, Z_i)\}_{i=1}^K$, where X_i denotes a time series and Z_i the class assigned to X_i and K is the number of time series cases in the case base.

With a time series case base at hand, the knowledge discovery process involves analyzing sequences that are included in the case base. A sequence in a time series is formally described in definition 3.

Definition 3. A sequence S in a time series $X = \langle x(1), x(2), \cdots, x(n) \rangle$ is a list consisting of elements taken from contiguous positions of X, i.e., $S = \langle x(k), x(k+1), \cdots, x(k+m-1) \rangle$ with $m \le n$ and $1 \le k \le n - m + 1$.

Usually there is a very large amount of sequences included in the time series case base. But only a quite small part of them that carry useful information for estimating consequences are in line with our interest. Such sequences are referred to as indicative sequences and defined in the following:

Definition 4. A sequence is regarded as indicative given a time series case base provided that

1) it appears in sufficient amount of time series cases of the case base;
2) the discriminating power of it, assessed upon the case base, is above a specified threshold.

A measure for discriminating power together with the arguments that lie behind this definition will be elaborated in the next section. The intuitive explanation is that an indicative sequence is such a one that, on one hand, appears frequently in the case base, and on the other hand, exhibits high co-occurrence with a certain class.

Obviously, should a sequence be indicative, another sequence that contains it as subsequence may also be indicative for predicting the outcome. However, if these both are indicative of the same class, the second sequence is considered as redundant with respect to the first one because it conveys no more information. Redundant sequences can be easily recognized by checking possible inclusion between sequences encountered. The goal here is to find sequences that are not only indicative but also non-redundant and independent of each other.

Having given necessary notions and clarifications we can now formally define our problem to be addressed as follows:

Given a time series case base consisting of time series instances and associated classes, find a set of indicative sequences $\{S_1, S_2, ..., S_p\}$ that satisfy the following two criteria:
1) For any i, j∈{1, 2, ...p} neither $S_i \subseteq S_j$ nor $S_j \subseteq S_i$ if S_i and S_j are indicative of a same class;
2) For any sequence S that is indicative, $S \in \{S_1, S_2, ..., S_p\}$ if S is not redundant with respect to S_j for any j∈{1, 2, ...p}.

The first criterion above requests compactness of the set of sequences $\{S_1, S_2, ..., S_p\}$ in the sense that no sequence in it is redundant by having a subsequence indicative of the same class as it. A sequence that is both indicative and non-redundant is called a key sequence. The second criterion further requires that no single key sequence shall be lost, which signifies a demand for completeness of the set of key sequences to be discovered.

3   Evaluation of Single Sequences

This section aims to evaluate individual sequences to decide whether one sequence can be regarded as indicative. The main thread is to assess the discriminating power of sequences in terms of their co-occurrence relationship with possible time series classes. In addition we also illustrate the importance of sequence appearing frequencies in the case base for ensuring reliable assessments of the discriminating power.

Given a sequence S there may be a set of probable consequent classes $\{C_1, C_2, ..., C_k\}$. The strength of the co-occurrence between sequence S and class C_i ($i=1...k$) can be measured by the probability, $p(C_i \mid S)$, of C_i conditioned upon S. Sequence S is considered as discriminative in predicting outcomes as long as it has a strong co-occurrence with either of the possible outcomes. The discriminating power of S is defined as the maximum of the strengths of its relations with probable classes. Formally this definition of discriminating power PD is expressed as:

$$PD(S) = \max_{i=1\cdots k} P(C_i \mid S) \tag{1}$$

In addition we say that the class yielding the maximum strength of the co-occurrences, i.e., $C = \arg\max_{i=1\cdots k} P(C_i \mid S)$, is the class that sequence S is indicative of.

The conditional probabilities in (1) can be derived according to the Bayes theorem as:

$$P(C_i \mid S) = \frac{P(S \mid C_i)P(C_i)}{P(S)} \tag{2}$$

As the probability $P(S)$ is generally obtainable by

$$P(S) = P(S \mid C_i)P(C_i) + P(S \mid \overline{C}_i)P(\overline{C}_i) \tag{3}$$

equation (2) for conditional probability assessment can be rewritten as

$$P(C_i \mid S) = \frac{P(S \mid C_i)P(C_i)}{P(S \mid C_i)P(C_i) + P(S \mid \overline{C}_i)P(\overline{C}_i)} \tag{4}$$

Our aim here is to yield the conditional probability $P(C_i \mid S)$ in terms of equation (4). As $P(C_i)$ is a priori probability of occurrence of C_i which can be acquired from domain knowledge or approximated by experiences with randomly selected samples, the only things that remain to be resolved are the probabilities of S in (time series) cases having class C_i and in cases not belonging to class C_i respectively. Fortunately such probability values can be easily estimated by resorting to the given case base. For instance we use the appearance frequency of sequence S in class C_i cases as an approximation of $P(S \mid C_i)$, thus we have:

$$P(S \mid C_i) \approx \frac{N(C_i,S)}{N(C_i)} \tag{5}$$

where $N(C_i)$ denotes the number of cases having class C_i in the case base and $N(C_i, S)$ is the number of cases having both class C_i and sequence S. Likewise the probability $P(S \mid \overline{C}_i)$ is approximated by

$$P(S \mid \overline{C}_i) \approx \frac{N(\overline{C}_i,S)}{N(\overline{C}_i)} \tag{6}$$

with $N(\overline{C}_i)$ denoting the number of cases not having class C_i and $N(\overline{C}_i,S)$ being the number of cases containing sequence S but not belonging to class C_i.

The denominator in (4) has to stay enough above zero to enable reliable probability assessment using the estimates in (5) and (6). Hence it is crucial to acquire an adequate amount of time series cases containing S in the case base. The more such cases available the more reliably the probability assessment could be derived. For this reason we refer the quantity $N(S) = N(C_i,S) + N(\overline{C}_i,S)$ as evaluation base of sequence S in this paper.

At this point we realize that two requirements have to be satisfied for believing a sequence to be indicative of a certain class. Firstly the sequence has to possess an adequate evaluation base by appearing in a sufficient amount of time series cases. Obviously a sequence that occurred randomly in few occasions is not convincing and can hardly be deemed significant. Secondly, the conditional probability of that class under the sequence must be dominatingly high, signifying a strong discriminating power. These explain why indicative sequence is defined by the demands on its appearance frequency and discriminating power in definition 4.

In real applications two minimum thresholds need to be specified for the evaluation base and discriminating power respectively, to judge sequences as indicative or not. The values of these thresholds are domain dependent and are to be decided by human experts in the related area. The threshold for discriminating power may reflect the minimum probability value that suffices to predict a potential outcome in a specific scenario. The threshold for the evaluation base indicates the minimum amount of samples required to fairly approximate the conditional probabilities of interest. Finally only those sequences that pass both thresholds are evaluated as indicative ones.

4   Discovering a Complete Set of Key Sequences

With the evaluation of sequences being established, we now turn to exploration of qualified sequences in the problem space. The goal is to locate all key sequences that are non-redundant and indicate. We first detail a sequence search algorithm for this purpose in subsection 4.1 and then we demonstrate simulation results on a synthetic case base with the proposed algorithm in subsection 4.2.

4.1   A Sequence Search Algorithm

Discovery of key sequences can be considered as a search problem in a state space in which each state represents a sequence of patterns. Connection between two states signifies an operator between them for transition, i.e. addition or removal of a single pattern in time sequences. The state space for a scenario with three patterns a, b, c is illustrated in Fig. 2, where an arc connects two states if one can be created by extending the sequence of the other with a following pattern.

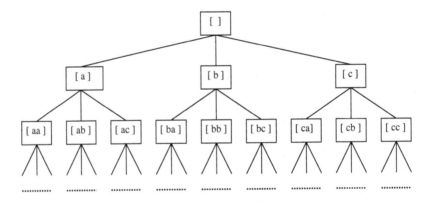

Fig. 2. The state space for sequences with three patterns

A systematic exploration in the state space is entailed for finding a complete set of key sequences. We start from a null sequence and generate new sequences by adding a single pattern to parent nodes for expansion. The child sequences are evaluated according to evaluation bases and discriminating powers. The results of evaluation determine the way to treat each child node in one of the following three situations:

i) If the evaluation base of the sequence is under a threshold required for conveying reliable probability assessment, terminate expansion at this node. The reason is that the child nodes will have even smaller evaluation bases by appearing in fewer cases than their parent node;

ii) If the evaluation base and discriminating power are both above their respective thresholds, do the redundancy checking for the sequence against the list of key sequences already identified. The sequence is redundant if at least one known key sequence constitutes its subsequence while both remaining indicative of the same class. Otherwise the sequence is considered non-redundant and hence is stored into the list of key sequences together with the class it indicates. After that this node is further expanded with the hope of finding, among its children, qualified sequences that might be indicative of other classes;

iii) If the evaluation base is above its threshold whereas the discriminating power still not reaching the threshold, continue to expand this node with the hope of finding qualified sequences among its children.

The expansion of non-terminate nodes is proceeded in a level-by-level fashion. A level in the search space consists of nodes for sequences of the same length and only when all nodes at a current level have been visited does the algorithm move on to the next level of sequences having one more pattern. This order of treating nodes is very beneficial for redundancy checking because a redundant sequence will always be encountered later than its subsequences including the key one(s) during the search procedure.

From a general structure, the proposed sequence search algorithm is a little similar to the traditional breadth-first procedure. However, there are still substantial differences between both. The features distinguishing our search algorithm are: 1) it does not attempt to expand every node encountered and criteria are established to decide whether exploration needs to be proceeded at any given state; 2) it presumes multiple goals in the search space and thus the search procedure is not terminated when a single key sequence is found. Instead the search continues on other prospective nodes until none of the nodes in the latest level needs to be expanded. A formal description of the proposed search algorithm is given as follows:

Algorithm for finding a complete set of key sequences

```
1. Initialize the Open list with an empty sequence.

2. Initialize the Key_List to be an empty list.

3. Remove the most left node t from the Open list.

4. Generate all child nodes of t

5. For each child node, C(t), of the parent node t

a) Evaluate C(t) according to its discriminating power
and evaluation base;
```

b) If the evaluation base and discriminating power are both above their respective thresholds, do the redundancy checking for $C(t)$ against the sequences in the *Key_list*. Store $C(t)$ into the *Key_list* if it is judged as not redundant. Finally put $C(t)$ on the right of the *Open* list.

c) If the evaluation base of $C(t)$ is above its threshold but the discriminating power is not satisfying, put $C(t)$ on the right of the *Open* list.

6. If the *Openlist* is not empty go to step 3, otherwise return the *Key_list* and terminate the search.

4.2 Simulation Results

To verify the feasibility of the mechanism addressed above we now present the simulation results on a synthetic case base. A case in this case base is depicted by a time series of 60 patterns and one diagnosis class as the outcome. A pattern in a time series belongs to {a, b, c, d, e} and a diagnosis class is either 1, 2, or 3. The four key sequences assumed are [a c e b], [d b a c], [b c b e], and [d d a e]. The first two sequences were supposed to have strong co-occurrences with class 1 and the third and fourth exhibit strong co-occurrences with classes 2 and 3 respectively. Each time series in the case base was created in such a way that both sequences [a c e b] and [d b a c] had a chance of 75% of being reproduced once in the time series cases of class 1, and with the same probability (75%) sequences [b c b e] and [d d a e] were added into class 2 and class 3 cases respectively. After stochastic reproduction of these key sequences, the remaining patterns in the time series of all cases were generated randomly. The whole case base consists of 100 instances for each class. Presuming such time series cases to be randomly selected samples from a certain domain, a priori probability of each class is believed to be one third.

The sequence search algorithm was applied to this case base to find key sequences and potential co-occurrences hidden in the data. The threshold for the discriminating power was set at 70% to ensure an adequate strength of the relationships discovered. We also specified 50 as the threshold of the evaluation base for reliable assessment of probabilities. The sequences found in our test are shown in table 1 below.

Table 1. Sequences discovered on a synthetic case base

Sequence Discovered	Discriminating power	Evaluation base	Dominating Class
[a c e b]	83.52%	91	Class 1
[d b a c]	82.80%	93	Class 1
[b c b e]	87.13%	101	Class 2
[d d a e]	80.41%	97	Class 3

As seen from table 1 we detected all the four key sequences previously assumed. They were recognized to potentially cause the respective classes with the probabilities ranging from 80.41% to 87.13%. These relationships with a degree of uncertainty are due to the many randomly generated patterns in the case base such that any sequence of patterns is more or less probable to appear in time series of any class. But this would reflect non-deterministic property prevalent in many real world domains.

5   Case Indexing Based on Key Sequences

The discovered key sequences are treated as significant features in capturing dynamic system behaviors. Rather than enumerating what happened in every consecutive time segment, we can now more concisely represent a time series case in terms of occurrences of key sequences in it. Let $\{S_1, S_2, ..., S_p\}$ be the set of key sequences. We have to search for every S_i ($i=1...P$) in a time series X to detect all possible appearances. Then case index for X can be established according to the results of key sequence detection. In the following three alternate ways to index X based on key sequences are suggested.

5.1   Naive Case Index

A naive means of indexing a time series case X is to depict it by a vector of binary numbers each of which corresponds to a key sequence. A number in the vector is unity if the corresponding sequence is detected in X and zero otherwise. This means that, by the naive method, the index of X is given by

$$Id_1(X|S_1, \cdots S_P) = [b_1, b_2, \cdots, b_P] \tag{7}$$

Where

$$b_i = \begin{cases} 1 & if \quad S_i \ is \ subsequence \ of \ X \\ 0 & otherwise \end{cases} \tag{8}$$

This index has the merit of imposing low demand in computation. It also enables the similarity between two cases to be calculated as the proportion of the positions where their indexing vectors have identical values. Suppose two time series cases X_1 and X_2 which are indexed by binary vectors $[b_{11}, ... b_{1P}]$ and $[b_{21}, ... b_{2P}]$ respectively, the similarity between them is simply defined as

$$Sim_1(X_1, X_2) = 1 - \frac{1}{P} \sum_{j=1}^{P} |b_{ij} - b_{2j}| \tag{9}$$

5.2   Case Index Using Sequence Appearance Numbers

With a binary structure the case index in section 5.1 carries a little limited content and would be usable only in relatively simple circumstances. A main reason is that the index can not reflect how many times a key sequence has appeared in a series of consideration. To incorporate that information, an alternate way is to directly employ the numbers of appearances of single key sequences in describing time series cases. By doing this we acquire the second method of indexing time series X by an integer vector as

$$Id_2(X|S_1,\cdots,S_P)=[f_1,f_2,\cdots,f_P] \tag{10}$$

where f_i denotes the number of occurrences of sequence S_i in series X.

Further, considering the case index in (10) as a state vector, we use the cosine matching function [15] as the similarity measure between two time series cases X_1 and X_2. Thus we have

$$Sim_2(X_1,X_2)=\frac{\sum_{j=1}^{P}f_{1j}f_{2j}}{\sqrt{\sum_{j=1}^{P}f_{1j}^2}\sqrt{\sum_{j=1}^{P}f_{2j}^2}} \tag{11}$$

with f_{1j}, f_{2j} denoting the numbers of occurrences of key sequence S_j in X_1 and X_2 respectively.

5.3 Index in Terms of Discriminating Power

Although the case index in (10) can distinguish two cases having a same key sequence but with different numbers of appearances, it still might not be an optimal representation to capture the exact nature of the problem. Recall that the value of a key sequence is conveying a degree of confidence in the sense of discriminating power for predicting a potential class, a time series X would be more precisely characterized by the discriminating powers of the appearances of single key sequences. Intuitively two times of occurrences of a key sequence would give a stronger discriminating power than occurring just once, but not twice in the quantity of the strength. From view of this we suggest indexing X as a vector of real numbers, representing discriminating powers for the appearances of single key sequences, as follows:

$$Id_3(X|S_1,\cdots,S_P)=[g_1,g_2,\cdots,g_P] \tag{12}$$

with

$$g_i=\begin{cases} DP(f_i*S_i) & \text{if } f_i\geq 1 \\ 0 & \text{if } f_i=0 \end{cases} \tag{13}$$

With $DP(f_i*S_i)$ we denote the discriminating power by sequence S_i appearing f_i times in X.

Let C be the class that the key sequence S_i is indicative of. We define the discriminating power $DP(f_i*S_i)$ as the probability for class C given f_i appearances of sequence S_i. Assuming the appearances of S_i are independent of each other, this probability can be obtained by applying the Bayes theorem in a sequential procedure. Considering a two class problem without loss of generality, this procedure is depicted here by a series of equations as follows:

$$P(C|S_i)=\frac{P(S_i|C)P(C)}{P(S_i|C)P(C)+P(S_i|\overline{C})P(\overline{C})} \tag{14}$$

$$P(C|2*S_i) = \frac{P(S_i|C)P(C|S_i)}{P(S_i|C)P(C|S_i) + P(S_i|\overline{C})P(\overline{C}|S_i)} \tag{15}$$

. . . .

$$P(C|t*S_i) = \frac{P(S_i|C)P(C|(t-1)*S_i)}{P(S_i|C)P(C|(t-1)*S_i) + P(S_i|\overline{C})P(\overline{C}|(t-1)*S_i)} \tag{16}$$

. . . .

$$DP(f_i*S_i) = P(C|f_i*S_i) = \frac{P(S_i|C)P(C|(f_i-1)*S_i)}{P(S_i|C)P(C|(f_i-1)*S_i) + P(S_i|\overline{C})P(\overline{C}|(f_i-1)*S_i)} \tag{17}$$

where the probabilities $P(S_i|C)$ and $P(S_i|\overline{C})$ can be estimated according to equations (5) and (6) respectively. The probability updated in equation (14) represents the probability for class C given one appearance of S_i, which is further updated in equation (15) by the second appearance of S_i producing a higher probability considering both occurrences. Generally, the probability $P(C|t*S_i)$ is yielded by updating the prior probability $P(C|(t-1)*S_i)$ with one more occurrence of S_i in equation (16). Finally we obtain the ultimate probability assessment incorporating all appearances, i. e. the required discriminating power, by equation (17).

We now give a concrete example to illustrate how a case index can be built in terms of occurrences of key sequences. Suppose a two class (C_1 and C_2) situation in which three key sequences S_1, S_2, and S_3 are discovered. Sequence S_1 appears twice in time series X and S_2 appears once while S_3 is not detected. S_1 and S_2 are both indicative of a C_1. The a priori probability for class C_1 is 40% and the probabilities of sequences S_1, S_2 in situations of class C_1 and C_2 are shown below:

$$P(S_1|C_1) = 0.5 \qquad\qquad P(S_1|C_2) = 0.2$$
$$P(S_2|C_1) = 0.8 \qquad\qquad P(S_2|C_2) = 0.3$$

With all the information assumed above, the discriminating powers for the appearances of S_1 and S_2 are calculated in the following:

1. Calculate the probability for C_1 with the first appearance of S_1 by

$$P(C_1|S_1) = \frac{P(S_1|C_1)P(C_1)}{P(S_1|C_1)P(C_1) + P(S_1|C_2)P(C_2)} = \frac{0.5 \cdot 0.4}{0.5 \cdot 0.4 + 0.2 \cdot 0.6} = 0.6250$$

2. Refine the probability $P(C_1|S_1)$ with the second appearance of S_1, producing the discriminating power for the appearances of S_1

$$DP(2*S_1) = P(C_1|2*S_1) = \frac{P(S_1|C_1)P(C_1|S_1)}{P(S_1|C_1)P(C_1|S_1) + P(S_1|C_2)P(C_2|S_1)} = \frac{0.5 \cdot 0.625}{0.5 \cdot 0.625 + 0.2 \cdot 0.375} = 0.8065$$

It is clearly seen here that the power of discrimination is increased from 0.6250 to 0.8065 due to the key sequence occurring for the second time.

3. Derive the discriminating power for the occurrence of S_2 by calculating the conditional probability for C_2 upon S_2 as

$$DP(1*S_2) = P(C_1|S_2) = \frac{P(S_2|C_1)P(C_1)}{P(S_2|C_1)P(C_1)+P(S_2|C_2)P(C_2)} = \frac{0.8 \cdot 0.4}{0.8 \cdot 0.4 + 0.3 \cdot 0.6} = 0.6400$$

Moreover, because S_3 is not detected in X, there is no discriminating power for it. Hence we construct the index for this time series case as:

$$Id_3(X|S_1, S_2, S_3) = [0.8065, \quad 0.6400, \quad 0]$$

With this case indexing scheme, we first calculate the dissimilarity between two time series X_1 and X_2 as the average of the differences in discriminating powers over all key sequences as follows:

$$Dis(X_1, X_2) = \frac{1}{P} \sum_{j=1}^{P} |g_{ij} - g_{2j}| \tag{18}$$

where g_{1j} and g_{2j} denote the jth elements in the case indexes (12) for X_1 and X_2 respectively. Since the dissimilarity measure in (18) is opposite to that of similarity, the degree of similarity between X_1 and X_2 is simply given by

$$Sim_3(X_1, X_2) = 1 - Dis(X_1, X_2) \tag{19}$$

6 Related Works

Representation and retrieval of time series cases has received increasing research efforts during the recent years. The primary idea is to convert time-varying profiles into somehow simplified and shorter vectors that still preserve the distances between time series cases. Fourier transform and Wavelet transform are two commonly used methods for such a conversion, and their usages for retrieving similar cases to support clinical decisions and industrial diagnoses have been shown in [10,12] and [13] respectively.

A more general framework for tackling cases in time dependent domain was proposed by [11], in which temporal knowledge embedded in cases are represented at two levels: case level and history level. The case level is tasked to depict single cases with features varying within case durations, while consecution of cases occurrences have to be captured in the history level to reflect the evolution of the system as a whole. It was also recommended by the authors that, at both of the two levels, the methodology of temporal abstraction [3, 18] could be exploited to derive series of qualitative states or behaviors, which facilitate easy interpretation as well as pattern matching for case retrieval.

This paper would be a valuable supplementary to the framework by Montani and Portinale in the sense that our key sequence discovery approach can be beneficially applied to the series of symbols abstracted from original time series. The point of departure is that, in many practical circumstances, significant transitional patterns in history are more worthy of attentions than the states or behaviors themselves associated with single episodes. It follows that the key sequences discovered will offer us useful knowledge to focus on what are really important in case characterization. Moreover, as the number of key sequences is usually is smaller than the number of elements in the series, indexing cases in terms of key sequences exhibits a further dimensionality reduction from series obtained via temporal abstraction.

Finally, finding sequential patterns was widely addressed in the literature of sequence mining [2, 6, 19], where the goal was merely to find all legal sequential patterns with their frequencies of appearances above a user-specified threshold. Identifying key sequences in our context differs from those in sequence mining in that we have to consider the cause-outcome effect for classification purpose. Only those non-redundant sequences that are not only frequent but also possess strong discriminating power will be selected.

7 Conclusion

This paper aims to identify significant sequences to interpret and deal with dynamic properties of time series cases consisting of discrete, symbolic patterns. A knowledge discovery approach is proposed for this purpose. This approach uses the whole case library as available resources and is able to find from the problem space all qualified sequences that are non-redundant and indicative. An indicative sequence exhibits a high co-occurrence with a certain class and is hence valuable in offering discriminative strength for prediction. A sequence that is both indicative and non-redundant is termed as a key sequence.

It is shown that that the key sequences discovered are highly usable to characterize time series cases in case based reasoning. The idea is to transform an original (lengthy) time series into a more concise representation in terms of the occurrences of key sequences detected. Three alternate ways to develop case indexes based on key sequences are suggested. The performance and applicability of these three case indexing methods will be tested in practical case studies within our medical project in future.

References

1. A. Aamodt and E. Plaza. Case-based reasoning: foundational issues, methodological variations and systems approaches. AI Communications, 7:39-59, 1994.
2. R. Agrawal and R. Srikant. Mining sequential patterns. In Proceedings of the 11th International Conference on Data Engineering, pages 3-14. 1995.
3. R. Bellazzi, C. Larizza, and A. Riva. Temporal abstractions for interpreting diabetic patients monitoring data. Intelligent Data Analysis, 2:97-122, 1998.
4. I. Bichindaritz and E. Conlon. Temporal knowledge representation and organization for case-based reasoning. In Proc. TIME-96, pages 152-159. IEEE Computer Society Press, Washington, DC, 1996.
5. K. P. Chan and A. W. Fu. Efficient time series matching by wavelets. In Proceedings of the International Conference on Data Engineering, pages 126-133. 1999.
6. M. N. Garofalakis, R. Rajeev, and K. Shim. SPIRIT: Sequential pattern mining with regular expressing constraints. In Proceedings of the 25th International Conference on Very Large Data bases, pages 223-234. 1999.

7. M. D. Jaere, A. Aamodt, and P. Skalle. Representing temporal knowledge for case-based prediction. In S. Craw and A. Preece, editors, Proceedings of the European Conference on Case-Based Reasoning, pages 174-188. 2002.

8. J. Jarmulak, S. Craw, and R. Rowe. Genetic algorithms to optimise CBR retrieval. In E. Blanzieri and L. Portinale, editors, Proceedings of the European Conference on Case-Based Reasoning, pages 136-147. Springer, 2000.

9. D. McSherry. Explaining the Pros and Cons of conclusions in CBR. In Proceedings of the European Conference on Case-Based Reasoning, pages 317-330. 2004.

10. S. Montani, et al. Case-based retrieval to support the treatment of end stage renal failure patients, Artificial Intelligence in Medicine, in press.

11. S. Montani and L. Portinale. Case based representation and retrieval with time dependent features. In Proceedings of the International Conference on Case-Based Reasoning, pages 353-367. Springer, 2005.

12. M. Nilsson, and P. Funk. A Case-based classification of respiratory sinus arrhythmia. In Proceedings of the 7th European Conference on Case-Based Reasoning, pages 673-685. Madrid, Springer, 2004.

13. E. Olsson, P. Funk, and N. Xiong. Fault diagnosis in industry using sensor readings and case-based reasoning. Journal of Intelligent & Fuzzy Systems, 15:41-46, 2004.

14. P. Perner. Incremental learning of retrieval knowledge in a case-based reasoning system. In K. D. Ashley and D. G. Bridge, editors, Proceedings of the International Conference on Case-Based Reasoning, pages 422-436. Springer, 2003.

15. G. Salton. Automatic information organization and retrieval. New York: McGraw-Hill, 1968.

16. R. Schmidt, B. Heindl, B. Pollwein, and L. Gierl. Abstraction of data and time for multiparametric time course prognoses. In Advances of Case-Based Reasoning, pages 377-391. LNAI 1168, Springer-Verlag, Berlin, 1996.

17. B. von Schéele. Classification Systems for RSA, ETCO2 and other physiological parameters. PBM Stressmedicine, Technical Report, Heden 110, 82131 Bollnäs, Sweden, 1999.

18. Y. Shahar. A framework for knowledge-based temporal abstractions. Artificial Intelligence, 90:79-133, 1997.

19. R. Srikant and R. Agrawal. Mining sequential patterns: Generalizations and performance improvements. In Proceedings of the 5th International Conference on Extending Database Technology, pages 3-17. 1996.

20. Y. Wu, D. Agrawal, and A. El Abbadi. A comparison of DFT and DWT based similarity search in time series databases. In Proceedings of the 9th ACM CIKM Conference on Information and Knowledge Management, pages 488-495. McLean, VA, 2000.

21. S. Zelikovitz and H. Hirsh. Integrating background knowledge into nearest-neighbor text classification. In S. Craw and A. Preece, editors, Proceedings of the European Conference on Case-Based Reasoning, pages 1-5. Springer, 2002.

Case-Based Reasoning for Autonomous Service Failure Diagnosis and Remediation in Software Systems

Stefania Montani and Cosimo Anglano

Dipartimento di Informatica, Università del Piemonte Orientale, Alessandria, Italy
stefania.montani, cosimo.anglano@unipmn.it

Abstract. Self-healing, one of the four key properties characterizing Autonomic Systems, aims to enable large-scale software systems delivering complex services on a 24/7 basis to meet their goals without any human intervention. Achieving self-healing requires the elicitation and maintenance of domain knowledge in the form of ⟨service failure diagnosis, remediation strategy⟩ patterns, a task which can be overwhelming. Case-Based Reasoning (CBR) is a lazy learning paradigm that largely reduces this kind of knowledge acquisition bottleneck. Moreover, the application of CBR for failure diagnosis and remediation in software systems appears to be very suitable, as in this domain most errors are re-occurrences of known problems. In this paper, we describe a CBR approach for providing large-scale, distributed software systems with self-healing capabilities, and demonstrate the practical applicability of our methodology by means of some experimental results on a real world application.

1 Introduction

The inherent complexity, heterogeneity, and dynamism of today's large-scale networked applications and services makes inappropriate, if not impossible, the traditional human-centered approach to system administration [15]. As a result, the attention of the industrial and academic communities has been driven towards novel solutions for the design of computer and software systems that can manage themselves in accordance with high-level guidance from humans. A common background for these contributions can be found in the definition of the *Autonomic Computing* paradigm [15,21], which introduces the concept of an Autonomic Computing System (ACS), an environment composed of (one or more) *managed elements*, whose behavior is controlled by an *autonomic manager*. The autonomic manager operates according to the so-called *autonomic cycle* [21], schematically depicted in Fig. 1, that encompasses four distinct steps:

- *monitoring* the managed element(s), in order to collect information concerning its (their) state and behavior;
- *analysing* the collected data, to determine possible deviations from the correct or intended functioning;

T.R. Roth-Berghofer et al. (Eds.): ECCBR 2006, LNAI 4106, pp. 489–503, 2006.

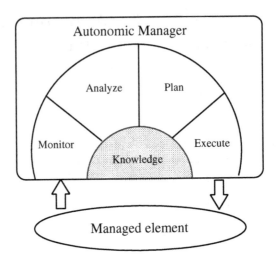

Fig. 1. The architecture of an Autonomic Manager, illustrating the *autonomic cycle*

- *planning* proper remediation strategies, to bring the system back into normal behavior;
- *executing* the plan by exploiting suitable actuation mechanisms that must be provided by the managed element(s).

The goal of the approach is to obtain a system that exhibits the so called *Self-** properties, namely:

- *Self-Configuration*: the ACS is able to (re)configure itself under varying and unpredictable conditions;
- *Self-Optimization*: the ACS is able to detect and to optimize suboptimal behaviors;
- *Self-Protection*: the ACS is able to protect itself from both external and internal attacks;
- *Self-Healing*: the ACS is able to detect problems and/or failures and to recover from them.

The achievement of each one of the *Self-** properties requires that all the steps of the autonomic cycle are carried out.

The Autonomic Computing paradigm is particularly attractive for large-scale software systems aimed at delivering on-line services on a 24/7 basis, as for instance those described in [12,27]. The very large size of these systems (that may typically include from hundreds to thousands of machines), and the adoption of customized application software and middleware, makes at the same time service failures relatively frequent and human-centered system administration very hard, if not impossible. Consequently, self-managing capabilities, and especially self-healing, represent a very attractive solution.

Providing a software system with self-healing capabilities requires the availability of specific knowledge about the ⟨service failure diagnosis, remediation strategy) patterns that may apply to the system at hand. Formalizing this kind of knowledge, e.g. by means of rules or models, is a difficult and time consuming task, and periodic revision od the knowledge base is required to always keep it up to date. These requirements are clearly in conflict with the goal of making the system as much as possible independent of human intervention. It is worth pointing out that this observation holds also when the task is the one of "retrofitting" self-healing behavior into existing legacy applications [20].

The Case Based Reasoning (CBR) methodology [3] is known to be well suited to those domains where formalized and widely recognized background knowledge is not available. CBR actually allows one to build a knowledge base of past situations (*cases*), which represent an "implicit" (i.e. operative) form of knowledge, that can be reused in present problems, possibly after an adaptation step. Representing a real-world situation as a case is often straighforward: given a set of meaningful features for the application domain, it is sufficient to identify the value they assume in the situation at hand; typically, a case also stores information about the solution applied and the outcome obtained. Due to the simplicity of this process, in many real world examples the knowledge acquisition bottleneck can be significantly reduced in comparison with the exploitation of other reasoning methodologies. Moreover, new knowledge is automatically stored in the case base during the normal working process; as the case library grows, more and more representative examples are collected, and it becomes easier to find a proper solution to a new problem by means of this paradigm.

CBR seems particularly appropriate to failure diagnosis and remediation in software systems, as in this domain most errors are re-occurrences of known problems [8,13,26]; the methodology also provides a unique framework in which failure diagnosis and remediation are performed jointly.

Nevertheless, to the best of our knowledge, the only investigation in this direction has been published in [13], where a case-based retrieval system for discovering software problems without requiring human intervention is presented. The approach is quite limited, as it consists of a pure retrieval systems, in which the other steps of the CBR cycle [3] are ignored, and the problem solution is not provided.

In the present paper, we describe a CBR approach to support self-healing in (possibly large and distributed) software systems, in which case-based retrieval supports service failure diagnosis, while the reuse-revise step supports remediation. This contribution extends the ideas described in [6], and further tests them through some experiments. Experiments were conducted on a test bed implemented by means of Cavy [7], a tool supporting the deployment and operation of testbeds tailored to self-healing infrastructures.

The rest of the paper is organized as follows. In Section 2 we present related work about self-healing achievements in software systems. Section 3 details the CBR approach to self-healing, while Section 4 provides some experimental results, obtained on a testbed built using Cavy. Finally, Section 5 concludes the paper and outlines future research work.

2   Related Work

Various approaches to fault diagnosis and remediation have been proposed in the literature. Sterrit [32] proposes an approach to fault diagnosis based on *event correlation*, where various *symptoms* of system malfunctions (represented by alarms triggered by the various system components that are collected during the monitoring phase) are correlated in order to determine the (set of) fault(s) that have occurred. An alternative approach is proposed by Garlan and Schmerl [16], where fault diagnosis is performed by means of a suitable set of models. Joshi et al. [18] use Bayesian estimation and Markov decision processes to probabilistically diagnose faults, and use the results to generate recovery actions. Littman [23] proposes *cost-sensitive fault remediation*, a planning-based technique aimed at determining the most cost-effective system reconfiguration able to bring the system back to full functionality. Planning is also the basis for the fault remediation strategy proposed by Arshad [8].

The main drawback of these approaches is that they require the availability of formalized and widely recognized background knowledge (henceforth referred to as *structured knowledge*) about the structure and/or the behavior of the system. For instance, planning-based techniques require a description of the domain, the states, and the correct configurations of the system, while event correlation requires the availability of a model describing how the various system components interact with each other. Unfortunately, as already observed, significant effort is usually required to build, maintain, and use structured knowledge, with the consequence that its applicability to large-size systems, exhibiting complex behaviors and interactions among their components, may be problematic. Another drawback of these approaches is their "fault orientation", that is they are triggered by individual component faults. Consequently, they attempt to correct a fault as soon as it is diagnosed (*preventive maintenance* [2]), even if it is not (yet) causing any service disruption because it is *dormant* [2], or it has been masked by the fault-tolerance techniques embedded into the system. Devising a repair plan for a fault that can be masked by the system is a waste of resources, and the same holds true for a dormant fault that, when it occurs, can be masked as well. Furthermore, from the perspective of service delivery, a dormant or masked fault has little or no importance until it causes a service failure (i.e., it becomes *active* [2]). However, while pro-active repair of dormant faults can be important in physical systems, for software systems it is much less important, as an unnoticed bug or a misconfiguration (which are, by definition, dormant faults) may never turn into an active fault causing a service failure. For instance, an unnoticed bug may be corrected as a side effect of a software update performed to fix another problem. Moreover, the correction of dormant or masked faults requires the availability of a model of the system, which brings us back to the problem of acquiring structured knowledge mentioned before. Finally, the proposals discussed before either address fault diagnosis or fault remediation, but none of them addresses both issues at the same time.

3   A CBR Approach to Self-healing

As discussed in the Introduction, achieving the self-healing property in a software system requires that the four steps of the autonomic cycle are carried out.

The CBR cycle fits very well into the autonomic cycle, since it naturally covers the *analysis* and *planning* phases by means of the *retrieval* and *reuse-revise* steps, respectively; moreover, the *knowledge* used by the autonomic manager is contained in the case base, properly maintained by applying the *retain* step policies.

The other two phases of the autonomic cycle (i.e., *monitoring* and *execution*) have to be covered by additional specific modules (see Fig. 2), giving birth to an architecture in which the running system (i.e. the managed element) is treated as a "black box", surrounded by a set of external modules that form a closed-loop controlling the "health" of the system itself, and performing proper repair actions in case of service failures (an approach known as *externalization* [16]).

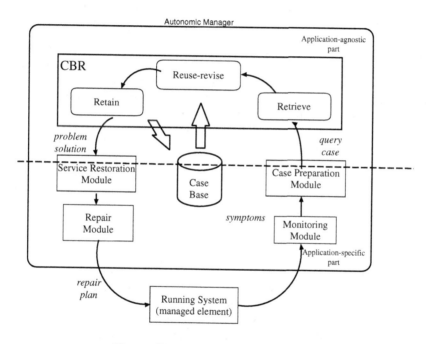

Fig. 2. CBR approach to Self-Healing

In our implementation of externalization, this closed loop includes:

- the *monitoring* module, which detects a service failure by means of specific tests (the list of which tests to execute has to be provided by a human expert in a *bootstrap* phase - see section 3.3);
- the *case preparation* module, which collects the set of symptoms identified by the monitoring module, and maps them to an application-specific case

structure. In this way, it properly defines a new case, which can be used as a query case by the three modules listed below, which implement the CBR cycle:

- the *retrieve* module, which retrieves past cases similar to the query one, thus implicitly providing a set of possible diagnoses for the current problem (see section 3.1);
- the *reuse-revise* module, which establishes what is (are) the candidate(s) solution(s) to the input problem, given the list of retrieved ones (see section 3.2);
- the *retain* module, which defines some policies about the opportunity of maintaining the current problem-solution pattern in the case base, possibly after a proper summarization strategy has been applied (see section 3.3);
- the *service restoration module*, that converts the above solution(s) into a (set of) repair plan(s);
- the *repair* module, which finally executes the repair plan corresponding to the selected solution, by using suitable application-specific mechanisms.

As shown in Fig. 2, the external modules can be classified either into *application-specific*, i.e. that must be tailored to the specific characteristics of the running system, or *application-agnostic*. While the monitoring and repair activities require the availability and usage either of knowledge and mechanisms provided by the running system or of adapted third-party components [19] (hence their classification as application-specific), the problem resolution activity (performed by the CBR modules) does not rely upon any particular system feature (although an adaptation strategy would require specific domain knowledge). The *case definition* and the *service restoration* modules do not fall in just one of the two cathegories, since they act as an interface between the two layers. Further details about the CBR modules can be found in the following subsections.

3.1   Retrieve

As already observed, case-based retrieval will cover the diagnostic task of the self-healing procedure. In a large and distributed software system, different kinds of failures, that need to be solved by applying completely unrelated solutions, might take place. The service failure observed in the query case could therefore be used as a means for identifying relevant subparts of the case base to work with.

We therefore propose to structure retrieval as a multi-step procedure, in which two steps have to be accomplished (see e.g. [25]):

1. a *classification/grouping* step, which selects from the case base the subset of past cases in which the same (or a similar - see Section 4) service failure as the one in the query case took place;
2. a proper *retrieval* step, which extracts the most similar (i.e. less distant) cases from the reduced search space identified at step 1.

As described by Kolodner [22], classification/grouping may be seen as a particular kind of the so-called *situation assessment*, which allows one to provide the context under which the input situation can be better interpreted.

The above classes/groups can be either implicit or explicit. In the first situation, there is no need to explicitly identify a set of predefined classes - a task that might be hard to be achieved without sufficient background knowledge, e.g. when an exhaustive list of possible service failures is not available. In this case, a k-NN step is used, in order to restrict the case library (through *k-NN retrieval*). Case features are used to obtain the set of most similar service failures: only cases related to such failures constitute the *group* which is then used in Step 2. In the second situation, a set of predefined explicit *classes* is required to be available. Cases belonging to the same class as the input case are identified this time through *k-NN classification* and they will be used as the search space for the subsequent retrieval step. The distance $d(c_i, c_j)$ between cases c_i and c_j is typically computed as a weighted average of the normalized distances among their various features.

3.2 Reuse and Revise

After past similar cases have been retrieved, their solutions have to be analysed, in order to verify if they can be reused in the present situation.

In the software failures domain, it can happen that the query situation is a combination of two or more past ones (i.e. two different service failures have taken place contemporaneously, or the same service failure has been caused by two faults, whose symptoms are described as feature values). If this condition holds, all the pertinent past solutions (i.e. remediation strategies) can be exploited, by applying all of them in sequence, until the service is restored (and all the remaining unapplied solutions are then discarded). The order in which solutions should be applied, and the possible need to undo the effect of an already tested remediation strategy before applying another, are application-dependent aspects, that should be provided as initial guidelines by the human experts. As a matter of fact, the details of even a simple adaptation strategy cannot be provided in a general fashion, but need to be tailored to the system under consideration.

3.3 Bootstrap and Retain

In order to behave as a really self-healing system, our infrastructure must be able to work as much as possible in an autonomous way, i.e. without human intervention. However, this can happen only if a case base containing enough instances of solved cases is available, but in general this does not hold true when the system is initially put into operation.

We therefore envision a *bootstrap* phase, enabling the collection of the initial cases, during which problem solution is performed by humans.

Background knowledge is needed also when the case base does not contain examples similar to the query case (due to the presence of competence gaps within the case base itself). In this situation, human intervention could be required on the fly.

However, it is worth noting that:

1. Competence gaps tend to be reduced while the system is being used, since CBR is a lazy learning paradigm which automatically collects new knowledge in an implicit form. A retain strategy could be applied to control case base growth, for example by resorting to techniques already published in the literature, like for instance the definition of suitable "prototypes" (see e.g. [31]), able to summarize the information carried by the ground cases they represent, that are stored in place of the cases themselves. These aspects may become more critical if a memory organization has been imposed on the case base, and has to be maintained while introducing new examples; proper startegies have to be devised to this hand;

2. If a reasonable amount of explicit knowledge is available in the beginning, it might be somehow integrated with the CBR system (especially in the revision phase), in order to improve the remediation strategies definition (see also Section 5).

4   Experimental results

We tested the CBR-based self-healing infrastructure by means of a testbed built using Cavy [7], a tool specically conceived to deploy and operate hardware/software testbeds aimed at testing self-healing infrastructures. Cavy provides failure injection and repair mechanisms, as well as monitoring and repair functionalities. In our experiments the testbed was used to inject a set of failures into Moodle [1], a Web-based widely adopted system supporting distance learning. Moodle's architecture encompasses a PHP-enabled Web server, that acts as a portal to access various kinds of services (typically Apache), and a Database Management System (typically MySQL), that stores all the relevant information about users and courses handled by Moodle.

Like any software system delivering complex services, Moodle exhibits a rather large set of service failures, that may be due to a variety of reasons including misconfiguration errors due to human operations, software bugs, and faulty hardware components and/or crashes of the operating system used on the various resources. These problems are well documented on the Moodle's web site, where a list of known problems and possible solutions is posted and constantly kept up-to-date. For our example, we analyzed this list of failures and mapped each failure to a set of individual faults, that were subsequently injected into the hardware/software components of the testbed. Details have been omitted in this paper because of space constraints (the interested reader may refer to [7] for a fuller explanation). This analysis resulted in the identification of the three service failure classes described below, each one containing several failures:

1. *Page display failures*: under this category fall all the cases in which the contents of a Moodle section are not displayed correctly on the web browser. Examples taken from the installation FAQ are:

- All the pages are blank
- Rather than its correct contents, the pages show errors such as "call to undefined function", the error string "headers already sent", or the error message "Failed open required /web/moodle/lib/setup.php"

2. *Resource access failures*: this category contains all the cases in which various objects contained in a Moodle section cannot be accessed correctly, such as the ones listed below (taken again from the installation FAQ):
   - When trying to access an uploaded file, Moodle replies with a "File not Found" error message
   - When trying to add a resource, Moodle replies with an error message

3. *User services failures*: under this category fall all the failures in delivering user-oriented services, such as:
   - When the user tries to log in, nothing happens and the login screen seems to be stuck
   - After logging in to the system, the user page is not shown and a "session_start" error is displayed
   - The messages posted on a forum managed by Moodle are not sent to the registered users

We structured the case base in different classes, each one corresponding to one of the three service failure classes described above. We were thus able to structure retrieval as a two-step procedure (see Section 3.1), in which a first classification step selects the subpart of the case library that will be then exploited for retrieval itself (second step).

As a first example, for the sake of brevity we will concentrate on the third class of service failures (namely *User services failures*), assuming that the classification step has already been completed. The class at hand includes five cases, listed in Fig. 3. In particular, the *Failure* feature describes the observed service failure (either session fail, or login fail, or forum email not sent). The *Error(msg)* feature contains a string corresponding to the error message shown on the screen (if any), or briefly describing the kind of error that can be observed (i.e. the screen seems to be stuck, or a timeout has been registered in the webserver log). The *Cron* features specifies whether the *cron* process is active or not at the time of the failure observation, while the *DBMS* feature indicates if the DBMS is responsive or not. Finally, the *Solution* feature has a self-explanatory meaning.

The case describing the input problem is shown in Fig. 4, and corresponds to a non trivial situation, that has been emulated through Cavy, in which both the DBMS process is not responsive because of an accidental kill, and network connectivity on the webserver machine is unavailable because of an operating system problem. Nevertheless, we suppose that the DBMS reachability has not been explicitly tested (therefore the *DBMS* feature value is NULL). Note that no case in the case base represents the co-existence of two problems at the same time.

Case	Failure	Error(msg)	Cron	DBMS	Solution
1	session fail	"session_start" "...no such file"	NULL	yes	update session.save.path in php.inifile
2	login fail	stuck	NULL	yes	set secureform to NO in config.php
3	forum email not sent	NULL	no	yes	setup Cron process
4	login fail	timeout in webserver log	NULL	no	restart DBMS
5	login fail	timeout in webserver log	NULL	yes	restart webserver machine

Fig. 3. Contents of the case base in the user services failures class. NULL means "not tested".

Failure	Error(msg)	Cron	DBMS
login fail	timeout in webserver log	NULL	NULL

Fig. 4. The case corresponding to the new service failure in the user services failures example

The new case c_n is then passed to the retrieve module (see Fig. 2) that computes its distance from each case c_i in the case base as:

$$d(c_n, c_i) = \frac{\sum_{k=1}^{N} w_k \cdot d(c_n(k), c_i(k))}{N} \qquad (1)$$

where $d(c_n(k), c_i(k))$ and w_k denote the normalized distance between feature k of cases c_n and c_i, and the weight associated with this feature, respectively. Different types of features obviously require the use of different distance functions. For the features describing cases in this example (all of which are of type either 'string' or 'boolean') we use the *overlap distance* [34], defined as:

$$d(c_i(k), c_j(k)) = \begin{cases} 0 & \text{if } c_i(k) = c_j(k) \\ 1 & \text{otherwise} \end{cases}$$

and we assume that all the features have weights equal to 1. We also define as 1 the distance between the NULL value and any other value.

The distances between the new case and all the cases in the case base are shown in Fig. 5, from which we can observe that the closest matches to the new case are Case 4 and Case 5.

In the event of a tie, as regards the Moodle application, we have implemented a policy in which the solutions from the two most similar cases are applied in sequence (this is a very simple form of adaptation; obviously, more complex adaptation procedures could be devised, depending on the application).

distance w.r.t.	Failure	Error(msg)	Cron	DBMS	Overall Distance
Case 1	1	1	1	1	1
Case 2	0	1	1	1	3/4
Case 3	1	1	1	1	1
Case 4	0	0	1	1	2/4
Case 5	0	0	1	1	2/4

Fig. 5. Distances between the new service failure and the cases in the case base in the user services failures example

In the example the reuse-revise module (see Fig. 2) first tries to restart the DBMS (technically, it sends to the service restoration module the solution of Case 4, which is mapped to the corresponding fault repair plan).

But just restarting the DBMS cannot solve the problem, as we know. The DBMS is now correctly responsive, therefore the input case becomes identical to Case 5. The further implementation of the Case 5 solution, foreseen by the adaptation policy, is obviously successful.

Note that, since both the DBMS and the webserver problems are represented in the query case at the same time, and they are technically independent, it would be equally possible to apply the two best match solutions in the opposite order, obtaining the desired result. In other words, in this situation the order of implementation of the solutions is not critical.

As a second example, let us refer to the *Page display failures* class. For this class, the *Failure* feature describes the observed service failure (either the displayed page is blank, or it is non-blank but contains error messages of various types). The *DirRoot Pathname* feature indicates the presence of an error in the PHP configuration file config.php, consisting of setting its *DirRoot* variable to a relative path name rather than to an absolute one. The *Missing Delimiter* feature indicates the presence of syntax errors (missing semicolon or quotes) at the end of some lines in the configuration file, while *Blank Line After End* indicates the presence of blank lines after the final delimiter of the configuration file, which is considered a syntax error by the PHP interpreter.

For this example, we assume that the case base contains the three cases reported in Fig. 6. As can be observed from the contents of the case base, all the failures are due to syntax errors unintentionally introduced in the config.php

Case	Failure	DirRoot pathname	Missing delimiter	Blank Line after end	Solution
1	page blank	relative	No	No	use absolute path name for DirRoot in config.php
2	Page shows errors	absolute	Yes	No	insert missing semicolon or ending quote in config.php line
3	Page shows errors	absolute	No	Yes	Remove blank lines after final '? >' in config.php

Fig. 6. Contents of the case base in the page display failures class

Failure	DirRoot Pathname	Missing Delimiter	Blank Line After End
Page shows errors	relative	No	No

Fig. 7. The case corresponding to the new service failure in the page display failures example

distance w.r.t.	Failure	DirRoot Pathname	Missing. Delimiter	Blank Line After End	Overall Distance
Case 1	1	0	0	0	1/4
Case 2	0	1	1	0	2/4
Case 3	0	1	0	1	2/4

Fig. 8. Distances between the new service failure and the cases in the case base in the page display failures example

file used by the Apache web server. The case describing the input problem is shown in Fig. 7.

The distances between the new case and all the cases in the *Page display* class are shown in Fig. 8, from which we can observe that the closest match to the new case is Case 1. Therefore, the reuse-revise module sends to the service restoration module the solution of Case 1, which is mapped to the corresponding fault repair plan. Observe that the retrieved past solution can be correctly reused, even if the past failure is different from the current one.

5   Conclusions and Future Work

In this paper we have presented a CBR approach for the achievement of self-healing in software systems that, unlike alternative solutions, avoids unnecessary repair actions. The repair procedure is indeed triggered by service failures rather than by individual component failures. Moreover, it does not require the availability of structured knowledge, such as models of the system behavior, thus easing its applicability to large-scale, complex software systems.

The suitability of this approach has been demonstrated in this paper by some tests conducted on the Moodle application, running on a distributed architecture. For this purpose, we built an ad hoc test bed using Cavy, a tool supporting the deployment and operation of testbeds tailored to self-healing infrastructures. Cavy allows to easily define testbeds with various characteristics. In the future we plan to exploit it for verifying our CBR approach to self-healing on additional real world applications.

Moreover, we also plan to test the advantages of our approach in applications in which some formalized background knowledge is available. Actually, CBR can be easily combined with other knowledge sources and with other reasoning paradigms, and is particularly well suited for integration with Rule Based or Model Based systems [17]. The interest in multi modal approaches involving CBR is recently increasing through different application areas [5,14], from planning [10] to classification [33] and to diagnosis [24], and from legal [11,29] to medical decision support [9,31,35]. Our goal will be to demonstrate the further advantages of relying on two different methodologies, by tightly coupling them, or alternatively by just switching between one and the other, when the aim is to provide a software system with autonomic diagnosis and remediation capabilities.

References

1. The Moodle project web site. http://www.moodle.org. Accessed on Jan. 15th, 2006.
2. A. Avizienis and J. Laprie and B. Randell and C. Landwehr. Basic Concepts and Taxonomy of Dependable and Secure Computing. *IEEE Transactions on Dependable and Secure Computing*, 1(1), January-March 2004.
3. A. Aamodt and E. Plaza. Case-based reasoning: foundational issues, methodological variations and systems approaches. *AI Communications*, 7:39–59, 1994.
4. D.S. Aghassi. Evaluating case-based reasoning for heart failure diagnosis. Technical report, sept. of EECS, MIT, Cambridge, MA, 1990.
5. D. Aha and J. Daniels, editors. *Proc. AAAI Workshop on CBR Integrations*. AAAI Press, 1998.
6. C. Anglano and S. Montani. Achieving self-healing in autonomic software systems: a case-based reasoning approach. In H. Czap, R. Unland, C. Branki, and H. Tianfield, editors, *Proc. International Conference on Self-Organization and Adaptation of Multi-agent and Grid Systems (SOAS), Glasgow, December 2005*, pages 267–281. IOS Press, Amsterdam, 2005.
7. C. Anglano and S. Montani. Cavy: a tool for the deployment and operation of Self-Healing testbeds, Jan. 2006. Submitted for publication.
8. N. Arshad, D. Heimbigner, and A. Wolf. A Planning Based Approach to Failure Recovery in Distributed Systems. In *Proc. of 2nd ACM Workshop on Self-Healing Systems (WOSS '04)*, Newport Beach, CA, USA, October 2004. ACM Press.
9. I. Bichindaritz, E. Kansu, and K. Sullivan. Case-based reasoning in care-partner: Gathering evidence for evidence-based medical practice. In B. Smyth and P. Cunningham, editors, *Proc. 4th European Workshop on Case-Based Reasoning*, volume 1488 of *Lecture Notes in Computer Science*, pages 334–345, Dublin, Ireland, September 1998. Springer.
10. P.P. Bonissone and S. Dutta. Integrating case-based and rule-based reasoning: the possibilistic connection. In *Proc. of 6th Conference on Uncertainty in Artificial Intelligence*, Cambridge, MA, USA, July 1990.
11. L.K. Branting and B.W. Porter. Rules and precedents as complementary warrants. In *Proc. of 9th National Conference on Artificial Intelligence*, Anaheim, CA, USA, July 1991. AAAI Press.
12. E. Brewer. Lessons from giant-scale services. *IEEE Internet Computing*, 5(4), 2001.
13. M. Brodie, S. Ma, G. Lohman, T. Syeda-Mahmood, L. Mignet, N. Modani, J. Champlin, and P. Sohn. Quickly finding known software problems via automated symptom matching. In *Proc. of the 2nd International Conference on Autonomic Computing*, Seattle, WA, USA, June 2005.
14. E. Freuder, editor. *Proc. AAAI Spring Symposium on Multi-modal Reasoning*. AAAI Press, 1998.

15. A.G. Ganek and T.A. Corbi. The dawning of the autonomic computing era. *IBM Systems Journal*, 42(1):5–18, 2003.

16. D. Garlan and B. Schmerl. Model-based Adaptation for Self-Healing Systems. In *Proc. of 1ˢᵗ ACM Workshop on Self-Healing Systems (WOSS '02)*, Charleston, SC, USA, November 2002. ACM Press.

17. K.J. Hammond. *Case-Based Planning: viewing planning as a memory task.* Academic Press, 1989.

18. K.R. Joshi, M.A. Hiltunen, W.H. Sanders, and R.D. Schlichting. Automatic Model-Driver Recovery in Distributed Systems. In *Proc. of 24th IEEE Symposium on Reliable Distributed Systems (SRDS 05)*. IEEE Press, 2005.

19. G. Kaiser, J. Parekh, P. Gross, and G. Valetto. Kenesthetics eXtreme: An External Infrastructure for Monitoring Distributed Legacy Systems. In *Proc. of 5ᵗʰ IEEE International Active Middleware Workshop*, Seattle, WA, USA, June 2003. IEEE CS Press.

20. G. Kaiser, J. Parekh, P. Gross, and G. Valetto. Retrofitting Autonomic Capabilities onto Legacy Systems. Technical Report TR CUCS-026-03, Department of Computer Science, Columbia University, 2003.

21. J.O. Kephart and D.M. Chess. The vision of autonomic computing. *IEEE Computer*, January 2003.

22. J.L. Kolodner. *Case-Based Reasoning.* Morgan Kaufmann, San Mateo, CA, 1993.

23. M. Littman, T. Nguyen, and H. Hirsh. Cost-Sensitive Fault Remediation for Autonomic Computing. In *Proc. of IJCAI Workshop on AI and Autonomic Computing: Developing a Research Agenda for Self-Managing Computer Systems*, Acapulco, Mexico, August 2003.

24. D. Macchion and D. Vo. A hybrid knowledge-based system for technical diagnosis learning and assistance. In S. Wess, K. Althoff, and M. Richter, editors, *Proc. 1st European Workshop on Case-Based Reasoning*, volume 837 of *Lecture Notes in Computer Science*, pages 301–312, Kaiserslautern, Germany, November 1993. Springer.

25. S. Montani and L. Portinale. Accounting for the temporal dimension in case-based retrieval: a framework for medical applications. *Computational Intelligence* (to appear).

26. D. Oppenheimer, A. Ganapathi, and D. Patterson. Why do Internet services fail, and what can be done about it? In *Proc. of 4ᵗʰ Usenix Symposium on Internet Technologies and Systems (USITS '03)*, Seattle, WA, USA, March 2003.

27. D. Oppenheimer and D. Patterson. Architecture and Dependability of Large-Scale Internet Services. *IEEE Internet Computing*, September-October 2002.

28. L. Portinale, P. Torasso, and D. Magro. Selecting most adaptable diagnostic solutions through pivoting-based retrieval. In D. Leake and E. Plaza, editors, *Proc. of 2nd International Conference on Case-Based Reasoning*, volume 1266 of *Lecture Notes in Computer Science*, pages 393–402, Providence, RI, USA, July 1997. Springer.

29. E. Rissland and D. Skalak. Combining case-based and rule-based reasoning: A heuristic approach. In N. S. Sridharan, editor, *Proc. of 11th International Joint Conference on Artificial Intelligence*, pages 524–530, 1989.

30. J.W. Schaaf. Fish and shrink. a next step towards efficient case retrieval in large-scale case bases. In I. F. C. Smith and B. Faltings, editors, *Proc. 3rd European Workshop on Case-Based ReasoningEWCBR*, volume 1168 of *Lecture Notes in Computer Science*, pages 362–376, Lausanne, Switzerland, November 1996. Springer.

31. R. Schmidt, S. Montani, R. Bellazzi, L. Portinale, and L. Gierl. Case-based reasoning for medical knowledge-based systems. *International Journal of Medical Informatics*, 64(2-3):355–367, 2001.

32. R. Sterrit. Autonomic networks: engineering the self-healing property. *Engineering Applications of Artificial Intelligence*, 17:727–739, October 2004.

33. J. Surma and K. Vanhoof. Integration rules and cases for the classification task. In M. Veloso and A. Aamodt, editors, *Proc. 1st Int. Conference on Case-Based Reasoning*, volume 1010 of *Lecture Notes in Computer Science*, pages 325–334, Sesimbra, Portugal, October 1995. Springer.

34. D.R. Wilson and T.R. Martinez. Improved heterogeneous distance functions. *Journal of Artificial Intelligence Research*, 6:1–34, 1997.

35. L.D. Xu. An integrated rule- and case-based approach to AIDS initial assessment. *International Journal of Biomedical Computing*, 40:197–207, 1996.

Tracking Concept Drift at Feature Selection Stage in SpamHunting: An Anti-spam Instance-Based Reasoning System

J.R. Méndez[1], F. Fdez-Riverola[1], E.L. Iglesias[1], F. Díaz[2], and J.M. Corchado[3]

[1] Dept. Informática, University of Vigo, Escuela Superior de Ingeniería Informática,
Edificio Politécnico, Campus Universitario As Lagoas s/n, 32004, Ourense, Spain
{moncho.mendez, riverola, eva}@uvigo.es
[2] Dept. Informática, University of Valladolid, Escuela Universitaria de Informática,
Plaza Santa Eulalia, 9-11, 40005, Segovia, Spain
fdiaz@infor.uva.es
[3] Dept. Informática y Automática, University of Salamanca,
Plaza de la Merced s/n, 37008, Salamanca, Spain
corchado@usal.es

Abstract. In this paper we propose a novel feature selection method able to handle concept drift problems in spam filtering domain. The proposed technique is applied to a previous successful instance-based reasoning e-mail filtering system called SpamHunting. Our *achieved information* criterion is based on several ideas extracted from the well-known information measure introduced by Shannon. We show how results obtained by our previous system in combination with the improved feature selection method outperforms classical machine learning techniques and other well-known lazy learning approaches. In order to evaluate the performance of all the analysed models, we employ two different corpus and six well-known metrics in various scenarios.

1 Introduction and Motivation

Internet has introduced a revolutionary way for communication issues. Some daily activities such as news reading or message sending has been innovated and facilitated. Now, an Internet user can send an e-mail through thousands of kilometres with no cost. Unfortunately, some people and companies with doubtful reputation had quickly discovered how to take advantage of this new technology for advertising purposes. Since then, they are constantly sending a lot of advertisement messages known as spam e-mails. These messages are damaging the rights of Internet users because they are paying the transfer costs of the spam messages. Moreover, spam collapses networks, routers and information servers belonging to the Internet Service Providers (ISPs) generating high costs and damages.

Although some legal actions have been introduced for combating the delivery of spam messages, at the moment anti-spam filtering software seems to be the most viable solution to the spam problem. Spam filtering software is often classified as *collaborative* or *content-based* [1]. In the context of collaborative systems, the message filtering is carried out by using judgements made by other users [2]. Although there is no doubt

T.R. Roth-Berghofer et al. (Eds.): ECCBR 2006, LNAI 4106, pp. 504–518, 2006.

that collaborative techniques can be useful to spam filtering, systems able to analyse in detail the intrinsic properties of the message (subject, body contents, structure, etc.) have a better chance of detecting new spam messages [3]. These approaches are included within the content-based approach and are studied in this work.

The main types of content-based techniques are machine learning (ML) algorithms and memory and case-based reasoning approaches. In ML techniques an algorithm is used to 'learn' how to classify new messages from a set of training e-mails. On the other hand, memory and case-based reasoning techniques store all training instances in a memory structure and try to classify new messages by finding similar e-mails to it. Hence, the decision of how to solve a problem is deferred until the last moment. Although ML algorithms have been successfully applied in the text classification field, recent research work has shown that case-based reasoning (CBR) and instance-based reasoning (IBR) systems are more suitable for the spam filtering domain [4, 5, 6].

In this paper we propose and analyse an enhancement over a previous successful anti-spam IBR-based system called SpamHunting [6]. The main objective is to discuss and test a new improvement over knowledge representation in SpamHunting to show the importance of instance representation in CBR/IBR approaches. Results obtained by different well-known spam filtering models and those obtained by our new approach are shown for benchmarking purposes. The models selected to carry out the evaluation are Naïve Bayes [7], boosting trees [8], Support Vector Machines [9], and two case-based systems for spam filtering that can learn dynamically: a Cunningham *et al.* system which we call *Odds-Ratio CBR* [4] and its improved version named *ECUE* [5]. Experiments have been carried out using two different well-known public corpora of e-mails and taking into account several measures in order to represent different points of view.

We are also interested in achieving new findings about the role of feature selection process when using CBR/IBR approaches on the spam filtering domain. Specially, our aim is centred in handling the concept drift problem [4] (inherent in the spam filtering domain) at this early stage. In this work we are showing the dynamical adaptation capacities of SpamHunting when the environment changes. We also describe in detail the role of the feature selection preprocessing step in this kind of situations.

The rest of the paper is structured as follows: section 2 we outline machine learning and case-based e-mail filters mentioned above. In section 3 the SpamHunting IBR architecture is described in detail while in section 4 we present our improved feature selection method for our previous SpamHunting system. Section 5 contains a description of some relevant issues belonging to the experimental setup while section 6 is focused in showing the empirical results obtained by the different models. Finally, in section 7 we expose the main conclusions reached as well as the future lines of our research work.

2 Spam Filtering Techniques

This section contains a brief description of the popular Spam filtering techniques. The following subsections are structured as follows: Subsection 2.1 contains a short introduction to classical ML models that has been successfully applied to the spam filtering domain. Subsection 2.2 is focused in summarizing newest models proposed in the most recent research work.

2.1 ML Classical Approaches

There is no doubt regarding the similarities of text categorization and the spam filtering domain. In fact, both research fields are included into the document automatic classification domain belonging to the Natural Language Processing (NLP) area. Both are based on distributing a collection of documents (or corpus) into several classes or categories. However, we should note that spam and legitimate classes are generally more imprecise, internally disjointed and user-dependant than text categories [1]. Moreover, there are some additional problems in the spam filtering domain such as noise level and concept drift [5, 10].

Due to the related similarity between text categorization and spam filtering domains, several commonly used models and techniques from the former have been successfully applied on the later. The traditional Bayesian method is a clear example of this issue. This kind of spam filters are based on computing the probability of a target message being spam taking into account the probability of finding its terms in Spam e-mails. If some words of the target message are often included in Spam messages but not in legitimate ones. Then it would be reasonable to assume that target e-mail is more likely to be Spam. Although there are several Bayesian approaches, it is Naïve Bayes that is widely used for Spam filtering [7].

Besides Bayesian models, Support Vector Machines (SVM) and boosting techniques are also well-known ML algorithms used in this domain [11]. SVMs [9] have become very popular in the machine learning and data mining communities due to its good generalization performance and its ability to handle high-dimensional data through the use of kernels. They are based on representing e-mails as points in an n-dimensional space and finding a hyperplane that generates the largest margin between the data points in the positive class and those in the negative class. Some implementations of SVM can be found in ML environments such as Waikato Environment for Knowledge Analysis[1] (WEKA) or Yet Another Learning Environment[2] (YALE). Particularly, WEKA includes the *Sequential Minimal Optimization* (SMO) algorithm that has demonstrated a good trade-off between accuracy and speed (see [12] for details).

Boosting techniques [8] classify a target e-mail by combining and weighting the outputs of several weak learners when they are applied over a new message. Weak learners are simple classification algorithms that can learn with an error rate slightly lower than 50%. Several boosting algorithms have been introduced for classification. Of these the AdaBoost algorithm [13] is commonly used.

2.2 Recent Trends in the Spam Filtering Domain

Recently, several new ML models have been introduced for e-mail classification such as Chung-Kwei [14], which is based on pattern-discovery. In this sense, recent research work are focused on improving or adapting current classification models used in spam filtering domain. In this sense, two improvements over Bayesian filtering are proposed in [15, 16] while in [17] Hovold presents an enhancement over SVM model enabling misclassification costs. Keeping in mind the continuous update of the knowledge and the concept drift problem, an incremental adaptive Bayesian learner is

---

[1] WEKA is available from http://www.cs.waikato.ac.nz/ml/weka/
[2] YALE is available from http://yale.sourceforge.net

presented in [18] while in [19, 20] an ensemble classifier able to track concept drift and a SVM enhancement for support this problem are proposed respectively. However, we highlight advances achieved by using CBR systems as they have started a revolution in Spam filtering applications.

Case-based approaches outperform classical machine learning techniques in anti-spam filtering because they work well for disjoint sub-concepts of the spam concept (spam about *porn* has little in common with spam offering *rolex*) whereas classical ML techniques try to learn an unified concept description [5]. Another important advantage of this approach is its ease of updating to tackle the concept drift problem in the anti-spam domain [21].

Cunningham *et al.* have proposed in [5] a successful case-based system for anti-spam filtering that can learn dynamically. The system (which we call *Odds-Ratio CBR*) uses a similarity retrieval algorithm based on Case Retrieval Nets (CRN) [22]. CRN networks are equivalent to the *k*-nearest neighbourhood algorithm but are computationally more efficient in domains where there is feature-value redundancy and missing features in cases, as spam. This classifier uses a unanimous voting technique to determine whether a new e-mail is spam or not. All the returned neighbours need to be classified as spam e-mails in order to classify the new e-mail as Spam.

In the work of Delany *et al.* [4], it is presented the ECUE system (*E-mail Classification Using Examples*) as an evolution from *Odds-Ratio CBR* preceding model. While the previous system uses an odds ratio method for feature selection, the ECUE model uses Information Gain (IG) [23].

Recently, a successful spam filtering IBR model called SpamHunting has been proposed [6]. The main characteristics and the model operation of this system are briefly outlined in the next section.

3 SpamHunting IBR System

The SpamHunting system is a lazy learning hybrid model based on an instance-based reasoning approach able to solve the problem of spam labelling and filtering [6]. This system incorporates an Enhanced Instance Retrieval Network (EIRN) model, which is able to index e-mails in an effective way for efficient retrieval.

Figure 1 presents the SpamHunting model architecture. As it shows, an instance representation stage is needed in order to correctly classify an incoming e-mail. In this step a message descriptor should be generated. This message descriptor consists of a sequence of N features that better summarize the information contained in the e-mail. For this purpose, we use data from two main sources: (*i*) information obtained from the header of the e-mail (see Table 1) and (*ii*) those terms that are more representative of the subject, body and attachments of the message.

In order to gather additional information, the pdf files, images and HTML documents attached to the e-mail are processed and converted to text. This text and the e-mail body are tokenised together by using space, carriage return and tabulator chars as token separators. Finally a stopword removal process is performed over identified tokens by using the stopword list given in [24].

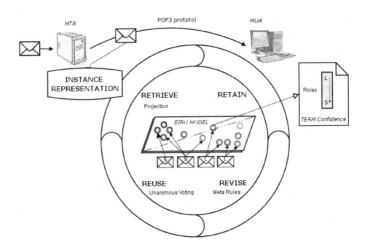

Fig. 1. SpamHunting model architecture

The selection of the best representative terms is carried out in an independent way for each training and testing e-mail. Therefore, each message has its own relevant features. The term selection process is done by computing the set of the most frequent terms which frequency amount is over a given threshold [6]. We have empirically found that best results are obtained by using a threshold of approximately 30% of the frequency amount.

Table 1. Representation of header features stored in the instance-descriptor of SpamHunting system

Variable	Type	Description
From	String	Source mailbox
Return Path	String	Indicates the address used for reply purposes
Date	Date	Delivery date
Language	String	Tongue of the language
Attached Files	Integer	Number of attached files
Content Type	String	MIME type

As Figure 1 shows, the relevant terms selected from the messages are represented in the EIRN network as term-nodes, while the instances are interpreted as a collection of weighted associations with term-nodes. The instance retrieval is carried out by projecting the selected terms from the target problem over the network nodes [6]. The set of messages sharing the maximum number of features with the actual target e-mail is selected as the closest e-mails. Finally, these messages are sorted keeping in mind the frequencies of each shared term between the retrieved e-mails and the target message.

The EIRN network is able to store some useful information about how words are affected by concept drift. In order to support this feature, a confidence measurement for each term-node is computed and saved. Expression (1) defines the confidence of a term w_i using the current knowledge K where $P(w_i \mid S, K)$ and $P(w_i \mid L, K)$ stands for the probability of finding the term w_i in spam and legitimate messages from K respectively.

$$c\left(w_i, K\right) = \frac{\left|P\left(w_i \mid S, K\right) - P\left(w_i \mid L, K\right)\right|}{P\left(w_i \mid S, K\right) + P\left(w_i \mid L, K\right)} \tag{1}$$

In the reuse stage, using a unanimous voting strategy taking into account all the re-trieved e-mails in the previous phase generates a preliminary solution. This approach has been previously used in other successful spam filtering CBR systems [4, 5].

The revise stage is only carried out when the assigned class is spam and it entails the utilisation of meta-rules extracted from e-mail headers. This re-evaluation is per-formed with the goal of guaranteeing the accuracy of the proposed solution.

Finally, when the classification process has been completed, a new instance mes-sage containing the instance-descriptor and the solution (assigned class) is constructed and stored in the instance base for future reuse. During this stage, confidence level of term-nodes affected by the message indexing should be recalculated in order to ade-quately track concept drift effects. A detailed description of the model operation can be found in [6].

4   SpamHunting Feature Selection Improvement

In this section, an improvement for the SpamHunting relevant terms selection algo-rithm can be found. A detailed explanation about the underground ideas behind our proposal and its main abilities are contained below.

A relevant issue related to the context of Artificial Intelligence is the need for ade-quately knowledge representation. Problem solving gets easier when a suitable knowledge representation is chosen. We think that modern and classical classifier models are not sufficient to achieve accurate classification results in spam-filtering domain. In other words, if the knowledge is not perfectly represented, the classifier will not achieve accurate results [25].

Our successful SpamHunting IBR system is based on an EIRN network which has been combined with: (*i*) an original method for selecting the most relevant features in order to improve the representation of the instances and (*ii*) some mechanisms de-signed to adequately handle concept drift during the instance representation stage. Using SpamHunting architecture, we had achieved better results than other current classifier models and other non-improved k-nearest neighbourhood approaches [6].

Shannon has introduced the use of probabilities for measuring the information amount provided by knowing a concrete feature [26]. Keeping in mind this approach, if we are trying to identify somebody, knowing the name is more useful than having knowledge about sex. This happens because the probability of finding somebody knowing the sex is lower than the probability of finding someone when name has been provided. In this context, Expression (2) is used to compute the amount of in-formation achieved by knowing a feature X, where $P(x_i)$ stands for the probability of each event x_i between the n possible values.

$$H(X) = -\sum_{i=1}^{n} P\left(x_i\right) \log P\left(x_i\right) \tag{2}$$

From the above discussion, we can deduce the following ideas: (*i*) the word (term) length is a relevant issue for categorization and filtering because largest words are unusual in documents (the probability of finding a document knowing that it contains a long word is higher) and (*ii*) we should introduce a measurement able to estimate the usefulness of knowing whether or not a keyword *w* is present.

Afore mentioned ideas are important and should be applied to improve the selection of relevant features and consequently the instance representation. The main target goal is to maximise the information contained in an instance.

In this sense, Expression (3) defines the Achieved Information (AI) measure when a term *w* is found in a message *e* having the current knowledge **K**. $P(w \mid e)$ represents the frequency of appearance of a word *w* in the considered message *e*, $P(w \mid S, K)$ and $P(w \mid L, K)$ are the frequencies of finding the word *w* in the current spam and legitimate stored instances (**K**) respectively, and finally, *length(w)* measures the number of characters of the word *w*.

$$AI(w, e \mid K) = P(w \mid e) \cdot \left[1 - \frac{1}{length(w)} \right] \cdot \left[\frac{\left| P(w \mid S, K) - P(w \mid L, K) \right|}{P(w \mid S, K) + P(w \mid L, K)} \right] \tag{3}$$

We highlight the importance of including variable **K** designed for addressing concept drift. In the presence of concept drift, some terms affected by the passage of time can loose its capacity of correctly classifying messages. Therefore, the measurement of this capacity for each word should not be previously calculated using only the training corpus. It must be computed when the target message arrives using all available knowledge at this time.

When a word *w* is not present in any instance stored in the SpamHunting instance base (**K**), the second part in square brackets belonging to Expression (3) will be replaced with 1. Therefore, when no information has been compiled about a term, we assume that it will be fully predictive. This decision prevents to stop discovering new predictive words and represents an important advance included in our SpamHunting system to handle concept drift.

The underlying idea is that the concept drift problem must be addressed at the instance representation stage. Using techniques designed for handling concept drift at this early stage can boost the accuracy of the models. As static feature selection methods (calculated before the training stage) are not able to handle concept drift in this way, we use a dynamical feature selection process.

The method proposed for selecting the most relevant terms is made by following two steps: (*i*) computing the AI measure for all words included in the target message and (*ii*) select the most helpful terms from the message having an AI amount greater than a percentage of the total AI of all terms belonging to the target e-mail.

In our forthcoming experimentation we have tested different percentage configurations varying between 20% and 65% with the aim of finding the best threshold. Finally, we have chosen 60% as it produced the best results on the related preliminary experimentation.

5 Experimental Setup

In this section we discuss several relevant decision related to the configuration of the experiments. Firstly, Subsection 5.1 contains a description of the available spam corpora for benchmarking purposes. Then, Subsection 5.2 is focused in message tokenising, preprocessing and representation issues.

Evaluation has been done by a comparative performance study of several classical ML models (Naïve Bayes, AdaBoost and SVM), two case-based reasoning approaches proposed by Cunningham (ECUE and *Odds-Ratio CBR*) and our previous successful SpamHunting IBR system (with and without applying our proposed feature selection improvement).

5.1 Available Corpus

A significant issue about experimental configuration is choosing a corpora of e-mails for benchmarking purposes. Despite privacy issues, a large number of corpus like SpamAssassin[3], Ling-Spam[4], DivMod[5], SpamBase[6] or JunkEmail[7] can be downloaded from Internet. Table 2 shows a short description of the related corpus focussing on the spam and legitimate ratio and the distribution form.

Table 2. Comparative study of the most well known corpus

Corpus	Legitimate%	Spam%	Format	Preprocessing steps applied
Ling-Spam	83.3	16.6	Tokens	Tokenised
PU1	56.2	43.8	Token Ids	Tokenised ID representation for each token
PU2	80	20	Token Ids	Tokenised ID representation for each token
PU3	51	49	Token Ids	Tokenised ID representation for each token
PUA	50	50	Token Ids	Tokenised ID representation for each token
SpamAssassin	84.9	15.1	RFC 822	Not preprocessed
Spambase	39.4	60.6	Feature Vectors	Tokenised Feature selection
Junk-Email	0	100	XML	Not preprocessed
Bruce Guenter	0	100	RFC 822	Not preprocessed
DivMod	0	100	RFC 822	Not preprocessed

In this work, we are using the SpamAssassin and Ling-Spam corpus. The former comprises 9332 messages from January 2002 up to and including December 2003. The later contains 2412 previously tokenised messages without any date information. Although these corpuses seem old, the Spam problem remains the same. We have used them since they are the most widely used public corpora in spam filtering domain.

---

[3] Available at http://www.spamassassin.org/publiccorpus/
[4] Available at http://www.iit.demokritos.gr/
[5] Available at http://www.divmod.org/cvs/corpus/spam/
[6] Available at http://www.ics.uci.edu/~mlearn/MLRepository.html
[7] Available at http://clg.wlv.ac.uk/projects/junk-e-mail/

5.2 Message Representation Issues

A relevant question in models applied to spam filtering is the internal structure of the messages used during the training and the classification stages. The knowledge representation is different in classical ML techniques and CBR/IBR models.

In the context of the classical spam filtering ML models, messages are usually represented as a vector $\vec{t} = \langle t_1, t_2, ..., t_p \rangle$ containing numerical values that represent certain message features. When we use this form of model, messages must be represented with the same features. The selected features are often representing the presence or absence of a term in the message. This idea has been inherited from the vector space model in information retrieval [24, 27].

CBR/IBR systems use a memory structure able to store all messages in the form of cases or instances. This structure is optimised to quickly carry out the retrieval stage (given a target problem, recover cases from memory that are relevant to solving it). As with SpamHunting, this kind of systems is able to work when messages are represented with distinct feature measurements.

A significant topic for message representation is feature extraction (identifying all possible features contained in a message). Feature identification can be performed by using a variety of generic lexical tools, generally by tokenising the text extracted from e-mails into words. At first glance, it seems to be a simple tokenising task guided by several characters as word separators. However, at least the following particular cases have to be considered with care: hyphens, punctuation marks and the case of the letters (lower and upper case) [25]. In the spam domain, punctuation marks and hyphenated words are among the best discriminating attributes in a corpus, because they are more common in spam messages than legitimate ones.

In our experimentation, text for tokenising was extracted from e-mail body and attachments. In order to process diverse formats of the attached files, we use different techniques in each case taking into account the "content-type" header information. So, HTML code was translated into text/plain using the HTMLParser[8] tool, images were processed using the Asprise OCR[9] software and the text inside pdf documents was extracted using the PDFBox[10] package. We tokenised the text extracted from e-mails using only blank spaces in order to preserve the original aspect of the words belonging to each message and finally, all identified words were converted to lower case.

When the tokenising step has been completed, stopword removal (which drop articles, connectives and other words without semantic content) and/or a stemming (which reduces distinct words to their common grammatical root) can be applied to identified tokens [24]. In our experiments we have used only stopword removal as it has shown to be the best choice for the majority of systems [25].

Once carried out the lexical analysis over the training corpus, a large number of features would probably have been identified. In our experimentation we use a feature selection method to select the most predictive ones. *Information Gain* (IG), *Mutual Information* (MI) and the χ^2 statistic are well-known methods used for aggressive feature removal in text categorization domain [23]. From them, we had chosen the IG

---

[8] HTMLParser is available for download at http://htmlparser.sourceforge.net/
[9] Asprise OCR can be downloaded at http://asprise.com/product/ocr/
[10] PDFBox is available for download at http://www.pdfbox.org/

method to select the most predictive features as it has been successfully used for feature removal in several spam filtering research works [3, 4]. This method is based on computing the IG measure for each identified feature by using the equation given in Expression (4) and selecting those terms having the highest computed value.

$$IG(t) = \sum_{c \in \langle l,s \rangle} P(t \wedge c) \cdot \log \frac{P(t \wedge c)}{P(t) \cdot P(c)} \tag{4}$$

We have kept the original feature selection method used by the *Odds-Ratio CBR* model based on computing an odds ratio measurement. Moreover, the number of selected features for each message needs to be decided. For our comparisons, we have selected the best performance configuration of each classical ML technique varying between 100 and 2000 features. In order to test the *Odds-Ratio CBR*, and ECUE models we have maintained their original feature selection configurations. The first one uses 30 words for representing spam class and 30 words describing legitimate category while an IG selection of 700 features has been recommended by the authors for using ECUE CBR system.

Finally, for testing classical ML models the weight of terms in each message e, need to be calculated. The measure of the weight can be (*i*) binary (1 if the term occurs in the message, 0 otherwise), (*ii*) the *term frequency* (TF) representing the number of times the term occurs in the message calculated by Expression (5) or (*iii*) the *inverse document frequency* (IDF) given by Expression (6) denoting those terms that are common across the messages of the training collection.

$$t_i(e) = \frac{n_i(e)}{N(e)} \tag{5}$$

$$t_i(e) = \frac{n_i(e)}{N(e)} \log_2 \frac{m}{df(T_i)} \tag{6}$$

In Equations (5) and (6), $n_i(e)$ stands for the number of occurrences of term T_i in e, $N(e)$ represents the recount of terms in e, m is the number of training messages and $df(T_i)$ stands for the number of training messages where the term T_i occurs.

A binary representation has been used for testing ML classical models. ECUE and *Odds-Ratio CBR* are also using a binary feature representation for organizing the case base by using Information Entity Nodes in a CRN Structure [4].

6   System Evaluation

Information about selected metrics and several minor details concerning the use of the different corpus for evaluation purposes are described in this section. Experimental results are also contained in Subsection 6.1.

Six well-known metrics [3] have been used in order to evaluate the performance of all the analysed models: *total cost ratio* (TCR) with three different scenarios, spam *recall*, spam *precision*, percentage of correct classifications (%OK), percentage of False Positives (%FP) and percentage of False Negatives (%FN).

Firstly, we had used the SpamAssassin corpus for analysing the improved version of the SpamHunting IBR system in action. Then, we have used the Ling-Spam corpus to demonstrate the significance of the achieved results. All experiments have been carried out using a 10-fold stratified cross-validation [28] in order to increase the confidence level of results obtained.

Finally, some details about classical ML models configuration is described. Decision Stumps [29] have been used as weak learners for AdaBoost classifier with 150 boost iterations and SVM has been tested by using a polynomial kernel.

6.1 Experimental Results

Initially, the performance of the analysed models was measured from a cost-sensitive point of view. For this purpose we compute the TCR metric in the above mentioned different situations. TCR assumes that FP errors are λ times more costly than FN errors, where λ depends on the usage scenario (see [3] for more details). 1, 9 and 999 values for the λ parameter have been used over the experiments.

Table 3 shows a TCR comparative of the analysed models when using the SpamAssassin corpus. The number of selected features used for each model is placed in square brackets. Results show that the classifications obtained by using the improved version of the SpamHunting IBR system is extremely safe and good (TCR λ=999). Moreover, the original version of SpamHunting, ECUE and *Odds-Ratio CBR* are also safer than classical ML approaches. From a different point of view, Table 3 also shows that only SVM model is able to go beyond the improved SpamHunting system in amount of correctly classified messages (TCR λ=1).

Table 3. TCR scores over 10 stratified fold-cross validation using SpamAssassin

	Model						
Metric	Naïve Bayes [1000]	AdaBoost [700]	SVM [2000]	Odds-Ratio CBR [60]	ECUE [700]	Spam Hunting [-]	Improved Spam Hunting [-]
TCR λ=1	2.647	5.011	22.852	1.382	6.792	7.498	12.255
TCR λ=9	0.416	1.688	5.225	1.345	2.658	5.331	9.293
TCR λ=999	0.004	0.020	0.057	0.990	0.036	0.874	6.573

Table 4. TCR scores over 10 stratified fold-cross validation using Ling-Spam

	Model						
Metric	Naïve Bayes [1000]	AdaBoost [700]	SVM [2000]	Odds-Ratio CBR [60]	ECUE [700]	Spam Hunting [-]	Improved Spam Hunting [-]
TCR λ=1	7.769	22.871	27.385	2.152	13.070	1.211	6.014
TCR λ=9	3.798	9.016	8.672	2.152	1.811	1.122	5.250
TCR λ=999	1.524	6.471	5.788	2.152	0.017	0.757	4.415

In order to contrast and validate the obtained results with a different corpus, Table 4 shows analysed models in action when using the Ling-Spam corpus. SVM, AdaBoost and the improved version of SpamHunting get the highest score for the relation between security (lower FP amount) and hits (correctly classified messages) (TCR λ=999). From this fact, we can realize that the improved SpamHunting system gets a higher security level independently of the selected corpus.

From a different point of view, Table 5 shows the recall and precision scores obtained for each considered experimental corpus. Analysing recall scores and keeping in mind the idea of maximizing the highest correctly classified amount, we can realize that sometimes classical models can slightly get better than the improved version of SpamHunting. However, precision scores clearly show that the improved SpamHunting IBR system always gets the best balance between correctly classified amount and security scores. The precision score achieved by using ECUE system and *Odds-Ratio CBR* model should be highlighted, as they are extremely good.

Table 5. Recall and precision scores using Ling-Spam and SpamAssassin

Measure	SpamAssassin		Ling-Spam	
	Recall	Precision	Recall	Precision
Naïve Bayes [1000]	0.876	0.774	0.884	0.975
AdaBoost [700]	0.850	0.943	0.954	0.977
SVM [2000]	0.974	0.976	0.971	0.973
Odds-Ratio CBR [60]	0.276	0.992	0.526	1
ECUE [700]	0.883	0.964	0.985	0.928
Spam Hunting [-]	0.862	0.992	0.177	0.942
Improved Spam Hunting [-]	0.921	0.994	0.831	0.993

Taking into consideration other measures, Table 6 shows the percentage of correct classifications, false positives and false negatives belonging to the experimental work with the seven analysed models over the defined experimental configuration and corpus. Analysing Table 6 we can see that SVM and AdaBoost algorithms usually achieve the greatest percentage of correct classifications.

Table 6. Percentage of correct classifications, FPs and FNs

Measure	SpamAssassin			LingSpam		
	%OK	%FP	%FN	%OK	%FP	%FN
Naïve Bayes [1000]	90.3	6.5	3.2	97.7	0.4	1.9
AdaBoost [700]	94.9	1.3	3.8	98.9	0.4	0.7
SVM [2000]	98.7	0.6	0.7	99.1	0.4	0.5
Odds-Ratio CBR [60]	81.5	0.1	18.4	92.1	0	7.9
ECUE [700]	96.2	0.8	3.0	98.5	1.3	0.2
Spam Hunting [-]	96.3	0.2	3.5	86.1	0.2	13.7
Improved Spam Hunting [-]	97.9	0.1	2.0	97.1	0.1	2.8

From a different point of view, Table 6 shows that *Odds-Ratio CBR* and all versions of SpamHunting model achieve the lowest FP error. Other models (like SVM or AdaBoost) are able to slightly increment the correctly classified messages amount but they achieve a greater number of FP errors. Finally, It is needed to highlight the FP ratio obtained using the *Odds-Ratio CBR* model over the LingSpam corpus. This fact supports the suitability of the CBR/IBR approaches to spam filtering.

7 Conclusions and Future Work

In this paper we have introduced an improvement to our previous successful Spam-Hunting IBR system. We have carried out a deep analysis by choosing a representative set of spam filtering models (including Naïve Bayes, AdaBoost, SVM, and two case-based systems) in order to benchmark their performance while corpus is changed.

The original and improved versions of the SpamHunting IBR system had shown to be the safest spam filtering models by obtaining a convenient ratio between the FP error and correctly classified rates. Moreover, the improved version of SpamHunting is the first model able to adequately handle concept drift at the early instance representation stage.

We highlight results obtained in both versions of SpamHunting IBR system. Improvements in the relevant term selection stage have allowed a significant enhancement over the obtained results. Moreover, concept drift should be kept in mind while the most relevant terms are being selected because some features can indicate its presence (and consequently they should not be removed).

The application of the Achieved Information (AI) measure has been suitable for selecting representative features in an e-mail. It has been designed for handling concept drift problem when the instance representation is computed. If instances are represented without taking care of concept drift, following stages of the CBR/IBR system will not be able to adequately support it.

Finally, as experimental results from this paper have shown, SVM and AdaBoost models get a great amount of correctly classified messages. We should note that these models are heavily focused in the feature selection issues. SVM model supports a second feature selection stage while the feature space is transformed into a new linearly separable space. In this process irrelevant features are discarded. In the other hand, AdaBoost constructs some weak classifiers by using subsets from all features and weights them according to its classification ability. When a weak classifier is assembled from inappropriate features it gets irrelevant because its weight will be very low.

Keeping in mind the previous related issues, future work should be focused in the relevant term selection process. Newer and original methods should be studied and probed with different e-mail corpus and preprocessing scenarios.

CBR/IBR systems have greatly contributed to the Spam filtering domain. As experimental results have shown, SpamHunting, ECUE, and *Odds-Ratio CBR* models are the most reliable choice for spam filtering. Therefore, we are aware of its probed capabilities for handling concept drift and manage disjoint concepts.

Acknowledgments

This work has been supported by the University of Vigo project SAEICS: *sistema adaptativo con etiquetado inteligente para correo spam / Adaptive system with intelligent labeling for spam e-mails*. The authors want to thank the considerable effort made by the reviewers in order to improve the quality of the paper.

References

1. Oard, D.W.: The state of the art in text filtering. User Modeling and User-Adapted Interaction, Vol. 7, (1997) 141–178
2. Wittel, G.L., Wu, S.F.: On Attacking Statistical Spam Filters. Proc. of the First Conference on E-mail and Anti-Spam CEAS, (2004)
3. Androutsopoulos, I., Paliouras, G., Michelakis, E.: Learning to Filter Unsolicited Commercial E-Mail. Technical Report 2004/2, NCSR "Demokritos", (2004)
4. Delany, S.J., Cunningham P., Coyle, L.: An Assessment of Case-base Reasoning for Spam Filtering. Proc. of Fifteenth Irish Conference on Artificial Intelligence and Cognitive Science: AICS-04, (2004) 9–18
5. Cunningham, P., Nowlan, N., Delany, S.J., Haahr, M.: A Case-Based Approach to Spam Filtering that Can Track Concept Drift. Proc. of the ICCBR'03 Workshop on Long-Lived CBR Systems, (2003)
6. Fdez-Riverola, F., Iglesias, E.L., Díaz, F., Méndez, J.R., Corchado, J.M.: SpamHunting: An Instance-Based Reasoning System for Spam Labelling and Filtering. Decision Support Systems, (2006), *to appear*
7. Sahami, M., Dumais, S., Heckerman, D., Horvitz, E.: A Bayesian approach to filtering junk e-mail. In Learning for Text Categorization – Papers from the AAAI Workshop, Technical Report WS-98-05, (1998) 55–62
8. Carreras, X., Màrquez, L.: Boosting trees for anti-spam e-mail filtering. Proc. of the 4th International Conference on Recent Advances in Natural Language Processing, (2001) 58–64
9. Vapnik, V.: The Nature of Statistical Learning Theory. 2nd Ed. Statistics for Engineering and Information Science, (1999)
10. Lee, H., Ng, A.Y.: Spam Deobfuscation using a Hidden Markov Model. Proc. of the Second Conference on E-mail and Anti-Spam CEAS, (2005)
11. Druker, H., Vapmik, V.: Support Vector Machines for Spam Categorization. IEEE Transactions on Neural Networks. Vol. 10 (5). (1999) 1048–1054
12. Platt, J.: Fast training of Support Vector Machines using Sequential Minimal Optimization. In Sholkopf, B., Burges, C., Smola, A. (eds.). Advances in Kernel Methods – Support Vector Learning, MIT Press, (1999) 185–208
13. Schapire, R.E., Singer, Y.: BoosTexter: a boosting-based system for text categorization. Machine Learning, Vol. 39 (2/3). (2000) 135–168
14. Rigoutsos, I., Huynh, T.: Chung-Kwei: a Pattern-discovery-based System for the Automatic Identification of Unsolicited E-mail Messages (SPAM). Proc. of the First Conference on E-mail and Anti-Spam CEAS, (2004)
15. Graham, P.: Better Bayesian filtering. Proc. of the MIT Spam Conference, (2003)
16. Hovold, J.: Naïve Bayes Spam Filtering Using Word-Position-Based Attributes. Proc. of the Second Conference on Email and Anti-Spam CEAS, (2005). http://www.ceas.cc/papers-2005/144.pdf
17. Kolcz A., Alspector, J.: SVM-based filtering of e-mail spam with content specific misclassification costs. Proc. of the ICDM Workshop on Text Mining, (2001)
18. Gama, J., Castillo, G.: Adaptive Bayes. Proc. of the 8th Ibero-American Conference on AI: IBERAMIA-02, (2002) 765–774
19. Scholz, M., Klinkenberg, R.: An Ensemble Classifier for Drifting Concepts. Proc. of the Second International Workshop on Knowledge Discovery from Data Streams, (2005) 53–64
20. Syed, N.A., Liu H., Sung. K.K.: Handling Concept Drifts in Incremental Learning with Support Vector Machines. Proc. of the fifth ACM SIGKDD international conference on knowledge discovery and data mining, (1999) 317–321

21. Widmer, G., Kubat, M.: Learning in the presence of concept drift and hidden contexts. Machine Learning, Vol. 23 (1). (1996) 69–101
22. Lenz, M., Auriol, E., Manago, M.: Diagnosis and Decision Support. Case-Based Reasoning Technology. Lecture Notes in Artificial Intelligence, Vol. 1400, (1998) 51–90
23. Yang, Y., Pedersen, J.O.: A comparative study on feature selection in text categorization. Proc. of the Fourteenth International Conference on Machine Learning ICML-97, (1997) 412–420
24. Baeza-Yates, R., Ribeiro-Neto, B.: Modern Information Retrieval. Addison Wesley, (1999)
25. Méndez, J.R., Iglesias, E.L., Fdez-Riverola, F., Díaz, F., Corchado, J.M.: Analyzing the Impact of Corpus Preprocessing on Anti-Spam Filtering Software. Research on Computing Science, (2005) 17:129–138
26. Shannon, C.E.: The mathematical theory of communication. Bell Syst. Tech. J. Vol. 27. (1997) 379–423 & 623–656
27. Salton, G., McGill, M.: Introduction to modern information retrieval, McGraw-Hill, (1983)
28. Kohavi, R.: A study of cross-validation and bootstrap for accuracy estimation and model selection. Proceedings of the 14th International Joint Conference on Artificial Intelligence IJCAI-95, (1995) 1137–1143
29. Oliver, J.J., Hand, D.J.: Averaging over decision stumps. Proc. of the European Conference on Machine Learning ECML-94, (1994) 231–241

Case-Based Support for Collaborative Business

Ralph Bergmann[1], Andrea Freßmann[1], Kerstin Maximini[1],
Rainer Maximini[1], and Thomas Sauer[2]

[1] University of Trier
Department of Business Information Systems II
54286 Trier, Germany
{ralph.bergmann, andrea.fressmann, kerstin.maximini,
rainer.maximini}@wi2.uni-trier.de
[2] rjm business solutions GmbH
68623 Lampertheim, Germany
t_sauer@rjm.de

Abstract. This paper describes the development of the generic collaboration support architecture CAKE incorporating case-based reasoning (CBR). CAKE provides unified access to knowledge available within an organization, and CBR technology is used throughout the system to distribute this knowledge to agents as required. Adaptive workflows and collaboration patterns selected by a CBR process are introduced for explicitly describing collaboration among agents. In order to guide the technical design of the architecture, a systematic analysis of the requirements for collaboration support has been performed in various application domains.

1   Introduction

While the first case-based reasoning systems have been designed and implemented as stand-alone applications addressing an isolated problem solving task, a current trend can be observed towards the integration of CBR techniques as one component into more complex environments. Within such environments CBR can play different roles in situations in which decisions are to be made based on previous experience. One such complex environment under investigation at the Business Information Systems II research group at the University of Trier is the support of collaborative business.

Since the 1980s *CSCW (Computer supported cooperative work)* [1,2] is the research field that deals with the analysis and the design of information technology to improve the way human beings are working together in a certain working environment. In such a collaborative working environment, support for *communication*, *coordination*, and *cooperation* must be integrated systematically with the business processes of the organization. Recently, it has been recognized that collaboration support must not be limited to humans but must also cover automated decision support systems and automated knowledge sources in a seamless fashion. This demands for a much stronger link between CSCW and research on decision support technologies like for example CBR.

One main goal of research was to develop a new generic collaboration support architecture that integrates access to automated knowledge sources and whose overall behaviour is guided by previous experience. Previous experience can be useful when

T.R. Roth-Berghofer et al. (Eds.): ECCBR 2006, LNAI 4106, pp. 519–533, 2006.

knowledge sources are selected or whenever successful ways of collaboration among human and automated collaboration partners must be determined. In order to guide the technical design of such an architecture, a systematic analysis of the requirements for collaboration support and particularly for the support by previous experience is necessary. In various R&D projects such analyses have been performed. It turned out that similar problems occur in quite different application domains: geographical information management, fire services, and software engineering. In all these domains there is a need to coordinate collaborative activities jointly together with the knowledge required for enacting these activities. Furthermore, the flow of these activities is very often quite dynamic and subject of change depending on the current context. Thus there is a strong need for a highly flexible CSCW solution incorporating CBR. The authors have identified the most important requirements in each application domain in detail, generalized them to a more abstract level, and addressed them during the development of a domain-independent system called *Collaborative Agent-based Knowledge Engine (CAKE)* [3,4,5,6]. CAKE provides unified access to knowledge available within an organization, and CBR technology is used throughout the system to distribute this knowledge to agents as required. Adaptive workflows and collaboration patterns selected by a CBR process are introduced for explicitly describing collaboration among agents.

This paper summarizes the experiences made during the development of the first prototype of CAKE and its application in three application domains, namely geographical information management, fire services, and software engineering. It starts with a presentation of the three application scenarios and a summary of the most important requirements for CAKE in Section 2. Section 3 shortly presents the CAKE architecture and lays a special focus on the role of CBR. How these technologies have been utilized to build up support systems for the three regarded application scenarios is sketched in Section 4. The paper closes with the presentation of related work in Section 5 and with a short conclusion in Section 6.

2   Requirements Derived from the Application Scenarios

In the following, three applications scenarios are described, with a special focus on the problems that the people face. After that, requirements for a software solution that can be used as a basis to develop support systems for all the application scenarios are summarized.

2.1   Workflow Support for Geographical Information Management

The company rjm business solutions GmbH has been assigned by the Monument Protection Agency of Hessen to conduct the long-term eGovernment project *DenkXweb*. DenkXweb provides a freely accessible Internet service to publicly access the monument register[1], that lists each building and site of historic interest together with its exact location and a rationale why it is subject to protection. That is advantageous for landlords, planners and architects, who have to ensure themselves that they comply with all

---

[1] A demonstration is available under http://www.denkmalpflege-hessen.de/denkxweb.

regulations that apply to the corresponding land parcels, including monument protection. During the development of DenkXWeb, rjm business solutions GmbH is facing several problems and the two most engraving ones are shortly sketched below. A more detailed description of that problems can be found in [6].

Inconsistency of data. Geospatial data is maintained by 41 regional authorities, that provide their data on CD once a year using separated files to describe map data in ALK^2 format and meta information in ALB^3 format. After having combined map data and meta information, the location and dimensions of monuments and protected sites have to be transferred from a printed map, often collected manually by specialists in the fields. Thus, data inconsistencies are quite common, e.g. map and meta information often cannot be merged because of missing or contradicting descriptions or different granularity of the data, or transferring monument related data can fail because of differences between digital and printed map editions. In all cases, inquiries to the authorities are required, and while waiting for answer– that may take up to half a year –, the area in question cannot be processed further.

Determination of the current processing status and open issues. Several programs and databases are currently used to document flaws and to store the duration needed for each piece of work: a time recording tool, a Wiki system, and Excel spreadsheets. This heterogeneous data storage makes it difficult to determine the exact status of progress, and it is hard to derive documentation for the project stakeholders. But especially such documentation is required to estimate efforts for future pieces of work.

A flexible support system should tackle these problems: the staff could be supported during data acquisition and publishing by coordinating and documenting inquiries to the authorities and by automatic flaw detection, and the project stakeholders could be supported by automatic documentation and open issue collection.

2.2 Support for Time-Critical Processes for Fire Services

In recent years, the demand for support systems for emergency services has increased significantly in order to optimize methods for all types of protection. Focus is put on training, qualifying, and supporting members of emergency services that can be characterized by time-critical processes on incident locations. In that scope, the AMIRA (Advanced Multi-modal Intelligence for Remote Assistance) project[4] was initiated to address innovative technologies and their combinations leveraged in high safety of time-critical application domains. Particular to fire services, a lot of knowledge is captured in several data sources in different forms, e.g. structured databases and unstructured text.

The overall goal of the AMIRA project is to provide a multi-modal solution that will significantly improve the accessibility of resources available to support urgent and critical decisions that must be taken by mobile workers. The envisaged AMIRA system makes knowledge available by integrating best practices for improving search

---

[2] ALK = "automatisierte Liegenschaftskarte", graphical representation of real estates.

[3] ALB = "automatisiertes Liegenschaftsbuch", textual information on real estates.

[4] AMIRA is funded by the EU. Project partners are Kaidara Software, Fast DataSearch, DaimlerChrysler RIC, University of Trier, Fire Service College, West Midlands Fire Service, and Avon Fire & Rescue.

processes. This project aims at developing a solution that provides a hands-free access (e.g. headset) for operatives whose hands and eyes are otherwise occupied. For achieving this goal the solution is developed basing on two mobile working domains, roadside assistance and fire services.

An envisaged scenario within fire services can be as follows: the *incident commander (IC)* is the only person who is in charge and responsible for the decisions made on location. Therefore, all fire fighters involved provide him/her precise known details of the incident. Consequently, there is a demand for supporting the IC when he/she lacks information necessary for decision-making and in estimating current resources. For example, a fire fighter comes to the IC talking about a burning van loaded with explosives and found on the incident ground. Therefore, the IC uses the mobile AMIRA system in order to receive information about what has been found on the location and how to deal with it, while staying close to the incident and close to the fire fighters. For supporting the information flow between IC and fire control, the incident control centre, and for improving collaboration on the incident the AMIRA systems pro-actively routes the IC's requests and corresponding answers to fire control.

2.3 Workflow Support for Agile Software Engineering

In the software engineering domain, workflow systems are an established technology for team coordination and cooperation. That is, workflow support covers overall structuring of activities (e.g. by providing project plans or to-do lists), reuse of task descriptions to efficiently handle situations encountered before, or effective scheduling to ensure that team members always work on the most important tasks. However, software development processes tend to be unknown, unrepeatable, and knowledge intensive, with changes occurring frequently and the team members can be supported by collaborating with other team members (*human agents*) and by usage of *computerized agents* like bug-tracking systems or automated test tools. Nevertheless, in many organizations there are norms [7] shaping the way of working within the organization. Hence, effective collaboration strategies following such norms are necessary to ensure that the efforts of individual team members are all aiming in the same direction.

During the course of defining and enacting business processes, finding appropriate agents is crucial. First, modellers have to make sure that tasks are performed by the most experienced team members. Second, there may be activities that are known to succeed only when an appropriate collaboration strategy is taken. Finally, an agent trying to enact a task might seek assistance from another agent.

An envisaged scenario within an agile development [8] is a follows: the team has proceeded to the first iteration, and an intermediate system has been deployed at the customer site. Negotiations with the customers throughout the first iteration have resulted in the customer preference that an e-commerce system should be added to the system. Now, the team members playing management roles have to settle on the most basic workflow, which will control the very next steps. The team starts to instantiate the very first business process and suitable team members playing the roles of a domain expert and a software developer are assigned. Thereby, organization-specific constraints have to be taken into account (by querying a human resources management information agent providing availability data and a Wiki system containing tentatively planned leaves). These team members can now autonomously decide how to proceed for fulfilling the tasks. E.g., the software developer starts work on the assigned task by adapting the actual business process. Because of not being familiar to the actual project the software developer is searching comprehensive information about this project with respect to similar tasks, to relevant Java references, and to relevant design rationales. That is, relevant information is presented to the developer that he/she can be familiarized to the work at issue. Additionally, the developer gets a link for searching a Java expert for booking systems if more explicit information is necessary. Primarily the idea is to support the developer through computerized agents but if this is not enough there is an option to ask human experts. Therefore, a search facility organizes retrieval on human Java experts, returning information about how to get in contact to such an expert. Surely, the developer can proceed further in adapting the assigned task. Either he/she uses best practices in terms of collaboration which already includes useful domain knowledge or he/she carries out own adaptations on the task for achieving the envisaged task artefact.

2.4   Requirements

The authors have identified the most important requirements in each application domain and generalized them to a more abstract level. These requirements have than been tackled during the development of a domain-independent software solution, in the following denoted as *envisaged system.*

Requirements for Integration. In all application scenarios the necessary knowledge is scattered over a rich set of heterogeneous information sources within the organization. Thus the envisaged system should provide functional features and services that are able to access different information sources and can be tailored to integrate the particular sources in a given application domain. The achievement of interoperability between existing tools, features, and services and the envisaged system is a general requirement in organizations in order to avoid restricting previous business processes.

In all application scenarios, people are collaboratively working together and a seamless integration of humans and machines is needed. This can be reached by implementing an agent architecture that is able to administrate human as well as machine agents. Such an agent architecture could also allow organizations to efficiently distribute business tasks among organization members with reference to their competencies.

Requirements for Business Process Support. All application scenarios are characterized by complex knowledge-intense business processes that are executed over and over again, but always with (slight) variations depending on the actual context and on user interaction. Even worse, in some cases the tasks of a business process cannot be specified at the time of business process modelling, so that late-modelling of processes is required as well. An appropriate workflow technology, allowing representing and executing such highly flexible business processes, must be developed for the envisaged system. It should allow using past experiences done within organizations that may help novices and inexperienced organization members in carrying out their jobs. For alleviating collaboration among humans and machines the envisaged system should also provide means for reusing best practices in terms of agent collaboration. This would allow the improvement of business processes within organizations with regards to time-saving and cost-optimizing purposes.

Requirements for Search Facilities. Regarding the two kinds of requirements described above a need for search facilities on business processes and agents becomes obvious. More precisely, search facilities can support the modelling of new business processes through reuse of business process or business task representations and the execution of business processes through reuse of old business processes, a key feature for adaptive workflows and late-modelling. Search facilities for agents, meaning humans and machines, are also needed to enable the execution of flexible, situation-dependent business processes, allowing assigning competent and currently available agents to a business task during runtime.

3   The CAKE Approach

The fundamental idea of the CAKE approach [3,4,5,6] is to realize CSCW technology through the combination of *workflow*, *agent*, and *CBR technologies*. According to the requirements summarized in Section 2.4, different key features were considered during the development of CAKE. It makes use of *agent technology* in order to integrate IT systems as well as humans as agents. It uses *workflow technology* for representing business processes and for specifying collaboration among agents which are following a common goal. Instead of supporting static and pre-defined processes, CAKE aims at supporting flexible and changing processes through adaptive workflow management. In order to realize the high flexibility, sophisticated search facilities for business processes, single tasks, and agents are required. A *Structural CBR (SCBR)*[9] approach, working on top of a domain-specific data model and considering the semantics and structural aspects, meets all requirements. An overview of CAKE's architecture, showing the interactions of the three key technologies is shown in Figure 1. These key technologies, set up on the underlying common data model, are explained in the following sections.

3.1   Workflow Technology

The goal of the workflow system is to model and execute processes to support business processes within organizations. CAKE conceptually distinguishes between the representations of such *business processes* ("real-world processes") and the "internal processes" *collaboration pattern* and *administrative process*. Business processes aim at producing an end-product and collaboration patterns produce a by-product of a final business process product. Furthermore, collaboration patterns focus on agent collaboration based on best practices. Administrative processes are CAKE-specific processes used for internal procedures. For example, sometimes a top-level workflow is needed that waits for initial user interactions. All of these processes are formally represented as *workflow definitions* that can be instantiated and executed in concrete situations at runtime. These workflow instances are in the following shortly denoted as *workflows* and the situations are represented in the so called *context* of the workflow.

Each workflow definition consists of initial context values, a *workflow characterization*, a set of *task descriptions*, and the control flow relationships between the task

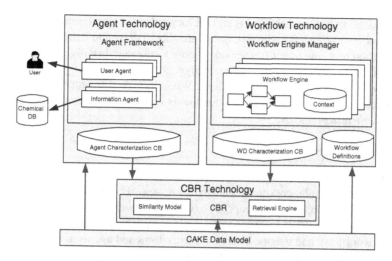

Fig. 1. CAKE System Architecture

descriptions. The latter allows arranging the tasks in sequence, in parallel, or in loops, but does not cover data flow at all; data exchange is realized by using the context. Workflow characterizations and task descriptions are structural CAKE data objects describing the workflow definitions or tasks. They are stored in a central repository called *WD Characterization CB*. One of the capabilities of a task is to trigger further workflow definitions, so hierarchical decomposition of complex processes is enabled.

Due to the domain requirements a further distinction of the workflows is done. *Short term workflows* are representations of short-lived (time-critical) business processes. The usage of such workflows aims at achieving dynamic changes and flexibility during enactment. *Long term workflows* represent processes without time limitations. As opposed to short term workflows, the support of these workflows requires maintaining the state of workflow executions.

3.2 Agent Technology

The CAKE agent framework provides a unified interface to couple external knowledge sources as well as user interfaces with the core system. Technically, the framework distinguishes between *information agents* and *user agents*. Information agents provide and may also change knowledge like search engines, databases, groupware calendars, human experts, data mining tools, classifiers, or dialogue strategy tools. User agents request knowledge and are in general interfaces to human system users, e.g. graphical user interfaces or natural language interfaces, but can also be other computer systems. Each agent is composed of a *technology component*, a *wrapper*, and an *agent characterization*. The technology component is the external knowledge system that is made accessible via CAKE. To enable the communication between CAKE and different technology components, wrappers are used as mediators that fulfill two tasks: firstly, to map between the technology components' ontologies and the CAKE domain specific ontology and secondly, to realize the technical interface. The agent characterization is a structural CAKE data object, characterizing the agent's competencies.

The flexibility of the workflows is carried forward to the agent framework by providing a dynamic set of agents whereas agents are able to enter and leave the CAKE *agent society*. Therefore, the agent framework is able to manage heterogeneous agents that have completely different purposes, knowledge, and capabilities [10]. This information can be captured by agent characterizations. When intending to enter the agent society an agent has to register its characterization that is stored into a central repository called *Agent Characterization CB*.

3.3   Structural CBR Technology

Within CAKE, CBR technology is applied for two different purposes. First, it is used for the selection of suitable workflows whenever a new workflow must be started. Second, it is used for the selection of appropriate agents, whenever an agent communication is initiated. CAKE uses CBR for these tasks to overcome the inflexibility of static assignments of workflows and agents. Therefore, workflows and agents are treated as cases, whose characterizations are stored in the *WD* and *Agent Characterization Case Base* (see Figure 1). A characterization of a particular workflow describes the situation in which this workflow can be (or has been) applied successfully. When a new similar situation occurs, the workflow is proposed again. A characterization of a particular agent describes the situations for which the agent is competent to answer a query. When a new similar situation occurs, the agent is used again as information source. Hence, two different similarity-based case retrieval tasks occur.

CAKE incorporates a single generic CBR component to implement both retrieval tasks. The requirements analysis strongly supported the need for a structured description of the respective application domains and for the need to construct an overall domain ontology. Its purpose is to add structure to the various information sources, items, and tasks that must be considered. Therefore we decided to implement the CBR component as a standard structural CBR approach [9]. The idea underlying the structural CBR approach is to represent cases according to a common structure called domain model. The domain model specifies a set of typed attributes (also called features) that are used to represent a case. In CAKE the domain model for the case bases are subsets of the overall Cake Data Model (see Figure 1). This data model supports full object-oriented data modelling including the modelling of class hierarchies as well as relational and multi-valued attributes [11]. For a particular application the overall domain ontology is encoded in this data model. Characterizations of workflows and agents are then constructed as instances of this data model. This data model is also used to represent the current working context in which workflows and agents must be selected.

The case retrieval step of the CBR component makes use of an explicitly modelled similarity measure. This similarity measure is a function that compares two instances of the data model (i.e. the current context and a characterization of a case) and assesses their similarity. We do not provide a single standard similarity, but enable the system developer to model the notion of similarity according to the requirements of the domain [11]. Similarity modelling is guided by the traditional local-global principle. For each attribute in the domain model the developer can chose a local similarity measure and for each class in the domain model the developer must assign a global measure that describes the aggregation of the similarity values obtain from the local measures.

3.4   Combination of the Three Key Technologies

The three key technologies can be combined to realize adaptive workflows and dynamic agent societies.

Adaptive Workflow Support. According to the requirements different kinds of workflow adaptations are required depending on changing contexts. Regarding time-critical situations a quick reaction on user actions is demanded, which is supported by short term workflows. As opposed to this, long term workflows are often subject to change when adaptations to ongoing business processes become necessary. From a more technical point of view, adaptations to workflows can be realized through both, instantiations of new workflows and insertion/deletion/modification of tasks during runtime. Therefore, CAKE integrates the following features:

1. Ability to search workflow definitions
2. Sub workflow instantiation during enactment
3. Ability to search task descriptions
4. Inserting tasks during workflow enactment

Those features have different impact on short or long term workflows. Due to short-lived constraints, short term workflows require automated adaptations based on the first two features. Automated adaptations can be viewed as situational workflow instantiation for a concrete context that may be changed after user interaction. Based on the current context information, CAKE starts a search for an appropriate business workflow or collaboration pattern. Then the most suitable workflow definition is instantiated as sub workflow. Different context constellations during enactment influence the selection of the next sub workflow to be enacted as depicted in Figure 2. Both features lead to an automated form of late modelling [12] of workflows which is a key feature for adaptive workflow management and it is well-known for long term workflows. Changes to such workflows are intended to be done manually, which means that the decision what kind of adaptation has to be done is left to users.

Dynamic Agent Societies. The second application field of CBR technology in CAKE is the retrieval on agent characterizations. Agent characterizations consist of attributes like the agent's role, the quality of data the agent provides, the area of expertise, the type of service it offers, and the data format. In order to support a dynamic agent society where agents can be registered and deregistered, CAKE allows dynamically agent allocation during workflow enactment. For exploiting these potentials, task descriptions only contain agent roles in order to specify what kind of agent should carry out the corresponding task. Based on these roles an appropriate agent characterization can be retrieved and the corresponding agent can be allocated to the task in an ad-hoc manner. Thus, user agents can be integrated in workflows for carrying out a particular job according to their competencies and information agents can be selected according to their knowledge and quality. In time-critical situations only registered agents, which are definitively available, are retrieved.

A difference to other agent-based approaches is that CAKE agents do not negotiate with each other. Instead, collaboration patterns are especially developed for organizations acting as loose contract among agents and capturing best practices about efficient

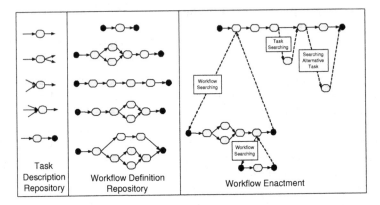

Fig. 2. Adaptive Workflows by CAKE

cooperation. Best practices often occur as organizational norms or past experiences, e.g. about what agents are working together efficiently.

4   Solutions for the Application Scenarios

In the following a description of how CAKE was put into practice in the three application scenarios presented in Section 2 is given. Due to space limitations, only the geographical information management scenario is described in detail. For the other scenarios, the solutions are only sketched in brief.

4.1   Workflow Support for Geographical Information Management

A group of five students from the University of Trier have used CAKE to develop a support system called *GIS-DOKU* [13,6] that improves the data acquisition and publishing processes and provides automated documentation and flaw detection. The first step during the development of GIS-DOKU was modelling the workflow definitions to describe the data acquisition and publishing processes for the closed area of a commune. As such a business process takes a while, long-term workflows are used. Because CAKE supports sub workflow modelling and execution, the students started with the very general top-level workflow definition shown in Figure 3, and refined each of the three process steps by further workflow definitions of its own.

Additionally, workflow definitions for open issue resp. flaw handling have been modelled. They are not part of each workflow, but the corresponding process steps are dynamically inserted in case of occurring failures, e.g., an inconsistency of ALK and ALB

Fig. 3. Top-Level workflow definition represented as an EPC

data. As the next step, 426 workflows have been instantiated, representing how each municipality in Hessen is processed. Thereby, each workflow indicates whether for a commune data acquisition could have been completed, data acquisition has not been started yet or the data acquisition is already running.

When preparing data for the DenkXweb Internet service, each commune requires an individual strategy in order to overcome ALK and ALB handling problems and issues arising from preprocessing and transferring monument related data. In addition, external events have to be handled, like communal authorities voting against publishing data for certain areas. Using CAKE, handling these deviations is supported well, since workflows can be altered using late modelling. Using CBR retrieval, CAKE helps to find appropriate workflow definitions which can be incorporated as exception handlers. That is, employees can tailor workflows easily as CAKE suggests appropriate workflow definitions for a given situation. Furthermore, the CBR engine helps to find appropriate agents to put these workflows into practice. That is, the numerous information agents can be leveraged best, and human team members can be selected based on their characterization profile as well.

Example. The sub workflow of the first process step "Import ALK and ALK data" of the Top-Level workflow definition includes a task called "Assure granularity of ALK and ALB data" that can be started after ALK and ALB data are available in electronical form. During the execution of this task, several problems may occur. They are arranged in a taxonomy, together with other problems that can occur during the whole data acquisition and publishing process. Figure 4 shows an excerpt of the whole taxonomy.

⊟ Problem
   ⊟ ALK
      • ALK-CD Reading Error
      • Wrong granularity of ALK
      • …
   ⊟ ALB
      • ALB-CD Reading Error
      • Wrong granularity of ALB
      • …
  • …

Fig. 4. Problem Taxonomy

Assume that an employee has problems in assuring the granularity. Then CAKE can find appropriate workflow definitions by the help of their characterizations. For the sake of brevity, the following example limits the latter to contain only two attributes: (1) problem description (an element of the Problem Taxonomy) and (2) an Integer type attribute describing how often the task has been executed for the same commune. In table 1, three characterizations for such workflow definitions (i.e. three cases) are given. The corresponding "solutions" are texts displayed to the employee. The words in brackets are representatives for real data: when applying the case, information agents retrieve the corresponding data from data bases already deployed at rjm business solutions GmbH and replace the representatives with the correct values.

Assume that the employee wants to start the acquisition of a new commune but finds that ALB does not match the corresponding ALK. His/her query would have the values Problem = "Wrong granularity of ALB" and NumberOfTries=0. By usage of a taxonomy similarity measure, Case 1 is retrieved with a similarity of 100% and the employee inserts it as a sub workflow within the workflow of the commune. Finally,

Table 1. Three Cases

ID	Characterization	Solution
1	Problem=*ALB* NumberOfTries=*[0,1]*	Contact <responsiblePerson> of commune <commune>. His telephone number is <telephoneNumber>. Ask him to re-send ALB data with correct granularity.
2	Problem=*ALB* NumberOfTries=*[3,8]*	Escalate problem to <superiorContact>, phone number is <telephoneNumber>. Explain what <responsiblePerson> has already tried in order to solve the problem and ask for assistance.
3	Problem=*ALB-CD* *Reading Error* NumberOfTries=*[0,∞]*	Contact <responsiblePerson> of commune <commune>. His telephone number is <telephoneNumber>. Ask him to re-send the CD because of CD reading errors.

he/she would call the responsible person as suggested. Two weeks later, a new CD is delivered, but ALK and ALB still won't match. Again, Case 1 is found, inserted and executed. However, the problem persists, and his/her next query would have the values Problem = "Wrong granularity of ALB" and NumberOfTries=2. As there is no perfect matching case in the case base, CAKE would propose Case 1 and Case 2, both with a similarity of 90%. Depending on the current situation (e.g. the deadline for publishing the commune is coming soon), the employee would insert Case 1 or Case 2.

4.2   Support for Time-Critical Processes for Fire Services

In order to tackle the envisaged scenario sketched in Section 2.2, CAKE supports the user agent in requesting information. First, CAKE assigns an initial workflow to the IC. This workflow captures the IC's incoming query about "explosives in a van" in the context and starts a retrieval for an appropriate collaboration pattern that describes collaboration among information agents in order to answer this particular query. In this case, this pattern proposes to ask two different information agents that work on high quality structured data in terms of explosives in vehicles. If no relevant results can be found, one other information source is requested capturing more general and unstructured data about explosives. When the query cannot be satisfied again, an information agent is requested searching contact information of an appropriate human expert. This collaboration pattern is instantiated as sub workflow. Before the sub workflow is completed it passes the response as context information to the corresponding superior workflow. This response is sent back to the user agent, which transforms the result into natural language for reading it to the IC. Furthermore, the initial workflow starts a context analysis. E.g., if hazardous materials like explosives are found there is a demand to inform the fire control. Another sub workflow is started that pro-actively notifies fire control about explosives that have been found. Additionally, the response is also added to the control's notification.

4.3   Workflow Support for Agile Software Engineering

Software development using a Scrum-like agile method is supported by CAKE in the following way: The development team starts by instantiating a baseline workflow definition (long-term workflow) for the first iteration. The team adds "pre-game", "sprint" and "post-game" sub workflow definitions to it, with each triggering a CAKE sub workflow of their own in sequence. The pre-game workflow definition covers the negotiations with the customer like "meetings on site" or "writing recommendation reports". Using SCBR, workflows outlining best practice learned from previous projects or iterations can be identified to ease workflow modelling. The "sprint" workflow definition acts as the Scrum backlog: While executing the tasks included within pre-game, the team will add tasks to the sprint workflow required to actually produce the system. For instance, after having executed pre-game, the sprint workflow would include tasks like "design database schema" or "create input forms". For each task, risk is estimated, and by placing control flow relationships between the tasks, the most risky tasks will be executed first. The risk estimation itself is knowledge-intense, thus CAKE supports this as well: By using an information agent which connects to a bug database, information about the reliability of a specific component may be retrieved.

5   Related Work

Although the CAKE combines agent, workflow, and CBR technology in an innovative manner some parallels in state-of-the-art approaches can be found. Workflow technology is mostly assigned to CSCW technology because of being the core technology of systems, which manage activities to be done by different persons within organizations. Jennings et al. [14] propose an approach to use autonomous agents for business process management, which is similar to agent-based workflow management. Here, responsibilities are split for enacting various components of business processes to agents leading to more flexibility, agility, and adaptability. Instead of supporting agent-based workflow management CAKE enables agent enhanced workflows [15] where an agent can be assigned to a task for carrying out this task. Thereby, CAKE is able to provide agents that are conform to the established agent definition [14]. Beyond that, in CAKE non-autonomous services can be integrated as agents as well.

A further parallel to CAKE is the CBRFlow approach [16], which combines workflow technology with conversational CBR (CCBR) in order to cope with changing and unpredictable processes. The CBR technology is used for acquiring new knowledge when exceptions within processes are encountered. Combining CBR and modelling/planning is not new: the workbrain approach [17] uses CBR for workflow modelling prior enactment whereas the HICAP approach [18] make use of CCBR for acquiring information from users and for adapting plans based on alternative proposals. As parallel for CAKE's agent retrieval, a process-based knowledge management approach [19] incorporates a search for appropriate information sources backed by CBR retrieval and a CCBR approach [20] is available where agents are characterized by questions, which they are able to answer. This could lead to a cumbersome task when many questions express one agent's suitability.

6   Conclusion

In this paper, the CAKE system has been presented and how CBR techniques are used by it to create a generic collaboration support architecture. This architecture has been already proven useful within three different application domains, namely geographical information management, fire services, and software engineering, where there is a need to coordinate collaborative activities and to automatically provide the knowledge required to enact them. By using the concepts of information and user agents, the CAKE architecture provides unified access to knowledge available within the organization, integrating already established information systems seamlessly. Collaboration and coordination between agents are described explicitly by using adaptive workflows, allowing tailoring whenever required.

As of this writing, a first prototype of CAKE was already implemented and successfully applied in the three presented application scenarios. The next steps in these scenarios will be extensive evaluations to assess the benefit that can be achieved by the usage of the newly developed supporting systems. First impressions revealed weaknesses in the usability of these systems. Thus, focus will be put on UI enhancements and on improvements regarding long-term workflow support. Two additional application domains are currently evaluated: CAKE will be used to support the design of nanoelectronic chips, aiming to improve design efficiency and to reduce design errors, and it will be used in a medical context, where it will optimize the diagnosis and therapy processes for stroke patients.

Further research interests include aspects of workflow and collaboration pattern evolution. For instance, by capturing information on real-world workflow enactment, workflow definitions may be tailored automatically without obliging a user. The latter may be considered a workflow definition itself, and CAKE could make use of CBR to retrieve a well-working tailoring strategy.

References

1. Grudin, J.: Computer-supported cooperative work: Its history and participation. IEEE Computer **27(5)** (1994) 19–26
2. Carstensen, P.H., Schmidt, K.: Computer supported cooperative work: New challenges to systems design. In Itoh, K., ed.: Handbook of Human Factors/Ergonomics, Asakura Publishing, Tokyo (2003) 619–636
3. Freßmann, A., Maximini, R., Sauer, T.: Towards collaborative agent-based knowledge support for time-critical and business-critical processes. In Althoff, K.D., Dengel, A., Bergmann, R., Nick, M., Roth-Berghofer, T., eds.: Professional Knowledge Management. Volume 3782 of LNAI., Kaiserslautern, Germany, Springer-Verlag (2005) 421–430
4. Freßmann, A., Maximini, K., Maximini, R., Sauer, T.: CBR-based execution and planning support for collaborative workflows. In: Workshop "Similarities - Processes - Workflows" on the 6th Int. Conference on Case-Based Reasoning (ICCBR 2005), Chicago, USA (2005)
5. Freßmann, A., Sauer, T., Bergmann, R.: Collaboration patterns for adaptive software engineering processes. In Czap, H., Unland, R., Branki, C., Tianfield, H., eds.: Self-Organization and Autonomic Informatics (I). Volume 135., Amsterdam, Netherlands, Frontiers in Artificial Intelligence and Applications (FAIA), IOS Press (2005) 304–312
6. Sauer, T., Maximini, K., Maximini, R., Bergmann, R.: Supporting collaborative business through integration of knowledge distribution and agile process management. In: Multikonferenz Wirtschaftsinformatik (MKWI 2006), Teilkonferenz "Collaborative Business". (2006)
7. Liu, K., Sun, L., Dix, A., Narasipuram, M.: Norm-based agency for designing collaborative information systems. Information Systems Journal **11** (2001) 229–247

8. Boehm, B.: Get ready for the agile methods, with care. IEEE Computer **35** (2002) 64–69
9. Bergmann, R., Breen, S., Göker, M., Manago, M., Wess, S.: Developing Industrial Case-Based Reasoning Applications: The INRECA Methodology. LNAI 1612. Springer (1999)
10. van Elst, L., Dignum, V., Abecker, A.: Towards agent-mediated knowledge management. In: Agent-Mediated Knowledge Management, International Symposium AMKM 2003, March 24-26, 2003, Revised and Invited Papers, Stanford CA, USA, Springer-Verlag (2004) 1–30
11. Bergmann, R.: Experience Management - Foundations, Development Methodology, and Internet-Based Applications. Volume 2432 of LNAI. Springer Berlin, Heidelberg, New York, Hong Kong, London, Milan, Paris, Tokyo (2002)
12. Heinl, P., Horn, S., Jablonski, S., Neeb, J., Stein, K., Teschke, M.: A comprehensive approach to flexibility in workflow management systems. In: Proceedings of the International Joint Conference on Work Activities Coordination and Collaboration. (1999) 79–88
13. Birkner, J., Ognyanova, M., Pütz, J., Rücker, A., Yao, Y.: Workflow-Unterstützung für Geoinformation. Technical report, University of Trier (2005) Endbericht.
14. Jennings, N.R., Norman, T.J., Faratin, P., O'Brien, P., Odger, B.: Autonomous agents for business process management. International Journal of Applied Artificial Intelligence **14(2)** (2000) 145–189
15. Judge, D., Odgers, B., Shepherdson, J., Cui, Z.: Agent enhanced workflows. BT Technology Jounal **16** (1998) 79–85
16. Weber, B., Wild, W.: Towards the agile management of business processes. In Althoff, K.D., Dengel, A., Bergmann, R., Nick, M., Roth-Berghofer, T., eds.: WM2005: Professional Knowledge Management Experiences and Visions, Kaiserslautern, Germany, German Research Center for Artificial Intelligence (DFKI GmbH) (2005) 375–382
17. Wargitsch, C., Wewers, T., Theisinger, F.: Workbrain: merging organizational memory and workflow management systems. In: Proceedings of KI'97: Workshop on Knowledge-Based Systems for Knowledge Management in Enterprises, Freiburg, Germany (1997)
18. Muñoz Avila, H., McFarlane, D.C., Aha, D.W., Breslow, L., Ballas, J.A., Nau, D.: Using guidelines to constrain interactive case-based HTN planning. In: Proceedings of the 3rd International Conference on Case-Based Reasoning (ICCBR 99), Springer (1999) 288–302
19. Holz, H.: Process-Based Knowledge Management Support for Software Engineering. PhD thesis, Department of Computer Science, University of Kaiserslautern (2003)
20. Giampapa, J.A., Sycara, K.: Conversational case-based planning for agent team coordination. In: Proceedings of the 4th International Conference on Case-Based Reasoning (ICCBR 2001). Volume 2080 of LNAI., Springer (2001) 189–203

A CBR-Based Approach for Supporting Consulting Agencies in Successfully Accompanying a Customer's Introduction of Knowledge Management

Mark Hefke and Andreas Abecker

Forschungszentrum Informatik (FZI), Haid-und-Neu-Straße 10-14,
76131 Karlsruhe, Germany
{hefke, abecker}@fzi.de

Abstract. This paper describes a case-based approach for supporting consulting agencies in accompanying an organisation's Knowledge Management (KM) implementation. Best Practice Cases (BPCs) of successfully conducted consulting services are captured by the system's ontology-based case base and reused for further KM introduction services. The system synergetically combines technologies of the Semantic Web with those of Case-based Reasoning. Seen from the KM point of view, the system follows the holistic approach of a KM introduction by considering technological, organizational and human aspects of KM in equal measure.

1 Introduction

A KM introduction has to overcome manifold barriers of an organizational, technical, or cultural nature [9]. For supporting such a complex endeavour, a KM consulting agency has to collect and capture as much as possible experiences from accomplished KM implementation projects in order to flexibly react on a new customer's knowledge problems. This can be done by, e.g., continuously performing project debriefings after the end of KM Introduction projects and finally trying to externalize, structure and somehow capture personally made experiences of senior experts in the form of so called best practice cases (BPCs). Based on that important knowledge, consultants have a chance to avoid mistakes that were made in the past. The practical problem is that existing BPC descriptions in the scientific literature (normally available as final project reports in the form of text documents) are usually not well-structured, and due to that not directly comparable, and not easily applicable to new customers' needs. Further, a "knowledge base" for KM introduction – which can easily be queried for typical KM implementation problems – does not exist. Our KMIR Framework (__KM__ __I__mplementation and __R__ecommendation) tackles these problems by providing an ontology-based, electronic repository of KM introduction BPCs. Its internal representation as well as its search and retrieval functionalities are implemented by combining approved methods from the CBR and the Semantic Web areas.

The motivation for bringing together CBR and Semantic Web is the assumption that the two different technologies have complementary strengths [7]. In addition

T.R. Roth-Berghofer et al. (Eds.): ECCBR 2006, LNAI 4106, pp. 534–548, 2006.

to the benefits of approved methods like CBR, an ontology-based case base (CB) can provide (1) the integration of a traditional CB with a background knowledge model, (2) an ontology-based querying and navigation interface for manual case browsing, as well as (3) a more flexible, refinable, and maintainable CB – due to an easy to understand and extend case structure which can easily be modified. Our framework has been realized by a web-based system providing organizational and technological recommendations, based on BPCs representing successful KM implementations.

This paper is structured as follows: In the remainder of this chapter, we sketch the KMIR framework. The software components of KMIR are described with some more detail along the processes of the adapted CBR-cycle in section 2. The paper concludes with related work (section 3) and some ideas for future research (section 4).

KMIR is methodologically based on the CBR Cycle by Aamodt & Plaza [1]. The four processes of the CBR Cycle comprise **Retrieval** of the most similar case(s) to a new problem, **Reuse** of information and knowledge from hat retrieved case in order to solve the new problem, **Revision** of the proposed solution, and finally **Retainment** of a newly originated case for solving new problems in the future. For technically supporting all these processes, we have designed and implemented the KMIR architecture, which consists of the following components:

1. A **case base** containing KM BPCs: BPCs are represented as interrelated bundles of instances of concepts described in an overall KM BPC ontology.
2. A **Case Editing Component:** supports a consulting agency (a) on one hand in the structured description of BPCs, or just single problem-solution pairs based on accompanied KM introduction projects, and facilitates (b) an organizational audit at the customer organisation in order to identify the organisation's general structure, technical infrastructure, knowledge problems and knowledge goals (cf. [19]).
3. An ontology-based **Matching Component:** returns most similar cases by matching a customer request with existing BPCs in the case base.
4. A **Solution Generator:** associates a customer's profile, knowledge problems and goals with existing solutions, methods and experiences of the most similar BPC in order to offer KM recommendations to a customer (i.e., about how to introduce KM, based on retrieved and adapted most similar cases).
5. A **Learning Component:** stores adapted, reused and revised best practices cases as a new case into the case base.
6. **Administration Functions:** support the configuration of similarity measures and filters, and provide further means for maintaining the CB.

More details about the KMIR framework components are given in section 3. KMIR is fully integrated with "KAON Portal", a framework for generating ontology-based web portals which is a stand-alone framework for the visualization of (multi-lingual) ontologies by supplying easy ontology navigation and searching [16].

2 Methodological Approach

The major contribution of our work is certainly not a breakthrough innovation in new CBR techniques, but mainly – besides some technical achievements through the combination with Semantic Web methods and tools – the application of a case-based approach in a more than difficult real-world consulting area. Hence we think it is valuable to describe our overall methodological approach and give an idea of the respective weights of BPC attributes as estimated by practitioners (Table 1). In order to develop the KMIR framework, we have performed the following steps:

1. Identification of indicators for the description / portability of KM BPCs.
2. Verification of identified indicators in form of an open survey.
3. Development of a "reference model" and ontology-based case base implementing the evaluation results.
4. Collection of (unstructured) episodic cases from different information sources which are describing "real" events.
5. Definition of "prototypical" cases in order to capture innovative technical solutions, new methods and practices into the CB that are not widely used in organizations (these hypothetical cases complement the "real" ones in order to sufficiently cover the space of possible organizational problem situations).
6. Development and implementation of the KMIR Framework Architecture.
7. Structuring and storing cases from 4.) and 5.) into the case base.

2.1 Identification and Verification of Relevant Indicators

At the beginning, we have analyzed KM methodologies and BPCs from literature and web pages (e.g. [19], [9], [12]). Based on that, we have created a preliminary list of indicators for the description and portability of BPCs. In order to verify the significance of the selected indicators and to endue significant ones with a specific relevance, we have performed an internationally accomplished open survey (n=103, cf. http://www.knowledge-management.de.tc), where we interviewed people who were in progress of implementing KM, had already implemented KM, or were just sensitized with that topic. As a result of both activities, we achieved the following list of indicators, which are sorted by relevance (cf. Table 1)[1]:

---

[1] Please note that we adhere with our terminology more to the KM community and consulting practice than to the CBR community. In terms of a typical CBR approach, "indicator" would become a feature or attribute of a case, and "relevance" of indicators goes, of course, directly into the weights of these attributes in a composite similarity function. Moreover, if we are talking about a "classification" of indicators, this means a (typically multivalued) attribute with a taxonomically structured co-domain.

Table 1. Indicators for the description and portability of BPCs and their relevance[2]

Indicator	Classification	Examples/ Range	Relevance
Knowledge problems; addressed core processes	organizational, technical, cultural	e.g., knowledge identification, acquisition	High
(Technical) solutions, methods, knowledge instruments	-	e.g., yellow pages, think tanks, lessons learned, knowledge marketplace, storytelling, knowledge mapping, …	High
Knowledge goals	normative, strategic, operative	e.g., systematization of service knowledge, knowledge transfer among employee generations, creation of a knowledge balance, …	High
Sustainability	-	-	High
Qualitative benefit	-	e.g., increased turnover or profit	High
Increased competitiveness	-	e.g., faster knowledge distribution	High
Implementation time	-	nonnegative integer	High
Involved department	-	e.g., R&D, IT, PR, HRM, …	High
Maturity level	-	depends on underlying maturity model	High
Organization sector	primary, secondary and tertiary sector	e.g., IT, Finance & Insurance, Automotive	High
Amortization time	-	nonnegative integer	Medium-High
Quantitative benefit	-	-	Medium-High
Implementation costs	technical, organizational, person-related	nonnegative integer	Medium
Company size		nonnegative integer	Medium
Organizational structure, involved processes	-	e.g. matrix organisation	Medium
Type of k.nowl. transformation	-	implicit, explicit	Medium
Affected organizational level	-	e.g., team, department	Medium

---

[2] Please note that the ordering according to the perceived relevance of indicators confuses a bit the inherent logics of indicators which can be grouped into characteristics of the company and affected department in general, the knowledge problems addressed, and the respective KM project undertaken. Of course, one should also note that some of the attributes are asymmetric in the sense that they would be used differently in a stored BPC and in a query. For instance, the "implementation costs" can be clearly specified as a feature of a stored BPC, but for a query, this attribute will be empty, or specify an upper bound, or an expected value.

Table 1. (*continued*)

Used software/ technologies and KM instruments	-	e.g., Lotus Notes, Sem. Web Techn.	Medium
number of in- volved KM work- ers	-	nonnegative integer	Low
Considered quality standards	-	e.g., EFQM	Low
Turnover and profit		integer	Low
External support	-	e.g., public funding	Low
Implementation status	-	completed, in progress	Low
Legal form	-	e.g. ltd.	Low

Based on the verification and relevance weighting of indicators, we developed a reference model for the description of KM BPCs. We distinguished between entities describing an organization profile in general (e.g., company size and sector, legal form, turnover, profit, software infrastructure, technologies, etc.) and KM-specific ones (e.g., KM goals and problems, solutions and methods, departments involved in the KM process, considered business processes, the number of employees that are actually involved in the KM process, planned / used implementation time, costs and status, regarded quality standards, and the current KM maturity level of an organization). We classified attribute values (e.g., company sectors are classified as "primary sector", "secondary sector" and "tertiary sector"; processes are classified by the Process Classification Framework of the American Productivity & Quality Center; KM problems are classified into organisational, technological and cultural problems; KM goals are divided into strategic, normative and operative ones). In a next step, we defined a measurable and above all comparable range for all entities (a stringent precondition for the later described case retrieval process). In addition, all entities are classified regarding their ability to describe the situation before, during, and after the introduction. Several entities can even change the value during the KM introduction process (e.g., turnover, number of employees, etc.). Finally, we modeled an ontology-based CB which serves as a data model for structuring and storing the BPCs.

3 The KMIR Framework Architecture

The KMIR framework architecture basically distinguishes the following core components: An *ontology-based case base*, a *case editing component*, an ontology-based *matching component*, a *solution generator*, a *recommendations component*, a *learning component* and several *administration functions* (cf. Fig. 1), which are described in detail in the following subsections.

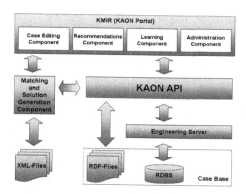

Fig. 1. KMIR Framework Architecture

3.1 Ontology-Based Case Base

Each BPC is stored as a set of interlinked "profile instances" in the ontology. There-fore, it comprises all above-named entities, as well as relations between them. The conceptual level of the CB ontology consists of the main concepts "Company", "Pro-file", "Problem", "Goal", "Solution" and "Method". The concepts "Company" and "Profile" are linked together by the property "Company_has_Profile". Knowledge Problems which the companies had to solve are sub-divided into organisational, tech-nical and cultural ones. A "Knowledge Goal" can either be normative, strategic or operative. Each profile is linked to one or more problem(s) or goal(s) by the proper-ties "Profile_has_Problem" and "Profile_has_Goal". A problem is linked to one or more achieved solution(s) with the property "Problem_has_Solution" and an inverse property "Solution_solves_Problem". Problems can address a specific core process of the Probst KM Model (i.e., knowledge acquisition, sharing, etc.) [19]. Problems are divided into sub-problems by the property "Problem_consists_of / is_part_of_problem".

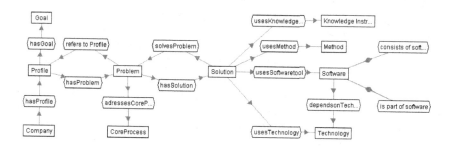

Fig. 2. Excerpt of the KMIR Ontology

In order to reflect the holistic KM approach, the concept "Problem" has the sub-concepts "Organisational Problem", "Technical Problem" and "Cultural Problem"., because the implementation of a KM system could depend, for instance, on a specific technology and, furthermore, require to solve a specific organisational problem, as well as a cultural change in the organization. The concept "goal" disposes of the more special sub-concepts "Normative Goal", Strategic Goal" and "Operative Goal". Every solution can be combined with a method (property: "uses_method"), a knowledge instrument (property "uses_knowledge_instrument"), a specific technology or software-tool, which again may depend on a technology (properties: "uses_Software_tool / Technology" and "depends_on_Technology"). Moreover, a solution, software, or technology can consist or be a part of other solutions (just as software tools and technologies). Several other concepts of the ontology are structured by a taxonomy in order to have the possibility for more precisely specifying the top concepts. The CB ontology has been realized with the KAON OI-Modeler (http://kaon.semanticweb.org), a tool for visually creating and maintaining ontologies. Figure 2 depicts an excerpt of the KMIR ontology's top concept level.

3.2 Description of KM Best Practice Cases

Selected and created episodic and prototypical BPCs are described by the use of a Case Editing Component (CEC), a web-based user interface, which is part of the KMIR framework architecture and allows for a template-oriented filling of all known attributes of a BPC. Attribute values are filled in as texts are numbers, or can be chosen from pulldown menus. The interface is automatically generated from the ontology defining the case structure. Finally, a described best practice case is directly stored as a set of instances, attributes and relations into the ontology store.

3.3 The Organisational Audit

The Case Editing Component is also used to later support a consulting agency in capturing a new customer's organisation profile, thus its organisational structure, technical infrastructure and economic aspects, as well as normative, strategic, and operational knowledge goals. Additionally, the organisation may define target costs for the implementation of a KM solution, may describe or select organisational, technical or cultural knowledge problems and requirements, and finally assign them with typical knowledge processes. Finally, KMIR supports the association of *weights* to all described aspects, in order to attach more or less importance to them. The received profile from the organisational audit is directly stored as a set of instances, attributes and relations into the ontology which structures the CB. In order to disencumber consultants from filling in all characteristic values of the customer profile that have to be used later for the case retrieval, several characteristic values are automatically created or transformed by the use of ***derivation rules*** and ***transformation rules*** before storing a new case into the case base. Derivation rules infer the organisation type (e.g., "Small and Medium Enterprise") from the characteristic values "turnover" and "company size", transformation rules are used to transform values between different scale units (e.g., time and currency).

Further, it is possible to only define one or more problems or problem-solution-pairs, because in practice, customers often have already accomplished several KM activities and now search for a solution to solve one or more new particular problem(s).

3.4 Case Retrieval Process

In order to retrieve BPCs that are most similar to a newly created customer profile achieved from the organisational audit, or just solutions for one or more requested problems, a matching component matches the profile or a given problem (set) against already existing BPCs or problems from the CB. This is done by combining syntax-based with semantical similarity measures [11]. Syntax-based similarity measures in our system are *distance-based similarity, syntactical similarity (edit distance* combined with a *StopWordFilter* and *Stemming)* and *equality* for comparison of values of numeric data types from the organization profile with those of existing BPCs. Additionally, the profile from the self-description process is matched against profiles of the CB using *semantic similarity measures.*[3] That is to compute the similarity between (sets of) instances on the basis of their corresponding concepts and relations to other objects (*relation similarity*) as well as *taxonomic similarity. Relation similarity* is used on one hand for comparing attribute values of instances that are no direct instantiations of the concept "profile", but of further concepts instantiations (e.g., of concept "problem" or "software") that are linked to the concept "profile" (using the relations "profile_has_problem" and "profile_uses_software"). On the other hand, the similarity type is used for, e.g., comparing instantiations of the concept "problem" that are linked to further instantiations of the concept "Core process" using the relation "(problem) addresses core process". *Taxonomic similarity* identifies similar software tools or technologies for the requesting organization, which base upon problem-solution pairs of BPCs similar to the defined problem(s) from the organization profile. For example, an organization is searching for an extension of its existing groupware system using an ontology-based tool solution. The matching component identifies a similar groupware system in the case base, which also served as a basis for such an extension. This finding is made by checking all instances of the corresponding software sub-concept "groupware" and recommending the assigned solution to the requesting organization. Furthermore, taxonomic similarity is used to additionally compare particular attribute instances based on the conceptual level in order to improve results of the syntactic similarity computation (e.g., matching the attribute "sector" of a profile based on the concept taxonomy "primary", "secondary" and "tertiary sector"). Finally, a weighted average determines the global similarity of all local similarities. Figure 3 depicts all regarded ontology concepts, attributes and relations of a profile that are applied in KMIR during Case Retrieval.

For the technical realization of the matching component, we have integrated an already existing Java-based framework for instance similarities in ontologies into the KMIR architecture. An additionally implemented user interface allows parameterizing

---

[3] A comprehensive discussion of the concept of "semantic similarity" goes beyond the scope of this paper. Since the advent of Semantic Web research, there is a growing confusion wrt. a reasonable usage of the word "semantic". We comprise here – in our current implementation – taxonomic and relational similarity – and in general – all similarity measures taking into account some kind of inference or background knowledge in the form of rules, a complex domain model, etc. – as opposed to simple datatype-value similarity which can be derived completely context-free with simple string or arithmetic operations or table look-up's. For further information, please refer to [11].

the user-defined selection and composition of (atomic) similarity measures, and their assignment with weights directly in KMIR. Settings are stored in an XML-File and processed by the underlying similarity framework. Depending on the selected similarity measure(s), attributes like maxdiff (distance-based similarity) or recursion depth (instanceRelationSimilarity) can be defined. Due to the complexity of computing ontology-specific similarity measures, the similarity framework provides two different types of filters, **pre-filters** and **post-filters** in order to constrain the number of instances to be considered for similarity computation. They can be individually combined from (atomic) filters. All filters are configurable either by a KMIR user interface or directly in the XML-File.

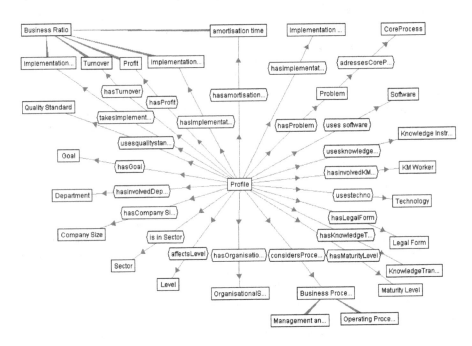

Fig. 3. Concepts, Attributes and Relations Regarded during Case Retrieval

Pre-filters are used before similarity computation. They allow the inclusion of one or more particular concept(s), as well as the exclusion of particular concepts that are later regarded during the similarity computation of corresponding instantiations. Further, it is possible to define KAON Queries[4] in order to reduce the amount of profiles in the CB that is used for computing the similarity. The KAON query language allows easy and efficient locating of elements in KAON OI-models.

Post-filters determine the number of instances that are returned after the similarity computation. There exist two filter types, *minSimilarityFilter* and *maxCountofInstancesFilter*. The first filter type defines the similarity threshold (between 0 and 1)

---

[4] Cf. "Developer's Guide for KAON", http://kaon.semanticweb.org/documentation

required for inclusion in the result list, the second one retains information about the maximum number of presented similar results.

In case of a negative case retrieval (no existing profile of the CB directly matches to a selected organization profile), the matching process can be constrained to only matching (all) single problems of the given organization profile with existing problems (independent of a particular profile) in order to at least identify solutions for given problems.

As an alternative for identifying similar profiles/ problems to a given one based on the integrated similarity framework, it is also possible to let the user of the system directly define KAON queries or construct with a query wizard. For instance, the query

[#Solution] AND SOME(<#usesKnowledgeInstrument>,!#Yellow-Pages!)

returns all solutions which are using the knowledge instrument "Yellow pages".

3.5 Recommendations and Solution Generation

The *Recommendations Component* provides recommendations based on identified most similar case(s). This is done by presenting one or more profile(s) retrieved within the matching process that correspond to the profile from the organisational audit – including similar problems, as well as interlinked solutions and methods to solve these problems. In addition, the system user can identify for each profile's problem-solution pair further relations to other KM aspects by browsing the structure of the ontology. The identified most similar case(s) also comprise information about implementation costs and time, qualitative and quantitative benefits, savings, sustainability, application to other fields, external support/ funding and others.

An example for a so called "holistic recommendation" would be the recommendation of using a specific tool, technology or knowledge instrument combined with a specific organizational method, as well as with a required organizational culture program.

Moreover, the system provides a *Solution Generation Component* which supports the automatic generation of solutions by merging problems with solutions of similar problems from the CB. This can be done for either single problems or all problems of a selected profile based on a predetermined minimal similarity value. When generating solutions for profiles, the solution generator only creates solutions for one or more problem(s), if a profile can be identified where the global similarity of all profile attributes has at least a predetermined value.

Moreover, we are currently developing *modification rules*, in order to realize automatic case adaptation in "easy situations". For instance, it is planned to implement a verification component which allows KMIR to check if a specific "software application" makes sense for a recommendation or solution generation, based on background information defined by further specific attributes (e.g., compatibility, interoperability, scalability and extensibility of the software tool to be recommended), and on this basis also adapt technical solutions from a BPC to specific needs of a new customer.

3.6 Feedback Loop and Learning

Successfully accomplished KM implementations are added as a new BPC into the CB. This is done by technically supporting the revision of the new constructed KM introduction solution (e.g., editing/ correcting existing information to the generated solution or providing additional information like for instance new experiences or benefits, etc.). After that, the adapted, reused and revised BPC is stored as a new learned case into the CB. The learning component collects lessons learned regarding successful or inappropriate given recommendations in order to refine or extend the BPCs as well as the general structure of the CB. This is done by providing an **evaluation function** to the requesting organization The consulting agency has the opportunity to describe experiences made with the given recommendations to the customer regarding their correctness and capability to solve a specific customer problem. The evaluation results directly flow into the learning component and are considered in the next case retrieval by using them for an internal ranking of the best practice cases in the CB. Based on that, the recommendations component is able to provide better recommendations to new requesting organisations in the future. Worse evaluated recommendations with a low ranking can be either optimized or thrown out of the CB.

3.7 Administration Functions

KMIR disposes of several administrative functions for maintaining and analyzing the case base which are shortly described as follows:

- **Importing Instance Lists**
  An Import Interface supports an easy import of instance lists from text files in order to instantiate concepts, where the concent changes over time, like e.g. "Technology", "Software" or "Knowledge Instrument" and thus avoids to model them laboriously with an ontology editor.
- **Case Completion**
  Case completion is used for automatically enriching cases with existing background knowledge. In KMIR, case completion is used to learn new relation instances by analyzing existing solution descriptions for the appearance of instances or synonyms of the concepts "software tool", "technology" or "knowledge instrument". Based on that, instances are interlinked with the concerning solution (e.g. "Solution S uses technology T"). The functionality is particularly suitable for updating existing cases after the enhancement of instance lists (e.g., the lists of existing tools, technologies or knowledge instruments). However, the case completion component is freely configurable for using it with any concept or relation in the ontology.
- **Case Disjunction Tester**
  The function identifies BPCs, problems or goals, that are very similar to each other in order to check on the one hand the relevance of specific attributes regarding case retrieval and on the other hand to identify redundant profiles, problems or goals (cp. [34])
- **Statistical Analysis**
  That function provides a "real-time analysis" of the existing case base by presenting frequencies, averages and standard deviations for all interesting concepts in order to support to examine the BPC's statistic distribution.

4 Related Work

We combined approaches from *CBR* and *Semantic Web* for structuring problem-solution pairs (cases) by the use of an ontology, thus being able to identify a solution for a new problem by retrieving the most similar case using syntactical and *semantical* similarity measures. All this is applied in the *Knowledge Management* area. Hence related work in these three areas is interesting.

Knowledge Management research: Typically, KM introduction is guided by "cookbook-like methods" (e.g., [17];[20];[14];[18]) or inspired by collections of anecdotically narrated – in the best case semi-structured – best practice cases (e.g., [9];[12]). Another systematic development of a big, homogeneously annotated, case base with an intelligent search facility is not known to us. Of course, the idea of applying CBR methods to *lessons learned* systems – which can be seen similar to best practice systems – is not new in the KM area [21]. However, typical applications in this spirit focus on a relatively narrow application domain and usually employ a *textual CBR* approach or *feature-based CBR* with a small attribute set, describing few metadata for each case. Tackling such a complex problem as KM introduction is a much more challenging task. Hence, the design of the appropriate attributes and their respective value domains – i.e., the design of the KMIR ontology – is a main contribution of our work.

CBR research: The observation that CBR and Semantic Web are closely related, with complementary strengths and characteristics, and should be combined synergistically, has already been made a few times ([14];[22]). However, this did not yet lead to a widespread take-up of the idea in the CBR community. The use of taxonomies as the basis for local similarities has, e.g., has been discussed by [24], and taxonomic similarities are widely used in many applications, like comparing chip designs [25], working contexts [26] or employee skill profiles [27]. However, such approaches often do not settle upon and exploit the possibilities of logic-based Semantic Web languages, and they do rarely exploit other domain knowledge structures than taxonomic ones, i.e. they do not offer relational similarity for comparing ontology instance bundles. As already mentioned above, it might be subject to future research to clearly define the boundaries as well as the interfaces of typical CBR approaches and more reasoning-oriented Semantic Web technologies. Some work might be worth to be rediscovered, such as Kamp's approach to knowledge-intensive CBR based upon Description Logics [33]. Generally, the use of extensive background knowledge models within CBR systems is not unusual, cp. [35];[36]. It seems interesting to identify efficient operating points with a good balance between upfront knowledge engineering, knowledge acquisition costs, system powerfulness, and system retrieval efficiency.

Semantic Web research: Case and similarity mark-up languages have been proposed by [8];[23]. Widespread use of ontologies as background knowledge in similarity assessment, has recently been proposed for several applications such as plan retrieval [28], buyer-seller matchmaking in eCommerce [29], or question answering [30]. [3] and [4] investigate ontology-based similarity of queries for ranking query results in information retrieval. They suggest several semantic similarity measures exploiting the structure of ontologies. [2] describes a CBR system implemented in LOOM exploiting Description-Logic reasoning to determine case similarities based on background knowledge. Settling upon the logic-based semantics of OWL and / or on information-theoretical approaches for analyzing concept expressions instead of traversing taxonomies, is also proposed by [31] and [32]. Very interesting recent work has been published in [5] and [6]. The authors discuss a large-scale experimental study showing the positive effects of similarity-based IR approaches on precision and recall. In particular, they evaluated the retrieval quality and the user-oriented adequacy of several semantic similarity measures. Similarly, [15] demonstrated the positive effects already of very simple semantic similarity measures on retrieval quality in bioinformatics. Altogether, these citations show that semantic similarity is often useful in complex retrieval situations, but that there is no "gold standard" for it. Hence our work does not implement one specific way of semantic similarity, but offers a generic framework which allows to declaratively specify arbitrary measures, combine them, extend, and rearrange them. This provides an ideal playground for experimental work and further integration with Semantic Web technology.

5 Future Work

We have described the KMIR framework which supports consulting agencies in successfully accompanying a customer's Introduction of Knowledge Management by providing recommendations based on CBR and Semantic Web Technologies. For the development of KMIR, an extensive collection, analysis and structuring of BPCs from different information sources was done. The analysis as well as the ontology for structuring the BPCs directly focus on human, technical and organizational aspects (holistic KM approach).

For the future, we intend to validate KMIR under real-life conditions which might be realized in the context of a concrete project with a consulting agency. Moreover, we will integrate KMIR with ONTOKNOM, an ontology-based software infrastructure for retaining and maintaining KM Maturity Models in order to better focus on the organization's needs with regard to a successful introduction of KM [13]. This will be done on one hand by associating BPCs in KMIR with a specific KM Maturity Level, and on the other hand by proposing BPCs in ONTOKNOM, depending on a calculated maturity level. A further research interest is to extract a reference maturity model based on all captured KMIR cases and, the opposite way around, to extract a reference BPC out of several KM maturity models in ONTOKNOM.

Acknowledgement

The work presented here has partially been co-funded by the German National Ministry for Education and Research (bmb+f) with the project "Im Wissensnetz – Vernetzte Informationsprozesse in Forschungsverbünden", by the Federal State of Baden-Württemberg with the project "Kompetenznetzwerk Wissensmanagement", and by the European Commission with the project "NEPOMUK - Networked Environment for Personalized, Ontology-based Management of Unified Knowledge".

References

1. Aamodt, A., Plaza, E.: Case-Based Reasoning: Foundational Issues, Methodological Variations, and System Approaches. AI Communications (1994) 7(i):39-59
2. Díaz-Agudo, B., González-Calero, P.A.: A Declarative Similarity Framework for Knowledge Intensive CBR. Int. Conf. on Case-Based Reasoning ICCBR-2001 (2001)
3. Andreasen, T., Jensen, P.A., Nilsson, J.F., Paggio, P., Pedersen, B.S., Thomsen, H.E.: Content-Based Text Querying With Ontological Descriptors. Data and Knowledge Engineering 48(2):199-219 (2004)
4. Andreasen, T., Bulskov, H., Knappe, R.: Modelling and Use of Domain-Specific Knowledge for Similarity and Visualization, 7th Int. Conf. on Terminology and Knowledge Engineering, TKE 2005 (2005)
5. A. Bernstein, E. Kaufmann, C. Bürki, M. Klein: How Similar Is It? Towards Personalized Similarity Measures in Ontologies. In: 7. Int. Tagung Wirtschaftsinformatik (2005)
6. A. Bernstein, E. Kaufmann, C. Bürki, M. Klein: Object Similarity in Ontologies: A Foundation for Business Intelligence Systems and High-performance Retrieval. In: 25th Int. Conf. on Information Systems (2004)
7. Bergmann R., Schaaf, M.: Structural Case-Based Reasoning and Ontology-Based Knowledge Management: A Perfect Match? J. Universal Computer Science 9(7):608-626 (2003)
8. Chen, H. & Wu, Z.: On Case-Based Knowledge Sharing in Semantic Web. In: 15th IEEE Int. Conference on Tools with Artificial Intelligence (ICTAI'03) (2003)
9. Davenport T.H., Probst, J.B.: Knowledge Management Case Book, Publicis Corporate Publishing and John Wiley & Sons (2002)
10. Davenport T. and Prusak L.: Working Knowledge. How Organizations Manage What They Know. Harvard Business School Press (1998)
11. Ehrig, M., Haase, P., Hefke, M., Stojanovic, N.: Similarity for Ontologies - A Comprehensive Framework. In: 13th European Conference on Information Systems (2005)
12. Eppler, M.J., Sukowski, O.: Fallstudien zum Wissensmanagement: Lösungen aus der Praxis. NetAcademy Press, St. Gallen (2001)
13. Hefke, M., Kleiner, F.: An Ontology-Based Software Infrastructure for Retaining Theoretical Knowledge Management Maturity Models. In 1st Workshop "FOMI 2005" Formal Ontologies Meet Industry (2005)
14. Lindstaedt, S., Strohmaier, M., Rollett, H., Hrastnik, J., Bruhnsen, K., Droschl, G., Gerold, M: KMap: Providing Orientation for Practitioners when Introducing Knowledge Management. In: 4th Int. Conf. on Practical Aspects of Knowledge Management (2002)
15. Lord, P., Bechhofer, S, Wilkinson, M., Schiltz, G., Gessler, D., Goble, C., Stein, L., Hull, D.: Applying Semantic Web Services to Bioinformatics: Experiences Gained, Lessons Learnt. In: Proc 3rd Int. Semantic Web Conference ISWC2004 (2004)
16. Maedche, A. and Staab, S.: KAON - The Karlsruhe Ontology and Semantic Web Meta Project. Künstliche Intelligenz (KI), 17(3):27-31 (2003)
17. Mentzas, G., Apostolou, D., Young, R., Abecker, A.: Knowledge Asset Management. Springer-Verlag, London (2002)
18. Peters, M. and Forzi, T.: A Decision Support Toolkit for the Selection of KM Methods and Instruments for Inter-organisational Networks. In: 15th eChallenges Conference (2005)
19. Probst G., Raub S., Romhardt K.: Managing Knowledge: Building Blocks for Success, Wiley, London (1999)
20. Tiwana, A.: Knowledge Management Toolkit: Orchestrating IT, Strategy, and Knowledge Platforms. Pearson Education (2002)

21. Weber, R., Aha, D.W., Becerra-Fernandez, I.: Intelligent Lessons Learned Systems. International Journal of Expert Systems Research & Applications 20(1) (2001)
22. Bichindaritz, I.: Mémoire: Case Based Reasoning Meets the Semantic Web in Biology and Medicine. In: ECCBR-2004: 47-61, Springer LNCS 3155 (2004)
23. Coyle, L., Doyle, D., Cunningham, P.: Representing Similarity for CBR in XML. Technical Report TCD-CS-2004-25, Trinity College, Dublin (2004)
24. Bergmann, R.: On the Use of Taxonomies for Representing Case Features and Local Similarity Measures. In: 6th German Workshop on Case-Based Reasoning GWCBR (1998)
25. Schaaf, M., Freßmann, A., Maximini, R., Bergmann, R., Tartakovski, R., Radetzki, M.: Intelligent IP Retrieval Driven by Application Requirements. Integration, the VLSI Journal (2004)
26. Shkundina, R. and Schwarz, S.: A Similarity Measure for Task Contexts. In: Workshop Similarities - Processes - Workflows at ICCBR-05 (2005)
27. Oldakowski, R. and Bizer, C.: SemMF: A Framework for Calculating Semantic Similarity of Objects Represented as RDF Graphs. In: 4th Int. Semantic Web Conference (2005)
28. Hung, L.C. Beng, L.H., Wah, N.G., Yin, H.K.: Plan Ontology and its Applications. In: 7th Int. Conference on Information Fusion (2004)
29. Bhavsar, V., Boley, H., Yang, L.: A Weighted-Tree Similarity Algorithm for Multi-Agent Systems in E-Business Environments, Computational Intelligence Journal, 20(4) (2004)
30. Vargas-Vera, M., Motta, E.: An Ontology-Driven Similarity Algorithm. Technical Report KMI-04-16. Open University, Milton Keynes (2004)
31. D'Amato, C., Fanizzi, N., Esposito, F.: A Semantic Similarity Measure for Expressive Description Logics. In: CILC 2005, Convegno Italiano di Logica Computazionale (2005)
32. Hau, J., Lee, W., Darlington, J.: A Semantic Similarity Measure for Semantic Web Services. In: Web Service Semantics Workshop at WWW (2005)
33. Kamp, G.: Using Description Logics for Knowledge Intensive Case-Based Reasoning. In Proc. of the 3rd European Workshop on Case-Based Reasoning, vol. 1168 of Lecture Notes in Artificial Intelligence, Springer-Verlag (1996)
34. Smyth, B. & McKenna, E.: Modelling the Competence of Case Bases. In Prof. of the 4th European Workshop on Case-Based Reasoning. Springer-Verlag (1998)
35. Aamodt, A.: Knowledge-Intensive Case-Based Reasoning in CREEK. In Proc. of the 7th European CBR Conference, Lecture Notes in Artificial Intelligence, LNAI 3155, Springer-Verlag (2004)
36. Minor, M. & Schmidt, K.: Automatic Transformation and Enlargement of Similarity Models for Case-Based Reasoning. In Modellierung-2006, Innsbruck (2006)

The PwC Connection Machine:
An Adaptive Expertise Provider

Mehmet H. Göker, Cynthia Thompson, Simo Arajärvi, and Kevin Hua

PricewaterhouseCoopers LLP
Center for Advanced Research
Ten Almaden Blvd, Suite 1600
San Jose, CA 95113
{mehmet.goker, cynthia.thompson, simo.arajarvi,
kevin.k.hua}@us.pwc.com

Abstract. The Connection Machine helps PricewaterhouseCoopers LLP (PwC) partners and staff to solve problems by connecting people to people. It allows information seekers to enter their question in free text, finds knowledgeable colleagues, forwards the question to them, obtains the answer and sends it back to the seeker. In the course of this interaction, the application unobtrusively learns and updates user profiles and thereby increases its routing accuracy. The Connection Machine combines features of expertise locators, adaptive case-based recommender systems and question answering applications. This document describes the core technology that supports the workflow, the user modeling and the retrieval technology of the Connection Machine.

1 The Power of Connected People

Information, knowledge and experience are key success factors and the most important competitive advantage for any business. However, most of this core corporate asset is in the heads of the employees and cannot be easily accessed, shared or distributed. Capturing and protecting it in documents (electronic or otherwise) is not only cumbersome, but the documents become rapidly outdated and the maintenance effort required to keep document collections up-to-date is formidable.

Furthermore, in the complex business scenarios of today's world, problem solving requires an increasingly large amount of specialized knowledge. It is nearly impossible for one individual to be an expert in every aspect of a company's business and deliver comprehensive solutions. Problem solving requires co-operation and the sharing of ideas and information. The size of a corporation and the collective knowledge of its employees are only valuable if these employees can share their information and cooperate. We believe that the best way to provide the most up-to-date and accurate information to those who seek it is by putting them directly in touch with the experts.

The PricewaterhouseCoopers Connection Machine is an application that enables employees to solve business problems by helping them obtain answers to their questions from knowledgeable colleagues. Rather than trying to extract information from experts and pointing information seekers to stale document directories, the

T.R. Roth-Berghofer et al. (Eds.): ECCBR 2006, LNAI 4106, pp. 549–563, 2006.
© Springer-Verlag Berlin Heidelberg 2006

Connection Machine matches incoming questions to the expertise profiles of users, routes questions to the experts with highest similarity, collects their answers and relays the answer back to the seekers. The application extends the personal network of employees to the entire firm and makes otherwise difficult to reach experts accessible.

2 Existing Approaches to Locating and Contacting Experts

2.1 Directory Systems

Most firms allow their employees to search for other colleagues by means of directories. Typically, these directories list the business unit, office phone numbers and addresses of employees, as well as some limited information about their background. Searches are usually performed by entering the (partial) name of the employee or by browsing to through the business unit structure of the firm. In terms of their functionality, these systems resemble phone books with a job categorization, similar to "yellow pages".

If we know which employee we are looking for, directory systems are very useful for finding their contact information. However, most of these applications do not help to determine which employee might be knowledgeable on a *specific* topic [c.f. 1] and able or willing to answer our question. They also do not help to relay the question to the right person, to obtain an answer in a given timeframe, or to create a network of employees. Additionally, the data that goes beyond office location, department, phone numbers etc. is typically not centrally maintained and requires manual updates by the employees themselves. As such, the information is mostly outdated and its reliability rather limited.

Also, in personal interactions, if experts are not able to give an answer to a question, they typically refer the inquirer to another specialist from their personal network. A user looking for an expert in a directory system has only access to one level of experts and is at the mercy of the expert he/she contacts. People who have no representative profile in the directory system are beyond the reach of the seeker entirely.

Since standard directory applications do not provide the functionality to find an expert and ask a question easily, employees typically revert to the rather inefficient practice of sending emails to broad audiences in the hope of finding someone who is able and willing to help them.

2.2 Expertise Locator Systems

To answer the need for being able to access experts and ask questions, companies have developed so called Expertise Locator Systems (ELS). These systems try to find experts that are potentially able to answer a user's question by matching the query to the expertise profiles of the employees [2, 3, 4, 5]. Some systems enhance the matching process by using the social connections between employees or collaborative filtering (e.g. [1, 6]). Depending on the application, they return a combination of potentially knowledgeable experts and related documents. It is up to the user looking for information to contact the experts and to get an answer to their question.

Employees are normally represented by an expertise profile which, depending on the application, contains a limited number of structured attributes coming from an enterprise directory, a list of documents published by the employee, and general background information in free text or in a list of terms/noun phrases. The experts can update their profiles manually by adding new documents, modifying their background information and, potentially, the structured data. Responses to queries can be published and added to the profile as new documents as well. Some systems generate profiles automatically by analyzing emails and authored documents and extracting a set of terms. Users have to go through the terms to specify which ones represent areas that they would feel comfortable answering questions in.

Current expertise locator systems are designed to search for *people*. They match the user's question with documents and expert's profiles and display the list of matching experts to the users. The users, in turn, have to pick an expert from this list and contact them with the question. However, the goal of users who submit questions to an expertise locator system is not to find the name of colleagues but to find answers to their questions! The fact that a user has found the name of a potentially knowledgeable person does not mean that his/her question has been answered.

An additional weakness in current expertise locator systems is the lack of division between interest and expertise. Existing expertise locators analyze documents that have been authored by users and their emails to generate a profile to represent each user's expertise. If a user subscribes to an electronic newsletter out of interest in the specific topic, or writes a "Request for Proposals" (RFP) for vendors to respond to, he/she will be presumed an expert in that field.

3   Overview of the PwC Connection Machine

The Connection Machine extends the concepts of directory systems and expertise locators beyond the pure search for *people* and helps PwC partners and staff to get *answers* to their questions and to solve problems together. It leverages the personal networks and intelligence of PwC employees, facilitates collaborative problem solving, and fosters a work environment in which people are truly connected.

By answering questions rather than just locating people, the Connection Machine acts as a virtual, adaptive expertise provider. It combines features of expertise locators with adaptive case-based recommender systems and question answering applications.

Figure 1 provides a general overview of the interaction between the information Seeker, potential Providers and the Connection Machine.

An interaction with the Connection Machine starts with an Information Seeker entering a question in free text format, as if he/she were asking a colleague a question via email. The Seeker is also able to specify the urgency of the question, the name of a client the question relates to as well as additional, optional, structured information (e.g. knowledge domain, line of service, industry) to be used to locate appropriate potential Providers (Figure 2).

The Connection Machine processes the query, finds a set of suitable potential Providers and contacts them. The system only contacts potential Providers whose expertise levels for the given question are higher than the Seeker's and whose maximum number of questions per week has not been reached.

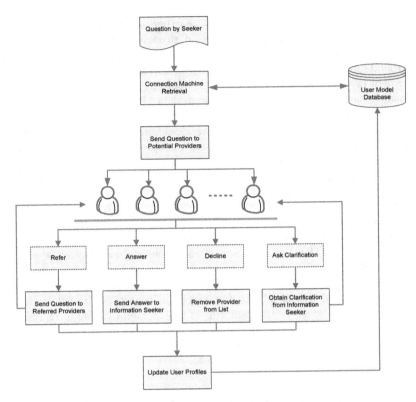

Fig. 1. Overview of the application workflow in the PwC Connection Machine

The number of potential Providers who will be contacted regarding a question is configurable. If the first set of potential Providers is not able to respond within the allocated time (a fraction of the time the Seeker needs the answer by), the system sends the question to a second batch of potential Providers. If no potential Providers can be identified or the Providers do not react, the question is sent to the Knowledge Administrator of the Domain for further processing.

Once the system identifies potential Providers, they are notified via email (Figure 3) and a visual indicator in the "Summary" page of the web interface, informing them that their expertise is needed. In addition to the question, the potential Providers are informed of the Seeker's contact information (e.g. name, line of service) and of the timeframe in which the question needs to be answered.

After receiving a question, the potential Providers may choose to respond either via web interface or via email. Potential Providers may offer an answer to the question; request additional information from the Seeker; refer the question to other potential Providers; or decline to answer. Once one of the potential Providers offers an answer or requests additional information, he/she becomes the "Provider" for the interaction. From this point on, the Connection Machine facilitates communicates between the

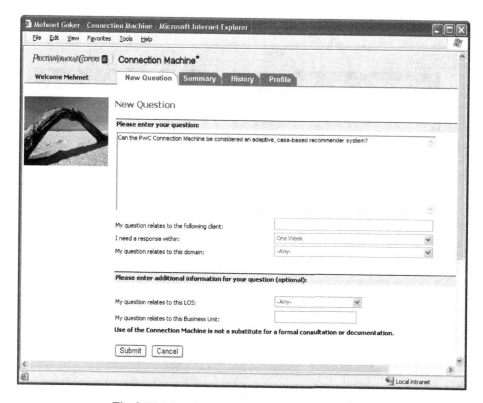

Fig. 2. Web interface of the PwC Connection Machine

information Seeker and the Provider and removes other potential Providers from the problem solving conversation by sending them email and removing the indicator in their "Summary" web page.

If a Provider chooses to answer the question, the Seeker is notified of the answer via email and a visual indicator in the web application (Figure 4). Upon receiving an answer, a Seeker can choose to accept it and close the request, ask a clarification question about the answer, or reject the answer and request a second opinion unless they have already done so.

The Provider can also ask for additional information that may be needed to answer the question. Once the Seeker provides additional information the Provider will be presented with the same options as when initially contacted by the Connection Machine (i.e. provide an answer, request question clarification, refer the question and decline to answer).

If a (potential) Provider decides that someone else from his/her personal network is better suited to answer the question, he/she may choose to refer the question. In this way the Connection Machine can learn about potential Providers who may have been missing from its initial set of profiles. The Seeker will not be made aware that the question was referred to another potential Provider as long as the initial Provider had not contacted the Seeker prior to referring the question (i.e. the provider did not request question clarification prior to referring the question).

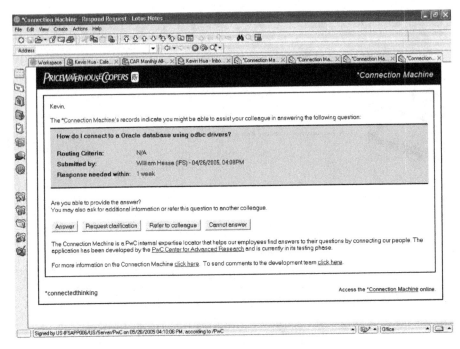

Fig. 3. Sample email from the PwC Connection Machine

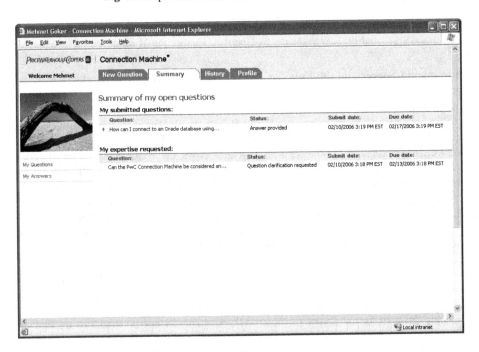

Fig. 4. Open question summary page

The Provider can also indicate that he/she is not able to provide an answer to the question and specify the reason for declining to answer (e.g. "Too busy", "Don't know the answer", "Independence conflict").

If the question was declined by all contacted Providers, it will be sent to the Knowledge Administrator of the domain for further processing. The use of a Knowledge Administrator as a "backup" for answering or referring questions ensures that all questions entered in the Connection Machine are answered in a timely manner.

4 Retrieval of Potential Providers in the Connection Machine

To execute the workflow described above the application needs to be able to determine who is potentially capable of answering the question by matching a user's query against information it has about other users. To achieve consistently high accuracy over a long period of time, the information of the users has to be updated with appropriate sections of the interaction on an ongoing basis. (Fig. 5)

The technology we used to implement these functions in the Connection Machine is similar to User Adaptive, Case-Based Recommender Systems [7, 8, 9]. However, most recommender systems are geared towards selecting the best match out of a set of (mostly static) items and presenting it to the user. In the case of the Connection Machine, the items in the case-base are continuously evolving user models where each model contains multiple profiles. Rather than being the final goal, the retrieval process is an intermediate step and users, whose expertise profile matched the query, are utilized in the workflow to route questions. The resulting interaction between the Seeker and Provider is the desired outcome for the application.

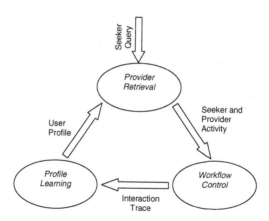

Fig. 5. Profile maintenance and usage in the Connection Machine

The user modeling in the Connection Machine is not geared towards influencing the similarity metrics, the user interaction or the user interface of the application. Neither can it influence the solutions a Provider may offer to a Seeker. The case-base of the Connection Machine is a collection of user models which are constantly maintained and updated by unobtrusively observing the user's interaction with the system [cf. 10] and, which are then used to select the users that will participate in the workflow as potential Providers.

5 The User Model of the Connection Machine

5.1 Interest, Expertise and Referral Profiles

A user model (i.e. case) in the Connection Machine contains three types of user profiles, each of which captures one aspect of a user's preferences or capabilities:

- The *interest profile* denotes the topics a user is interested in. It is updated from the questions a user asks and the associated clarifications.
- The *expertise profile* represents the topics that the user is knowledgeable in. This profile can be initialized from documents the user authored, a resume, prior engagement histories or similar. It is updated with the questions a user could answer, the answers he/she provided, and all associated clarification conversations.
- The *referral profiles* represent the topics in which the user is able to refer questions. It is updated with the questions, any clarification conversation associated with them, and any referral comments.

We also make a distinction between *positive* and *negative* profiles. Negative profiles contain information that the user does not want to be associated with. Users of the Connection Machine can choose to "Opt out" from a question by stating that they no longer wish to receive questions similar to the current one. This information is used to update the negative profiles. The use of negative profiles thus brings the total number of profile types available to six. In the following, we focus on "positive" profiles but all techniques apply to negative profiles as well.

Having six different profile types in a user model allows us to route questions with higher accuracy. It also enables us to generate reports on the distribution of interest, expertise and referral capabilities within the firm, to generate communities of interest or expertise and to route relevant documentation to inform group members or for review.

5.2 Data Sources for User Models

User profiles of directory systems and expertise locators are typically generated from structured data from sources such as enterprise databases, or from unstructured sources such as documents authored or read by the user. The resulting user profiles can be structured (e.g., a list of attributes and their associated values), unstructured (e.g., a list of terms, a collection of documents), or a mix of these representations.

While structured representations provide benefits in terms of retrieval accuracy and standardized vocabulary, they are very difficult to create and to maintain (both for the company and the individual). Since the Connection Machine operates in an environment where structured information is already generated and maintained for directory systems, we can utilize this information where available and concentrate our research on the generation of profile information from unstructured data sources and on the best way to represent it.

The information source we consider for the generation of user profiles is the set of documents (e.g., resumes, whitepapers, emails) that the user has authored, read or received. As such, the problem we are targeting is how to use *unstructured* data to generate and represent an expressive, flexible, and easy to create and maintain user profile.

5.3   Representation of Document or Term Based User Profiles

The representation that is used to store the content of the user models has a significant impact on the capabilities, flexibility, maintainability and learning abilities of the system.

In today's expertise locator systems, information from unstructured source documents is typically captured in profiles that are either based on term statistics extracted from discrete documents, or from term statistics based on the union of all documents associated with a user. In the first approach, the profiles are collections of term statistics per document and experts are ranked based on their respective total number of documents that are similar to the user's query. In the second approach, the profile is a set of term weights extracted from the union of documents for an expert and the similarity is computed between the query and the term weights for this collection.

We observed that the focus on discrete documents and their terms neglects the fact that the documents associated with a person can represent different facets of a bigger picture. A person who discusses the topic of "Hybrid Engine Performance" in one document and "Engine Emissions" in another is highly likely to be knowledgeable on "Hybrid Engine Emissions" or potentially "Engine Performance and Emissions" as well.

We also found that basing the profiles purely on terms (from discrete documents or the collection of documents) and neglecting the impact of phrases and relationships between terms can reduce accuracy and results in routing errors. For example, a person mentioning "Captive" at the beginning of a document, "Insurance" in the middle and "Bermuda" at the end may not be knowledgeable on the topic of "Captive Insurance arrangements in Bermuda". On the other hand, a person who wrote a document with exactly this title and who did not frequently mention "Bermuda", "Captive" and "Insurance" in the body of the document might be better able to help the Seeker than the travel agent who wants to sell an additional "insurance policy for a captivating trip to Bermuda".

5.4   Lattice Based User Profiles

To address the problems described above, we devised a profile representation in which interest, expertise and referral profiles of users can each be incrementally learned and that captures a unified summary of the individual's knowledge, crossing document boundaries. Using the documents associated with an individual we generate a profile for them that contains each term in these documents as well as the distance based co-occurrence weight between terms. Graphically, this represents a lattice[1] in which the nodes are the terms with their associated term weights and the links between the nodes are the co-occurrence weights between two terms. Below, we call any such group of linked terms a phrase.

Table 1. Notation used in the Lattice Representation

For Terms	For Phrases	Description
N	N	Number of profiles of a particular type
$f_p(i)$	$f_p(i,j)$	Frequency (occurrence count) of term i or phrase i-j in profile p
$f_{max\,p}$	$f_{max\,p}$	Maximum term (or phrase) frequency in profile p
$pf(i)$	$pf(i,j)$	Profile frequency: number of profiles containing term i or phrase i-j
$ipf(i)$	$ipf(i,j)$	Inverse profile frequency of i th term or phrase i-j
$w_p(i)$	$w_p(i,j)$	weight of term i or phrase i-j in profile p

One lattice is built for each of the six profile types to represent a given user. We generate a lattice by starting with the available documents, appropriate for the profile type being built, that are associated with each user. Each document is divided into tokens, synonyms are processed, terms are stemmed, and stop words are removed. Once the documents have been pre-processed, we compute term weights, phrase distances, and other relevant statistics needed to create the profiles. Note that any document can be processed in this manner, including questions, answers, and other conversations between users.

Table 1 shows the notation used here to describe the process of computing the weights for each term and phrase. We begin with the terms. Each term in each user's profile is associated with a term weight. Our process for computing individual term weights is the same as standard TF-IDF (term frequency / inverse document frequency) approaches used in information retrieval (IR) [11], but is applied to profiles containing multiple documents rather than individual documents as in IR. Thus, the weight of term i in profile p is calculated as:

$$w_p(i) = tf_p(i) \times ipf(i) \tag{1}$$

In this equation, the normalized term (or phrase) frequency $tf_p(i)$ and the inverse profile frequency ipf_i are calculated as follows:

$$tf_p(i) = \frac{f_p(i)}{f_{max\,p}} \tag{2}$$

$$ipf(i) = \log(1 + N/pf(i)) \tag{3}$$

To generate links between the terms (the "phrase" weights) we gather all pairs[2] of terms that occur together in a sentence, usually using a window size to restrict the

---

[1] This is not a lattice in the mathematical sense.
[2] This idea can be extended to phrases containing more than two words.

number of pairs considered. Each link is then connected by a weight proportional both to the number of times the terms occur together in the profile and the number of intervening words between the terms. Thus, in the formulas above $tf_p(i)$ becomes $tf_p(i,j)$ and $ipf(i)$ becomes $ipf(i,j)$ with all formulas being adapted according to Table 1. For the case of phrases, we compute the frequency $f_p(i,j)$ by using a distance-based frequency count:

$$f_p(i, j) = \sum_{k=1}^{N} \frac{1}{d_k(i, j)} \qquad (4)$$

where n is the number of occurrences of the phrase containing the terms i and j in the same sentence and within a window of w terms in the profile p, and $d_k(i,j)$ is the distance for a given occurrence of the two terms, i.e. one plus the number of terms intervening between i and j. Thus, adjacent terms would have $d_k(i,j)=1$, and so on. While the formula above assumes a linear weight decrease over distance, we could consider other ways for the distance between terms to impact the weight computation (e.g. exponential).

As an example of the computations above, let us assume we have a single document for a given user, containing only a single sentence: "The Connection Machine models the interest, expertise and referral capabilities of each user." Then the term and phrase frequencies computed would be as in Table 2. Note that this shows only normalized frequency, not overall term weight, which would depend on the inverse document frequency factor, and is not illustrated here for simplicity.

Capturing link strength between terms allows the detection of associations between terms in a sentence, no matter their syntactic relationship; allows term association detection to cross document boundaries by following paths in the lattice; and allows precise calculation of term association strength. Instead of using the number of times terms occur together, we use the totaled inverse distance between them. Thus both frequency and closeness of association are captured.

Table 2. Sample lattice built from one sentence

	connec	machin	model	interest	expert	referr	capabl	user
connec	1	1	1/2	1/3	1/4	1/5	1/6	1/7
machin	0	1	1	1/2	1/3	1/4	1/5	1/6
model	0	0	1	1	1/2	1/3	1/4	1/5
interest	0	0	0	1	1	1/2	1/3	1/4
expert	0	0	0	0	1	1	1/2	1/3
referr	0	0	0	0	0	1	1	1/2
capabl	0	0	0	0	0	0	1	1
user	0	0	0	0	0	0	0	1

Similar ideas have been reported in information retrieval (IR) where co-occurrence statistics have been used for thesaurus construction [12] and for relevance feedback [13]. Distance-based collection and use of co-occurrence statistics have also been used at the character level for Japanese word segmentation [14]. We believe the utilization of link strength for enhancing user profiles is a new approach, integrates easily with the framework of the Connection Machine, and provides benefits over approaches that extract noun-phrases and require parsing.

5.5 Profile Updates in the Connection Machine Workflow

The initial user profiles in the system will be created based on the information provided in corporate and business databases, resumes and direct input from the users. While these initial profiles are not necessary for the system's operation, they will reduce the number of referrals needed until a suitable Provider is found during the initial phases of the application.

Once the system starts being used, the interest, expertise and referral profiles will be updated directly from the interactions as outlined in Table 3.

The user will also be able to manually update and manage his/her profiles by adding relevant documents or keywords. The profile changes caused by a user's interactions with the Connection Machine are visible in the profile section of the application as well and can be removed by users if they should choose the do so.

These updates all affect the term and link weights in one or more user's lattice-based profile. For example, the TF-IDF weights of the terms in an added document are adjusted. This could cause changes in the IDF values of terms that appear across multiple profiles. Also, if a deletion removes all information from a profile, then N, the number of profiles changes, and N also changes when a new profile is added. Adjustments such as these are not needed in typical stable document repositories.

5.6 Profile Retrieval and Ranking

As mentioned above, our approach to finding the best expert that matches a user's query is to match queries to user's profiles. We thus need to retrieve people whose expertise profiles are in some way similar to the query, and rank the profiles from most to least similar. We can also incorporate into this process the exclusion or reduction in ranking of users whose negative profiles match the query.

We base the process on the terms and phrases in the query and in the profiles. First, all profiles with terms that intersect the query terms are retrieved. This is done for computational efficiency, since profiles that do not contain any of the terms in the query are obviously irrelevant. Computation can be further optimized by sorting the returned set of profiles according to the number of terms and phrases that overlap with the query and cutting off the profiles which fall below a threshold. Then, we calculate similarity between the query and each retained profile. Recall that each term and phrase in the query carries a weight, as does each term and phrase in a profile. Based on these, we compute the similarity between a query and a profile by determining the cosine of the angle between the profile's weight vector and the query's weight vector [11]. Other similarity metrics could be used as well.

Table 3. Profile update specifications

Situation	Interest Profile Changes (Seeker)	Expertise or Referral Profile Changes (Provider)
Seeker submits a question	Add question to interest profile regardless of the outcome (i.e. whether it's answered, withdrawn, not answered).	No update
Provider refers a question	No update	No update until new provider (aka. referee) provides an answer. If referee answers question, add to referral profile the conversation up to the point of referral. If referee refers to someone else, no update.
Provider requests question clarification	No update	No update
Seeker provides question clarification	Clarification question and clarification answer are both added to interest profile.	No update
Provider supplies an answer	No update	No update until answer is accepted by Seeker
Seeker accepts the answer	No update	Add entire conversation including any clarification or (other provider's) referral comments to expertise profile.
Provider declines to answer with "Don't know the answer"	No update	Remove question from expertise profile.
Provider declines to answer with "Too busy" or "Independence conflict"	No update	No update
Provider or referrer checks "don't send similar" box after receiving a question	No update	Add question to negative expertise profile.

6 Future Work and Summary

As next steps, we are planning to utilize the user models of the Connection Machine for tasks such as targeted content distribution to interested parties, routing content to experts for verification, personalization of portals, as well as the creation of communities of interest and expertise. By analyzing interest, expertise and referral profiles for the entire organization, gap analyses could be performed and areas of concentrated expertise or interest highlighted. The continuously changing weight and link distribution of the lattice allows capturing trends in interest and expertise.

We are also interested in experimenting with different similarity metrics that take multiple profiles and feedback ratings into account and to evaluate the applicability of Case Retrieval Nets [15] for our purposes. We are also planning to look at the limited feedback mechanisms of the Connection Machine within the broader framework of a reputation system and as a means to motivate users to participate and share their knowledge [16, 17]. Other topics we consider worth pursuing are the link between social networks and expertise location [7,18] and how the information in the lattice can be interpreted with Social Network Analysis techniques [19] to determine synonyms, antonyms and value ranges.

In summary, the PricewaterhouseCoopers Connection Machine allows information seekers to enter their question in free text, finds knowledgeable colleagues, forwards the question to them, obtains the answer and sends it back to the seeker. In the course of this interaction, the Connection Machine unobtrusively updates and refines the interest, expertise and referral profiles of each user. Rather than just locating *people*, it extends the concepts of directory systems and expertise locators and acts as a virtual (adaptive) expertise provider and *answers questions*.

References

1. Kautz, H., Selman, B. Milewski, A., "Agent Amplified Communication", in Proceedings of the Thirteenth National Conference on Artificial Intelligence, AAAI-96, Portland, Oregon, 1996, pp. 3-9, AAAI Press, Menlo Park, 1996
2. Ackerman, M., Pipek V., Wulf V. (Eds), "Sharing Expertise: Beyond Knowledge Management", MIT Press, Cambridge, Massachussetts and London, England, 2003
3. American Productivity & Quality Center (APQC), "Expertise Locator Systems: Finding the Answers", Benchmarking Report, APQC Publications, Houston, Texas, 2003 (www.apqc.org)
4. Becerra-Fernandez, I., Wang T., Agha G., Sin, T., "Actor Model and Knowledge Management Systems: Social Interaction as a Framework for Knowledge Integration", in K.D.Althoff et.al. (eds.), WM 2005 - Professional Knowledge Management, Proceedings of the Third Biennial Conference, Kaiserslautern, Germany, LNAI 3782, pp. 19-31, Springer Verlag Berlin Heidelberg 2005
5. McDonald, D. Ackerman, A. "Expertise Recommender: A Flexible Recommendation System and Architecture", in proceedings of the 2000 ACM conference on Computer Supported Cooperative Work (CSCW 2000), Philadelphia, pp. 231 - 240 , ACM Press, New York, 2000
6. Kautz, H., Selman, B. Shah, M., " ReferralWeb: Combining Social Networks and Collaborative Filtering", Communications of the ACM, vol. 40, no. 3, pp. 63-65, March 1997.
7. Thompson C., Göker M., Langley P., "A Personalized System for Conversational Recommendations", Journal of Artificial Intelligence Research (JAIR), Volume: 21 (2004), pp 393-428
8. Bridge, D., Göker, M., McGinthy, L., Smyth, B., "Case-based Recommender Systems", The Knowledge Engineering Review, 2006, Cambridge University Press, to appear.
9. Burke, R., "Hybrid Recommender Systems: Survey and Experiments". User Modeling and User-Adapted Interaction. 12(4), pages 331-370.
10. Göker, M, 'Dimensions of Personalization and their Effect on the Knowledge Containers in a CBR system', in Göker, M. (ed.) ,'Proceedings, Workshop on Case Based Reasoning and Personalization', at the 6th European Conference on Case Based Reasoning", Aberdeen, Scotland, September 4th, 2002
11. Salton, G., McGill, M.J., "Introduction to Modern Information Retrieval", McGraw-Hill, New York, 1983
12. Schütze, H. , Pedersen, J., "A cooccurrence-based thesaurus and two applications to information retrieval" Information Processing and Management, 33(3), 307-318, 1997.

13. Jing, Y., Croft, B., "An Association Thesaurus for Information Retrieval" Proceedings of {RIAO}-94, 4th International Conference ``Recherche d'Information Assistee par Ordinateur", New York, pp. 146-160, 1994.
14. Nobesawa, S., Tsutsumi, J., Jiang, S., Sano, T., Sato, K., Nakanishi, M. , "Segmenting Sentences into Linky Strings using D-bigram statistics", COLING, Copenhagen, 1996.
15. Lenz, M., Burkhard H.D., "Case Retieval Nets: Basic ideas and extensions", in Görz G. and Hölldobler S. (Eds.), "KI-96, Advances in Artificial Intelligence", LNAI 1137, pp 227-239, Springer Verlag, Berlin, Heidelberg, 1996
16. Resnik, P., Zeckhauser, R., Friedman, E., Kuwabara, K., "Reputation Systems", Communications of the ACM, December 2000, Vol 43, No 12, pp. 45-48
17. Beenen, G., Laing, K., Wang, X., Chang, K., Frankowski, D., Resnick, P., Kraut, R., "Using Social Psychology to Motivate Contributions to Online Communities", Proceedings of the CSCW'04, November 6-10, 2004, Chicago,Ill, ACM Press, 2004
18. McDonald, D., "Recommending Collaboration with Social Networks: A Comparative Evaluation", Proceedings of CHI 2003, April 5-10, 2003, Ft. Lauderdale, ACM Press, 2003
19. Wasserman, S., Faust, K., " Social Network Analysis: Methods and Applications", Cambridge University Press, Cambridge, UK, 1994

Author Index

Lecture Notes in Artificial Intelligence (LNAI)

Vol. 3890: S.G. Thompson, R. Ghanea-Hercock (Eds.), Defence Applications of Multi-Agent Systems. XII, 141 pages. 2006.

Vol. 3885: V. Torra, Y. Narukawa, A. Valls, J. Domingo-Ferrer (Eds.), Modeling Decisions for Artificial Intelligence. XII, 374 pages. 2006.

Vol. 3881: S. Gibet, N. Courty, J.-F. Kamp (Eds.), Gesture in Human-Computer Interaction and Simulation. XIII, 344 pages. 2006.

Vol. 3874: R. Missaoui, J. Schmidt (Eds.), Formal Concept Analysis. X, 309 pages. 2006.

Vol. 3873: L. Maicher, J. Park (Eds.), Charting the Topic Maps Research and Applications Landscape. VIII, 281 pages. 2006.

Vol. 3863: M. Kohlhase (Ed.), Mathematical Knowledge Management. XI, 405 pages. 2006.

Vol. 3862: R.H. Bordini, M. Dastani, J. Dix, A.E.F. Seghrouchni (Eds.), Programming Multi-Agent Systems. XIV, 267 pages. 2006.

Vol. 3849: I. Bloch, A. Petrosino, A.G.B. Tettamanzi (Eds.), Fuzzy Logic and Applications. XIV, 438 pages. 2006.

Vol. 3848: J.-F. Boulicaut, L. De Raedt, H. Mannila (Eds.), Constraint-Based Mining and Inductive Databases. X, 401 pages. 2006.

Vol. 3847: K.P. Jantke, A. Lunzer, N. Spyratos, Y. Tanaka (Eds.), Federation over the Web. X, 215 pages. 2006.

Vol. 3835: G. Sutcliffe, A. Voronkov (Eds.), Logic for Programming, Artificial Intelligence, and Reasoning. XIV, 744 pages. 2005.

Vol. 3830: D. Weyns, H. V.D. Parunak, F. Michel (Eds.), Environments for Multi-Agent Systems II. VIII, 291 pages. 2006.

Vol. 3817: M. Faundez-Zanuy, L. Janer, A. Esposito, A. Satue-Villar, J. Roure, V. Espinosa-Duro (Eds.), Nonlinear Analyses and Algorithms for Speech Processing. XII, 380 pages. 2006.

Vol. 3814: M. Maybury, O. Stock, W. Wahlster (Eds.), Intelligent Technologies for Interactive Entertainment. XV, 342 pages. 2005.

Vol. 3809: S. Zhang, R. Jarvis (Eds.), AI 2005: Advances in Artificial Intelligence. XXVII, 1344 pages. 2005.

Vol. 3808: C. Bento, A. Cardoso, G. Dias (Eds.), Progress in Artificial Intelligence. XVIII, 704 pages. 2005.

Vol. 3802: Y. Hao, J. Liu, Y.-P. Wang, Y.-m. Cheung, H. Yin, L. Jiao, J. Ma, Y.-C. Jiao (Eds.), Computational Intelligence and Security, Part II. XLII, 1166 pages. 2005.

Vol. 3801: Y. Hao, J. Liu, Y.-P. Wang, Y.-m. Cheung, H. Yin, L. Jiao, J. Ma, Y.-C. Jiao (Eds.), Computational Intelligence and Security, Part I. XLI, 1122 pages. 2005.

Vol. 3789: A. Gelbukh, Á. de Albornoz, H. Terashima-Marín (Eds.), MICAI 2005: Advances in Artificial Intelligence. XXVI, 1198 pages. 2005.

Vol. 3782: K.-D. Althoff, A. Dengel, R. Bergmann, M. Nick, T.R. Roth-Berghofer (Eds.), Professional Knowledge Management. XXIII, 739 pages. 2005.

Vol. 3763: H. Hong, D. Wang (Eds.), Automated Deduction in Geometry. X, 213 pages. 2006.

Vol. 3755: G.J. Williams, S.J. Simoff (Eds.), Data Mining. XI, 331 pages. 2006.

Vol. 3735: A. Hoffmann, H. Motoda, T. Scheffer (Eds.), Discovery Science. XVI, 400 pages. 2005.

Vol. 3734: S. Jain, H.U. Simon, E. Tomita (Eds.), Algorithmic Learning Theory. XII, 490 pages. 2005.

Vol. 3721: A.M. Jorge, L. Torgo, P.B. Brazdil, R. Camacho, J. Gama (Eds.), Knowledge Discovery in Databases: PKDD 2005. XXIII, 719 pages. 2005.

Vol. 3720: J. Gama, R. Camacho, P.B. Brazdil, A.M. Jorge, L. Torgo (Eds.), Machine Learning: ECML 2005. XXIII, 769 pages. 2005.

Vol. 3717: B. Gramlich (Ed.), Frontiers of Combining Systems. X, 321 pages. 2005.

Vol. 3702: B. Beckert (Ed.), Automated Reasoning with Analytic Tableaux and Related Methods. XIII, 343 pages. 2005.

Vol. 3698: U. Furbach (Ed.), KI 2005: Advances in Artificial Intelligence. XIII, 409 pages. 2005.

Vol. 3690: M. Pěchouček, P. Petta, L.Z. Varga (Eds.), Multi-Agent Systems and Applications IV. XVII, 667 pages. 2005.

Vol. 3684: R. Khosla, R.J. Howlett, L.C. Jain (Eds.), Knowledge-Based Intelligent Information and Engineering Systems, Part IV. LXXIX, 933 pages. 2005.

Vol. 3683: R. Khosla, R.J. Howlett, L.C. Jain (Eds.), Knowledge-Based Intelligent Information and Engineering Systems, Part III. LXXX, 1397 pages. 2005.

Vol. 3682: R. Khosla, R.J. Howlett, L.C. Jain (Eds.), Knowledge-Based Intelligent Information and Engineering Systems, Part II. LXXIX, 1371 pages. 2005.

Vol. 3681: R. Khosla, R.J. Howlett, L.C. Jain (Eds.), Knowledge-Based Intelligent Information and Engineering Systems, Part I. LXXX, 1319 pages. 2005.

Vol. 3673: S. Bandini, S. Manzoni (Eds.), AI*IA 2005: Advances in Artificial Intelligence. XIV, 614 pages. 2005.

Vol. 3662: C. Baral, G. Greco, N. Leone, G. Terracina (Eds.), Logic Programming and Nonmonotonic Reasoning. XIII, 454 pages. 2005.

Vol. 3661: T. Panayiotopoulos, J. Gratch, R. Aylett, D. Ballin, P. Olivier, T. Rist (Eds.), Intelligent Virtual Agents. XIII, 506 pages. 2005.

Vol. 3658: V. Matoušek, P. Mautner, T. Pavelka (Eds.), Text, Speech and Dialogue. XV, 460 pages. 2005.

Vol. 3651: R. Dale, K.-F. Wong, J. Su, O.Y. Kwong (Eds.), Natural Language Processing – IJCNLP 2005. XXI, 1031 pages. 2005.

Vol. 3642: D. Ślęzak, J. Yao, J.F. Peters, W. Ziarko, X. Hu (Eds.), Rough Sets, Data Mining, and Granular Computing, Part II. XXIII, 738 pages. 2005.

Vol. 3641: D. Ślęzak, G. Wang, M. Szczuka, I. Düntsch, Y. Yao (Eds.), Rough Sets, Fuzzy Sets, Data Mining, and Granular Computing, Part I. XXIV, 742 pages. 2005.

Vol. 3635: J.R. Winkler, M. Niranjan, N.D. Lawrence (Eds.), Deterministic and Statistical Methods in Machine Learning. VIII, 341 pages. 2005.